WOMEN
TRANSFORMING
COMMUNICATIONS

Dedicated to

Roberta Applegate
Cathy Covert
Muriel Cantor
Marilyn Fife
Frances Grinstead
Helen Hostetter
Marian McBride
Helen Patterson
Anne Pride
Madge Rush
Martha Stuart
Elizabeth Yamashita
and especially MaryAnn Yodelis Smith whose chapter would have been in this book—we will always wish it were.

Their respective energies flow around and through us, as they did when they were identifiable bodies. In that sense, we miss talking to them and being with them. But we continually draw upon their knowledge and wisdom, and their constant courage and strength to keep going and encouragement to keep us going.

We encourage readers of this book to add names to our beginning list of those who have gone before us, leaving an indelible mark on each of us and our abilities to have our voices heard. Their voices and ours must never be silenced. Send the names to Co-Chairs, Commission on the Status of Women, Association for Education in Journalism and Mass Communication, 121 LeConte Street, University of South Carolina, Columbia, SC 29208-0251.

WOMEN
TRANSFORMING
COMMUNICATIONS
GLOBAL INTERSECTIONS

**DONNA ALLEN
RAMONA R. RUSH
SUSAN J. KAUFMAN**

EDITORS

SAGE Publications
International Educational and Professional Publisher
Thousand Oaks London New Delhi

For information address:

SAGE Publications, Inc.
2455 Teller Road
Thousand Oaks, California 91320
E-mail: order@sagepub.com

SAGE Publications Ltd.
6 Bonhill Street
London EC2A 4PU
United Kingdom

SAGE Publications India Pvt. Ltd.
M-32 Market
Greater Kailash I
New Delhi 110 048 India

Printed in the United States of America

Library of Congress Cataloging-in-Publication Data

Main entry under title:

Women transforming communications: Global intersections / editors,
    Donna Allen, Ramona R. Rush, Susan J. Kaufman.
        p.   cm.
    Includes bibliographical references and indexes.
    ISBN 0-8039-7266-0 (acid-free paper).—ISBN 0-8039-7267-9 (pbk.:
acid-free paper)
    1. Mass media and women.   I. Allen, Donna.   II. Rush, Ramona R.
III. Kaufman, Susan J.
P94.5.W65W683   1996
302.23′082—dc20   96-4467

This book is printed on acid-free paper.

96 97 98 99 00 01 10 9 8 7 6 5 4 3 2 1

Sage Production Editor: Astrid Virding
Sage Typesetting: Andrea D. Swanson
Sage Cover Design: Candice Harman

Contents

Part III: Transformative Communications

Preface

Decadent and Magnificent Socially Constructed Realities

What a difference a decade makes . . . we can see clearly now . . . magnificent realities that were only yearned-after visions as we started in the early to mid-1980s working on the forerunner to this book, *Communications at the Crossroads: The Gender Gap Connection.*

One of the most delightful things to literally hold on to are the many books and materials on multiculturalism, race, class, and the media of communication—all in one. No longer do we have to painstakingly find and draw together from alternative sources a literature to represent us all. "Full inclusion" education and educational materials are at our fingertips more and more every day, sometimes even in the traditional media. It is a logical place for our next wave of awareness, study, encouragement, publication, and activism.

The multitude of writings now found on women's issues, including those concerned with all aspects of communications, is a sight of choices to behold. In fact, it is sometimes overwhelming, especially because of our knowledge of the earlier scarcity and silence of such voices when we were envisioning *Crossroads. Crossroads* took a few hits as well as many praises: hard hits from white male administrators returning low merit evaluations for an edited, nonmainstream (read: not important) piece that took five years to complete (two of ours and three of the publisher's); soft hits from a younger white female scholar who, at that time newly replete with feminist theory and research training, reviewed it favorably but wanted more theory; and accurate hits from a feminist scholar of color who criticized the book for not including more multifaceted perspectives such as culture, race, and class issues, as she did in a more recent book.

Most of us now know that it depends upon standpoint dependency, a feminist perspective about controlled and controlling information and knowledge. Feminist theologian Elizabeth Dodson Gray (1982; author of a chapter in both *Crossroads* and this book) was an early writer in this current wave of feminism about male standpoints as part and parcel of a conceptual, patriarchal trap. As Reinharz (1992) points out: "At first, the very act of discovering sexism in scholarship was revolutionary . . . it was radical simply to study women" (p. 11). *Crossroads* was challenging and exciting because we were actually writing about women and communications and being published, period. Women have learned from and about each other since then because of the increased extensiveness *and* inclusiveness of women's writing. Women of color are agents of some of the most provocative and important literature available for students of society, culture, and communications.

The "literature of all voices" did not just spring immaculately from a conceptual chasm during the latter part of the twentieth century—the dominating structure of society finally could not contain the swell of voices that have repeatedly demanded to be heard over time.

If the voices seem fragmented in resistance against a dominant, socially constructed reality in a postmodern sense, they are. They are about the business of establishing their own identities and agendas, not having it continually done for them by the mass media and economic structures of society. But what seems to be missed by the "inquiring minds who want to know" is that the voices are now in interactive dialogue with one another and connecting as they never did in the past. And, yes, we are concerned. Those "angry white males," equipped at the center-right in the United States at the time of this writing with a Newt World Order, a Contract on America, and heavily armed paramilitary groups composed of fascist elements of the Ku Klux Klan, skinheads, neo-Nazis, and survivalists, are not a winsome sight.

Women especially now recognize many standpoint dependencies, and such understanding has further served to empower and liberate us. As an example of a decadent standpoint perspective that has taken a long time for the light of awareness to illumine is the following: more traditional males, especially those in leadership positions at universities, in religious organizations, and in the mass media (read: advertising and pornography), might well turn their energies to the study of their own dominating, masculinist cultures of violence and power instead of criticizing, co-opting, or circumventing the substantial body of literature of feminist and women's studies. Few men study their behavior from this perspective—they merely keep tight, standpoint control over the societal institutions that perpetuate traditional/generic (one mold fits all) men's studies. Many of them instead have learned to pitch a multicultural game, earning lots of praise, good will, promotions, and consultants' fees as they "sub" for women and minorities who, of course, are often missing or, if present, not allowed to speak for themselves.

Decadent constructions of reality can and do change over time, which offers hope. As an example, this book might not be here today if the publishing house of Ablex had not been the first and continued voice of encouragement for *Crossroads* to be completed. We recounted in its preface the lack of support we found for women's books, and included a letter of rejection from one of the growing, major publishing houses. The letter itemized the "reservations" (ah, censorship by any other name would still be repugnant) of the publications board through the channel of an empathic associate editor who happened to be female. We didn't reveal the identity of the publishing house then, for various reasons, including the job security of that associate editor. But now—for the first time, and on these pages—we can reveal that the publishing house was none other than . . . Sage, the publisher of this book. Sage has grown, at least in its proliferation of titles, to cover many facets of society and culture. We suspect that it was a sound marketing decision to combine both political aspects of the U.S. society—efficiency *and* equality. But that is Sage's story to tell.

It is the people, as well as members of other species, who still silently give and are taken from, often without their knowledge or consent, that our book wishes to acknowledge. Too many of us have died without acknowledgment of either our work or our existence. So many of us still are kept in stages and cages of frustration, oppression, repression, depression, legislation, litigation, isolation, humiliation, mutilation, while waiting and hoping for far more than "just a moment, please" of recognition.

Not One of Us Deserves Imposed Anonymity

Some burdens must be taken "off our backs" because they truly were not and are not of our own making. But some loads must be placed on our backs when our writings and speech begin to exist in perpetuity. These "outer talks" and "outer writings," once only figments of our imagination and dreams, are now in society's reality, no matter how it is constructed or our words are construed. We do owe silenced others their day in court—their right to speak, to be heard and listened to—we *are* responsible for their historical, diverse, and unique existence and experience, which, in unity, are also our own. As we connect and construct bridges from the era of so-called postmodernism to the environmental justice and global eco-communications possibilities of the twenty-first century, we do so pledge thee our troth.

To the others who usually would have been specifically acknowledged on these pages—you know who you are, and so do we, and so do others. And isn't that the point we are trying to make here, anyhow? Most of us have had our 15 minutes of fame—we're going to save our breath, energy, pages, and trees so that others might have theirs, if they wish, and by name, if they so desire.

rrr da sjk
(Lexington, KY; Washington, DC;
Charleston, IL; 1995)

References

Gray, E. D. (1982). *Patriarchy as a conceptual trap.* Wellesley, MA: Roundtable.

Reinharz, S. (1992). *Feminist methods in social research.* New York: Oxford University Press.

Rush, R. R., & Allen, D. (Eds.). (1989). *Communications at the crossroads: The gender gap connection.* Norwood, NJ: Ablex.

Introduction: Websters and Spinsters

Ramona R. Rush

Decide to Network

Decide to network
Use every letter you write
Every conversation you have
Every meeting you attend
To express your fundamental beliefs and dreams
Affirm to others the vision of the world you want
Network through thought
Network through love
Network through the spirit
You are the center of a network
You are the center of the world
You are a free, immensely powerful source
of life and goodness

Affirm it
Spread it
Radiate it
Think day and night about it
And you will see a miracle happen:
the greatness of your own life.
In a world of big powers, media, and monopolies
But of four and a half billion individuals
Networking is the new freedom
the new democracy
a new form of happiness.

Robert Muller

AUTHOR'S NOTE: This Introduction draws material from Ramona R. Rush (in press), "Networking: Being, Through Being Connected," in Kramarae and Spender (Eds.), *The Women's Studies Encyclopedia.* Harvester Wheatsheaf, International Book Distributors, Simon & Schuster International, Campus 400, Maylands Avenue, Hemel Hempstead, Herts. HP2 7EZ, England. Attn: Clair Chaventre, Reference Development Editor. The poem by Robert Muller is used by permission of the author.

A look through *Women Transforming Com-munications* soon establishes the central theme running through the various chapters: *net-working*. The coeditors and authors each have, for the most part, lived and verbalized this noun.

This is a "nuance difference" in compari-son with our earlier book, *Communications at the Crossroads: The Gender Gap Connec-tion* (1989). There we were concerned with women's voices—women speaking up and out, women writing—breaking the imposed si-lences forced on women by men and society. Networking there was but an implicit theme.

An ultimate, perhaps the ultimate, out-come of networking is to feel connected by being connected. Most humans are social animals and come together, group together, for a variety of logical, survival, and quality-of-life reasons.

The so-called good old boys' network has been in effect for most of humans' literate history because men have controlled most of the public communications and information technologies at any period in history, includ-ing the current ones as the twenty-first cen-tury opens. Men also have domineered the private networks of communications and in-formation under the economic construction of the "individual" entity within the business and corporate world that allows co-optation of the masses through a structural "father" image.

Such economically, legally, and socially sanctioned networking among men in their singular human and corporate skins has kept adult women and primarily female children as wards of the state and the property of all males. This condition was most likely to persist as long as women and children were restricted to and isolated in the domestic sphere of the males, whether husbands, fa-thers, sons, priests, teachers, judges, and/or bankers.

Women historically came together in in-terpersonal networks for collective produc-tion events: clothes making and alterations and food preparation, such as drying and preserving. Social collectives created through religious and educational study and teaching also brought women together in meaningful groups.

The collective efforts of men through wars to acquire more possessions often through territorial acquisitions brought some disrup-tion to the ordinary, "normal" state of affairs. Women were often allowed or forced to step into official male "roles" such as working outside or inside the home in male occupa-tions as men did battle. Thus women for brief periods of time, including when men died or were disabled through natural causes, liter-ally became the "breadwinners" as well as the breadmakers. The "superwoman syndrome" has a long history.

Various technologies, although largely created and controlled by men in their own images and for their own uses, often have been used after the fact by women for intel-lectual stimulation, education, occupation, and liberation. The printing press, for exam-ple, affected women through the bookstore, the library, and the school, where they were seen as clerks, librarians, and nurturing ele-mentary teachers (Kramarae, 1988). The type-writer and computer likewise have affected women, but often with gendered role stereo-types dictating the use for women (e.g., sec-retarial pools where clattering machines could do little toward the connection of women except for the remote possibility of group bargaining for higher financial gains). The telephone, an electronic connection for women, also has been described as an oppressive technology for women.

Nonetheless, networking among women brought basic elements of individual empow-erment by sharing information and knowledge through direct and mediated communication messages and channels, and by discovering commonality of social treatment and status as a group. Most important, networking for and by women has allowed this multisplen-dored and multicultured group to work toward social equality with men as women and per-sons of color have deconstructed the social

reality erected by men for primarily a materialistic reward system (i.e., positions of hierarchical power with economic, educational,
and social levels of comfort and dominance
beyond individual and even group needs).

Networking is what it sounds like: working the net, which is like working the web.
We are all websters and spinsters, according
to feminist theologian Mary Daly, and thus
one might conclude that we are all networkers, and are usually networking. Daly (1987)
defines the Network as "the Gyn-Ecological
context: tapestry of connections woven and
re-woven by Spinsters and Websters; the Net
which breaks the fall of Journeyers experiencing the Earthquake Phenomenon and
springing us into New Space"[1] (p. 149).

Women have had to figure out, time and
time again, that although each one of us is
unique, our experiences have common threads
to link us, which allow us to share our common, unusual, and unique experiences. Threads,
webs that we recognized, that we could relate
to, tithe to, bond to, and connect to, sharing
a common web. Women's webs. Wild women's
webs. Women's worldwide webs. Women's
worldwise webs. As the twenty-first century
envelopes us, computer networks appear to
be the technological world primarily of elites
who have the time, skills, and resources to
have and use them. Women are increasingly
using electronic networks as a way of identifying political, social, and economic groups,
but with a lagged-use pattern because science
and technology are primarily sanctioned as the
invention and activity domain of men. One
estimate is that in the mid-1990s only 15%-
30% of Internet users were women.

Informal networks, because of their allow-
ance in domestic/private spheres, have been
important to women. These include those
that have become institutionalized at varying
levels of politics, from nongovernmental organizational (NGO) activities (e.g., violence
hot lines and centers) to local sociocultural
spaces, such as the poor urban neighborhood
that Riaño (1994, p. 39) discusses. She points
to the works of Alfaro (1994),

who examines how women have transformed
their motherhood (individual level) into a social
maternity (the public). The neighborhood consti-
tutes a symbolic and material space in which their
social motherhood is exercised by supporting informal networks of exchange and collective
strategies of survival. (Riaño, 1994, p. 39)

Alternative networks and media are also
the "stuff" of communications for those usually outside the mainstream (malestream) of
most traditional media. Riaño (1994) points
to the importance of such group communication processes in reclaiming cultural and ethnic concerns, "to facilitate the recovery of
indigenous knowledge and historical memory" (p. 35). She describes the work of Mata
(1994), who

explores how the discourses created through
grassroots communication are not about the
Other but about a We. . . . [T]he recognition of
the otherness (of gender, race, and class) is
achieved in grassroots communication through
the dynamic building of group bonds; through
identifying a common project, a sense of belonging (ours); and through the recognition of the
participants as a collective subject (we). (p. 35)

Riaño and others, when discussing regional
and international levels of networking, usually note that the establishment of 1975 as
International Women's Year and the declaration of the United Nations Decade for Women
(1976-1985) increased the momentum of the
importance and nature of women's issues
through the increase, enlargement, and beginnings of many current women's organizations and media. The Beijing Conference for
Women in 1995 evolved even more. More
webs spun, more narratives evolved, weaved,
and displayed by the websters.

Other combinations will also emerge as
environmentalists and feminists attempt to
join together for what seems to be one of the
more inclusive and diverse mergings in which
Mother Nature—Gaia—is being looked to as
the most complete and comprehensive network to which all living and nonliving matter

can attend. At least two groups now immersed in this planetary philosophy and ethical debate are generally known as deep ecologists and eco-feminists. It is an ongoing discussion well worth "surfing the nets" of communication and information technology to join.

Humans are entering the twenty-first century with a far greater potential for networking, being websters, "beings being through connection," than at any time in literate history because of powerful advances in communication and information technologies.

As an example, the coeditors of this book used a variety of communication technologies for this book (in order of the frequency of use): e-mail, fax, snail mail, plane-to-ground express mail delivery, and the usual person-to-person telephone. In comparison, when doing *Crossroads,* we used the computer for word processing and regular mail most often, with telephone conferences as often as we thought we could afford them. And we had the knowledge that in either case we wouldn't have done a book if we had had to use a typewriter. We, as women, did not have access to (other women for) manuscript typing as did our male counterparts.

What did we gain with all kinds of technology at our disposal this time around? Time and money, as e-mail and fax whipped around the world and waited for someone to answer it, without either party dialing back again and again in perpetual wasted motion. What did we lose? Time and money, if time is money, as more of the word processing and disc translation became ours to do, freeing the book publisher to (perhaps?) get the book out faster, which is one of our goals this time. Either way, and with three coeditors this time instead of two, each book took two years, start to publisher.

Yet, the social construction of reality of a relatively few elites—usually male, usually white, usually heterosexual, usually highly educated, usually wealthy in monetary terms, usually of elevated class status—creates great chasms of mistrust and lack of respect for and among the less powerful and have widened gaps in natural discourse. And there are serious disruptions in the genetic diversity of all species largely due to man-made interventions in nature.

This paradoxical connect/disconnect situation is known by many names and is a centerpiece focus for a worldwide sub-elite agenda for discussion and action. It appears that as community entities become seemingly less important and economic elites become more concentrated in monolithic market economies, financial networking becomes the veneer of the planet. It is a thin information cover encircling and girding the planet Earth, much like a wooden veneer covers a table top. About 10% of the world's elite, mostly financial, communicate rapidly back and forth and around through this veneer of information channels.

Under this thin cover of technocrats, however, are about another 10% to 20% sub-elites—educators, students, scientists, religious and spiritual leaders, and leaders of voluntary and nongovernmental organizations. There are many fragmented networks of social movements that are connecting here—they include first nations; peace; environment; women; people of color, disability, homelessness; and migrants and refugees, to name a few. People in social movements within the second layer of rapid, interactive, and informative communications transcend and connect across class, race, gender, and age barriers more often than those within the economic veneer, due largely to the educational and technological sub-elites whose expertise is primarily directed toward social action research and praxis. These social movements network often through local, state, national, regional, and international conferences, whether they are electronic or traditional organizational structures. Important to the networking across social movements are crossover members and cooperating groups.

Most of the world's peoples, an estimated 70% to 80%, are not connected in any widespread, interactive, and meaningful communication of information, except perhaps for distance learning and radio or shortwave transmissions. If being connected is being, then those persons do not/will not exist in the reality of today. Their daily bread, their hallowed heads, their squalor, their poverty, their abuse, their desolation, isolation, rejection, existence, death are noticed by only a handful of people in each instance. And they are not the same few handfuls of people who ultimately control the wealth, the resources, the networking of this planet—the ultimate gap, the ultimate distance in the universe, the ultimate bridge in networking.

Thus we have our work cut out to help people "be all they can be" (see Rush's Chapter 15). The three following suggestions might lead us together through the uncharted route of diversity and inclusivity if we are able to (a) systematically and systemically remove all barriers to the access and use of the communication of information, (b) locate and fill the communication and economic gaps in biocommunities with user-friendly and appropriate technology and information, and (c) advance global civil development by "being, through connecting."

Although all chapters in *Women Transforming Communications* sooner or later lead to networking, the chapters in Part III by Hosken, Kassell, Sreberny-Mohammadi, Suarez, and Werden must surely emphasize to all of us the difficulties, impacts, and benefits of networking.

How This Book Is Organized

Women Transforming Communications is shaped as a trilogy—that is, a set of three related parts that together form an extended, unified work, though each has its own unity.

The three parts are "Communication Visions," "Communication Chasms," and "Transformative Communications."

Part I, "Communication Visions," brings together envisionary writings for communications, whether from the past, the present, or somewhere out there.

Rush leads off with 10 tenets for deeper communications, bringing together myriad societal and cultural forces, including mass and alternative communications, eco-communications through diversity and inclusivity, sexuality and spirituality, healing and liberation. Bulkeley then uses some of Rush's tenets to examine the partnership of the press and religion, suggesting that perhaps lambs can reside at-one with carnivores.

Eisler highlights the role of communication in the partnership paradigm that she continues to develop here. Valenti pulls together yet another partnership paradigm with the idea of environmental communications being friendly terrain for women. Einsiedel puts visions to praxis in demonstrating the use of social action research when applied to gender and development concerns.

Hutton reminds us of our heritage in building our communication future through the vision of Afrocentric archetypes. Wilson Schaef beguiles us with the old idea to be careful what you wish for, in case you might become it.

Part II, "Communication Chasms," reminds us to pick our way carefully through the field of visions and transformations because, at any moment, we can drop out of sight and sound into those conceptual crevices of socially constructed realities.

Where better to start this s/hero's journey than in a democratic information depository as the trio of Lengermann, Niebrugge-Brantley, and Kirkpatrick discuss the relationship of the feminist public to public libraries in the information age. Lose this information at your own peril!

Steinem begins the mass media saga as she journeys with and through one of her books, finding that inner revolutions have to continually contend with imposed externalities. Samuels furthers the theme of the media as dysfunctional, especially in relation to ethnic and racial groups. The lesson seems similar when lesbians are reflected, employed, and used by the mass media, according to Cramer and Nelson in their respective chapters. These "touched-up" pictures from the media seem most chilling as Kaufman and Dworkin, with contrasting writing techniques and content in their respective chapters, tell much the same media story—the debasement and defilement of human beings, as Holocaust survivors and pornography victims.

Rush, Cirksena, Stocking and Newton, de Uriarte, Russell, and Creedon lead us into and out of the "enchanted halls" of academe, where one can be damned if you do and damned if you don't, much like the history of the mass media: • Dirty tricks in *academe*? • Why the delay of the wedding and embedding of feminist and women's scholarship to and in traditional literature? • Why (circle one) is/sometimes is/is not/sometimes is not/don't know/don't care/not applicable the promotion and tenure process like/not like living a fable? • Are we teaching our future communication leaders the same old-same old hegemonic, dominant paradigm? • Why do I feel like I am talking to myself about appropriate instruction methods? • Can I grow up to be "other" than a nearsighted administrator?

Part III, "Transformative Communications," allows a multifaceted examination of how communications have been, are being, and will be transformed into equitable, inclusive, and, yes, diverse relationships.

Kassell, Hosken, Werden, Suarez, and Sreberny-Mohammadi show us intriguing and complex constructions of regional, national, and international networks for, of, and by women—the very stuff of this book.

Miller and Swift, Dates and Stroman, Reed, Dodson Gray, and Rosario-Braid demonstrate how structures such as language, literature, a print medium, an electronic medium, and a nation in development can slowly but surely transform. Simpson shows the transformative activity of professional women journalists, and how to ensure their individual stories will not be lost, co-opted, or distorted. Stuart and Bery place technology in the hands of women—and lo and behold! Fine theo-

rizes about transformations through the learning of multicultural literacy. And last but not ever least or leased, Allen transforms *equality* and *democracy* into twenty-first-century verbs, injecting women's voices and actions where the dominant paradigm's money and mouths currently communicate.

Note

1. "Earthquake Phenomenon: 1. the experience of cosmic shakiness, trembling, and dislocation, during which time Gyn/Ecologists share with our sister the Earth the agony of phallocratic attacks 2. Ordeal experienced by Crones engaged in the Otherworld Journey beyond patriarchy which involves confronting one's Aloneness as the ground splits open, and the Spanning the chasm by Acts of Surviving, Spinning and Weaving Cosmic Connections" (Daly, 1987, p. 72).

"New Space: Space on the boundary of patriarchal institutions; Space created by women which provides real alternatives to the archetypal roles of fatherland; Space in which women Realize Power of Presence" (Daly, 1987, p. 84).

References

Alfaro, R. M. (1994). Women as social agents of communication: Social maternity and leadership. In P. Riaño (Ed.), *Women in grassroots communication: Furthering social change* (pp. 260-278). Thousand Oaks, CA: Sage.

Daly, M. (in cahoots with Caputi, J.). (1987). *Webster's first new intergalactic wickedary of the English language.* Boston: Beacon.

Kramarae, C. (Ed.). (1988). *Technology and women's voices keeping in touch.* New York: Routledge Kegan Paul.

Mata, M. (1994). Being woman in popular radio. In P. Riaño (Ed.), *Women in grassroots communication: Furthering social change* (pp. 192-211). Thousand Oaks, CA: Sage.

Riaño, P. (1994). Gender in communication: Women's contributions. In P. Riaño (Ed.), *Women in grassroots communication: Furthering social change* (pp. 30-44). Thousand Oaks, CA: Sage.

Rush, R. R., & Allen, D. (Eds.). (1989). *Communications at the crossroads: The gender gap connection.* Norwood, NJ: Ablex.

PART
I

Communication
Visions

1

Ten Tenets for Deeper Communications
Transforming Communications Theory and Research

Ramona R. Rush

Vice President Al Gore, of the United States, in speeches in 1994 appropriately circulated via "information highways," envisioned a National Information Infrastructure (NII) and the Global Information Infrastructure (GII) as metaphors for planetary unity. Universal service, in this model, is viewed as a democratic enhancement to the envisioned development of such globe-crossing electronic networks by commercial firms, regulated by governments.

One cannot read about such activities without a certain amount of cynicism: I wrote several years ago that "communication revolutions come and go but the actors remain the same" (Rush & Allen, 1989, p. 9). Today, control of the world's communication and information technological channels, messages, and, no doubt, minds is concentrated in the reach of fewer and fewer corporations. Indeed, it appears that the number of such corporate "individuals" could be counted on

AUTHOR'S NOTE: Preliminary versions of this chapter were presented as papers during "A New Decade for Women: An International Colloquium," sponsored by Texas Christian University and the Association for the Advancement of Policy, Research, and Development in the Third World, Fort Worth, Texas (March 1993), and the 6th Annual MacBride Roundtable, Honolulu, Hawaii (January 1994). Colleague Pamela Creedon showed me the power of "deeper editing" on this manuscript and thus taught me more about my own "shallow communications" than I will ever be able to define for others. So did other colleagues including Carolyn Byerly, Christy Bulkeley, Carolyn Cline, Judy Cramer, Don Stacks, Judy Tipton, Elizabeth Toth, and the coeditors of this book—Donna Allen and Susan Kaufman. To all, I owe innumerable, begrudging-but-necessary transformations in my thinking and writing: a wonderful exercise in deeper communications— it is not for the weak of spirit.

3

the fingers of a real person's two hands shortly after the turn of the upcoming century (see any of Ben Bagdikian's books and other writings on the topic).

Be that as it may, there seems to be that time-honored eternal hope and promise, for a society at any level, that emerging and advanced technological tools of communications and information will lead, in tandem, to an improvement and advancement of the human condition. There is also a related hope for the acceptance and/or understanding of multicultural diversity[1] because of, not in spite of, communications (as can be seen in contemporary and concomitant backlash accusations of "political correctness"). But somewhere out there in the discounted biosphere, there still exist voices that seem to have no immediate or ultimate importance to the conduct of global affairs as usual. It's as if these articulations, in whatever form, have no realistic applications to the world about us. And largely for that reason, they don't, and too many of those voices of all species shrivel up and die without any notice or record that a living thing had been in that particular place at that particular time. It seems to me and others that this worldview is not what civilization, especially that one under the particular purview of human beings, is or should be about.

The Need for Integration of Communication Theory and Research as if Women Mattered[2]

> While both sexes may have been making theories for as far back as we can trace, only one sex is seen as the theorists, one sex has its theories accepted as legitimate, only one sex owns the realm of theory. (Spender, 1983, p. 1)

We in graduate schools learned from our Master Scholars (capitalization here indicates mostly generic, mostly white, mostly scholarly appearing males) about theories and research: There's nothing as practical as a good

theory . . . there's nothing as good as a practical theory . . . the simplest theory should explain the most . . . a law is the most exact formulation of what we know . . . a hypothesis is an educated guess—try it out . . . a theory has accumulated many observations, much evidence about how things work.

Many of the Scholars told us that there was a considerable leap in knowledge (and faith, some of us later suspected) between the "hard" (physical) and "soft" (social and behavioral) sciences, between inanimate and animate matter (especially the humankind), and between system levels (in generalizing research results about individuals to groups or nations, for example). No one indicated, perhaps did not notice, that most of this teaching had little to do with women's own observations, experiences, and understanding of the nature of things (what Elise Boulding, 1976/1992, calls the "underside of history"). But mostly men and a few women helped the Scholars distribute those half-minded observations (women often were excluded from the study samples either as researchers or subjects) to our children and students, to mankind *(sic)*, as predominant worldviews without the presence of other, different perspectives.

The light dawned. So while Spender (1983) and other feminists were illuminating three centuries of key women thinkers, others of us were advocating that communications scholars stop replicating research from the dominant scholarly establishment so that women could add our own voices, our own theories (Rush & Allen, 1989). And while women's studies in academic fields were starting and slowly networked in the late 1960s and early 1970s, graduate female students in university classrooms began to develop the most recent feminist studies and theories from the throes of descriptive research indicating women's diminished value as part of the human race.

Spender's quotation cited above was one of the first used in introducing *Communications at the Crossroads: The Gender Gap Connection* (1989). Rush and Allen, the

Crossroads editors, and some of the contributors intuitively knew that we would come back to this quote. And we did, each in our own time and way until there was sufficient connection again to begin plans on a *Crossroads II,* as we fondly called this book. There is no obvious starting point when an individual begins to weave her or his own worldview, but there is a time when it must be committed to oral and written communications if it is to have a life of its own.

Women have known for some time, depending upon which wave of our civil rights movement was occurring, that our voices have been silenced or, if heard, not listened to and recorded in meaningful ways. What eludes many women and most men are the extreme and extensive societal and planetary consequences that these selective silencings have had on more than one-half of the world's population *plus* their male and female children for a long, long time. The consequences are being etched slowly, perhaps too slowly for human survival and certainly for quality of life standards, into our consciousness. Perhaps the cruelest indicators of the effects of sanctioned silence are high infant mortality (intended and unintended) rates, domestic terrorism and violence, societal and institutional controls over women's bodies (including clitoridectomy), the lack of research about women's vital organs, and on and on (see French, 1992).

The silence is a lack of theoretical and worldview inclusiveness: When earthly *women-space* is excluded from theoretical and research writing, the silence results in deadening and deadly consequences.

What Is Theory?

A *theory* is a mental viewing, as *Webster's* (1988) so simply puts it in its first definition. It is how each of us "sees"/perceives or "mentally maps" the world, through our own unique blend of nature and nurture:

A theory is my world. It is how I envision the world, as organized and structured through the sight/cite/site of my own mind's eye. A long time ago, some people near and dear to me told me that the world didn't always look that way. And then, one by one, lots of people I met on my journey told me how the world *really* looks. I have layers and layers of their pictures stacked upon the one I hid away in a secret place in my mind's eye. I bring the original out once in a while just to re-member. I like it best. (Ramona's inner self, 1990)

Bunch (1987) divided theory into four interrelated parts: description (describing what exists), analysis (analyzing why that reality exists), vision (determining what should exist), and strategy (hypothesizing how to change what is to what should be). Theory, Bunch wrote, is more than an assemblage of fact and personal opinion; "theory enables us to see immediate needs in terms of long-range goals and an overall perspective on the world" (pp. 43-45).

Models of scarcity (Henderson, in press), power and greed, exclusionary and enforced silences seem to be what have guided the mind-sets, standpoints, ideologies, theories, worldviews from the time that mankind *(sic)* swung into the saddle (apologies to R. W. Emerson) to the twenty-first century. Women's theories, mental viewings, are age-old but have had to be remembered, recollected, and recorded again and again. The twenty-first century must be viewed as "that new age one more time" when we gather together women's writings, our theories, for yet another beginning, another wave of the women's movement, another collective connection about what we know, what we should know, and where in the world we should be now.

Tenets for Deeper Communications

Deeper[3] Communications is the term finally selected by this author prompted by my work on "Global Eco-Communications"

(1989b, 1992) as well as the writings of many "others" to bring to traditional mind-sets different ways of "viewing" phenomena within and around each of us. *Deeper Communications is the notion that all forms of life have something important to say, each in its own way, day by day.* Deeper Communications is based on the premise that each unique life-form continually receives, stores, distributes, redistributes, and imparts information—tries to communicate its experiential knowledge, in other words.

When each life-form has an ecological flow of internal and external information such that it can process information to situate and sustain itself to the maximum potential for its life-form, and thus its positive and unique contribution to the life chain, then it is in a state of Deeper Communications. Deeper Communications, simply stated, is the maximization of external and internal information and communication processing to allow full enhancement or actualization (Abraham Maslow; see Huffman, Vernoy, & Vernoy, 1994) of a life-form's situational (Haraway, 1991) and sustainable knowledge.

Deeper Communications is the verb, the action, the "hum" of the communication of information that continually adjusts and integrates vast biotic and often chaotic universal systems and processes. This descriptive phrase is unfortunately and increasingly reminiscent of the teaser: "Why do hummingbirds hum?" Answer: "Because they don't know the words." It is likely that intraspecific and interspecific members do not "know the words" because we are not really or realistically listening to each other's attempts to communicate, let alone trying to understand and accept the uniqueness of knowledge that each adds to this planet.

Is Deeper Communications the scenario that Vice President Gore and others "see" when they envision the global information infrastructure as a metaphor for planetary unity? Do they see business as usual; or do they hear the hum of Deeper Communications? Do they know the words? Is it a medi-

ated version or literally straight from the horse's mouth?

Deeper Communications is influenced by the "Deep Ecology" work of Norwegian philosopher Arne Naess (1973, 1992) who, during a lecture in Bucharest in 1972, attempted to distinguish between shallow and deep ecology movements. A summary of the lecture noted: "Ecologically responsible policies are concerned only in part with pollution and resource depletion. There are deeper concerns which touch upon principles of diversity, complexity, autonomy, decentralization, symbiosis, egalitarianism, and classlessness" (Naess, 1973, p. 99). He notes that the Shallow Ecology movement is a fight against pollution and resource depletion with a central objective of the health and affluence of people in the developed countries. The Deep Ecology movement, he writes, "is a rejection of the man*[sic]*-in-environment image in favor of the *relational, total-field image . . .* and of *biospherical egalitarianism*—in principle" (p. 95).

As ecofeminism, deep ecology, social ecology, and other variations of ecology are current topics for discussion and definition (see, for example, *Society and Nature,* vols. 1-5), there are many concerns and criticisms about each of them, especially the variations that have Nazi German roots (Biehl, 1994) or mythic, paganistic orientations (discussed often in terms of ecofeminism; see Gaard & Gruen, 1993, pp. 25-32). Deep or Deeper Communications, whatever this perspective is named and however it evolves, will likely have these criticisms and more. It is in keeping with the nature of Deeper Communications to nurture an inclusive "flow-keeping" (Rush, 1989a) agenda rather than the traditional and exclusive gatekeeping one. Naess (1992) notes:

The values that supporters of the Deep Ecology movement share in common cannot necessarily be formulated in terms of a single set of propositions or expressed in a single language. They are the product of a dynamic social movement and therefore cannot be pinned down as if they belonged to a painstakingly formulated philosophy of the relationship between humans and nature, or as if they formed a coherent body of doctrine. Deep Ecologists do not have a discrete philosophy or religion in common—a definite credo, a set of ultimate "norms and hypotheses"—and why should they? . . . Why monolithic ideologies? We have had enough of those in both European and world history. Supporters of Deep Ecology aim to conserve what is left of the richness and diversity of life on Earth and that includes human cultural diversity. (p. 108)

Naess goes on to write that the current crisis in the relationship between humans and nature has revealed a surprising amount in common between the different supporters of Deep Ecology, perhaps even enough to elaborate a set of principles—a "platform"—for Deep Ecology. The platform includes the following:

1. The flourishing of human and non-human life on Earth has inherent value. The value of non-human life forms is independent of the usefulness of the non-human world for human purposes.
2. The richness and diversity of life are also values in themselves and contribute to the flourishing of human and non-human life on Earth.
3. Humans have no right to reduce this richness and diversity except to satisfy vital needs.
4. The flourishing of human life and cultures is compatible with a substantial decrease of the human population. The flourishing of non-human life requires such a decrease.
5. Present human interference with the non-human world is excessive, and the situation is rapidly worsening.
6. Polices must therefore be changed. The changes in policies affect basic economic, technological, and ideological structures. The resulting state of affairs would be deeply different from the present and would make possible a more joyful experience of the connectedness of all things.
7. The ideological change is mainly that of appreciating life quality (dwelling in situations of inherent value) rather than adhering to an increasingly higher standard of living. There will be a profound awareness of the difference between "big" and "great."
8. Those who subscribe to the foregoing points have an obligation, directly or indirectly, to participate in the attempt to implement the necessary change. (Naess, 1992, p. 114)

Shallower Communications (defined here as, "on the surface"; "superficial" in human terms, for example, "beauty is only skin deep") is to Deeper Communications what traditional environmental risk assessments (e.g., locating and counting hazardous or toxic waste dumps) are to ecological evaluations that include assessment concerns about the human condition through social science measurements (Wilkins, 1994). In this regard, Shallower Communications is like counting movie seats and radio and television sets as has been done across countries in international communication studies. Shallower Communications can be as simple as the "maze of pleasantries" that we go through each day, such as "Hi, how are you?" without expecting, or wanting for that matter, an answer; Deeper Communications as a universal process is as complex as the global mapping of information and communication processes that have contributed to the well-being of, for example, a human's daily life including, and most important, each person's own assessment.

Shallower Communications are also represented in the superficial, late-breaking "news nibbles" we get from television; Deeper Communications are frequently contained in strategic social policy evaluations by the alternative press (see a research accounting of this in Gutierrez-Villalobos, Hertog, & Rush, 1994). Shallower Communications among humans tell us mostly about the who, what, and where—the stuff of elite communications for the masses; Deeper Communications include the how and why—the stuff of elite communications currently and unwisely reserved primarily for the elite. The former adds to our McNews cocktail trivia; the latter to our understanding and knowledge about who we, each of us, are in relation to the world within and around us.

What follows, then, are tenets of Deeper Communications, to guide and I hope transform the theories and research of communications and information for the twenty-first century—to assure the silenced that what they say this time will be heard by enough people so that their ideas and experiences will be heard and held—that is, sustainable communications and knowledge. The suggestions include that a theory and its research will

be concerned about human spirituality and sexuality;

be healing and liberatory;

employ realistic frameworks and social action research;

assess the traditional mass media, in their current corporate state, as demographic investigators and reporters of societal trends and progress;

include the alternative media as scenario sketchers for strategic, social policy surveillance;

emphasize peace, equality, and justice as dynamic growth forces;

develop an envisionary media;

have a global civil society worldview with concern and respect for the information, communication, and integration of its citizens.

(1) A theory and its research will be ecologically based, inclusive, and thus diverse. Each of us is and is within an ecosystem. And each of us works within and toward a *global eco-communications system.* I have defined eco-communications, which stands for the ecology of communications, as the mutual communicative and informative relations among humans, as a species, and between us and our environment (1989b, 1992).

Eco-communications is an integrative, realistic, networking force among humans and their concerns for the inclusion and well-being of all planetary species' information and communication systems. The process of human eco-communications as envisioned and when fully operative in a community will help people to secure important and relational places in a changing, ongoing society, challenging and enhancing their unique contributions. A truly integrative eco-communications system will prevent any long-term estrangement or dysfunction or displacement, except for temporary and necessary adjustments, between the individual and its state (of being). A global eco-communications system, in application, provides a map of communication and information flows and gaps, and continually works to improve delivery methods, channels, and content for filling the lacunae. It is what this author has elsewhere called a "flow-keeping" agenda (1989a, p. xxxiii).

Global[4] has at least two meanings. One is the traditional definition of international or intercultural, which has messages, data, or people going across or through some kind of barriers, boundaries, or constraints, largely man-made, whether it is the encoding-decoding process from one human being to another, or the artificial borders between nation-states. The other *global* defines issues that are common enough to any group(s) of people that they share similar problems and/or meanings. Such global issues often transcend traditional boundaries. A good example of this latter definition are women's issues, preferably those defined by women (see Rush, 1993).

(2) A theory and its research will go beyond dualistic thinking and action. We now appear to be in a stage of human development where old traditions intervene in progress toward a truly associative civilization. Some powerful members of the human species, through habitual mental views of territoriality and sanctioned violence, are exhibiting societal maladaptation and cultural lag. The man-versus-nature and nation-state theories are outworn paradigms (see any of Hazel

Henderson's writings, but especially *Paradigms in Progress,* 1991) in view of the potential of advances in communication technologies, predominantly and ironically developed by men in war and boardrooms.

The first major obstacle to discard is old, outworn paradigms that make many of us Janus-faced humans, habitually thinking and acting in dualistic, competitive, either-or, black-or-white, win-or-lose, me-against-you terms. This is hardly the relational, total-field image that Naess (1973) writes about; he sees that "live and let live" is a more powerful ecological principle than "either you or me" under the principles of diversity and of symbiosis.

The second, related obstacle is the segregation of "other" experiences and information/communication channels and messages. "Other" people are primarily those who do not fit, for whatever reason, into a patriarchal, hierarchical, capitalistic, organizational culture. This worldwide system has largely been constructed by elite males, with power extraordinarily greater than their proportional numerical representation in any society. Resource-poor people, people of color, women, and children mostly belong to "other" groups of people (see, e.g., Andersen & Collins, 1992; Dines & Humez, 1995). If "other" people have communication capability, it is usually through alternative media channels that reach fewer people less often in comparison to those with access to the mainstream media often through the latest communication technologies. Our challenge is to learn a multicultural sensitivity and literacy (see Fine's Chapter 33), while often standing in and knowledgeable about primarily one culture. It is our species' task and turn to learn, practice, and appreciate unity through diversity.

(3) A theory and its research must basically be concerned about human spirituality and sexuality—sometimes interchangeably, often interactively. If humans are expected to go beyond duality in thinking and action, then

our conceptual frameworks and research investigations must acknowledge, explore, and try to understand the dimensions of two basic human elements. Humans are known to be deeply concerned with both spirituality and sexuality, for they are frequently the stuff of legend, mythology, culture, religion, sociology, communications, politics, law, economics. Dictionary definitions indicate that *sex* means to divide, cut, as in male/female with reference to our reproductive functions. Current connotations have elaborated on that primitive, biological designation. Our worldview now concentrates on social, economic, psychological, and political gender roles and structures, which, in large part, have to do with "power-over economics." That is, there are a powerful few who think they need to be "served" whether it is with sex, food, work, information, money, leisure, recreation; "others" are expected to be the servers. To keep that distinction, some persons have had to be persuaded through "commodification" efforts (e.g., controlled and restricted monetary and human resource systems, advertising, commercialization) that their roles were and are to be that of servers (poor, consumers, prostitutes, maids, welfare mothers, staff assistants). Even the homeless and families in poverty are servers in the sense that the power brokers need to "demon-strate" them so that they can exercise even more control through overt comparisons of their obvious God-given status and thus superiority.

To the extent that a person's spirituality and sexuality could be separated and owned, controlled by those in power (persuaded that the nuances of particular religious, political, economic, and/or social ideologies meant it to be so), could a mythology of dualism arise. Personal and cultural symbols and accounts of peaceful, cooperative cultures that went before these transgressions, including those that later recorded the vicious acts of external control, were conveniently lost, stolen, buried, burned, destroyed. Archaeomythologists (a field that includes archaeology, comparative mythology, and folklore) have written on this progression from the time of Indo-European invaders to the present (see Gimbutas, 1989, especially the introductory pages). Our personal centers of security, peace, and justice have either been co-opted or are in hiding from the societal centers of controlled violence pollution. Too often today, addiction, co-optation, isolation, or death are the ways these two centers of externalities and internalities, of sexuality and spirituality, come together. They might instead be viewed as a centered continuum, like a community and bioregion, of life and living.

(4) A theory and its research will be healing and liberatory. bell hooks (1992) has an explanation for the relationship of healing to liberation. She says simply, *"I came to theory because I was hurting."* A powerful statement under any circumstance, hooks explains how living in childhood without a sense of home with a young black couple as parents, who struggled to realize the patriarchal norm, provided her a sanctuary in "theorizing," where she could imagine possible futures:

> This lived experience of critical thinking, of reflection and analysis, became a place where I worked at explaining that theory could be a healing place. When our lived experience of theorizing is fundamentally linked to processes of self-recovery, of collective liberation, no gap exists between theory and practice. But theory is not inherently healing, liberatory, or revolutionary. It fulfills this function only when we ask that it do so and direct our theorizing toward this end. (p. 80)

It might seem strange to expect theory and research to be healing and liberatory, but those who have been victims of societal and individual abuse and those who feel trapped by their human condition will have no trouble understanding this inclusion. As more becomes known about the vast, historical, continuing, and permanent damage done to all species by so few (in comparison) information power brokers entrenched in self-serving societal structures and ideologies, the more people and devices (such as the mass media) will be used to diffuse and distribute ultimately empowering, self-actualizing knowledge about such pollution of the mind. For example, the control of information regarding life-threatening diseases (e.g., AIDS, breast and vaginal cancer) to certain classes of people (gays, bisexuals, and lesbians; women); normalizing and generalizing scientific information about a few to many (e.g., diseases studied only in men applied to mankind *[sic]*, including women and children); maintaining a tightening loop of elite information and decision making (e.g., top levels of business, government, and academe); changing policy under the name of increased and/or different productivity to remove older and more experienced critical thinkers and speakers (early retirement; downsizing, post-tenure review); labeling and deriding dissension as "political correctness" and "victimization."

Let us count the ways to fragment, objectify, commodify, and media-scapegoat the powerless—all ways to confuse, divide, conquer, and reconquer those who do not have the necessary resources of all kinds to withstand the feeding-frenzy attack, which speak back to self-serving, constructed models of marketplace scarcity and greed.

One solution is for national watchdog groups, accreditation bodies (see Rush, 1993), governmental (all levels) human resource agencies, and international groups (such as nongovernmental organizations) to publicly demand that public and private employers with documented discrimination put a hold on any policy, production, and employee formulation and changes (in other words, bar the door) until the structural inequality/ideology is demonstrably removed.

(5) A theory will employ realistic frameworks and will not be disregarded or discounted if it supports social action research. Social policy research, mostly about humans, drives much of the U.S. social science research agenda; social *action* research (see Einsiedel's Chapter 5) has not received the

same attention. Tenet 5 proposes that the process of theory and research should be applied to improve the conditions of the human and other species, especially for those most in need of the applied results. Such an agenda is usually present in critical, feminist, humanist, qualitative theories and research methods. This tenet does not discount *hard* (a masculine word often indicative of impersonal approaches and methods) science research, or research for the sake of research. However, what is behind the ivory towers of the increasingly corporate public and mainly private (including religious) colleges and universities needs to be rethought. Behind these walls we still find predominately patriarchal, hierarchical, white male-dominated institutions where top-down decision making has kept theory and research narrow and discriminatory, both in its topics and through its investigators. There now exists a big discrepancy, a big gap, between theory and reality, between theory and application, between theory and social action research, *between those who observe and those who are studied.* Along this line, Folbre (1993) took a look at the myth of the middle class. She argues for moving away from the focus on class structure in theory and instead studying CRAG: class, race, age, and gender. It is a current gridlock where many of the conflicts and realities of today are played out, but according to the thesis of this book could become a "commons" area for enrichment, a global intersection.

When we are going through periods of transitions in which the civil rights and freedoms of many "other" groups are being forwarded into the mainstream of society, models and theories are needed that allow these freedoms to be a part of everyday life. How far removed are most of us from those policymakers called presidents, vice chancellors, and deans of universities; chairmen and publishers of boards and organizations (often residing in metropolitan areas hundreds and thousands of miles away in corporate headquarters); politicians, popes, and other ap-

pointed and anointed ministers and holy men who issue didactical dicta from afar. People need to be able to cross rigid CRAG lines, to push across constraints and barriers, to seek and find that information most helpful to them when they most need it.

In large part, the old idea of praxis is being picked up and recycled by researchers, including those in communications and especially by those concerned with grassroots, indigenous, and women's issues. *Praxis* is simply practice, as distinguished from theory. In this tenet of Deeper Communications, practice informs theory, and theory informs practice: an interactive cycle. The current relationship of practice and theory can be seen as where the tire meets the pavement, where the round meets the linear; in contemporary theory, praxis is a friction point instead of a global intersection.

Peck (1993) has an interesting standpoint about praxis:

> To escape heresy, we must accept paradox. Thinking with integrity is paradoxical thinking. And it is not only necessary that we think with integrity, it's also necessary that we act with integrity. Behaving with integrity is "praxis," a term that was popularized initially by Marxists, and since then has been picked up by liberation theologists. Praxis refers to the integration of your practice with your belief system. As Gandhi said: "What is faith worth if it is not translated into action?" Obviously, we have to integrate our behavior with our theology in order to become people of integrity. Too often that is not done, whatever the religious belief. (p. 209)

(6) "A theory and its research will assess the traditional mass media, in their current corporate state, as demographic investigators and reporters of 'who we are.' " Concentration of ownership has brought the media under the control and direction of a few and diminished the voices of the many. Thus, studying what the media do best—sell—which is a tactical role, not a strategic, social policy orientation, could help us understand "who

we are." The traditional media through their advertisers and corporate owners have a heavy financial investment and reward structure built into counting and understanding consumers, not citizens. They do this through expensive marketing research, quite often and well. This same information could also be used to help society understand itself through surveillance of educational, social, economic, political, and even communication trends that now primarily informs those corporations and advertising firms selling products. Thus, in Tenet 6, a theory will take into account global civic responsibility, and perhaps a new theory of the press can be developed. The new theory is a *"prosumer" approach to a society's knowledge, in which democracy and capitalism can often reside comfortably together.* Efficiency and effectiveness of the mass media and their messages do not have to bring with them a damned or praised dualist image if the media would help to deliver citizen empowerment, diversity, and equality along with the entertaining "goods." The current materialistic, externally concentrated and controlled locus of power in national or multi- or transnational corporations renders the working journalists' traditional center of defined balance—objectivity or presenting all sides fully—not one of their own making. But certainly neither is the current usage of "objectivity" the creation of most of the world's population. The individual passion of journalists for fairness and justice seems to have been separated from their relational, total-field image, in Naess's description. In the premise of this chapter, mainstream journalists practice Shallower Communications more often than Deeper Communications.

Howard Ehrlich, cofounder of the Prejudice Institute (Center for the Applied Study of Prejudice and Ethnoviolence) and author of several books on the subject, had contact with about 200 reporters over a five-year period and 100-150 clips a week from nearly 500 newspapers and newsmagazines to inform him about stories of conflict and ethnoviolence. He notes that the clips make

transparent the operation of the American newspaper (Ehrlich, 1994, p. 53), and why "objectivity" has achieved mystical status in professional journalism (p. 55). His article is well worth reading as it talks about what is missing as well as what is practiced: the missing parts are "the sociological perspectives that tell you that the news of race and ethnic affairs is reported so as to validate the power relations among groups in society" (p. 59). He observes that within the context of the large corporate newspaper, reporters and columnists, including those widely syndicated, the advocacy of genuine social reform is rare. He points to a study that found that the most widely distributed columnists are clearly to the right, articulating a consistent conservative perspective—that a consistent progressive position is entirely absent. Critical aspects of enthnoviolent incidents are never reported, according to Ehrlich, including substantive psychological devastation details of victim suffering, underlying issues, public agenda legitimation, and so on (pp. 59-60).

He continues:

> The underlying effect of the newspaper reporting of prejudice, group conflict, and ethnoviolence is to reaffirm the subordinate status of women, of the "traditional" minorities, and of the political and cultural dissidents. In doing so, it fragments and distorts the news of intergroup problems and generally alienates the underrepresented, minorities, and those members of the dominant groups who are genuinely civically concerned. (p. 60)

He concludes by noting that

> given the wrong information, including no information, people can't think very constructively about the issues of race and ethnicity. Given the wrong information, people are often left with the illusions of knowledge. Those media-generated illusions do not lead to knowing. (p. 60)

Deeper Communications in this chapter's premise and this tenet's challenge are the traditional media's best chance to thrive while keeping people literally and fully alive. The visualization of this challenge is that of a circle with the media at center-spoke and the demo/cratic/graphic of the people interwoven throughout the whole wheel: The prosumers are all the people who need efficient (now usually market-driven) and egalitarian (inclusive diversity) information to live full lives. They need to speak in their own voices about their own agendas through society's main channels. In this challenge, the traditional media mind-sets can either lead, follow, or get out of the way, as one old saw would have it, and as one well-known business mogul was wont to periodically proclaim through mainstream media channels of advertising.

(7) The alternative media will be included in a theory and its research as scenario sketchers in the strategic role they assume. Although their circulation and distribution are limited because of financial, legal, and institutional restraints, these media carry news and opinions about the human condition not often seen in depth in status quo media. Their alternative (women's, minority, humanistic, realistic media) roles are seldom theoretically examined for their societal importance, and thus such information and communication roles are continually diminished, if included at all, within traditional theories and research. This social policy surveillance function of the press being attributed to the alternative media is used in a similar meaning to the Deeper Communications or Global Eco-Communications that this author understands/ advocates. Particularly in the United States, *Ms.* magazine, *Z* magazine, *Utne Reader,* the *Progressive, In These Times,* the *Advocate,* the *Nation, Media Report to Women, Sojourner: The Women's Forum, Mother Jones,* and others give us viewpoints of inclusion and diversity that we wouldn't have otherwise.

(8) A theory and its research will emphasize peace, equality, and justice as dynamic growth forces through peace education and the pro- *cesses of conflict resolution, especially mediation. Peace* can be defined as constructive communication; *equality* as the availability of and information about opportunities in a society; and *justice* as being treated fairly, including by oneself. Few people would argue against these values, although some might say these definitions of peace and equality overprivilege communication (Hackett, 1993). We have to recognize and relearn cognitive processes that see *peace* as a verb, a dynamic force as powerful as violence. Even *nonviolence* contains the word that many of us are trying to restructure in our thought processes (as Naess's use and distinction of *human* and *nonhuman* above seems to take away from the visibility, credence, and inherent value of all other living species that he so earnestly advocates). Our learned behaviors, emanating largely now from competition, sports, military, the entertainment media, the traditional news media, and imitative, repetitive acts from the family and other agencies of socialization, weigh heavily on the side of violence.

We need attitudinal, cognitive, behavioral, and linguistic adjustments that, when we think, speak, and act, come from a dynamism of peace, equality, and justice. Some of the societal adjustments—the civil rights movement, the women's movement, the older citizens' movement, the persons with disabilities movement, the gay-lesbian-bisexual-transsexual-family diversity movement, the environmental movement—gathered renewed force in U.S. society in the 1960s-1990s and have been met with increasing and often altruistic, terroristic violence.

Peace education and conflict resolution skills will help (Rush, 1993):

Proactive approaches to the twenty-first century. Important approaches include the integration of conflict resolution and peace education materials into communication curricula, research, and media content. (The Center for Teaching Peace in Washington, D.C., for example, was founded and is directed by newspaper columnist

Colman McCarthy.) *Mediation, arbitration, and negotiation skills might well be as important to professionals, professors, and students in our field as are written and oral communication skills.*

The flip side of war and violence is peace and cooperation; we just need to think, act, talk, and write that way and etch these cultural transmissions into our consciences for thousands of years as we have etched the cultural transgressions of abuse, violence, war, and war periods, often cited as historical time demarcations (e.g., "Since World War II . . ."). Along these lines of thinking, we can use terms such as "peace correspondents" instead of "war correspondents" or "global correspondents" instead of "foreign correspondents" [as most women and minorities know, to name or rename is to claim]. (p. 79)

Theory and research about communication and information in this tenet will account for and try to integrate many "other" worldviews, for ultimately we must intend, as humans, to interact in ways conducive to a healthy, ecologically, communicatively, and informationally enhanced planet.

(9) Envisionary media are possible when theory and research include both destructive and constructive roles and functions of communications. Galtung and Vincent in *Global Glasnost: Toward a New World Information and Communication Order* (1992) offer proposals for a peace-oriented news media and for environment-oriented news media (pp. 127, 174). They note that if the news media focus on violence and on events rather than processes, the primacy of newness would direct attention toward direct violence rather than structural violence:

People will be trained to conceive of the world in terms of the former rather than the latter. In order to see political or economic structural violence at work—commonly referred to as injustice, repression, or exploitation—a higher level of education would be needed to compensate for the difficulties in reporting and conceiving of structural categories undergoing slow processes of change. (p. 15)

It takes a long time to get out of the room that Elizabeth Dodson Gray wrote about in *Patriarchy as a Conceptual Trap* (1982), which, once inside, you cannot imagine a world outside of (p. 17). Miedzian (1991), in *Boys Will Be Boys: Breaking the Link Between Masculinity and Violence,* takes a whole chapter to point out why the media will not identify what I call a violent male population syndrome (VMPS) that is responsible for most of the brutality in society:

Imagine the reaction if close to 90 percent of all violent crimes were committed by women! If tabloid headlines carried stories, with some regularity, of man-hating women leaving behind them cross-country trails of murdered men; bodies of ex-wives, driven by fits of jealousy, killing their former husbands and their children; of groups of women killing each other in rival gang fights. Imagine the scorn that would be heaped on women for killing each other off at such high rates! How quickly such behavior would be perceived as an aberration, a deviation from the norm of male behavior, a "women's problem" to be dealt with urgently! Think of the fuss made about menstrual emotional stress and menopausal hot flashes as reason for keeping women out of top political decision-making situations—this in a century which has given us Hitler and Stalin and more recently Khomeini, Idi Amin, and Saddam Hussein. But when so many men commit violent crimes, or when nations led by men engage endlessly in armed conflict, there is no awareness that we are faced with a "man's problem." (pp. 11-12)

We might have a more equitable, holistic approach if we could blend traditional and alternative press, electronic and print journalism, interpersonal and mass communication disciplines, and on and on. But it's not going to work until there is a global envisioning, accounting, and hearing of all voices "in here and out there." Male authors (and that's most of them) of books advocating peace studies, conflict resolution, and feminist scholarship as a means to these ends seldom include either the feminists speaking for themselves or their scholarship.

Miedzian (1991) writes that

a norm is by definition a standard for judging; it is not itself subject to judgment. So while individual men can be found defective in light of a paradigm of manhood, they cannot be found defective by comparison with women who stand outside the paradigm and are seen as secondary and defective to begin with. (p. 12)

Since male behavior is the norm, warfare and violence are not only accepted as central, normal parts of human experience but they are transformed into heroic, exciting events. (p. 12)

Galtung and Vincent (1992) state that "a *new* journalism, a *global* journalism, a problem-conscious, socially conscious journalism, at home in the world as a whole, is still far away" (p. 23). Orr (1992), in his listing of academic disciplines with a suggested environmental focus for each, merely leaves out journalism and communications (pp. 135-136). My advocation of Deeper Communications as a working process for Global Eco-Communications as a possible theoretical framework (in progress) relies heavily on resolving the dualism, the cognitive dissonance of humans with other life-forms, with their communities, societies, and planets. The study of the intersection and interaction of capitalism and democracy currently seems paramount in this integrative paradigm with keystone reliance on peace studies and conflict resolution. In this, however, my primary focus is on mediation as a constructive communication process for it is, or can be, the *conflict resolution of choice for common people* (one in which those wanting conflict resolution are guided, not directed or forced, to make their own decisions; they don't have to be of elite status to participate in this process). It is with this tool, then, that envisionary media might finally listen to the constructive criticism of Hazel Henderson in a 1969 *Columbia Journalism Review* (also included in Henderson, 1989), who notes that the mass media have had a role to play in dysfunctional communication for they "are only a poor shadow of what they could be—not for lack of technology, but because of our imperfect understanding of their potential power" (Henderson, 1989, p. 295).

As an example, the media can become mediators instead of gladiators. At first blush, it seems to be what the media have purported to be or wanted to do in their quest for "objectivity," but for which they did not appear to have the "communicatively correct" process. As Baumann and Siebert (1993) point out in their article "The Media as Mediator," "The media mediates conflict, whether it intends to or not" (p. 28). They also urge the media to note that violence is grist for the media—to see the process, not just the outcome: "If violence is an outcome, then the media needs to learn much more about the process, or continuum, of conflict leading to such violence" (p. 29). Baumann and Siebert (1993), editor and associate editor, respectively, for the *Cross Times* magazine of Cape Town, South Africa, write that "principles of sound mediation are basically principles of sound journalism." They note some of the core principles or lessons that journalists can learn from mediation:

- see the process, not just the outcome
- move parties beyond positions
- watch your language (the volatility of language in journalists' work, how misleading or inflammatory it can be—the mediation principle of laundering your language, being more aware of culturally exclusive language; of racist, sexist, fascist, militant language: stay away from stereotypes that reinforce pain)
- how to win trust, build credibility, and challenge secrecy and authority at the same time. (pp. 29-30)

The Mediation and Conflict Training for Journalists Project (MPJ) was initiated in early 1990 by the *Cross Times* Trust:

The intent behind the MPJ is not to transform journalists into mediators per se, but to make them much more sensitive to conflict dynamics, to the impact of their work, and to the potential for managing conflict—by defining antagonists' mutual interests and getting to the genuine causes of conflicts. Through a series of workshops and publications, we challenge the myth of "objective" journalism, urging journalists to look at the ruts and biases in which they are trapped— the same stale and limited sources they use, the parties' positions they reiterate, the body counts and graphic scenarios of violence they perpetuate.

The project urges them to maximize one of their key advantages—nearly unparalleled access to parties in a conflict. They can ask antagonists in a conflict questions that parties would not ask each other. They can promote dialogue. They can widen agendas. They can help manage conflict towards just resolution, rather than merely get the story and run. (Baumann & Siebert, 1993, pp. 29-30)

Envisionary media? Mediators instead of gladiators? What we can do is envision what they might/should be. They can be at once the best of the traditional mainstream channels of communication and information (usually concentrated exclusivity and tactical efficiency), the alternative press ("other" issues with strategic, inclusive social policy), the academic journals (concentrated precision, largely reductionistic), the professional press (trend and market analysis), the technological media (unlimited, often elite connectivity), and face-to-face and small group discussion (limited, often common connectivity). They, separately and collectively, must be considered a potential link to the understanding and improvement of the condition of all species.

(10) A theory and its research will have a global civil society worldview with concern and respect for the information, communication, and integration of its citizens. Several international communication scholars (e.g., Frederick, 1993; Galtung & Vincent, 1992; Hamelink, 1991; Rush, 1992; Tehranian & Tehranian, 1992) are turning toward a new "one world concept" in the sense that ad-

vances in technology make possible global conversations and communication. This new/old concept is often called a "global civil society," a concept by John Locke (Frederick, 1993, p. 270), the English philosopher and political theorist, but without the current "global" reaches of communications and other technology. The society consists of those individuals and groups who work together beyond, outside, parallel with the operations of the state and corporate business but always well within the scope of their broad influence, as Frederick (1993, p. 270) points out. One of the often cited examples are the nongovernmental organizations (NGOs), groups around the world that share common interests and work together to solve common problems (Boulding, 1976/1992). The NGOs during the final 1985 meeting of the U.N. Decade for Women in Nairobi had their own busy and extensive agenda as formal meetings convened; a later example was the presence of the NGOs during the global environmental meeting in Brazil in 1992, known as the Earth Summit. The traditional media and large business interests exerted their tremendous capitalistic influence on the outcomes of each meeting, however, and placed the role of NGOs in a dubious position of influence (Boggs, 1994).

Increasingly important to this associative global society are new technologies, some of them most likely undeveloped or underdeveloped. Playing important current roles as the twenty-first century approaches are the VCR, fax machine, direct broadcast satellites, shortwave broadcast, and electronic mail. These technologies have the earmarks of *envisionary* media. Such envisionary media must in some way allow persons to speak for themselves in their own times in their own way about their own needs, hopes, ideas, worldviews—this scenario is exemplified in a two-generation, mother-daughter team with their intercultural work on the democratic use of video formats, recounted in the *Crossroads* book (Stuart, 1989; see Sara Stuart and Renuka Bery's chapter in this book).

A global civil society is certainly a reasonable expectation if we have the means with which to share information, and try to communicate and cooperate with all of humanity. Sooner or later, our issues are similar because we share human condition concerns. To arrive at those initial crossroads of communication and information—these global, community, bioregional intersections of Deeper Communications—we can ponder the words: "To be together without being afraid of each other—that's the beginning of the revolution" (sermon by Flood, February 28, 1993). Although most of us can hum or "guess that tune" of a couple of immensely popular commercial songs like "It's a Small, Small World" and "I'd Like to Teach the World to Sing," few of us, it seems, have made "worldview sense" of the words.

Perhaps that is because we are trapped in our own limited and, too often, violent and miserable worldview of humanity; we're not allowing ourselves to become a part of the bigger picture. We have relations yet to be recognized within a community and bioregion. I think those other living forms are awaiting a family reunion—much like young children and domesticated animals are eager to see us after work so that they might once again go outside to stand in the sky (Ackerman, 1990, p. 237) and listen to the grass grow. For a while at least, as we practice the tenets of Deeper Communications, perhaps we should call the process "atonement communication." That is, at-one(ment) communication.

Notes

1. That diversity (i.e., inclusive of all species and, particularly here, persons of all hues of color and experience) in fact exists should no longer be a point for consciousness-raising.

2. E. F. Schumacher is acknowledged by paraphrasing the subtitle from his important work, *Small Is Beautiful: Economics as if People Mattered* (1973).

3. I am indebted to Stephen Duplantier (1995) for his discussion of deep ecology and deep communication in

The Full Ecology of Communication, presented to the "Communication and Our Environment" Conference (1995). I took seriously his suggestion that "the pair 'deep: shallow' are dualistic and an unfortunate either/or choice: 'deeper' might have been a more processual term" (p. 6) and, indeed, changed references to *Deep Communication* in this text to *Deeper Communication*. A process keeps evolving and changing; how easy it is to be into the "seminal" frameworks of patriarchy, naturism, and all other forms of oppression we know by brute (w)rote. I frequently use the term *vaginal* work or framework in the sense that *vaginal* means a sheath or covering. Often, the writings of feminists and women are holistic as well as determinedly, emphatically, and pointedly inclusive. The images of the boundaries and interior design (multiplicity of voices in a cross-cultural context) of a quilt depicted in the writings of ecofeminist Karen Warren (1993, p. 331) seem to apply here.

4. Duplantier (1995) criticizes "global" as a metaphor gone out of control and instead suggests the bioregional way of community and communications (p. 5).

References

Ackerman, D. (1990). *A natural history of the senses.* New York: Random House.

Andersen, M. L., & Collins, P. H. (Eds.). (1992). *Race, class and gender: An anthology.* Belmont, CA: Wadsworth.

Baumann, M., & Siebert, H. (1993, Winter). The media as mediator. *Forum,* pp. 28-30 (Washington, DC: National Institute for Dispute Resolution).

Biehl, J. (1994). Ecology and fascism [Nationalism and the New World Order issue]. *Society and Nature: The International Journal of Political Ecology, 2*(2), 130-170.

Boggs, C. (1994). Social movements [Nationalism and the New World Order issue] *Society and Nature: The International Journal of Political Ecology, 2*(2), 91-129.

Boulding, E. (1992). *The underside of history: A view of women through time* (rev. ed.). Thousand Oaks, CA: Sage. (Original work published 1976, Boulder, CO: Westview)

Bunch, C. (1987). *Passionate politics.* New York: St. Martin's.

Dines, G., & Humez, J. M. (Eds.). (1995). *Gender, race and class in media: A text-reader.* Thousand Oaks, CA: Sage.

Duplantier, S. (1995, March). *The full ecology of communication.* Paper presented at the "Communication and Our Environment" Conference, Chattanooga, TN.

Ehrlich, H. J. (1994, June). Reporting ethnoviolence: Newspaper treatment of race and ethnic conflict. *Z magazine,* Media Watch section, pp. 53-60.

Flood, K. (1993, February 28). [Sermon, Unitarian Universalist Church, Lexington, KY; words from Ignazaio Silone. (1937). *Bread and wine*. New York: Signet Classics.]

Folbre, N. (1993, July 26). The center cannot hold. *In These Times*, pp. 14-17.

Frederick, H. (1993). *Global communication and international relations*. Belmont, CA: Wadsworth.

French, M. (1992). *The war against women*. New York: Ballantine.

Gaard, G., & Gruen, L. (1993). Ecofeminism: Toward global justice and planetary health [Feminism and Ecology issue]. *Society and Nature: The International Journal of Political Ecology, 2*(1), 1-35.

Galtung, J., & Vincent, R. (1992). *Global glasnost: Toward a new world information and communication order*. Cresskill, NJ: Hampton.

Gimbutas, M. (1989). *The language of the goddess*. New York: Harper & Row.

Gray, E. D. (1982). *Patriarchy as a conceptual trap*. Wellesley, MA: Roundtable.

Gutierrez-Villalobos, S., Hertog, J., & Rush, R. (1994, Autumn). Press support for the U.S. administration during periods of external conflict: A test of three theories. *Journalism Quarterly, 71*(3), 618-627.

Hackett, R. (1993, November). [Written communication, Department of Communication, Simon Fraser University, Burnaby, Canada.]

Hamelink, C. J. (1991). Global communication: Place for civil action. In B. Hofsten (Ed.), *Informatics in food and nutrition* (pp. 5-8). Stockholm: Royal Academy of Sciences.

Haraway, D. J. (1991). *Simian, cyborgs, and women: The reinvention of nature*. New York: Routledge Kegan Paul.

Henderson, H. (1969, Spring). Access to the media: A problem in democracy. *Columbia Journalism Review*, pp. 5-8.

Henderson, H. (1989). Eco-feminism and eco-communication: Toward the feminization of economics. In R. R. Rush & D. Allen (Eds.), *Communications at the crossroads: The gender gap connection*. Norwood, NJ: Ablex.

Henderson, H. (1991). *Paradigms in progress: Life beyond economics*. Indianapolis, IN: Knowledge Systems.

Henderson, H. (in press). Information: The world's new currency isn't scarce. In *World business academy perspectives*. San Francisco: Berrett-Koehler.

hooks, b. (1992, July-August). Out of the academy and into the streets. *Ms.,* pp. 80-82.

Huffman, K., Vernoy, M., & Vernoy, J. (1994). *Psychology in action*. New York: John Wiley.

Miedzian, M. (1991). *Boys will be boys: Breaking the link between masculinity and violence*. New York: Doubleday.

Naess, A. (1973). The shallow and the deep, long-range ecology movement: A summary. *Inquiry, 16*(1), 95-100 (Blindern, Oslo, Norway: Universitetforlaget, Norwegian Research Council for Science and the Humanities).

Naess, A. (1992, September-December). Deep ecology and ultimate premises [Philosophy of Ecology issue]. *Society and Nature: The International Journal of Political Ecology, 1*(2).

Orr, D. W. (1992). *Ecological literacy: Education and the transition to a postmodern world*. Albany: State University of New York Press.

Peck, M. S. (1993). *Further along the road less traveled*. New York: Simon & Schuster.

Rush, R. (1989a). Communications at the crossroads: The gender gap connection. In R. R. Rush & D. Allen (Eds.), *Communications at the crossroads: The gender gap connection*. Norwood, NJ: Ablex.

Rush, R. (1989b, May). *Global eco-communications: Assessing the communication and information environment*. Paper presented to the International Communication Association, San Francisco.

Rush, R. (1992, August). *Global eco-communications: Grounding and refinding the concepts*. Paper presented to the International Association for Mass Communication Research, Guarujá, Brazil.

Rush, R. (1993). Being all that we can be: Harassment, barriers prevent progress. *Journalism Educator, 48*(1), 71-79.

Rush, R. R., & Allen, D. (Eds.). (1989). *Communications at the crossroads: The gender gap connection*. Norwood, NJ: Ablex.

Rush, R., Buck, E., & Ogan, C. (1982, July-September). Women and the communications revolution: Can we get there from here? *Chasqui* (Quito, Ecuador: Centro Internacional de Estudios Superiores de la Comunicacion para America Latin [CIESCPAL]).

Schumacher, E. F. (1973). *Small is beautiful: Economics as if people mattered*. New York: Harper & Row.

Spender, D. (Ed.). (1983). *Feminist theorists: Three centuries of key women thinkers*. New York: Pantheon.

Stuart, M. (1989). Social change through human exchange: Listening moves people more than telling. In R. R. Rush & D. Allen (Eds.), *Communications at the crossroads: The gender gap connection*. Norwood, NJ: Ablex.

Tehranian, K., & Tehranian, M. (1992). *Restructuring for world peace: On the threshold of the twenty-first century*. Cresskill, NJ: Hampton.

Warren, K. J. (1993). The power and the promise of ecological feminism. In M. E. Zimmerman et al. (Eds.), *Environmental philosophy: From animal rights to radical ecology*. Englewood Cliffs, NJ: Prentice Hall.

Webster's new world dictionary. (1988). (3rd College ed.). New York: Simon & Schuster.

Wilkins, J. S. (1994). *The public involvement challenge and comparative risk*. Unpublished master's thesis, Antioch New England Graduate School, Keene, New Hampshire.

2

Transforming Faith in the First Amendment

Christy C. Bulkeley

The 10 tenets of deeper communication described by Ramona Rush in Chapter 1 of this book parallel and reinforce the ideal of inclusive, egalitarian community seen in Christianity's governing scriptures by feminists and other liberation theologians. Traditional practitioners of the press and of religion today studiously avoid and sometimes pointedly disown each other. But connections extend from both disciplines into imperatives for vitality and validity of democracy. Thus the press and religion, considered from the perspectives of deeper communications and liberation theology, have more in common than their cohabitation of the First Amendment to the U.S. Constitution. Whatever the conscious reasoning of those who joined them in the Bill of Rights and whatever the reasoning of those who have torn them asunder in modern times, the core values they share, if joined with faith in the principles they preach, offer the prospect of

transforming society. The mutual mission becomes clear when the tenets of Rush's deeper communications are considered with principles of feminist theology.

Basics

The Bible grounds Christianity, its Old Testament anchored in the Hebrew Scriptures; the New in stories and letters witnessing to the life of Jesus of Nazareth and of his early followers. The Bible's stories survived orally for generations, even centuries, in hierarchical and patriarchal culture. Over more centuries, they were written down, collected, combined, and, finally, adopted in the form we have today. The text has been used as a guide and defense of hierarchy and patriarchy for centuries. But it works that way only when read and interpreted selectively and narrowly. Read and heard by "the others,"

19

the Bible suggests inclusive egalitarian democracy as the ideal. Given its time—and ours—it thus calls for radical transformation of society. The imperative survived, even given the hierarchical nature of the church organization that evolved to claim custody over (sometimes even captivity of) the Bible and of most academic institutions where biblical scholarship is done. That survival tells us how strong the original impulse to egalitarian society must have been at the times and places its stories originated.

The discussion in this chapter refers to the work of three women who are leading Anglo, Christian feminists (see Johnson, 1992; Schneiders, 1991; and Schussler Fiorenza, 1992). Their books show the practice of Rush's tenets: Each author acknowledges some privilege associated with her position in dominant society (and each now in a major university), but each also is marginalized more than enough to relate at some points to lives and experiences of women (and men) with no privilege or standing in the dominant culture. Each feminist also draws on work of feminists from other cultural locations, citing culture-based differences in their situations and thinking as appropriate. Their example shows inclusion and diversity as enriching assets rather than the threats dominant culture believes them to be. Similarly, each reviews the evolution of related theological traditions and contexts, effectively providing thorough documentation and references for readers who want to go beyond points and conclusions cited here.

My recent three-year immersion in graduate study of theology and religion in a Protestant/Christian seminary informs this project. Most faculty members are liberation theologians, whatever their specialty; the students, a diverse and inclusive group of many cultures from throughout the world, of many ages, various denominations and life experiences. Those of my classmates who tend to read the Bible literally suffered, they said, from loss of voice and credibility. Some transferred to complete their education elsewhere; some registered occasional protests; some remained silent.

My background, like that of the theologians cited, combines privilege with marginalization. I grew up in a Protestant-dominated midwest city of 3,500. My first job was on that community's weekly newspaper in the 1950s (founded and owned by women, Gene Cunningham and Mary Lou Stover, and run by them at that time). My journalism education (in the formative years of television, in the midst of manual typewriters, carbon paper, and hot type) added to my belief that journalism was part of the process of democracy, not an end in itself. The combination sent me into the world thinking that things worked approximately the way they would if the principles Rush describes were in effect—as if journalism (and the society it reports, reflects, and serves) were open to and respectful of all voices and situations in society. Seen that way, utility to the readers and other people was a necessary part of stories. Questions asked the powers-that-be were to relate directly to the immediate context of the public; content was to help give meaning to everyone's day. Possible impact and consequences of the information on all people and the institutions within reach of the particular medium were part of the routine considerations. The "journalist's creed" by Walter Williams, first dean of the first school of journalism, was (and is) clear about those points, as it is clear that advertising is within the "public trust," not apart and subject to some other standards (Rucker, 1964, opposite p. 31).

I learned soon that beyond the little town and my journalism school, controlling authorities divide most facets of life into separate, unconnected parts and divide people into the few who are seen and heard, and the many unheard and mostly invisible pawns. Patriarchy and hierarchy dominate the modern news business just as they've dominated Western systems of government, religion, business/commerce, and so forth from some prehistoric time. For journalists, the reasons include the fact that traditional media are businesses operating within the dominant culture; but, additionally, journalists (like most people in the Western world) are (carefully) taught to think, respond, and act as if hierarchy and patriarchy were natural, even inborn.

History recorded by the dominant authorities shows too that the Bible, teaching attributed to it, and institutions derived from it have figured into the evolution of the hierarchical and paternalistic culture's dominance of the Western world and its relationships with other societies on the globe. So it's easy to dismiss Christianity as a source of affirmation of egalitarian, democratic community life. Which really came first is immaterial for this discussion; the spiritual wasn't considered separate and distinct until relatively modern times. Christian liberationists acknowledge the contradiction between scripture as defense for hierarchy and as inspiration for radical transformation away from hierarchy. Their discussions dealing with the contradiction are beyond the scope of this chapter.

At its most basic, the work of theology is "reflecting on God and all things in light of God" (Johnson, 1992, p. 5). *Liberation theologies,* in this context, encompass work coming from a variety of "the others"—people outside the dominant authorities of Christianity—although some theologians use the term only for theologies growing out of Third World experience. Christianity is those religions confessing Jesus as the Christ, the son of God, but also a man who lived in a particular place and a particular time to share with humanity the abiding interest of God in the well-being of the creation.

The Bible, the primary text of Christianity, witnesses in words to the various ways people believe they have experienced revelations of God, and God's creation. Some Christians generally regard the Bible as a living document offering new and different insights and inspiration to those who read or hear its words in other times and places. Others consider the Bible as the precise, unchanging/unchangeable words of God to be read and understood literally.

As Christian liberation theologies re(dis)-cover the scripture's insistence on a radically

egalitarian society, the strong patriarchal/hierarchical elements of the text can't be ignored, but the survival of material supporting a radically different kind of society, if modern experience is any indication, strengthens the significance of that call. The evidence becomes apparent when the Bible is read/heard from the stance Rush describes as deeper communications—with recognition of the source's context and authentic voice, interaction and connectedness, multiple perspectives (rather than dualistic), and so forth.

The Conversation

Rush's first tenet establishes an ecological base for communications theory and research, requiring respect for all the Earth's species with mutual sharing of information necessary for ongoing adaptation and well-being of all (human and the environment). The sources and recipients of communication thus are inclusive and diverse. Even though powers-that-be claim a scriptural basis for their (ab)use of whatever exists, including humans who differ from themselves, clues abound in the Old Testament especially that God claims responsibility for all of creation and expects humans to exercise responsible stewardship over all, and not destructive dominance.

Liberation theologians, including specialists in creation and environmental theology, have recovered much of that holistic aspect of the Christian scripture. (Some other religions—the most familiar probably that of Native Americans—never lost the connections or the respect due the creation.) For instance, a close reading of the Exodus story shows that the God who directs the action claims involvement with all of creation and over all the Earth. The holistic theology stands out in the details—not in visions of Moses/Charleton Heston standing on a mountainside or the cast of thousands moving across the desert.

Rush cites next the need to go beyond dualistic thinking and action. Dominant Christian practice reads the scripture as if each story, each episode, each action were about opposites, about either-or, winning and losing, one-up/one-down, bigger/more as the measures of success. Such readings and resulting interpretations have helped hide the radical meaning behind/before the text and even within it. The hierarchical techniques truncate processes, compartmentalize, stereotype, devalue, and denigrate difference. Those techniques affected the text in its formative generations and interpretation of the text after it was completed. Thus "the text" has been used to build the earthly stature and authority of relatively few (mostly men and mostly Anglo—even though few of any Caucasians were among the many peoples in the eastern Mediterranean landscape at the time of the Christ event).

But such use also has sapped the scripture and its derivative organization—the church in many forms—of relevance and vitality in the same way traditional communications, news, and information media lose relevance when they function with severe limits on what's legitimate, appropriate, worthy of respect and recognition. If those institutions don't describe or relate compellingly to the reality people live, people invest their time, their energy, their passion elsewhere. Or they give up and submit to the opiates of soap operas and other seemingly nonthreatening time fillers. The powers-that-be apparently see such opiates as relatively harmless vehicles to surround or draw pawns to their advertising or as ways to reinforce their limiting view of reality. Yet some television programming manages to present the radical messages of diversity as enriching, change as empowering, and other liberating ideas.

Such unintended consequences help illustrate the modern origins of liberation theologies. The umbrella term originated from the experience of Christian base communities among peasants of Latin America. As they read/heard the scriptures, they identified with the oppressed peoples liberated by God or God's action. They recognized their story, for instance, in the story of the Exodus. The peasants identified with the Hebrew slaves freed from Pharaoh's control and with the slaves' struggle in the wilderness to find new ways to be community after generations of domination by an oppressive hierarchy. That's a common connection, seen among religious refugees from Europe in the Reformation, among African American slaves in the United States before the Civil War, and in myriad other circumstances. But traditional readings carry the slaves/their descendants forward ultimately into control of their own hierarchies/patriarchies and consider that to be the successful end of the story and its lessons. That kind of trajectory repeats, for instance, in development of the Roman Catholic Church in postbiblical times. From only modest, metaphorical hints in the New Testament, the Catholic Church has become a massive, patriarchal bureaucracy with layer on layer of tradition reinforcing it.

Liberation theologians see a different trajectory. It starts in biblical texts describing how the Hebrews became enslaved by the Egyptians and reads through the development of oppressive, hierarchical patriarchies by descendants of the former slaves. Time and again, the systems and rulers were subject to prophetic criticism and, ultimately, were destroyed because they abused people and other resources. They lost the land; the people were scattered. That destruction parallels the realization that the Exodus represents political action—removal of the slaves needed to maintain the Pharaoh's economic system. To villagers in contemporary Latin America, the story says that those who are oppressed can respond politically, as the Hebrew slaves did, whether the sinning rulers are descended from the Pharaohs or are descended from the formerly oppressed. In the modern Latin American context, then, abusive rulers (sometimes including those of the church) are the descendants of Pharaoh, not of the Hebrew slaves at the point when they achieved freedom. Action, possibly including revolution, seems an appropriate response to the sins of the powers-that-be.

Less dramatic but a current reality reflecting limited or narrow reading of the text is the work of the so-called Christian Coalition, a political organization claiming a biblical basis for policies it promotes, many limiting access to information and services of this democracy and narrowly defining the potential of some people. Schussler Fiorenza cites Margaret Atwood's *The Handmaid's Tale* as a visionary modern projection of the same kind of limited interpretation (Schussler Fiorenza, 1992, pp. 2-4). Atwood's book (1987) carries Rush's next point forward as well.

Dominant powers use sexuality and spirituality as limits and controls—usually irrelevant—as Rush describes in her third tenet. Both should be considered appropriately and constructively. They are of the essence of an individual's identity. Feminist theologians, as part of reclaiming the scripture as liberating text, show ways language has been used to read and interpret into scripture sex-based distinctions that weren't always present (Schussler Fiorenza, 1992, pp. 24-26, 39-52, among others). The resulting limits on the many then became—and in some religions and Christian denominations remain—institutionalized in religious practices, inappropriately and unjust(ifiab)ly validating dominance and oppression. When unjustified use of the masculine is removed, many inappropriate limits or controls disappear or are reneutralized. Divine-sanctioned being, voice, and agency are established in or for those who had been left out, marginalized, or subjugated. (Some feminists are investing enormous energy in liturgical reform beyond questions of written and spoken language, working with visual images, dance, song, and other nontraditional forms to restore wholeness and respect for many ways of praying, praising, and worshipping.)

Spirituality—how individuals regard themselves and their relationship to the ultimate good, whether that ultimate good is something seen, measured, and tangible on Earth or something other—affects their relationships with other people and the rest of the creation. A person whose ultimate good is money or measured by money will relate to all of the creation in ways quite different than the ways of a person whose ultimate good is an invisible divine known only in part but believed to care about the wellness of the whole creation.

Some people today (as always) do regard their spiritual life as something personal and private, somehow separate from the rest of their lives—perhaps mystical, perhaps a one-to-one relationship with something/one representing the ultimate good (Schussler Fiorenza, 1992, p. 44). The comprehensive understanding Rush implies is the more nearly standard theological meaning (Richardson & Bowden, 1983, pp. 549-550). Regardless, when communications theory doesn't acknowledge the spiritual, it assumes that we all are motivated by the here-and-now, visible-and-measurable. Then it can't ask the right questions, let alone interpret effectively or accurately the information its questions generate. Similarly, ignoring the spiritual ignores a variety of worldviews and stances, misses vital connections, and fails to provide compelling meaning for possible readers.

Holistic communications theory and research also bring into consideration possibilities that are healing and liberatory, as Rush describes for her fourth tenet. Healing may have to do with overcoming bodily, physical ailments or with an individual's (or group's) overcoming dis-ease or dysfunction with its part of the world reality. The relatively new discipline of pastoral counseling, whether by pastors or counselors basing their work in Christian theology, works to restore individuals' wholeness and ability to return to the world with agency for spreading such wholeness (Clinebell, 1984, chap. 2). In Christian theology, people who understand and accept the Divine's offer of unconditional love realize their own completeness and freedom to be regardless of the state of their body and situation in worldly terms. If they are led to think that the healing process stops when

they are made whole, as the traditional trun-
cation of biblical text often suggests, critique
of text as opiate is fulfilled. For instance,
traditionalists lose or obscure the connections by treating most New Testament healing stories as self-contained miracle stories.
Study and worship aids that split the text by
episodes usually stop at the point of the healing. Paragraphs or verses and subheads assigned to the text in modern times contribute
to the "authority" of these limits. Yet feminists show through structural or literary analysis that healings are often, in fact, part of a
process of restoring the person to community, to full standing and agency among peers
or in society (Schneiders, 1991, chap. 7).
Seldom are the healings (physical and spiritual) simply a matter of adding to the creden-
tials or credibility of the one who appears to
be the instrument of healing.

The realistic frameworks and the valid possibility of social action research Rush discusses as the fifth tenet are as necessary for
theology or theological ideals to become part
of reality as they are for communications
theory and research to be of value beyond the
individuals directly involved. Indeed, as already noted, human reality and experience
that differ from the versions the establishment
would have us believe, inform and even drive
much liberation theology. Christian scriptures as read/heard by feminists show correction of injustice as a primary response to
realization of God's saving grace. The realization of God's unconditional love and offer
of life after death (however that happens)
compels individuals to join the work of the
Creator, to try to move life where they live it
toward the Creator's expectations so that others might benefit too.

Just as Rush sees a valid and constructive
role for, rather than elimination of, traditional mass media in deeper communications
research and theory, so liberation theologians
work to build on, not displace, traditional
practices of religion. By rejecting dualism as
dominant in society (Rush's second tenet),
deeper communications and liberation the-

ologies reject the notion that traditional communications and religions must lose if other
practices are to be accepted. Applying their
own standards, deeper communications and
liberation theologies accept and identify possible ongoing roles for what has been traditional and dominant practice. A religious
congregation need not give up ancient chants
or church music composed by northern European white men in order to use music created
by African American slaves or in the barrios.
Personal and private use of religious text and
belief need not be abandoned to achieve liberating action.

And similar to the way Rush describes the
developmental potential alternative media offer, so, too, the liberation theologies. First,
the Old Testament prophets, whose words
Christians most often hear as forecasting the
coming of a messiah, in context were criticizing the dominant authorities for abuse of
people and resources. Second, just as liberation theologies came from alternative practice, so they encourage believers to adopt
new ways of learning from and sharing with
each other. Some Roman Catholics and their
congregations and some Protestant denominations (including those called "conservative" in current use) are adapting the concept
of small groups to form communities or "families" within the larger congregations. They're
one way to achieve scale in which individuals can relate to and look out for each other,
to have scripture-based discussions that move
beyond the coffee-hour superficial into depth
not possible in congregation worship and
sermons. At their best, the groups radiate
new life and energy back into the larger
church community and into the whole reality
of participants.

Rush links peace, equality, and justice as
dynamic growth forces. Her eighth tenet especially cites peace education and conflict
resolution processes, especially mediation,
to help bring this about. But, by implication,
the other tenets of deeper communications
contribute as well. First, the practice of deeper
communications and of liberation theology

both eliminate "otherness," abuse of others, winning at the expense of others, and excess accumulation of property (land and material things) as values to be lauded—and defended. Individual violence, group violence, and even war then become remote or deplored rather than the primary accepted actions and reactions. Although the Old Testament scripture appears to condone violence (one of the contradictions liberation theologians continue to grapple with but quite probably a result of forces during centuries of text formation), the New Testament abounds in illustrations of peaceful resolution of differences.

Second, as the various tenets combine to help affirm alternate ways of being, they empower and energize individuals and groups who benefit. For instance, ecology, healing, and liberation connect with such energy that Johnson (1992) writes lyrically of Spirit-Sophia's overcoming "human imbecility," "destructive ill will," and sin (pp. 135-139). She sees signs of transforming energy and potential benefits in the spring renewal of Earth, in renewal of social and political structures so that they can combat social injustice. Johnson credits Jewish scripture with identifying the Spirit as the shaper and source of gifts for building community (p. 139), an understanding carried into Christianity as an imperative of life intended by the creator.

Spirit, then, signifies the presence of the creator with the creation and its creatures, the breath of life, the transforming energy that overcomes barriers created by human beings and that flows from the renewal and reuniting as the barriers and divisions fall. As Rush notes, peace is more than just the absence of violence, the passive safety in an enclave or other place out of harm's way. Feminist theology shows peace as a circumstance both growing from the end or reduction of sin and evil and as a source of the energy that propels people and communities toward their intended potential—in Christianity, God's realm on Earth or however close to that potential (as we understand it) life on Earth can come.

Envisionary media may emerge in communications, perhaps as a result of deeper communications theory, research, and action, Rush says. Envisionary content in traditional media is a strong possibility too, given what many see as the traditional media's failure so far to make content gains in the quantum leaps possible because of the freeing impact of new technology and new learning.

Likewise, Christianity may evolve in ways that only the most imaginative can envision or sense emerging from the new voices joining the God talk, the ideas and experiences of the whole/holy they bring. Church in the sense of a steepled building however plain or grand may, one day, be obsolete (not all of the world's religions tie their participants to structures). But traditionalists, some not particularly concerned about dropping numbers of members and financial support, consider as threats those who are simply changing to auditorium-style seating or drive-in/sit-in-the-car worship, singing hymns by watching the bouncing ball mark the words, and hearing members of the congregation describe their encounters with the Spirit. And, as this world goes, those are practices of thriving congregations called "conservative" in current religious nomenclature.

Third, as illustrated by the Johnson citation above, liberation theologians recognize systems and institutions created by humans as sources of sin, destruction, abuse, and violence against individuals, society, and the environment. Deeper communication holds open that possibility, enhancing the prospects for correction.

Together, all of these tenets make more likely the global civil society Rush describes as a "new/old concept." That worldview is not unlike what first journalism dean Walter Williams described in his journalist's creed: a journalism "profoundly patriotic *while sincerely promoting international good will and cementing world-comradeship* . . . a journalism of humanity" (Rucker, 1964, opposite p. 31, italics added). Christianity, its largest organization based in a palatial edifice/compound in Rome, literally manned in layers and layers at the top, was born at the trading crossroads of the eastern hemisphere, the meeting ground of Asia, Africa, and southern Europe. The stories talk literally of birth, God personified as Jesus, born of woman Mary; Jesus, called the Word of God made flesh, delivered by a woman. The person Jesus hung out with the poor, the outcasts, the marginalized women and men of the time. He sought out the despised for companionship, sharing meals with many. He openly ignored, even defied, socioreligious convention as he wandered the countryside with his followers. He baited officials and, when questioned, bested them or left them openly puzzled—a move hierarchicals consider insubordinate and insulting today. Jesus taught and encouraged women as well as men. He engaged women as well as men in his work. That work focused on liberating the poor, the captives, the blind, the oppressed, widows, and others from the situations that diminish them. Spelled out in what scripture describes as his first scripture reading and theological discussion in the synagogue, that statement of mission was met with the threat of violence. Jesus also frequently failed to teach or convince some of his closest followers of his role and expectations. In some versions of the story, the men named as closest to him were the last to learn. Indeed, most abandoned him before he was put to death in a political execution. Some of the women stayed. In some versions, women were the first to encounter the risen Christ and were asked by him to carry the word to the others. The story ends as they leave the encounter. ("See?" some men say. "The women couldn't be trusted to do the job." But if not, how did we get the story of the encounter? The end isn't the end.)

Conclusions

So why is all of this important for any communicators, let alone feminist communicators? Can't it be just coincidence or ordi-nary (feminist) commonsense prediction that women (and some men) intellectuals and academics would arrive at the same or similar propositions when they examined the outside of age-old systems dealing with human reality, truth, and potential? Maybe. But I think not.

Consider: Belief in a Divinity confessed by theologians isn't necessary to seek partnerships with them. Rather, respect for belief is the criteria (as it is with other aspects of inclusive and diverse community).

Theology, with ancient texts as the starting point, is consciously multidisciplinary, interdisciplinary. History, sociology, political science, anthropology (in many forms), archaeology, psychology, the various disciplines of learning, knowing, and literature all engage theologians at critical thought levels. That offers a running head start to communications theorists and practitioners who realize the need to reach beyond their own discipline and to do it in more than a superficial (next deadline) way—the need for deeper communications rather than shallow.

Feminist (and liberation) theologies have learned long since to listen to and hear what the interested nonexperts—the people—are saying and thinking. Feminist communicators, most still surrounded by colleagues who openly sneer at research involving the public's interest (never mind actual engagement with interested nonexpert people!), will discover theologians ready and willing to share the skills of engagement.

Feminist theologians generally take great care to explain their own worldview and stance, to document sources of ideas and inspiration, to show thought patterns used to transfer information from one discipline to another, to specify what's known from nontraditional evidence and what's known from fact acceptable to the dominant establishments. Given the relative wealth of published work in theology and religion, their work offers both practical models and the ability to follow any step in more depth.

Pragmatic or applied theology and religion—bringing the text alive for the folks in the pews and helping them make use of it all week long—connects theory and research in many ways still unfamiliar or only little practiced in communications. This is another opportunity to move ahead quickly.

Similarly, some of the establishments of theology and religion and their publics rush to apply new technologies. Those whose theology and resulting social values would be considered conservative, in fact, were among the earliest to use television teleconferencing for training and other information sharing, to develop broadcast and cable networks to communicate with their own adherents and other people too, to develop computer and compact disc-based Bible study and study aids, and to provide access to publications in online services for the general public.

Thus the partnership of press and religion, implicit in their sharing of First Amendment protections, already is being used by some who would transform society by severely limiting what's possible. Indeed, these partnerships and their impact on traditional media and political systems show what can be done by making selective and narrow breaches in the barriers dominant society continues to defend. Envision the transformative potential of partnerships built on faith in and respect for all peoples and the rest of creation.

This era of unprecedented social change driven by technology and human curiosity leaves us without handed-down stories and patterns that provide step-by-step guides for life. Rather, we go forward seeking ways to adapt and apply the best of what is and to avoid the worst. If we can learn from each other rather than letting dominant practices of separation keep us apart, we can hasten the transformation and liberation of communications and theology for the good of the whole creation. For 40 years (a biblical number symbolizing two generations), the Hebrew slaves lived in the wilderness trying to work out new ways of being a people. Our situation is not unlike theirs: Wherever we are, it probably is Egypt. The way out and into the promised land is through a wilderness we can traverse best if we do it together (Walzer, 1985, p. 149).

References

Atwood, M. (1987). *The handmaid's tale*. New York: Ballantine.

Clinebell, H. (1984). *Basic types of pastoral care and counseling: Resources for the ministry of healing and growth* (rev., enlarged ed.). Nashville, TN: Abingdon.

Johnson, E. A. (1992). *She who is: The mystery of god in feminist theological discourse*. New York: Crossroads.

Richardson, A., & Bowden, J. (Eds.). (1983). *The Westminster dictionary of Christian theology*. Philadelphia: Westminster.

Rucker, F. W. (1964). *Walter Williams*. Columbia, MO: Missourian Publishing Association.

Schneiders, S. M. (1991). *The revelatory text: Interpreting the new testament as sacred scripture*. New York: HarperSanFrancisco.

Schussler Fiorenza, E. (1992). *But she said: Feminist practices of biblical interpretation*. Boston: Beacon.

Walzer, M. (1985). *Exodus and revolution*. New York: Basic Books.

3

Communication, Socialization, and Domination
The Replication of Violence and the Partnership Alternative

Riane Eisler

Why in face of warnings from scientists that the "conquest of nature" use of modern technology is not sustainable—and even despite growing consciousness that nuclear and chemical warfare makes violence to resolve conflict potentially suicidal—are these dysfunctional patterns so resistant to change? Why despite the rise in violent crime and terrorism—and even despite many studies showing that television and other mass media are powerful socialization tools—do the mass media still present violence as not only manly, but fun? And why, when the most basic human impulse is to avoid pain and instead seek pleasure, does so much of what is presented as news on the media focus on pain, either through natural disasters or through human agency?

This chapter looks at these questions through the prism of cultural transformation theory (see, e.g., Eisler, 1987a, 1987b, 1993a, 1993b, 1994, 1995), which proposes that underlying the great diversity of human societies are two basic possibilities for social and ideological organization. The dominator model of rigid hierarchies of domination—beginning with the ranking of half of humanity over the other half—is characterized by the interactive configuration of rigid male dominance, political, economic, and religious control by a small

---

AUTHOR'S NOTE: Portions of this chapter are adapted from *Sacred Pleasure: Sex, Myth, and the Politics of the Body* (San Francisco: HarperSanFrancisco, 1995).

male elite, and a high degree of institutional-ized violence, ranging from child and wife beating to chronic warfare. The partnership model is characterized by a very different core configuration of mutually reinforcing elements. First is an equal valuing of the female and male halves of humanity, which serves as a prototype for the valuing of diversity rather than its equation with superiority or inferiority. Sec-ond is a generally equitable and democratic po-litical, economic, and familial structure. Third, because the infliction or threat of pain is not required to maintain institutions that rank man over woman, race over race, tribe over tribe, and nation over nation, there is a much lower degree of violence.

Cultural transformation theory also pro-poses that underlying the many currents and crosscurrents of our time is the struggle be-tween a powerful movement toward a more just and peaceful society orienting primarily to a partnership model, countered by massive dominator systems' resistance and regression.

In the pages that follow I will place the contemporary struggle over the control and content of our mass media in the context of this larger struggle. I will begin with the changes in consciousness that in the last 300 years have gone along with cumulating chal-lenges to entrenched traditions of domina-tion. I will then examine how the mass media have been co-opted to counter these chal-lenges through a number of means, including their intensive focus on the infliction and/or suffering of pain. I will detail how the main-tenance of hierarchies of domination is inex-tricably connected with the maintenance of gender stereotypes appropriate for a domina-tor social and ideological organization and how the mass media have perpetuated and reinforced these stereotypes. I will then look at the grassroots struggle against violence and domination. And I will close with some issues that need to be addressed if we are to accelerate the shift to a partnership social and ideological organization and prevent recur-ring dominator regressions.

The Modern Revolution in Consciousness and the Subversion of the Mass Media

Over the last 300 years, there have been major changes in consciousness: in how peo-ple see themselves, their relationships, and the world. Although these changes began in the West as far back as the Renaissance and the end of the Middle Ages, they were vastly accelerated during the later stages of the In-dustrial Revolution, which brought massive technological and economic changes that in turn forced major changes not only in work habits but in habits of thinking and living. These changes in turn required much social and economic restructuring as well as a re-evaluation of many long-established "truths." In the process, many things that had been thought inevitable—such as slavery, the di-vine right of kings to rule, and the idea that women's subservience to men is God's will—began to be reexamined and rejected.[1]

In the seventeenth century, the leading philosopher of political democracy, John Locke, proposed that freely chosen representative governments based on responsibility and trust replace autocratic monarchs who for millen-nia had ruled through force and fear.[2] In the next century, the leading philosopher of capi-talism, Adam Smith, offered the "invisible hand" of the free marketplace as a way to end top-down economic control. In the following century, the framers of scientific socialism, Karl Marx and Friedrich Engels, wrote of a time when the state itself might wither away and all power would be in the hands of the people. During that same century, Frederick Douglass, Sojourner Truth, and other leaders in the struggle against racism challenged the idea that "superior" races should dominate, exploit, and even enslave "inferior" races. Also in the nineteenth century, Elizabeth Cady Stanton, Hedwig Dohm, Matilda Joslyn Gage, Emmeline Pankhurst, and other leading phi-losophers of modern feminism wrote of a society where the female and male halves of humanity would no longer be forced into dominator-dominated rankings.[3]

The nineteenth-century abolitionist and pacifist movements and the twentieth-century anticolonialist, civil rights, peace, economic justice, and women's movements shared this cumulating goal of building systems of relations free of painful domination and exploitation. And so also have the far less publicized eighteenth-, nineteenth-, and twentieth-century movements toward a more egalitarian and companionate form of marriage, as well as the movement during this same time—often against vehement secular and religious opposition—to leave behind long-standing traditions of painful punishment of children.

In other words, at the same time that people began to awake to the brutality and injustice of political, economic, and racial rankings backed by force and fear in the so-called public sphere, there was also, albeit more slowly, a gradual awakening to the brutality and injustice of rankings backed by fear and force in the private sphere of parent-child and man-woman relations.[4]

The analytical tools provided by cultural transformation theory make it possible to see these developments in an even larger context. What we then see is that the underlying struggle in modern history has not been between religion and secularism or capitalism and communism, but between a powerful partnership resurgence and strong dominator resistance from entrenched institutions—including the media of communication.

I say "resurgence" because there is a growing body of archaeological data showing that the institutionalization of force-backed rankings of domination—beginning with the ranking of the male half of humanity over the female half—was a relatively late development in the history of civilization.[5] And I say "strong dominator resistance" because, as the works of systems' theorists such as the biologists Humberto Maturana and Vilmos Csanyi (Csanyi, 1989; Maturana & Varela, 1987) demonstrate, like other living systems, social systems seek to maintain themselves.

And this they do not only by replicating the kinds of families, religions, economics, and politics required for their maintenance, but also by replicating the kinds of ideas and images that present a particular type of social system as not only desirable but inevitable.

In our time, the technological, social, and economic changes that mark the onset of the so-called postindustrial age are further destabilizing what were once thought to be firmly established beliefs and institutions, thereby opening the door for even further changes in consciousness—as evidenced by the worldwide growth of grassroots organizations to change entrenched patterns of violence. But at the same time, the powerful electronic technologies of communication have also ever more intensively replicated the message that cruelty, abuse, exploitation, domination, and violence are only normal, and even "entertaining."

Indeed, so powerful has this message been that it has for many people obscured something we see by simple observation: that whether in the public sphere of our schools, workplaces, and governments or in the private sphere of our sexual, family, and other intimate relations, human relations can be structured democratically or tyrannically, peacefully or violently, with respect for human rights, or in ways that chronically abuse, exploit, degrade, and terrorize others. And one of the most effective means of obscuring this obvious fact has been the constant replication of gender stereotypes in which "real" masculinity is equated with "heroic" violence and domination.

There are economic reasons behind some of the violent programming that increasingly permeates the world's airwaves. It is cheaper to produce violent formula shows, and such shows are more easily exported, as they require little translation. But contrary to what we are often told, violent programming is not what most people in the viewing audiences want. The most highly rated programs are usually not violent (Gerbner, 1995). Not only that, polls show that a majority of Americans feel "personally bothered" by violence and, according to a 1993 Times Mirror poll, 80%

believe entertainment violence is harmful to society (Gerbner, 1995).

From a logical standpoint, the use of television—a medium that is rapidly replacing parents and schools as a primary socialization agent—to present brutality as normal, manly, and fun makes no sense. After all, those who decide what will or will not be included as entertainment and news, for their own sake and the sake of their children, must also want a safer, saner, fairer, or (as a speechmaker for George Bush put it) kinder and gentler world. Yet, as epidemiologist Brandon Centerwall's (1992) work shows, television has in country after country where it was introduced quite literally produced epidemics of violence. For example, in both the United States and Canada, violent crimes increased almost 100% within a generation after television was introduced, whereas during some of these same years in South Africa, violent crime rates actually dropped—only to also more than double after the introduction of television in 1975 (Centerwall, 1992). There are also hundreds of studies confirming the obvious: that television programming does not affect only buying behaviors (the explicit goal of the advertisers who fund it) but all kinds of behaviors—including whether children (particularly boys, because most violence modeled on television is by males) are more aggressive (which, not surprising, they then are; Williams, 1986) and whether adults behave in hurtful or helpful ways (as shown by a research project directed by social psychologist David Loye during the 1970s at the UCLA School of Medicine; Loye, Gorney, & Steele, 1977).

So the growing public perception that television violence is extremely harmful, teaching children (and adults) not only violence but insensitivity as a way of life, is extremely important. But what is not yet generally discussed—and urgently needs to be—is how the way our world is portrayed on television serves to maintain entrenched power imbalances, and how this fits into a long history of the use of public displays of violence to maintain rankings of domination that are ultimately backed up by fear and force: rankings in which stereotypical definitions of "masculine" and "feminine" roles and relations play a major part.

The Public Exhibition of the Power to Inflict Pain

In rigid dominator societies, violence starts very early, with the confluence of caring and coercive touch in a child rearing where obedience to authority is a condition for parental love (Eisler, 1995). It continues through the erotization of domination and violence that is characteristic of the social construction of sexual relations in such societies (Eisler, 1995). And until modern times in the West, and in many places still today, it also has been through the use and/or threat of violence that despotic rulers have maintained control over their "subjects."

In the West, this control was often ritually dramatized—as it still is in some places today—through public exhibitions of the most brutal infliction of pain, not only to dissidents but to members of socially disempowered groups, such as the women labeled "witches" publicly executed as late as 300 years ago in Europe and some American colonies. These public exhibitions of the power to inflict pain served a number of social functions. They were warnings to those who might want to question the status quo. They taught people how vulnerable they were, as well as signaling who could be scapegoated with impunity (such as the 100,000, and by some estimates millions, of "witches" burned by Christian inquisitors at the stake; Barstow, 1994). They also served to desensitize people to suffering, and even to view it as entertainment—thus deadening empathy.

After the eighteenth-century Enlightenment, such public exhibitions of brutality gradually stopped in the West at the same time that more democratic families, along with more democratic governments, began to emerge. Nonetheless, as part of the continuing struggle between partnership resurgence and dominator resistance, there continued to be violent backlashes in both the private and the public spheres—for example, the rise in private or "domestic" violence against women in the wake of both nineteenth- and twentieth-century feminism (see, e.g., Faludi, 1991; Roszak, 1969; Russell, 1988; Sanday, 1990) as well as various forms of violent public scapegoating, from the Nazis' persecution and genocide of 6 million Jews and the neo-Nazi "skinhead" terrorism we see today in the West to the religious, tribal, and ethnic massacres we find in other regions of the world. And although in the West efforts to again institute public displays of brutality (for example, the bill introduced in the California legislature in 1994 to institute public whippings for graffiti paintspraying on walls and cars) have not been successful, a new way of focusing attention on the power to inflict pain continues unabated: its almost constant display on television and other mass media.

This electronic display of violence is a vast improvement over the real-life executions through public crucifixions, drawings and quarterings, and other barbarities commonplace in the West in earlier times. Still, the amount of brutality dispensed to us through both television news and "entertainment" on our home screens is staggering. As David Barry (1993) writes, it is estimated that in the United States "the average child is likely to have watched 8,000 screen murders and more than 100,000 acts of violence by the end of elementary school"—a figure that will again double by the end of his or her teen years (p. 10). Moreover, as George Gerbner (the former dean of the Annenberg School for Communication) and others have pointed out, much of this violence is "cool violence"—violence that has no visible consequences, as in cartoons where severely bludgeoned characters simply get up and walk away—helping to explain the recent phenomenon of children killing children seemingly with no sense that what they have done is inhuman, antisocial, or even wrong.

This constant mass media focus on violence is of course another way of ritualizing the public exhibition of the power to inflict pain, which serves to maintain dominator-dominated human relations. It serves to deaden empathy, and to condition people to view the infliction of pain as entertaining. Furthermore, because women, minorities, the aged, and other socially disempowered groups are disproportionately cast in the role of victims of violence, it identifies those who can be victimized—that is, those who, unlike American white males in the prime of life, are also generally on television restricted to a stereotypical range of roles and activities where they have, in Gerbner's (1994) words, "less than their share of success and power" (p. 136).[6]

As Gerbner, Larry Gross, Michael Morgan, and Nancy Signorielli (1994) have pointed out, there is in television "an overall pattern of programming to which total communities are regularly exposed over long periods of time," in which repetitive themes that cut across all types of programs are "inescapable for the regular (and especially heavy) viewers" (pp. 20, 25). And part of this inescapable message is the constant presentation, and even idealization, of the "masculine" power to inflict pain—whether in prime-time shows or in children's cartoons (where there are on the average no less than 25 violent incidents per hour; Barry, 1993, p. 10).

All of this not only makes violence seem a very important, indeed indispensable, element in human relations; it also models the use of violence as a means of dealing with problems or conflicts, whether in international or intimate relations. Moreover, as I develop in depth in *Sacred Pleasure: Sex, Myth, and the Politics of the Body* (1995), the constant association of male violence with sex—in other words, the erotization of domination and violence—further conditions both men and women to associate the capacity to inflict pain with sexual arousal, at the same time that it deadens empathy for those on whom pain is inflicted by association of it with sexual excitement, rather than concern for other people's suffering.

Pain can be not only physical but psychological. And here too the mass media have been subverted to perform a dominator systems-maintenance function. For instance, television "situation comedies" or "sit-coms" frequently present verbal abuse as funny, with laugh tracks reinforcing this message. Once again, this serves to deaden empathy to the pain of others. It also communicates the message that those who do not have this amused reaction are "bleeding hearts" or, worse still, "do-gooders"—odd people who misguidedly believe that it is everyone's responsibility to help create a more compassionate and humane way of relating.

How effectively these "humorous" messages have penetrated the American unconscious is evidenced by much of what we see today: the wholesale acceptance by the mass media, politicians, and American public of vicious political campaigns, and of even more vicious talk shows, such as those of Rush Limbaugh and G. Gordon Liddy. Moreover, many "funny" programs serve to identify those who can be psychologically abused with impunity—and those who cannot. For instance, with the exception of a few programs such as Norman Lear's *All in the Family* and Linda Bloodworth-Thomason's *Designing Women*, bigotry against women is rarely made fun of. Quite the contrary, women who complain of violence or discrimination are frequently ridiculed as "male-bashing extremists" or "whining feminists." Similarly, instead of making fun of "macho" men, the media have tended to idealize "heroic" or "good" violence—which, given the privileged position of white males in American society, is on television primarily perpetrated by white males.

Once again, this type of programming has been all too effective in reinforcing the notion that domination and violence are normal in human relations. Because it presents violence in the service of "good" causes as heroic, it has fueled terrorism, helping those who today all over the world maim and murder randomly chosen children, women, and men justify their inhuman behavior. It has also helped pave the way for the epidemic of scapegoating of socially disempowered groups,

such as minorities and women worldwide, diverting attention from our real problems, and thus from more effective and creative ways of addressing them.

For example, in the United States, where the postindustrial revolution is in its first stages, the scapegoating of feminists along with mothers living in poverty diverts attention during this time of economic dislocation from the fact that politicians funded by big business are dismantling safety nets that have since the Great Depression helped raise the general standard of living—causing even more suffering and dislocation as well as severe long-range social and economic problems. Similarly, just as during the end of the Middle Ages, when the Industrial Revolution was in its first stages in the West, "deviant" women—that is, women who did not live in a male-headed household—were the primary target for scapegoating as "witches" by the medieval church (which then exercised a virtual monopoly on the media of communication), in parts of the developing world where feudal theocracies exercise despotic rule through terror, men are again blaming all social and economic ills on women who step out of their "traditional" roles in rigidly male-controlled families.

The Invisible Subtext of Gender

Scapegoating, or the diversion of anger and frustration from those who dominate to socially disempowered groups, is a built-in feature of dominator systems. The conditioning for scapegoating in dominator societies begins in families that condition children to suppress feelings of anger and frustration against the "superior" authority figures who cause them pain, and instead deflect it against those considered inferior. It is expressed in the bullying of smaller playmates in childhood, and then continues with the often violent vilification and persecution of socially disempowered groups (Eisler, 1995, particularly chap. 10).

But there is a related mechanism for conditioning people for venting anger and frustration on socially disempowered out-groups: In dominator societies, people are taught from childhood on to internalize a basic template for superior in-group versus inferior out-groups—the division of humanity into a male-superior in-group and a female-inferior out-group.

This division teaches people from early childhood on to unconsciously equate difference with either superiority or inferiority. Even beyond this, it leads people to unconsciously regard out-groups as not quite human, and therefore dangerous. Thus, as our legacy from much more rigid dominator times, we have the archetype of Eve—the primal woman— blamed for nothing less than all of humanity's ills. And we also have a plethora of newer "scientific" dogmas that present women as genetically inferior to men—as in the nineteenth-century claims that women are of inferior intelligence, and the twentieth-century claims that biological differences (which keep changing, as earlier assertions are disproven) show that men are inherently superior.

Obviously this dominator model of our species radically restricts the life choices of the female half of humanity. But what is still rarely noted is that the way a society structures the relations between the two halves of humanity—women and men—is not just a so-called women's issue, which in dominator ideology is automatically relegated to a secondary or peripheral place. As more and more men are beginning to recognize, dominator stereotypes of masculinity also restrict men's life choices, forcing them to suppress in themselves those characteristics and behaviors stereotypically labeled feminine. Most critically—and this is one of the central findings of my work over the last two decades— the way gender roles and relations are structured affects the social construction of every institution, from the family and religion to education, economics, and politics.

For instance, in societies oriented primarily to the dominator model, women are excluded from positions of religious authority, and thus deprived of moral authority to de-fine what is right and wrong, including what is right and wrong in family and sexual relations. Work such as feeding children and maintaining a clean environment is not considered economically productive—as reflected in calculations of gross national product that to this day do not include these activities as "productive work"—despite the fact that without this "women's work," human society would die out. Moreover, so-called feminine values and activities, such as nonviolence, empathy, caretaking, and environmental housekeeping, are not given fiscal priority. By contrast, particularly in times of dominator regression, there is always enough funding for stereotypically masculine activities—as dramatically illustrated by the astronomical budgets for weapons to wage wars that have practically bankrupted the world during the last several decades, at the same time that funding for the feeding of children and other stereotypically feminine activities has been systematically cut in accordance with policies formulated by government leaders as well as the International Monetary Fund (IMF) and the World Bank on the rationale that such cuts are necessary for fiscal health.

This centrality to social and ideological organization of how the relations between the female and male halves of humanity are structured—and with this, how masculinity and femininity are defined—helps explain why those who would today push us back to a much more rigid dominator social order so fiercely focus on returning women to their "traditional" place. It also explains why fundamentalist-rightist leaders who would like to reimpose extreme punishments for any deviation from their "God-given orders" are so intent on reimposing "traditional" family values—that is, an authoritarian, male-dominated family where women must obey men, and children of both genders must obey orders from above, no matter how unjust or unloving they may be. For this effectively conditions people to deflect frustration and anger from those in control to the scapegoating of socially disempowered out-groups such as women, gay people, and racial or religious minorities.

Viewed from this gendered perspective, it is possible to see that the so-called fundamentalist religious resurgence of our time has little to do with core religious teachings, such as Jesus's teachings of nonviolence and empathy (stereotypically feminine behaviors) that are at the core of Christianity. But it has a great deal to do with the maintenance of a system where—beginning with the control of half of humanity over the other—rankings of domination are presented as necessary, and even decreed by God.

Certainly if the men who head the so-called Christian right succeed in seizing power, we will see extreme social and sexual controls—as well as the escalation of culturally condoned violence, which we already see to some extent in the West in the bombing of Planned Parenthood clinics and to a much larger extent in the fundamentalist violence against women in parts of the Muslim world, where young girls have been killed merely for the "crime" of standing at a bus stop with their heads uncovered.[7] For in essence these people would impose on us a religious form of fascism in which the ultimate strongman is a wrathful divine father who countenances neither freedom nor equality, and whose power (like that of the men who rule in his name) is imposed and maintained through threats (and intermittent acts) of the most painful violence.[8] And they would also reimpose on us strict and, if "necessary," violent control over women and women's sexuality, because this control is both a symbol and a linchpin for all other forms of domination and control.

But this struggle for our future is today also taking place in far more subtle and ubiquitous ways than the "culture wars" launched by those who call themselves religious fundamentalists, even though their hate-mongering and incitements to violence go against the fundaments of partnership teachings (emphasizing love and peace rather than hate and holy wars) that are the core of most world religions. And perhaps the most critical arena

for this struggle is in the mass media of communication. For it is here that we find a pattern of programming that by and large reinforces *traditional* gender roles and relations (a code word for the social construction of masculinity and femininity to fit the requirements of a dominator model), rather than highlighting the immense variability of both men's and women's traits and behaviors. And it is also here that we find the sensationalizing and/or trivializing of women's problems as purely personal rather than socially, politically, and economically significant;[9] the ghettoizing of "women's issues" to a handful of articles or shows rarely on front pages or during television prime time; and the almost constant subliminal message that men and the "masculine" are much more important than women and the "feminine."

A striking, though still rarely discussed, example is the blatant numerical gender imbalance characteristic of television programming, where male characters outnumber female characters two to one—effectively communicating the higher social valuation of men and "masculinity" (Gerbner, 1994). And still another example, as noted earlier, is the constant media focus on violence, along with the chronic association of masculinity with "heroic" violence and domination.[10]

This idealization of violence is not a new phenomenon. On the contrary, it is a major theme in our heritage from 5,000 years of dominator history, in which violent men have regularly been idealized as heroic and noble—whether Ulysses in Homer's *Iliad* or Samson in the Judeo-Christian Bible. Similarly, as I develop elsewhere, the linking of sex with violence that is today marketed by a billion-dollar pornographic industry is only a much more explicit and ubiquitous repetition of earlier dominator themes—as evidenced by the many legends about Don Juan (a man who seduced and/or raped women) and Casanova's memoirs about all the women with whom he had sex, not, as he himself writes, out of love or even the pursuit of sexual pleasure but to impose upon them his will (see Eisler, 1995, chap. 13).

What *is* new is the scale of violence due to new technologies of a magnitude not so long ago found only in science fiction tales. And what is also new is the documentation by social scientists of how destructive the idealization and erotization of a "masculinity" of violence and domination is. For example, social psychologist David Winter (1973) found a rise before or during periods of imperial expansion and war of Don Juan-type stories—that is, stories about men who "conquer" women by seducing and/or raping them. Similarly, social psychologist David McClelland's (1975) study of literary materials in modern U.S. and British history shows that periods when there is a rise in stories emphasizing what he called "n Power" or "the imperial power motivation" (the stereotypically masculine definition of power as conquest and domination) almost invariably culminated in wars. Conversely, a rise in stories emphasizing what McClelland called "n Affiliation" or the "affiliation motive" (more stereotypically feminine values of compassion and nonviolence) generally preceded more peaceful times. Just as significantly, "high n Power combined with low n Affiliation has been associated among modern nations with dictatorships, with ruthlessness, suppression of liberty, and domestic and international violence" (McClelland, 1975, p. 319).

These findings are not surprising from the perspective of cultural transformation theory. They confirm the centrality of how the roles and relations of the two halves of humanity are structured to whether a time or place orients primarily to a dominator or partnership model. They are also congruent with the findings of feminist scholars that, as Wendy Kozol (1995) writes, "cultural values regarding gender roles and the appropriateness of violence as a solution to problems create an environment in which society tolerates the routine brutalization of women and children" (p. 655, citing Jones, 1994). And they highlight the extreme urgency—at a time when all over the world we find the threat of regressions to more rigid male dominance, and with this to the dominator

configuration of more violence, inequality, and repression—of making visible the hidden subtext of stereotypical gender roles and relations that in today's mass media so often makes brutality and violence look like "real masculinity."

The Grassroots Struggle Against Violence and Domination

Considering how much of mass media programming is violent, what is remarkable is not the rise of violence, particularly among young people—such as the men arrested for the April 1995 Oklahoma City bombing that so shocked America and the world—but how many people, young and old, are repelled by violence. Similarly, considering how much of our media (not only the pornography industry, but mainstream publications and programs) condition people to eroticize domination and violence, what is remarkable is not that many people are insensitive to the pain of victims of rape and other sexual violence, but that so many women and men are taking a stand against all forms of intimate violence (Kimmel & Mossmiller, 1992; Loye, *Moral Transformation,* work in progress; Stoltenberg, 1990).

But if we are to succeed in moving to a less violent and more equitable future, we must bring about a broad realization of the centrality of gender issues to the struggle between the worlds of the dominator and the envisioned worlds of the partnership society. The dominators "get it"—they have spent billions against the Equal Rights Amendment, against reproductive freedom, against affirmative action, and other means of pushing women back. We've got to "get it" too.

We also need fundamental changes in the composition of the boards of directors and other policy-making bodies of the mass media to rapidly move toward the equal representation on them of the female half of humanity. We need many more women's caucuses in all the mass media, from television networks and film studios to publishing houses and newspapers. And we also need far stronger alliances with men (both inside and outside the media) whose consciousness has been, or can be, heightened to these basic gender issues.

In those cases where we meet a brick wall, one strategy could be the introduction of resolutions by holders of shares of stock to require that guidelines for programming discourage the glamorization of violence and the linking of sex with violence and domination—resolutions that would be worded so as to explain the harmful effects of these types of programs. Because corporations are generally required by law to include resolutions introduced by shareholders in the packets sent out to all shareholders for annual elections, even if these resolutions are not passed, they too would serve as consciousness-raising tools.

If we are to truly democratize our mass media, we will also have to form new umbrella coalitions and networks, such as the Women's Institute for Freedom of the Press in Washington, D.C., and the Cultural Environment Movement in Philadelphia, to bring more diverse, and healthier, ideas and images to the billions of people for whom television and other mass media are today the major force shaping attitudes, beliefs, and behaviors.[11] Moreover, we need to address the growing concentration of media ownership in the hands of a few individuals and organizations, by more effectively using antimonopoly legislation. We also need to obtain much more financing for alternative television, newspapers, and other media that give the authentic voices of women, people of color, and other traditionally disempowered groups full representation.

This is particularly urgent at this time when new interactive communication technologies offer the possibility of replicating partnership rather than dominator images and ideas. For unless we are successful in radically changing the cultural environment created by the mass media, these new technologies will again be used to spread messages of fear, hate, and scapegoating—as through the highly organized male supremacist militia computer net-

works already in existence worldwide. Moreover, unless we invoke all the legal, economic, and political means available, these new media too will be subverted to meet dominator systems-maintenance requirements, so that what looks like diversity will only be a repeat of what happened with the multiplication of television cable channels, which are for the most part merely clones of one another.

We also need to address some difficult legal issues, including even the concept of freedom of speech, which needs to be realigned to the intent of the framers of the U.S. Constitution. This intent was to protect freedom of speech (including even incitements to violence) against despotic rulers. It was not to protect those who incite hate and violence against traditionally disempowered groups such as women, minorities, and gays.

Obviously we need to be wary of government bodies that assume a censorship role through prior restraints or prohibitions against publishing certain kinds of materials. But we can focus on civil remedies that hold those who incite violence, scapegoating, and hatred accountable for the consequences of their words—a legal trend that has already brought economic sanctions against individuals who incited ethnic, religious, and antireproductive choice violence.

Finally, we need to find ways of using the mass media to bring to public consciousness the reality of our economic situation as we shift from an industrial to a postindustrial world. We are entering an era when more and more blue-collar jobs will continue to be lost in manufacturing due to automation, more and more pink-collar secretarial and receptionist jobs will be replaced by computers and other forms of automation, and the middle class will continue to shrink as middle management is gradually phased out. Unless we find ways of bringing these developments to people's attention, we cannot effectively change the cultural climate of mean-spirited scapegoating that today, under the guise of freedom of speech, is being promulgated by bigots posing as defenders of freedom and equality—as in recent political campaigns that in the United States fanned old prejudices and hatreds leading to a massive attack on affirmative action programs under the guise of "reverse discrimination."

Even more critically, we need to find ways to use the mass media to raise fundamental economic questions—such as how to redefine productive work in an era of jobless economic growth. And here again we come back to the hidden subtext of gender. Although automated new technologies are today creating a major economic crisis, this can also be our opportunity to find creative ways of at long last giving economic value to the caretaking and cleaning work traditionally performed by women either for very low pay or for free. For only by giving the work that is essential if human society is to survive real economic value can we realistically expect to change the dominator pattern of creating artificial scarcities not only through economic policies and laws that widen the gap between haves and have-nots, but through the allocation of ever larger sums for weaponry, and the public acceptance of ever deeper cuts in funding for traditional "women's work" such as caring for children, the sick, and the elderly.

Obviously it will take more than changes in the media to complete the shift from a dominator to a partnership system of social and ideological organization. It will require fundamental changes in economics, politics, and other institutions—including our educational system worldwide.

But the media can play a critical role in this shift. They can change their programs so that they no longer spread the message that the capacity to inflict pain is the most important factor in human relations—for example, by no longer glamorizing violence, and instead glamorizing nonviolent conflict resolution. They can launch an intensive global human rights education campaign to help people learn to recognize chronic violations of human rights in the "private sphere" of our sexual and family relations through programs that model intimate relations where there is empathy and respect

for people's human rights. They can create programs showing how this affects all other relations—in other words, how the so-called public and private spheres are inextricably intertwined. They can highlight how the dominator model and high technology are a potentially lethal mix in our age of nuclear/bacteriological warfare and terrorism, when "man's conquest of Nature" dangerously degrades and pollutes our natural habitat.

Above all, they can help us avoid continuing dominator regressions by providing a model of our species where partnership rather than domination is presented as normal in the basic relations between the female and male halves of humanity.

Notes

1. See Eisler (1987a, particularly chaps. 10 and 11) for an examination of this process.

2. Although this idea is usually said to originate with Western philosophers such as Locke, Native American tribal societies such as the Iroquois antedate it. An essay relating to this subject, focusing on the eighteenth-century Shawnee Nation leader Queen Coitcheleh, is Gregory L. Schaaf's "Queen Coitcheleh and the Women of the Lost Shawnee Nation" (1990). Schaaf brings out how to the extent that some of the American tribal societies were more democratic, women in these societies also had higher status.

3. Our school curriculum prominently mentions (and offers whole courses about) men such as John Locke, Adam Smith, and, even in the anticommunist U.S. political climate, Karl Marx and Friedrich Engels. But if we want such in-depth treatment of Frederick Douglass, Sojourner Truth, and other African American leaders, we have to go to the intellectual ghetto of Black Studies. Similarly, to find out about the major contributions of the feminist thinkers and theorists who led the struggle for women's human rights, one has to go to the intellectual ghetto of Women's Studies. For information on some of these thinkers, see Dale Spender (1983), Alice S. Rossi (1974), and Miriam Schneir (1972, 1994).

4. This had already begun at the end of the Middle Ages (Gies & Gies, 1987).

5. For example, the works of archaeologists such as James Mellaart, Marija Gimbutas, Lucy Goodison, and Nicolas Platon present evidence that the first cradles of Western civilization were not, as we have been led to believe, chronically violent and warlike, rigidly male-dominant, and characterized by rigid hierarchies of domi-

nation ultimately backed up by force or the fear of force, ranging from child and wife beating to the institutionalized form of male violence we call warfare—the basic dominator system configuration. What these data indicate is that the earliest cradles of Western civilization (now known to go back approximately 8,000 years to the beginnings of the Neolithic or first agrarian age) were actually societies characterized by a more equal partnership between women and men, a more generally egalitarian social and economic structure, and (because it is not required to maintain rankings of domination) a low degree of institutionalized violence—the basic partnership configuration. In short, what these data show is that many of our most ancient stories, which deal with an earlier more peaceful and egalitarian time, while already very idealized, are based on folk memories of a time before, as the ancient Greek poet Hesiod writes, a "golden race" who lived in peaceful ease were replaced by a "lesser race" who brought in Ares (the Greek god of war). See, for example, James Mellaart (1967), Marija Gimbutas (1982, 1991), Nicolas Platon (1966), R. F. Willetts (1977). See also Riane Eisler (1987b, 1995) for a description of these earlier, more partnership-oriented societies and a discussion of the prehistoric shift during a period of great systems disequilibrium to societies orienting primarily to the dominator model.

6. This problem of power imbalance, both in the media and in real life, is a major subject of feminist writings. For some works on this subject, see Gayle Tuchman (1978), bell hooks (1984), Ramona R. Rush and Donna Allen (1989), Patricia Hill-Collins (1990), Colleen Roach (1993), Pamela J. Creedon (1993), Angharad N. Valdivia (1995).

7. *Women and Vision* (published by Isis International, P.O. Box 1837, Quezon City, Luzon, the Philippines; June 1994) reported that two young women, ages 19 and 20, were killed by gunmen while waiting at a bus stop in Algeria, to punish them for not wearing the veil. This violence against women by Muslim fundamentalists has claimed the lives of many other women. For example, the July 27, 1994, *Alert for Action of Women Living Under Muslim Laws* (Boite Postale 23-34790, Grabels, Mont Pelier, France) reported that more than 550 women have been murdered in Kurdistan on "moral" pretexts.

8. In his classic cross-cultural work on ideology and values, social psychologist Milton Rokeach found that fascism is the one modern ideology that still openly devalues both freedom and equality, thus justifying the suppression of both (Rokeach, 1973, particularly pp. 172-173). In other words, even though the suppression of freedom and equality is characteristically justified in "pure" dominator ideologies, for example, in the monarchism that to varying degrees held sway in the West until the Enlightenment, fascism is the only contemporary ideology that still justifies their suppression. Yet, although fascism has been massively discredited in this century by the brutality and inhumanity of the fascism in

Germany, Japan, and Italy that led to World War II, the subordination of both freedom and equality to "higher" goals still remains entrenched in the authoritarian factions of some of the world's religions. (This is analyzed in more depth in Eisler, 1995, and David Loye, *The River and the Star,* work in progress. See also Chapter 11 of *The Chalice and the Blade,* 1987a, for a discussion of modern fascist regimes as a regression to a "pure" dominator society, using modern technologies for more effective domination and destruction.)

9. For a recent article on these issues, see Deborah L. Rhode (1995).

10. For an in-depth discussion of this, see Eisler (1995, particularly chap. 12).

11. For an important discussion of these issues, see Donna Allen (1991). The Cultural Environment Movement (P.O. Box 31847, Philadelphia, PA 19104) was organized by George Gerbner in coalition with other organizations to deal with some of these approaches.

References

Allen, D. (1991). *Media without democracy and what to do about it.* Washington, DC: Women's Institute for Freedom of the Press.

Barry, D. S. (1993, Summer). Growing up violent: Decades of research link screen mayhem with increase in aggressive behavior. *Media and Values, 62,* 8-11.

Barstow, A. L. (1994). *Witchcraze: A new history of the European witch hunts.* London: Pandora.

Centerwall, B. (1992). Television and violence: The scale of the problem and where to go from here. *Journal of the American Medical Association, 267,* 3059-3063.

Creedon, P. J. (Ed.). (1993). *Women in mass communication.* Newbury Park, CA: Sage.

Csanyi, V. (1989). *Evolutionary systems and society: A general theory.* Durham, NC: Duke University Press.

Eisler, R. (1987a). *The chalice and the blade: Our history, our future.* San Francisco: Harper & Row.

Eisler, R. (1987b, April). Woman, man, and the evolution of social structure. *World Futures: The Journal of General Evolution, 23*(1-2), 79-92.

Eisler, R. (1993a). From domination to partnership: The foundations for global peace. In C. Roach (Ed.), *Communication and culture in war and peace* (pp. 145-174). Newbury Park, CA: Sage.

Eisler, R. (1993b). Technology, gender, and history: Toward a nonlinear model of social evolution. In E. Laszlo, I. Masulli, R. Artigiani, & V. Csanyi (Eds.), *The evolution of cognitive maps: New paradigms for the 21st century* (pp. 181-203). New York: Gordon and Breach.

Eisler, R. (1994). From domination to partnership: The hidden subtext for sustainable change. *Journal of Organizational Change Management, 7*(4), 35-49.

Eisler, R. (1995). *Sacred pleasure: Sex, myth, and the politics of the body*. San Francisco: HarperSanFrancisco.

Faludi, S. (1991). *Backlash: The undeclared war against American women*. New York: Crown.

Gerbner, G. (1994). The politics of media violence: Some reflections. In C. J. Hamelink & O. Linne (Eds.), *Mass communications research* (pp. 133-145). Norwood, NJ: Ablex.

Gerbner, G. (1995). Television violence: The power and the peril. In G. Dines & J. M. Humez (Eds.), *Gender, race and class in media: A text reader* (pp. 547-556). Thousand Oaks, CA: Sage.

Gerbner, G., Gross, L., Morgan, M., & Signorielli, N. (1994). Growing up with television: The cultivation perspective. In J. Bryant & D. Zillmann (Eds.), *Media effects: Advances in theory and research*. Hillsdale, NJ: Lawrence Erlbaum.

Gies, F., & Gies, J. (1987). *Marriage and the family in the Middle Ages*. New York: Harper & Row.

Gimbutas, M. (1982). *The goddesses and gods of old Europe*. Berkeley: University of California Press.

Gimbutas, M. (1991). *The civilization of the goddess*. San Francisco: HarperSanFrancisco.

Hill-Collins, P. (1990). *Black feminist thought: Knowledge, consciousness, and the politics of empowerment*. New York: Routledge Kegan Paul.

hooks, b. (1984). *Feminist theory: From margin to center*. Boston: South End Press.

Jones, A. (1994). *Next time, she'll be dead: Battering and how to stop it*. Boston: Beacon.

Kimmel, M. S., & Mossmiller, T. E. (Eds.). (1992). *Against the tide: Pro-feminist men in the United States 1776-1990*. Boston: Beacon.

Kozol, W. (1995). Fracturing domesticity: Media, nationalism, and the question of feminist influence. *Signs, 20*(3), 646-665.

Loye, D. (work in progress). *Moral transformation*.

Loye, D. (work in progress). *The river and the star*.

Loye, D., Gorney, R., & Steele, G. (1977). Effects of television: An experimental field study. *Journal of Communications, 27*(3), 206-216.

Maturana, H., & Varela, F. (1987). *The tree of knowledge*. Boston: New Science Library, Shambhala.

McClelland, D. (1975). *Power: The inner experience*. New York: Irvington.

Mellaart, J. (1967). *Çatal Hüyük*. New York: McGraw-Hill.

Platon, N. (1966). *Crete*. Geneva: Nagel.

Rhode, D. L. (1995). Media images, feminist issues. *Signs, 20*(3), 685-710.

Roach, C. (Ed.). (1993). *Communication and culture in war and peace*. Newbury Park, CA: Sage.

Rokeach, M. (1973). *The nature of human values*. New York: Free Press.

Rossi, A. S. (Ed.). (1974). *The feminist papers*. New York: Bantam.

Roszak, T. (1969). The hard and the soft: The force of feminism in modern times. In B. Roszak & T. Roszak (Eds.), *Masculine/feminine*. New York: Harper Colophon.

Rush, R. R., & Allen, D. (Eds.). (1989). *Communications at the crossroads: The gender gap connection*. Norwood, NJ: Ablex.

Russell, D. (1988). Pornography and rape: A causal model. *Political Psychology, 9*, 41-73.

Sanday, P. R. (1990). *Fraternity gang rape: Sex, brotherhood, and privilege on campus*. New York: New York University Press.

Schaaf, G. L. (1990). Queen Coitcheleh and the women of the lost Shawnee Nation. In F. R. Keller (Ed.), *Views of women's lives in Western tradition* (pp. 158-167). New York: Lewiston.

Schneir, M. (1972). *Feminism: The essential historical writings*. New York: Vintage.

Schneir, M. (Ed.). (1994). *Feminism in our time: The essential writings, World War II to the present*. New York: Vintage.

Spender, D. (Ed.). (1983). *Feminist theorists: Three centuries of key women thinkers*. New York: Pantheon.

Stoltenberg, J. (1990). *Refusing to be a man*. New York: Penguin.

Tuchman, G. (1978). *Hearth and home: Images of women and the media*. New York: Oxford University Press.

Valdivia, A. N. (Ed.). (1995). *Feminism, multiculturalism, and the media*. Thousand Oaks, CA: Sage.

Willetts, R. F. (1977). *The civilization of ancient Crete*. Berkeley: University of California Press.

Williams, T. M. (1986). *The impact of television: A natural experiment in three communities*. Orlando, FL: Academic Press.

Winter, D. (1973). *The power motive*. New York: Free Press.

4

Environmental Communication
A Female-Friendly Process

JoAnn Myer Valenti

Effective communication involves dialogue; understanding is achieved through interactive listening and discussion. Environmental communication as a process integrates audience predispositions and differences, establishes the basis for a relationship between people and their environment, and offers a means to enhanced environmental literacy. Environmental communication requires dialogue. The premise in this chapter is that most everyone recognizes the risk of environmental crisis, our poor record of environmental literacy, and the obvious need for policy and practice reflecting environmental sustainability. David Orr (1992) and other environmental scientists acknowledge that public understanding is prerequisite to a

goal of sustainability, to avoid continuing environmental crisis. Walter Lippmann (1922) was right a long time ago when he said, "Until we know what others think they know, we cannot truly understand their acts."

Perhaps the primary goal of environmental communication is ecological literacy, which Orr defines as an understanding of the interaction of dynamic technological, economic, political, social, and natural systems. Public understanding of this web of relationships is the prerequisite to environmental sustainability. A broader, more inclusive approach to understanding science and how the environment works, offers greater potential stimulus for increasing information-seeking about science in general. Environmental literacy—or

AUTHOR'S NOTE: A version of this chapter was originally presented as an invited topical lecture at the 1993 annual meeting of the American Association for the Advancement of Science (AAAS) in Boston, and appeared in revised form in the proceedings of the Conference on Communication and Our Environment, Big Sky, Montana (July 1993).

41

ecological literacy—may be the more likely first step toward what has been called science literacy.

Orr offers six foundations for ecological literacy, "whether the public understands the relations between its well-being and the health of the natural systems":

1. All education is environmental education.
2. Environmental issues are complex and cannot be understood through a single discipline or department.
3. Education occurs in part as a dialogue and has the characteristics of good conversation.
4. The way education occurs is as important as its content.
5. Experience in the natural world is both an essential part of understanding the environment and conducive to good thinking.
6. Education relevant to the challenge of building a sustainable society will enhance the learner's competence with natural systems (Orr, 1992, p. 90).

Ecological literacy requires knowing, caring, and practical competence. Environmental communication, grounded in communication skills and theory, and focused on environmental content, provides the renaissance, how-to-do-something course Orr envisions. Environmental communication, the process by which the environmental agenda is set and acted on by the public, begins with a recognition of the need to transfer information effectively. I believe women do this well.

Gender Advantage

I do not want to belabor women's strengths in relationship expertise. But to borrow from Linda Steiner's conclusions in her study on the construction of gender in news reporting: Gender is neither everything, nor does it count for nothing (Steiner, 1992). Empirical studies in communications have repeatedly confirmed gender-based differences in ways of knowing and conversing, audience re-

sponses, leadership and consumer behaviors, decision-making processes, and more. Not seeing gender leaves blind spots in our understanding in spite of otherwise "fully equipped conceptual toolboxes" (Jansen, 1993). Generally, conflict characterizes men's style, while women opt to negotiate, a more resolution-seeking style. Men tend to look at communication as a means to establish and maintain control or dominance, whereas women (possibly have learned to) look at communication as a means to develop and maintain relationships. Women may therefore be advantaged if the focus (sustainability) turns to building and strengthening relationships. A review of the feminist perspective of "situated knowledge" (Haraway, 1988) reinforces such a suggestion.

The perspective of situated knowledge reminds us that "[seeing] from below is neither easily learned nor unproblematic, even if 'we' 'naturally' inhabit the great underground terrain of subjugated knowledges" (Haraway, 1988, p. 575). Shared conversations and webs of connections have a way of getting past barriers. Situated knowledge is about understanding communities, not isolated individuals. The logic is not discovery but a social relation of "conversation." Whereas men have problems seeing relations between people and experiences, women often fail to see the differences (Flax, 1987). Clearly, we should expect to lose a complete sense of audience if we assume gender neutrality. Rather than digressing into a rich literature on women's instinctive and acquired communication strengths, see Rawlins (1989) for a summary of research on gender dialectics in communication.

Any gender-based argument, especially if confused with sex rather than gender, rouses anxiety among folks. Today's theorists examine gender through a more cultural perspective, not disregarding biological or psychological influences but focusing on the larger cultural influence. Tannen (1993) has described female-male communication as intercultural communication. It's risky business to make too much of gender advantages, lest the disadvantages become the next focus. Yet, to ignore gendered advantages or disadvantages is to neglect possible strengths and methods of improving how we behave and how we might better accomplish set goals.

In the case of environmental communication, I am willing to risk reliance on some rather common "scholarly" anecdotal evidence. You may, for example, have noted the number of scholars who happen to be women, and who have made enormous contributions to public understanding of science. One might easily argue that the "Mother" of environmental communication was Rachel Carson, who birthed the environmental movement and demonstrated the power of effective communication of environmental issues with the publication of *Silent Spring* in 1962. Over the subsequent three decades, attention to instruction about the environment has been evident in K-12 curricula, where women educators have a strong presence. Clearly, job opportunity has as much to do with this occurrence as does the gender of teachers.

But let me suggest that even in our "play" in retirement years, women offer leadership and enthusiasm about environmental issues. In the West, many take heart in the very existence of organizations like Great Old Broads for Wilderness. Women in their seventies and eighties, called "Canyon Crones," offer continuing, ageless role models for those seeking involvement with the environment. At least we can dismiss age as a critical factor in environmental expertise.

Those uncomfortable with anecdotes or personal experience can take respite in the research on women's right-lobe functions specialization. The right lobe is the site of greater aptitude for imaginative and artistic activity and holistic, intuitive thinking including some advantaged spiritual and visual tasks. Additional recent research appears to support an assumption of greater verbal strengths resulting from women's larger bundle of nerves connecting the hemispheres of the brain. (See Maccoby, 1990; Phillips, Steele,

& Tanz, 1987; Wood, 1994, for example.) Monsma (1994) summarizes: "The causal connection is not clear, but it does appear that men utilize only one lobe for language while women utilize both lobes and that women can draw upon the unaffected lobe when the other is medically impaired" (p. 4). Lobal advantages may account for why women describe events with greater detail and more color, certainly an advantage in communicating about the environment.

Now, before pushing this or any other gender advantage argument further, you should be cognizant of wisdoms, cautionary signs, established by other female scholars. In her careful defrocking of E. O. Wilson and sociobiologists' sexist assertions, biologist and general demystifier of women's health issues Ruth Hubbard (1995) writes:

> When it comes to sex differences, it is questionable whether anyone can hold opinions, or do research, that express anything other than her or his beliefs about how society operates, or should operate, because everything about our lives, including our language, is gendered. In as loaded and value-laden an area as sex differences, everything becomes political, a way of persuading others to promote what we believe to be correct ways for the society to function. Under these circumstances, it is wrong to ignore, or even deny, one's biases and pretend that one is doing objective research or dispensing objective information. (p. 120)

Nonetheless, women are historically recognized as educators, communicators, persuaders, and translators. One wonders why there are not more women not only in biology but in engineering; women would seem to be superior bridge builders. Some would say women have had to work very hard to help men "get it" in reference to what seems obvious to women but is utterly missed in the male vision.[1] Some men join in this general criticism of gendered communication weakness. Lawlor (1991), who has penned a wonderful book called *Earth Honoring: The New Male Sexuality,* writes:

We have lost the inner vision by which we might observe the role language plays in giving birth to our perceived world. As a result, language, particularly that which is broadcast by mass media, functions like a sorcerer's spell, hypnotizing us into a fraudulent, ungrounded sense of reality. (p. 385)

A feminist viewpoint, on the other hand, classifies power and concepts horizontally, joins intellectual and emotional work, reasons in context, employs multidimensional processes, recognizes perspective in every source, and breaks down false barriers (Preston, 1994). The feminist perspective knits webs of related concepts, people, and places; theirs is a holistic, ecosystemic focus. Compare such joy in simultaneous thought patterns with the more male linear progression and dissection of subjects into parts for separate scrutiny. The "woman question" begins by framing decisions/situations as being about caregiving. Women are more likely to listen to stories and personal narratives, and give these perceptions as much or more legitimacy as the more masculine abstractions, statistics, and quantifiable data. In professions such as journalism, this difference translates into easier male claims of neutrality and objectivity, while male journalists recognize the necessity or confess to worrying about "crossing over" into advocacy or, worse, public relations. Reporting differences might take the form of reliance on experts or authorities as sources (male) instead of seeking different voices in the community and those who share power in partnerships (female). Just as women have been deemed better listeners in human dialogue—leaning into the speaker, maintaining eye contact, responding with comments to encourage communication (Pearson, Turner, & Todd-Mancillas, 1991)—women may also better hear the voices in environmental discourse.

Means and Process

Environmental journalism—mass mediated information about the environment—provides the means for increasing awareness of environmental issues or problems. The effect or long-term goal of environmental messages is generally to persuade action or influence beliefs through the information provided. Environmental communication is the process of providing the best available knowledge to those involved or interested in environmental matters.

The goal of environmental communication is to affect perceptions, attitudes, and behaviors through improved knowledge. The long-term objective is to enhance the possibility of informed decision making. Environmental communication provides the frame or connection for environmental messages. When the goal is effective environmental communication, shared fields of knowledge and paying more attention to feedback from the intended audience become critical. It means we—as message senders and message developers—have made an initial effort to know who we're talking to, and assume the responsibility for listening; we take the lead in initiating a dialogue; and we acknowledge our interest in building a relationship.

The communication process depends on an understanding of audience, a relationship between the sources of information and the intended receivers. We've come a long way since the early linear communication models proposed in the 1940s. We've spent a great deal of time studying interactions among senders, messages, gatekeepers, and audiences, as well as considering the effects of noise. We've probed each element in the process. One of the greatest remaining challenges in effective communication about scientific or environmental issues is the failure to stimulate dialogue: information processing and information seeking. A two-way flow between senders and receivers is rarely achieved. Students, readers, viewers, and listeners may sometimes pay attention, and occasionally actually learn some of what they're being told. We fall short of effective communication, however, if we only measure specific knowledge learned, and ignore the missing applause for encores—the enthusiasm for an ongoing relationship.

Environmental communication requires a continuing relationship where the exchange of ideas is two-way, not just top-down or between experts, and certainly not driven by what only one partner or the other in the relationship thinks is needed. Educators, scientists, and journalists believe they have something worth communicating to audiences, something important for the public to consider, oftentimes critical information if we are to have a fully informed democracy. But the public more often than not lets us know that what experts are trying to communicate is not particularly compelling, relevant to their lives, or what they wanted to know.

I worked not too long ago with a graduate student who as a teacher and broadcast professional wanted to explore ways to use television in her classroom to enhance environmental literacy. In an experiment testing the effects of the television news documentary format, we found subjects could demonstrate greater knowledge about the specific information presented. They could more accurately answer knowledge questions about wetlands ecosystems than a control group, but there was no evidence of further information seeking. We failed to find evidence of a continuing interest in understanding water systems. They liked the video. It was entertaining and they remembered some fairly pertinent facts, even over time. But we found no indication that these students were inspired to look for more or similar information on their own. They had not committed to an ongoing relationship with the science of water (Baker, 1991).

When we review the common barriers to effective communication, it's easy to see why those charged with delivering messages about science or the environment have a hard time. Sources lack credibility. Information is too complex, not clearly relevant to daily life, and so on. What intrigues me is that the barriers we imagine all involve the receiver of the information.

If this is so, we ought to be attending more to understanding the intended audience's predispositions, preparation, and perceptions before we attempt to foist our ideas on them. We also know there is no "general public." Whether the intended receiver is sitting in a classroom, visiting a facility, reading, viewing, or listening to stories, unless the message is tailored to that individual, unless she or he feels as if there is enough in common to consider building a relationship, there will be no interaction, no dialogue, and probably no learning in the direction the sender had hoped. Rejection. Misunderstanding. The wrong signals, and the date is off. What I'm proposing goes beyond a marketing concept of audience demographic and psychographic factors. We stand to learn more from Jim Grunig's expansion of John Dewey's philosophy of what makes a public an active social unit. Grunig says people need, first, to know that they need information. Second, people need to think they can make a difference in a problem situation, and therefore they seek information. And, third, people need to see themselves as involved and affected (Grunig, 1983).

Environmental Communication

I have taught environmental communication at both the undergraduate and the graduate levels over the past two decades, currently at Brigham Young University in Utah, initially at the University of Michigan's School of Natural Resources, when we saw an emphasis expansion following Earth Day 1970. Then, along with forestry or wildlife management, one could specialize in environmental education and outdoor recreation, or environmental communication, and, even, environmental advocacy. During my tenure in the 1980s at the University of Tampa, a science writing course broadened into an interdisciplinary course to bring biology majors and journalism majors together to learn communication skills and build science literacy through a shared experience. More recently, prior to my arrival at BYU, I taught environmental communication as an undergraduate and graduate course at the University of Florida.

The last I heard, Florida doesn't offer environmental communication any longer and that's a shame. The administrative letter explaining to students why the emphasis would no longer be available made reference to my departure, but then went on to note that no one at Florida communicates with the environment anyway, except perhaps for renowned environmental systems scientist H. T. Odum, whose students, they were sure, talked to trees. What Florida administrators failed to understand is the importance of an opportunity for Odum postdocs, environmental engineering majors, chemistry majors, journalism and public relations students, and future teachers to learn from each other. Students in environmental communication read from a lengthy list of book titles and articles. They canoed what remains of the Oklawaha River. They spent a day on Seahorse Key with a marine ecologist and a science editor. They pored over toxicological profiles together. They met with government policymakers. They discussed. They debated. They wrote a lot. And they asked for more. As the instructor, I learned a lot from them, and I am convinced they have gone on to become more effective as environmental journalists, science writers, environmental education teachers, and scientists because they've learned how to talk with each other. They established relationships.

Adding environmental communication courses to our curricula or mobilizing a flurry of workshops on environmental communication is oversimplifying the solution. But I do think we can build a better understanding of those we're trying to reach, and place more emphasis on understanding the public in what each of us already does. We need to divest some of the self-importance, and by that I refer to the importance of what we know, and learn to think better of those who don't have

the benefit of our learning. Talk to people, listen to them. Try to relate to them. Some of you are no doubt acquainted with *Science and Society: Past, Present and Future* (1977). In it you'll find Cottle's "Show Me a Scientist Who's Helped Poor Folks and I'll Kiss *Her* Hand." I've added the pronoun's emphasis.

Some of us credit past greats for bringing science and environmental issues into our own lives: Rachel Carson, Aldo Leopold, and sometimes personal mentors. For me, Florida's Marjorie Carr, wife of naturalist Archie Carr, who spent a great deal of time asking students what ecology meant, inspired an interdisciplinary approach to the environment. Dr. Carr, a naturalist and award-winning writer, was a good listener, just before he told you why you were wrong. His biologist-environmental activist wife Marjorie Harris Carr, knew how to inspire learning, get people involved in science or environmental actions, primarily through a scientist and citizen organization she founded to stop the notorious Cross Florida Barge Canal. When Florida Defenders of the Environment faced what seemed to be unsurmountable odds battling the Army Corps of Engineers, pork-barrel politicians, and pre-EPA environmental impact statement (EIS) mandates, Marjorie assured us repeatedly, "This too shall pass," and set about mobilizing local scientists to compile our own EIS. Knowing how to relate to your audience is what makes naturalists and writers like Terry Tempest Williams so effective. I'm sure few people, even in Utah, understood about the ecological systems, the ebb and flow of the Great Salt Lake, before reading *Refuge* (1991). It's only when the lake's history is presented alongside the story of a family struggling with cancer that people begin to understand their relationship to the natural environment.

Summary

When a communicator understands the importance of human relationships, she or he has a place to start to expand understanding of other important relationships: the relationship between nature and our behavior, the relationship between us and our environment, the relationship between what happens to us and what science tells us. Communication with the public must begin with a readiness for dialogue, preparation for a good two-way interaction. That's simply not the same as being told what is known and therefore what you ought to know in order to be considered literate. Consider what might happen if we remember to reframe our task as understanding the public first, rather than forcing public understanding of what we think we know, and what we believe they "ought to know." Isn't the basic difficulty a broken, or never established, relationship between people and nature? Barriers between the public and science? Don't we face a public asking: So what?

Why do we need to know about physics, chemistry, or even biology? And, then, when we do pay attention, why can't anyone give us a straight, complete answer? Isn't a first rule of building relationships getting to know each other? Have we taken enough time to get to know "the public," or are we trying too hard to force our good intentions on them?

As Ruth Hubbard suggests, to be understandable and useful, scientific inquiry should be grounded in the needs and questions of ordinary people. My 16-year-old complained to me that high school science is "just memorizing a lot of boring stuff," but he found geometry totally relevant, even fun. He also liked psychology, political science, history, even journalism. Not surprising, he especially valued drivers' education. Consider how easily this teenager could be introduced to physics in his drivers' ed course. My son's basic complaint about his science classes, and the instructors, and his frustrations with the material is the Lois Gibbs's question at Love Canal: So, why don't they know the answers to my questions? My daughter's experience in chemistry, and in her pursuit of higher math and science classes, was one of criticism for "asking too many questions" in general. Her male teachers failed in dialogue.

Communication is a reciprocal process that takes place within the context of relationships and the larger social setting. According to a recent Worldwatch Institute assessment (1992), a new relationship between environmental concerns and business interests will be a major factor in reducing unemployment, reversing natural resource degradation, leading us to a healthy merger of development policies and conservation, an environmentally sustainable society, or to economic collapse. If business and environmentalists can "do lunch," hope exists for all sorts of new relationships. We can improve public understanding of the environment and science by understanding each other. What makes the process of environmental communication effective is the prerequisite understanding of what makes environmental knowledge persuasive to an audience. Dialogue within established relationships makes such understanding possible. A feminist perspective illuminates future possibilities.

Note

1. Feminist scholars note even in poetry and literary symbolism that whereas women see nature as female, feel her power, and are respectful or nurtured, men see nature as female and are compelled to conquer her.

References

Baker, P. Q. (1991, May). *The effects of a television news documentary in enhancing environmental science literacy among viewers: Florida Public Television's Crossroads program on the Cross Florida Barge Canal.* Unpublished thesis, University of Florida, Gainesville.

Carr, A. F. (1956). *The windward road.* New York: Knopf.

Carr, A. F. (1964). *Ulendo.* New York: Knopf.

Carr, A. F. (1967). *So excellent a fishe.* Garden City, NY: Natural History Press.

Carr, A. F. (1973). *The Everglades.* New York: Time Life.

Carson, R. (1962). *Silent spring.* New York: Harper & Row.

Carson, R. (1984). *The sense of wonder.* New York: Harper & Row.

Cohn, V. (1989). *News and numbers: A guide to reporting statistical claims and controversies in health and related fields.* Ames: Iowa State University Press.

Cottle, T. J. (1977). Show me a scientist who's helped poor folks and I'll kiss her hand. In N. H. Stenck (Ed.), *Science and society: Past, present, and future* (pp. 216-227). Ann Arbor: University of Michigan Press.

Flax, J. (1987). Postmodernism and gender relations in feminist theory. *Journal of Women in Culture and Society, 12*(4), 621-643.

Grunig, J. E. (1983). Communication behaviors and attitudes of environmental publics: Two studies. *Journalism Monographs, 81,* 9-14.

Haraway, D. (1988). Situated knowledges: The science question in feminism and the privilege of partial perspective. *Feminist Studies, 14*(3), 575-599.

Hubbard, R. (1995). *Profitable promises: Essays on women, science and health.* Monroe, ME: Common Courage Press.

Jansen, S. C. (1993). The future is not what it used to be: Gender, history, and communication studies. *Communication Theory, 3*(2), 136-148.

Lawlor, R. (1991). *Earth honoring: The new male sexuality.* Rochester, VT: Inner Traditions.

Leopold, A. (1971). *A Sand County almanac.* New York: Oxford University Press.

Lippmann, W. (1922). *Public opinion.* New York: Harcourt Brace.

Maccoby, E. E. (1990). Gender and relationships: A developmental account. *American Psychologist, 45,* 513-520.

Monsma, J. W. (1994). *Her talk/his talk: Addressing some key issues in gender communication.* Paper presented at the Western Social Science Association Annual Meeting, Albuquerque, NM.

Odum, H. T. (1971). *Environment, power, and society.* New York: John Wiley.

Odum, H. T. (1987). *Environmental systems and public policy.* Gainesville: University of Florida Press.

Orr, D. W. (1992). *Ecological literacy: Education and the transition to a postmodern world.* Albany: State University of New York Press.

Pearson, J. C., Turner, L., & Todd-Mancillas, W. (1991). *Gender and communication.* Dubuque, IA: William C. Brown.

Phillips, S. U., Steele, S., & Tanz, C. (1987). *Language, gender, and sex in comparative perspective.* New York: Cambridge University Press.

Preston, C. B. (1994, July). [Presentation at Brigham Young University Women's Studies Annual Workshop, Snow Bird, UT.]

Rawlins, W. K. (1989). A dialectical analysis of the tensions, functions, and strategic challenges of communication in young adult friendships. In J. A. Anderson (Ed.), *Communication yearbook* (Vol. 12, pp. 157-189). Newbury Park, CA: Sage.

Steiner, L. (1992, October). Construction of gender in newsreporting textbooks 1890-1990. *Journalism Monographs,* p. 135.

Tannen, D. (Ed.). (1993). *Gender and conversational interaction.* New York: Oxford University Press.

Williams, T. T. (1991). *Refuge: An unnatural history of family and place.* New York: Random House.

Wood, J. T. (1994). *Gendered lives.* Belmont, CA: Wadsworth.

Worldwatch Institute (Brown, L. R., Flavin, C., & Kane, H.). (1992). *Vital signs: The trends that are shaping our future.* New York: Norton.

5

Action Research
Implications for Gender, Development, and Communications

Edna F. Einsiedel

The tradition of separating theory from practice has had a long existence. This separation is echoed in the distinction often made between basic (or theory-building) research and applied research, the latter often seen as the poor cousin of the former, sometimes atheoretical in nature, sometimes the practical ground on which theoretical seeds are tested. Action research affords a different lens with which to view the theory-practice relationship, one that explores the realm of experience and practice as potential sources of theoretical ideas, particularly those relating to social change. It is a framework that offers fruitful ways of examining gender issues in development practice, recognizing that the knowledge-building process proceeds and is strengthened by understanding the world of practice and experience and, particularly, experience that is motivated by efforts for social transformation.

This chapter will explore the nature and origins of action research and will examine how women's experiences in the realm of development practice have contributed to enriching theoretical ideas on development. The possibilities for expanding our understanding of communications in the context of gender and development issues will then be explored.

What Is Action Research?

Action research has been described in various ways and the following statements are illustrative rather than comprehensive:

Action research . . . has as its central feature the use of changes in practice as a way of inducing improvements in the practice itself, the situation in which it occurs and the rationale for the work, and in the understanding of all of these. (Brown, Henry, & McTaggart, 1988, p. 84)

Inevitably, the action researcher becomes involved in creating change not in artificial settings where effects can be studied and reported dispassionately, but in the real world of social practice. In action research, the intention to affect social practice stands shoulder to shoulder with the intention to understand it. (Kemmis & McTaggart, 1988, p. 33)

Action science is an inquiry into how human beings design and implement action in relation to one another. Hence, it is a science of practice [that] calls for basic research and theory building that are intimately related to social intervention. (Argyris, Putnam, & Smith, 1985, p. 4)

The focus on social practices and the ways that research and reflection leading to theoretical insight might inform the process of social change is called "praxis." Action research's historical roots extend back to Aristotle and his notion of self-reflection as a way of informing practice (Grundy, 1987). The term *praxis,* introduced by the Greeks, was equated with the idea of "critically informed practice." Praxis requires reflection on three levels: the exact nature of the action as conducted (and as it is perceived and understood by its practitioners), the impact or consequences of the action, and its context. This reflection is meant to transform the knowledge base so as to guide further action.

Another important dimension to praxis is its guidance by a moral disposition to act for the enhancement of truth and justice, a disposition labeled "phronesis" by the Greeks. Without such a moral imperative, one was left with technique and the possibility of perpetuating self-deception and injustice (Grundy, 1987). Praxis is, in essence, building "theories" of understanding from practice for social transformation.

It is the *praxis* dimension of action research that distinguishes the latter from *applied* social science. An applied science is normally the counterpart to basic science and the applied scientist is typically seen as one who puts into practice the principles uncovered by basic scientists. Argyris and his colleagues (1985) have argued that "this division of labor reinforces a pernicious separation of theory and practice" (p. 5). What action research emphasizes instead is the importance of practical knowledge, the knowledge of the practitioners or the community of individuals with whom the researcher interacts, and the need for harnessing this knowledge to inform social theory and to achieve social change.

John Dewey provided an early impetus for action research by suggesting that a philosophy isolated from the rest of life was sterile and that social practice was an important focus of scientific inquiry (Dewey, 1929). His argument that teachers, educational researchers, and community members might collectively address educational problems to bring about reform was a way of demystifying and democratizing the conduct of research. In this regard, it was his contention that practical judgments shared common attributes with theoretical judgments. Foreshadowing the action-reflection process of action research, he viewed inquiry as a continuous, self-corrective process, with every contention or knowledge claim open to further criticism and discussion (Bernstein, 1971).

For Dewey, the usefulness of research findings in the realm of practice was the final arbiter of the research's "value":

Educational practices provide the data, the subject matter, which form the problems of enquiry. . . . These educational practices are also the final test of value and test the worth of scientific results. They may be scientific in some other field, but not in education until they serve educational purposes, and whether they really serve educational purposes can be found out only in practice. (Dewey, 1929, p. 47)

Viewed from this perspective, his analysis of scientific inquiry was clearly not value-neutral. Moreover, he saw praxis as a base for genuine social reconstruction (Bernstein, 1971), a view strongly echoed by other action researchers' work emphasizing the need for research to become the base for social understanding and social change (see, for example, Lewin, 1946, 1952).

The essence of action researchers' ideas might be summarized as having the following attributes: It was an effort that focused specifically on the amelioration of some social problem; such a focus would also provide the impulse for inquiry and the articulation of social theory; the effort was a collaborative one, or a joint project between social actors and researchers; its process was characterized by cyclical elements of action-reflection, consisting of analysis, fact-finding, conceptualization, planning, execution, more fact-finding, and evaluation. However, the successful maintenance of this process and resolution was one that required systematic efforts at training.

The work of a number of Third World scholars under the rubric of participatory action research provides additional perspectives on action research. Particularly relevant is the work of Paulo Freire (1970), whose notion of conscientization referred to a process of raising self-awareness via collective inquiry and reflection to promote empowerment and change. He brought home the idea that the "peasants" were not illiterate but brought with them to the learning situation their own life experiences, their own valid stocks of knowledge: "It is sufficient to be a person to perceive data of reality, to be capable of knowing, even if this knowledge is mere opinion. There is no such thing as absolute ignorance or absolute wisdom" (p. 43).

The work of Orlando Fals-Borda similarly rests on the action-reflection principle and the importance of praxis, with its twin prongs of practice, or experience, and commitment: "Through the actual experience of something, we intuitively apprehend its essence. . . . In participatory action research, such an experience, called vivencias in Spanish, is complemented by another idea: that of authentic commitment" (Fals-Borda & Rahman, 1991, p. 4).

Finally, the contributions of feminist theory as embodying the major principles of action research need to be underlined. Two elements of feminist theory are particularly relevant. First, its starting points for investigation are the situations and experiences of women in their social contexts. It is through understanding of these experiences—through the vantage points of the women themselves—that theoretical understanding can be developed. Second, it sees itself as critical and activist on behalf of women. The rejection of social science as value-free and the outright incorporation of advocacy as part of the research process as well as the involvement of the research subjects in the organization of understanding and the organization of action bring feminist research into the realm of action research.

Action Research in Development Contexts: Issues of Gender and Development

The development arena in the last few decades has been the site of debates over approaches to modernization and economic development. In our examination of the specific context of gender, development, and communications, the process has been informed by several decades of development experience and research. Within this larger context, however, the interactive influences of feminist development researchers and practitioners and communities (national or local), particularly the women of these communities, are central to our interest.

Accommodated within much of the development work are a variety of theoretical models that have predominated at various times: modernization, dependency, and, more recently, people-centered (Korten, 1990) or communitarian (Tehranian, 1994) models. The protagonists within each of these models have varied: the state and its bureaucratic power, the transnational or multinational corporation with its international power base, or the homogeneous mass simply called "the people" or "the community" (i.e., in the last two and a half decades). Only recently has there been recognition of women and the different perspective of development afforded by women's experiences.

New conceptions about the place of women within the development sphere began with the same general question posed by feminist theory (Lengermann & Niebrugge-Brantley, 1992): And what about the women? Indeed, this was the starting point for Boserup's (1970) work on women and development, the first effort to systematically delineate the sexual division of labor in agrarian economies at an international level. She further analyzed the changes that occurred in traditional agricultural practices as societies modernized and the differential impacts of modernization processes on men and women. Remarkably, the data she analyzed had long been available but hers was the first effort to examine gender as a differentiating variable. Subsequent work examined the place of women in such diverse economies as agriculture and fishing, and in these cases, the consistent findings remained as follows:

• Women's work was underpaid if not unremunerated and, consequently, undervalued. Yet, women were responsible for fuel, water, child rearing, sanitation, family health— essentially the entire range of so-called basic needs.

• Women's work in the production economy remained unrecognized for a long time, or was regarded as "supplemental" to that of men. The result was lower wages for women, fewer training opportunities, more difficult working conditions, or less protection in the labor market, to name only a few problems. In looking at women's work, feminist development researchers and practitioners essentially posed this set of questions:

• Where are the women in the development situation?
• If not present, why? If present, what exactly are they doing?
• How do they experience the development situation? What do they contribute to it?
• What does it mean to them?[1]

Why were women invisible in the development process? At the macro level, the emphasis on gross economic indicators such as GDP, GNP, per capita income meant overlooking the informal economy populated mostly by women. It also meant devaluing the productivity within the private sphere— the home—where women were responsible for household health, nutrition, sanitation, child rearing.

This emphasis on paid productive work, and the concomitant neglect if not ignorance of what women did in the productive sector, resulted in development processes and outcomes that not only favored men (e.g., emphasis on agricultural technology that promoted faster harvesting) but did little to improve aspects of the work that involved women (e.g., weeding, marketing of fish); in some instances, women's work situations were exacerbated by this neglect or inequitable attention. For example, when common lands have been privatized and traditional tree cover exploited for commercial purposes, women's workloads have been found to increase in such areas as fuel gathering and water collection (see, for example, Dankelman & Davidson, 1989). Some land reform programs have resulted in women losing some of the traditional land rights when titles have been awarded to male heads of households.

In examining the intersections between theory and practice in the area of gender and development, it is clear that theoretical shifts have been influenced as much by conceptual changes of heart or paradigmatic preferences as by lessons from the field. A brief recapitu-

TABLE 5.1 Communication Practices From Theory and Policy Perspectives

Theory	Policy Approach	Communications Approach
Modernization	Welfare	Big media, top-down, Effects perspective
Dependency	Equity	Alternative media
		Bottom-up
Grassroots/Communitarian	Empowerment	Appropriate media
		Horizontal, vertical

lation of these patterns in the gender and development area and their implications for communications theory and practice will demonstrate this.

The Western-based development programs that sprung out of the emergency relief and reconstruction efforts after World War II targeted aid to "vulnerable groups," with women among the prime beneficiaries. This development model, imported to developing countries with development assistance efforts, similarly provided relief and assistance to people in Third World countries, primarily to women and children. These efforts were premised on the notions of women as passive players in development, with their primary responsibilities being motherhood and child rearing. The top-down approach of handing out free goods and services was, not surprisingly, buttressed by communication activities that were in support of national modernization efforts (known as "development support communications").

The modernization model was quickly challenged by dependency theorists who maintained that capitalist development models were even more likely to exacerbate inequalities between men and women. This model—known in policy shorthand as Women and Development—recognized women's active participation in the marketplace and women's need to earn a viable livelihood. The economic independence of women was therefore stressed at the same time that such independence was premised on reducing the status of insubordination at home. The equity approach for development entailed bringing women's status

up to par with men in both the domestic and the public spheres, implying a clear redistribution of power and resources (see Moser, 1990).

Such an approach carried with it a model of communications that viewed media systems as no more than ideological apparatuses of international capitalist structures. The approach promoted by equity proponents instead argued for delinking of communication vehicles from their multinational ties and focusing on alternative or indigenous media.

The equity approach encountered resistance if not hostility from aid agencies for reasons ranging from a lack of measurable indicators to the perception of interference with local traditions.

The policy approach of empowerment emerged primarily from the experiences of field-workers at the grass roots. Among Third World women, this approach was elucidated in the recognition that women's activism in Third World contexts had long historical roots independent of the women's movement in the West. It was embedded in historical struggles for nationalism and workers' rights as well as peasant struggles. This approach recognized the importance of looking at the status of women and men, and that women's circumstances were as much a function of such factors as class, race, ethnicity, and historical context as they were of gender. This policy approach became known as the Gender and Development (GAD) approach and was characterized by researchers from the University of Sussex as having the following characteristics:

• GAD is an approach preoccupied with gender relations in a variety of settings. It is not concerned with women per se but with the social construction of gender.

• GAD sees women as agents of change, and not as recipients of development assistance.

• GAD privileges a holistic perspective, which means it focuses on "the fit between family, household or the domestic life, and the organization of both political and economic spheres."

• GAD sees development as a complex process for the betterment of individuals and society itself. Therefore, in examining the impact of development, a proponent of the GAD approach would ask: Who benefits? Who loses? What trade-offs have been made? What is the resultant balance of rights and obligations, power and privilege between men and women, and between social groups?

• The GAD approach is skeptical about the role of the market as the distributor of benefits; rather, it stresses the need for women's self-organization so as to increase their political power within the economic system (Young, 1988).

Although sharing the interest of the equity approach in the transformation of structures of subordination, it avoided the confrontational activities characteristic of the equity approach and worked for legislative changes via political mobilization and popular education.

The communication approach embedded within the empowerment model combines the use of appropriate media. This means using the range of channels from big to little media, indigenous media, local to international media systems.

The shifts in theory, policy, and practice were important from an action research perspective because these reflected considerations of lessons from the field and collabora-

tive efforts to share and organize understanding. An early reflection of this process was a 1976 conference on women and development held at Wellesley College that brought together people from both North and South, from the policy and field sectors and academics, interested in issues confronting women in Asia, Latin America, Africa, and the Middle East as these regions went through significant socioeconomic, political, and cultural changes (see Wellesley Editorial Committee, 1977). Such a meeting, and subsequently many others like it, saw some of the lessons from the field translated into policy directions that were, at the same time, reflections of different theoretical emphases.

Implications for Development Communication

In the preceding discussion, we made the case that action research's foundation of viewing practice as the base for theoretical understanding offers another useful arena for theory-building on development and, more particularly, on development communications around issues of gender.

The area of women and development has provided an arena within which to address questions of praxis. The evolution of different theoretical frameworks represents the interweaving of theory and practice. Such an evolution has demonstrated two elements in particular: that theoretical changes that explain the human condition or address social problems in the interest of larger social transformations can fruitfully result from lessons from the field, and that such frameworks can result from beneficial collaborations between academics as field-workers and grassroots women, between North-South partners.

The lessons from the area of gender and development suggest that all development issues have gender implications. Such implications occur in both public and private spheres; hence communication issues ought to be con-

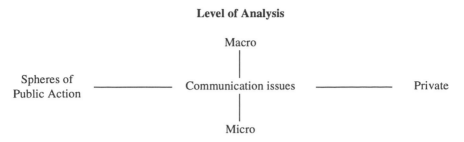

Figure 5.1. An Analytical Model for Women, Communications, and Development

sidered with this in mind. In terms of levels of analyses, experiences with gender issues in development demonstrate the fruitfulness of considering both macro and micro levels. The implications for communications are thus represented in the model in Figure 5.1.

This model suggests that development communication issues surrounding gender need to be examined at both macro and micro levels, in both public and private spheres. Much of the writing on gender and development has not addressed communication issues directly while those in the communications area have often examined communications in narrower contexts: for example, how media channels (such as video) might be used to communicate ideas, how communication strategies might be used to address issues that have direct impacts on women (health), how message design processes might include women's participation, and so on. The need to locate our understanding of gender, development, and communications issues in the context of micro and macro levels as well as at the intersection of public and private spheres is underlined in the following observations:

Since political structures and political ideas shape and set the boundaries of public discourse and of all aspects of life, even those excluded from participation in politics are defined by them. Non-actors . . . are acting according to rules established in political realms; the private sphere is a public creation; those absent from official accounts partook nonetheless in the making of history; those who are silent speak eloquently about the meanings of power and the uses of political authority. (Scott, 1988, p. 24)

In examining both streams of literature, it is useful to consider how analyses of communication issues within the realm of action research might occur. Three areas suggest themselves.

Focus on Communication Processes

The issues of communication as dialogue and communication processes involved in participation are important. They are particularly important within the public and private spheres, at the micro level of analyses. What aspects characterize communication and decision making within the household? How are these replicated within the public arena vis-à-vis such activities as civic (or religious or cultural) participation?

As women carry out the variety of social interactions that mark their worlds of experience, they are acting on meanings located in discursive practices that are produced and reproduced, contested, and transformed. How the discourses intersect with women's material lives is an important realm for investigation in order to understand how women locate themselves in different sites, whether in the household, the marketplace, or the civic arena, and the meanings they attribute to these locations in the context of power differences.

What communication patterns are evident in the dialogic processes surrounding learning for social transformation? A number of action researchers have depicted this dynamic and participatory learning process with parallel concepts. Argyris and Schön (1978), for example, suggest "deutero-learning" as a concept describing participants learning how to learn. Freire (1970, p. 136) argues for a dialogic relationship characterized by "subjects who meet to name the world in order to transform it." Korten (1981) has used the notion of "social learning" in an organizational sense to describe "a well-developed capacity for responsive and anticipatory adaptation" (p. 498), a capacity that involves recognizing and learning from errors, collaborating with community groups, and joining knowledge-building with action.

Communication in the context of social mobilization locates any communication and development project squarely in the realm of action research. Such efforts at social mobilization have underlined group communication processes for developing leadership skills, mobilizing social cohesion, and engendering collective action. The experiences of the Grameen Bank and the Self-Employed Women's Association in South Asia, for example, have involved social organizing to facilitate women's understanding of their legal entitlements and to bargain collectively for the provision of credit.

Communication as Social Practice

In many development projects, the communication issue has been reduced to a technical one: "What messages, through which channels, for which audiences?" Even those sensitive to the use of appropriate information technologies have sometimes tended to isolate the communication process. We suggest that another exploratory arena is afforded by interpretivist ethnographic accounts of communication practices that exist within a community, and particularly among women,

that serve as inhibiting conditions for change or, alternatively, may serve to enrich efforts at information diffusion. If communication patterns are expressions of one's cultural identity, what endogenous communication practices of women might be incorporated into development practice? It is in the realm of everyday life that individual and sociocultural communication systems and practices are elaborated. These practices include the indigenous modes of knowledge transfers, the use of community media (or, more broadly, cultural sites for information exchange such as the local barbershop, the marketplace, or the stream where women gather to do the wash), and the linguistic or discursive practices underlying local communication processes.

The experience of Heath in a southern rural community in the United States is instructive.[2] She lived and worked in an Appalachian community for nine years, living multiple roles as ethnographer, consultant to a local school system, and university professor, an experience laid against the backdrop of the implementation of a national desegregation policy in the United States.

Communication was a central concern for both black and white parents, the teachers, and the personnel in local mills where many of the parents worked. Many in the community felt the need to understand better how others communicated, why teachers and students often could not understand each other, why questions were sometimes not answered, or why habitual ways of talking and listening did not always seem to work. Heath began by conducting extensive communication ethnographies in the rural black and white communities. Informally, she also gathered information about surrounding middle-class communities. She discovered systematic differences between the communities in the use of print, the rules of interaction around print, and the degree to which reading and writing were bound up with community members' identities. While uncovering the fact that some teachers were aware that children in different communities exhibited differences, she also noted that they were unable to identify or explain these differences.

Heath shared this information with the teachers, raising their consciousness about the different uses and meanings of print that characterized the different communities. The teachers and Heath then discussed her own methods about learning, with the idea that the teachers themselves would incorporate, adapt, and themselves translate their ethnographic knowledge to their classrooms. In the end, they became learning researchers, who used knowledge from ethnographies of communication to build a two-way channel between communities and their classrooms (Heath, 1983).

Communication as a Social Right

In this context, macro- and microstructures are implicated in terms of structures that promote access. We define *access* on several levels: access to the various modes of communication (or "technologies"), access in terms of appropriate skills, access in terms of ownership possibilities, and access with regard to content production. This democratization of communication for women needs to be examined and understood at these various levels of access, even at the most basic level of literacy, a level often overlooked in feminist work. As Bunch argues, literacy is more than a skill; it is a key to the practice of freedom, to use a Freirean phrase.

Reading and writing are valuable in and of themselves, and women should have access to their pleasure. Beyond that, they are vital to change for several reasons. First, they provide a means of conveying ideas and information that may not be readily available in the popular media. For example the idea of women's liberation first spread through mimeographed articles. . . . Second, reading and writing help develop an individual's imagination and ability to think. . . . Third, an individual's access, through reading a variety of interpretations of reality, increases that person's capacity to think for

herself, to go against the norms of the culture, and to conceive of alternatives for society—all of which are fundamental to acting politically. Fourth, reading and writing aid each woman's individual survival and success in the world, by increasing her ability to function in her chosen endeavors. (Bunch, 1979, p. 2)

These communication areas are not mutually exclusive categories. If the larger political structures do not support the rights to speak, to mobilize, and to organize, how have women workers created more democratic processes under these conditions? Case studies have shown that the creation by women of democratic spaces in varied contexts has extended the meanings of organization and communications by situating these processes within the women participants' personal and social existence (see, for example, Rowbotham & Mitter, 1994).

This theme of communications as the bridge for women within and between the public and private spheres is one that needs to be explored more systematically. Many accounts of women's roles in social movements invariably point to the significance of the personal and the difficulty of disentangling the public and private spheres. This is already evident in feminist attempts to modify and expand the notion of the communication "public sphere" (McLaughlin, 1993), with its publishing, dissemination, and dialogic routines through grassroots publishing companies, film and video distribution networks, lecture series, on-line discussion groups, research institutes, and so forth.

It is clear that our theoretical understanding of communication issues in development as these affect women can be usefully embedded within the world of practice. The rich variety of case studies available on communication practices (see Riaño, 1994) are a useful start. It is also clear that research on women, communication, and development must be integrated with studies of the development process itself. What the lessons from the field point to will finally need to be integrated with our theories of understanding for social action.

Notes

1. These questions were adapted from Lengermann and Niebrugge-Brantley's (1992) general questions for understanding women's situations.

2. I, obviously, am using the term *development* generally here to describe sites or cases not limited to "Third World" contexts.

References

Argyris, C., Putnam, R., & Smith, D. M. (1985). *Action science.* San Francisco: Jossey-Bass.

Argyris, C., & Schön, D. (1978). *Organizational learning.* Reading, MA: Addison-Wesley.

Bernstein, R. J. (1971). *Praxis and action.* Philadelphia: University of Pennsylvania Press.

Boserup, E. (1970). *Women's role in economic development.* London: George Allen and Unwin.

Brown, L. C., Henry, J., & McTaggart, R. (1988). Action research: Notes on the national seminar. In S. Kemmis & R. McTaggart (Eds.), *The action research reader.* Victoria: Deakin University Press.

Bunch, C. (1979). Feminism and education: Not by degrees. *Quest, 5*(1), 1-7.

Dankelman, I., & Davidson, G. (1989). *Women and environment in the Third World: Alliance for the future.* London: Earthscan Publications.

Dewey, J. (1929). *The sources of a science of education.* New York: Livewright.

Fals-Borda, O., & Rahman, M. A. (1991). *Action and knowledge: Breaking the monopoly with participatory action research.* New York: Apex.

Freire, P. (1970). *Pedagogy of the oppressed.* New York: Herder and Herder.

Grundy, S. (1987). Three modes of action research. *Curriculum Perspectives, 2*(3), 23-34.

Heath, S. B. (1983). *Ways with words.* Cambridge, MA: Cambridge University Press.

Kemmis, S., & McTaggart, R. (1988). *The action research reader* (3rd ed.). Victoria: Deaking University Press.

Korten, D. (1981). Community organization and rural development: A learning process approach. *Public Administration Review, 40*(5), 480-511.

Lengermann, P. M., & Niebrugge-Brantley, J. (1992). Contemporary feminist theory. In G. Ritzer (Ed.), *Contemporary sociological theory.* New York: McGraw-Hill.

Lewin, K. (1946). Action research and minority problems. *Journal of Social Issues, 2*(4), 34-46.

Lewin, K. (1952). Group decision and social change. In G. E. Swanson, T. Newcombe, & E. Hartley (Eds.), *Readings in social psychology* (pp. 459-473). New York: Holt.

McLaughlin, L. (1993). Feminism, the public sphere, media and democracy. *Media, Culture, and Society, 15,* 599-620.

Moser, C. (1990). *Gender planning and development: Theory, practice and training.* London: Routledge Kegan Paul.

Riaño, P. (1994). *Women in grassroots communication: Futhering social change.* Thousand Oaks, CA: Sage.

Rowbotham, S., & Mitter, S. (1994). *Women encounter technology: Changing patterns of employment in the Third World.* New York: Routledge.

Scott, J. (1988). Gender: A useful category of historical analysis. In J. Scott, *Gender and the politics of history* (pp. 24-50). New York: Columbia University Press.

Tehranian, M. (1994). Communication and development. In D. Crowley & D. Mitchell (Eds.), *Communication theory today.* London: Polity.

Young, K. (1988). WID: A retrospective glance into the future. *Worldscape, 2*(1), 3-5.

Wellesley Editorial Committee. (1977). *Women and development.* Boston: Ailey Publishers.

6

Afrocentric, Archetypical Perspectives
Four Black Female Journalists

Frankie Hutton

African American women have been said to fit uneasily into feminist praxis and theory because they have historically endured the dual rejections of race and gender. According to mass communication educator Paula Matabane, the isolation and oppression experienced by these women has led to a "very consistent" primary identification with race, not gender (Matabane, 1989, p. 118). Black feminist bell hooks makes the point that while women of color have been reluctant to express solidarity with white feminists, it is resistance to white female domination that is the real issue (hooks, 1989, p. 179). According to hooks, the resistance to domination issue must be separated from black female refusal to engage in the feminist struggle. Be that as it may, historically, black female journalists ostensibly have been associated in theory and in practice with race more than gender.

Although the relationship between black women and feminism has been sensitive and debatable, the Afrocentric or race-centered model brings exciting possibilities for new mass communication research on black women. The Afrocentric model seems particularly apropos where the contributions of black women to American journalism are concerned largely because it is positive. This chapter introduces the Afrocentric model as a foundation to analyze and explore the work of four archetypical African American female journalists: Mary Shadd Cary, Ida B. Wells, Hazel Garland, and Phyl Garland. These women represent each period of American journalism since blacks have been involved in the profession.

As a concept, Afrocentricity fits uneasily into mainstream academia primarily because it is misunderstood and, for the misguided, is associated with militancy, disturbance of the status quo, and anti-Eurocentrism. The Eurocentric foundation of higher education causes it to suffer from uninclusiveness (Schiele, 1994). Moreover, African Americans are still plagued by negative images that have transcended their perpetuation in the nation's early literature and mass media to become strong threads of the contemporary sociopolitical fabric. Black women have been victimized by these negative images. In praxis and in scholarship, journalism, as well as the mass media, need to do much more to address and to correct the long-standing negative images that define and depict blacks in America.[1]

Although Afrocentricity has not been without debate and scathing criticism,[2] Ayele Bekerie, Afrocentric scholar at Temple University, has explained that in its true sense Afrocentrism is anything but anti-Eurocentric. Bekerie assesses the Afrocentric model as purely positive and says it is the "generative theme" that makes it a "hot and captivating paradigm" (Bekerie, 1994, p. 137):

> One of the most salient features of Afrocentric theory is a belief in a creative approach to problems or conditions of life and living. Creative here refers to the ability to freely voice and revoice, symbolize, sign, and design a whole range of human activities. Afrocentrism strives to generate, sustain, and perpetuate viable and dynamic communities of African peoples. (pp. 133-137)

Jerome H. Schiele of Clark Atlanta University has been one of a number of other respected scholars to embrace and broaden the concept of Afrocentricity. Schiele addresses the concept's implications for higher education and explains that it is more far-reaching than mere exposure of schoolchil-

dren to historical accomplishments of people of African descent; Afrocentrism seeks to do more than expose white racism and culpability (Schiele, 1994, p. 151). For instance, a preeminent proponent of Afrocentricity, scholar-author Molefi Asante of Temple University, has assessed black male leaders through the ages with regard to their Afrocentricity—their humanizing, caring work, and genuine devotion to help their race. Asante (1992) points to the Afrocentric ideology of victorious thought and avows that "Afrocentricity is the centerpiece of human regeneration."[3] Asante explains that the African ancestors have given signs through "songs, poems, stories, sermons, and proverbs" that demonstrate their "inexorable movement toward the humanizing function" (p. 6). Recent research has shown that humanitarianism was in fact a significant aspect of the development of the early black press in America (Hutton, 1993, pp. 36-52).

Still, journalism and related disciplines also seem to suffer an uneasiness where Afrocentrism is concerned. This is suggested to be the case because there is a dearth of the positive, humanizing, and regenerative aspects of Afrocentricity in journalism praxis and scholarship. The profession is still tremendously driven and marred by its avaricious nature and more recently its proclivities toward pathological coverage, especially where African Americans are concerned. Accordingly, as a first line of attack in changing this pathology, higher education in general and journalism in particular need to lead the way with thoughtful, creative curriculum development that is focused not solely on inclusiveness but on more positive, humanistic, community-building paradigms. Such curriculum development fits the concept of Afrocentricity because it would render journalism positive and intended for the good of the whole of humanity, rather than for any select group. Specifically, in attempts to bring Afrocentrism to journalistic praxis, more attention could be paid to coverage that quells negative, stereotypical images in favor of more balanced reporting of African Americans and other groups that have been marginalized in American society. The benefits of such an overhaul are obvious. There seem to be other tremendous possibilities for the humanizing and regenerative aspects of Afrocentrism to be spread throughout journalism—in higher education and in media practice.

The focus here is an analysis of the work of four archetypal journalists through the prism of Afrocentrity through the ages. Beginning in the second quarter of the nineteenth century with the life and work of Mary Shadd Cary, the analysis in this chapter spans the whole of black female involvement in American journalism, including Ida B. Wells and Hazel Garland and her daughter Phyllis Garland. Although their personalities, tactics, and lifetimes differed, what all of these exceptional women have in common is their commitment to race centeredness and humanitarian approaches to journalism. These women seem also to share a regenerative nature; that is, they not only helped the race but had some sense that they were role models with the inherent mission of passing along their skills, abilities, and exemplary, hardworking lifestyles to help other generations. Hence journalism and Afrocentricity become two interactive elements that bind these women together in history.

Mary Shadd Cary

Born October 9, 1823, in Wilmington, Delaware, Mary Shadd represents the primal force of black women in American journalism. She was even seen as courageous and race-conscious during her nineteenth-century lifetime; ever since then, her journalistic work and contributions to African American life have been studied in earnest.[4] From all indications, Mary Shadd was greatly influenced by her father and followed the race-conscious, humanitarian example set by him, although there is no evidence that Abraham D. Shadd had ambitions for his daughter. Abraham

Shadd was by profession a shoemaker; by moral, social conscience, he was active in the National Convention for the Improvement of Free People of Color in Philadelphia in the early 1830s and was an operative in the Underground Railroad. His home and financial means were used clandestinely to aid fugitive slaves. By standards of that time, the Shadd family was well-to-do and could have lived insularly in some degree of comfort, offering little or no aid to their race. It is clear that the foundation for Mary's path in life was set at home during her early years in Wilmington and in West Chester, Pennsylvania, where the family moved to take advantage of more accessible education. In West Chester, Mary Shadd attended a private school run by Quakers, who probably also influenced her preference for an unfrivolous, industrious lifestyle.

When Mary returned to Wilmington as a young woman teacher and organizer of a school for black youth, she began a focus on black equality and integration that paralleled her professional life. As a naysayer to materialism and conspicuous consumption, Mary Shadd rejected segregation or isolation as being the right path for blacks though it was a reality that continued in America and in Canada, where she lived in exile for a while during the turbulent 1850s. Any analysis of Shadd's approach to helping her people would probably note that the tactics she used were debatable, although her race work was ostensibly earnest and constant. At a glance, her goal and dogged striving for the integration of blacks both in Canada and in the United States would seem also to be antithetical to what is described here as Shadd's Afrocentric commitment, but this is not necessarily the case. Afrocentric theorists describe Afrocentrism as concerned with centeredness, humanitarianism, and commitment to race. Specifically, Molefi Kete Asante points to it as "an idea that gives agency to African ideals, customs and people so that they become subjects, agents, actors in history and are viewed as such rather than as mere spectators" (personal communication, April 3, 1995). Mary Shadd was an agent, a catalyst for change. As such, the Afrocentric concept well embraces Shadd's persistence in her journalistic work, begun in earnest and continued primarily to help her race rather than to earn a living. It is immaterial whether she helped her people in the diaspora, as she did when she moved about in Canada beginning in 1851, or in slavery, or in so-called freedom; her journalistic work and her life reflected a commitment to her people, however and wherever she found them.

Mary Shadd's was not a malleable character; clearly, aspects of her life and the tactics she used were as disquieting to people of color as to whites. She does not fit the fantasy image so often associated with white women of the time or of the beleaguered, overworked domestic, the job classification most often relegated to free women of color. Mary Shadd was a good-looking, bright, and articulate woman, but these attributes did not provide her with immunity to criticism. A pamphlet published in 1939 about America's black heroes described Shadd as "progressive and energetic," a woman whose marriage to Thomas F. Cary of Toronto did not cease her pattern of extensive travel in connection with race-conscious work (Bragg, 1939, p. 14). Although she most certainly was admired, the ideals and the dreams she had for her people were at times repressed by them. She seemed to require some kind of perfection of blacks in the aggregate that they could not live up to given the harsh realities of what they had experienced in America and in the continued racism of the time. Nevertheless, Mary Shadd Cary's moves were carefully designed to be what she earnestly thought was of greatest aid to her people and this fact is clear at various stages of her life. When, for instance, as a young woman she left West Chester to return to Wilmington, it was with a mind to teach black children and to begin her own school.

In 1849, Mary Shadd Cary wrote and published what could be described as her first real journalistic endeavor, a race-conscious pamphlet titled "Hints to the Colored People of the North." What she had to say in the pamphlet was abundantly self-righteous and angered a lot of black people. She chastised her people for their vanity, expensive entertainment, and extravagance. One of the agents who agreed to help sell the booklet admitted in a letter to Frederick Douglass's newspaper, the *North Star*, that blacks were so put off with the pamphlet's content that they would not even "have had it as a gift" (Unnamed, 1849). Mary Shadd Cary had charged that too many blacks were "making a grand display of themselves" and "were too much in attendance at public dinners, excursions, and the like" (Cary, 1849, p. 1). There was simply too much self-elevation work to be done to waste time on entertainment, in the view of Mary Shadd Cary.

Likewise, when she moved to Canada in 1851, she appears to have selected places of residence strategically so as to be of greatest aid to her race. This fact has been noted by one of her biographers, Jason Silverman (1988), who explained: "She chose Windsor as the place to begin helping elevate the immigrants because it was one of the most destitute Black communities in Canada West" (p. 90). It was in Windsor that Mary found great opposition to her ideals of integration as she attempted to garner support to start a private school for black and white children. Her sense of the matter was that an integrated school would go a long way toward community building and toward the acceptance and total integration of blacks in Canada. Nevertheless, in this regard, Mary's view falls in line with Afrocentricity, which does not negate integration and the peaceful coexistence of races of people. What Afrocentricity rejects is the domination of one race by another. As led by abolitionist Henry Bibb and his wife Mary, most of the leading blacks in the Windsor area favored separatism and were in opposition to Mary's efforts for an integrated school. As can be imagined, white Canadians who already had the benefit of public schools for their children were also in opposition to Mary's endeavor.

In fact, obstacles and opposition were never foreign to Mary; in this way, her life was immensely difficult, but she seemed never completely broken or deterred. In Toronto, Canada, she also received opposition as the head of her own newspaper, the *Provincial Freeman,* which she began publishing in March 1853. This endeavor made her the first black female to publish a newspaper in North America. In an attempt to defray what some thought of as too bold an undertaking for a woman, Mary Shadd called upon Samuel Ringgold Ward, another abolitionist expatriate, to lend his name to the masthead of her integrationist newspaper. This move was instrumental in the paper's shoestring survival as were a number of lecture trips the plucky female editor made to solicit subscriptions to support the newspaper. That she managed to publish the *Provincial Freeman* for nearly six years was quite a feat given opposition from some of her own people. As the mastermind behind the *Provincial Freeman,* Mary Shadd was remarkably race-centered and business-minded. This led her to eventually move the newspaper to Chatham, the site of a larger community of blacks. Nevertheless, sustaining the *Provincial Freeman* became increasingly difficult, so much so that Mary was forced to cease publication of the weekly in 1859. We can only surmise that the lack of support for the newspaper resulted from the economic depression of the time, but the newspaper's failure probably also harks back to her integrationist politics and outspokenness, aspects of her nature for which she had many detractors as well as admirers.

It must be emphasized that Mary Shadd Cary's selection of newspapers as a channel to help her race was a bold undertaking during her lifetime because only a very few women, most of them white, ventured into journalism. The brilliant, outspoken Margaret Fuller was one such woman and, it could be ventured, a contemporary of Mary Shadd Cary's. Although Fuller died in an accident

at sea in 1850 and there is no evidence that she and her black counterpart, Mary Shadd Cary, ever made acquaintance, the two courageous, audacious women both came particularly under their fathers' provocative influence. Each must have been aware of the other's work.

After her own *Provincial Freeman* folded, Mary wrote occasionally—always from a race-conscious perspective—for other receptive newspapers such as Frederick Douglass's the *New National Era.* In April 1872, while living in Washington, D.C., she wrote a second "Letter to the People" published in Douglass's weekly in her usual outspoken manner. This time the focus was the lack of opportunity for advancement of black tradesmen and contractors, who were being pushed aside by whites and denied work and recognition for their skills. Mary Shadd lamented that "the lessons of slavery are not so readily unlearned by White Americans," who seemed to relish keeping blacks down in "a mean, uncertain and cruel spirit" (Cary, 1872, p. 1).

It should be noted that although she was outspoken and could be described as petulant at times, Mary Shadd Cary's work to help her race was wide ranging and she was a "first" in several areas. In addition to being the first black woman to edit a newspaper in North America, she was probably also the first (or among the first) black female recruiter of troops during the Civil War. She was the first woman to attend Howard University's law school, a feat she accomplished part-time over a decade. She graduated at the age of 60 in 1883.[5] Mary Shadd Cary died of cancer in Washington, D.C., on June 5, 1893.

Ida B. Wells

Ida B. Wells was born into slavery in Holly Springs, Mississippi, in 1862, 39 years after Mary Shadd Cary. In fact, the influence of industrious, relatively successful fathers is but one of a number of similarities between the women. Both women seemed not to slow down their race-conscious work after marriage. Both were tremendously active women who traveled and lectured a great deal, relative to other women of their time. Whereas Mary's dad was a successful shoemaker, Ida Wells's dad was a well-respected master carpenter. And like Mary Shadd, Ida Wells could also be persistent and self-righteous about race matters when she perceived an injustice.

Ida Wells's birth and formative years were overshadowed by the Civil War and the subsequent exciting Reconstruction era. The latter offered hope for her people that was soon crushed by the South's violent redemptive temper as evidenced by the rise of the Ku Klux Klan and vicious, cowardly lynchings and murder of black men and women by southern whites. A horrific yellow fever epidemic wiped out half of her family when it hit Holly Springs in 1878. Parentless at age 14, Ida was destined to raise what was left of her brothers and sisters and to pursue a career of journalism and teaching just as Mary Shadd Cary had done before her. Ida Wells's life and work have been the subject of her autobiography, *Crusade for Justice,* edited by her daughter Alfreda M. Duster (1970), and a more recent biography by Mildred Thompson (1990a). Her autobiography is a classic in American post-Reconstruction literature.

In fact, much of Ida Wells's courage and boldness of approach as she sought ways to help her race parallel Mary Shadd Cary's although the two were not contemporaries in the true sense. Apparently both women realized the worth of their work in helping their race overcome despotism and injustice, because they were unrelenting in their efforts to fight these ills over their lifetimes. Neither woman was deterred by the incredibly violent, intolerant times during which she lived. This fact would seem to render both of them all the more valuable as models of Afrocentricity and of a status to be continuously revered both in journalism and in American history.

By her own admission, Ida Wells had a "hard beginning" made particularly so by the yellow fever epidemic that overtook Holly Springs. Because of her own determination and will to do so, Ida raised six brothers and sisters, including one who was handicapped. Briefly, she was aided in this pursuit by a 70-year-old grandmother and later an aunt. Eventually, Ida moved her family to Memphis, Tennessee, where she was able to secure a better teaching job than the one she had in rural Mississippi. It was while teaching in Memphis that she had her first bout with racism and injustice while riding in the nonsmoking railroad car designated for whites. Ida was dragged out of the car and forced to sit in a smoking car designated for blacks. For this maltreatment, she sued the Chesapeake and Ohio Railroad and won, although the case was later overturned. She remembered well that in trying to get the railroad to stop its mistreatment of blacks she was also victimized in the majority white press and imaged as a troublemaker.[6]

The case against her was significant in a number of ways. It was the first case of a black plaintiff to appeal to a state court in the South after the repeal of the Civil Rights Bill by the U.S. Supreme Court in 1883. Equally important is the fact that the case began Ida's race-conscious commitment to fight injustice, which she elected to do primarily as a journalist. The case is also noteworthy because black people did not rally to support her in this civil rights struggle. She persisted, however, paying her attorney in installments out of her small teacher's salary, and knowing full well that the landmark case would have significant implications for black people later. This fact is crucial in understanding the nature of Ida Wells as a race-conscious, forward-looking journalist: If she genuinely felt that she was right about something and that what she was doing was of general benefit to the race or humankind in the long run, she did it and risked the consequences and often her life.

Ida Wells seemed actually to delight in the journalism profession and in helping her people through her profession. She probably also relished the power she found in journalism to influence and enlighten her race. After writing briefly for Kansas City's *Gate City Press* and editing the *Evening Star,* which she described as "spicy" journalism, Ida began to catch on to the nature of journalism, and her byline was sought after. In her biography, she credits the Reverend William J. Simmons as providing the real breakthrough opportunity for her in the journalism profession. In terms of regional black leadership, Simmons was prominent, president both of a state university in Louisville, Kentucky, and of the National Baptist Convention as well as editor of the Negro Press Association. In Ida Wells he saw a capable writer and social activist who would serve the race well in the newspaper business. Ida seemed also duly impressed with him:

> He was truly a big man, figuratively and physically. He wanted me as a correspondent of his paper and offered me the lavish sum of one dollar a letter weekly. It was the first time anyone had offered to pay for the work I enjoyed doing. I have never dreamed of receiving any pay. For the next three years I was on the staff of the American Baptists. I went to Louisville to the first press convention I had ever attended and was tickled pink over the attention I received from those veterans of the press. I suppose it was because I was their first woman representative. (Duster, 1970, pp. 31-32)

Ida's excitement for journalism grew tremendously after this experience and in 1889 she was asked to be a writer for the *Free Speech* of Memphis. This she resolved to do only as part owner and editor. The journalistic experience more than any other revealed that Ida Wells was in her element—had found her niche. Traveling extensively, including trips back to Mississippi, she was tremendously well received and likewise gained more support through subscriptions for the newspaper than she had ever imagined. Ida Wells delighted in this success and was proud that she was actually earning a living from journalism, although she also managed to get

into a few editorial scrapes in the black community that resulted from her self-righteous, no-nonsense nature as much as anything else.

On a subscription-gathering lecture trip for the *Free Speech* in May 1892, Ida Wells got the news that racist whites had lynched three black men, including a dear friend of hers in Memphis. This atrocity, more than any other occurrence in Ida Wells's life, brings into focus her unrelenting courage and marks her as a superior crusading journalist. It is presented in synopsis here to make the point salient that not even the threat of death deterred Ida Wells from exposing the lynching of innocent black men as one of the gravest, most heinous crimes in the United States of her time. Ida Wells's antilynching journalism is legendary, and yet it has not been captured and taught as standard fare in American journalism history, or in minorities and the media courses, to the extent that it deserves to be. The model set by her work could be of tremendous value to journalism students, not because she was black and a woman and her exciting story needs to be told, but because what she wrote was provocative and muckraking as it treaded the ground of humanitarian, socially responsible, and committed journalism. Moreover, Ida Wells's commitment to her race through antilynching commentary was life-threatening.

The three of Ida's friends lynched in Memphis in 1892 were grocers and partners in the People's Grocery Company. There had been growing resentment in whites that the three black men successfully operated a business in direct competition to a white-run grocery establishment. A white grocer had previously enjoyed a business monopoly in a predominately black neighborhood. The resentment over the increasingly successful black grocery business apparently brewed and then boiled over as a result of an apparently unrelated scrap between young boys of both races. After standoffs and violent episodes in the black neighborhood where the grocery stores existed, the three black grocers were arrested and later taken by mob force from jail and murdered. According to Ida Wells, the same mob "took possession of People's Grocery Company, helping themselves to food and drink, and destroyed what they could not eat or steal" (Duster, 1970, p. 51). The city and county authorities did nothing. Before being lynched, Ida's friend urged his people to leave Memphis. Despite the vehement objection of whites who depended on black labor and business support, Ida wrote editorials and commentary in *Free Speech* urging her people to leave Memphis and head West. This they did in droves. Meanwhile, Ida, fearing for her life, bought a gun and psychologically prepared herself to use it when necessary. Remembering the tension-filled time in her autobiography, Ida wrote:

> Although I had been warned repeatedly by my own people that something would happen if I did not cease harping on the lynching of three months before. I had bought a pistol the first thing after Tom Moss was lynched, because I expected some cowardly retaliation from the lynchers. I felt that I had better die fighting against injustice than to die like a dog or a rat in a trap. I had already determined to sell my life as dearly as possible if attacked. I felt if I could take one lyncher with me, this would even up the score a bit. (Duster, 1970, p. 62)

It was Timothy Thomas Fortune who urged Ida not to return to Memphis when he met her a few weeks later during her first trip to the Northeast. The illustrious editor of the *New York Age,* the North's leading black newspaper, Fortune gave Ida Wells solace and a job with his weekly that she was obliged to take. In Memphis, Ida's own newspaper was wrecked, her partners scattered.

During and following Ida Wells's stint with the *New York Age,* she unfurled a strategy of antilynching journalism and lecture tours that took her throughout the Northeast and Chicago. The voluble Wells received tremendous support from the black club women in Brooklyn and the New York City area. She then went abroad to England, Scotland, and Wales to spread the word of the horrific

lynching of blacks, particularly in the southern United States. Wherever she spoke in Great Britain, Ida Wells sought support to continue her single-handed crusade to stop the hideous practice of lynching. She wanted the world to know of this profound flaw in America's character, and looked for ways to press the issue. The discrimination against blacks at the 1893 World's Colombian Exposition in Chicago annoyed her so greatly that she took that opportunity to write a pamphlet titled "The Reason Why: The Colored American Is Not in the World's Colombian Exposition." In this pamphlet, she explained the history of lynching in the United States and showed how it had been perpetuated under the thin guise of appropriate justice for black men who raped white women: Publishing her pamphlet in the summer of 1893, she estimated that more than 1,000 men, women, and children had been lynched over a 10-year period:

> The first 15 years of his [the black man's] freedom he was murdered by masked mobs for trying to vote. Public opinion having made lynching for that cause unpopular, a new reason is given to justify the murders. . . . He is now charged with assaulting or attempting to assault white women. This charge, as false as it is foul, robs us of the sympathy of the world and is blasting the race's good name.[7]

Wells's race-conscious journalism and muckraking continued when she moved to Chicago and married attorney Ferdinand L. Barnett. Soon after her marriage, she purchased the *Chicago Conservator,* a small weekly newspaper, from her husband and his partners. As a towering woman of her race and as an American, Ida Wells was involved in numerous social-civic activities and women's rights organizations as she lived the rest of her life in Chicago. She died there of uremia in 1931.

Hazel Garland

Hazel Garland's Afrocentric approach to journalism and to helping her race through journalism was far different than that of Mary Shadd Cary and Ida Wells Barnett. Hazel Garland's journalistic work did not lend itself so much to controversy and danger as it did to community building and civic service in the segregated, Negro world of the Pittsburgh area in the 1940s and 1950s.

Born Hazel Hill in 1913 in a small farming community near Terre Haute, Indiana, at an early age she moved with her family to the Pittsburgh area. There she married photographer Percy Garland, made a home and apparently a significant difference in the tri-city area of McKeesport-Clairton-Duquesne. Residing in the McKeesport, Pennsylvania, community and working at the *Pittsburgh Courier* in various capacities for over 40 years, Hazel Garland was an extraordinary journalist who was the recipient of numerous journalistic and civic awards. Although Garland's journalistic career and contributions to the discipline have not received the kind of scholarly, pedagogical attention they deserve, some writers and scholars have taken note that she is archetypical in American journalism history.[8]

What kept Hazel Garland in touch, and indeed in tune, with her community was membership and activity in a number of church and social-civic groups, including the National Council of Negro Women, the Girl Friends, Inc., and county, state, and national Associations of Colored Women's Clubs, Inc. One of her colleagues, city editor Frank Bolden, remembered the caring aspect of the journalism she practiced and how she managed to find something good in every echelon of the community:

> She would give a wedding in the housing projects the same attention she would give a wedding that occurred in the upper echelon of what was then called Negro society. When I asked her about it, she'd say, "They're all human, and as long as I'm doing this, that's the way it's going to be."[9]

Hazel Garland seemed to thrive on civic activity and service and this aspect of her life was transposed into her journalism career. Her approach to journalism was undeniably race-conscious and sensitive to the needs of the community of which she was so much a part. For this caring and sensitivity, her community bestowed respect and recognition through numerous awards and citations, including a National Headliner Award in 1975 and the Jane Swisshelm Award, named for the first newspaper woman in Pittsburgh and presented by the Pittsburgh Chapter of Women in Communication in 1976. From a Jewish women's group in Pittsburgh, she was given a citation for "bridging the gap between races."[10]

Garland's journalistic instincts were ostensibly clear and vital: Stay in touch with the community, and work to make it a better place to live. With this attitude as a foundation, she rose from stringer to reporter to women's editor to columnist to city editor to editor-in-chief in her 40 years with the *Courier* organization. Her community-building instincts carried over into one of her most wide-ranging journalistic endeavors, a column known as "Video Vignettes." A unique media criticism endeavor, "Video Vignettes" was the first column of its kind written by a woman of color. In it Garland did not mince words when she tackled topics relating to the short shrift blacks received in the television industry. In 1970, for example, she urged the commercial television industry to become more socially responsible in addressing the inadequacies "that society has forced upon Black people" (Garland, *Pittsburgh Courier,* January 10, 1970, "Video Vignettes" column, p. 12). She praised shows that made attempts to correct the negative images of blacks in the media. And with a hint of sarcasm in 1972, she commented, "So, how long will it be before a Black will anchor a network news show is anybody's guess because I haven't the slightest idea" (*Pittsburgh Courier,* February 5, 1972, p. 14). She deplored the token number of blacks in local and national television and criticized "lily white" shows such as *Ozzie and Harriet* and *My Three Sons* (January 8, 1972, p. 14). In

January 1975, she gave encomiums to new FCC Commissioner Benjamin Hooks in "Video Vignettes." Hooks, at that time, was the first and only black member of the Federal Communications Commission. In Garland's assessment, he "came well prepared for his position on the FCC" because he was "one of the country's most eloquent orators" and had a fine legal mind (January 25, 1975, p. 14).

When interviewed about her journalistic work, Garland remembered that, like herself, the *Pittsburgh Courier* was a viable part of the community. She reminisced that at times the entire *Courier* organization rallied around a humanitarian cause:

> Once I did a story about a little girl who had some sort of ailment that caused her to need extra oxygen. It cost eight dollars and forty-nine cents a day, so we called her "the eight forty-nine girl." We had a special room built onto her parents' house because she had to have pure air—no germs or anything. We built this room and furnished it, and the paper paid for the oxygen until she died. When you do things like that, it makes you feel you're accomplishing something. (Collins, 1980, pp. 103-118)

When she died at age 75 in 1988, Hazel Garland was already legendary in the Pittsburgh area for her expansive, community-conscious brand of journalism. Although she was not a college graduate, Garland engineered her own education through insatiable reading and a series of courses taken whenever she could. She was the only female journalist ever to serve two consecutive years as a juror to select winners of the Pulitzer prizes in New York City. Phyl Garland, Hazel's only offspring, is the chief testament to her mother's regenerativeness. Early in her career, Phyl, like numerous other novice journalists, came under her mother's tutelage at the *Courier*. Phyl says of her mother: "If I'd had to pick a mother, Hazel Garland would have been it; she was a wonderful, kind and talented woman."[11]

Phyl Garland

The erudite, gutsy journalist daughter of Hazel Garland, Phyl Garland has also made her mark in journalism primarily in the black press. Distinguishing herself as a music and entertainment journalist covering black artists, Phyl sees herself as a writer-reporter who also happens to teach. Phyl Garland, in a most unlikely progression from her work almost exclusively with the black press, was in 1995 a respected full professor at the prestigious Graduate School of Journalism at Columbia University in New York. It is her conscientious, Afrocentric selection and support of the black press—even though she could have moved away from it in the 1970s when most journalists of color did—that makes her unique in mainstream journalism education. By hiring Phyl Garland in a full-time faculty position in 1973, the selection committee at Columbia University saw beyond the typical misassessments of the black press to the heart of Phyl's excellent, credible journalistic ability gained other than through mainstream journalism. Phyl, who is also said to be the first full-time female member of the journalism faculty at Columbia, explained her sense of the black press vis-à-vis how it has been viewed in the mainstream:

> Unlike the other Blacks or women who had taught within the high ceilinged building endowed by Joseph Pulitzer, my total orientation has been the Black press, commonly considered unquestionably inferior or tangentially insignificant by both journalistic and academic establishments. Yet it had been my breeding ground and my source of inspiration. (Garland, 1974, p. 169)

Contributing a chapter to Henri LaBrie's *Perspectives of the Black Press,* Phyl well remembers her precarious prejournalism career period following graduation from Northwestern University's Medill School of Journalism in Evanston, Illinois:

I deliberately did not seek a job in the mainstream though I'm certain none of the publications to be found there would have hired me anyway, back at the tail end of the 50s. In fact, I wanted to remain as far removed from the establishment as possible. My first job after leaving Northwestern was as a maid and attendant in a beauty shop, located in a stuffy little prefabricated suburb of Evanston, IL. (Garland, 1974, p. 177)

One has but to read Phyl Garland's feature articles and writings on black musicians and music to sense that she herself is a music buff and a musician who knows and feels the pathos of her race through both music and journalism. She has carefully, sensitively profiled numerous musicians from pianist and composer Fats Waller, to jazz great Wynton Marsalis, to world renowned opera singer Jesse Norman.[12] In her posthumous profile on "stride pianist" Fats Waller for *TV Guide* during the revival of his work *Ain't Misbehavin'*, Phyl educated her readers:

It was not long before he [Waller] discovered Harlem's flourishing jazz clubs and rent parties where the "stride pianists"—whose technique made the piano alone sound like a full jazz band—held sway in stride, the pianist would swing the left hand, alternating a bass octave with a chord played toward the middle of the piano, while the right hand played the melody and variations in a ragged tempo. Stride players commonly engaged in "cutting" contests, taking turns at the keyboard, trying to outdo each other in speed and musical complexity. (Garland, 1982, pp. 33-34)

Although Phyl is versed in all types of music, soul is her specialty and for her it bares all—the pain and suffering, the good times, the injustices, and the resilience of her people in the face of all odds. Soul music is, according to Phyl, "manifest in the overlapping forms of blues, jazz, gospel and popular music" whose very "essence is indisputably Black." Associate editor and music critic for *Ebony* magazine when she wrote *The Sound of Soul* in 1969, Phyl admitted to no attempt

at "Olympian objectivity" as she addressed soul music as the aesthetic property of blacks. In her soul music sourcebook, Phyl was clear about an Afrocentric approach from the outset. She explained: "My perspective is a Black one, and I have concentrated on the work of Black musicians simply because I believe them to be the most vital factor in the development of modern music." Spanning nearly 250 pages of history, facts, and interpretation of soul music, Phyl explains in *The Sound of Soul* that the seeds of what is known as the blues in America began in 1619 when the Dutch *Man of War* deposited 20 or so Africans in Jamestown, Virginia, and continued as black slave labor rendered the nation the "richest the world has ever known."

As a young woman looking for female role models outside her own household, Phyl found one in journalist Evelyn Cunningham. Phyl described Cunningham, who left journalism to become special assistant to Nelson Rockefeller, as "a swinging sophisticate who commuted between Pittsburgh and New York." What impressed Phyl most about Cunningham was that she carried herself with dignity and was both worldly and down to earth (Garland, 1974, p. 175).

Phyl Garland is in fact an extraordinary role model herself. New York *Daily News* columnist Richard G. Carter profiled her as a "natural" role model in 1988 when she was 52 years old, after 15 years at Columbia.[13] Carter said Garland's own career is a "barometer" of what can happen in the face of the real struggle of getting blacks into decision-making positions in the media (Carter, 1988). Garland, an award-winning, earthy journalist, does not seem too impressed with herself or the fact that she has trained hundreds of journalists at Columbia. Although she avoided mainstream journalism in preference for work mostly for the black press, Garland is aware of her regenerative nature, her place in helping the race and the journalism profession as role model and teacher of journalists. Phyl Garland's former students run the gamut. She has taught, for instance, race-conscious journalist Jill Nelson whose national best-selling book *Volunteer Slavery: My Authentic Negro Experience* is a compelling account of her somewhat troubled life and time as a *Washington Post* journalist (Nelson, 1993). Another of her students, Sheryl Hilliard Tucker, savvy former editor-in-chief of *Black Enterprise* magazine who is now editor of *Your Company,* a *Money Magazine* business quarterly, well remembers Garland as a role model at Columbia University. Tucker, who deplores the proclivity of many white Americans to lump all blacks together in pathological assessments, says she came from a good family and has had an excellent education and a good life both at Cornell as an undergraduate student leader and at Columbia as a graduate journalism student (S. Tucker, personal communication, April 23, 1995). For Tucker, Garland was an extraordinary role model who "embodied the responsibility that I felt Black journalists have" to bring others along. Of Phyl Garland's teaching and advising style, Tucker said she didn't know whether to call it teaching or training, but what Phyl Garland did for her at Columbia certainly was not preaching.

> I felt that I was in a newsroom situation and that Phyl was my editor when she critiqued my work. She didn't just look at how you wrote something, she looked at how you thought about it. She wanted her students to succeed, black or white. (S. Tucker, personal communication, April 23, 1995)

As archetypical black female journalists, Phyl Garland and her mother Hazel, Ida B. Wells-Barnett, and Mary Shadd Cary have in common a firm commitment to race through journalism. Respectively, they confronted the potent issues of violence, racism, and oppression as women and as journalists. Ostensibly, all four of the women, from different periods in American journalism history, serve as exemplary role models for the race and for the whole of the journalism profession. Al-

though their tactics and styles differed greatly, their race-first journalism places these women in the quintessential Afrocentric category, a concept that has exceptional potential as it is concerned with positive, humanitarian, regenerative forces that could have tremendous implications for journalism praxis and theory.

Notes

1. A number of new studies have focused on the treatment of minorities by the media and also the negative images of blacks in particular. See, for instance, Clint Wilson and Felix Gutierrez (1995) and Camille O. Cosby (1994). Cosby recommends that the increased involvement of African Americans in television programming may result in a more accurate portrayal of African American images. See also Jannette L. Dates and William Barlow (1990). This anthology explores the difference between the way mainstream media images African Americans, and black image makers' response to continued distorted stereotypical portrayals. Also of interest, specifically regarding the portrayal of blacks in the newspaper industry, is Jill Nelson (1993), an autobiographical account of her frustrations in her efforts to get more positive images of blacks projected in the *Washington Post Magazine* during her stint as a reporter/writer there in the 1980s. From a historical perspective, see the chapter "Women" in Frankie Hutton (1993), which suggests that the synergy between black women and black press editors resulted practically from the need to uplift the race and particularly women from negative images of them that were pervasive in nineteenth-century American culture. Also of interest is Rodger Streitmatter's book, *Raising Her Voice: African-American Women Journalists Who Changed History* (1994).

2. See, for instance, Linda Chavez (1987). Also of interest is the book *Not Out of Africa: How Afrocentrism Became an Excuse to Teach Myths as History* (1996) and an overview of the debate over Afrocentricity presented for general readership in a *Village Voice* cover story by Greg Thomas (1995).

3. In Asante (1992, p. 20), the author points to seven Kiswahili principles of nationhood, which are *umoja* (unity), *Kujichagulia* (self-determination), *ujima* (collective work and responsibility), *ujamaa* (cooperative economics), *nia* (purpose), *kuumba* (creativity), and *imani* (faith), based on Nguzo Saba as revealed in America by Maulana Karenga.

4. See, for instance, a discussion of Mary Shadd Cary's work in Freeman Bragg's *Heroes of the Eastern Shore* (1939). Also of interest is Jim Bearden and Linda Jean Butler's work for younger readers, *Shadd: The Life*

and Times of Mary Shadd Cary (1977). A staple article in the research of Shadd is Alexander Murray's "The Provincial Freeman: A Source for the History of the Negro in Canada and the United States" (1959). More recently, an excellent biographical essay written by Jason H. Silverman is "Mary Shadd and the Search for Equality" (1988). Silverman also focuses on Shadd's work in Canada in *Unwelcome Guests* (1985).

5. There is a minor discrepancy in terms of her graduation date from Howard's law school. Freeman Bragg gives the year as 1884, while Shadd's biographer, Jason Silverman, cites 1883.

6. Ida Wells addresses this issue in her autobiography *Crusade for Justice* (Duster, 1970, p. 19).

7. See the pamphlet in the appendix to the biography on Wells (Thompson, 1990b).

8. See, for instance, Jean E. Collins's (1980) chapter devoted to Hazel Garland. Although intended for young readers, this chapter is important because it is based on an interview with Garland during the twilight of her life. Garland's story is told in her own words. Also of note are Roland Wolseley's (1990) brief mention of Garland as well as Marianna Davis's (1995) feature on Garland. Because black journalist Ethel Payne's life and work parallel Hazel Garland's, also of note is Rodger Streitmatter's article, "No Taste for Fluff: Ethel L. Payne, African-American Journalist" (1991).

9. This quotation is from private unpublished notes on Hazel Garland, property of Phyl Garland.

10. See Garland's obituary in the *Daily News* (McKeesport, Pennsylvania), Wednesday, April 6, 1988.

11. Phyl Garland about her mother (interview by author, April 23, 1995, New York City).

12. As examples of Phyl Garland's entertainment journalism, see in *Ebony*, "Jessie Norman: Diva" (March 1988), "Wynton Marsalis: Musical Genius Reaches the Top at 21" (March 1983), "The Lady Lives Jazz: Mary Lou Williams" (October 1979), and in *Stereo Review*, "Al Jarreau" (February 1978).

13. See Richard G. Carter's column, "As a Role Model, Phyl Garland's a Natural" (1988).

References

Asante, M. K. (1992). *Afrocentricity*. Trenton, NJ: Africa World.

Bearden, J., & Butler, L. J. (1977). *Shadd: The life and times of Mary Shadd Cary*. Toronto: University of Toronto Press.

Bekerie, A. (1994). The four corners of a circle: Afrocentricity as a model of synthesis. *Journal of Black Studies, 25*(2), 133-137.

Bragg, F. (1939). *Heroes of the eastern shore*. Baltimore: Author.

Carter, R. G. (1988, January 9). As a role model, Phyl Garland's a natural. *Daily News* (New York), p. 9.

Cary, M. S. (1849, June 8). [Letter to the editor]. *North Star* (Rochester, NY), p. 1.

Cary, M. S. (1872, April 11). [Letter to the editor]. *New National Era* (Washington, DC), p. 1.

Chavez, L. (1987). *Alternatives to Afrocentrism* (Monograph). New York: Manhattan Institute.

Collins, J. E. (1980). *She was there: Stories of pioneering women journalists*. New York: Julian Messner.

Cosby, C. O. (1994). *Television's imageable influences: The self-perspective of young African-Americans*. New York: University Press of America.

Dates, J. L., & Barlow, W. (Eds.). (1990). *Split image: African-Americans in the mass media*. Washington, DC: Howard University Press.

Davis, M. (1995). *Contributions of black women to America*. New York: P. Lang.

Duster, A. M. (Ed.). (1970). *Crusade for justice*. Chicago: University of Chicago Press.

Garland, P. (1974). Staying with the black press: Problems and rewards. In H. La Brie (Ed.), *Perspectives of the Black press*. Kennebunkport, ME: Mercer House.

Garland, P. (1982, June 19). Ain't misbehavin'. *TV Guide*, pp. 33-34.

hooks, b. (1989). *Talking back: Thinking feminist, thinking black*. Boston: South End Press.

Hutton, F. (1993). *The early black press in America: 1827-1860*. Westport, CT: Greenwood.

Lefkowitz, M. (1996). *Not out of Africa: How Afrocentrism became an excuse to teach myths as history*. New York: HarperCollins.

Matabane, P. (1989). Strategies for research on black women and mass communication. In P. J. Creedon (Ed.), *Women in mass communication* (pp. 117-122). Newbury Park, CA: Sage.

Murray, A. (1959, April). The Provincial Freeman: A source for the history of the Negro in Canada and the United States. *Journal of Negro History*, p. 4.

Nelson, J. (1993). *Volunteer slavery: My authentic Negro experience*. New York: Penguin.

Schiele, J. H. (1994). Afrocentricity: Implications for higher education. *Journal of Black Studies, 25*(2), 150-169.

Silverman, J. H. (1985). *Unwelcome guests: Canada West's response to American fugitive slaves, 1800-1865*. New York: Associated Faculty Press.

Silverman, J. H. (1988). Mary Shadd and the search for equality. In L. Litwack & A. Meier (Eds.), *Black leaders of the nineteenth century*. Chicago: University of Illinois Press.

Streitmatter, R. (1991). No taste for fluff: Ethel L. Payne, African-American journalist. *Journalism Quarterly, 68*(3), 528-538.

Streitmatter, R. (1994). *Raising her voice: African-American women journalists who changed history*. Lexington: University Press of Kentucky.

Thomas, G. (1995, January 17). Who's winning the black studies war? *Village Voice, 40*(3), 23-29.

Thompson, M. I. (1990a). *Ida B. Wells-Barnett: An exploratory study of an American black woman, 1893-1930.* Brooklyn, NY: Carlson.

Thompson, M. I. (1990b). *The reason why: The Colored American is not in the World's Colombian Exposition* [Pamphlet, August 30, 1893]. In the appendix to *Ida B. Wells-Barnett: An exploratory study of an American black woman, 1893-1930.* Brooklyn, NY: Carlson.

Unnamed correspondent. (1849, June 8). [Letter to the editor]. *North Star* (Rochester, NY), p. 1.

Wilson, C. C., & Gutierrez, F. (1995). *Race, multiculturalism and the media.* Thousand Oaks, CA: Sage.

Wolseley, R. (1990). *The black press U.S.A* (2nd ed.). Ames: Iowa State University Press.

7

Return of a
Native Daughter

Anne Wilson Schaef

For Native Peoples, truth is in the storytelling and can be discovered in the listening. Native women will, by default, transform communications if and when we communicate in the forms that are congruent with who we are. One of the most effective forms of communication for a Native woman is storytelling. I, therefore, want to tell a story of my experience with the media.

The Story of a Return
of a Native Daughter

I was born in Arkansas right close to the Arkansas-Oklahoma border near the seat of the Cherokee nation. I never knew my father. He and my mother separated before I was born. My first years were spent in Oklahoma living with my mother and my great-grandmother. I was born during the Great Depression and we had little money. As a conse-quence of being "poor" and my mother's being very close to the Cherokee, we lived very simply and very close to the earth. Much of our food was gathered from nature's bounty and medicines were herbs and healing plants. I continue to be amazed with how much I remember of those early days.

Even after we left the "land of our roots," my mother always insisted on going back every year and reconnecting with "our land." And, wherever we lived—my stepfather did research for the government—my mother always insisted that we live in the country and learn about the Native people who belonged there.

I marvel now at the freedom and safety I had in that little town and the way my mother let me "roam" the woods with my dog when I was 5 and 6 years old. She always taught me that nature was safe when we respected it and were one with it. It was people with whom we had to be careful. She also raised me to trust myself and to have my own thoughts, ideas, and opinions. I knew to respect and value other people's opinions, and mine were just as important. In fact, my mother was a one-woman civil rights movement in Arkansas and Oklahoma back in the 1930s. My admiration for her grows with age. I chose a good parent in her. It was only natural that I get involved in the civil rights movement in the 1960s.

During the 1960s, I resistantly and stubbornly learned about my racism and my whiteness. I learned that racism wasn't just judging persons by the color of their skin—in some ways that was the easy part to grasp. Racism was a systems issue. I, as a white person, wasn't just racist because of my privilege and my advantage. I thought white. I felt white. I perceived white. I was trained to think out of the white, Western worldview and only when I knew and admitted this bias could I begin to perceive the issues of racism. Because of my training, background, and assumptions as a white person, I could never really understand what it meant to be black.

During those painful years, all I wanted was to be told I was "different"; I was on the right side of the fence; I was not like those "others." Luckily, I had a few black friends who would not let me get away with this slipperiness. The argument that I understood the black experience because I was a woman in a male-dominated society did not even hold water. Goodness knows, I sure gave it a try. I had to face what it meant to be a "trained white." Those lessons came hard and painfully. Then came feminism.

Feminism

Feminism answered a need. There was definitely something wrong with the inequality I felt and experienced as a woman. Luckily (or maybe not!) I was an intelligent and articulate woman, well educated and trained in white Western culture. My "putting it all in a nutshell" example of what it meant to be a woman in this culture is this: Often, when I was in a meeting with other people, mostly males, I would say something that was very deeply felt and very important to me. I could tell by the responses and the feeling in my gut that no one understood what I was attempting to communicate—often when it was clear that they very much wanted to understand me. I would then say, "You don't understand what I was saying." This statement would be met by, "Yes, I do." Then I would say, "If you understand what I am saying then you tell me what I just said." What I would then hear is their version of what they thought I said, which was clear to me not what I had been saying at all. I then would say: "That's not it," and the response was usually, "Yes it is!"

In *Women's Reality* (1981), I wrote about the tendency of the dominant system to think that it is the center of the universe and to interpret everything in terms of itself with no knowledge whatsoever that other realities exist and that they are valid. Although the myth is that the dominant system knows and understands everything, the reality is that what we call minority systems know and understand more because they have to know and understand the dominant system in order to survive and they have to understand their own system for their souls to survive. Unfortunately, some from the nondominant system have wanted acceptance in the dominant system so desperately that they have tried to unlearn their own system and, in so doing, I believe, jeopardized their souls and what their system has to contribute to the society.

Feminism has been an important part of my journey. And I have experienced much pain when I have seen feminists, at times, act and think like the dominant system so that their *content* focused upon women and their *process* was indistinguishable from what I have elsewhere called the White Male System. Unfortunately, when belief becomes dogma, oppression is not far behind.

Addiction

It was an easy leap from naming the White Male System to seeing the system in which we live as an Addictive System. Clearly, the system in which we live functions like an active addict and has the same processes and characteristics as an active addict. The characteristics of dishonesty, isolation (or nonparticipation or the myth of objectivity), the illusion of control, self-centeredness, and self-will that characterize the addict are or have become accepted characteristics of the system in which we live.

During this phase of my development, I began to see how I had been trained into the myth of objectivity and how this had resulted in nonparticipation with myself, with others, with nature, with the planet, and with my deep spirituality. I could see the difference between religion and dogma and my spirituality and how I had been asked to leave my spirituality behind in my head somewhere under the rubric of theology.

Participating in a recovery program moved me deeper into myself. A recovery paradigm gave me tools to live in a participatory way with myself, my world, and my creator; it gave me a conceptual and feeling framework to understand the insanity surrounding me in the culture.

The Mechanistic, Modernist, Western Scientific Paradigm

As I became clearer in myself and my investigations took on more of a global perspective, I began spending time with Native Peoples throughout the world and simultaneously began investigating the scientific paradigm that drives Western culture.

I was not surprised that the assumptions that underlie the science of Western culture are identical to those underlying what I had called the White Male System and the Addictive System. The fulcrum was different.

The fulcrum on which Western science turns is that of the myth of objectivity or nonparticipation. To be a good "scientific" member of Western culture, it is necessary to be "objective." "Objectivity" requires that we remove ourselves from ourselves and make ourselves "objects" to be observed (and manipulated). It requires that we remove ourselves from the "other" (persons, nature, countries, peoples, our creator) and make "the other" objects to be manipulated and controlled.

Western science has created a system that is based upon control and nonparticipation. Western culture needs addictions in order to exist! Unfortunately, this issue does not stop with control and nonparticipation. We have created a system in which the requirement to be in that system is that we have to be out of contact with ourselves and the wisdom of our inner beings and with our creator or our spirituality. We need this illusion of control to tolerate what we have created. We are supporting a system that must devour itself and everything with which it comes in contact in order to maintain itself.

Native Peoples

I have always lived among Native Americans, and during the process I have described, I found myself spending more and more time with Native Peoples throughout the world. With them was where I felt most at home.

Whenever I spoke at a university or convention, the Native people in the audience would always come up and tell me that I was one of them. In my heart I felt a resonance of truth and I did not want to be a "wannabe." I had seen so many people try to be Native through dress, beliefs, taking ceremonies, or just plain play-acting that I wanted no part of this. Hence, I always responded, "What you say feels true and I was born white." At times, I thought this "knowing" was because I was a woman and we had all experienced oppression.

Yet, I continued to feel the need to be with Native people. I did not want just to "take" from them as I believed enough had been taken from them. I always offered whatever I had to give that they might need and I became a listener—a respectful listener. In spite of the fact that I have earned my living as a speaker and writer, there were several years (and they continue) when I almost became mute. I just wanted to listen and soak in what I was hearing. The words, ceremonies, and prayers seemed to go directly into my hungry soul.

Gradually, I began to be invited to sit with and listen to Native Elders throughout the world as they spoke and taught. I have met with Native Elders from Alaska, Canada, the United States, Hawaii, Fiji, New Zealand, Australia, and Africa. Most were not glamorous shaman or medicine women and men (though some were). Most were just people who had grown old, learning and expanding along the way. All were those who had contact with the "old ones" who remembered the "old ones." All were deeply spiritual. All were my teachers and mentors. I began to see that being with these "wise ones," whoever they were, had become the core of my spirit. I had no preconceived notions about what they would teach me. I did not want to learn their "secrets" or their "ceremonies." I only wanted to hear whatever they wanted to share.

After some years, I could see that I was hearing the same message from Native Elders the world over. The language may be different, the myths may be different, the focus may be slightly different, but the message was the same from Native Peoples the world over.

The messages that were being repeated were as follows:

1. Our myths and legends have told us that a time would come when we have to tell what we know in order to save the planet. That time is now.
2. Centuries ago, the white people decided to go the way of mechanistic science and technology. That way will destroy the planet.
3. We have to operate in such a way that we participate with all things. We cannot stand outside of nature or we will destroy it.
4. We need to be grateful to the earth, the sky, and the sun and see that everything that we have comes from the creator through them.
5. We all have the same mother and the same father. We are all children of the same creator.
6. We need to respect all spiritualities. The creator has given each people a way to come near to the creator. No one way is "right." "I don't care how a person prays. I only care *that* he or she prays. Then, I can stand beside her or him."
7. We are one with all things. It's absurd to believe we are not.

I was deeply affected by all these teachings and knew them to be true in the deepest recesses of my being.

The more time I spent with Native people, the quieter I became inside and I more and more felt myself living my spirituality every moment. Sometimes, I would be so tenderly aware of my oneness with the creator that I would just sit and cry.

I also felt myself coming full circle back to a focus upon racism. I became hypersensitive to racism and painfully intolerant of it. I just could not understand how it could exist. If we are all one, how can we be racist? I could see how Western mechanistic science and culture isolates and divides. Analysis breaks down and breaks apart, moving toward isolation, while Native science moves toward oneness and wholeness.

I remember the first time I went to Australia and sat down with a group of Australian Aboriginal Elders. Even though they had invited me to come to be with them, when I arrived, they put me through the third degree. "Why are you here?" "What do you want?" "You're not trying to get your Ph.D. are you?" I was not sure why I was there and I said that. Finally, I said, "I'm here to find out why I am here." They liked that and then they said, "What kept you so long? We expected you in 1986!" I was planning to make my first trip to Australia in

1986 and the plans did not work out! "Then we thought you were coming in 1988." Again, I did plan to go and had an emergency appendectomy. By this point, I was wondering what else they knew.

"Oh, well, you're here now [1990] so let's get started." And they then proceeded to talk among themselves and ignore me. They talked about their lives, their beliefs, and their families. As I listened to them, tears began to roll down my cheeks and deep sobs clamored up from my belly. All this sobbing seemed just fine with them. I realized that what I was experiencing was relief—total physical relief. They were talking about what I knew! They knew what I had been trying to teach in the Living Process System. I had never been with a group that knew more about what I was trying to teach than I did. I had been with individuals, Elders and others in Native groups, who seemed to think more "white" than I did. Yet, here was a whole group of people who already knew what Living in Process was really about!

Most of the groups with whom I find myself in a teaching position are white Westerners. The very fact that they have chosen to enter my training groups and work with me indicates their openness. And working with them is a lot of work. For most of them, it takes several years before they begin to get a gut-level awareness of what another paradigm might be. These people in Australia already knew it! I thought about how exhausting it must be for Native Peoples to teach something so vital as their message to people who thought they already knew and understood everything. My body racked with exhaustion and relief. After I left that group of Australian Aboriginal Elders, I was not sure I could stay away. I actually felt a physical pull to return.

Native Wisdom for White Minds

Several years ago, a man who was an important mentor of mine and a great spiritual leader of the American Indian people said that he was giving me the responsibility to bring healing to the white people. I had no idea what that meant and was a bit overwhelmed by the whole idea so I gently put it aside until the time was right.

As I sat with Native Peoples and especially with their Elders, it was clear to me that the wisdom they were sharing with me was needed by the world, especially the Western culture or "You White People" as so many of them put it.

I talked with them about doing a daily meditation book using the words of Native Peoples and sharing my own reactions and responses to what I was learning. I planned to call the book *Native Wisdom for White Minds*. Almost all with whom I talked gave me their blessing and shared their thoughts. I also gathered quotations from writings I found in my travels. I wanted to put the book in a daily meditation format because I wanted the wisdom to be "like water on sandstone" and seep into our consciousness. I didn't want it to be like a "quick fix"—skim through the book and put it down.

I started writing the book and was excited about the format and information. I continued to check in with various Elders about it and was given their prayers and support. It was clearly something I wanted to do, and I certainly did not see it as one of my major theoretical books—even though an important book to me.

A short time before it was completed and in the publisher's hands, I received a letter from the publisher with whom I was working saying that the title was totally unacceptable and I would have to come up with a new title. I was shocked! The contract had been negotiated with this title and nothing was ever said until this late date.

I took some time and sat with this confusing development. I prayed and I consulted with some of the Elders. After some careful thought, intense consultation with Native Elders, and heartfelt prayer, I came to the conclusion that I was not at liberty to change the title. In the Native System, one does not break one's word to the Elders. It simply isn't done! The Elders had shared their wisdom and knowledge with me given the information that it was to come out in a book called *Native Wisdom for White Minds*. They had prayed about it and consulted on it. I had no way of contacting some of these Elders and some were dead. I could not renegotiate. The title of the book was a matter of integrity and a spiritual matter. Surely, this publisher could understand the importance of these issues in a Native System!

I sat down and wrote the publisher a sincere, honest letter about this being a spiritual issue for the Native Elders and for me. I stated the issues involved from a Native perspective as best I could and sent it off feeling that I had expressed the issues well.

What I received back essentially said, "I don't care whether it's a spiritual issue or not, do as I say—you bad girl." I couldn't believe it. Again, I prayed and consulted with the Elders and participated in some ceremonies to get clear. In the process, I thought about the reality of sacredness to Native Peoples. I thought about the sacredness of art objects that were chosen for the first Maori art exhibition sent to the United States. I remembered how the objects chosen were prayed over and accompanied as they were gathered together. Then, powerful Maori people went with them to see that they were handled appropriately and to see that proper prayers were given at every stop on the way. I tried to imagine what, if anything, we have in Western culture that has that kind of sacredness. I couldn't think of anything except money, perhaps.

I realized how many times Native Peoples have said, "This is a spiritual issue. This is a spiritual place," only to be ignored and have experienced Westerners running rough-shod over their ideas, their ceremonies, their land, and their spirituality because there is no grasp of what "the spiritual" means to them. I ached with the listening of nonunderstanding. I felt in my body the sacrilege and the violation of centuries. I cried and I prayed.

I also felt stuck. The book was ready to move into a quick production schedule. I needed the money and I had promised some of the money to Native projects and had already funded some. I experienced myself between the proverbial rock and a hard place.

I began to doubt myself. I began to doubt my perceptions. Whenever authors get in conflicts with publishers, we always have the phrase *author ego* leveled at us. (I don't know what the counterpart term for publishers is. Maybe this situation is analogous to there being a term in a sexist society for a man whose wife sleeps with someone else—*cuckold*—but no term for a wife whose husband sleeps with someone else.) I didn't want to be unreasonable and I certainly did not want to appear closed-minded (even though it appeared to me that my publisher was!). I asked friends and Elders to help me with possible solutions.

My publisher wrote me asking me to generate new titles. I answered that this was difficult for me because I did not know what was wrong with the original title, I did not know what the publisher wanted in a title, and I thought this was a very good title. Perhaps the publisher could suggest titles.

By this time, the manuscript had been completed and sent in, and I thought when they saw it, they could see that it was the best title. No such luck.

Finally, the publisher suggested titles. I could not believe what I was hearing. The titles were all so New-Agey that the Native people who had trusted me would hate them. I faxed back that these titles were setting me up to be mistrusted by Native Peoples, which was one of the concerns voiced by the publisher.

My agent and I were both confused by the intensity of the response to this title. This book was supposed to be just a little meditation book of Native wisdom and, a surprise, it was turning out to be the most controversial book I had ever written.

Returning Home

One week after *Native Wisdom for White Minds* was submitted, I went to a family reunion of the Irish (my mother's) side of the family. On a side trip to visit my mother's grave, my aunt—my mother's sister—was chatting and giving me information about the family. Without warning, she casually threw over her shoulder, "You knew your father was an American Indian, didn't you?" My world stopped. I felt frozen in time—suspended between realities. "No, I didn't," I said. "I can't believe she never told you," she said. "Well he was. Cherokee, I think."

I had a sensation of the tumblers of my being falling into place and my life suddenly making sense. I knew who I was. I was not who I *thought* I was. I was who I had always felt I was. Everything made sense.

I had a sudden flash of anger with my mother. "Why hadn't she told me?" Then, I had a quick flash of recognition. My stepfather and the society were very racist. She was protecting me from that. She chose to raise me with white privilege and she raised me like an Indian. She taught me the history of my people. I cried over the Trail of Tears before I went to school. I visited the first church in the Cherokee nation at the end of the Trail of Tears, where my family and my mother chose to be buried. Wherever we went, my mother dragged me through Indian museums, she saw that I spent time with Indian people, and she insisted that I learn American history from an Indian perspective. My first research paper in college was on the Mesa Verde Indians. Yet, she never told me.

I could see that she had saved me from the terrible racism I would have grown up with and she had kept me from knowing my roots, my tribe, as one of the tribe. The information felt like a precious, fragile piece of dragonfly wing that I was carrying in my cupped hands right at chest level. It danced and vibrated yet it seemed so fragile that if I let anyone even see it, it might shatter. At first, I couldn't tell anyone. Then, I began calling my closest American Indian friends. Every one of them said, "I knew that. I knew you were Indian. Don't ask me how, I just knew it."

One of my closest Elder friends asked me what my father's name was. When I said "Paul Ragsdale," he said, "I knew some Ragsdales. We went to Haskell Indian School together . . . but they were tall and blond and lived over on the Arkansas-Oklahoma border." All I ever knew about my father was that he was tall and blond and was born in Siloam Springs, Arkansas. I gasped. "They were tall and blond?" "Yes," he said. "They were part of what we called the 'civilized tribes' that had come from the East over the Trail of Tears. They mixed early with the Scotch and Irish and some of them were tall and blond but they were Indians, all right." I am having my heritage researched and, yet, my being, my Indian friends and teachers, and some white folks too know who I am.

Back to Racism

Ironically, when I had written *Native Wisdom for White Minds,* I had thought it was important that I was white because I could be a bridge. Suddenly, I was both white and Indian. Meanwhile, the struggles went on about the title of the book. Faxes were sent, phone calls were made, meetings were held, and prayers were offered. I decided to hang in with the negotiations because I wanted to wait until I discovered what the real issues were. I knew that whatever was going on was more than met the eye.

We set back publication dates and kept at it. In the meantime, the publishers suggested that we go ahead with the editing process as my books usually did not need much editing and we could move quickly as soon as we agreed on a title.

When I received the manuscript back, I knew what the problem was. I was dealing with racism. It was difficult to see it was racism because I thought I was white and they thought I was white. Throughout the manuscript, there were subtle little changes that whitewashed what was being said. *Native peoples* was changed to *Native people* (the rationale was there is only one native people). *Native people* was changed to *Natives.* (Insulting, wouldn't you say?) Other subtle changes were made so as to make the book more "attractive." What I wanted to say with integrity was subtly and skillfully being altered. Even the direct quotes from Elders and Native writers were edited!

I saw that racism is not just discrimination due to skin color. Racism is ideas and wanting those ideas to conform to one worldview. Racism is wanting the entire world to share a white, Western mechanistic worldview. Racism is bigger than patriarchy. Racism is not just what we think; it is how we think it. Racism is being asked to betray principles and beliefs and to defile the sacred.

I called the only person of color in publishing I knew and found someone who loved the book and the title. My spirituality was intact. I had not broken my word to the elders.

Summary

What does "freedom of the media" mean? Is it only to voice white, Western, mechanistic, patriarchal ideas? Why are so many Indians who publish with major publishers having problems like being picketed or being called "New Age" by their own people?

The process of treaty making and breaking is happening on a regular basis today and it is not just in government. It is taking place on the battleground of the media. People in the media may mean well, and they are hampered by their own system, combined with ignorance and arrogance and smugness. The pressures of publishing and the media leave no time to "talk story" and teach in a native way.

In *Women's Reality,* I talked about the pseudopodic ego of the White Male System. I likened the ego of the White Male System to the pseudopod or false foot of the amoeba that goes out and pulls whatever it encounters into its food vacuole, where it is either spit out or becomes absorbed and indistinguishable from the amoeba. This is a media process of the dominant system. Differences are either discarded or absorbed and changed so they become the system.

If women are to change communications, we must have support to resist becoming an absorption of a pseudopodic ego and have opportunities to contribute our differences.

A world without differences will not be a world.

Reference

Schaef, A. W. (1981). *Women's reality.* Minneapolis: Winston (San Francisco: Harper-Collins).

PART

II

Communication
Chasms

8

Democracy, Technology, and the Public Library
A Feminist Sociological Analysis

Patricia Madoo Lengermann
Jill Niebrugge-Brantley
Jane Kirkpatrick

This chapter offers a sociological analysis of the public library in the contemporary global system. Our focus is on the challenges posed to the public library by the new information technologies produced by that system, and takes as its referents the public library in the United States and Canada. Our analysis makes five points. First, the public library has traditionally served as a mediator between the immediate local community in which it is situated and the larger extralocal world in which that community is located. Second, in this mediation, the public library has acted as a democratic force, ensuring the corollary to First Amendment rights of free expression—the right of free and equal access to information. Third, this democratic mediation is now challenged by the new in-

formation technologies created in the global system that threaten to transform access of information in the same undemocratic ways that innovations in the production of media have transformed free expression, making both expression and access not "citizen rights but economic rights" (Allen, 1989, 1991). Fourth, the public library's mediation between local and extralocal knowledge traditionally has been done out of a professional ethic of service based in a feminine understanding of what service must be. Fifth, this ethic of service can guide the public library in its current struggle for a democratic incorporation of the new information technology.

Our analysis is based on feminist sociological theory. Like all sociological theory, feminist sociological theory attempts to "see through" existing claims and situations to the human relationships creating those situations and claims. Like all feminist theory, feminist sociological theory sees human relationships in terms of patterns of gender and power. Thus we focus on the relationships of gender and power that shape the library, the librarian, the library user, and the forces creating and marketing the "information revolution" of late twentieth-century capitalism. Like all feminist theory, feminist sociological theory seeks not only to describe and explain but to propose strategies for change in the world-in-place to make the world-in-place more humane, just, and joyful. We conclude with a discussion of opportunities for the public library to direct the course of change in information technology.

In presenting our argument, we draw on three principal sources: the feminist theory of sociologist Dorothy E. Smith in *The Everyday World as Problematic* (1987), *The Conceptual Practices of Power* (1990a), and *Texts, Facts, and Femininity* (1990b); the feminist analysis of library science scholars Roma Harris, *Librarianship: The Erosion of a Female Profession* (1992), and Sydney Chambers and Carolynne Myall, *Women and the Values of American Librarianship* (1994); and the media analysis of Donna Allen, *Media Without Democracy—and What to Do About It* (1991). (See also Allen's chapter in this volume.)

The Library in the World-in-Place

The World-in-Place

Dorothy E. Smith (1987) describes the world of late capitalism as divided into two overlapping spheres—the "local actualities of lived experience" and the "extra-local apparatus of ruling." The local actuality of lived experience is the sphere in which the "dailiness" of producing our social world occurs through the work of individual, embodied human beings. It is the world of personal relationships and concrete coping activities.

Work in this sphere produces the material products sustaining human life—food, shelter, and clothing and modern material structures such as appliances and transportation—and also keeps the world clean, meets emotional needs, provides recreation and education, satisfies sexual desire, gives meaning through religious and aesthetic and athletic activities.

The "extra-local apparatus of ruling" is the sphere of organizations and practices that control and appropriate the production done in the local actualities. Smith sees this world of "the apparatus of ruling" as operating today primarily through what she calls "texts." Texts are documents of control; they include contracts, laws, agency regulations, legal opinions, transcripts, diplomas, tax codes, media portrayals of ideals of conduct and being, news reports of "fact" and opinion, and professional practices—codes of behavior, licensing and certifications, journal articles, directives for clients.

These two spheres permeate each other in varying degrees of visibility. People primarily positioned in the local actualities see the actions of the world of texts as they try to fill out a tax form, prepare a meal paying attention to food additives and calories, decide what octane of gas to buy, renew a driver's license, pay home insurance, monitor the toxic content of cleaning products, seek a doctor's prescription, read the daily newspaper for a sense of what is "going on in the world." People primarily positioned in the extralocal apparatus of ruling can treat much of the individual activity that sustains their world as "invisible" and "trivial," noticing it only if—like the proverbial housework—it does not get done. Thus the corporate leader dictating terms for a contract does not think about the condition of the word processor on which the secretary will type it. The secretary may be only marginally concerned with the actual content of the contract but very focused on the actuality of the word processor on which she is working. But the contract may have impact on the lives of people around the globe as it moves jobs from one local actuality to another.

The apparatus of ruling is shaped by two historic and now-related arrangements of control: capitalism and patriarchy. Capitalism has as its primary goal the appropriation of wealth from the productive process. Its primary alignment of control—that is, of order-givers and order-takers—is to be found in the class system. Patriarchy has as its primary goal the control of society by men. Its primary alignment of control is gender stratification. Capitalist patriarchy is the control of society by powerful males who appropriate the production of women and less powerful males. Capitalism and patriarchy combine in the prevailing ideologies of the apparatus of ruling, which describe who has power and value and reproduce male dominance of capitalist structures. Borrowing from the language of world systems theory (Wallerstein, 1989; Ward, 1994), we can describe the sphere of the extralocal apparatus of ruling as located in "core" geosocial areas, that is, geosocial entities of concentrated power in the global system; and we can describe the sphere of the local actuality as "peripheral" geosocial areas, that is, geosocial entities where production occurs but there is no power. Increasingly, with the emergence of the contemporary global economy, these two areas—core and periphery—may coexist in any nation or any city. Thus, the United States remains a core country but has peripheral areas of agriculture and manufacture controlled from its own core cities and the core cities of other nations—New York City, Tokyo, London—which in turn have their core and peripheral areas.

There is a gender subtext in the consciousness with which individuals attend to experience in each of these spheres. These gendered traits of consciousness have been described by Jessica Benjamin (1988), Nancy Chodorow (1978), Carol Gilligan (1982; Gilligan et al., 1988), and Sara Ruddick (1990), among others. The consciousness of the apparatus of ruling or the core is essentially what we think of as masculine—not that all men possess it but that it represents the traits the culture ascribes to masculinity. Core con-

sciousness attends to the world through texts, relates to the world through generalization and abstraction rather than through concrete and situated experiences, makes moral and ethical judgments on the basis of those principles, thinks in terms of hierarchy, imagines a world in which people set clear plans and move through rational choices to the completion of those plans, distances from emotion, and has control as a basic relational style.

The consciousness of those anchored in the local actualities tends to be more "feminine." The local actuality or peripheral consciousness attends to the world through immediate situated events and actions, prefers situated and contextualized knowledge to abstraction and generalization, makes moral and ethical judgments in terms of relational knowledge and outcomes, thinks of relationships in terms of a web rather than a hierarchy, sees life as marked by "incidentalism" rather than planfulness, is emotionally open, and has mutuality of recognition as a basic relational style.

The Public Library

Within the model just presented, the public library can be seen as a mediator between the sphere of the extralocal apparatus of ruling and the sphere of the local actuality. The nature of this mediation is affected by three primary factors: the library user's consciousness of purpose in entering the library, the user's culturally acquired understanding of the library, and the librarian's culturally and professionally acquired sense of norms of service, of the appropriate relational stance to take toward the user. The library user who approaches the library for recreational reading is actively seeking to discover extralocal worlds, worlds beyond the horizon of her or his daily life. He or she probably approaches the library and the librarian with an attitude of open-minded anticipation and pleasure and feels relatively able with minor guidance to find what will please. In contrast, the instrumental user of the library is trying to access "texts" (that is, documents of control) that, in the way Smith describes, control and pattern her or his daily existence. The instrumental user is guided by specific questions and the need for practical action, and may approach with anxiety this encounter with an impersonal (and potentially incomprehensible) textual authority. The recreational library user may seek only a friendly point in the right direction. The instrumental user may need help in framing questions in a way that allows access to library holdings and in interpreting texts once they are found. Especially important in the latter case may be a sense that the librarian is seeing the user's need in a sympathetic manner, that is, in the same way the user is defining that need. In all cases, library users probably wish to remain in control of the "research" process—at least to the extent of defining what is sought and evaluating the worth of the materials found. (Librarian scholarship shows an ongoing concern with monitoring the effectiveness of the librarian in helping the user in research; for example, Belkin, 1987; Humber, 1995; Kobziar, 1995; Lancaster, 1993; Rice, 1995; Saracevik, 1987.)

The library user in the local actuality defines the staff encountered in the library as a "librarian"—however librarians may classify their various ranks and functions. And in the library user's mind, based on past experiences, the ideal typical librarian is a woman. This typification in part reflects the fact that 85% of all librarians are women—a percentage that has stayed relatively constant for nearly a hundred years (Chambers & Myall, 1994). But it also reflects a sense of the ethos or culture of the library as "feminine." Above all, the library user sees the library as a facilitating government agency—going to the library is not the same as going to the police station or through customs.

This cultural understanding of the library is explicated by Chambers and Myall in the representative statement of the 1991 Compact of the Friends of the Library USA (FOLUSA):

We believe in the Library, for its
  Nurturing of our children and youth,
  opening doors to the wonder and
  excitement of the world of ideas;
Dedication to literacy,
  giving to all a key to fulfillment;
Commitment to diversity,
  a foundation of pluralism, democracy, and
  peace;
Reservoir of memory,
  linking records of yesterday with the
  possibilities of tomorrow;
Continuum of knowledge,
  ever open to the changing form and flow
  of information;
Treasury of reading,
  where muse and spirit enrich the soul, and
  dreams excite discovery.

This statement is rich in feminine or womanly imagery: the library (and by extension the librarian) is "nurturing," "giving," "a key to fulfillment." It suggests an ideal of caring for others, as finding one's own calling in others' growth and fulfillment, a focus on spirit. In practice it seems that most librarians, male and female, have seen themselves in this model of service: They have sought to include and empower others by nonobtrusively mediating the link between embodied subjects in local actualities and wider worlds and textual practices.

Professional librarianship grew up during the tremendous expansion of the U.S. economy in the last quarter of the nineteenth century. This expansion made it possible for women to seek college educations and professional employment. Librarianship—like nursing, teaching, and the soon-to-follow social work—was a profession that society saw as right and proper for women. As Dee Garrison (1979) has argued in *Apostles of Culture: The Public Librarian and American Society 1876-1920,* librarianship could be made to fit certain ideals people had of women and women's work: The "feminine mind and nature were innately suited" to perform service tasks that required that one be "kind, sympathetic . . . delicate of touch, [have] love and charity . . . [and be] . . . industrious, sober, and nimble-fingered" (Garrison, 1979, pp. 177, 184). Women themselves accepted this definition—either because it genuinely fit their self-concept or because they saw it was a useful way to meaningful employment. When women entered a field, they brought this idea of service with them. And women entered librarianship in vast numbers. Chambers and Myall (1994) report that as early as 1895 the *Library Journal* proclaimed "she is the impersonal pronoun in library science" (p. 13). By 1910, almost 80% of library workers were women; in 1970, 84% of librarians were women; and in 1988, 85% of librarians were women (Chambers & Myall, 1994, p. 13).

The professional organizations and self-identification of librarians are, however, divided about this feminine identity. Many within the field of librarianship blame this female idea of service for the profession's marginalization and failure to attain what they would define as full professional status (Garrison, 1979; Hole, 1990). Hole (1990) has even argued that women librarians have so "feminized" the library as to create an environment that is either actively hostile or uninteresting to males. Hole's argument is refuted by statistics on library users; the most recent survey, a 1991 study of educational attainment, found that 47% of the men interviewed and 57% of the women had used the library at least once in the last year (Lynch, 1995). These percentages accord with librarians' own observations of a fairly even division between men and women (Humber, 1995; Kobziar, 1995; Rice, 1995). In *Librarianship* (1992), Harris argues that women's professions have low status because women have low status. She cautions against the most frequently proposed solution to low status in professions dominated by women—"to adopt the values and definitions of the higher prestige male professions in order to advance their own status." Harris recognizes the danger that "professionalism may almost inevitably lead to a movement away from service,

which for many people, represents the core of the female-intensive professions" (pp. 16-17). Harris's and Chambers and Myall's discussions, while reaffirming feminine or feminist values within librarianship, also point to the division within the profession as it seeks increased prestige and power. In fact, this division may have intensified since the 1970s as women librarians have seen other women move in significant numbers into the traditional male professions such as law, business, and medicine. The "information revolution" intensifies this division.

The Library and the Information Revolution: Dangers and Opportunities

The Information Revolution in the Library

The information revolution in the public library is part of the general technological revolution so effectively marketed to people through mass media that today nearly everyone in United States and Canadian societies works or consumes in a computerized environment.

The information revolution in the library has been occurring incrementally and up to the last five years has been in step with the pace of information change in the society at large. Richard DeGennaro, director of the New York Public Library, traces the first major technological innovation to the 1950s and the accelerated use of microfilm, which though crudely in place since the 1930s had been greatly improved by better ways of viewing and printing. In the 1960s, the photocopier became a standard part of library operations; users at a library could easily copy a document and people at a distance could request a copy of a document the library might own. From the 1970s on, this technological innovation accelerated. Most library users' first traumatic encounter with the new technologies was the switch from the traditional—and often much beloved—card catalogue of library holdings to the on-line catalogue with its terminal stations. Even in 1995, librarians still reported complaints from people who do not know how to work this initial computerization of library service (Humber, 1995; Kobziar, 1995; Rice, 1995). The on-line catalogue allowed the library and library patron to access collections beyond the immediate holdings of the library and allowed the library—and eventually the patron—to keep an increasingly up-to-date report on the status of its holdings.

The next major innovation, even now coming into many libraries, is the growth in the use of the CD-ROM to provide access to serials of all sorts. As DeGennaro (1989) notes, this "new optical disc technology would make possible the storage, retrieval, communication, and manipulation of vast quantities of research resources" (p. 42). Audrey N. Grosch (1995) sees as a central issue for libraries the pace at which they will "move to a CD-ROM-based file environment" (pp. 85-86). The average library user encounters the CD-ROM today in accessing *Books in Print,* indexes of articles in current periodical literature, and abstracts and sometimes full reprints of many of those indexed articles. In an increasing number of libraries, CD-ROM is the main way for a library user to find out what newspapers and magazines around the country may have reported on a given topic, and many encyclopedias are offered in this form. The CD-ROM is becoming the basic staple of the reference collection. Reading the CD-ROM requires a computer station where this electronically stored data can be translated to a screen. Thus, although the CD-ROM enormously increased the amount of information a local public library can offer, users' ability to access that information depends in part on the number of stations the library can offer for reading the CD-ROMs.

The newest technology the library must decide about has two components—on-line databases and various on-line communication networks, including e-mail, electronic bulletin boards, and news groups. These two components are today most widely combined and accessed via the much-heralded "Internet," the vast network that now encompasses, according to Grosch (1995), 2,218 distinct regional networks (at its most basic level, a network or a lowercase *internet* is a connection between a host computer and terminal servers).

Through the on-line databases, this technology offers the library and the library user access to information that is being created and changed almost as one connects with it (e.g., some of the business on-line databases advertise on screen that they are updated every 12 or 24 hours). In the mid-1980s, the on-line databases increased the range of information they offered in response to increased competition from the CD-ROM collections. In the 1990s, governments are increasingly using the Internet, in various forms such as the World Wide Web, to present legislation currently under consideration or recently enacted. For instance, an on-line IRS could have allowed taxpayers to learn immediately that the Congress had extended the standard health care tax credit for the self-employed for tax year 1994; the hard copy of the tax forms simply warned the taxpayer to "watch out" as such a change might happen—and, indeed, did in April 1995 only days before filing was due.

Electronic interaction with other users on various news group and "chat" lines or through e-mail makes possible a sharing of nontextual information, a reporting from the local actualities to the apparatus of ruling or, more important, to other local actualities. Paul Evan Peters (1995), executive director of the Coalition for Networked Information, goes so far as to say that the idea of "using the Internet to access and consume resources and services provided by other folks is a tired subject. Using the Internet to produce and operate resources and services that you want other folks to consume is a wired one" (p. 34).

The challenge for librarians is to decide the best ways to use their limited resources to guarantee open and equal public access to these extraordinary technological possibilities.

Dangers and Opportunities of the Information Revolution for the Public Library

The Chinese ideogram for *crisis* conveys two ideas: "danger" and "opportunity." The public library faces both dangers and opportunities as it confronts the challenge of the information revolution—and its ability to meet this challenge will profoundly affect the future of the democratic process in the United States and Canada. Dangers are that (a) the library will follow market pressures rather than user needs in applying the new technology, (b) the new technology will override the egalitarian service relation between librarian and library user, and (c) the new technology's commoditization of knowledge will undermine the library's traditional principle of free access to information. But opportunities are there for public librarians to emerge as champions of the public interest in the information revolution by saying plainly what is going on, by acting to maintain an egalitarian relationship between librarian and library user, and by refusing to capitulate on the principle of free access to information.

What Is Really Going On

Any major technological revolution confronts a society with the problem of what is "really going on" because they are not absolute like natural upheavals such as earthquakes nor are they totally socially created like artistic and culture movements. The information revolution in society is socially produced, distributed, and interpreted—and yet has a material facticity. The interpretation of the information revolution by the mass media is that it is an almost "grassroots" response to a felt need for improved communication and information handling, that everyone is now participating in it, that par-

ticipation is easily affordable, and that the technology itself is easily accessible. The source of this interpretation is the corporate-controlled mass media, part of the apparatus of ruling that produces the texts that increasingly control our daily lives. The new technology is a market-driven phenomenon—not a grassroots response—in which the apparatus of ruling has found ways to sell both access to existing texts and a new technology to access those texts; this technology of access calls into being yet another text, computer literacy. The ability of the apparatus of ruling to enforce this textual revolution is well illustrated by the way the government "published" the 1995 Clinton budget: a print hard copy cost the reader $56; a CD-ROM, $30; but on-line Internet access copies were "free"—if one, of course, already had on-line access ("What the Budget Costs," 1995).

The public library confronts the paradox that although not everyone is able to participate at the current time, the insistence by the apparatus of ruling that everyone is, can, and should participate is a self-fulfilling prophecy to which the library must respond for the sake of its users. While avoiding a Luddite response, the public librarian must recognize that *not everyone is participating*. In 1991, only 4% of U.S. households were "on-line." Even optimistic mass media estimates predict only 25% of households being on-line by 1999 (Neuborne, 1994). This estimate coincides with Herman and Chomsky's (1988) analysis that about 20% of the population belong to what we have described as the core group of text producers working within the apparatus of ruling.

One of the reasons not everyone is participating is cost. The individual alone, without a connection to the apparatus of ruling through a government, corporate, or educational institution, must negotiate for access to a computer, a commercial on-line contract, and a telephone connection. This involves getting the right hardware and software, paying for a contract that offers very limited basic service and accelerating rates for any connections or time above this basic service, and in many parts of the country budgeting for a long-distance phone connection to the computer service. Especially significant to the information revolution in the public library is the fact that accessing many on-line databases involves additional fees and licenses. *Computerization on an individual basis in a start-up year* would average (including fees for equipment) minimally $100 a month. This figure is beyond the reach of the vast majority of people's discretionary income pool. And, ironically, the people most able to pay it typically already have access via their work within organizations involved in the apparatus of ruling.

Further, *the technology, once purchased, is not easily accessible.* Computer literacy in general is not an easily or immediately acquired skill, and the communication networks are especially difficult programs to learn (Landis, 1994; Steiner, 1995; "Teachers Need More Training," 1995). Acquired literacy can quickly become redundant as both hardware and software manufacturers practice a version of "planned obsolescence." And there is a significant gender gap in computer literacy. A 1994 MIT study showed that at age 17, 60% of boys but only 46% of girls had used a computer to solve a math problem and 42% of boys but only 26% of girls had written a computer program. The study further showed that the percentage of degrees in computer science awarded nationally to women is declining annually, from 37% in 1984 to 30% in 1990. Women tend to drop out of computer science faster than any other field in science (Hale, 1995). This computer gender gap crosses with the facts that 85% of all librarians are women and that, while schools of library science struggle and reorganize, programs in computer science and "information technology" continue to grow and to pluck jobs that once went to librarians (Grosch, 1995, pp. 356-358).

Dangers

First, public librarians must resist the danger outlined by Harris (1992) of seizing this new and complex technology as a means to build professional status by serving as gatekeepers to information. Harris sees the challenge to relate to this new technology as part of the librarian's struggle for professional status. The danger, Harris argues, is that the librarian may shift from a feminine or feminist notion of professional service to a masculine or paternalistic notion. With the best intentions, this could happen within the public library if the librarian becomes the expert in manipulation of information access through the new technology. Harris says that such a shift conforms to the "expert" or paternalistic model of professionalism in which the professional knows what is best for the client, and so on.

One important difference, then, between the female-intensive professions and the traditionally male professions lies in the degree of control exercised over the helping process. The female fields have been stigmatized for being helpful and "non-assertive in nature, rather than authoritative in . . . provision of service" (McDermott, 1984, p. 20). Unfortunately, the nonpaternalistic type of service orientation that has traditionally characterized librarianship is currently under siege by those who wish to advance these fields by embracing the model of professionalism exemplified by lawyers and physicians (Harris, 1992, p. 19).

The new information technologies, especially on-line database searching and communication through news groups on the Internet, are sufficiently complex to make it seem "reasonable policy" that only the librarian be allowed actually to do the hands-on navigation of the various programs. But such a policy contributes to the continuing de-skilling and disempowerment of the so-called information have-nots.

A second danger in this professional shift is that information will become increasingly commoditized and librarians will join in this entrepreneurial trend. DeGennaro argued in 1989 that a number of trends might be pushing librarians in this direction;

The trends being described in the library and information field are parallel to and part of the major economic, social, and political trends of the last two or three decades. . . . We are experiencing a number of historic swings in our society. Government ownership is out, privatization is in; government planning is out, business and free enterprise are in; welfare is out, self reliance is in; . . . free is out, fee is in; cooperation is out, competition is in. I am not saying that all these changes are good, but they are happening, and the reason they are happening is attributable largely to the high-tech revolution. (p. 43)

Librarians and the public must see how this information revolution can spark these social changes. DeGennaro takes as an example the photocopier that libraries at first tried to offer as a free service but that they were quickly forced to shift to fee because of the cost of heavy reader usage. The photocopy service is, however, a service not of access to information but of ease in recording information once accessed. The new technologies, especially the on-line databases, present a very new threat. Access to knowledge itself can be charged for every time any individual user effects such access. Unlike traditional hard copy mediums or even the CD-ROM technologies, the on-line databases are never "owned" by the library—they are always potentially being rented out and they can be rented out on a fee-for-access basis each time access is sought. Further, the access can be sold through special cards and passwords so that one library user might have the economic capacity and contractual right to access a particular database while another library user might not be able to afford this right. The commercial database companies even now are writing contracts that restrict access to many of their on-line databases. The fierceness of this new contractual enterprise is indicated by the fact that several of the sources we interviewed about contracts requested anonymity.

If librarians and the public are not on guard, the information revolution may follow the course of change produced by technological innovations in print production during the Industrial Revolution—innovations that essentially eliminated the individual news-sheet producer and distributor because of the increased costs and space of the high-speed presses. As Donna Allen (1989, 1991) has repeatedly stressed throughout her career as founder of the Women's Institute for Freedom of the Press, First Amendment rights have been transformed—beginning with nineteenth-century technological innovations in printing—from "citizen rights to economic rights." The ability to freely express oneself in various media now depends on one's economic control of the production of that media, an economic control that has become increasingly complex, corporate, and capital-intensive because of changes in technology. These corporations have claimed for themselves, as Allen says, rights originally guaranteed to citizens and have now presumed to speak "for the people" while in reality serving as the voice of corporate capitalism. The same challenge faces us today as technological innovation threatens to change free access to information from a "citizen right to an economic right."

In the politics that surround library funding, libraries constantly fight against the demands that they "pay-their-own way" by charging "user fees." This new technology, with its fee-for-access contracts, opens up the possibility of the principle of fee for access becoming part of public library philosophy. James F. Govan (1988) is one of many librarians warning that

some governing boards and administrations . . . are now instructing directors to produce income. Librarians will have little defense against this kind of pressure unless they are able to clarify their thinking on the issue. . . . To the degree that libraries become retailing shops, to that degree will librarians cease to be professionals and will become shopkeepers, of necessity. . . . This new enthusiasm for entrepreneurship is ill-founded. The market is not sufficiently valued to create income equal to the loss of public support for libraries that fees for service will prompt. (pp. 36-38)

Opportunities

The challenge to the public library is to cut through the paradox of the self-fulfilling prophecy described above and "speak truth to power." Public librarians have the chance to express with a new and self-consciously feminist voice the values that have long undergirded their profession. The extent of the feminist movement in librarianship is suggested by Christine Baum's (1992) study *Feminist Thought in American Librarianship.* The work of Harris and of Chambers and Myall translates traditional values of librarianship into feminist principles. Chambers and Myall (1994) offer their own statement of the feminist values they see imbuing both librarianship and the attitudes of the public toward the library:

> responsibility to community and sense of responsibility for maintaining community;
>
> cooperation rather than competition;
>
> concern for children and weaker members of the community;
>
> objectivity, a nonjudgmental appreciation for multiple points of view, which we regard as an important aspect of what some would call "selflessness";
>
> concern for consequences of actions;
>
> holistic view of human beings;
>
> local scope of action . . . ;
>
> connectedness as both fact of life and value to encourage. (p. 6)

In practice as well as theory, librarians are speaking out for freedom of access to information as a citizen right and not an economic right, and for freedom of access including the empowerment to access on one's own. We take for analysis one example, the 1995 testimony of Janet Steiner, director of the Tompkins County Public Library (located in Ithaca, New York), before the New York State Legislature, which was considering grants to public libraries to provide for connections to the Internet. In her testimony, titled "Regarding Libraries as Points of Public Access to the Information Superhighway," Steiner addressed hidden infrastructure costs, the absolute need for training, the concerns of the disempowered and the average library user, and the problems of deciding which services to offer on-line.

> How will citizens access this new form of information? If you dial in, if you have a computer and a modem, you can do it from home or office. If you don't, the first location that everyone identifies is the public library. The library is perceived as a neutral place, where information of all kinds can be accessed freely and openly. The library is a natural choice of everyone involved in this planning effort. . . .
>
> [T]he chair of the county's Budget and Fiscal Policy Committee, said that his goal was Internet access for everyone. . . . It will not be cheap. Radical renovations of my building will be needed, computer hardware and software acquired, and training staff added. For example, my library built in 1967 does not have one extra square foot of flow space available for another computer terminal nor do we have one spare electrical outlet. Rewiring . . . involves drilling through cement floors and foot-and-a-half brick walls. . . . Suppose the public access to the Internet is provided by the library. If a Tompkins County resident could make a local phone call to the library's computer catalog and then get on the Internet, I predict that I would need hundreds of incoming phone lines to handle the traffic. If a Tompkins County resident came into the library, walked up to a terminal and could access the Internet, I would need hundreds of terminals, lots of space and lots of electrical outlets. I would also need scores of people to offer training assistance and help, because one thing we do know about the Internet is that it is not yet user-friendly. . . .
>
> Having just finished a series of focus groups with library users, I can tell you that users want and need more help in using . . . our computer catalogue, which is one of the best in the industry. Library users uniformly report frustration and unhappiness with electronic resources and desperately need help. We will not add Internet access unless it is accompanied by exemplary

user training and education. (Steiner, 1995, pp. 3-4)

The opportunities for the public library are already being seized in statements like Steiner's, which speak the truth about what will be needed to achieve this technological revolution. Public librarians must insist on keeping the public library a supportive environment, focused on the needs of individuals in the local actualities of lived experience. They must seek ways to exert pressure on the vendors from the apparatus of ruling. For instance, Harris suggests that librarians refuse to buy from vendors who do not offer hard copy as well as on-line databases. Librarians must resist the pressure to switch to a totally electronic environment or they will find themselves at the mercy of these vendors and will increasingly value the technological specialists in their own ranks rather than the traditional service providers. Librarians must keep empowerment rather than control as their service goal. And feminist publics must support librarians as they work to realize in a more self-conscious way than in the past the feminist values of public library service. We hope this chapter contributes to an understanding that will translate into support of the public library as it argues for democracy on the information superhighway.

References

Allen, D. (1989). From opportunity to strategy: Women contribute to the communication future. In D. Allen & R. Rush (Eds.), *Communications at the crossroads: The gender gap connection.* Norwood, NJ: Ablex.

Allen, D. (1991). *Media without democracy—and what to do about it.* Washington, DC: Women's Institute for Freedom of the Press.

Baum, C. (1992). *Feminist thought in American librarianship.* Jefferson, NC: McFarland.

Belkin, N. (1987). User/intermediary interaction analysis. In J. Varlejs (Ed.), *Information seeking.* Jefferson, NC: McFarland.

Benjamin, J. (1988). *The bonds of love.* New York: Pantheon.

Chambers, S., & Myall, C. (1994). *Women and the values of American librarianship.* Las Colinas, TX: Ide House Press.

Chodorow, N. (1978). *The reproduction of mothering.* Berkeley: University of California Press.

DeGennaro, R. (1989, October). Technology and access in an enterprise society. *Library Journal,* pp. 40-43.

Garrison, D. (1979). *Apostles of culture: The public librarian and American society 1876-1920.* New York: Free Press.

Gilligan, C. (1982). *In a different voice.* Cambridge, MA: Harvard University Press.

Gilligan, C., et al. (Eds.). (1988). *Mapping the moral domain.* Cambridge, MA: Harvard University Press.

Govan, J. F. (1988, January). The creeping invisible hand: Entrepreneurial librarianship. *Library Journal,* pp. 35-38.

Grosch, A. (1995). *Library information technology and networks.* New York: Marcel Dekker.

Hale, E. (1995, February 25). Girls left off superhighway. *Ithaca Journal,* p. 12A.

Harris, R. (1992). *Librarianship: The erosion of a female profession.* Norwood, NJ: Ablex.

Herman, E. S., & Chomsky, N. (1988). *Manufacturing consent.* New York: Pantheon.

Hole, C. (1990). The feminization of the public library. *American Libraries, 21*(11), 1076-1079.

Humber, A. (1995, April 26). [Telephone interview, Ithaca, NY].

Kobziar, T. (1995, April 21). [Author interview, Ithaca, NY].

Lancaster, F. (1993). Librarians, technology and mediocrity. In A. H. Helal & J. Weiss (Eds.), *Opportunity 2000: Understanding and serving users in an electronic library.* Essen, Germany: Essen University Library.

Landis, D. (1994, January 21). Computers are just too darn difficult. *USA Today,* p. 1D.

Lynch, M. J. (1995, April 27). [Telephone interview, Ithaca, NY].

McDermott, J. C. (1984). The professional status of librarians. *Journal of Library Administration, 5*(3), 17-21.

Neuborne, E. (1994, March 22). Online goes on offensive. *USA Today,* p. 1D.

Peters, P. E. (1995, March 15). Information avatars. *Library Journal,* pp. 32-34.

Rice, R. (1995, April 24). [Telephone interview, Ithaca, NY].

Ruddick, S. (1990). *Maternal thinking: Towards a politics of peace.* New York: Ballantine.

Saracevik, T. (1987). Cognitive patterns in online searching. In J. Varlejs (Ed.), *Information seeking.* Jefferson, NC: McFarland.

Smith, D. E. (1987). *The everyday world as problematic.* Boston: Northeastern University Press.

Smith, D. E. (1990a). *The conceptual practices of power.* Boston: Northeastern University Press.

Smith, D. E. (1990b). *Texts, facts, and femininity*. New York: Routledge.

Steiner, J. (1995, March 15). *Regarding libraries as points of public access to the information superhighway*. Testimony to the New York State Legislature, Albany, NY.

Teachers need more training on computers. (1995, April 4). *USA Today*, p. 1D.

Wallerstein, E. (1989). *The modern world system* (Vol. 3). New York: Academic Press.

Ward, K. (1994). Reconceptualizing world system theory to include women. In P. England (Ed.), *Theory on gender/gender on theory*. New York: Aldine de Gruyter.

What the budget costs. (1995, January 28). *USA Today*, p. 1A.

9

Revolutionary Circles Within Larger Political Patterns
An Afterword to Revolution From Within

Gloria Steinem

A book, like a person, is born with the genetic imprint of the past, shaped by parental dreams and society's politics, launched at a certain time in history—and then goes off to lead a life that none of those things could have predicted.

That was certainly true of *Revolution From Within*. From the beginning, it was readers who made me see the folly of prediction. Their responses were so diverse and interesting, so understanding of the book's spirit and yet so surprising in its uses, that I realize each person was bringing a unique reality to her or his half of the conversation. Not only did they supply all the elements I'd been stewing about not including, but they

carried the book's thesis into countries I never could have imagined.

In the first weeks of my book tour, for instance, I noticed this offspring was introducing me to an unusually varied group of friends. Though I had thought its acceptance would be limited by its radical thesis—that systems of authority undermine our self-authority to secure obedience, to them, which makes self-esteem the root of revolution—readers seemed never to have heard that what is radical can't succeed, and what succeeds can't be radical. If it was empowering in their daily lives, that was enough. In long informative letters, they shared their own experiences of self-esteem in response to the book's parables; told what actions they were taking as a result of putting the internal and external together, especially if they hadn't been activists before; and described what new self-understanding had arrived, especially if they confused motion with action in the past. They responded on street corners and in supermarkets, at lectures and book signings, in radio call-in shows and women's reading clubs, on a national computer network of male executives and in a local self-help group for women prisoners, in a discussion on the future of democracy and a television forum on the Los Angeles rebellion—most personally at dinners where old friends told me about their lives in new ways.

Nevertheless, I doubted that critics would praise a book with *self-esteem* in the title; my reporting on the reception of other self-esteem efforts had convinced me of that. The liberal intellectual establishment seemed to find this subject too soft and intangible to be taken seriously; on the other hand, a newly influential right wing was clear that it was too subversive of authority to be tolerated.

But at least I had a sense of humor about it. In old notes, I found scribbled this parody of what a reviewer might say: "*Revolution from Within* has two flaws, both fatal. First, it portrays the individual as infinitely redeemable, a romantic notion that flies in the face of history. Second, it describes self-esteem as a birthright that can only be preserved by transforming our methods of education and childrearing; by abandoning patriarchy, racial caste systems, monotheism, and hierarchy as the main form of human organizations; indeed, by transforming Western civilization itself."

That would have been tough—but fair. After all, it was what this book was saying.

But life and reviews are always a surprise. I certainly hadn't anticipated seeing myself described as "the Ivan Boesky of Nookie" (more about that in a minute), and I'd forgotten that when the message is unwelcome the messenger becomes the focus. Though reviewers for less prestigious publications called the book a pioneering blend of the personal

and the political—in fact, the more obscure the review, the more favorable it was—critics for renowned publications here and in England had three main points:

1. That my interest in the internal must mean I had become weaker and/or regretted my earlier years of activism.
2. That including struggles of my own would disillusion female readers, who preferred women in public life to stay on pedestals; or, that my having any struggles at all was evidence that feminism had failed.
3. That the pages most deserving of attention were the three personal ones in a romance section: Who was my unidentified lover anyway? Why had I included this story at all? Or why wasn't it longer?

The usually impersonal *New York Times Book Review* headlines: "*She's Her Weakness Now.*" *Newsweek* described it as a "squishy exercise in feeling better." A television interview about the book was edited into such a frivolous "profile" that its woman producer eventually quit in protest. Journalists on both sides of the Atlantic assumed I must have deserted serious political pursuits to write a self-help book for personal gain. A reporter for the *Washington Post* misread a romance parable as my "falling in love with someone who treated her badly," added accounts of other feminists' supposedly unacceptable marriages or love affairs (one because her life was too conventionally heterosexual, another because hers wasn't heterosexual enough), and wrote a nationally syndicated article headlined "LEADERS' HYPOCRISY KILLED FEMINIST MOVEMENT." A reporter for the *New York Post* decided that it was I who had treated my lover badly, and called this reversal bad for feminism, too. It was in support of this theory that I must have been interested only in this man's money, a writer for the *New York Observer* described me as "the Ivan Boesky of Nookie."

Okay, some of this is funny now. But at the time, it was painful. Not only did such trivializing words hurt, but they obscured the book's content, purpose, and politics. The serious disagreement I had anticipated—and would have welcomed—gave way to points like those above. Unserious, I could find no major review that noted the book's criticism of traditional child-rearing and education, gender and race roles, separation from nature, or even monotheism. There was none that supported, opposed, or ever noticed its striving for inclusiveness across lines of sex and race, class, sexuality, and ability; none that mentioned its linking of social justice and self-realization movements; and no examination, pro or con, of self-esteem as a source of revolution. Though reviewers were heavy into the new parables from my personal life, none acknowledged the larger points they had been included to make. When I responded to interviewer's inevitably personal questions by explaining that an increased inner awareness had made me more effective as an activist—that I felt stronger, not weaker—this, too, was roundly ignored. No major publication analyzed this book's feminist worldview, or took a look at self-esteem as a serious subject.

This chasm between what authorities believe and what people experience was similar to the distance I'd been encountering between reviewers and readers—sometimes also between intellectual women reviewers and everyday women readers. It was the greatest such distance I'd witnessed in my 30 years as a writer.

So there I was, feeling quite "crazy" and not a little depressed. It was as if my intentions—and even the reactions of readers—had become invisible. I was doing readings that had to be moved to movie theaters, churches, school gyms, town libraries, and shopping malls to accommodate those who were interested, and hearing people talk about the book as energizing, activating, a needed unity of internal and external, not as a retreat from activism—on their part or mine. Yet I was reading critics and facing interviewers who assumed that I had repudiated my activ-

ist past, that I was suddenly attributing women's problems to individual weakness rather than a woman-hating society, or that my personal stories were the book's sole content.

I confess that most of what I've told you about the quality and quantity of reader response was not what I was absorbing at the time. I remember sitting in a Chicago hotel room, feeling negated by weeks of being told with great public authority that I meant what I didn't mean. Though I understood by then that those blows were hitting a not-quite-healed bruise of neglect in childhood that sometimes made me feel less real than other people, they were not imagined. I had become stronger, yet I was being called weaker; I had included many kinds of subjects and people in these pages, yet only a narrow few were treated as visible; I had written a book with serious political implications, yet I was being accused of deserting politics in general and feminism in particular. Though I had been as surprised as reviewers when this book had begun to appear on national bestseller lists a few weeks after publication, even those numbers meant little to me then. When a friend called to congratulate me, for instance, I remember saying, "But you don't understand—that just makes more people who won't like it." He laughed—but I did not.

Fortunately, Susan Faludi's *Backlash,* an important book about the mainstream media's distortions and defensiveness in the face of feminist advances, had been published just a few months before mine. I hadn't read it—I understood its value, but felt that my own years of dealing with the backlash meant I didn't need to learn more—until wise readers explained that it had helped them understand why they also felt the media was describing some book other than the one I had written.

Only a few chapters into it, I began to relearn a classic feminist lesson: I was rescued and affirmed by other women's experiences. By naming and documenting the political patterns behind our common experiences, Faludi reminded me (and thousands of other readers) that we could trust our perceptions: there was a great will to misunderstand out there. I suddenly realized that, if I'd been watching another woman getting media treatment parallel to mine, I would have understood in a minute and been angry on her behalf; yet it's amazing how being the subject of something painful can keep you wondering what you did to deserve it. Only reading Faludi's well-documented case histories made me realize that I wasn't alone, and so might not be the cause.

In detailed example after example, Faludi shows how statistics and studies have been shaped, perhaps unconsciously, to support the message of the backlash: *Feminism is not the cure for women's problems; it's the cause.* Even when the problems being discussed were those that only the women's movement had been trying to solve—violence against women, for instance, or women's double burden of working both in and outside the home— they were still said to stem from changing old roles, not from the need to change them even more. Her most famous example, the 1986 study in which researchers from Harvard and Yale statistically minimized women's chances of finding a husband if they delayed marriage, had been exaggerated by the media in very big stories, and clarified, if at all, in very small ones. (As *Newsweek* so famously put it, such women became "more likely to be killed by a terrorist" than to marry.) Though Faludi had first exposed the false statistical premises and reporting of this study in an article for *Ms.* magazine, I hadn't thought that the same kind of bias might apply to this book's reception until I read it again after my own media experience, and in the context of Faludi's many other examples. The message I'd been getting from mainstream media began to make sense: *If I or other women had self-esteem problems, they were a personal failing at best, or proof of feminism's failure at worst. In either case, it was feminism's fault for not solving them, not the fault of an unjust system for creating them.*

No wonder there was such a will to personalize everything, to focus on examples from my life that made up only a small part of the book, while ignoring the larger points they made. Instead of seeing shared experience as proof of the political patterns, it was an admission of individual weakness.

No wonder my inclusion of male readers was mostly ignored. If men came to see male superiority as an impossible goal that undermined their self-esteem, too, they would have an incentive to rebel against it. What if a critical mass of men decided to trade in "masculinity" for humanity?

No wonder the media was obsessed with the three pages of my romance story, yet had totally ignored the equally personal but happy love story a few pages later. (Not one single reviewer or interviewer ever asked me or wrote about the positive parable—the only personal one they had excluded. Amazing.) Clearly, the first one could be used to support the backlash belief that feminists can't have good relationships with men. The second could not.

No wonder there was such a will to believe that I had become weak, that examples from my own life would disillusion the readers, or that I was leading women away from activism. The backlash reason was simple: wishful thinking.

Once I got a grip on the political rationale behind otherwise mysterious and contradictory responses, I stopped talking back to the media in my head and began talking back in reality. I stopped feeling uncertain and started getting angry. In the course of the next few months of book touring, I spoke my mind, as I have in these pages. Getting unsaid words out in the air where they belonged not only helped objectively—after all, "the media" is only composed of people who are also struggling with social mythology, and who can't read our minds—but it cleared a space in my head to hear readers. I began listening, really *listening*. These stories are typical of what I heard:[1]

• In Detroit, a woman with a factory job and three children under eight stayed after a book signing to tell me about her burnout as a single mother. The killing workload hadn't changed, she said, but something almost as basic had: she no longer felt she deserved it.

"I may or may not get this promotion, but at least I won't have screwed myself by not asking for it," she explained. "When things don't work now, I get mad instead of depressed—a big change for me. I only slip backwards on the days when I forget to meditate and take time for myself. . . .

"I thought I couldn't take time for an inner life. The truth is, I can't afford *not* to."

As I listened to that woman's story, the link between self-esteem and action seemed so natural that all the notions of inward exploring as weakness began to lose their sting . . .

• In Chicago, I met the administrator of a special program for adolescent boys with dropout or criminal records. He had known for years, he said, that strengthening self-esteem was the only way to change self-destructive behavior, but unfortunately, the conventional answers were still discipline, inflexible rules, and other enemies of self-authority. "Self-esteem is seen as self-indulgent," he explained. "They think we're trying to excuse past behavior when really, we're just trying to change future behavior. But since your book wasn't written in educationalese—and since you started out being a skeptic yourself—I'm giving it to the most hidebound officials I know to try to loosen them up."

• In Denver, a young woman gave me a slender manuscript in which she had written her first memories of sadistic sexual abuse by her father. "When it was going on, I used to feel as if I were watching from outside myself," she explained, "and I pretended it was happening to somebody with a different name, a bad girl who deserved it. I never told anyone—not until I read what you said about multiple personality in your chapter. It meant so much that you included this in a book for

'normal' people, and that you said we who are survivors might be 'prophets of human possibilities.' It's the first time I've seen myself as strong or a survivor, and that I even have something to teach. I've started to tell a few friends instead of hiding all the time, and I'm beginning to get some help from one of the few therapists who understands. We're all encouraged to be false selves by injustice—maybe I'm not so separate after all. Maybe we're all part of a continuum."

The gift she gave me was far greater than mine to her.

But by far the most consistent responses came from women who had been active feminists for years before retreating, or from women who'd been turned off by the women's movement. They sounded remarkably alike. Both said feminism had come to seem distant, impersonal, and only for the strong: a way of helping "other" women when they themselves were barely hanging on. Both said the movement had been neglecting the personal and internal half of the persona/political equation.

I was surprised that both groups expressed relief at discovering that I shared many of the same experiences and problems. If I wasn't immune either, they said in various ways, then perhaps they were not personally at fault, there really was a sexual caste system at work. Together, we could change it. I hadn't realized that I'd ever seemed invulnerable—one more lesson in how public life distances the few in order to disempower the many—but I began to be very glad that I'd heeded the feminist adage of the personal as political (and the political as personal) by including personal parables, no matter how the backlash had used them.

By the time I neared California and the last of a three-month book tour, reader responses had multiplied. Lines snaked around the blocks at book stores and readings, people introduced themselves and organized in line, and the fact that this book had climbed to number one on the best-seller list and remained there, in spite of opposition, seemed to be their own triumph. As I moved West to warmer climates, readers began to phone and ask if they could bring sleeping bags to wait in line overnight. I'd never witnessed anything like it. There seemed to be a new critical mass of people who had learned the hard way, as I had, that activism without introspection and self-discovery turns into imitation at best and burnout at worst; and that introspection without activism leads to isolation and passivity. There seemed to be a community of full-circle consciousness with nowhere to go, no institutions of its own or even places to gather, and so it had assembled around this current ad hoc signal.

At Cody's, the largest bookstore in Berkeley, for instance, there were people crowded into an upstairs room and a balcony, sitting on the staircase, and standing downstairs in the aisles around loudspeakers. Susan Faludi, whom I had not met before and who lived in San Francisco, had been invited to introduce me. She explained to the crowd that she was going to read the experience of a 22-year-old college student, written in response to my parables about my mother. I can only characterize that long narrative here, in part because this young woman's violent father has forbidden the printing of her name or anything that would make her recognizable. It was the story of this student's own mother, "a beautiful and fiercely intelligent woman," who had been ignored or abused for so much of her life that she spent years in a violent marriage, and eventually tried to commit suicide.

"At the hospital," Susan said, reading this young woman's words, "my mother stayed in a quasi-coma for weeks, not responding to a word or gesture I made. I decided to read to my mother about you and your mother. Even though she was sleeping long and white in a cold room, I knew she could hear me. I read until the nurses started repeating phrases and themes to each other. But my mother didn't respond. Finally, I gave up and just sat there with her, a certain silence and smell filling the room, and started to prepare myself for her death.

"And then suddenly her eyes opened. . . . She often tells me that when she was 'asleep'

in the hospital, she was actually thinking about your words, about your mother, about all the songs so many women never get a chance to sing."

The sequence of her recovery after this crisis was like a "rebirth," as her daughter put it. "Now, my mother is a business major in college, raises protest signs with me in pro-choice marches, and is dating as often as she likes with whomever she likes. In her own words: 'The younger the better.' She goes hiking, reads voraciously.

"As for myself, I'm graduating soon with a major in English, and dating one of the few good men on earth, and have embarked on a writing career with a short-story collection dedicated to my mother and to you. I know this sounds hopelessly melodramatic, but I know that if it wasn't for you, both my mother and I would not have survived. It is not often that language transforms itself into a true healing device—but it did one morning with a mother and a daughter."

The crowd had been quiet at the beginning of this long story, then laughed with surprise at the mother's signs of spirit, then grown silent again with a new kind of quiet. Instead of anonymous people filling disparate spaces on two floors, there was now a group whose links to each other brought the spaces together. Instead of the silence of strangers, there was a willingness to turn toward each other, smile, and make room.

Stories are medicine for our individual spirits. They are also powerful makers of community.

That was the turning point of my post-book journey. Instead of feeling discouraged and confused, I felt the strength of readers coming back to me. Instead of losing something when this book left home, I understood that it was bringing me the learning, comfort, and magic of community.

Of course, I wouldn't want to leave you thinking that controversy was over. While writing this many months later, I picked up a copy of *Newsweek* and found *Revolution*

From Within still referred to as "an embarrassment." Even feminist journals published long after mainstream reviews also reflected the difference of opinion. In some ways, it was a rerun of the seventies division between "politicos" and "cultural" or "spiritual" feminists. I had been on the political side in those days, but even then it seemed to me there was a need for both—if only for the tactical reason that leaving out big chunks of women's experience left them with nowhere but patriarchal places to go. By the *1980s* when I was thinking about writing this book, I'd come to agree with feminist theologian Mary Daly that the internal would grow out of the external. As she wrote more than 20 years ago, "Women should be sensitive to the fact that the movement itself is a deeply spiritual event which has the potential to awaken a new and post-patriarchal spiritual consciousness."

I confess, however, that I still have a harder time empathizing with those male intellectuals who seem to believe a serious political message can't be conveyed in a personal, accessible way. They treat self-esteem as "selfish," especially when sought by groups on whose self-sacrifice they have been depending. Nonetheless, I can see that anyone schooled in *either/or* might fear that I was just beginning a new hierarchy in which the internal was on top. They might mistake my *synthesis* for an *antithesis* of their *thesis*—if you get what I mean.

A critical mass of us may have to experience the full circle—internal exploring as a continuing source of energy, not just as emergency therapy—before we can ditch either/or thinking. If so, there's an individual reward. Even if we are not among those who trigger the critical mass, each one of us is still helping to create it.

I tell you all this about these experiences because you, too, may be finding resistance from those around you or within yourself; a similar fear that looking inward will negate action instead of nourishing it.

I also offer suffering responses because I've come to the conclusion that each reader will have to be the authority on whether I was clear enough about self-esteem as a source of positive action, and about positive action as a source of self-esteem. It is this never-ending spiral that I meant and still mean, with all my heart.

As for getting clear and getting angry, I offer my postpublication experience as proof that a book is also a process that never ends. I'm thinking in particular of a reviewer who said I had "forgotten to get angry" about sexism. I don't agree: this book is about the step after getting angry, which is finding a center of power within ourselves to change an unjust system.

And if you find that you, too, are talking back to disembodied critics in your head, consider getting your words out in the air. That silent dialogue only allows someone else to be the prime mover. Once you speak, you become a force on your own. More important, getting the words out leaves room in your head to hear your own inner voice as well as understanding voices around you.

Because our books had turned into such unexpected best-sellers, for instance, Susan Faludi and I were interviewed after that session at Cody's by two women editors from *Time* magazine, though its reviewers had originally been skeptical of Faludi's thesis and found mine not personal enough. As it turned out, it was less what was said than the depth of interest they heard from readers that impressed them.

When our joint interview became part of a cover story analyzing the popularity of our two feminist books, Susan and I found ourselves together on the cover of *Time*. It was a pairing that made sense—her book was documenting what was wrong; mine was exploring ways to make it right—but the heart of *Time*'s cover story came straight from readers. For instance:

"Something must have happened in the climate of relations between men and women

for these books to have such an impact. . . .
Faludi's book has set off firecrackers across
the political battlefield. . . . She has inspired
men and women to take a new look at the
messages they absorb, messages that act as
barriers to understanding or to justice."

"Many reviewers . . . virtually ignored the
political implications of [Steinem's] thesis in
order to elaborate on the minimal amount of
personal details she chooses to divulge. . . . But
with ordinary readers, Steinem's message has
broken through. They don't ask her about the
personal much. They want to know about self
and how to gain and trust their own. It is a fine
triumph for this woman . . . to succeed in holding the feminist course while expanding its
horizons to include everyone."

What more could any writer ask?

I've been traveling around the country talking to women in shopping malls and bookstores, school gyms and community centers,
universities and living rooms—learning that
there's a great impatience out there to put the
internal and the external together into one
revolutionary whole.

I stumbled on this by writing what I was
experiencing: the need to connect self-authority to standing up to authority, self-esteem to
revolution. Unexpectedly, the book struck a
chord that was both wide and deep. It was as
if two great movements of our time, those for
social justice and for self-realization, were
halves of a whole just waiting to come together. And as if the feminist movement that
pioneered the connection between the personal and the political had been under such
political pressure for so long that the personal
part of the equation had been neglected—and
had left a deep longing.

Of course, there was also resistance to
bringing up the personal; a fear that it would
be energy taken away from the political. This
isn't surprising given that either/or culture
we live in, not to mention the cases in which
turning inward really *is* hiding out. But the
truth is that once we get out of "either/or"
thinking and into an "and" state of mind, we
can combine what we've learned about po-

litical effectiveness *and* inner growth over
the last 25 years, and inspire a response from
women that is beyond anything I've witnessed since the movement's early years.
Before talking solutions, however, here are
examples to help explain the problem:

• Though an overwhelming majority of
women now support feminist issues, they often
feel distant from feminist organizations. That's
especially true for women of color, poor
women, and young women. *Yet when a women
does try to connect—which often happens, I've
discovered, by such simple methods as looking
up "women's movement" or "feminism" in the
phone book—she probably finds nothing that
general, and if she persists, she finds groups
that are often too specialized or hard-pressed
to welcome her.*

• Some women don't identify with feminism because it's seen as a danger to their
existing support system, or an obligation to
help other women—while they themselves
are barely hanging on. *Yet few movement
groups offer the mutual, personal support
that is the strength of feminism.*

• More and more hardworking activists
find themselves saying, "Oh, god, I have to
go to another meeting." *Yet instead of turning those meetings into something that would
be helpful to them personally, they either go
to the same old meetings out of duty, or burn
out and stay home.*

• Some feminists are alarmed by the growth
of 12-step, "inner child," and other recovery
movements. *But instead of looking at what
those very apolitical groups are providing
that feminist ones may not be, they just dismiss them.*

• Many feminists in academic and other
traditional professions have learned to write
and speak in a way that excludes the uniniti-
ated, and sometimes condescends toward all
that is experiential, emotional, or even popu-

lar. *Yet knowledge that is understood by a few can only be acted upon by a few, and excluding what doesn't fit into the professions leaves most of women's experience with no place to go.*

• Antiequality leaders, from Washington rightwingers to fundamentalist preachers, have used words like "family values" to subsume the rights of women and children under a patriarchal unit. *But women tend to use "family" to mean any people they love and depend on, related or not, and "family values" to mean mutual support, caring, and other things they desire. As one woman said to me, "What I need is a family of women—why can't the women's movement be that?"*

• Women of all races, classes, ethnicities, ages, sexualities, and abilities are still the only oppressed group that doesn't have a nation, a neighborhood, or usually even a bar. In our own homes, we may be sabotaged in our deepest sense of self, used as servants, and treated with violence. *Yet we have lost the psychic families—the groups variously called "consciousness-raising," "rap," or just "women's groups" in the late 1960s and early 1970s—that offered both the support system and the revolutionary insights of feminism; the personal/political means of transformation.*

Of course, there are many reasons why all of us, women and men, are also missing small, diverse groups together. The nuclear family, a new and cruel event in human history, has replaced the extended family that once sustained us. (Think of the contrast, for instance, between the isolation of the two-parent household and the wisdom of the African proverb, "It takes a whole village to raise a child.") When we do manage to create a chosen family from among our neighbors, friends, and colleagues, modern mobility means we'll probably have to remake it several times. The old town-meeting way of getting information and making decisions has narrowed

to the isolation of a living room or polling booth.

The small, full circle, personal/political groups we're yearning for are neither small in importance nor rare in history. They've been the major means of sustaining daily life in older cultures and of personal/political transformation in modern ones. It was the "testifying" meetings in black churches in the South that allowed personal experiences to be shared, and gave birth to the civil rights movement. The Chinese revolution against centuries of despotism was nurtured in small groups where people were finally allowed to "speak bitterness to recall bitterness," and to begin digging out the deep roots of self-defeating tradition—including that of male dominance and female subservience. In the late sixties and early seventies, women's consciousness-raising groups were inspired by both those examples, especially by the civil rights one, and they spread like wildfire. Women told the stories of their lives, analyzed shared patterns, gave names to injustices once just called "life," and turned them into public issues through speak-outs and political action. In many ways, it was those early c-r groups that gave feminism its heart, depth, and lasting legacies.

There were meetings about which we never said, "I can't believe I have to go to another meeting," because they were the highlights of our week. We brought our problems and experiences, from what to do about a racist/sexist boss to tensions with mothers and lovers. We went around the room with serious personal themes and also with outrageous jokes. We talked about sex with an honesty few had ever heard before. We listened, really *listened* to each other for clues to our mutual welfare. We unearthed archaeological fragments of our lives that turned out to be parts of larger political patterns. The result was personal exhilaration, and an amazing political impact.

In the last dozen years, however, the very success of the feminist movement has created a backlash, and the resulting necessity of fighting hard to hang on to external gains had often caused us to neglect internal goals. Over and over in this year, I've heard women wish for more time, space, and energy for themselves; more links to other women for support, community, and growth.

Our first job is to envision a full-circle, extended-family-size group. Our second is to know we have a right to it. Otherwise, we will go right on turning to big organizations, narrow interest groups, and nuclear family units that can't take the pressure of all our hopes and needs. Look at it this way: if each cell within our bodies is a whole and indivisible version of those bodies, and each of us is a whole and indivisible cell of the body politic, then each of us has an organic need to be part of a group in which we can be our whole and indivisible selves.

So, as a result of what I've learned from readers, here is a suggestion for a goal by the year 2000: *A national honeycomb of diverse, small, personal/political groups that are committed to each member's welfare through inner and outer change; both self-realization and social justice.* It doesn't matter whether we call them testifying or soul sessions as in the civil rights movement; consciousness-raising or rap groups as in early feminism; covens, quilting bees, or women's circles as in women's history; or revolutionary cells, men's groups, councils of grandmothers, or "speaking bitterness" groups as in various movements and cultures. Perhaps they will have an entirely new name, since combining the elements of diverse communities will make them different from all of them. I think of them just as "revolutionary groups," for a revolution is also a full circle. The important thing is that they are free, diverse, no bigger than an extended family—and everywhere.

It doesn't matter on which side we begin this personal/political, internal/external journey. It matters that we complete the circle. It doesn't matter whether we begin with the individual or the group. We need both.

Note

1. Some of the details in the following stories are disguised, since I did not ask permission to publish them while they were being told.

Resources

These books may be helpful in creating groups, not all of the books listed below are in print and may take a trip to the library.

Allen, Pamela. (1973). "Free Space," *1970, Notes from the Third Year.* Reprinted in *Radical Feminism,* Anne Koedt, Ellen Levine, and Anita Rapone, editors. New York: Quadrangle/New York Times Book Co., pp. 271-279. Philosophy and goals of consciousness-raising.

Evans, Sara. (1979). *Personal Politics: The Roots of Women's Liberation in the Civil Rights Movement and the New Left.* New York: Knopf. The birth of small-group feminism.

Hagan, Kay Leigh. (1993). "Co-dependency and the Myth of Recovery," "The Habit of Freedom," *Fugitive Information: Essays from a Feminist Hothead.* San Francisco: Harper. Two essays: a feminist critique of co-dependency groups, and the necessity of women sharing experience as an escape from the colonized mind.

Kasl, Charlotte. (1992). *Many Roads, One Journey.* San Francisco: HarperCollins. A feminist psychologist replaces "recovery" with "discovery" of the self, and adapts the twelve steps to women.

Kimmel, Michael S., and Thomas Mosmiller, editors. (1992). *Against the Tide: "Pro-Feminist Men" in the United States: 1776-1990, A Documentary History.* Boston: Beacon Press.

Kivel, Paul. (1992). *Men's Work: How to Stop the Violence That Tears Our Lives Apart.* Center City, Minnesota: Hazelden. A personal journey, with exercises and group topics at the end of each chapter, by a co-founder of the Oakland Men's Project.

Kleiman, Carol. (1980). *Women's Networks.* New York: Lippencott & Crowell. The gamut of women's support, self-help, and networking groups.

"NOW Guidelines for Feminist Consciousness-Raising." (1982). National Organization for Women, 1000 16th Street N.W., Suite 700, Washington, D.C. 20036, (202) 331-0066. Process and topics used by NOW in groups with leaders, of eight to ten weeks duration. Many chapters offer these groups for anyone, not just

NOW members. Join one—or order this $10.00, 93-page guide to help start your own.

Pennebaker, James W. (1991). *Opening Up: The Healing Power of Confiding in Others.* New York: Avon.

Sarachild, Kathie. (1976). "A Program for Feminist Consciousness-raising." *Notes from the Second Year.* Reprinted in *Women Together,* Judith Papachristou, editor. New York: Knopf. Outline of subjects and process as presented to an early women's liberation conference by a pioneer.

Self-Esteem for Women, 1079 West Morse Boulevard, Suite A, Winter Park, Florida 32789. (800) 531-2208. Three-day weekends, 25 women each, in various parts of the country, for a fee, scholarships available. Also help with creating continuing groups.

Stambler, Sookie, editor. (1970). *Women's Liberation.* New York: Ace Books. Although out of print, this book is worth tracking down at a library for its essays by June Arnold and Susan Brownmiller on their experience with consciousness-raising groups. Also of interest are excerpts from an essay by Patricia M. Robinson, "A Historical and Critical Essay for Black Women of the Cities," which explores connections between race and sex, women and nature.

Stettbacher, J. Konrad. (1991). *Making Sense of Suffering: The Healing Confrontation with Your Own Past,* with Foreword and Afterword by Alice Miller. New York: Dutton. A four-step program—usable by groups or individuals—for confronting and interrupting cycles of childhood trauma.

10

Women, Ethnic and Language Minorities, and Mass Media

Annette J. Samuels

"Congress," the First Amendment of the U.S. Constitution declares, "shall make no law respecting an establishment of religion, or prohibiting the free exercise thereof; or abridging the freedom of speech, or of the press; or the right of the people peaceably to assemble, and to petition the Government for a redress of grievances."

In effect, the Constitution empowers each of us with the right to communicate with one another using our power of speech, the ability to petition, and to assemble and distribute our message. Effective communication provides an opportunity for an exchange of ideas and opinions in an effort to better understand and develop respect for the beliefs of others. Unfortunately, the philosophy of effective communication does not match the reality of women and ethnic and language minorities in the United States who view themselves as outside of the mainstream of the nation's communications systems. Mass media do little to dispel that sense of disconnection, and most Americans have little understanding of the role and responsibility of mass media.

Mass media are reflections of our society. The good, bad, beautiful, and ugly are splashed across the front pages of our newspapers, played backed during 30-second sound bites on our television screens, and blasted at us over our radio waves. Those visions we see and voices we hear do not always tell us a pleasant story. They also do not tell us the whole story.

In 1968, the Kerner Commission on civil disorders charged that major news media had not adequately analyzed and reported on "racial problems in the United States and, as a related matter, to meet the Negro's legitimate expectations in journalism" (National Advisory Commission on Civil Disorders, 1968/1988, p. 366). The Kerner report also pointed out that the images portrayed of black Americans in newspapers and on television did little to assist white Americans in understanding and accepting black Americans.

The Kerner Commission's criticism was no surprise to the African American community. For more than 140 years, beginning with the publication of *Freedom's Journal* in New York in 1827, African Americans had depended upon the black press to provide them with information about their community and present their case to the American public. "We wish to plead our cause," said *Freedom's Journal*'s two editors, John B. Russwurm and Samuels Cornish. "Too long have others spoken for us" (Editorial, March 16, 1827).

Until the end of the Civil War, black newspapers were published exclusively in northern communities. Slaves were forbidden to learn to read, and freed men and women found themselves constantly threatened if slave owners suspected them of funneling information to their slaves.

After emancipation, scores of black newspapers appeared in the states that once constituted the southern Confederacy. Today, despite great financial difficulties, the National Newspapers Association in Washington, D.C. (the organization that represents black newspapers), says it has more than 225 members and claims there are about 300 African American newspapers being published.

Prior to the advent of television, there were a number of mediums by which Americans gained a sense of whom they were—newspapers, magazines, books, radio, and film. In the early twentieth century, the only *mass medium* was newspapers. For the most part, the major newspapers, and there were many of them, ignored blacks or only covered them when egregious crimes were allegedly committed against whites.

In 1915, films such as *Birth of a Nation,* the classic of the motion picture world of that day, heralded the efforts of white America, represented by the Ku Klux Klan, to rid itself of the black man. And the majority of the films produced during the early decades of the twentieth century depicted African Americans as lazy, shuffling, happy-go-lucky, devil-may-care people. Black women were highly sexed and black men hungered for and raped white women. Native Americans were portrayed as savages who scalped white men and raped white women. The Irish were depicted as uneducated thugs determined to populate the Earth with thousands of little Catholic children who would take over the world and give it to the Pope. Jews were conniving, sneaky, stingy people who killed Jesus and should be banished from the earth. Hispanics, usually decked out in sombreros, were depicted as lazy, ignorant, and macho. Asians and other ethnic minorities were usually cast in subservient roles. Women, of course, were depicted as sex kittens, devious, crazy, and money-hungry.

Magazines, for both men and women, upheld the status quo: Business and sports were issues for men. And magazines for women, published by men, served a steady diet of housecleaning, cooking, child rearing, and keep-your-husband-happy tips. Blacks were ignored completely, and needless to say, other minorities were also ignored.

By the 1930s, film and radio made newspapers less affordable and necessary. Radio, for the most part, was the purveyor of news and music and, in a sense, was color-blind. Savvy radio station owners—most, if not all, of whom were white—quickly came to realize that in certain areas of the country they could make money if their programming was directed toward the black community. During the late 1930s, programs such as *Amos and Andy* and *Beulah,* played by whites over the radio waves and claiming to depict the black experience in America, became very popular. Later, during the early days of television, both of those programs were rewritten and cast with black actors for television viewers.

During the 1950s, as television grew in influence, things began to slowly change—but not enough to make a difference in how white America viewed African Americans and other minorities. And women, during that time, were being encouraged to stay at home, raise their children, and become the ultimate consumers of every conceivable kind of gadget imaginable. Studies of that era showed that 1 character in 50 was Hispanic, fewer than 1 in 100 was Asian, and 1 in 200 was black. Once in a while, you would catch a glimpse of a black delivery man, porter, or waiter. Black professionals and businessmen were virtually nonexistent.

In 1954, when the Supreme Court declared in *Brown v. Board of Education* that "separate, but equal schools" for blacks and whites were unconstitutional, white America was not ready for integration. For those of us who lived through the 1950s, 1960s, and early 1970s, there are scenes of horror etched into our collective memories: Lester Maddox with his hatchet in hand declaring "segregation today, segregation tomorrow." Four young people bravely walking the gauntlet of angry, screaming whites as they integrated Little Rock High School. The bombing of the church in Birmingham, Alabama, that killed four little black girls. The march across the Freetis Bridge, where young civil rights workers were greeted by police dogs and water hoses. The killings of three civil rights workers in Mississippi. The election of President John F. Kennedy, whose handlers saw the wisdom in having him telephone Coretta Scott King and offer whatever help he could provide to free Dr. Martin Luther King, Jr., from jail. The 1963 March on Washington. The assassination of President John F. Kennedy. The assassinations of Dr. King, Malcolm X, and Robert Kennedy. The uprisings in major cities throughout the country. Tanks rolling through the streets of our nation's capital. The women's movement, which used many of the strategies of the civil rights' movement to bring about change. Those were turbulent times.

Despite almost 20 years of turbulence and dramatic social change, a 1972 study of television commercials, sponsored by the Wash-

ington, D.C., Chapter of the National Organization of Women (NOW), found that women were characterized as housekeepers, household workers, adjuncts to men, dependent on men, submissive, unintelligent, and sex objects (Butler & Paisley, 1972, pp. 72-73). And why not? The early 1960s had ushered in prime-time television's "idiot" sitcom. *Dennis the Menace,* the *Real McCoys,* the *Beverly Hillbillies, Mr. Ed,* and *McHale's Navy* followed a lighthearted, noncontroversial style. There were no minorities, little discussion of ideas and values. The message of commercial television was to laugh your head off, work hard, and don't think about what's going on around you.

The "idiot" era came to an abrupt halt with the escalation of the civil rights movement that, at first, demanded attention with peaceful demonstrations that were marred by violence perpetrated by the opposition. By the end of the 1960s, violence erupted within the black community as a result of an accumulation of unresolved grievances and increasing tension. Television and print media scurried to find, and hire, African Americans to cover a community that they had long ignored or reported on from the perspective of a white man's world.

Out of that effort came NBC's Gordon Graham, Norma Quarles, Robert "Bob" Teague, and such correspondents as the late Lem Tucker and Bill Matney. At CBS, there was Joan Murray in New York, Chris Borgen, Stanley Duke covering sports, George Foster in Chicago, and network reporters Ponchita Pierce and Hal Walker. ABC's lineup carried Gil Noble in New York and Layhmond Robinson and Melba Tolliver as network reporters. The presence of minorities in television programs and commercials increased dramatically during those years. In the 1980s, we saw the increase of participation of other minorities, Hispanic and Asian in particular, as reporters and anchors on news shows.

By the late 1970s, television shows entered a reformist era with shows like *All in the Family, Maude,* and *Good Times.* Black-oriented shows such as *The Jeffersons, Sanford and Son,* Flip Wilson's variety show, *Chico and the Man,* and *Rhoda,* one of the rare series since the 1950s to feature strong Jewish characters, balanced the vinegar of social conscience with the honey of laugh lines. Family viewing time brought *Happy Days* and *Laverne and Shirley.* And women's issues were given a brief viewing with the airing of *Charlie's Angels* and *Three's Company.*

Giant leaps forward, wouldn't you say? Blacks, Hispanics, Jews, women, issues. Clearly, media, particularly television, was moving toward a recognition of the coloring and feminization of America. Maybe. Maybe not.

In 1942, Langston Hughes's fictional character "Simple" observed that "the only time colored folks is front page news, is when there's been a lynching or a boycott or a whole bunch of us have been butchered or is arrested."

Is it fair to use an observation that was made by a fictional character dealing with a real situation more than 50 years ago to evaluate where we are today? Let's see.

Herbert J. Gans, author of *Deciding What's News* (1979), noted that by 1975 most racial news stories zeroed in on black rioters, gangs, criminals, and disaster victims. National news stories, for the most part, featured middle- and upper-middle-class blacks who had overcome racial, economic, and political obstacles. And black business and cultural activities had effectively been relegated to the back-of-the-book sections of most magazines.

In 1990, the *Los Angeles Times* spent four months doing a nationwide review of how the press portrayed African Americans, Latinos, Asian Americans, and Native Americans. Not much had changed since 1975. Most of the respondents complained about the overwhelmingly negative nature of stories about people of color—especially blacks and Latinos—and the absence of people of color from the mainstream of daily news coverage. Television, with its emphasis on crime and violence at the local level and public policy at the network level, were es-

pecially susceptible to the above criticisms (Shaw, 1990).

In 1995, white Americans were startled and dismayed at the response of a broad section of the black community to the "not guilty" verdict in the O. J. Simpson double murder trial that had been dubbed the "trial of the century." Mr. Simpson had been charged with the stabbing murders of his former wife, Nicole Brown Simpson, and a friend, Ron Goldman. The tragic, more than 15-month saga leading up to the jury decision was played out over television stations throughout the world.

A wide variety of polls showed that more than a majority of blacks agreed with the jury's verdict, and more than three-fourths of them thought the jury was fair and impartial. Although a little over half of whites disagreed with the jury's not guilty verdict, about one-third agreed with it, about one-half of whites thought the jury was fair and impartial, and about 35% thought it was not (see *Newsweek,* October 1995, p. 30; *U.S. News and World Report,* October 16, 1995, p. 32). It was clear that blacks and whites had seen the same trial but from diametrically opposite points of view. There was no question that the "colored people" were still "front page news, when there's . . . a whole bunch of us have been butchered or is arrested."

The situation is further exacerbated by the fact that, according to the Federal Communications Commission, Office of Consumer Assistance and Small Business Division, less than 3% of the 1,104 television stations in the nation are owned by people of color. Moreover, we are no longer dealing with just local and network news shows. There's C-Span with its gavel-to-gavel coverage of Congress, Court TV, Cable News Network, which broadcasts around the clock, and Black Entertainment Television. In addition, we continue to see a decline in the number of local newspapers that are available to provide a more in-depth point of view of our communities and the events and issues that we face as our country becomes more diverse.

Maintaining democratic mass media that are open and accessible to the public is an almost impossible task in a capitalistic society that encourages individualism. On the other hand, it would be helpful if the citizens of our country had a clearer understanding of the role and responsibility of mass media. Despite these seemingly insurmountable challenges, women and ethnic and language minorities have developed mechanisms for addressing these issues with some measure of success.

Where do we go from here? There are no clear-cut answers.

We have seen a tremendous growth in the variety and publication of magazines for women, several of them published by women. Also, the number of black and other ethnic and language minority magazines has increased.

Newspapers, whose editorial desks are still mainly headed by white men, attempt to address the issues facing women and ethnic and language minorities. But many of those stories continue to show the bias and lack of appreciation of the roles and responsibilities of women and ethnic and language minorities in American society.

Television has shown itself to be a follower, a documenter rather than a leader. It is likely that it will continue in that direction being pushed and pulled forward into dealing with a changing nation and world.

Change is never easy. Nor does it occur swiftly. The future holds great potential. It is not clear whether or not our nation's mass media will be able to meet the challenge.

References

Butler, M., & Paisley, W. (1972). *Women and the mass media: Sourcebook for research and action.* New York: Human Sciences Press.

Gans, H. (1979). *Deciding what's news.* New York: Vintage.

National Advisory Commission on Civil Disorders. (1988). *Report of the National Advisory Commission on Civil Disorders.* New York: Pantheon. (Original work published by Bantam in 1968)

Shaw, D. (1990, December 11-14). Minorities and the press [series]. *Los Angeles Times,* pp. A1 ff. (each date).

11

Uncovering the Media Coverage of Sport

Judith Cramer

The sport stars of my youth were typically white men, people like Joe Namath, John Havlicek, Carl Yastrzemski, Jack Nicklaus, and Rod Laver. The representation of successful women athletes was rare. Role models for young female athletes, such as Billie Jean King, Chris Evert, and Donna de Varona, were limited because their performances received such little media coverage.

When I was growing up, springtime meant playing softball and soaking up the media coverage of high school, college, and professional baseball, none of which had anything to do with me. With the exception of some *Wide World of Sports* coverage of the Japanese women's volleyball team, there was no validation for who I was and what I was doing as a college volleyball player other than through my own participation and the women's matches I saw in person. It was not until the summer of 1994 that the mainstream media covered a sports event—Gay Games

IV—that more closely related to who I am and to the experiences I've had as a 38-year-old white, educated, middle- to upper-middle-class lesbian. Although there is little question that media coverage of women athletes and women's sports has changed from the time I was a child, I still do not see regular, representative coverage of the girls and women I know/have known who participate and compete in sport.

Historically in American culture, the majority of people holding positions of power have been educated middle- to upper-middle-class white men, or what Barbara Ehrenreich (1995) calls the "professional middle class," creating the dominant ideology, setting the public agenda. People of different gender, class, race/ethnicity, sexual orientation, ability, and age are regarded as Others, Outsiders (Becker, 1963; Fuss, 1991), Border Dwellers (Anzaldúa, 1987), individuals who work and play on the margin (hooks,

1990). They are the social unequals of those who dominate; their power is less not because they are intrinsically so but because that is the way the dominant group views and treats them and the way they, in turn, view and treat themselves. The dominant group creates this hierarchy to maintain "existing differences and inequalities . . . [out of] fear . . . [those inequalities] will diminish" (Pieterse, 1994, p. 26).

Because we can't personally experience every event, person, or place, we rely heavily on the media, which interpret events and determine what is important for us to know. Journalists, also members of the "professional middle class" who sit atop the hierarchical ladder, traditionally have determined that violence and politics are of greater value than education and health, for example; that men are more important than women; that whites are of greater interest than people of color and different ethnicities; and that, more often than not, the lives of white middle- to upper-middle-class individuals have greater import than those of the working class. The worldview the media constructs is not an accurate representation of us, but nevertheless plays a significant role in shaping our individual worldviews.

Underrepresentation and misrepresentation are two ways in which the mainstream media consciously and unconsciously magnify differences between people like themselves and those Others who might threaten their power, their "top dog" positions. The invisibility, underrepresentation, or misrepresentation of women in sports coverage by the media is well documented. A two-year content analysis (Bryant, 1980) found that women's sports coverage constituted just 4.4% of the total column inches in two newspapers. A study of *Sports Illustrated* covers from 1954 to 1978 (Boutilier & SanGiovanni, 1983) revealed that sportswomen constituted less than 5% of all coverage accorded athletes. In 1984, Rintala and Birrell analyzed *Young Athlete* magazine and found that female athletes were subjects of fewer than a third of all photo-graphs published in that magazine between 1975 and 1982, and that the more prominent the photograph, the less likely it was to be one of a female athlete, thus creating the impression that few girls and women play sports. An analysis of *Sports Illustrated* feature articles between 1954 and 1987 (Lumpkin & Williams, 1991) found that 91% of all coverage was given to male athletes and their accomplishments, lending support to the results of the earlier research.

The most recent studies suggest that there has been no improvement in the representation of women athletes and women's sports. Duncan, Messner, and Williams (1990, 1991) found extreme gendering, including gender marking (e.g., the men's championship game was called "the national championship game," while the women's was called "the women's national basketball championship") and infantilization ("girls" or "young ladies") in the local television coverage by a Los Angeles station. They also found the station misrepresented women's sports and women athletes by trivializing (the focus on a woman athlete's appearance and attractiveness) their performances. In addition, research conducted by Kane (1989) suggests that women athletes who participate in individual sports such as gymnastics, tennis, and skating, which emphasize traditional feminine characteristics (e.g., grace), rather than team sports are more likely to be reported on by the sports media, and that individual and team "masculine" (e.g., shot putting and softball) sports are less likely to be covered.

People of color and different ethnicities also have received less sports coverage. Historically, much of the focus of women's sports coverage has been on upper-/middle-class whites (Cahn, 1994; Williams, 1994), suggesting that the experiences of black women athletes were similar (virtually all of the research done on the coverage of women athletes of color has focused on black women). Unlike white women athletes, however, black women enjoyed the early support of their community and the Negro press (Williams,

1994) for their participation in black basketball leagues during the early twentieth century. While the media coverage of white women, especially those who are middle to upper-middle class, has been minimal, mainstream coverage of black women athletes has been just about invisible. Lumpkin and Williams (1991) found that of the women athletes presented on 114 of the 1,835 *Sports Illustrated* covers from 1954 to 1989, black sportswomen appeared on just five of them (Althea Gibson; Jackie Joyner-Kersee, twice; and Florence Griffith-Joyner, twice). All three featured athletes who participate(d) in individual sports (e.g., tennis, track and field). Other research (Condor & Anderson, 1984) suggests that white female athletes receive more and longer feature articles than black women athletes in *Sports Illustrated* and that although women athletes are extremely underrepresented in *Sports Illustrated*'s coverage (327 of 3,273 feature articles), black sportswomen are even less visible, appearing in only 25% of the articles on women athletes (Lumpkin & Williams, 1991).

As with people of color, lesbians have been underrepresented and misrepresented in sports coverage. What has been reported by the mainstream sports media has been minimal, often endorsing narrow, negative stereotypes. Books such as Susan Fox Rogers's *Sportsdykes* (1994) and Mariah Burton Nelson's (1991) *Are We Winning Yet?* address the issue of lesbians in sport but devote little space to the media representation of lesbian athletes. In *Coming on Strong* (1994), a history of women in sport, Susan Cahn discusses the saliency of sexual orientation as a news criterion. She writes that journalists since the 1920s have questioned the sexual orientation and femininity of women athletes. Track star and golfer Babe Didrikson was one of the first to face such scrutiny. With the exception of contemporary tennis greats such as Martina Navratilova and Billie Jean King, and women such as Juanita Harvey, whose participation in Gay Games IV was chronicled by the New York media (Cramer,

1995), "named" lesbian athletes have been invisible in mainstream sports coverage. In part, this is because of their unwillingness to break their own silence and because of a reticence and uneasiness the mainstream sports media feel about addressing homosexuality in their reports. As a result of their homophobia, the popular sports media have used heterosexual lenses to consistently focus on women athletes they describe as exceptionally attractive (e.g., Chris Evert, Florence Griffith-Joyner, Jan Stephenson, and Katerina Witt) or very masculine (e.g., European athletes such as Martina Navratilova and East German swimmers). The journalists' vision also creates pictures colored by nationalism and ethnocentrism.

The dominant group controlling the worlds of sport and media, like society-at-large, are (mostly) white, (mostly) middle-aged, (mostly) male, (mostly) middle- and upper-middle-class (Gross, 1991, p. 21) elitists who work to subordinate those groups that potentially threaten the dominant group's position. In the case of sport, men and those women who have adopted the dominant ideology have traditionally preserved their turf by showing much greater support for those women who participate in the more "feminine" individual sports (e.g., tennis, ice skating, golf, gymnastics, track). It costs a lot more money to play and train in those individual sports than it does to play on a more "masculine" softball or soccer team. And implicit in this message is another—that most working-class women, and most women of color, are not welcome to compete in the majority of individual sports— and that the system favors the wealthy, white, and privileged.

In covering individual sports much more frequently than team sports, the media add further support to the idea that if women are going to play sports, they should play those that are "more becoming." They should not play those that "encourage" and "develop" lesbians, that detract from their femininity, masculinize them, and develop the status so often associated with masculinity. The media, however, are doing more than just conferring status on those who compete individually. They are reflecting their own value system in suggesting that factors in addition to gender—class, race/ethnicity, and sexual orientation—significantly influence their construction of coverage. In the end, what this does is keep gender, race/ethnicity, class, and sexual orientation separate from each other and from those constructing the coverage. The media create the illusion of representation by including primarily women athletes who compete in individual sports. This is an exclusionary media practice. Inclusive practice requires representations of women of color, of working-class women, of women of differing sexual orientations participating in team sports as well.

We may be seeing the beginning of a shift in the value the sports media place on women athletes and women's sports from mostly reporting on individual sports to the increasing coverage of intercollegiate basketball, a team sport in which women of different colors, class, and sexual orientation play. A sports writer recently told me that women's basketball is "about to explode," and when I asked him why, he said that it is because "the level of the women's game has really improved." What did he mean by "about to explode"? He was predicting that women's basketball would soon "explode" in mainstream media coverage even though media such as *USA Today,* and campus newspapers and radio stations, have been reporting on women's intercollegiate basketball on a somewhat consistent basis for more than a decade.

Some theorists believe that media ownership plays the most important role in determining what is reported about whom and how they are reported on. But the "routines" theorists such as Herbert Gans say ownership is not that important. Rather, to varying degrees, "organizational constraints, economic constraints, the journalists' own class positions, ideologies, career pressures, and general 'values' in the news" (Eliasoph, 1988, p. 314) combined with reporting/writing routine limitations (e.g., stressing event reporting, controversy, and telling rather than explaining a story) have a more significant impact. The stories that are reported, according to Gans, incorporate dominant ideas and therefore are most often those that affect large numbers of people or are unusual. Impact and novelty have always ruled sports news.

The mainstream sports media are not willing to take much financial risk when it comes to devoting space/airtime to something they perceive to be out of the mainstream. Women's intercollegiate basketball, however, is demonstrating that it can draw a large audience and so the media decision makers are increasing their coverage of that sport, thinking that with improved coverage will come profit. Today's women basketball players are competing at a much higher level, the genesis of which can be traced to the contemporary American women's movement and demands made by its leaders for Title IX legislation that was enacted in 1972 to create more athletic scholarships and opportunities for young women athletes. Much more athletic and competitive performances have pushed other events to happen that have contributed to women's intercollegiate basketball becoming a hot commodity in today's sports media market. These include NBC's mid-1970s and early 1980s broadcasts of the Association of Intercollegiate Athletics for Women (AIAW) championship games; a change in the governance of women's intercollegiate athletics in 1982 from the AIAW to the larger, more financially powerful National Collegiate Athletic Association (NCAA); sports editors who now have daughters old enough to be playing high school and college basketball; women's teams in media population centers that have improved and are winning; and a women's intercollegiate basketball coaches' poll that Mel Greenberg introduced in 1976.[1] Greenberg, a writer with the *Philadelphia Inquirer* and editor of the daily file to the Knight-Ridder (owner of the *Philadelphia Inquirer*) News Tribune wire service, says,

The poll is the singular, most important thing to happen in terms of media because it unified the country. Prior to us coming along, you could go two months before you knew who beat who in another part of the country. We instantly united the country . . . the poll then created the coverage because people had something to look at. (personal communication, February 28, 1995)

Greenberg, as well as Ohio State University women's basketball coach Nancy Darsch, say the fact that the 1984 Olympic women's basketball competition took place in a major city, Los Angeles, and that the women's team won the gold medal helped focus worldwide media attention on the sport. Darsch, an assistant coach on that team, says that although there wasn't as much coverage of women's basketball after the 1984 Games as there was during the Games, at least coverage didn't stop.

But it is *USA Today*'s coverage of women's intercollegiate basketball—including a weekly coaches' poll, scores, and articles, starting in 1982 when it began publication as this country's only national newspaper—that Greenberg and Darsch cite as the genesis for much of the increased coverage. "We finally have a national publication that gives daily coverage of, through the season anyway, women's basketball. And for people who want to follow women's basketball, that is the publication that they lean on for their information" (Darsch, personal communication, February 16, 1995). *USA Today* is viewed by women's basketball coaches, athletes, and fans as an alternative to local dailies such as the *Columbus Dispatch* (Ohio) and the *Stockton Record* (California). Greenberg believes *USA Today* has pushed local dailies to include more women's basketball more frequently in their sports coverage: "It forced other papers to start paying attention to women because out in the sticks people were saying to their local paper, 'Hey, I don't have to read you. I'm getting my women's stuff from *USA Today*'" (personal communication, February 28, 1995). If mainstream journalists had looked through

different lenses in the mid-1980s, they would have seen something more than the comparatively small crowds and lesser ability (by major men's basketball program standards). A closer look would have provided them with information about the kinds of fans women's basketball drew and continues to attract in increasing numbers. WOSU Radio Sports Director Herb Howenstine can remember going to Ohio State women's basketball games in the mid-1970s when on a good day there might be 200 or 300 people to watch a game in St. John Arena (personal communication, January 31, 1995). Then, in the early 1980s, there were crowds of 400 or 500 that grew to maybe 1,000 to 2,000 on a very good day. Now, the Lady Buckeyes regularly have a two-game weekend total of 17,000, and average 8,500 fans a game.

So who is filling the stands? Mostly women, with a good number of men watching as well. And families. Howenstine says,

You see a lot of fathers bring daughters to games. . . . For example, a good friend of mine, Rusty Miller, goes from broadcasting a regional championship game in 1985 to bringing his daughter's Brownie Troop into St. John Arena to watch the Buckeyes beat Illinois on Sunday. (Howenstine, personal communication, January 31, 1995)

Mothers and their sons and some older people are also women's intercollegiate basketball fans.

In the mid-1980s, as a public radio broadcaster who wanted very much to broadcast those games, I remember paying attention to who was covering them—people (mostly white men) from the opposing teams' campus radio stations. Herb Howenstine and I had made efforts to broadcast the women's games but we'd been told by WOSU station management that finding organizations to underwrite the broadcast costs would be all but impossible because there was so little listener interest. Two years after I left the station, in 1988, Howenstein began broadcasting the women's games, both home and away.[2] So what value did Howenstine and thousands of fans believe women's basketball had that most of the mainstream media did not? Darsch says, "For the men, they enjoy it because it's basketball the way they played it, the way they remember it, played below the rim and it's a sport they can relate to. I've heard a lot of men say that it's more finesse than power" (personal communication, February 16, 1995).[3]

Darsch does not think media coverage reflects the differences in the women's and men's games. She says, "I think that for the most part we get reporters who just report the game. Women's basketball writers are not the media's premiere writers, are not their best writers, and I think that they pretty much report the score." The article the next day, according to Darsch, is not as thorough, "not as long and I don't think it's as insightful." In explanation, Greenberg says,

> A lot of people doing the women's games are just new. What they've basically done is the men's games so that's what they're used to seeing. . . . Part of it too is you're writing for the public that may know nothing. If you say that somebody is like somebody on a women's team, maybe the women will know who you're talking about but most of the public won't. If you say so-and-so is like Shaquille O'Neal. . . . I don't think it's a compliment to the female player to be in that image, but it's something that at least the public can appreciate because it's something they can [identify] with. (personal communication, February 28, 1995)

Greenberg believes there will be more knowledgeable reporting and fewer comparisons between women and men players when ESPN, in the 1995-1996 season, begins to carry out the terms of its contract with the NCAA, spinning off programs like a highlights show that introduces viewers to more players and stories (Kurt Pires, Communications Department, ESPN, personal communication, March 8, 1995).[4]

There has been a noticeable shift away from women's sports coverage that focuses almost exclusively on individual sports to that which includes the representation of women's intercollegiate basketball. The sports media now need to take care that they present the intersections of gender, race, class, and sexual orientation in coverage of sports other than intercollegiate basketball. They also need to be aware that within their coverage girl and women athletes must be represented accurately; women athletes must be treated as individuals, not representative of particular groups. When commentators are broadcasting a women's soccer game, for example, they must use adjectives to describe the play of women and not men, and commentators and writers must avoid infantilization or trivialization of the women and their play.

The impetus for change must come from the top, from sports editors/directors who set policy, do the hiring, and influence story assignment and copy (content). However, hiring and appointing more women, people of diverse backgrounds, as sports editors/directors and reporters, and changing source lists so that they are more inclusive will not, alone, bring about change in sports news content (van Zöonen, 1988). Women and all others who value difference must demand that the journalists themselves appreciate diversity and those whose individual experiences differ from their own. Unlike in my youth, girl and women athletes will have an abundance of role models from which to choose. Only then will sports coverage truly celebrate difference and so become more reflective of the athletes and the sports they play.

Notes

1. In 1994, Mel Greenberg sold the rights to his poll to the Associated Press. In buying those rights, the Associated Press changed the poll to one in which 34 sports writers plus Greenberg vote on the best Division I women's basketball teams in the country.

2. In 1993, WBNS, a commercial radio station in Columbus, won the contract to broadcast all Ohio State men's *and* women's basketball games, Howenstein, who

continues as sports director at WOSU-AM, is also the "Voice of the Lady Buckeyes" for WBNS-AM.

3. Ticket prices, which are about half the cost of the men's, and ticket availability have also contributed to the rise in popularity of the Ohio State women's program and women's intercollegiate basketball in general. In addition, the Big Ten has a long-standing tradition of playing Sunday afternoon games, making women's basketball a family activity or one for those who don't want to be out late at night.

4. ESPN's contract with the NCAA runs from 1995-1996 through 2001-2002. The agreement calls for ESPN to televise 23 Division I games: eight games from the round of 32, the eight regional semifinal games, all four regional championships, the two national semifinals, and the national championship game. For the first time, the women will have a day of rest between the semifinals and the national championship game, all of which began being televised during prime time starting in 1995-1996. ESPN will also continue to televise the "NCAA Women's Selection Show" and will televise highlight shows during the Division I tournament.

Mel Greenberg points to the National Hockey League strike in 1994-1995 and the need for newspaper sports departments, in particular, to fill that sports news hole as contributing to such improved coverage of women's intercollegiate basketball this year.

References

Anzaldúa, G. (1987). *Borderlands: LaFrontera, the new nesticia.* San Francisco: aunt lute books.

Becker, H. S. (1963). *Outsiders.* New York: Free Press.

Boutilier, M. A., & SanGiovanni, L. (1983). *The sporting woman.* Champaign, IL: Human Kinetics.

Bryant, J. (1980). A two-year investigation of the female in sport as reported in the paper media. *Arena Review, 4,* 32-44.

Cahn, S. (1994). *Coming on strong.* New York: Free Press.

Condor, R., & Anderson, D. F. (1984). Longitudinal analysis of coverage accorded black and white athletes in feature articles of *Sports Illustrated* (1960-1980). *Journal of Sport Behavior, 7*(1), 39-43.

Cramer, J. (1995, May). *Gay Games IV: A preliminary look at the coverage of two New York newspapers.* Paper presented at the annual meeting of the International Communication Association, Albuquerque, NM.

Duncan, M. C., Messner, M., & Williams, L. (1990). *Gender stereotyping in televised sports.* Los Angeles: Amateur Athletic Foundation of Los Angeles.

Duncan, M. C., Messner, M., & Williams, L. (1991). *Coverage of women's sports in four daily newspapers.* Los Angeles: Amateur Athletic Foundation of Los Angeles.

Ehrenreich, B. (1995). The silenced majority: Why the average working person has disappeared from American media and culture. In G. Dines & J. M. Humez (Eds.), *Gender, race and class in media* (pp 40-42). Thousand Oaks, CA: Sage.

Eliasoph, N. (1988). Routines and the making of oppositional news. *Critical Studies in Mass Communication, 5,* 313-334.

Fuss, D. (1991). *Inside/out: Lesbian theories, gay theories.* New York: Routledge Kegan Paul.

Gans, H. (1979). *Deciding what's news.* New York: Vintage.

Gross, L. (1991). Out of the mainstream: Sexual minorities and the mass media. In M. A. Wolf & A. Kielwassen (Eds.), *Gay people, sex and the media* (pp. 19-46). Binghamton, NY: Haworth.

hooks, b. (1990). *Choosing the margin as a space of radical openness: Yearning: Race, gender and cultural politics.* Boston: South End Press.

Kane, M. J. (1989). The post Title IX female athlete in the media: Things are changing but how? *Journal of Physical Education, Recreation, and Dance, 60*(3), 58-62.

Lumpkin, A., & Williams, L. D. (1991). An analysis of Sports Illustrated feature articles, 1954-1987. *Sociology of Sport Journal, 8,* 1-15.

Nelson, M. B. (1991). *Are we winning yet? How women are changing sports and sports are changing women.* New York: Random House.

Pieterse, J. N. (1994). White negroes. In G. Dines & J. M. Humez (Eds.), *Gender, race and class in media* (pp. 23-27). Thousand Oaks, CA: Sage.

Rintala, J., & Birrell, S. (1984). Fair treatment for the active female: A content analysis of *Young Athlete* magazine. *Sociology of Sport Journal, 1,* 231-250.

Rogers, S. F. (1994). *Sportsdykes: Stories from on and off the field.* New York: St. Martin's.

van Zöonen, L. (1988). Rethinking women and the news. *European Journal of Communication, 3,* 35-53.

Williams, L. D. (1994). Sportswomen in black and white: Sports history from an Afro-American perspective. In P. Creedon (Ed.), *Women, media and sport: Challenging gender values* (pp. 45-66). Thousand Oaks, CA: Sage.

12

Suing the Sacred Cows That Fed Her

Sandy Nelson

When I sued the *News Tribune* of Tacoma, Washington, for removing me from reporting in September 1990 because of my off-duty political activities, I hoped the case would resolve the perennial issue of whether reporters must surrender their rights to free expression to keep their bylines.

That case, at the time of this writing, was headed for the Washington State Supreme Court, which will decide if the newspaper violated the state constitution as well as a 1992 state law prohibiting job discrimination on the basis of political activities or if the paper enjoys immunity from such laws to preserve its appearance as an "impartial" medium.

The case is being litigated at a time when the newspaper industry is reexamining its tradition of detachment from the public, and growing numbers of journalists are questioning the industry's standard and definition of "objectivity."

Evolution of a Showdown

I was hired by the *News Tribune* as a features writer in 1983 after three years learning the trade at the *Daily World* in Aberdeen. I felt ready for the professional and political challenges of working at the state's third-largest daily (after the Seattle *Times* and *Post-Intelligencer*) and living in the state's second-largest city.

Best of all, the family-owned paper had a collective bargaining agreement between the Pacific Northwest Newspaper Guild Local 82 and the publisher. That contract ensured reporters and other journalists the right to do as we pleased on our own time. When I wasn't working, I was organizing on behalf of two socialist-feminist organizations, Radical Women and the Freedom Socialist Party, in community coalitions to defend abortion rights and oppose police brutality. I was escorting women into clinics blockaded by anti-abortion activists, attending community meetings and rallies to protest police brutality, marching against U.S. intervention in Central America and the Middle East, organizing grassroots support for gay and lesbian rights, and attending monthly union meetings. To me, this vital work made me a better journalist. It brought me into the community, into the vortex of social change, not just as an observer but as a mover and actor.

Although I took care not to report on matters with which I was directly involved, my years of activism had acquainted me with issues and individuals overlooked by my more detached colleagues. My stories about such people and their causes won awards from the Society of Professional Journalists and even the Daughters of the American Revolution and the Freedoms Foundation at Valley Forge. Year after year, I continued to receive excellent evaluations and praise from my supervisors.

In 1986, McClatchy Inc. bought the *News Tribune* in an asset sale, fired many newsroom workers, and abrogated all labor contracts. The Guild immediately began negotiating a contract with the new owners from Sacramento, California. Meanwhile, top newsroom managers quickly attempted to impose a code of ethics on newsroom workers that included sweeping prohibitions against all political involvement. In newsroom meetings, many coworkers and I denounced aspects of the code that interfered with our off-duty freedoms. The proposal finally was referred to collective bargaining, where the employer let it languish until the Guild was decertified as union representative in 1991.

The Gay Rights Fight

In May 1989, the Tacoma City Council passed a law prohibiting job and housing discrimination on the basis of sexual orientation. Their action was the result of years of work by gay and lesbian activists, feminists, and our allies in other social movements. A month later, I helped found the Committee to Protect Tacoma Human Rights to defend the new law against a repeal campaign. My role, as I saw it, was to help the gay community reach out to our allies in the people of color, feminist, and labor movements and the Left.

A united front was the only hope for our emergent gay movement in the face of a better organized and well-financed opposition. Our efforts yielded historic endorsements from the Pierce County Labor Council, the Black Collective, and numerous religious and community groups. Even though we lost the gay rights law by about 800 votes out of some 33,000 in November 1989, we had changed qualitatively the lives of gay men and lesbians in Tacoma.

Emboldened by the narrowness of our defeat, activists reorganized the committee in early 1990 and launched a campaign to restore the law by initiative in 1990. After months of signature gathering, we got a place on the November ballot and began knocking on doors all over the city to win support for our cause. In August, newsroom managers suddenly pulled me aside to tell me I was being moved indefinitely to a nonreporting, copyediting job because they thought my work on the gay rights campaign might jeopardize the paper's appearance of objectivity. Even though I never wrote about the campaign and took great pains to ensure that my political and professional lives didn't overlap, I was told the potential for a conflict of interest was too great to risk.

I protested the move, as did many of my coworkers and dozens of people in the community, including a school board member, a legislator, the president of the state teachers' union, and my comrades in the gay rights campaign. "It is discriminatory to exile a respected, award-winning reporter for her constitutionally protected efforts to end housing and employment discrimination on the basis of sexual orientation," Karla Rudy, chair of the Committee to Protect Tacoma Human Rights, wrote to the *News Tribune* managing editor. "And it's an attack on the labor movement, which endorses Proposition 1 [the gay rights initiative] as a labor issue." But newsroom bosses refused to budge and I was sent packing to a night job on the copy desk untrained and unhappy. After the gay rights initiative failed at the polls in November 1990, top newsroom managers told me I would have to forgo all off-duty political activism before I could return to reporting—a condition not required of other reporters and editors engaged in civil and political activities off the job. I refused to do so.

Taking a Stand

After we had exhausted our internal remedies, the Guild took my case to the National Labor Relations Board's (NLRB) regional office in Seattle, arguing that the *News Tribune* management had committed an unfair labor practice by unilaterally imposing an ethics code that was subject to collective bargaining.

The Guild further argued that management's proposed code unnecessarily infringed on the political and personal freedoms of newsroom workers. But the NLRB refused to issue a complaint and the NLRB's national board rejected two appeals of its decision in early 1991 without considering the merits of the case. And, after a five-year antiunion campaign by *News Tribune* management, the Guild was narrowly decertified in 1991, leaving newsroom workers with few legal protections against arbitrary and capricious behavior by management.

In June 1993, I sued the *News Tribune* with backing from the American Civil Liberties Union (ACLU) of Washington.

"That Sandy Nelson is a reporter does not change the fact that she deserves to live her private life as she sees fit," state ACLU director Kathleen Taylor said. "This case is important for all workers in Washington who do not want their employers controlling their off-the-job activities. We hope the Washing-

ton courts will use this case to secure employees' rights to off-duty political activities that do not interfere with job performance."

In my corner were veteran civil rights attorneys James Lobsenz and William Bender as well as Bender's young associate Paul Chuey. Lobsenz made a name for himself when he won a lawsuit against the Pentagon for its dismissal of gay Army Sergeant Perry Watkins. Bender was known in the Northwest for bringing conspiracy charges against antiabortion activists in Everett, Washington, who were affiliated with a man convicted of firebombing an abortion clinic.

My lawyers argued that the *News Tribune,* by transferring me to the copy desk, violated free speech and freedom of assembly provisions of the state constitution. They charged the newspaper with breaking a state law prohibiting job discrimination on the basis of political activities and with violating its own conditions of employment, which required just cause for termination or discipline. Furthermore, ACLU lawyers argued, the permanent nature of my transfer amounted to a wrongful discharge from reporting. In two separate summary judgment rulings in 1995, Pierce County Superior Court Judge Vicki Hogan dismissed the constitutional claims and instead accepted the newspapers' argument that previous court rulings have not extended constitutional guarantees of free speech and political participation to private sector employees. She ruled in the newspaper's favor on the statutory claim, agreeing that newspaper publishers can prohibit political participation by newsroom employees to protect their appearance of neutrality.

The Double Standard

From the very beginning of the case and in earlier newsroom discussions on the proposed ethics code, I was struck by the irony that an industry founded upon precious First Amendment freedoms would demand that its employees surrender those liberties to maintain an image of the newspaper as a neutral medium of information no matter how insubstantial that image may be. In depositions and court, the *News Tribune* claims a need to require its employees to meet a standard of detachment off the job in the interest of neutral coverage on the job. Yet dozens of my coworkers are involved in organizations such as the Boy Scouts, Little League, Big Brothers, United Way, and so on. Some sit on boards of community organizations for the homeless and disabled. Others belong to churches that have an activist political agenda. Publisher Kelso Gillenwater belongs to the Executive Council of Tacoma/Pierce County, an organization of bankers, public officials, and CEOs of the region's most powerful businesses. The council is involved in numerous urban redevelopment projects that are covered extensively by the newspaper, and it lobbies state government for funding and legislation that further its goals.

How could the standard of detachment apply to me but not to the publisher or other coworkers? The only difference between us was that their off-duty involvements bolstered the status quo and mine challenged it. Obviously, their standard of objectivity was a double standard.

As a lesbian and socialist, I couldn't afford to abstain from the fight for my civil rights. If I could be fired or evicted for being a lesbian or a radical, how secure was my job or my home? It was apparent to me that management's rules against reporter involvement were a pretext to discriminate against the most vulnerable people in the newsroom—gays, people of color, and political minorities.

My case further challenges management's argument that I am an affront to the "tradition" of the reporter as a disinterested observer. We are prepared to offer testimony from several experts that ethics codes are a relatively recent phenomenon in the industry and continue to be one of the most hotly debated. Maybe that's because journalists remember our revolutionary roots. We re-

member Thomas Paine, whose newspapers incited rebellion against England; Ida B. Wells, who alerted the nation to the horror of lynching; John Reed, whose book *Ten Days That Shook the World* offered an eyewitness account of the 1917 Bolshevik Revolution; and Upton Sinclair, who exposed the appalling conditions in Chicago meatpacking plants in a series of articles later published as *The Jungle*. The tradition of objectivity is only as old as the mass marketing of newspapers and came about as a way to avoid offending advertisers and readers.

The *News Tribune* argues that its First Amendment right to determine newspaper content entitles it to make unrestricted personnel decisions about whom it may employ and on what terms. My lawyers counter that press freedom doesn't grant the media a license to override employee rights, labor law, and antidiscrimination law. We say newspapers must fashion ethics codes narrowly, so journalists' First Amendment rights aren't violated. The *News Tribune,* for example, could order me to quit working as the mayor's press secretary if I'm covering city hall. But the paper can't bar me from writing altogether because I spend my free time working for social change.

Going Public

In the tradition of all precedent-setting civil rights battles, I am pursuing my case simultaneously in court and in the community. Since the Sandy Nelson Defense Committee formed in October 1990 to lead a community campaign for my reinstatement, the case has become a cause célèbre among labor and political activists. Even my peers in the mass circulation media are endorsing my effort to expose the myth of objectivity and open the profession to people who differ from the detached, disinterested, prototypical journalist.

"I hope Nelson wins," *Seattle Times* editorial board member Terry Tang wrote in a

July 1993 column. "It takes people like her to build communities worth living in. And it takes people like her to make newspapers reexamine their roles in those communities" (p. 59).

"With hardly a whimper, reporters have become political eunuchs," Frank Wetzel, retired managing editor of the Bellevue, Washington, *Journal American,* wrote in a column for *Eastside Week* in October 1994. "They need someone to say that giving up off-duty First Amendment rights is too great a price to pay for being a reporter. Nelson is saying just that" (p. 14). Roger Simpson, associate professor of communications at the University of Washington and an expert on ethics, was an early supporter. He said in a 1992 article in the *Freedom Socialist* newspaper,

> Sandy Nelson is unusual among a growing number of chastised and punished journalists for her determination to make a public claim that she is entitled to exercise all the rights of any person. It is her opinion about reporter loyalty, about speech and political activity, that has to endure if journalism can play any role at all informing us. (p. 5)

Nationally syndicated columnist Norman Solomon spoke on my behalf at a Seattle forum in September 1994 sponsored by the Sandy Nelson Defense Committee. At that forum, he said,

> She is not only exercising First Amendment rights that we all have to support, she is also engaging in an endeavor that creates an essential gateway to the future. The possibility of overturning the hostilities toward lesbians and gay men holds a key for lifting a great weight from everybody.

Most gratifying of all has been the support of my coworkers, four of whom signed affidavits in March 1995 urging Judge Hogan to reconsider before September 1996 her decision not to summarily return me to reporting. My coworkers testified that management's crackdown on the civil rights of one reporter has had a chilling effect on the newsroom, causing many to restrict their own community involvements.

As the case winds its way through the courts, I've settled in for a long fight to rid journalism of draconian conduct codes that stand in the way of developing a more open and responsive relationship with our readers. Readers value reporters who understand the issues that affect their lives. And they are rightfully suspicious when powerful and wealthy media corporations claim to be "unbiased." They see the newspaper's detachment from the community and its deference to advertisers and large corporate business. Organizations such as the Washington State Labor Council, the National Lawyers Guild, and the American Federation of State, County, and Municipal Employees and individuals including feminist writer Kate Millett and black feminist Flo Kennedy have voiced their support of the case. In addition, 15,000 people—nearly 2,000 of them from 12 countries outside the United States—have signed petitions demanding my reinstatement.

Their support should help the courts to recognize that I am fighting for journalists to enjoy the same political rights as the people we serve.

References

Reed, J. (1960). *Ten days that shook the world.* New York: Random House. (Original work published 1912)

Simpson, R. (1992, May-July). UW professor defends embattled journalist. *Freedom Socialist,* p. 5.

Sinclair, U. (1946). *The jungle.* New York: Viking.

Tang, T. (1993, July 16). When ethics, citizenship collide in the newsroom. *Seattle Times,* p. 59.

Wetzel, F. (1994, October 5). Blows against the status quo: Challenging newspapers' First Amendment violations. *Eastside Week,* p. 14.

13

Surviving Auschwitz and the Media
A Mengele Twin's Media Voyage

Susan J. Kaufman

First Remembrances of Media Power

Eva Kor was born January 30, 1935, in Portz, Transylvania, a village in the upper northwestern corner of what is now Rumania.[1] When she was 9 years old, Eva, her twin Miriam, two other sisters, and her mother and father were deported to Auschwitz.[2] Eva and Miriam became human guinea pigs experimented on by the infamous "Angel of Death," Dr. Josef Mengele.

"Before the war there was no media. We had a little boy, like a drummer, who beat the drum, and he would say, 'Hear ye! Hear ye! This is what is happening in the news . . .' The other thing that I was aware of, though, my father bought a battery operated radio. He

EDITORS' NOTE: The author, then a graduate teaching assistant at Indiana State University, first met Eva Kor in 1979 when Kor was working on her bachelor's degree. Assigned to give a "speech to inform," Kor spoke to the author's class about surviving Auschwitz. It was one of the first times she'd spoken in public about her experiences. Later, as a newspaper columnist and city editor, the author saw to it that Kor's stories were brought to public attention. In the 1980s, the author helped Kor form an organization that brought together twins who had survived medical experiments performed by Dr. Josef Mengele. Most recently, the author helped assemble a video crew to document Kor and her children's return to Auschwitz 50 years after liberation. There, Kor and her son and daughter met with SS Nazi physician Hans Münch and his children in a continuation of a half-century-long process of forgiveness and healing. Upon returning from that trip, the author interviewed Kor about her evolutionary relationship with media. Kor's story illustrates what some women have found it necessary to do if their voices are not to be silenced by the failure of the malestream mass media to recognize the importance of their existence.

wanted to know what was going on in the war," Eva recalled.[3]

"My parents would lock the door and they didn't want the children to hear. I put my ear to the door and could hear Hitler yelling; the voice coming from our radio was extremely threatening. Obviously, media in Hitler's regime was absolutely controlled by the people in power.

"The other thing that I remember, quite probably about 1942 or maybe 1943, was some people at school telling us that they were going to show us some big pictures of the war. I didn't really know what that was, but I definitely was curious about it. They said it would be shown after sunset. It had to be dark. It was the first film that I ever saw. I don't know what they called it—but all the children called it 'jumping pictures on the wall' because these were films where people were moving . . . the film was about how to kill, or to catch and kill, a

Jew. So my first experience(s) with the media were definitely very dangerous, very threatening, and a reflection of the people in power on how to destroy me. The other first things I remember [about media] were the liberation pictures."

When the Soviet film crews arrived with the Soviet troops to liberate the Auschwitz-Birkenau camps on January 27, 1945, Eva said the soldiers instructed the children to march along the corridor separating the two walls of barbed wire that outlined the vast expanse of the death camp.

Eva didn't know it that cold day in Poland, but what the Soviet filmmakers captured in their lenses would eventually bring her into focus as the object of worldwide mass media attention. For years the media showed the film, and prints were carried in newspapers and magazines. The two chubby-cheeked[4] little girls clutching each other's hand as they

EVA
MOZES
KOR

MIRIAM
MOZES
ZEIGER

PICTURE TAKEN IN AUSCHWITZ
SAME PLACE AS THE LIBERATION
PICTURE WAS TAKEN
DECEMBER, 1991

walked through the barbed wire corridor were eventually seen by thousands. An enlargement of that frame now covers a barrack's wall in the Polish museum of horrors that Auschwitz has become.

It would be almost 40 years before Eva would find that film and the world would begin to know that the two unnamed children were Eva and Miriam Mozes.

"I was not very aware and never thought that the media would be interested in my story, or that I would have anything to say that they would be interested in. I looked upon them, probably, as some group of people who were entrusted with the world's confidence, and whatever I read, I believed it always like one of the Ten Commandments. I would have never ever dared to doubt something that I thought was the news or for that matter even sometimes what I read in a book," Eva recalled.

But doubt inevitably crept in. "My first doubt came when I saw a book that was published about the Holocaust by Harry James Cargas. In there were some pictures of us from the liberation. At the bottom of it, it said that we, the liberated children, well-fed, must have been arriving at the camp because no children survived the camp, that we all ended up in the gas chambers. How could somebody write a book—and the book was endorsed by Elie Wiesel [a widely quoted survivor and Holocaust scholar/activist]—and it's in the libraries and everywhere—and it's a complete lie! When I contacted the writer, he said, 'Well, I received this picture from Yad Vashem and nobody told me what happened with these children; I put it in the book and I thought that these children died.' "

Eva wanted the writer to publish a new edition to correct the errors.

"It angered me for two reasons: I realized immediately that those children [who were thought to be dead] made a much bigger impact on the media than those who survived it. And, so I thought, 'I survived it, you are not going to kill me in your book. I am not going to let you do that.' And, that was actually the first time that I decided I must at least form an organization that would reflect the feelings and the truth about what happened to the children, because I realized another big problem: that children, women, and minorities were casualties, patronized groups of society. They are patronized and society decides what happens to them. The children are taught what they are supposed to say, what they are supposed to be doing. Those people who are running the media are usually not children nor sometimes they are not women. They are fabricating what the rest of the world should be reading about and they are

helping to form the opinion of the world. The more I think about it and study it, the more I realize that the media at times is almost as evil as [the] political power[s I had known]."

Learning the Ways of the Mass Media

It all began in 1977 when Eva had seen a network television series about the Holocaust. The series brought back vivid memories. It was a defining moment. Regardless of the pain, Eva wanted to remember.[5] "Since then the flow of memories has never stopped."

In fact, Eva did not really "re-member"[6] her own story until several years later in the early 1980s. Like so many of the children who have been survivors of other forms of abuse, whether sexual, physical, or psychological, she had to reclaim her past and put herself in context.

The first time that Eva created media publicity was in 1984.

"I went to Israel and I put together the organization Children of Auschwitz Nazi's Deadly Lab Experiments Survivors, Inc. (C.A.N.D.L.E.S, Inc.).[7] The media helped when we, the Mengele twins, wanted to get the story out that we were looking for other twins. I realized that most of these children whom I remembered so clearly in my mind and whom I had seen in the pictures that I had developed from the liberation film had to be alive somewhere. At the museum in Auschwitz, all they really had was a partial list of those who had survived and registered after liberation, but they had no idea what their names were now. Many of them had changed their names to the countries that they moved to. The women got married and of course their names changed. There were no records. The only way I could locate them [the surviving twins, of whom Eva has identified some 126] was with the help of the media, because people do read papers, people do see the news reports, and the print media became actually a lot more important in that case."

Gaining and Losing
the Media Spotlight

As Eva and the twins, through their organization, began to tell their story again and
again to media in various parts of the world,
the mass media began to pick it up. Suddenly
the media was excited about the "Mengele
Twins," as Eva had dubbed them, and the
story grew. The mass media of the world
were captivated by Eva and her twin Miriam
Mozes Zeiger[8] and, as a result, they did find
other twins and went on to lead them through
the 1985 reunion at Auschwitz and on to a
press conference in Tel Aviv. Eva, Miriam,
and the twins wanted the Israeli and U.S.
governments to press for release of their
medical records. Many of the twins were ill,
and they wanted to know what Mengele and
his assistants had injected into their bodies.

When Eva returned to the United States,
she was the toast of the media. Now everyone
was interested in the whereabouts of Dr.
Mengele, who was thought to be somewhere
in South America. Then what were purported
to be Mengele's bones were uncovered in
Brazil.

"The bones had been found; he was dead,
and the media reported it," Eva remembers
matter-of-factly. Not too many people were
interested in an open hearing to determine
conclusively whether those bones were really Mengele's. Eva pushed ahead and conducted a hearing at her own expense in Terre
Haute. What she was able to come up with in
that effort was most interesting. Dr. Werner
Loewenstein, a Terre Haute physician who
had graduated, coincidentally, from the same
medical school as had Dr. Mengele, made a
startling discovery: The bones found in Brazil showed no sign of osteomyelitis. Mengele's
SS records indicated he had osteomyelitis.
To this day, there remain questions about
whether Mengele is indeed dead, and exactly
whose bones were found in Brazil. But at that
time it didn't matter. The Mengele twins
were pushed off page 1, and the Mengele
bones story took their place. The govern-

ments and the media had agreed that Mengele
was dead—end of story. "We were dropped
like a hot potato."

The media had portrayed the survivors as
wanting revenge on Josef Mengele, but Eva
began to realize it wasn't revenge she was
seeking, "I was a lot more interested in getting Josef Mengele to come forward and tell
us what he injected into our bodies, because
that would make a difference to many of the
survivors and, I demand the right to know
what I was injected with."

What Happens When Someone
Decides You're Not News

On Memorial Day, May 6, 1986, Eva was
in the Capitol Rotunda for services in memory of the Holocaust. President Reagan was
honorary chairman. Vice President Bush was
there. All the senators and members of Congress were there. Eva Kor was there and she
was carrying a poster-size sign. The poster
stated that Memorial Services were not enough:
"We need an open hearing on Mengelegate.
I am on hunger strike."

When the ceremonies started, Eva held up
the poster. "I hardly lifted the poster over my
head when a policeman came. Obviously he
was watching me, and said, 'Ma'am, you
have to come with me.'

"But before that, I was handing out press
releases, and a woman came up to me and
asked, 'Who are you?' And, I said, 'I am a
Mengele twin.' 'What are you doing here?'
I said, 'I am here to protest the fact that there
is no hearing in regard to the Mengele investigation,' and I said, 'Here is a press release.'
And she said, 'You cannot do that.' 'Who are
you?' I asked. 'I am with the U.S. Holocaust
Museum and we are in charge of this event.'
I said, 'But this is a Holocaust Memorial Day
to the Holocaust event. I am a survivor of the
Holocaust. Why can't I be here? You can
hand out your press releases, and I cannot
hand out my press releases? Why is that?
This is the Capitol Rotunda, the heart of

United States democracy. Where else can I go?' And, so, she walked away.

"I realize now that as soon as I said that, they put people watching me so when I lifted my poster, a policeman came up to me. The room was dark, Elie Wiesel was speaking, and the policeman said, 'Ma'am, you have to come with me.'

"I thought to myself, 'I don't know where to go.' He didn't say, 'You are under arrest' and he didn't read me my rights . . . I was petrified, I was so scared—there was no way to describe it. If somebody was too close to me, they could have heard my heart beating, I was so scared. And, as I was trying to figure out how to react to this, I didn't move, I will tell you that much. I didn't move. He grabbed my poster. And then somebody came from the other side, he was standing to my left, and . . . the secret police in civilian clothes, pushed me to the ground with such brutality that I began screaming at the top of my voice, 'This is not Auschwitz! You cannot do this to me! This is not Auschwitz!'

"Emotionally this brutality threw me back to the selection platform at Auschwitz when my mother and I were ripped apart. They wanted me to get up, but I didn't want to get up. Then they stopped it. There was a camera man, a black, a good looking black guy with a video camera, who started recording and these two policemen—there was another policeman—the two of them were holding up my legs, and the other one was holding up my arms, digging into my muscles, with awful brute force. They were dragging me on the floor. My dress was hanging over my head, and I knew I was very embarrassed. And the camera kept going and going, and they finally took me in an elevator. And I quit the screaming. We arrived into a basement office and I looked at my arms and they were all blue from the way he was holding on and digging into my muscles. My back was hurting very badly, and I was sure that they were going to kill me. But, do you know, the whole Capitol Rotunda was filled—President Reagan, Vice President Bush—all the senators,

all the VIPs, all the media—everybody was there . . . Nobody [from the media] ever talked with me to find out what on earth was going on; ultimately, the version of the story was given by Wiesel, who was asked what I was doing. How on earth did he know? He never talked to me!"

Police in the basement first told Eva she was being arrested for disturbing the peace. "Excuse me! I was not disturbing the peace. I was not raising my voice. If you stood by me, you could have heard my heart beat I was so quiet and so scared."

The police then told her she was protesting without a permit. "That is true, but you obviously do not know what you are arresting me for." Police told Eva they thought she was a terrorist. "With both of my arms up holding a cardboard poster, I was a terrorist? I have already passed security check, so obviously I didn't have any bombs with me. I wasn't pointing a gun, I wasn't pointing a bomb. I didn't do anything except hold up a cardboard poster."

Eva was held for close to an hour, but never charged. Despite a telephoned death threat, Eva stayed in Washington. She organized a press conference at the National Press Building, but thought that the handful of reporters who showed up had dismissed her story. "I did not know that there was anything in the newspaper until I think—it was later when I went to testify at the congressional hearing against Elie Wiesel and against Simon Wiesenthal and against the U.S. Holocaust Council—that my friend [said to me], 'Oh, you are going to make the front page again?' And, I said, 'Excuse me?' He said, 'Last year you made the front page.' I said, 'What do you mean, the front page?' 'The *Washington Post* had a front page story on you and you ought to go to the library and look it up. You will find it.' And it was all Elie Wiesel's version of what happened. None of it true, but it was printed. It was printed. Doesn't the press have any obligation to find out from the person what is happening? Not one reporter ever contacted me. Not one reporter. I came home [and when] I walked into the house the telephone rang twice, and the caller said, 'You dirty, so and so, you make us ashamed that you live in Terre Haute, Indiana.' And that is what the press did to me."

Eva's demands to open the medical records went unheeded. Even when she went on a hunger strike for 13 days, in November 1988, placing herself in front of the Israeli Knesset, begging them to intercede and help obtain the medical records, the press ignored her. "Most of the members of the Knesset looked at me as if I had leprosy. The media was nowhere to be seen for these 13 days of hunger strike. There were two very small articles written in some of the Israeli papers, none written in the overseas press even though we had contacted them all repeatedly. And then the Israeli minister of justice was a little bit concerned, being a religious Jew, that I would appear to be making self-sacrifice. That's not accepted in the Jewish religion and they were going to do anything for me to stop my hunger strike. That was the most attention that I had gotten in those 13 days and I didn't even want to stop it. And they said, 'We will let you go on live television in Israel for half an hour to tell your story.' " Eva explained. "So, you can see right here how the politics and the media work. How can the politicians tell the Israeli television you are going to have these people there for half an hour? But that is exactly what happened."

As years passed, Eva continued in her pursuit of the medical records. From the time of her visit to the Capitol in 1986, Eva carefully followed up on lead after lead about records and documents Mengele had kept on the experiments he performed on twins and others at Auschwitz. She continued to pressure the world medical community, the media, governments, and even the Mengele family for information that would assist her in uncovering the twins' medical histories. Her path led her to the doorstep of Dr. Hans Münch, an SS Nazi doctor who had worked at the camp and was a friend of Josef Mengele's. Dr. Münch had headed the Institute for Hy-

giene at Auschwitz. He had been tried for war crimes in a trial in Krakow after the war, but had been found innocent. Former prisoners testified on Dr. Münch's behalf that the doctor had faked experiments so as to preserve prisoners' lives, and had otherwise attempted to help prisoners survive until their liberation in January of 1945.

As the 50th anniversary of the liberation of Auschwitz approached, Eva began to make plans. This time she wanted to bring her son, Dr. Alex Kor, an Evansville, Indiana, podiatrist, and her daughter Rina, who works at the University of Michigan, Ann Arbor, to Auschwitz. She wanted them to meet and experience that place with Dr. Münch and his children. Münch was to travel back to the camps for the first time in 50 years, bringing with him his son, Gigo, a pediatrician in Munich, his daughter Ruli, now a Canadian citizen, and his granddaughter, a resident of Vancouver, B.C. They had only recently learned of their father's role as an SS doctor in the Auschwitz camp. And, of course, Eva wanted the media to be there.

Eva had been on talk shows from Larry King on CNN, to Oprah Winfrey and Geraldo Rivera. *60 Minutes* had been to her home. She served as coproducer of a documentary produced by Kent State University that won her a regional Emmy. Eva in 1995 thought she was media savvy. But that did not help get coverage of her walk through Auschwitz with Dr. Münch.

Dutch, German, Swedish, and Polish TV and print media as well as the *Wall Street Journal* international editions carried the story of the survivor and the Nazi doctor and their families walking arm and arm through Birkenau and Auschwitz. European and Israeli media captured Eva's reading of a declaration of amnesty to all Nazis, and Dr. Münch's reading of his experiences in viewing Jews being selected for death in the gas chambers, as well as his remembrances of watching the Zyclon B being dropped into simulated exhaust vents outside the gas chamber. Dr. Münch, like other physicians, watched the gassings through a peephole so that he could certify that the victims inside the gas chamber were dead. It took about three to five minutes, Dr. Münch said. The victim-survivor read her document and one from the SS Nazi doctor as they stood side by side surrounded by their families just in front of the bombed-out remains of a Birkenau crematorium. "This is the nightmare I continue to live with 50 years later," Münch's document stated.

Eva had made the event known to all her media contacts, but the news agenda setters weren't into stories of healing and forgiveness in 1995. Lech Walesa's Polish government had staged a political event, and the international media focused on what politicians from across the globe were saying about this place and what had happened there half a century ago. The cameras rolled when a Mengele twin survivor wiped a tear away, and again as one twin survivor attempted to climb over the gates to watch the formal ceremonies. The press's attention was splintered and journalists were physically cut off from one another in different hotels in various locations stretching from Warsaw to Krakow. Only a few departed from the carefully prepared script for the day issued to them by the Polish government.

Upon returning to the United States, Eva talked about the lack of media attention on her death camp walk with Dr. Münch: "I had written to the same people I did in 1985, which is all the New York newspapers; the magazines; NBC, CBS, CNN, C-SPAN; I have sent to all the Jewish press—letters, I think it was in September of 1994, with what we were trying to do. In addition to that, I even faxed the week before I left, a complete itinerary and included the two documents to be signed by Dr. Münch and me in front of the gas chamber. I faxed them to NBC, CBS, ABC, *Newsweek, Time,* and CNN because I had these fax numbers. I do not understand how these decisions are made. I still do not understand.

"I would love to be able someday, somehow to find out who decides and how do they decide what is newsworthy. While the United States press decided that sending a message of peace, that forgiving the SS, and documenting the gas chambers and just the mere fact that this is the first SS that came back to the camps, walking with a survivor, had no merit whatsoever, [the world press quoted] Elie Wiesel stating that he would never forgive. I think it is a very sad statement for what the press is doing.

"What the press prefers to have is something ugly, something criminal, something bad rather than something good. Why? I do not know. I would hope that the people who are involved in the big media are human beings who want to have world peace, because people will do what the media is telling them to do. The majority of the people are very, very influenced by television. It is very powerful, the media.

"At Auschwitz in 1995, would I have fainted or would I have been on the railroad tracks and on the selection platform, saying, 'Oh, God, never forgive these criminals!'—had I carried on or would I have even taken a gun and shot Dr. Münch, everybody would have justified what I did and would have wanted to talk to me. But, I have not lived up to an image that they [the media] have painted of a survivor—an image that I can stand on my two feet; I can intelligently express myself— if I can rise above my past pain and say to them, 'Here, 50 years later, 50 years is enough of suffering. Let's try. I am trying and I have reached a conclusion that I am going to deal with my pain by forgiving the Nazis, the politicians, everybody, and it sets my soul free.' "

Eva Kor has grown in her understanding of mass media. She began, as most of us have, as a media consumer. Her survivor status objectified her. Her work with mass media radicalized her to what she has become today: media owner, producer, and publisher. In April 1995, Eva Kor opened a Holocaust Museum in Terre Haute. She hopes to make it a multimedia center. She has published, through C.A.N.D.L.E.S., Inc., her biography and the first of what she hopes will be a series of children's books. She is working with WEIU-TV, Charleston, Illinois, to complete the documentary of the 1995 trip to Auschwitz that she funded.

Notes

1. Hungary took over Transylvania in 1940 and was a German ally. By July 7, 1944, 437,000 of Hungary's Jewish population of approximately 650,000 had been deported to Auschwitz (see Kor, as told to Wright, 1995).

2. Eva had believed that with the exception of herself and Miriam, all her family had died at Auschwitz. As Nazi records continue to come to light, she continues to try to learn exactly what happened to her family. In 1992, she appealed to the Red Cross Holocaust and War Victims Identification Center for help. On July 21, 1995, she received a letter from the American Red Cross that indicates her sister Aliz may be alive. At this writing, she has traveled to her home in Transylvania and has queried Hungarian officials in search of news of her sister, who was, according to the Red Cross, transported from Auschwitz to Buchenwald in July 1944. Aliz Mozes was still in Buchenwald on October 17, 1944, and arrived in Budapest May 29, 1945. There is no information on the whereabouts of her father, Alexander, or her mother, Jaffa. She is still waiting for a response regarding her sister Edit.

3. Eva believes her father bought the radio in 1940. In writing this chapter, Eva and the author talked for more than two hours with both an audiotape and videotape running. Eva's biographer, Mary Wright, a retired high school newspaper adviser and English teacher from Danville, Illinois, transcribed the tapes. All quoted material from Eva comes from that taped discussion and she, Mary Wright, and Eva's daughter Rina have read through and helped proof this chapter.

4. The children looked chubby-cheeked, as can be seen in the photos of Eva and her twin Miriam. When the Nazis abandoned the camp, children were free to roam and "organize" (steal) food from Nazi supplies. For two or three weeks, they had stuffed themselves with everything they could find. Some children died because their starved digestive systems could not take the sudden influx of food.

5. To understand this process, the writings of Kate Millett and Judith Lewis Herman, M.D., are of immense help (see Herman, 1992; Millett, 1994).

6. Feminist theologian Mary Daly defines *re-membering* as a "healing of the dismembered Self" (Daly & Caputi, 1987).

7. Eva first identified herself in the film in 1983. While attending a Holocaust gathering in Washington, D.C., she saw the frame blown up to poster size. She and another twin she met at the conference started planning a reunion and founded C.A.N.D.L.E.S., Inc. (Children of Auschwitz Nazi's Deadly Lab Experiments Survivors).

8. Miriam Mozes Zeiger died in 1992, despite Eva's donating a kidney to her. She died of cancer.

References

Daly, M., & Caputi, J. (1987). *Webster's first new intergalactic wickedary of the English language*. Boston: Beacon.

Herman, J. L. (1992). *Trauma and recovery: The aftermath of violence—from domestic abuse to political terror*. New York: Basic Books.

Kor, E. M., as told to Wright, M. (1995). *Echoes from Auschwitz: Dr. Mengele's twins, the story of Eva and Miriam Mozes*. Terre Haute, IN: Children of Auschwitz Nazi's Deadly Lab Experiments Survivors (C.A.N.D.L.E.S.), Inc.

Millett, K. (1994). *The politics of cruelty: An essay on the literature of imprisonment*. New York: Norton.

14

Against the Male Flood
Censorship, Pornography, and Equality

Andrea Dworkin

To say what one thought—that was my little problem—against the prodigious Current; to find a sentence that could hold its own against the male flood.

Virginia Woolf

1. Censorship

Censorship is a real thing, not an abstract idea or a word that can be used to mean anything at all.

In ancient Rome, a censor was a magistrate who took the census (account of the male population and an evaluation of property for the purpose of taxation done every fifth year), assessed taxes, and inspected morals and

EDITORS' NOTE: In her determination to articulate the experiences of poor, lower-class, marginal, and prostituted women, Dworkin has deepened public awareness of rape, battery, pornography, and prostitution. In 1965, when Dworkin was 18 and a student at Bennington College, she was arrested at the United States Mission to the United Nations, protesting the Vietnam War. Sent to the Women's House of Detention, she was given a brutal internal examination. Her testimony about the sadism of that experience—reported in newspapers around the world—helped bring public pressure on the New York City government to close down the Women's House of Detention. A community garden now grows in Greenwich Village where that prison once stood. Dworkin's radical-feminist critique of pornography and violence against women began with her first book, *Women Hating,* published in 1974 when she was 27. In 1978, she addressed the historic rally at the first feminist conference on pornography when 3,000 women held the first Take Back the Night March and shut down San Francisco's pornography district for one night.

conduct. His power over conduct came from his power to tax. For instance, in 403 BC, the censors Camillus and Postimius heavily fined elderly bachelors for not marrying. The power to tax, then as now, was the power to destroy. The censor, using the police and judicial powers of the state, regulated social behavior.

At its origins, then, censorship had nothing to do with striking down ideas as such; it had to do with acts. In my view, real state censorship still does. . . . Where police power is used against writers systematically, writers are seen as people who by writing do something socially real and significant, not contemplative or dithering. Therefore, writing is never peripheral or beside the point. It is serious and easily seditious. I am offering no brief for police states when I say that virtually all great writers, cross-culturally and transhistorically, share this view of what writing is. In countries, like ours, controlled by a bourgeoisie to whom the police are accountable, writing is easier to do and valued less. It has less impact. It is more abundant and cheaper. Less is at stake for reader and writer both. The writer may hold writing to be a life-or-death matter, but the police and society do not. Writing is seen to be a personal choice, not a social, political, or esthetic necessity fraught with danger and meaning. The general view in these pleasant places is that writers think up ideas or words and then other people read them and all this happens in the head, a vast cavern somewhere north of the eyes. It is all air, except for the paper and ink, which are simply banal. Nothing happens.

Police in police states and most great writers throughout time see writing as act, not air—as act, not idea; concrete, specific, real, not insubstantial blather on a dead page. Censorship goes after the act and the actor: the book and the writer. It needs to destroy both. The cost in human lives is staggering, and it is perhaps essential to say that human lives destroyed must count more in the weighing of horror than books burned. This is my personal view, and I love books more than I love people.

Censorship is deeply misunderstood in the United States, because the fairly spoiled, privileged, frivolous people who are the literate citizens of this country think that censorship is some foggy effort to suppress ideas. For them censorship is not something in itself—an act of police power with discernible consequences to hunted people; instead, it is about something abstract—the suppressing or controlling of ideas. Censorship, like writing itself, is no longer an act. Because it is no longer the blatant exercise of police power against writers and books because of what they do, what they accomplish in the real world, it becomes vague, hard to find, except perhaps as an attitude. It gets used to mean unpleasant, even angry frowns of disapproval or critiques delivered in harsh tones; it means social disapproval or small retaliations by outraged citizens where the book is still available and the writer is entirely unharmed, even if insulted. It hangs in the air, ominous, like the threat of drizzle. It gets to be, in silly countries like this one, whatever people say it is, separate from any material definition, separate from police power, separate from state repression (jail, banning, exile, death), separate from devastating consequences to real people (jail, banning, exile, death). It is something that people who eat fine food and wear fine clothes worry about frenetically, trying to find it, anticipating it with great anxiety, arguing it down as if—if it were real—an argument would make it go away; not knowing that it has a clear, simple, unavoidable momentum and meaning in a cruel world of police power that their privilege cannot comprehend.

2. Obscenity

In the 19th and 20th centuries, in most of Western Europe, England, and the United States, more often than not (time-out for Franco, for instance), writing has been most consistently viewed as an act warranting prosecution when the writing is construed to be

obscene. The republics, democracies, and constitutional monarchies of the West, now and
then, do not smother writers in police violence; they prefer to pick off writers who
annoy and irritate selectively with fairly token prosecutions. The list of writers so harassed is elegant, white, male (therefore the
pronoun "he" is used throughout this discussion), and remarkably small. Being among
them is more than a ceremonial honor. As
Flaubert wrote his brother in 1857: "My persecution has brought me widespread sympa-
thy. If my book is bad, that will serve to make
it seem better. If, on the other hand, it has
lasting qualities, that will build a foundation
for it. There you are! I am hourly awaiting
the official document which will name the
day when I am to take my seat (for the crime
of having written in French) in the dock in
the company of thieves and homosexuals."[1]
A few months later that same year, Baudelaire was fined 300 francs for publishing six
obscene poems. They also had to be removed
from future editions of his book. In harder,
earlier days, Jean-Jacques Rousseau spent
eight years as a fugitive after his *Emile* was
banned and a warrant was issued for his
arrest. English censors criminally prosecuted
Swinburne's *Poems and Ballads* in 1866.
They were particularly piqued at Zola, even
in translation, so his English publisher, 70
years old, went to jail for three months. In
1898, a bookseller was arrested for selling
Havelock Ellis' work and received a suspended sentence. This list is representative,
not exhaustive. While prosecutions of writers under obscenity laws have created great
difficulties for writers already plagued with
them (as most writers are), criminal prosecutions under obscenity law in Europe and the
United States are notable for how narrowly
they reach writers, how sanguine writers tend
to be about the consequences to themselves,
and how little is paid in the writer's lifeblood
to what D. H. Lawrence (who paid more than
most modern Western writers) called "the
censor-moron."[2] . . . In our world, the writer
gets harassed, as Lawrence did; the writer

may be poor or not—the injury is consider-
ably worse if he is; but the writer is not
terrorized or tortured, and writers do not live
under a reign of terror as writers, because of
what they do. The potshot application of
criminal law for writing is not good, nice, or
right; but it is important to recognize the
relatively narrow scope and marginal character of criminal prosecution under obscenity
law in particular—especially compared with
the scope and character of police-state censorship. Resisting obscenity law does not
require hyperbolic renderings of what it is
and how it has been used. It can be fought or
repudiated on its own terms.

The use of obscenity laws against writers,
however haphazard or insistent, is censorship and it does hold writing to be an act. This
is a unique perception of what writing is,
taking place, as it does, in a liberal context in
which writing is held to be ideas. It is the
obscene quality of the writing, obscenity itself, that is seen to turn writing from idea into
act. Writing of any kind or quality is idea,
except for obscene writing, which is act.
Writing is censored, even in our own happy
little land of Oz, as act, not idea.

What is obscenity, such that it turns writing, when obscene, into something that actually happens? . . . There is the legal answer
and the artistic answer. Artists have been
consistently pushing on the boundaries of
obscenity because great writers see writing
as an act, and in liberal culture only obscene
writing has that social standing, that quality
of dynamism and heroism. Great writers tend
to experience writing as an intense and dis-
ruptive act; in the West, it is only recognized
as such when the writing itself is experienced
as obscene. In liberal culture, the writer has
needed obscenity to be perceived as socially
real.

What is it that obscenity does? The writer
uses what the society deems to be obscene
because the society then reacts to the writing
the way the writer values the writing: as if it
does something. But obscenity itself is socially constructed; the writer does not invent

it or in any sense originate it. He finds it, knowing that it is what society hides. He looks under rocks and in dark corners.

There are two possible derivations of the word *obscenity:* the discredited one, what is concealed; and the accepted one, *filth.* Animals bury their filth, hide it, cover it, leave it behind, separate it from themselves: so do we, going way way back. Filth is excrement: from down there. We bury it or hide it; also, we hide where it comes from. Under male rule, menstrual blood is also filth, so women are twice dirty. Filth is where the sexual organs are and because women are seen primarily as sex, existing to provide sex, women have to be covered: our naked bodies being obscene.

Obscenity law uses both possible root meanings of obscene intertwined: it typically condemns nudity, public display, lewd exhibition, exposed genitals or buttocks or pubic areas, sodomy, masturbation, sexual intercourse, excretion. Obscenity law is applied to pictures and words: the artifact itself exposes what should be hidden: it shows dirt. The human body, all sex parts and excretory acts are the domain of obscenity law.

But being in the domain of obscenity law is not enough. One must feel alive there. To be obscene, the representations must arouse *prurient* interest. *Prurient* means *itching or itch:* it is related to the Sanskrit for he burns. It means sexual arousal. Judges, lawmakers, and juries have been, until very recently, entirely male: empirically, prurient means *causes erection.* Theologians have called this same quality of obscenity "venereal pleasure," holding that "if a work is to be called obscene it must, of its nature, be such as actually to arouse or calculated to arouse in the viewer or reader such venereal pleasure. If the work is *not* of such a kind, it may, indeed, be vulgar, disgusting, crude, unpleasant, what you will—but it will not be, in the strict sense which Canon Law obliges us to apply, obscene."[3] A secular philosopher of pornography isolated the same quality when he wrote: "Obscenity is our name for the

uneasiness which upsets the physical state associated with self-possession. . . ."[4]

Throughout history, the male has been the standard for obscenity law: erection is his venereal pleasure or the uneasiness which upsets the physical state associated with his self-possession. It is not surprising, then, that in the same period when women became jurors, lawyers, and judges—but especially jurors, women having been summarily excluded from most juries until perhaps a decade ago—obscenity law fell into disuse and disregard. In order for obscenity law to have retained social and legal coherence, it would have had to recognize as part of its standard women's sexual arousal, a more subjective standard than erection. It would also have had to use the standard of penile erection in a social environment that was no longer sex-segregated, an environment in which male sexual arousal would be subjected to female scrutiny. In my view, the presence of women in the public sphere of legal decision-making has done more to undermine the efficacy of obscenity law than any self-conscious movement against it.

The act that obscenity recognizes is erection, and whatever produces erection is seen to be obscene—act, not idea—because of what it makes happen. The male sexual response is seen to be involuntary, so there is no experientially explicable division between the material that causes erection and the erection itself. That is the logic of obscenity law used against important writers who have pushed against the borders of the socially-defined obscene, because they wanted writing to have that very quality of being a socially recognized act. They wanted the inevitability of the response—the social response. The erection makes the writing socially real from the society's point of view, not from the writer's. What the writer needs is to be taken seriously, by any means necessary. In liberal societies, only obscenity law comprehends writing as an act. It defines the nature and quality of the act narrowly—not writing itself, but producing erections. Flaubert apparently did produce them; so did Baudelaire, Zola, Rousseau, Lawrence, Joyce, and Nabokov. It's that simple.

Men have made this public policy. Why they want to regulate their own erections through law is a question of endless interest and importance to feminists. Nevertheless, that they do persist in this regulation is simple fact. There are civil and social conflicts over how best to regulate erection through law, especially when caused by words or pictures. Arguments among men notwithstanding, high culture is phallocentric. It is also, using the civilized criteria of jurisprudence, not infrequently obscene.

Most important writers have insisted that their own uses of the obscene as socially defined are not pornography. As D. H. Lawrence wrote: "But even I would censor genuine pornography, rigorously. It would not be difficult . . . [Y]ou can recognize it by the insult it offers, invariably, to sex, and to the human spirit."[5] It was also, he pointed out, produced by the underworld. Nabokov saw in pornography "mediocrity, commercialism, and certain strict rules of narration . . . [A]ction has to be limited to the copulation of clichés. Style, structure, imagery should never distract the reader from his tepid lust."[6] They knew that what they did was different from pornography, but they did not entirely know what the difference was. They missed the heart of an empirical distinction because writing was indeed real to them but women were not.

The insult that pornography offers, invariably, to sex is accomplished in the active subordination of women: the creation of a sexual dynamic in which the putting-down of women, the suppression of women, and ultimately the brutalization of women, is what sex is taken to be. Obscenity in law, and in what it does socially, is erection. Law recognizes the act in this. Pornography, however is a broader, more comprehensive act, because it crushes a whole class of people through violence and subjugation: and sex is the vehicle that does the crushing. The penis is not

the test, as it is in obscenity. Instead, the status of women is the issue. Erection is implicated in the subordination, but who it reaches and how are the pressing legal and social questions. Pornography, unlike obscenity, is a discrete, identifiable system of sexual exploitation that hurts women as a class by creating inequality and abuse. This is a new legal idea, but it is the recognition and naming of an old and cruel injury to a dispossessed and coerced underclass. It is the sound of women's words breaking the longest silence.

3. Pornography

In the United States, it is an $8-billion trade in sexual exploitation.

It is women turned into subhuman, beaver, pussy, body parts, genitals exposed, buttocks, breasts, mouths open and throats penetrated, covered in semen, pissed on, shitted on, hung from light fixtures, tortured, maimed, bleeding, disemboweled, killed.

It is some creature called female, used.

It is scissors poised at the vagina and objects stuck in it, a smile on the woman's face, her tongue hanging out.

It is a woman being fucked by dogs, horses, snakes.

It is every torture in every prison cell in the world, done to women and sold as sexual entertainment.

It is rape and gang rape and anal rape and throat rape: and it is the woman raped, asking for more.

It is the woman in the picture to whom it is really happening and the women against whom the picture is used, to make them do what the woman in the picture is doing.

It is the power men have over women turned into sexual acts men do to women, because pornography is the power and the act.

It is the conditioning of erection and orgasm in men to the powerlessness of women: our inferiority, humiliation, pain, torment; to us as objects, things, or commodities for use in sex as servants.

It sexualizes inequality and in doing so creates discrimination as a sex-based practice.

It permeates the political condition of women in society by being the substance of our inequality however located—in jobs, in education, in marriage, in life.

It is women, kept a sexual underclass, kept available for rape and battery and incest and prostitution.

It is what we are under male domination; it is what we are for under male domination.

It is the heretofore hidden (from us) system of subordination that women have been told is just life.

Under male supremacy, it is the synonym for what being a woman is.

It is access to our bodies as a birthright to men: the grant, the gift, the permission, the license, the proof, the promise, the method, how to; it is us accessible, no matter what the law pretends to say, no matter what we pretend to say.

It is physical injury and physical humiliation and physical pain: to the women against whom it is used after it is made; to the women used to make it.

As words alone, or words and pictures, moving or still, it creates systematic harm to women in the form of discrimination and physical hurt. It creates harm inevitably by its nature because of what it is and what it does. The harm will occur as long as it is made and used. The name of the next victim is unknown, but everything else is known.

Because of it—because it is the subordination of women perfectly achieved—the abuse done to us by any human standard is perceived as using us for what we are by nature: women are whores; women want to be raped; she provoked it; women like to be hurt; she says no but means yes because she wants to be taken against her will which is not really her will because what she wants underneath is to have anything done to her that violates or humiliates or hurts her; she wants it, because she is a woman, no matter what it is, because she is a woman, that is how women are, what women are, what women are for.

. . . If it were being done to human beings, it would be reckoned an atrocity. It is being done to women, it is reckoned fun, pleasure, entertainment, sex, somebody's (not something's) civil liberty no less. . . .

4. Pornographers

Most of them are small-time pimps or big-time pimps. They sell women: the real flesh-and-blood women in the pictures. They like the excitement of domination, they are greedy for profit; they are sadistic in their exploitation of women; they hate women, and the pornography they make is the distillation of that hate. The photographs are what they have created live, for themselves, for their own enjoyment. The exchanges of women among them are part of the fun, too: so that the fictional creature "Linda Lovelace," who was the real woman Linda Marchiano,[7] was forced to "deep throat" every pornographer her owner-pornographer wanted to impress. Of course, it was the woman, not the fiction, who had to be hypnotized so that the men could penetrate to the bottom of her throat, and who had to be beaten and terrorized to get her compliance at all. The finding of new and terrible things to do to women is part of the challenge of the vocation: so the inventor of "Linda Lovelace" and "deep-throating" is a genius in the field, a pioneer. . . .

Even with written pornography, there has never been the distinction between making pornography and the sexual abuse of live women that is taken as a truism by those who approach pornography as if it were an intellectual phenomenon. The Marquis de Sade, as the world's foremost literary pornographer, is archetypal. His sexual practice was the persistent sexual abuse of women and girls, with occasional excursions into the abuse of boys. As an aristocrat in a feudal society, he preyed with near impunity on prostitutes and servants. The pornography he wrote was an urgent part of the sexual abuse he practiced, not only because he did what he wrote, but also because the intense hatred of women that fueled the one also fueled the other. . . .

One reason that stopping pornographers and pornography is not censorship is that pornographers are more like the police in police states than they are like the writers in police states. They are the instruments of terror, not its victims. What police do to the powerless in police states is what pornographers do to women, except that it is entertainment for the masses, not dignified as political. Writers do not do what pornographers do. Secret police do. Torturers do. . . . Intervening in a system of terror where it is vulnerable to public scrutiny to stop it is not censorship; it is the system of terror that stops speech and creates abuse and despair. The pornographers are the secret police of male supremacy: keeping women subordinate through intimidation and assault.

5. Subordination

In the amendment to the Human Rights Ordinance of the City of Minneapolis written by Catharine A. McKinnon and myself, pornography is defined as the graphic, sexually explicit subordination of women whether in pictures or in words that also includes one or more of the following: women are presented dehumanized as sexual objects, things, or commodities; or women are presented as sexual objects who enjoy pain or humiliation; or women are presented as sexual objects who experience sexual pleasure in being raped; or women are presented as sexual objects tied up or cut up or mutilated or bruised or physically hurt; or women are presented in postures of sexual submission; or women's body parts are exhibited, such that women are reduced to those parts; or women are presented being penetrated by objects or animals; or women are presented in scenarios of degradation, injury, abasement, torture, shown as filthy or inferior, bleeding, bruised, or hurt in a context that makes these conditions sexual.

This statutory definition is an objectively accurate definition of what pornography is, based on an analysis of the material produced by the $8-billion-a-year industry, and also on extensive study of the whole range of pornography extant from other eras and other cultures. Given the fact that women's oppression has an ahistorical character—a sameness across time and cultures expressed in rape, battery, incest, and prostitution—it is no surprise that pornography, a central phenomenon in that oppression, has precisely that quality of sameness. It does not significantly change in what it is, what it does, what is in it, or how it works, whether it is, for instance, classical or feudal or modern, Western or Asian; whether the method of manufacture is words, photographs, or video. What has changed is the public availability of pornography and the numbers of live women used in it because of new technologies: not its nature. Many people note what seems to them a qualitative change in pornography—that it has gotten more violent, even grotesquely violent, over the last two decades. The change is only in what is publicly visible: not in the range or preponderance of violent pornography (e.g., the place of rape in pornography stays constant and central, no matter where, when, or how the pornography is produced): not in the character, quality, or content of what the pornographers actually produce; not in the harm caused; not in the valuation of women in it, or the metaphysical definition of what women are; not in the sexual abuse promoted, including rape, battery, and incest; not in the centrality of its role in subordinating women. Until recently, pornography operated in private, where most abuse of women takes place.

The oppression of women occurs through sexual subordination. It is the use of sex as the medium of oppression that makes the subordination of women so distinct from racism or prejudice against a group based on religion or national origin. Social inequality is created in many different ways. In my view, the radical responsibility is to isolate the material means of creating the inequality so that material remedies can be found for it.

This is particularly difficult with respect to women's inequality because that inequality is achieved through sex. Sex as desired by the class that dominates women is held by that class to be elemental, urgent, necessary, even if or even though it appears to *require* the repudiation of any claim women might have to full human standing. In the subordination of women, inequality itself is sexualized: made into the experience of sexual pleasure, essential to sexual desire. Pornography is the material means of sexualizing inequality; and that is why pornography is a central practice in the subordination of women.

Subordination itself is a broad, deep, systematic dynamic discernible in any persecution based on race or sex. Social subordination has four main parts. First, there is *hierarchy,* a group on top and a group on the bottom. For women, this hierarchy is experienced both socially and sexually, publicly and privately. Women are physically integrated into the society in which we are held to be inferior, and our low status is both put in place and maintained by the sexual usage of us by men; and so women's experience of hierarchy is incredibly intimate and wounding.

Second, subordination is *objectification.* Objectification occurs when a human being, through social means, is made less than human, turned into a thing or commodity, bought and sold. When objectification occurs, a person is de-personalized, so that no individuality or integrity is available socially or in what is an extremely circumscribed privacy (because those who dominate determine its boundaries). Objectification is an injury right at the heart of discrimination: those who can be used as if they are not fully human are no longer fully human in social terms; their humanity is hurt by being diminished.

Third, subordination is *submission.* A person is at the bottom of a hierarchy because of a condition of birth; a person on the bottom is dehumanized, an object or commodity;

inevitably, the situation of that person requires obedience and compliance. That diminished person is expected to be submissive; there is no longer any right to self-determination, because there is no basis in equality for any such right to exist. In a condition of inferiority, and objectification, submission is usually essential for survival. . . .

Fourth, subordination is *violence.* The violence is systematic, endemic enough to be unremarkable and normative, usually taken as an implicit right of the one committing the violence. In my view hierarchy, objectification, and submission are the preconditions for systematic social violence against any group targeted because of a condition of birth. If violence against a group is both socially pervasive and socially normal, then hierarchy, objectification, and submission are already solidly in place.

The role of violence in subordinating women has one special characteristic congruent with sex as the instrumentality of subordination: the violence is supposed to be sex for the woman too—what women want and like as part of our sexual nature; it is supposed to give women pleasure (as in rape); it is supposed to mean love to a woman from her point of view (as in battery). The violence against women is seen to be done not just in accord with something compliant in women, but in response to something active in and basic to women's nature.

Pornography uses each component of social subordination. Its particular medium is sex. Hierarchy, objectification, submission, and violence all become alive with sexual energy and sexual meaning. A hierarchy, for instance, can have a static quality; but pornography, by sexualizing it, makes it dynamic, almost carnivorous, so that men keep imposing it for the sake of their own sexual pleasure—for the sexual pleasure it gives them to impose it. In pornography, each element of subordination is conveyed through the sexually explicit usage of women: pornography in fact is what women are and what women are for and how women are used in a society premised on the inferiority of women. It is a metaphysics of women's subjugation: our existence delineated in a definition of our nature; our status in society predetermined by the uses to which we are put. The woman's body is what is materially subordinated. Sex is the material means through which the subordination is accomplished. Pornography is the institution of male dominance that sexualizes hierarchy, objectification, submission, and violence. As such, pornography creates inequality, not as artifact but as a system of social reality; it creates the necessity for and the actual behaviors that constitute sex inequality.

6. Speech

Subordination can be so deep that those who are hurt by it are utterly silent. Subordination can create a silence quieter than death. The women flattened out on the page are deathly still, except for *hurt me*. *Hurt me* isn't women's speech. It is the speech imposed on women by pimps to cover the awful, condemning silence. . . . The women say the pimp's words: the language is another element of the rape; the language is part of the humiliation; the language is part of the forced sex. . . . The silence of the women not in the picture, outside the pages, hurt but silent, used but silent, is staggering in how deep and wide it goes. It is a silence over centuries: an exile into speechlessness. One is shut up by the inferiority and the abuse. One is shut up by the threat and the injury. In her memoir of the Stalin period, *Hope Against Hope,* Nadezhda Mandelstam wrote that screaming "is a man's way of leaving a trace, of telling people how he lived and died. By his screams he asserts his right to live, sends a message to the outside world demanding help and calling for resistance. If nothing else is left, one must scream. Silence is the real crime against humanity."[8] Screaming is a man's way of leaving a trace. The scream of a man is never misunderstood as a scream

of pleasure by passers-by or politicians or historians, nor by the tormentor. A man's scream is a call for resistance. A man's scream asserts his right to live, sends a message; he leaves a trace. A woman's scream is the sound of her female will and her female pleasure in doing what the pornographers say she is for. Her scream is a sound of celebration to those who overhear. Women's way of leaving a trace is the silence, centuries worth: the entirely inhuman silence that surely one day will be noticed, someone will say that something is wrong, some sound is missing, some voice is lost; the entirely inhuman silence that will be a clue to human hope denied, a shard of evidence that a crime has occurred, the crime that created the silence; the entirely inhuman silence that is a cold, cold condemnation of what those who speak have done to those who do not.

But there is more than the *hurt me* forced out of us, and the silence in which it lies. The pornographers actually use our bodies as their language. We are their speech. Our bodies are the building blocks of their sentences. . . .

This is the so-called speech of the pornographers, protected now by law.

Protecting what they "say" means protecting what they do to us, how they do it. It means protecting their sadism on our bodies, because that is how they write: not like a writer at all; like a torturer. Protecting what they "say" means protecting sexual exploitation, because they cannot "say" anything without diminishing, hurting, or destroying us. Their rights of speech express their rights over us. Their rights of speech require our inferiority: and that we be powerless in relation to them. Their rights of speech mean that *hurt me* is accepted as the real speech of women, not speech forced on us as part of the sex forced on us but originating with us because we are what the pornographers "say" we are.

If what we want to say is not *hurt me,* we have the real social power only to use silence as eloquent dissent. Silence is what women have instead of speech. Silence is our dissent during rape unless the rapist, like the pornographer, prefers *hurt me,* in which case we have no dissent. Silence is our moving, persuasive dissent during battery unless the batterer, like the pornographer, prefers *hurt me.* Silence is a fine dissent during incest and for all the long years after.

Silence is not speech. We have silence, not speech. We fight rape, battery, incest, and prostitution with it. We lose. But someday someone will notice: that people called women were buried in a long silence that meant dissent and that the pornographers . . . chattered on.

7. Equality

. . . It has plagued us to try to understand why the status of women does not change. Those who hate the politics of equality say they know: we are biologically destined for rape; God made us to be submissive unto our husbands. We change but our status does not change. Laws change, but our status stays fixed. We move into the market place, only to face there classic sexual exploitation, now called sexual harassment. Rape, battery, prostitution, and incest stay the same in that they keep happening to us as part of what life is: even though we name the crimes against us as such and try to keep the victims from being destroyed by what we cannot stop from happening to them. And the silence stays in place too, however much we try to dislodge it with our truths. We say what has happened to us, but newspapers, governments, the culture that excludes us as fully human participants, wipe us out, wipe out our speech: by refusing to hear it. We are the tree falling in the desert. Should it matter: they are the desert.

The cost of trying to shatter the silence is astonishing to those who do it: the women, raped, battered, prostituted, who have something to say and say it. They stand there, even as they are erased. Governments turn from them; courts ignore them; this country disavows and dispossesses them. Men ridicule, threaten, or hurt them. Women jeopardized by them—silence being safer than speech—betray them. It is ugly to watch the complacent destroy the brave. It is horrible to watch power win.

Still, equality is what we want, and we are going to get it. What we understand about it now is that it cannot be proclaimed: it must be created. It has to take the place of subordination in human experience: physically replace it. Equality does not coexist with subordination, as if it were a little pocket located somewhere within it. Equality has to win. Subordination has to lose. The subordination of women has not even been knocked loose, and equality has not materially advanced, at least in part because the pornography has been creating sexualized inequality in hiding, in private, where the abuses occur on a massive scale.

Equality for women requires material remedies for pornography, whether pornography is central to the inequality of women or only one cause of it. Pornography's antagonism to civil equality, integrity, and self-determination for women is absolute; and it is effective in making that antagonism socially real and socially determining.

The law that Catharine A. MacKinnon and I wrote making pornography a violation of women's civil rights recognizes the injury that pornography does; how it hurts women's rights of citizenship through sexual exploitation and sexual torture both.

The civil rights law empowers women by allowing women to civilly sue those who hurt us through pornography by trafficking in it, coercing people into it, forcing it on people, and assaulting people directly because of a specific piece of it.

The civil rights law does not force the pornography back underground. There is no prior restraint or police power to make arrests, which would then result in a revivified black market. This respects the reach of the First Amendment, but it also keeps the pornography from getting sexier—hidden, forbidden, dirty, happily back in the land of the obscene, sexy slime oozing on great books. Wanting to cover pornography up, hide it, is the first response of those who need pornography to the civil rights law. If pornography is hidden, it is still accessible to men as a male right of access to women; its injuries to the status of women are safe and secure in those hidden rooms, behind those opaque covers; the abuses of women are sustained as a private right supported by public policy. The civil rights law puts a flood of light on the pornography, what it is, how it is used, what it does, those who are hurt by it.

The civil rights law changes the power relationship between the pornographers and women; it stops the pornographers from producing discrimination with the total impunity they now enjoy, and gives women a legal standing resembling equality from which to repudiate the subordination itself. The secret-police power of the pornographers suddenly has to confront a modest amount of due process.

The civil rights law undermines the subordination of women in society by confronting the pornography, which is the systematic sexualization of that subordination. Pornography is inequality. The civil rights law would allow women to advance equality by removing this concrete discrimination and hurting economically those who make, sell, distribute, or exhibit it. The pornography, being power, has a right to exist that we are not allowed to challenge under this system of law. After it hurts us by being what it is and doing what it does, the civil rights law would allow us to hurt it back. Women, not being power, do not have a right to exist equal to the right the pornography has. If we did, the pornographers would be precluded from exercising their rights at the expense of ours, and since they cannot exercise them any other way, they would be precluded period. We come to the legal system beggars: though in the public dialogue around the passage of this civil rights law we have the satisfaction of being regarded as thieves.

The civil rights law is women's speech. It defines an injury to us from our point of view. It is premised on a repudiation of sexual subordination which is born of our experience of it. It breaks the silence. It is a sentence that can hold its own against the male flood. It is a sentence on which we can build a paragraph, then a page.

. . . Women have a right to be effective. The pornographers, of course, do not think so, nor do other male supremacists; and it is hard for women to think so. We have been told to educate people on the evils of pornography: before the development of this civil rights law, we were told just to keep quiet about pornography altogether; but now that we have a law we want to use, we are encouraged to educate and stop there. Law educates. This law educates. It also allows women to do something. In hurting the pornography back we gain ground in making equality more likely, more possible—someday it will be real. We have a means to fight the pornographers' trade in women. We have a means to get at the torture and the terror. We have a means with which to challenge the pornography's efficacy in making exploitation and inferiority the bedrock of women's social status. The civil rights law introduces into the public consciousness an analysis: of what pornography is, what sexual subordination is, what equality might be. The civil rights law introduces a new legal standard: these things are not done to citizens of this country. The civil rights law introduces a new political standard: these things are not done to human beings. The civil rights law provides a new mode of action for women through which we can pursue equality and because of which our speech will have social meaning. The civil rights law gives us back what the pornographers have taken from us: hope rooted in real possibility.

Notes

1. Flaubert, G. (1950). *Letters,* trans. J. M. Cohen (p. 94). London: George Weidenfeld & Nicolson Limited.

2. Lawrence, D. H. (1953). *Sex, Literature and Censorship* (p. 9). New York: Twayne Publishers.

3. Gardiner, H. (S. J.) (1958). *Catholic Viewpoint on Censorship* (p. 65). Garden City, NY: Hanover House.

4. Bataille, G. (1969). *Death and Sensuality* (p. 12). New York: Ballantine Books, Inc.

5. Lawrence, *Sex, Literature and Censorship,* p. 74.

6. Nabokov, V. (1977). "Afterword," *Lolita* (p. 284). New York: Berkley Publishing Corporation.

7. Linda was forced into the 1974 film "Deep Throat" as well as many other pornography films. See Linda Lovelace with Mike McGrady (1980). *Ordeal.* Secaucus, NJ: Citadel Press.

8. Mandelstam, N. (1978). *Hope Against Hope,* trans. Max Hayward (pp. 42-43). New York: Atheneum.

15

A Systemic Commitment to Women in the Academy
Barriers, Harassment Prevent "Being All That We Can Be"

Ramona R. Rush

A preconference session during the Association for Education in Journalism and Mass Communication's (AEJMC) 1992 annual meeting in Montreal might have escaped attention if it hadn't been for the title. "Old Issues—Unresolved: Women Educators' Status in the Academy" pushed enough old buttons to cause an involuntary utterance, "Isn't that the godawful truth!"

A ground-breaking 1972 study of discrimination in communications, "More Than You Ever Wanted to Know About Women in Journalism Education" (Rush with Carol Oukrop and Sandra Ernst, 1972), had imprinted forever, within some mass communication researchers, baseline data for comparison. Even though the academy and profession have made much progress for women in the two decades since that initial study, they have, in my professional judgment, fallen short. The inclusive and diverse academic units and media organizations needed to serve as societal leaders in the 21st century are not there in numbers sufficient to make a difference. What hubris related to old unresolved issues still has to be cleared away so that the next century won't be as lacking in civil society and human development as has this one?

"Being all that we can be" (a rejoinder from Marilyn Kern-Foxworth) can be studied as a cost benefit and time incentive for the capitalist part of our political and economic experiment; and as a fulfillment of a social and civic contract for the other, democratic, side of life in these United States. How many hours, days, years could many of us have devoted to the community, education, family, self-actualization, the mass communication profession, if so much of our energy had not been poured into being superwomen, liberationists, feminists, poverty parents, who were angry, frustrated, hurt, afraid, tired or fired . . . instead of just . . . being? Being free of senseless harassment, discrimination, abuse, and the myriad forms of malignant violence.

We have a few short years to 2000 to make major cognitive and behavioral adjustments in the way we view, write about, and use our gender relationships within one small world. If those of us in higher education and the media professions make a systemic and systematic commitment to equity we could arrive in the 21st century being all that we can be.

What follows, then, are some suggestions which might strengthen that possibility.

The Issues to Be Investigated

The following issues are interdependent and need to be approached with policy decisions and research methods:

1. Sexual harassment still exists but is unacknowledged and misunderstood as was demonstrated by the Anita Hill-Clarence Thomas case.

2. Political power harassment takes over in many places where sexual harassment is difficult to initiate. Structural inequities prevent women from having access to opportunities, information, and rewards necessary for professional and personal achievement, actualization, and acknowledgment.

3. Search procedures and hiring practices for females remain fraught with inadequacies, inconsistencies, and irregularities; and retention rates of women is nearly an unassessed area. Exit interviews are nearly unheard of in academe.

4. Academic and professional dirty tricks— our own Scholargate and Mediagate—seem

to be a stable, renewable resource in the socialization process, a process in serious need of intervention.

Barriers and Resources

How are these interlocking issues approached? First, there has to be an awareness and admittance that most of us usually deal with a heterosociety largely comprised of white male-dominated standards that establish realities through closed-loop decision-making strategies supported by hierarchic, patriarchic organizational cultures.

Within scholarly, professional, and media organizations, existing regulations can be acknowledged, applied, and expanded. For example, the Accrediting Council on Education in Journalism and Mass Communications (ACEJMC) represents both education and media organizations. Its Standard 12 on minority and female representation in academic units as part of the accreditation process was added in the late 1980s, and has placed women and minorities on many faculties for the first time.

The crucial point that now needs enhancement in the accrediting statement is how women are treated after they are hired. The method and extent of assessing the climate for women in academic units appear to vary across accreditation teams. If team members follow Standard 12 language, then they rely on campus affirmative action officers and administrators for the perceptions and results of unit plans; each unit is encouraged to research its own situation about women and minorities. This means that two levels of administrators, a dean and a chairman, could play key roles in such assessment.

If it is a closed loop, decision-making situation, the climate control might be chilling. A more realistic assessment might come from interviews by team members with senior, tenured female professors within all the communication units and across campus in related disciplines (there won't be that many female full professors), as well as exit interviews with female and male faculty members who have left the unit between the reaccreditation periods.

AEJMC, for example, strengthened the organizational efforts of women in 1990 by creating the Commission on the Status of Women (the Commission on the Status of Minorities was created at the same time). This Commission can do the necessary head counting of females on faculties and in administrations. The process also needs to include tracking, monitoring, mentoring, and networking of women (including those coming out of high schools and undergraduate programs) to assess the extent of sexual and political power harassment, and academic and professional dirty tricks which feed the two-headed harassment monster.

Approaching, Researching

Even though the levels of hierarchy and patriarchy seem to have spewed intact out of the black hole of creation, interdisciplinary studies in archaeomythology indicate that as recently as about seven to six thousand years ago we most likely had a peaceful, nonviolent, earth-centered prehistoric culture in which gender roles were balanced and natural (for examples, see Riane Eisler, *The Chalice and the Blade*, 1987; and Marija Gimbutas, *The Language of the Goddess*, 1989). But the historical, latter-day domination of quasi-religious and militaristic societies is difficult to disassemble for purposes of diversity and equality. This domination must be recognized and dispersed by applying various "points of pressure" (e.g., professional and scholarly organizations, and the media industry).

Once the decision-makers have about 60% or more of higher management, administration, and/or senior faculty in a tightly-held, well-rewarded closed loop, it is nearly impossible to access. The Outsiders (mostly untenured and tenured females and minorities, and entry-to-middle-level employees)

either "get with the program" or remain silenced, isolated, and usually under-rewarded. The untenured outsiders in academe and the under-employed in the media are often spun out of the system quickly if they are outspoken (abrasive and uncooperative in the jargon of the "looped"; also angry, as in "she's angry . . . that's why she acts like that"). If not, they are held in service until their usefulness is expended (i.e., immediately before tenure, or when requesting a promotion to an executive level) if they are submissive and/or passably quiet in their views.

The fastest way to take out sexual and political power harassment as well as academic and professional dirty tricks is to hire, promote, and tenure women in numbers that cannot be silenced or co-opted by policy, group, and/or individual coercion and harassment. A commitment by national communication organizations (such as AEJMC, the Accrediting Council, and the administrators' association, ASJMC) should encourage the rotation of chairpersons, deans, CEOs, and managers after one or two terms in order to increase the practice and experiential education of diversity and equity in leadership. This rotation policy should be immediately enforced if a substantial gain (for example, using AEJMC's Standard 12 together with the Global Communications and Information Freedom 2000 resolution passed by the AEJMC conference in 1989) is not demonstrated in the numbers of female hires and retentions, or document to the satisfaction of any official internal or external agency why they have not succeeded.

Also, university presidents and media owners need to be apprised about a serious lack of standards and demonstration in diversity and equity because of their own officers. Obviously, national organizations cannot hire, fire, or rotate administrators and managers. But supra-organizations (such as the Accrediting Council and its 20-plus national media and education organizations, and the numerous other communication affiliates listed in the annual AEJMC directory) are the power groups within the mass communication field. They can, for example, formally challenge higher administrations within universities by placing academic units and administrators on formal and informal probation until diversity and freedom of expression are not only achieved but maintained as valuable contributions to an academic, associative culture. To do this, national power groups must begin their own assessment and monitoring of structural equality, frequently at the start until standards are established.

The state of inequality is not the sole responsibility of organizations like AEJMC, BEA (Broadcast Educators Association), AAF (American Advertising Federation), and the PRSA (Public Relations Society of America) Educator's Academy. But research reports (one of the best repositories for this research has been the *Media Report to Women*, published since 1972) untiringly indicate that the mass communication industry and academy, where societal action is supposed to be happening and societal blame is unflinchingly applied, do discriminate in favor of males. In stark contrast to the upper echelons of seniority and authority are the great numbers of white females enrolled in journalism and mass communications classes, and working in "enabling" positions in the industry; currently these women are in desperate need of realistic career role models. If universities and the media hold the key to our future leadership, the closed decision-making power loops within universities and industry have to be opened.

Investigating insidious forms of abuse. For example, while ACEJMC's Standard 12 is being modified to add the words "demonstrate and/or rotate" for administrators to its "recruit, retain, and advance" litany for women and minorities, ongoing research could assess the extent to which sexual and political power harassment as well as academic tricks are contained within member academic units and affiliates.

Sexual harassment is a way of life for many and a burden for all. Immediate base-line data needs to be established within the communication academy and industry. Sexual harassment research guidelines, as a next step in the process, can follow work already done by the National Council for Research on Women. Summaries of current research and additional resource information is available in the NCRW's 48-page *Sexual Harassment: Research and Resources, A Report in Progress* (47 East 65th St., New York, NY 10021).

Political power harassment is often difficult to assess since its purpose is to make some persons seem superior to others through a continuous rejection and lowering of acknowledgment, earned rewards, and subsequent self-esteem for those ordained to be subordinate by the power brokers. These are often covert persuasions by those well-practiced and/or socialized in their power/over procedures and, as such, are the most insidious forms of abuse in a democracy. Trained, tenured, and high-level employees within communication organizations are needed to follow established procedures for the observation, collection, and analyses and reporting of such practices. The type of data and collection methods need to be carefully developed so that they are consistent across academic units and media organizations if possible.

For example, salary reports for a period of five-to-seven years can often reveal a pattern of misuse of salary fund distribution, especially when cost-of-living indices are used as baseline guides for fair and equitable financial distribution.

Salary inequities are frequently indicative of power-loaded distributions of efforts (DOEs) and merit review formulations. These can vary greatly across faculty and/or administrators. The variability of the DOEs as the result of acknowledged different strengths of individuals across the three categories of teaching, research, and service is a truly realistic approach to faculty assessment. However, merit evaluations based on DOEs can often be a powerful financial reward distribution system in which the Outsiders carry a heavier

Scholargate's Dirty Tricks: Initial Laundry List

• Lowering some merit ratings and, thus, salaries under the pretext of bringing down merit rating score inflation.

• Unit chairperson and/or dean arbitrarily handing out occasional financial awards coming from the university president or chancellor (such as faculty incentive grant money) primarily to the senior male professors and administrators.

• Selectively including or excluding in important (and historical) documents the names of persons receiving awards and honors, attending conferences and seminars, holding editorships and professional/scholarly offices, presenting papers, and so on.

• Initially preparing unfair and/or inconsistent contractual agreements or attempting to change the agreements later, including letters of agreement or appointment concerning promotion/tenure review, salary, committee and teaching assignments, sabbatical leave, etc. The vicious cycle begins placing the person at risk as s/he tries to untangle the situation instead of working at the tasks for which s/he was hired and thus will be evaluated.

• Ill-advising graduate students by recommending only particular persons as instructors and thesis/doctoral committee chairs or members, and making sure that certain persons are stereotyped as "political outcasts" and "loose cannons" in the academic unit.

• Consistently giving particular professors the "plum" and well-scheduled graduate seminars while others receive over-subscribed undergraduate courses. Also, advising students out of particular courses and into others and/or canceling courses before they have a chance to "make," such as before new graduate students show up to enroll. This keeps some professors out of the graduate teaching program and therefore reduces their research productivity and visibility. If this occurs on a consistent basis, the latter professor(s) most likely will receive lower merit evaluations and, thus, money for not being more active in the graduate program—another vicious cycle.

• Closing, restricting, distorting, controlling the flow of crucial information, such as for grant applications, teaching and other awards, fellowships, important meeting times or places, travel money and other financial availabilities, and so on. This practice has to rank as the highest irony in an academic unit having communication and/or information in its title.

• Not inviting or electing one or more qualified persons to be members of a team or committee (such as for grants, new programs, searches, faculty councils, reviews) even though they are as or more qualified than those so named.

• The grand scheme scenario: the in-group presents a plan at a faculty or other meeting in sketchy detail with obstacles seemingly overcome. Those not in the "lunch bunch" can end up voting for something that ultimately might be in opposition to their personal and/or professional ethics and perhaps own security.

• The stealth maneuver: bringing orchestrated, last-minute information into a review for promotion/tenure or other important meeting about the individual or issue under consideration with the purpose of tainting, biasing, or enhancing the decision.

(Excerpts from "All Things (Not) Considered: A Prologue About the Advancement of International and Intercultural Communications—and Communications in General—As a Field of Study and Practice," International Communication Association, Dublin, 1990).

Men's Work: Toward Systemic, Systematic Equality

National communication organizations such as the Accrediting Council and its member organizations must force the change from structural inequity to structural equality by the 21st Century. To do so, individual baseline data for promotion, tenure, and salary must be assessed and evaluated within and across academic units that request accreditation or reaccreditation:

• Collect and analyze each year between reaccreditation periods the following materials directly from each individual within an academic unit: an updated resume; a completed distribution of effort in written remarks and percentages; teaching evaluations, research, service and other essential, supporting documents; the administrators' evaluation in written remarks and ratings; the assigned salary figure and percentage. When normative standards and structural equality are assured, such documentation can be called for only in random but routine checks much in the same way that IRS purportedly "flags" tax returns.

• The materials from individuals must be collected from all communication units in which mass communications is located, such as a school or a college with departments as the basic structural units. Where there is a stand-alone school or department within, say, a liberal arts college, ACEJMC will petition the university to allow the Accrediting Council to collect individual materials from the most closely-related academic unit/discipline (such as speech communication) to the unit being accredited.

• Confidential interviews will be conducted at least once during the period between reaccreditations by the Accrediting Council with: (a) all full-time faculty members or staff members who leave the larger academic communications entity; (b) all staff members of the larger academic communications entity; and (c) all senior, tenured women within the largest academic communications unit and/or female full professors within the social sciences.

• Faculty members within the largest academic communication unit will be encouraged to send, in confidence, any documentation to the Accrediting Council that is related to the next accreditation review of the basic unit.

• The Accrediting Council will hire trained interviewers, researchers, human resources and legal staff as necessary to handle the annual collection, analysis, and interpretation of data concerning structural equality.

internal teaching, research, and service load so that the Power/Overs may have more time for "visibility involvement" in university governance, obtaining and reaping the benefits of funded research, paid and unpaid consulting, and community and professional leadership positions.

Unit and university service efforts for power subordinates (including those proportionately well-paid for their co-opted loyalty, apparent in the Queen Bee syndrome, for example) are too often equivalent to unpaid administration.

The membership composition of policy-making committees within and across academic units and media organizations over time can also reveal patterns of power and abuse (e.g., search committees have many of the same or same-thinking people appointed, selected, or elected time after time). How the minutes of meetings or self-study reports are constructed, reconstructed, and/or revisioned can be quite revealing under analysis. If details are vague or sketchy, most likely history has just been reconstructed (e.g., watch for "unanimous" votes, or about the same number of votes each time, for unsigned and undated reports).

It is important in assessing political power harassment that two or more well-trained, in-house researchers serve as observers, collectors, and reporters of salary schedules, newsletters, meeting minutes, review reports, committee and governance structures, recruiting and maintenance procedures, and so on. Or, in the succinct language of one graduate student: ethnographic research of organizational communication grounded in a feminist materialist framework.

Searching for, hiring, and retaining females is an essential employment process weakened by the lack of motivation, cooperation, understanding, and time spent by those ultimately in charge of policy. National communication organizations must join together interactive, integrated centralized databases of prospective talent so that the process is comprehensive and inclusive. Also, guidelines need to be developed at the national level for the mentoring process of women and minorities; salary and/or tenure appeal procedures; conducting national searches; successful retention, tenure, and promotion, or exit interviews for those terminated; and other guides as needed. Finally, preconference workshops (which should be considered mandatory for owners, managers, administrators, and senior professors) on prevention and elimination of sexual and power harassment, and academic and professional dirty tricks, can be conducted at annual and regional meetings of communication organizations.

Related Issues

Further recommendations include encouraging the implementation of the "Global Communication and Information Freedom 2000" resolution passed in 1989 by the AEJMC so that mass communication organizations, including academic units, might have a comparable standard for diversity and equality. Often, internal affirmative action offices have been co-opted by the higher administration and management, and/or their guidelines are too general for realistic assistance.

AEJMC's guidelines, for example, are more aligned with goals and missions of specific academic units; where the university's guidelines are clear and specific, the two sets can be interwoven. Guidelines for appealing harassment and salary actions need academic and professional interactive integration and application. Current guidelines are usually contained in legally vague administrative policy and regulations; managers and administrators can and do use the vagueness or lack of appeal procedures to their own advantage.

Perhaps the last groups to bash in public and private arenas for this century are gays, lesbians, and those persons involved in furthering family diversity. During the 1992 AEJMC meeting in Montreal, the Commission on the Status of Women sponsored the organizational meeting of a task force on gay, lesbian, and family diversity. Later in the year, the task force petitioned and was given Interest Group status, which means that it has its own programming capability within AEJMC.

With these actions, AEJMC has been slowly (it is one of the last academic associations to form such a group) but persistently inclusive in its direction, especially after it revised constitutional bylaws in 1990. "The association will not discriminate on the basis of gender, race, religion, ethnic origin, physical disability, or sexual orientation. In efforts to achieve this goal of diversity of membership and participation, the association will monitor the status of women and minorities in the profession and the association on a regular basis, report its findings to the membership, and take affirmative steps to rectify problems."

Lesbian, gay, and bisexual caucuses and groups within organizations such as the Speech Communication Association and the Interna-

Global Communications and Information Freedom 2000

The Association for Education in Journalism and Mass Communication (AEJMC), having early established a Division of Minorities and Communication and a Commission on the Status of Women, is proud of its record in pioneering strong affirmative action/equal opportunity activities to advance human rights in journalism and mass communications. But we know that the efforts have been too slow and too little, especially as we see the rapidity of advances and changes in communication and information technology, which are impacting us in ways we are only beginning to study and understand. It is therefore crucial that we encourage and utilize the experiences and knowledge of each unique person in the access, participation, study, and understanding of communications.

Preamble: As we approach the year 2000, affirmative action and equal opportunity programs need proactive approaches so that by the turn of the Century all vestiges of discrepancies and discriminations because of gender, race, and ethnicity have been removed.

Therefore, be it resolved that the Association for Education in Journalism and Mass Communication (AEJMC) encourages its members and affiliates to have at least 50 percent of their faculties and administrations comprised of females and minorities by the year 2000.

Further, we encourage working rapidly toward full societal population representation of women, African Americans, Hispanics, Asians, and Native Americans as we enter the 21st Century.

(Passed by the Association for Education in Journalism and Mass Communication, August 1989.)

tional Communication Association; the recently formed National Lesbian and Gay Journalists Association, the American Society of Newspaper Editors (which has demonstrated major interest in research and discussions about lesbians and gays in journalism); and AEJMC's Lesbian, Gay, and Family Diversity Interest Group must search for opportunities for cooperation. The turn of the 21st century should serve as the academic, professional, and media milestone to reach 100% inclusivity.

Proactive Approaches

Important approaches include the integration of conflict resolution and peace education materials into communication curricula, research, and media content. (The Center for Teaching Peace in Washington, D.C., for example, was founded and is directed by newspaper columnist Colman McCarthy.) AEJMC, in conjunction with the Commission on the Status of Women, should conduct

a public information campaign designed to (a) raise awareness that problems persist, (b) tell members what they personally can do to make a difference in this area, and (c) encourage increased levels of activism. Preliminary research that could serve as the foundation for such a campaign is currently being conducted.

Mediation, arbitration, and negotiation skills might well be as important to professionals, professors, and students in our field as are written and oral communication skills.

The flip side of war and violence is peace and cooperation; we just need to think, act, talk, and write that way and etch these cultural transmissions into our consciences for thousands of years as we have etched the cultural transgressions of abuse, violence, war, and war periods, often cited as historical time demarcations (e.g., "Since World War II . . .").

Along these lines of thinking, we can use terms such as "peace correspondents" instead of "war correspondents" or "global correspondents" instead of "foreign correspondents" [as most women and minorities know, to name or rename is to claim]; a Summer 1992 *Journalism Quarterly* article on "After Journalism" by Jurgensen and Meyer indicates how the information technology explosion has pulled us from journalism as a craft to the social and behavioral sciences process of mass communication; a doctoral student is working with this author on a Quality of Academic Life Assessment (QUALA) inventory; and this author has been working since 1988 on an all-inclusive, grounded, conceptual framework called "global eco-communications."

Off Our Backs

"Women's work is never done." This time, at the turn of this new century, women's work in its current form must be done. Now is the time for men to begin to correct the structural inequities and societal symbols they have erected, often in the name of God, institution, and knowledge. Men now need to pour their time, their energy, their money, their knowledge of the construction and maintenance of structural inequities into disassembling and restructuring those same systems.

Women have nearly and finally learned our lessons, and learned them well: we are beginning to understand that women have served the world as receptacles of the waste and ruin left over from those masculine memorials. (See Marilyn French's *The War on Women,* 1992.) Each one of us, men and women alike, will and must never be the same again. We have hurt each other and we mistrust each other. And in turn, and worst of all, we hurt and mistrust ourselves.

Many women and some men have discovered intersystemic connections, in which a dysfunctional family of nations has symptoms similar to a dysfunctional domestic family, a dysfunctional state contains dysfunctional private and public academic units. Now women, together with the few good men who have kept their sense of moral justice, are prepared to be the architects and on-site supervisors of a new, associative civil society, keeping the best of capitalistic efficiency and democratically channeling it into quality circles and networks of equality.

Women and men must heal themselves of old patriarchal wounds by *supervisioning* the creation, perhaps for the first time, of structural equality. The perpetrators of territoriality mindsets must heal themselves through the understanding that comes through breaking apart and down their old patterns, and reweaving their yarns into a mosaic of inclusiveness, diversity, and equality: an interweave of unique and varied experiences, valuing the whole rather than the parts—holistic.

The way to "being all that we can be" is to create gender-balanced and seamless communication academic units, not in our own images, but in the reality of our combined and spontaneous creativity.

16

Feminism After Ferment
Ten Years of Gendered Scholarship in Communications

Kathryn Cirksena

In recent years, there has been increased debate about gender and communications, in both scholarly and popular discourses. When a 1983 published symposium on the paradigm shift in communications, "Ferment in the Field" (Gerbner, 1983), omitted the flourishing of feminist theory in the humanities and social sciences, scholars contended that feminist approaches could and should radically shift the ground and methods of communication (Dervin, 1987; Rakow, 1986). How much ferment over gender ensued? How much impact did feminist ideas have in the subsequent decade? This study documents and evaluates the growth of scholarship on feminism, women, and gender in communications since 1983, describing in particular some of the issues that surround the adoption and application of feminist paradigms.

For the most part, the amount of gender-related research in communications has indeed increased. Studies loosely grouped as anti-sexist, pro-feminist, or concerned with gender equity issues also increased since the early 1980s. However, these changes are not consistent across different subdisciplines: interpersonal communication, organizational communication, mass communication, political communication, popular culture, new technologies, and so on. For example, a substantial number of new studies of gender differences in interpersonal communication have been produced. In mass communication, most of the attention has been on traditional content analyses and qualitative, interpretive studies of media texts, with a smaller number of works on reader/viewer uses and responses to mass media. In political communication,

153

human communication technology, and health communication, the growth in gender-related scholarship has been minimal. Research with an explicit "gender equity" focus continues to be predominantly concerned with the media.

The proposals of several key feminist critiques of communication theory can be used as criteria to assess the extent to which recommendations for integrating feminist perspectives into the study of communication, relative to other paradigms for understanding women and gender, have affected research trends in these subdisciplines. Although research on gender has grown a great deal, feminist theory has had an impact in some areas, but not others, and some approaches to incorporating feminist ideas are more common than others. Issues of gender parity or equity surface in a number of studies, but it is frequently within a framework that is philosophically embedded in the liberal democratic/capitalist/masculinist dominant paradigm of noncritical communication research. Structural and ideological factors in these discursive trends are explored.

In communications, the inherent conservatism of a field with so many ties to the corporate sector of society (in mass communication, interpersonal communication, and public relations, for example) may have converged with larger trends with academia to constrain and forestall the acceptance of feminist paradigms across large domains of communication studies.

Gender Research in Communications Since 1983

The editors of two key edited volumes of new feminist communication theory have offered conflicting assessments of the effects of feminist ideas on the field of communications since the "paradigm dialogues" were joined in 1983. Writing in 1991, Rakow remarked that the field can no longer ignore feminist scholarship and that feminists are making inroads into the basic paradigms that

are used (Rakow, 1992). Creedon, in her 1993 edition, retreated from her previous claim of a "gender shift" in mass communication and instead is much more dubious in her assessment of the overall impact of women and feminists on mass communication (Creedon, 1993). In the quantitative and qualitative analyses presented here, Creedon's more pessimistic assessment receives greater empirical support.

A number of feminist scholars in other social sciences have similarly reviewed their fields for evidence of feminist studies' impacts, with mixed results. Anthropology has, compared with other disciplines, more or less embraced feminist anthropology while Stacey and Thorne in their 1985 article took note of the "missing feminist revolution" in sociology. Ingraham (1994) has recently pointed out the problematics and contradictions of the feminist sociology that has grown since then. The main strands of my inquiry are the extent to which the field of communications has been influenced by the feminist intellectual revolution and what issues and themes have dominated discourse on gender in communications since 1983.

Analysis of public texts such as a key reference work in communications offers a vantage point on the field as a whole when one understands such texts as "constituent of social relations [that] offers access to the ontological ground of institutional processes which organize, govern, and regulate" (Smith, 1990, p. 122). Barriers to access to feminist criticisms, arguments, and exemplars of feminist communication research can result in part when that work is absent from the most widely consulted reference works for the field. As the main index to articles and books in communications, *Communication Abstracts* provides a gauge of whether these ideas are widely available in journals and books published over the 10 years since "Ferment in the Field."

Communication Abstracts publishes between 1,000 and 1,500 abstracts per year in the areas of mass communication, advertising, TV, radio, rhetoric, interpersonal com-

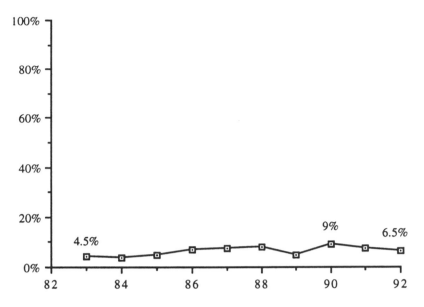

Figure 16.1. Percentage of *Communication Abstracts'* Entries in "Women's/Gender Studies," 1983-1992

munication, nonverbal communication, tele-communication policy, and communication law, among others. It draws on 150 to 200 journals per year including a few (two to five) women's studies journals, usually *Psychology of Women Quarterly* and *Sex Roles.* The journal *Women's Studies in Communication* was not indexed until 1990, although it's been publishing since the late 1970s.

This analysis of *Communication Abstracts* helps to answer three questions: (a) What is the trend in the volume of communication scholarship about women and gender (in the most inclusive definition of that category)? (b) What is the pattern of gender subtopics of the abstracted articles? (c) What are the trends in feminist studies within the subdisciplines?

To answer the first question, I selected all the abstracts that had anything to do with gender, women, sex difference, sex roles, or feminism in each of the 10 years. (Although many scholars don't accept the idea that sex differences research is inherently feminist, the aim here was to draw upon the widest range of relevant studies.) The abstracts that were counted for this tabulation included everything from corporate-oriented research on sex differences in managerial style and how to market to female consumers, to essays on radical feminist epistemology.

As shown in Figure 16.1, the overall trend is a relatively small increase in the number of abstracts having to do with gender over these 10 years. Proportionally, the percentage doubles between 1983 and 1990. But even in 1990, when the largest number were found, just 9% of all abstracts fall into the gender/women category. In 1991-1992, the trend appears to be reversing itself, with a decrease of 2.5%. (One factor that artificially inflates the percentage in 1990 is the inclusion in that year of abstracts from three edited volumes of feminist communication scholarship: More than 20 of the 136 abstracts in 1990 are from chapters of those books.) Although some renditions of the development of communication studies in these years would attribute undue influence to feminist critiques and reworkings, and others would hope to claim that feminist ideas have received increasingly wide discussion and use, the volume of work found in this analysis does not suggest that either is occurring. The pervasive-

TABLE 16.1 Citations per Keyword by Year

Keyword	Year										Total
	83	84	85	86	87	88	89	90	91	92	
Sex differences	5	10	12	17	8	15	17	3	7	3	97
Sex roles	21	4	9	25	41	31	21	16	23	9	200
Gender	—	4	5	—	5	8	16	48	40	48	174
Gender relations	—	—	—	—	—	—	—	—	2	—	2
Gender differences	—	—	—	—	—	—	—	2	2	1	5
Women	5	6	10	14	20	8	21	33	28	23	132
Women's representation	7	10	11	—	17	17	6	19	—	9	96
Women & media	2	4	6	1	—	9	2	—	15	—	39
Women in TV	2	—	—	12	1	—	1	—	—	—	16
Women's TV	1	—	—	—	—	—	—	—	—	—	1
Women's magazines	—	—	—	—	—	—	—	—	—	1	1
Sexism	2	—	—	—	—	—	—	1	—	5	8
Sex discrimination	—	—	—	—	—	—	1	1	—	—	2
Gender discrimination	—	—	—	—	—	—	1	—	—	—	1
Gender bias	—	—	—	—	—	—	1	—	—	—	1
Sexual harassment	—	—	—	—	—	1	—	—	—	—	1
Feminism	—	1	—	—	—	6	—	—	5	4	16
Feminist theory	—	—	—	—	—	—	—	1	—	—	1
Feminists	—	—	—	1	—	1	1	2	3	3	11
Suffragists	—	2	—	—	—	—	—	—	—	—	2

ness of feminist re/formations of communications is not a claim that can be supported by these data.

Table 16.1 is a list of keyword descriptors that are used to index the abstracts, giving the number of abstracts in each year that were assigned this keyword. The most common descriptor is "sex roles," with "gender" and "women" the second and third most frequent, and "sex differences" a distant fourth. Among the top five most frequently assigned keywords, only "women's representation" is inherently suggestive of a reconsideration or critique of gender relations. Of the 806 instances where any of these keywords was assigned to an abstract, just 43 explicitly refer to gender equity or feminist issues. One

confounding factor is that edited volumes of feminist scholarship and chapters within them are not necessarily assigned a "feminist" keyword descriptor. (This explains why there are not 20 or more feminist-related keywords counted in 1990.) For example, Carter and Spitzack's (1989) book on researching women's communication is described by the keywords "gender," "mass communication research," and "women" despite the fact that numerous chapters are explicitly feminist in their approach, including the editors' introduction.

The high incidence of particular keywords related to sex differences supports the claim that most of the work done since 1983 has been of this type. This is interesting, if not encouraging, because a number of feminist communication scholars have explicitly argued that sex differences research is not feminist—a point of view shared by feminist psychologists and sociologists. The student in search of new scholarship on gender might easily come away with the impression that "differences" research is substantially the same as feminist research.

Even though its use has declined in the past few years, the "sex differences" keyword continues to be applied to a number of studies. But its decline is deceiving because what appears to have happened is that researchers have adopted a different language, in particular *gender* and *gender differences,* to describe research studies that substantively are very close to traditional sex difference research. For example, a "gender differences in information processing" article with the keyword as "gender" notes that neither information processing style is inherently superior, but that these styles have implications for how advertisers can effectively target women versus men.

Very few keywords directly referencing feminism have been put into use, and these only relatively recently. For the most part, they are used to index the aforementioned theoretical critiques rather than studies that exemplify the type of scholarship that might result when alternative feminist proposals are applied.

The keyword "women" should not be assumed to refer to women from a feminist perspective, because the articles are often those that use a sample of women exclusively, such as one investigating age difference in the ability to decode facial expressions. One problem is that the feminist-related keywords seem to be assigned only to the articles that have the word in the title or where feminism is a featured part of the abstract. Taken together, the overall trend toward an increased number of articles and some shifts and changes in how keyword descriptors are applied can hardly be said to constitute a feminist revolution, although increased attention to gender is clearly demonstrated in this analysis.

A subset of the abstracts, selected based on examination of both the descriptors assigned and the content of the title and abstract, yielded 300 abstracts that dealt in some broad way with sexism, feminism, gender equity, media stereotypes of women/gender, and gender in relation to other dimensions of social identity (most usually race). A sample of half of these abstracts was selected to reduce the number of abstracts to a manageable group of 150.

Overwhelmingly, these articles dealt with media representations of women and women as media workers. Only 18% dealt with subjects other than mass media: 9% discussed feminist interpersonal communication studies, 6% were feminist theory and methods of a general sort, and 3% involved rhetorical and discourse analysis.

Of interest, in the three years from 1990 to 1992, more than one-third of the 69 feminist/anti-sexist abstracts examined were for books or book chapters. This suggests another barrier to access to feminist ideas: for those who keep up with the field primarily by perusing journals' tables of contents, the impact of feminist studies in communication would be greatly underestimated.

Feminist Paradigms and Their Proposals for Communication Studies

Admittedly, after the analyses discussed above, the body of work applying feminist recommendations as the basis for research will be small. Nonetheless, it is worthwhile to review what these recommendations are and some of the issues surrounding their implementation. Substantive articles that exemplify the different perspective that can be achieved through adopting feminist frameworks, that demonstrate the shift in the knowledge base and ground, may be a stronger impetus to increased influence in the field than explications of basic theoretical issues.

In any case, scholarship traditionally follows from theory, should test assumptions and claims, and should demonstrate the applicability of the new paradigm.

Overview critiques of communication from a feminist perspective that attempt to define a feminist paradigm seem to converge on the following five points:

1. Communication studies should give explicit and critical attention to the inequitable power dimensions of gender relations in all human communication.
2. Communication studies should "put women at the center" of research.
3. Scholarship should not attempt to abstract gender from other aspects of identity, especially, but not limited to, identity based on race and class.
4. It should be "action oriented"; a part of the research agenda should be linked to improving the status of women.
5. The "researched" (those people at the center of the investigation) should have some input into the framing of the issues and the research process.

To what extent have these recommendations been incorporated by communication scholars? Not terribly much by the end of the period covered by the 1992 volume of *Communication Abstracts*. There are very few studies, a handful at most, that meet more than one of the above criteria. Some newer studies seem, at least in their rhetorical strategies, to be putting women at the center and/or taking gender as a central conceptual category and even implicitly addressing gender-based inequities. But precious few published pieces are taking account of women's standpoints of multiply determined identities, and fewer still propose or include any activist orientation or involve the people being studied in the determination of the research process. Such recommendations are easier to formulate than to enact. Within the time frame of this study, few examples of research that fulfill these criteria are available.

In light of the dearth of such studies, it might be useful to speculate about what the barriers are to their production and circulation. Feminist scholars in communication as in other fields face the explicit and implicit sanctions of the graduate education, tenure-track, and funding source mainstream. Any of these institutions can unilaterally prompt hesitation on the part of the individual scholar and taken together form a formidable set of factors that can inhibit nonmainstream research. Structurally, there are venues that support and endorse feminist scholarship within the major professional associations of U.S. and international communication research. But the move from conference presentation to published article may be more difficult for feminist scholarship. Many journals remain under the control of mainstream/malestream scholars who are not particularly sympathetic to feminist ideas. The process of peer review can be used as a gatekeeping structure that works against submissions based on an alternative set of standards of academic quality. Such considerations may explain the predominance of feminist work found in book chapters compared with journal articles. Finally, the initial time frame of this study may not be long enough to account for the more recent work that has been done. Although a few individual scholars have produced a body of feminist work in a variety of venues, the majority of those who see the value of feminist paradigms as a central orientation to scholarship often express concern about the professional viability of such a path.

Conclusion

Although the amount of research on gender has increased in these 10 years, what this assessment suggests is that, compared with some other disciplines, communications remains relatively unaffected by the feminist intellectual revolution. What might explain this condition?

Communications has a history of applied research, especially in the subdisciplines of organizational and mass communication, where early landmark studies were conducted to serve managerial, corporate, and other status quo (patriarchal) interests. Communications as a field seems to have a recurring (or even perennial) identity crisis. In 1959, it was declared that all the interesting questions about the process of communication had been answered, while in 1991, the field was deemed inevitably pluralistic. It may be that the contested nature of communications' disciplinary identity creates an atmosphere that fosters resistance to incursions by a fundamentally transformational program such as feminist scholarship. If the legitimacy of the discipline (and departmental budgets in colleges and universities) has to be constantly defended within the larger arena of academic turf wars and competition for scarce resources that characterize contemporary higher education, marginalized and subaltern approaches may be the first casualties. Still, there may be some more focused, less sweeping observations that can be made on the basis of the analyses presented here.

The research agenda in organizational communication by and large continues to reflect a "top-down" corporation perspective, with gender-related studies implicitly based on a "parity within the hierarchical system" model. Such gender differences research has as its goal helping women succeed within the corporate structure and fails to question whether that structure is problematic for women. It is interesting that the same assumption of parity appears to dominate the literature of interpersonal communication, especially given the feminist aphorism that the "personal is political."

Feminists have long held the view that the role of the media is key in shaping gender relations and in reinforcing women's oppression. This view no doubt has had an influence on the large proportion of research on media images found in this study. But it is also true that the ability to do textual analysis without any problematic interactions with "subjects" can make this type of research more attrac-

tive. The influence of postmodernism has in part involved emphasizing text and narrative and sees the individual as already discursively inscribed. Issues of text and of representation aren't so intractable as women who are the subjects of their own lived experience: Texts can be more amenable to interpretive control than people and their activities. The irony is that the seductions of the text may be antithetical to a feminist praxis that sees scholarship as a contributor to improvements in women's condition. They may present easier questions than the noisome issue of what is to be done or needed in the way of useful information for feminist action.

In another vein, the problem of the accessibility of marginalized work such as feminist writing deserves mention. There is a perennial problem of fugitive documents— small or local publications that are difficult to locate. Frequently, such publications offer examples of writing that more adequately fulfill the criteria of feminist paradigms discussed above. Relatedly, there are problems of labeling and defining work in a dynamic discourse such as feminist studies when new terms and labels for referencing feminist scholarship must wait to be adopted until there is a substantial body of work completed. Although separate feminist indexes and reference works expand the accessibility of such work on one level, they may also become a marginalized resource in tight economic times. Such seemingly arcane issues of librarianship are significant in understanding the processes of constraint under which feminist scholarships are establishing themselves.

Access to scholarship on communication from a feminist perspective increasingly becomes one of a number of issues concerning the rapid adoption of electronic database technology, which is depicted as a panacea but in practice reproduces and exacerbates issues of access as priorities are set for making some kinds of documents easily available electronically. For those with access to the Internet and other advanced technological resources, documents may be more readily retrievable than previously, but this does nothing to open first-level doorways into computer-based communication among those not already privileged.

Feminist paradigms may still affect the field of communications to a much greater degree than they had by the end of 1991, when the last articles for the 1992 volume of *Communication Abstracts* were written. However, it should be clear to those concerned with implementing feminist ideas across the academic community and with making academia relevant to global concerns with social justice that feminist projects will require active advocacy and the promotion and legitimation of alternative discourses to grow and flower.

References

Carter, K., & Spitzack, C. (1989). *Doing research on women's communication: Perspectives on theory and method.* Norwood, NJ: Ablex.

Creedon, P. (1993). *Women in mass communication* (2nd ed.). Newbury Park, CA: Sage.

Dervin, B. (1987). The potential contribution of feminist scholarship to the field of communication. *Journal of Communication, 37*(4), 107-120.

Gerbner, G. (1983). Ferment in the field [Special issue]. *Journal of Communication, 33*(3).

Ingraham, C. (1994). *The heterosexual imaginary: Feminist sociology and theories of gender.* Troy, NY: Russell Sage College.

Rakow, L. (1986). Rethinking gender research in communication. *Journal of Communication, 36,* 11-26.

Rakow, L. (1992). *Women making meaning: New feminist directions in communication.* New York: Routledge Kegan Paul.

Smith, D. E. (1990). *The active text: A textual analysis of the social relations of public textual discourse* (Texts, Facts, and Femininity). London: Routledge Kegan Paul.

Stacey, J., & Thorne, B. (1985). The missing feminist revolution in sociology. *Social Problems, 32*(4), 301-315.

17

The Wren, the Eagles, and the Assistant Professor

Susan Holly Stocking
Julianne H. Newton

For as long as women have known other women, they have shared stories. On the shores of streambeds, over firelight, on the paths of meadows and mountains, they have told tales filled with wisdom and warnings for life's journey. Often they have offered such stories as gifts—from mothers to daughters, aunts to nieces, older sisters to younger sisters, and older friends to younger friends.

Academic women are no exception. As a group, we have collected many stories about our experiences in the academy, stories that we often have offered to those less experienced than ourselves. Typically, we have told our stories privately and informally—in hallways, in cafeterias, in the corridors of academic meetings. In recent years, however, we seem increasingly willing and able to share our tales in public and formal forums

of the academy—in sessions on the official programs of professional meetings, for example, and in anthologies such as this one. These developments suggest a growing use of stories as tools for institutional as well as individual transformation.

The following story, though fictional in many of its particulars, is reflective of these developments. It expresses important truths about our experiences and those of other academic women we have known. The story is about a woman who enters the academy naive to its ways. Eager to win a permanent professional home, she heeds the directions of an older woman who has traveled the road before her. In so doing, the younger woman strikes out on a path that leads her into a dark and unexpected place, a place that has little to do with the number of refereed articles she has published, or the number of citations others have given her work—and everything to do with the discovery, survival, and celebration of her deepest self.

We offer this story as a gift to our mothers, daughters, sisters, and friends who have chosen the academic path as one road on their personal journey. We hope that our story will nudge you in a deep-down place, indeed, that it will rattle a rib or two (or three), and nudge you to give voice to your own stories. Such stories—we now know—have the power to reveal and to heal, and to help lead you where you are meant to go.

In offering this gift, we acknowledge our profound debt to Clarissa Pinkola Estés, author of *Women Who Run With the Wolves: Myths and Stories of the Wild Woman Archetype* (1992). Estés reached us as we were at intersections in our own life journeys. Her gift of stories about women who cut themselves off from their intuition and creativity (or "wildness," as she puts it) inspired us to reach for our own healing wisdom. Estés's gift helped us recognize our unique paths—and one another. It also helped us summon the courage to speak in the voice of a teller of tales and myths, a voice that we have long yearned to hear in academic contexts such as this one.

The Tale

Once there was, and once there wasn't, an untenured woman whose skirts were long and flowed like a river. Her hair was the color of strawberries, and sometimes it stuck out in several directions at once, like the twigs in a nest. Her office was cluttered with posters, and plants, and cartoons, and other things that struck her fancy: a blue bird's feather, and a postcard of a nun gyrating in a hula hoop, and a soap bubble wand, and a Chinese fan. And in one corner flowered floor pillows, and an electric pot for tea.

In the beginning, the woman didn't hear the whispers that flapped like bats up and down the hallways outside her door. Her colleagues kidded her when she bought the flowered floor pillows, but it didn't bother her because she knew she needed a place that sang to her, of home. So when her colleagues made their good-natured jibes, she laughed, and invited them in for tea.

The woman had gone into teaching because she wanted to release the spirits of the young. But, of course, she never told that to anyone. Once, when the words wanted to fly from her lips, she stuck her fist into her mouth and forced them back, deep down into her heart, where she imagined souls leaping from students' bodies and dancing on the desks and the ceiling and the tops of the blackboards, and flying out the windows like birds. Instead, the words that issued from her mouth were about guiding students to become critical and creative thinkers and moral persons—words as sensible as her mother's shoes.

At first, the hallway whispers of her colleagues were simply about her office and her clothes. But soon, they concerned more important things like her research ("political . . . and . . . ssshhhhh . . . insignificant"), and her writing style ("too . . . sshhh . . . personal"). Most surprising to the woman, they also concerned her teaching. The woman taught in ways the elders did not understand. In her office, she passed out cookies and tea, and in the classroom, students scratched the earth with their toes, and laughter exploded like a flock of starlings breaking for the sky. Once, an elder in the department, hearing the laughter, stopped the younger teacher after class. "Whatever happened to decorum?" he asked. The woman puzzled over his choice of words: *decorum.* She looked it up: "The requirement of correct behavior in a polite society. Propriety, especially in behavior and conduct." She had crossed some invisible line.

As time went by, the woman found it harder and harder to ignore the whispers. The flapping in the hallways grew louder and louder to her ears. Finally, one of the elders in the department took her aside. She was a kind elder, a small woman who reminded the younger woman of a wounded wren who once had hopped forlornly on the ground outside her window. But the wren-elder knew things the younger woman did not; her eyes were wells of knowing. Quiet, but determined, she had managed to continue down the path where many other women had faltered and lost their way; she had even managed to secure a place in the far reaches of the Circle of Forever. And now she was hearing the whispers about her young friend—whispers that to her finely tuned ears sounded like the flickering tongues of poisonous snakes.

"You might want to try harder to fit the mold," the wren-elder counseled, and as she said this, a soft rattling shook her tiny ribs. The younger woman, hearing these words, thought she heard the voice of her mother calling out to her as she scrambled to the highest branches of a tree in her childhood: "Be careful, dear one, be careful you don't fall." And suddenly she remembered a day when she had not been careful (or when she had been too careful—she could no longer remember which), and she had fallen what seemed like the height of 12 treetops. And the young woman grew anxious and confused.

That night, returning to her home, the woman asked her partner what she should do. And her partner, loving her, urged the young woman to learn all the subtle knowings of the place: "Listen to what the elder has to tell you," the partner counseled, "for she has survived, and she knows." Hearing this, the young woman's eyes grew wide. And then, almost as quickly, they slid shut. The young woman was ambitious and anything but stupid. The wren-elder was right: She would learn to be careful; she would learn how to fit the mold.

So in the months that followed, the young woman sought the wren-elder's counsel. The older woman told her stories of coral snakes basking in the sunlight, and she advised her to study the long shadows cast by the other elders. And so the younger woman did: She scrutinized the huge coil-shaped shadows of the elders as they researched and wrote their papers, and she studied the long, slithering shadows of the elders as they instructed their classes. And before long, the young woman began to do research she thought the elders would deem important—and not "political." She began to write in a less personal voice that she thought the elders would hear. She cropped the nest of curls on her head, cleared the clutter and floor pillows from her office, and hemmed up her long, flowing skirt. She also stopped inviting students in for cookies and tea, and in the classroom, she laughed less, and she lectured more, and her students stopped scratching the earth with their toes.

For two years, the young woman labored harder than she could ever remember. She labored so hard that her thoughts grew heavy as stones, and her bones, bearing them, burned with the aching. But the kind wren-elder urged her along, and, after a while, the younger woman's shadow coiled and lengthened, and the whispers in the hallway fell silent.

At first, the young woman was relieved by the silence. But soon she began to hear other whispers rising, fluttering—this time from her ribs. In the beginning, she felt only a murmuring tickle, then larger and larger flutters. Alarmed, the young woman pushed them back down inside her with both of her fists. And she went on in this way, heavy and aching, with her fists flying to her mouth at the oddest moments, until she grew numb.

Then one day the young woman woke up and couldn't speak at all. She met with her students and tried to speak, but what flew out of her mouth were bats. Terrified, the woman tried again, but all that came out of her mouth were more black wings. More terrifying still, her students didn't notice. They were hunkered over their desks drawing bats—bats, bats, and more bats, all over their pages, and still they didn't notice. Finally, one of the students looked up and asked how many bats he ought to draw. Only then, listening to her student and eyeing the bats flapping up and down in her shadow, did the woman realize what she had done—to her students and herself.

In the days that followed, the younger woman allowed herself to feel the deep flutters inside her. She no longer pushed them back down with her fists. She opened her throat and mouth to release them—but now nothing came forth. She made a decision: If the whispers in the hallways returned, she would listen to them for the warnings they might sound, but she would not silence herself to silence them. She would let these whispers roll off like water on a wing, and she would tilt her head to better hear the soul-whispers deep down below. And so she did.

She tilted her head and listened to her soul. And she stopped copying the shadows of the elders. And she let down her skirts, and let some of the clutter return to her office, and once again, she offered her students cookies and tea.

Noticing the changes, the kind wren-elder asked the younger woman what she was doing. And the younger woman, her voice clear and strong, replied, "I am only doing what I must. I love you for your concern, but your mold is not mine. Every time I try to fit into it, I lose more and more of myself. If there must be molds at all," she added, "I will have to create my own."

And as the wren-elder heard these words, she began to weep, and her tired old bones began to rattle, softly at first, then louder and louder, until they rattled so loudly that the building shook, and the ground shook until it seemed the very earth would split in two.

Over time, the younger woman's nest of curls grew back, and the laughter in her classroom returned, and her office, which had grown as silent as a wall, sang to her again of home. And before long, she was thinking thoughts she had never thought, and writing words she had never written, and laughing in the oddest places. Her thoughts grew easy to carry, and her bones no longer ached, but felt strong and sure, and her research and her writing winged across the canyons of the academy. And the work was joyful and caressed her soul.

Seeing these things, the wren-elder was amazed. And slowly, picking her way as the earth shuddered beneath her feet, she, too, began to think thoughts she had never thought and to say things she had never said and to laugh in odd places. And before long she imagined that her ribs had sprouted wings, and she could soar like an eagle. Sometimes, when she thought hard enough, she would even soar on a thermal and she would look down and see how small everything really was. From this distance, her sharpened eyes could see that her colleague-elders were not hissing snakes at all. Rather, they were eagles like herself, some of whom had tumbled from their nests and now hopped, broken wings flapping, down the academy's long, echoing corridors. And for the first time since she had joined the academy, the wren-elder understood that her throat could open and she could sing with the wind, and others would listen. And they did.

The following year, when the younger woman received the letter granting her admission to the Circle of Forever, the wren-elder went to the younger woman, and once again, she wept. This time, though, the younger woman wept, too, and their cries ascended into the clouds—cries of relief and gratitude and sorrow for all the women, all the mothers and daughters, and elders and youngers, who, listening to others' whispers, had silenced their own. And hours later, when they had finished their weeping, the women began to laugh, and they laughed and laughed and laughed some more, until their hearts grew light as mist.

Then the younger woman returned to her classroom and invited her students to dance. She stood on the desktop, and swirled, and she felt her heart crack open, and a bright blue spirit—her spirit—leapt out of her body and flew. And that day and every day after that, when the elders paused at the door to her classroom, they beheld no decorum at all—only laughter bursting through the doorway and flying out the windows, and a room full of students, up on birds' feet, scratching the earth with their toes, and dancing.

The Tale's Untelling

In recent years, it has become common-place for women to speak about the many ways they feel themselves silenced in the academy. Less common is for academic women to speak about the ways they silence them-selves. Still rarer are conversations about how women have shut down—or sold—their very souls in exchange for security and aca-demic respectability. Like Faust, many of us, in our ambition, have made bargains with the devil. We have colluded with a terrible force that drains us of well-being.

Fortunately, with the publication of books such as *Women Who Run With the Wolves,* many of us are at last discovering what this bargain, this collusion, has cost us. In writing groups and support groups and, increasingly, in academic meetings and academic writing, many of us are delving deep down into the creative or intuitive parts of ourselves (what Estés calls the "wild" parts of ourselves)—the parts we usually cut out or silence when we enter the corridors of the academy. Con-sider that a recent session on spirit and the teaching of writing at a national conference on the teaching of composition drew a stand-ing-room-only crowd. An even more recent session on wild women in the academy, at the International Communication Association meeting in Sydney, filled a lecture room, even though the session was scheduled for the last time slot of the last day of the week-long meeting. Like wolves, we find ourselves padding down dark hallways, sniffing out danger, and joining in packs to comfort and defend ourselves and to find our ways back to the wild, to our deepest, authentic selves.

The way is not without risks. But for many of us, avoiding these risks is to walk know-ingly into a cage, just waiting for the bars to slam shut.

The academy is a highly conservative in-stitution—a so-called civilized place that val-ues tradition and decorum, tidy desks, and quiet, highly reasoned voices. That is what many women see and hear when they enter the academy. What they may not see as well—because it is hidden behind the rhetoric of traditional accomplishment that shines a too-bright light into their eyes—is that the acad-emy also is a place that values invention, and, in fact, invites invention, and even wildness and chaos, so long as they can be explained and understood.

Explaining and understanding are the keys. Often those new to the academy are unable to explain themselves. They may not yet have acquired the right vocabulary that en-ables them to speak in ways others can hear. They may be tongue-tied. Or they may tell stories only a close friend would love. Their own development may take unfamiliar turns, and they may, in their innocence, too readily confess to their own losses of direction. Con-versely, flushed with excitement, they may speak too boldly of their goals and accom-plishments. Many need—and yearn for—wise elders to speak on their behalf, and to help them learn how to explain themselves, so that when the entire tribe of elders gets together, they can fathom and value the wild, inventive apparition in their midst. Many new to the academy also need and yearn for an elder who can speak to them, teaching them which forms are important (and which can be cast away) for either one's position or one's self.

Sadly, there remain many young women in the academy who do not have women-elders to speak for them, or to them, and in doing so guide them on their way. Sometimes women-elders do exist, but they have so cut themselves off from themselves, or they are so absorbed in their own climbs, that they do not read the cries of the young as cries of distress, or they do not heed them. Some even recoil from the younger women who join their group, feeling threat-ened in ways they do not understand or would deny. Others, though perhaps more willing to honor the new voices, have unexpected diffi-culty understanding the younger, less ruly ver-sions of themselves.

The woman-elder in our tale at first is in no position to explain the wildness in her young charge. She is in no position because she has buried her own wildness; she has long ago closed and double-bolted the door to her soul. She is savvy. She plays it safe. All of us who have spent time in the academy have known such women. Indeed, some of us have been this woman, or at least have tried to become this woman. The savvy academic chooses her work with care, working on projects that cannot be construed as political but will be construed instead as "objectively" and "hardheadedly" representing the world. She erases the *I* from her vocabulary, a way of speaking that is deeply truthful and connecting for all people, but especially, perhaps, for women whose talk with one another so often depends on the personal. She learns the rhetoric of academic "significance" leavened by just the right amount of modesty, an amount that is generally greater for women than for men. She stifles her laughter (the Navajo believe that humans are not born as social beings until they emit their first laugh), and in so doing severs her connections with others. In doing all these things, she proves herself to be "solid" and "serious." Like the woman-elder in our tale, she learns well to "fit the mold" that appears before her. Her weary bones may rattle with the knowing of what she has lost, but chances are it is a soft rattling, until—if she's lucky—someone comes along whose refusal to fit the mold wakes her up; then her bones may rattle so furiously that the building, indeed the vast terra firma of assumptions that have grounded her in the academy, may begin to shake and break apart.

The rattling of bones in this story is significant. When we say we know something in our bones, we are saying that we know something deeply, intuitively, without the kinds of doubts that swirl around knowledge that inhabits other parts of the body (as in the ear, for example, when we say, "I hear what you're saying"). Knowledge that resides in the bones endures. Even when our heads deny such knowledge, our bones know. They rattle, and before they release their timeless wisdom, they clack softly, making tiny little bone-whispers.

Indeed, as Clarissa Pinkola Estés has noted, even when all that is left of the physical body is bones, the bone-knowledge lives on. When the bones of the woman-elder rattle with knowing, they rattle with this deep-down intuitive knowledge that the woman-elder has repressed. Only when the younger woman refuses to follow the path the elder has chosen is the older woman's bone-knowledge released. As her bones let go, they heave with a force that has built up and up until one day it bursts forth in a giant, trembling shudder.

Bone-knowledge is powerful. Released, it is like an earthquake, creating giant fissures in the known world, fissures that swallow entire structures, foundations and all, and transform forever the ground on which we walk. Creation, of course, always demands breaking with— or through—old forms. When a bird pecks out of its egg, the egg cracks open. Shaken, the wrenlike elder in our tale comes to see the academic mold for what it is, not a reptilian mold with scales, but a bird's shell that a tiny beak must crack in order to be born and for the family of birds to continue. With this realization, she begins to see possibilities she has long denied herself. She is no longer afraid. She understands her colleagues as herself. She knows that her colleagues, too, yearn to soar, and knowing this, she can speak with a kind of authority that will compel them to listen.

With the help of the transformed wren-elder, who can now speak effectively on her behalf, the younger woman in this tale ends up earning a permanent place—both in the academy and in the world of spirit. But it might not have ended so. Early in the tale, the younger woman is naive in the ways of the academy. She doesn't understand the invisible lines that have been drawn by tradition. She believes she can be a free, creative spirit without needing to explain herself. Soon, however, her desires are misunderstood, and her ambition and fear combine in a way that almost crushes her spirit, leaving her aching in that part of life that deeply matters.

Most of us who have made it this far know only too well this deadly chemistry. We want to succeed, but we grow afraid, sometimes so afraid that we believe that a single misstep could send us tumbling. Listening to the voices of warning—the well-intentioned, but fear-filled voices that strive to protect us from falling—we may lose our confidence and fail to reach the topmost branches that we seek to touch. How many of us have witnessed women—and yes, men, too—who, listening to the well-intentioned voices of senior colleagues, have tried to do what they thought was expected, only to clatter to their demise? It does no good to listen to the voices of others if we are not at the same time listening to our own—voices that seek to express, indeed that live to express, our thoughts, ideas, and questions. For that is what we are here for—to express, not to impress others, to express what we care about and deeply know.

The young woman in our tale shuts her eyes on her own soul. Almost cunning, no longer seeing what she really needs, she begins to peel away the flesh of her deepest self: first, the subjects of her research and writing; then the laughter in her classrooms, the clutter of her lived-in office, her flowered floor pillows, her flowing skirts, her twigs of hair, even that most civilized of institutions in other settings—afternoon tea. She strips them all away, hoping to silence the whispers, and to cast long shadows like the elders, which, of course, she does, shedding her own skin like a snake, giving in to dark, reptilian ways that are not her own.

In this tale, as in many myths, snakes are bearers of evil. They cast shadows, but they aren't human. In the commonly accepted interpretation of the biblical tale of Adam and Eve, the snake hands over knowledge, but not wisdom. Dispirited academics pass on knowledge, too, but seldom the kind of wisdom that students need to survive and flourish as human creatures. To provide that kind of wisdom in many academic settings today requires not only deep intuitive knowing, but courage.

The young woman in this story at first lacks such courage, and so she makes a truly Faustian bargain. Part of the reason she is motivated to make this bargain is that she still carries within her the muffled screams of her own frightened mother. If the powerful voice of the mother has been overprotective or overly critical, a voice that reminds us of hers can plant seeds of doubt about our abilities. On the ladder of life, this mother's voice may not only fail to prevent missteps, but actually create them. Well-meaning partners too—if overprotective or overly critical—can clip the wings of those who are meant to fly. With the best of intentions, they can encourage us to bargain off our souls.

Interestingly, it is not until the negative judgments of others are finally silenced that the young woman in our story begins to hear the callings of her deeply buried Self. By then, she has so come to fit the revered mold of academe that when she tries to stuff back down the whispers of her Self, she has to use not one fist (as in the beginning of the story when she wisely chose not to speak of "spirits" in the academy), but both fists. In spite of all the woman's efforts, however, the bone-whispers will not be stuffed back. Strong, healthy soul-whispers are like that. They will not remain contained, at least not for long. They grow and grow, in great flutters, like a child growing and kicking inside a woman's belly. So, in our tale, they grow and grow—until one day they emerge . . . as bats.

Bats arose unbidden and unbridled in the writing of this tale. And, as we are two minds writing this tale, we are of two minds about them. What the young woman wants to fly out of her students' mouths, and her own, of course, is spirit; when bats issue forth instead, it could be because the woman's spirit, like a fallen angel, has gone over to the "dark side." From this perspective, bats are symbols of dark forces in our culture, the forces of ambiguous knowing. From another perspective, the bats emerge as messengers of the spirit. Messengers of the spirit are often like that; they come disguised, sometimes as something quite ominous; in this case, the bats flying from the young woman's mouth, while terrifying, give rise to the arrival of dusk, the swirling, inexplicable dawn of night, the enchantress moon, the deep knowing of the Woman-Self. Looked at this way, even the snakes in this story can be viewed as symbols of the life force and regeneration, which they are in many traditions. (In some Native American tribes, for example, poisonous snakes were regarded with great reverence, as potentially life-threatening spirits that also contained within them the power to create new life.)

Whatever the reading, the bats shock the woman to her senses. In an instant of eternal knowing, she understands: It is one thing to be appropriately cautious as one forages for survival in one's environment, to avoid walking into the jaws of one's predator, to avoid sacrificing one's career, as many women do in the academy. It is another to completely shed one's skin and become enveloped in the skin of an alien other, to hide in the rocks or slither along the ground (though, of course, that may be exactly what one needs to do before one is ready to come to one's senses and give birth to a new and different self).

The fact that students take no notice of what issues from their young professor's mouth is a sad commentary on how dead students can become in spirit-deprived classrooms. A lecture is a note is a bat *[sic]*; one is indistinguishable from another in the mind of a student who, without guidance, often remains scribbling frantically in emotional and intellectual darkness. Seeing where her actions have led for her students, the young woman recoils in horror.

She determines the route to her salvation: She will listen less to the whispers of others; she will listen more to the whispers of her own soul rattling her bones like wings against the open door of a cage. (Notice, though, that she does not stop listening altogether to the whispers of others; the whispers contain warnings, which women may need to heed.)

While listening to her bones, the young woman of our story comes to know that she is not meant to fit the traditional mold; she is meant to create a new one, and create it she does, recovering her ability to laugh and connect with others and releasing her own brilliant spirit. In doing so, she frees her own students to laugh and to fly, proving right those wise elders who have said that you can only take others as far as you have taken yourself.

* * *

This story obviously has a happy ending. The young woman salvages both spirit and position. Like the women of popular culture, she comes to have it all. While we like this ending to our story, it is important to point out that in real life, honoring one's soul does not always win a permanent place in the academy. Indeed, especially if one lacks the skills or support to explain oneself and to negotiate some kind of "fit" with the institution, honoring one's own voice can jeopardize the prized position one is seeking. That is a hard truth. It is one many of us don't wish to face. But it must be faced, and it must be understood. If we choose to follow our soul-path, if we choose intuition over the injunctions and advice of institution, we are choosing for our Self, first; our institution may or may not follow.

In fact, it is important to notice the paradox that the young woman in our current tale didn't get tenure until she had accepted the fact that earning tenure mattered less than honoring her soul. Only when she gave up needing a permanent place in the academy did she gain one. Only when the young woman spoke up for herself, after she discovered what her soul required to survive, was the wren-elder able to rise to her defense. Finally, only when the young woman was willing to risk losing her place in the institution was she able to write and teach from her deep-down place. Her life energy poured forth, and her work—propelled by that energy—glided across the canyons of the academy. Laughter, the wings that bear one soul to another, flew up and out of her heart, and the woman was free to teach her students and to love her partner without suffering and inflicting the suffering of a deadened spirit.

This particular version of the story ends happily because Julianne, an assistant professor at this writing, wanted to end it that way, and because Holly, an associate professor at this writing, was willing to rewrite an earlier version—one in which the young untenured woman fails to gain tenure in the university, though she does earn tenure with her soul.

For Holly, who has seen too many souls crumple in the academy in recent years, rewriting the tale was surprisingly healing, for it helped her to conjure up an old but discarded vision of the academy—a vision of people helping one another (and, of course, themselves) in a way that deeply honors and nurtures their unique, creative powers. Indeed, with her soul intact, and with profound gratitude to the wild and wise elder who told her to

follow her heart (but "know there may be consequences"), and to the other senior women (and men) who reassured her and helped her to explain and defend herself, she herself has been granted tenure at her university.

Julianne, who is also deeply grateful to those who have advised her, has not yet reached the tenure crossroads. But for the moment, she chooses to believe that her colleagues, as Holly's have done, will recognize and value the wildness she has brought forth, and invite her to join them in the Circle of Forever. Whatever happens, she has begun to know that she will survive, for her wings are flapping and her eagle-feet are dancing even as we speak.

Reference

Estés, C. P. (1992). *Women who run with the wolves: Myths and stories of the wild woman archetype.* New York: Ballantine.

18

Demonstrations in Intellectual Diversity
Applied Theory to Challenge Campus Press Hegemony

Mercedes Lynn de Uriarte

For all the modern communications technology and college-educated newsrooms, the essence of the personal often escapes that which is conveyed. We write in terms of what happens to others and overlook what happens close at hand. So it is on the University of Texas, Austin, campus, which found itself on the front pages of the *New York Times* just before spring commencement in 1995.

On May 18, that paper reported, "Segregation in Higher Education Persists, Study of 12 States Says." The Southern Education Foundation (1995), citing some of the na-

tion's top scholars and educators, found that most flagship universities in the South remain more than 89% white. The University of Texas is one of those institutions. Others include Alabama, Florida, Georgia, Kentucky, and Louisiana.

The findings provided no surprises for minority students and faculty. For most students, social and intellectual isolation shrouds the classrooms of these institutions. In the midst of traditional institutional bustle, there is a certain silence. "I look all around that first day of class," one black graduate student in journalism at the University of Texas said

EDITORS' NOTE: Raised in Mexico, the author is recognized as a Latina who has been, throughout her professional and academic life, a woman transforming communications. The reader will notice that throughout the chapter, the number of Latina students and Latina professionals appears to be quite small. de Uriarte points out that at last count there are 11 Latina and about 13 Latino journalism educators in the United States of whom very few are tenured. In the profession, only 3% of all journalists are Latinos.

to me recently upon reading the news report, "but I don't see anybody like me. And I don't hear anybody either in the assignments."

"To achieve equal representation of blacks among college graduates, each of the 12 states would have to more than double the number of black graduates. For Hispanic students the challenge is even greater," the Southern Education Foundation study said. Meanwhile, there is a pervasive silence, an oppressive silence.

"The study said that [41 years ago] society had promised equal access to institutions of higher education regardless of race but that not a single state 'can demonstrate an acceptable level of success' in reaching that goal" (Applebome, 1995, p. C18).

Texas is the third largest state in the nation, experiencing a significant growth surge in the 1980s that continues today. The state has the second-largest Latino and the third-largest black population among the 50 states. In the 1990s, three of every five new residents are black or Latino. Based on the health, education, and welfare of its children, the state of Texas ranks 28th according to studies by the Annie E. Casey Foundation (Southern Education Foundation, 1995).

The southern college lag affects national participation. The workplace, the political, judicial, educational arenas—all intellectual endeavors—are shaped by this absence. Media, including campus press, structures this absence. In 1992, almost 1 million whites received B.A.s. But only 72,326 blacks did; 40,761 Latinos and 46,720 Asian Americans also received undergraduate degrees. American Indians received only 5,176 B.A.s. The numbers narrow further in graduate education. Fewer than 18,200 African American students received M.A.s and only 1,106 received Ph.D.s in 1993 at U.S. universities, compared with 268,371 white M.A.s and 23,202 Ph.D.s. Latinos received only 9,358 M.A.s and 834 Ph.D.s. Asian Americans earn slightly more degrees in both categories than do Latinos. American Indians are most severely underrepresented (American Council on Education, 1995).

And these advanced degrees are not distributed across the fields. Except for Asian Americans, minorities are disproportionately grouped in education.

Despite these sobering figures, shortsighted arguments support genetic diversity only, without understanding the critical importance of intellectual diversity. Without arenas of community fostered by shared histories and experience, without the commonalty of popular culture, the solitary minority student in college and university classrooms is denied an academic dialogue of inclusion. Such situations also shortchange majority students. Lacking a comprehensive history past and present, they graduate as cultural illiterates. In that denial resides future problems for a population that will become evenly balanced between minority and majority populations within the next 30 to 50 years. Nevertheless, we remain a society resistant to preparation for change. The situation recalls the words of Mort Rosenblum (1981), former editor of the *International Tribune,* speaking about media: "Because of the system—and in spite of it—most Americans are out of touch with events that directly affect their lives" (p. 1). That observation might equally be made of universities, where curriculum and campus media ignore diversity.

Pervasive absence censors by omission. Communicators, those who work or who prepare others to work in the press, assume a special charge that requires willingness to uphold First Amendment guarantees extended—at least in theory—to everyone within U.S. borders. Freedom of expression requires access and inclusion. Absence in curriculum and media fosters environments of victimization—to say nothing of intellectual dishonesty. In communication studies, this silencing is often evident in theory as well as practice. The study of communication theory and methodology that excludes minority scholars, multicultural methodologies, deconstruction, and cross-cultural analysis produces intellectual segregation.

Minorities, especially those on major southern campuses, daily navigate through a system that excludes their peers, ignores their scholars, overlooks their history, and otherwise diminishes contributions of these populations across a continuum anchored in the pre-Columbian Americas.

This pattern of exclusion within communication education is a distortion of history as well; the first printing press in the Americas arrived in Peru in 1534. The earliest preserved example of reporting describes a 1541 storm and earthquake in Guatemala, written by Juan Rodriguez and published in Mexico City by Juan Pablos (Emery & Emery, 1984, p. 3). This nation also has a long history of the black and Latino press.

Journalism education fosters particularly troubling elements. First, it remains a segregated field with fewer than 3% tenured or tenure-track minority faculty. Further, in 1995, its largest organization of faculty and professionals, the Association for Education in Journalism and Mass Communication, had only about 100 minorities among its more than 2,500 members. Journalism classroom materials dealing with diversity are virtually nonexistent.

In terms of hegemony—the theory that describes a homogeneous perspective in the interest of the prevailing ideology that undergirds social institutions and the basis of governance—journalism education is a key cog, folklore of press freedom notwithstanding. The role of the press in service to hegemony acts as a *conveyor,* not a *setter,* of agenda. Too consistently those in power determine the agenda, from politicians to newsroom gatekeepers.[1] "Governments may deny it, but it is inevitably their expectation that the news media will play their role as agents of social control and support the government in carrying out its domestic and especially its foreign policies" (Altschull, 1995, p. 426).

As part of press culture, ethnocentricity remains one of its primary values (Gans, 1980, p. 42). Thus the further the event or individual is socially, culturally, racially, economically, or politically from mainstream America, the less likely to be covered in media. The news page, in other words, remains segregated—except in coverage of crime and other deviant behaviors.

> With some oversimplification, it would be fair to say that the news supports the social order of public, business and professional, upper-middle-class, middle-aged, and white male sectors of society . . . the news is generally supportive of governments and their agencies, private enterprise, the prestigious professions, and a variety of other national institutions, including the quality universities. (Gans, 1980, p. 61)

As press ownership compresses into increasingly huge monopolistic corporations, these values become both entrenched and expanded.

To the extent that journalism education prepares students to fit comfortably into the corporate press model by stressing routine over inquiry, consistency over exploration, conformity over originality, it colludes with the silencing that invariably occurs when diverse voice seeks expression. Moreover, absent minority scholarship, oppositional media analysis, and "Third World" perspective, students are socialized more than educated about the field. The most serious implication of this practice is the failure in this regard for journalism education to measure up to standards and ethics laid out by the 1944 Hutchins Commission, which explored the role of the press in a democracy, and the 1967 Kerner Commission, which explored the role of the press in race relations. The former, a group of 13 renowned scholars who spent two years in study and interviewed scores of journalists, politicians, and business leaders, set five standards that the public could expect from an ethical press:

1. a truthful, comprehensive, and intelligent account of the day's events in a context which gives them meaning;
2. a forum for the exchange of comment and criticism;
3. the projection of a representative picture of the constituent groups in the society;

4. the presentation and clarification of the goals and values of the society;
5. full access to the day's intelligence.

At the very least, a clear grasp of standards 1 and 3 are central to preparing students to cover the diverse America of the twenty-first century. But educators may also find other observations to be valuable.

The Hutchins Commission recommendations require the press to be inclusive, comprehensive, interactive, and representative. Their work, *A Free and Responsible Press,* rests within American traditional ideals of service and stewardship brought to the defense of the First Amendment:

> It goes without saying . . . the responsibilities of the owners and managers of the press to their consciences and [to] the common good for the formation of public opinion. . . . The relative power of the press carries with it relatively great obligations. (Commission on Freedom of the Press, 1947, pp. vi-vii)

Those obligations were to the society and its citizens.

The commission recognized that freedom of expression belongs to the people. In relation to media, this freedom is exercised through access to the press, which generates forums for debate that contribute to a refinement of ideas. At the same time, these white, Ivy League men acknowledged that there exists a potential that such expression would be blocked by media.

"The press is not free," they wrote, "if those who operate it behave as though their position conferred on them the privilege of being deaf to ideas which the processes of free speech have brought to public attention" (Commission on Freedom of the Press, 1947, p. 9).

Central to the commission's conclusions was a deep commitment to freedom of expression. Their report also reflects a firm respect for intellectual engagement.

Civilized society is a working system of ideas. It lives and changes by the consumption of ideas. Therefore it must make sure that as many as possible of the ideas which its members have are available for its examination. . . . Moreover, a significant innovation in the realm of ideas is likely to arouse resistance. Valuable ideas may be put forth first in forms that are crude, indefensible, or even dangerous. They need the chance to develop through free criticism as well as the chance to survive on the basis of their ultimate worth. Hence, the man who publishes ideas requires special protection. (p. 6)

The power of the press, thought the commissioners, made the press both endangered by those who would silence it to protect their own ambitions and opinions and dangerous to those who might be vulnerable to manipulation through the ideas and by the agendas of others.

"As freedom of the press is always in danger, so it is always dangerous. The freedom of the press illustrates the commonplace that if we are to live progressively we must live dangerously" (Commission on Freedom of the Press, 1947, p. 7).

The National Advisory Committee on Civil Disorders appointed by President Lyndon Baines Johnson after more than 100 violent race-related protests in 1967, and headed by then-governor of Illinois, Otis Kerner, became known as the Kerner Commission. In one of its major findings, the commission said:

> The news media have failed to analyze and report adequately on racial problems in the United States and, as a related matter, to meet the Negro's legitimate expectations in journalism. . . . the media report and write from the standpoint of a white man's world. (National Advisory Committee, 1968, p. 366)

Further, the commission said, "This may be understandable, but it is not excusable in an institution that has the mission to inform and educate the whole of our society" (p. 366).

This observation is certainly equally applicable to journalism education.

Because of these and other press failings, the commission concluded: "By failing to portray the Negro as a matter of routine and in the context of the total society, the news media have, we believe, contributed to the black-white schism in this country." That analysis can be equally applied to all minorities in the United States. Those who are about to become 50% of the total population of the nation remain virtually unknown to the other half of Americans.

Journalism educators clearly play a part in the diminished civic role of the press. The academy exercise appears to have grown distant from the social responsibility with which the press is charged and for which it is provided constitutional protection—that of informing the citizens in a democracy so that they might be better prepared for self-governance. Indeed, Keith Stamm (1985) points to direct links between relevant newspaper coverage and the socially and politically dynamic community. Beyond that, the absence of intellectual diversity directly affects the construction of consciousness in which media engage by the framing and packaging of its content. A white, male-dominant point of view still prevails—even in the traditional campus press.

Given the power of media to influence our perceptions of others and to define reality, members of the press should be educated to communicate with and about diversity. But too often that is not the case, despite accreditation standards that impose guidelines on educators (such as Standard 12, which addresses diversity) and current professional requirements anchored in the reality of diminishing newspaper circulation and television network audience. Journalism education remains minimally integrated, both intellectually and within its participant body of faculty, students, and administrators.

Although we tend to think of censorship as a process of silencing protected by the laws of an oppressive political system, actual informal systems of censorship function efficiently in other arenas. The end result is the same: Certain ideas are routinely eliminated from public discourse.

A clear pattern of censorship by omission exists across history in the United States. Minority voices, ideas, events, and issues seldom appear in the mainstream press. Any number of studies document that finding. So it is not surprising that the campus press, which seeks to emulate the mainstream models, reflects a similar absence of Latinos, African Americans, American Indians, and Asian Americans. The model is flawed.

> The dominant media constantly devalorize the lives of people of color while regarding Euro-American life as sacrosanct, as when massive fratricidal killing in Miami's inner city is seen as less serious than the murders of a few European tourists, or when the talismanic phrase "saving American lives" is invoked as a pretext for murderous incursions in Third World countries. (Shohat & Stam, 1994, p. 24)

So students, encouraged to follow traditional routines, are trained in discriminatory repetition.

Too frequently, students first bump into press shortcomings in the campus paper. Indeed, it can be argued that the level of professionalism evident in any campus media is a measurement of the intellectual vigor of that campus's journalism educators, whether or not there is a direct link between the department and the publication. Most reporters and editors on campus papers pass through at least several required journalism courses. The quality of their reporting about minority matters and individuals should be enhanced by courses that teach ethics and standards directly related to coverage of underrepresented groups, individuals, and ideas. Beginning with the Hutchins Commission, there is a history of ethical concerns about the coverage of minorities. An understanding of these established press standards should eliminate arguments about affirmative action and focus students on professionalism. This is critical to the evolution of both corporate and campus media. In both arenas, few minorities participate. Among mainstream print journalists, for instance, about 7% are African American, 2.3% are Latino, 1% are Asian American, and .03% are American Indian. In other words, U.S. newsrooms are white. Nevertheless, greater numbers alone do not ensure diversity. Diversity requires an intellectual expression as well.

Understanding how to shape an ethical press requires an ethno-inclusive curriculum across the disciplines. Intellectual tokenism that forces students to consider multiculturalism in one course in order to earn a degree affects a compartmentalization of reason that defeats cognitive development. In other words, intellectual inclusiveness should not be affected solely by the genetic pool of the participants.

Studies by journalism professors indicate that campus newsrooms claim only 10% minority participation. However, when campuses with very high minority enrollment are eliminated from consideration, the percentage drops dramatically. Absent minority voice, the campus press distributes silence. That silence makes the press susceptible to an arrogance of ignorance that distorts minority issues and events, which, in turn, devalues students of color.

This was the case at the University of Texas at Austin in 1987, when a series of coverage problems led first to meetings between minority organizations and editors of the *Daily Texan,* then to protests, forums, and confrontations. At the time, I was the only minority professor in the College of Communication, which houses the departments of advertising, journalism, radio-television-film, and speech. (Today, I am the senior minority professor in the College of Communication and in the Journalism Department, where I am also the senior female faculty member. Across the entire faculty population of more than 100, about a dozen are minorities, including three blacks.)

After months of frustrating meetings with *Daily Texan* editors, Latino undergraduates gave up efforts to encourage inclusive coverage. A delegation of representatives from 15 Latino student organizations asked me to serve as the faculty sponsor for a Latino student publication. I declined that request with a counteroffer to establish a classroom laboratory publication that would provide them course credit, minority voice, and quality journalism training. I admit to an ulterior motive. It was my intent to attract more minority students to print journalism and to provide them clips that would allow them to compete for scholarships, internships, and jobs. At that time, almost no UT minority students could do so.

The University of Texas Journalism Department recruited me as I was about to leave on a Fulbright to Peru, after eight years with the *Los Angeles Times* as an assistant editor of the Opinion section and as a staff writer. I was hired by the *Times* while working on my dissertation in American Studies at Yale University; I became the third Latino on a staff of more than 800 journalists at the paper. So I learned well the importance of diversity in the newsroom.

Because most minority students both draw financial aid and work, they do not have time for the long hours of unpaid newsroom involvement on student papers. On some campuses, those that can may be driven out by newsroom insensitivity—if not open hostility—to diversity. Moreover, definitions of newsworthiness that exclude minority events and issues—found in traditional newsroom environments—generate an unwelcoming situation. So, many campus papers have fewer minority staffers by the end of the academic year than at the start.

As a result of that discussion, *Tejas* was born. It was the first multicultural classroom laboratory publication in the nation produced in an accredited mainstream journalism department. From the start, the publication faced a lack of support from journalism faculty, which went so far as to deny the course the use of computer laboratory classrooms except on certain weekends, to fail to assign regular classrooms in which to hold class, and to withhold other routine assistance. The editors and writers confronted a significant amount of conservative student hostility, including organized attempts to have the course discontinued. These struggles were covered in the *Chronicle of Higher Education,* the *New York Times,* as well as the Austin *American-Statesman* and other Texas newspapers. *Tejas* owes its success to the courage of such early students as Prescilla Barrera, Louis Lopez, Laura Muñoz, Jorge Renaud, Marissa Silvera, and Enrique Torres and to their determination to add minority voice to campus discourse.

In establishing *Tejas,* I seized an opportunity for applied theory. Attractive (and obedient) in texts, the real challenge of theory rests in its real-world application. What happens to hegemony faced with active resistance? Can the Hutchins and Kerner Commissions' recommendations become newsroom guidelines? I also drew upon my decade of professional experience and my academic training in American Studies with a comparative focus on Latin America (interdisciplinary training in history, literature, and sociology)— and, of course, on my life experience as a Mexican American.

The success of *Tejas* is most directly related to the enthusiasm of the students who, faced with an opportunity to give voice to their own concerns, spent long hours working on stories and battling old equipment to produce a diverse news feature tabloid. The process, however, led to more than a publication. With their efforts came empowerment and a sense of community in an institution where the students said they felt marginalized. With story assignments, students became willing to ask questions of authority. Given an arena for voice, their leadership skills emerged. Prescilla Barrera, an assertive first female editor, was also the first Hispanic UT student ever selected in national competition to attend the six-week stu-

dent editors program at Poynter Institute for Media Studies. She became an advocate for educational programs in "at-risk" neighborhoods. As a teacher/administrator in these programs, she has taken groups of teenagers to educational conferences in the Northeast— despite a serious dislike of flying.

Laura Muñoz, who succeeded Barrera, left journalism to work at the University of California, Berkeley, while preparing for graduate school. She recently won a substantial cash award as most valuable employee of the year on the UCB campus. Marissa Silvera, whose investigative bent as an editor and reporter for *Tejas* emerged early, graduated as the Outstanding Journalism Graduate of 1991, with honors degrees in both Journalism and Latin American Studies. She now holds a sports writer position on a San Antonio paper, where she is currently also pursuing international stories.

These women and several other *Tejas* alumni maintain close ties. For example, last semester, *Tejas* reporter Stella Chavez was selected in this year's national competition as a participant in a monthlong investigative reporting seminar at Poynter Institute for Media Studies. The current graphic artist, Alana Taylor, was selected to attend the six-week art direction training program there.

Under the auspices of a professional colleague, Chuck Halloran, who has succeeded me as classroom laboratory teacher, *Tejas* has won several competitive national awards, including the prestigious R. F. Kennedy Memorial Award for Oustanding Journalism in 1996. But not before the tabloid served as a model for similar publications elsewhere, including the outstanding *Native Directions* by American Indian students in the journalism department at the University of North Dakota, directed by Lucy Ganje.

My intent in teaching J352 Community Journalism was to serve several purposes: to teach strong writing and editing skills, to provide minority voice, to provide perspectives that would energize the news scene, and to draw into journalism careers individuals who might never have considered the field. Simultaneously, it was intended to build community where leadership skills could emerge. To stimulate exploration of the press, Community Journalism is cross-listed in several departments.

Opportunities to acquire clips are critical if minorities are to make their way into the press. Without clips, students cannot easily compete for scholarships, internships, and jobs.

Five years later, I was asked to talk about the history of that publication for Latino Media Day Celebration, an event planned by the new dean of the College of Communication, Dr. Ellen Wartella. What follows is that retrospective.

In Celebration of *Tejas* History

Buenas noches. Good evening.

This is the sort of event that many minorities, myself included, approach with very mixed feelings. For *Latino USA,* which has national visibility and a significant award-winning track record already in its short history, and for Maria Martin,[2] who is responsible for journalism with substance—this kind of recognition is well deserved. My reactions are not an indication of anything less.

But celebrations are too often used to mask the realities of ongoing struggle—and many minorities grapple with uncomfortable feelings for very good reason when they find that despite their own sentiments they have been swept into them. On the one hand, everyone—including myself—loves a party. On the other hand, celebrations can be painful if celebrants collude in a denial of reality.

For a journalist, accuracy must remain a key measure of professionalism—reality checks are critically important. Minorities are historically asked to live, learn, and work in institutions that deny their reality, fail to teach everyone their history, dismiss their perspectives as "irrelevant." Celebrations that disconnect from those daily problems risk

becoming strictly symbolic—often disingenuous—events.

And one thing *Tejas* students learn is that journalism ethics require context. It is an important lesson—especially in this age of sensationalist tabloid journalism and soft "feel good" publications that avoid issues.

So in honor of the real heroes of *Tejas,* the students, and in honor of Demitrio Rodriguez,[3] who also knows struggle, a little reality.

First, let me clarify the publication's identity. Although *Tejas* began as a Latino publication, it quickly became a model of multiculturalism. We are pleased that its typical newsroom includes African Americans, Asian Americans, gays, international students, and Anglos.

Tejas was born as the result of a visit from 15 students representing almost as many Latino organizations on campus. For the previous two years, they had objected to racist coverage or to the total exclusion of minorities by the *Daily Texan.* There had been endless meetings with editors, arguments with reporters, all the usual "going through channels" behaviors. And then the *Daily Texan* distinguished itself by publishing a cartoon so racist that it drew protest from various newsrooms across the nation. In 1989, writers from the *Washington Post* used the cartoon at a national conference to illustrate the problem of racism in the college press.

The 15 students who visited me asked me to serve as their sponsor for a student publication. I declined to do that, but offered instead a class that would generate a publication of Latino voice, and teach them how to do real journalism in the process. Recruiting minorities to journalism has been the goal of every major journalism association in the nation since first called for by the American Society of Newspaper Editors in 1979. Still, fewer than 3% of all journalists are Latinos. Only about 7% are black, 1% are Asian American, and .03% are Native American. Historically, campus publications have not welcomed diversity. Today, fewer than 8% of all campus journalists are minorities, except at predominantly minority institutions.

There are only about two dozen full-time Latino journalism professors in the nation. Increasingly, a Ph.D. is required to teach journalism. UT's Journalism Department has never had a U.S. Latino Ph.D. student, and only two Mexican Ph.D. students in the seven years that I have taught here. Older professors tell me that they can remember no U.S. Latino Ph.D. graduate in journalism in the past 20 years.

Tejas is a diverse newsroom today—the goal newsroom of tomorrow. We have had African American editors and writers, Asian American editors, writers, and graphic artists, gay writers and editors. The content reflects that diversity. Although *Tejas* at first carried a logo reading "Serving the Latino Community," that was dropped as diversity expanded.

The real heroes of this evening are the Latino students of those early years who ignored all of the obstacles put in their paths to producing *Tejas*. These include a hostile department, which for several semesters "forgot" to assign the class a classroom, denied the class use of the labs delegated for teaching journalism, and referred publicly to *Tejas* work as inferior. For students to survive such unkindness requires a firm grasp on reality and on the worth of their own identities. To talk about less tonight would be to disrespect them and their history.

All work was first done on one old Mac computer in my office, which crashed regularly in protest to overuse. So, we soon developed a routine. Twice a semester, come Friday 5 p.m., we moved with our polished drafts into the College of Communication, for a nonstop weekend lab-use marathon at the only times we were allowed access to the labs. I brought huge Crock-Pots of homemade chili and stacks of fresh tortillas. Chuck Halloran, a professional journalist then working for Mayor Henry Cisneros, flew in as a volunteer assistant on a ticket provided by the UT Mexican American Studies Center, to help out for the weekend. We worked around the clock. Students sometimes slept with their

foreheads on the video monitor. But come Monday morning, only the lingering odor of chili in the department of journalism was evidence of another deadline met.

Those students—Luis Lopez, now an assistant district attorney in El Paso; Enrique Torres, who will become the legal advocate for Advocacy Incorporated in Farr, Texas, in June; Andrea Guerra, who recently graduated; Prescilla Barrera, who is now Coordinator and grant writer at the Austin Housing Authority Learning Centers; Arnoldo Montemayor, who uses his legal education as coordinator for the Historically Under Utilized Businesses of Texas seeking contracts from the Texas Natural Resource Commission; Greg Cancelada, back in graduate school after three years reporting on politics and economics in Mexico; Lane Navarez, who works and writes from Europe; Marissa Silvera, our Outstanding Journalism Graduate of 1991, already beginning to win awards as a journalist in California; Jorge Renaud, who used to come from his weekend job at the *Statesman* to work on *Tejas* deadlines; Danny Vargas, now the *Statesman* Round Rock bureau chief; Laura Muñoz, who works in administration at the University of California at Berkeley; and so many others—they are the heroes of change. Some of these individuals are here tonight.

Nor can we overlook Jose Luis Benavides, now a Ph.D. student in Radio, Film and TV, who has been the teaching assistant to this class for three years. He has been a linchpin and role model in the community that is the *Tejas* newsroom. Professor Chuck Halloran's efforts have been acknowledged in an award for Teaching Excellence.

It would be disrespectful to those early student efforts, to their legacy, and to their real courage to overlook their struggle or the fact that things have not yet changed significantly.

Let me share a tiny piece of that experience so that we might understand why I use the word *courage*. When the campus right wing organized to eliminate the class that taught *Tejas,* the students began to get threatening phone calls. The newspapers we put out in designated stands were immediately picked up and destroyed. And some of us got nasty anonymous cards and letters. Before I came to UT, I never got anonymous hate mail. I found my first one in my restricted-access faculty mailbox soon after I came here to teach in 1987. The second batch came three years later. Let me share two.

One that I received said: *"Tejas is no more and no less than a continuation of the Mexican enema that you and those like you, continue to give to the people who are not Mexican. Peace is not so sweet that we will pay for it with chains on our minds and our bodies."*

Another said: *"Chuck, I read that you are a consultant to Tejas. Scum has some purpose. Do you?"*

Receiving such messages gives even the most experienced adult something of a jolt. Imagine the effect on our young students who got similar messages in the mail and on their answering machines. But they kept on working, writing, editing—and sleeping deadline weekends in the college.

Tejas owes its survival to them and to a number of other worthy warriors:

• To Chuck Halloran, who now teaches the class.

• To Roxanne Evans, president of the local chapter and the National Association of Black Journalists, which challenged the accreditation of the UT Journalism Department, drew national attention to recalcitrant journalism departments here and elsewhere, and brought about a brief "honeymoon period" of *Tejas* support during which time we won the right to regular lab time and space. Evidence of that change is marked by the "new look" of *Tejas,* which began in 1991, when Professor Halloran took over the class while I spent a year on a residence fellowship in New York.

Tejas has gone on to win national awards for two consecutive years—a low-budget classroom laboratory newspaper competing against expensive glossy university publications.

• To former Dean Robert Jeffrey, who supported the idea of *Tejas* from the start, who provided me six years of moral support, mentoring, and encouragement, and who paid all minorities the courtesy of listening and of learning the history and the context of issues.

• To Maggie Balough, editor of the *Austin American-Statesman,* who has been a professional colleague and friend. Maggie and I began working on these issues when she moderated the 1989 campus debate, "The *Daily Texan,* Is It Meeting Our Needs?" She then moved those issues into her own newsroom. She was among the first editors in the nation to provide intensive diversity management and coverage training top-down to editors and writers. This is still rarely done, and she remains one of the only editors to maintain this training as an ongoing activity.

• To Dr. Gene Burd, who was the first professor to bring courses about minorities to the UT College of Communication more than 20 years ago. During that time, Gene started a course called J352 Community Journalism. It had not been taught in some years. But when the right wing tried to force suspension of *Tejas,* the University of Texas was able to designate it as a J352, because it met all of the requirements established so many years before by Dr. Burd.

You may ask, so why the details? Because the recovery of history is key to minority recognition and to the respect these populations have earned in this nation. A major distinction between a sincere commitment to diversity and a liberal knee-jerk reaction to political correctness is a knowledge of history.

The difference between equity and tokenism requires that action be taken within the context of history. Good journalism, ethical journalism is the first recording of solid history. It is key to ensuring that social justice is possible. It is a mark of respect for the journalism profession to reject the cosmetic in favor of accuracy with all its blemishes and complexities. History obscured or denied is a form of oppression. There is no more serious insult than to deny a people their history or to dismiss their reality as irrelevant.

I tell my students to beware the concept of "objectivity." Whenever anyone defines something as objective, all they have done is define their own parameters of bias. History provides context.

There is no intellectual growth in comfortable feelings of "objectivity." In any educational institution, intellectual comfort must be challenged. A solid knowledge of history is a critical underpinning to intellectual integrity.

Studies show that minority journalists leave publications that exclude or stereotype minority news. About 50% of all minority journalists leave the field within the first five years, largely because of this struggle. Indeed, one of our early *Tejas* editors, Prescilla Barrera, gave up ideas of joining the press after a summer internship at a newspaper in her own hometown, where she ran head-on into conflicts over minority coverage.

Today, more institutions of higher education are reviewing their curriculum to broaden its base by including the history and literature of *all* Americans. To do less is to insist that minorities collude in their own mistreatment. Journalism is often the first gatherer of these stories, the first teller of these tales. So covering underrepresented communities is critically important.

Among the first classes of *Tejas* students, some parents held second jobs as maintenance workers to help meet family expenses. So there has always been a particular warmth, camaraderie, and common language between *Tejas* students and the college maintenance crews—evident in the 5 p.m. exchanges when that crew comes to work. In the late hours as we worked on *Tejas,* we had an extended community throughout the building that we appreciated. This was especially the case in those early years before UT once again raised entrance SAT score levels, and eliminated students largely along class lines. This interaction between students and workers serves as an im-

portant reality check. It is this anchor in reality, this connection with the most eclipsed voices in the community, that *Tejas* strives to keep.

Assimilation has always been a one-way experience promoted as movement into a "better" society. Yet across this nation, business management and economic experts tell us that assimilation is now dysfunctional for a nation that must draw from diverse perspectives and talents to compete in a globalized world.

Affirmative action that does not bring about intellectual diversity is simply the current assimilation formula.

Because institutions often spend more effort on symbolic activities than on substantive change and behavior modification, many minorities, including those early *Tejas* heroes, view celebrations with skepticism unless they include the strategy of harnessing energy for real change efforts. So, I hope that this evening marks the lead paragraph of a story of substantive change in the arenas where we are empowered to make it.

¡Felicidades a mis compañeros de la prensa Latina aquí presente!

My strong admiration for the *Tejas* heroes.

I thank you all for listening to the history of *Tejas.*

Notes

1. This concept is discussed in the works of many media scholars including Herbert Altschull, Herbert Gans, Edward Herman and Noam Chomsky, Oscar Gandy, Antonio Gransci, Stuart Hall, Jesus Martin-Barbero, Armand Mattelart, Michelle Mattelart, Geoffrey Reeves, Herbert Schiller, and others.

2. Maria Martin is the executive producer of *Latino USA.*

3. Demitrio Rodriguez was responsible for filing *Demitrio Rodriguez/Edgewood Elementary School v. the State of Texas* seeking equity in educational funding.

References

Altschull, H. (1995). *Agents of power: The media and public policy.* New York: Longman.

American Council on Education. (1995). *Minorities in higher education.* Washington, DC: Author.

Applebome, P. (1995, May 18). Segregation in higher education persists, study of 12 states says. *New York Times,* pp. A1, C18.

Commission on Freedom of the Press. (1947). *A free and responsible press.* Chicago: Chicago University Press.

Emery, E., & Emery, M. (1984). *The press and America: An interpretive history of the mass media* (5th ed.). Englewood Cliffs, NJ: Prentice Hall.

Gans, H. (1980). *Deciding what's news.* New York: Vintage.

National Advisory Committee on Civil Disorders. (1968). *Report of the National Advisory Committee on Civil Disorders* (Advance copy of Government Printing Office report). New York: Bantam.

Rosenblum, M. (1981). *Coups & earthquakes: Reporting the world to America.* New York: Harper.

Shohat, E., & Stam, R. (1994). *Unthinking Eurocentrism: Multiculturalism and the media.* London: Routledge Kegan Paul.

Southern Education Foundation. (1995). *Redeeming the American promise: Report of the Panel on Educational Opportunity and Post Secondary Desegregation.* Atlanta, GA: Author.

Stamm, K. (1985). *Newspaper use and community ties.* Norwood, NJ: Ablex.

19

A Challenge to Traditional Media Technology in the Form of a Dialogue With an Absent Other

Sharon A. Russell

When I think about how classrooms are organized and especially how we learn about technology, I want to talk to my colleagues who teach, and ask them why they make the choices they do. If you are interested in what goes on in the classroom or if you are concerned about how traditional ways of thinking and acting are perpetuated, you may join me in these concerns. I imagine conversations I might have with my colleagues.

How can I show them the connections between what is taught and the way it is taught? What happens to the student who is worried about dealing with equipment? After

all, how many nonprofessionals can easily program their VCRs? I think many of my teacher colleagues have made contact with equipment part of an obscure world that you can enter only if you can "talk the talk." I can't teach you how to program a VCR in this piece, but I can suggest some reasons people may not be able to do it. Many of us are in the position to control the way we teach and are taught. If we learn together about alternatives, we can all challenge schools to reconsider what is being done to, not for and with, people.

I began to rethink my teaching when I started working in the Women's Studies pro-

AUTHOR'S NOTE: Many people have helped me arrive at the ideas presented in this chapter. Principal among them are the students and faculty of my seminar group in the Democracy and Diversity project at Indiana State University: Heather Claypool, Gary Daily, Richard Johnston, Howard Ishisaka, Terry O Connor, and Ann Rider. I first began to restructure my class after communicating with Susan Frykberg of the School of Communication, Simon Fraser University, Burnaby, British Columbia, who has in turn been influenced by Starhawk.

gram. Although the concept of a feminist method of teaching that transforms traditional classroom practice is usually accepted in Women's Studies programs and in courses taught by their faculty in other disciplines, teaching approaches that attempt to alter the power structures in other classrooms have not spread widely in the academy. Women's Studies courses try to recognize the diversity in the classroom in terms of gender, age, race, and/or sexual orientation, and explore methods of involving all of the students in the work of the class. Most of these classes are also concerned about how power operates in the class. No one group, no one person, should be allowed to dominate the class, but many people also think a democratic classroom should also involve the students in the decision-making process itself. Teachers discuss how power operates in the classroom and how in most classes the power structure of the class mirrors that of society as a whole.

Domination is not necessarily based on individual worth or skill. Those groups who are most comfortable with the power they have in the world outside of the classroom want to reproduce that world in the classroom.

Many Women's Studies classes begin by discussing how power is distributed in society and try to determine the equity of that distribution. We see most society organized in a top-down structure, or a kind of funnel, with a powerful figure (most often a white male) at the top. The people at the bottom of the funnel have no role in deciding how the organization of society should be structured. They participate in decision making only at the lowest level. They learn the only way to rise in the organization is to step over other people or become a member of a network of similar people who help each other rise.

In Women's Studies, we try to see if there are other ways we can work together without constantly competing and yet not favoring one group over another. We try to find ways to avoid repeating these oppressive power structures in the classroom. Some classes make rules to give everyone the chance to talk and have their opinion valued. Some teachers discuss their place in the power structure. They may decide not to use their title in the classroom. They may find ways to share more of the responsibility for the conduct of the class with the students.

I wondered if these methods could be applied to another area where I teach—film production. I have been working with some of these techniques in the classroom, and every semester I carry the experiment a little farther. I have tried to think of ways of discussing what I am doing with my colleagues and others. I see this piece as the beginning of that kind of dialogue with those of you who have not thought of how classrooms might be changed and those of my colleagues who don't know this kind of change is possible. As I share my ideas with them, you may think of how these techniques might work in areas other than the classroom. How did you approach learning to program your VCR or working out how to deal with your computer? Where do you enter in this dialogue?

Most faculty members are content to rely on traditional lecture structures where they stand up in front of the class and present all of the information to their students. Some may add the spice of the occasional group report as a gesture toward class interaction. Ironically, those subject areas that are the most advanced technologically often remain the most conservative in teaching methodology. Departments that offer radio/television/ film production courses seldom challenge traditional approaches to teaching subjects that involve an understanding of technology. These fields are also still largely dominated by male professors with few women faculty but an increasing number of female students.

Too often in production courses, interactive teaching is equated with hands-on use of equipment. But as we have learned from contact with Women's Studies teaching methods, the basic power structure in the classroom must be challenged. We need to raise questions about how use of equipment is taught and how technical definitions are presented. How does a fact become a fact? Why is it a fact? These are the kinds of questions we need to ask in courses with a high technological content. We need to develop approaches that challenge the status of facts by exploring definitions together.

Only if students start to learn to ask and answer questions on their own, not as the result of hearing definitions come down from on high that they must then parrot back, will they master the equipment and find new ways of using it. In this kind of classroom setting, they can also understand how the same structures that organize society construct technologies that reproduce those structures.

In traditional classes, much of the information is presented in a lecture format where students listen to definitions, observe the operation of the equipment, and then repeat the definitions in quizzes and use the equipment in a series of exercises. "Do you find this to be a pretty accurate picture of your class?" I ask my absent colleague. "Aside from the increasing concern about the long-term retention of lecture material, why should I question this approach?" the more aware professor might respond. The lecture that carefully explains the technology seems to be an efficient means of presenting such complex material. The teacher's explanation would seem to be the neatest solution to the pressures of providing all of the information in a content-driven course. Most of us honestly believe the students have to get through all of the material, and all of the content of a course must be covered, especially in programs where advanced skills build on basic classes. After all, this method would seem to have worked well for most of our graduates who have been placed successfully in the industry.

The first crack in this tradition-based pedagogy occurs if I ask whether all students come to these courses equally prepared. Again, concerned faculty will agree some students may exhibit a certain apprehension about technology. One colleague told the story of having to physically place a student's hands on a computer. But even given this recent

example, I am certain most teachers believe these differences among students aren't as much of a problem these days when so many students have families with camcorders, when students use computers. These students should be prepared to deal with this technology. Let's not worry about the obvious elements of class, gender, and race bias obvious in these assumptions. Well, only students whose parents or adult caregivers have reached a certain income level may have this equipment. Some parents may still believe women can't work computers or camcorders. My responding colleague may even concede the point about certain students having problems dealing with the equipment and tell me: I have developed techniques to deal with these problems. I try to be very gentle in introducing the equipment and allow for individual experience. Of course, dealing with certain students in a special way can also set up certain kinds of relationships in the classroom and reinforce race and gender stereotypes while assuming other members of the class have no problems. Remember, I add, assumptions about traditional (what we can also call patriarchal) power structures create untenable roles for all. But our real concern must be with how these assumptions prevent us from questioning our approach to the subject. Are we privileging certain approaches to learning about the equipment?

Our teaching actually isn't so monolithic, my colleague counters. The industry's always changing, and we deal with how to adapt to those changes. We show the students that some rules can be broken. We can talk about classical periods in television and film lighting and editing. Many media educators do present a kind of education of the painter approach to teaching, editing, and the construction of narratives: If a student first learns to draw in the traditional way, if this student learns the rules, then this student can advance to the point when a more fully developed aesthetic sensibility will suggest moments when this student can stray into the abstractions of modern art. But we don't want students to explore too far, you add. Just remember we're dealing with commercial forms; people still have to understand what the students are doing once they're out in the world. I have to give the class a couple of lectures about jump cuts (breaks in the action with no change in camera position to cover the break) and the 180-degree rule (a rule about how action should be covered to maintain screen direction) so they can communicate with their audiences.

I don't want to get into questions about creativity and how and why we begin to challenge tradition (another dialogue, certainly). But what about those students out there working on their first project struggling with the equipment and trying to remember what the teacher said about avoiding a jump cut? Are they reasoning through the rules and evaluating their relevance to their current situation? Most likely, they either blindly follow the rules or are confused and forget them. But those students who actually see the problems created by their errors have a much greater chance of understanding the need for the rules. They will also be relieved to learn there are ways to make the action flow more smoothly.

Much of what we teach in production classes is subject to natural laws that are not open to alternatives anyhow, you now counter. I have to present these laws to the students. The rules covering depth of field aren't open to discussion. But I am concerned: If we present the technology in such a monolithic manner, are we leading students to make certain assumptions about the physical world that only reinforce the patriarchy? If students learn our perfectly crafted definition of depth of field, they have assimilated more than just a string of words. They have also internalized the concept that a single definition exists for a complex concept and that only one definition is necessary to master the concept. Pedagogically we are promoting blind acceptance and patriarchally we are assenting to a single authority, a single voice as the source of knowledge.

Well, my definition is a little different than what they will find in their text, you suggest. Now they have to reconcile the differences between two authority figures, I suggest. Do you help them reconcile these two definitions, or do they have to decide whether to go with the teacher or the text? What might govern their choice; the text isn't giving the quiz or the grade. If we only give one definition or provide multiple sources of authority, why are we surprised when students can't identify slightly different expressions of the term on a quiz because it doesn't match the version in their memories.

What is your reason for giving a quiz, I further wonder. Do you give quizzes to force students to memorize the material or to master it? We're all hoping for that elusive mastery of the material. And we all want to catch the person who hasn't bothered to study. But what kind of attitude are we demonstrating toward the class when catching the bad student or forcing students to study is the major goal of one of our standard academic practices. If students only learn under the threat of the test, the final, and the pop quiz, how are they going to behave when they have to use this knowledge in their jobs? Maybe we need to analyze what we are asking them to learn and how we are presenting the material. Is it possible to make them understand why they need to learn something?

What about some of the larger questions suggested by the kinds of teaching methods we have been discussing? I have to cover the material so they will come out of my class with the knowledge they need to get jobs in the industry, you repeat. They're just going to have to get it. You raise some interesting points, but these students need direction. We can deal with these questions in courses that don't have to give them all of this useful information they'll need in their careers. Leaving aside the fact that the majority of students do not have production-related career goals, I wonder about the attitudes your approach reinforces for them. A methodology that has all information coming from either the professor or the text teaches students to look to authority for answers. They soon understand the best solution to a problem is to ask the teacher or look it up in the book. Because these sources also provide the answers on tests, they do trust the voice of authority and doubt other solutions that might occur outside these sources. They are lost when they encounter situations for which their sources offer no information; they rely on authority.

We are teaching not only a technology but also an attitude toward that technology that constantly reinforces the patriarchy as the correct source for information about that technology. On a practical level, we are promoting memorized solutions to a constantly changing industry and technology. On a theoretical level, we are telling students who are already colonized that the only way to achieve parity with the patriarchy is to blindly absorb its rules, when we all know those in power are the ones who have the confidence to challenge these rules. Doesn't the patriarchy promote these rules as a form of power?

Historically, those who have challenged the rules in the film industry have remained outside the existing power structure working in the independent or avant-garde cinema. In this system where power is so often equated with money, techniques developed by outsiders have been appropriated from time to time, but the outsider is only brought inside if there is a fit with patriarchal goals.

If we continue to teach technology in a traditional manner, we are complicit in promoting the hegemonic practice of the film and television industry. Our students may be able to find entry-level positions in these fields, but once in the door they will be subject to the patriarchal structures of these industries and will be trapped into reproducing these structures. Will revisioning the structure of the classroom smash this cycle? Probably not. But is there a chance for change? Maybe. There are many means of transforming a production class. Each teacher will have to work out her or his method. We must remember the old concept about real change

not occurring overnight. I have found in my own experience that change is constant experimentation in the classroom. There is no magic answer. We all have to fight through to our own level of comfort with these changes. I do know I have felt a tremendous sense of renewal, exhilaration, and excitement when I try new techniques in the classroom.

I don't want to reproduce the very structures I am critiquing by providing anyone with a plan. I would just like to suggest a few areas where my colleagues might consider beginning to change their approaches to the production class. For me, any change begins with the students. I am always open with them about not only what I am doing, which is different than the usual approach, but also why I am doing it a certain way. A wonderful experience recently occurred in my Basic Film Production class that illustrates what I mean. I have tried during a semester to suggest the difference in the various terms we encounter, the difference I have already suggested between convention and physical law. This year, I decided to apply a technique suggested by one of my colleagues and have the students self-grade the quiz over this material. I used a standard fill-in-the-blank format for the quiz. I have been giving slightly different versions of this same quiz for years.

Usually when I hand the quiz back after I grade it, a few members of the class question the answers when I give them the correct ones. I can see the reason for their answers and give them credit for a different answer. The next time I write the quiz I try to be more specific with the definition or statement that produced multiple answers, but there is always a chance for an unforeseen response when dealing with statements on such topics as editing terms (cross cut, angle-reverse angle, and so on). This time I had the class self-grade the quiz. Many more students suggested alternate answers because their responses had not already been declared by the voice of authority. Everyone in the class participated. Students had to justify their answers, and I asked the class to help decide if the answer was right or wrong. The class, with some suggestions from me, was also able to see those questions that had many different responses and those for which only a single word would work. We discussed why this pattern was occurring, and I finally felt they were really understanding the idea of the relationship between convention and physical law. A happy side effect of this process is that no one was angry with any decision I had made about whether or not to accept an answer. The range of scores was no different than in previous classes, but it will be interesting to see if there is a change in the range in future quizzes.

I have given an example of one small change I made. Those of you who do not teach should think about these approaches. What is happening in the classrooms in your community? How have you suffered from some of these traditional approaches? Can you help the educators in your community make some of these changes? If you work in a company, you might think of how a new person is introduced to a piece of equipment. What could you do to make that a more positive, less threatening situation? Have you made assumptions based on gender or other categories when dealing with equipment? On a more fundamental level, how have traditional teaching methods affected your attitudes? You can go back on your own, think about these techniques, and try them out in your own lives. Don't be afraid, get out the instruction manual and play with the equipment.

If you are an educator, you may have noticed I have referred to suggestions from colleagues in making changes. I would hope that none of you who want to experiment in the classroom have to do it alone. It is wonderful to have people to share your ideas and your successes and failures with. We are all still victims of the pedagogy of the patriarchy, and we need help from others to break through the isolation that is a result of the role of this structure in our academic lives. Don't think you must find someone in your own discipline or even your own campus. Many of the best ideas I have found have come through the Internet.

Change is never easy for any of us. I have tried to frame this piece as a discussion so we can all locate ourselves, our colleagues, and our associates along its continuum. For those of you who are farther along on the journey than I am, I hope to learn from you. I sit at home, isolated, working at my computer, but I am strengthened by the powerful force for change I sense in all of us. As you can see from the acknowledgments, all of this work is connected to experiments done by others. Although I have felt comfortable with alternative methods in my Women's Studies classes, or in classes that have comparable room for discussion and student interaction, I have only recently begun this transformation in courses not usually identified with these approaches. But the point is not that I feel better because I can translate my beliefs into action in all of my classes; such an action taken in isolation and with damage to the teaching of the subject would actually end up betraying my beliefs. The great revelation for me is that students actually learn differently, and that difference makes them better students, prepares them for a changing world, and allows them to see alternatives to the power structures that are omnipresent. Only when we all learn to question and see the possibility of alternative responses can we effect any transformation of the larger world.

20

The Rib Syndrome
Rebels, Servants, and Victims

Pamela J. Creedon

I have ridden in your cart, driver,
waved my nude arms at villages going by,
learning the last bright routes, survivor
where your flames still bite my thigh
and my ribs crack where your wheels wind.
A woman like that is not ashamed to die.
I have been her kind. (Sexton, 1960)*

Pulitzer prize-winning poet Anne Sexton often opened her readings with a three-stanza poem, titled "Her Kind," from her first book. The central character in the poem is a witch who speaks of her experience. The poem is often interpreted as a metaphor for the decline of a woman's power—from rebel, to servant, and finally to victim (Colburn, 1989).[1] In its first stanza, the witch takes the world as her own and haunts the air at will. In the second stanza, she is domesticated and settles into a cave, where she acquires worldly goods and cooks supper for creatures of the woods. In the final stanza reprinted above, she has become the battered, bruised, and broken victim of conformity.

When I originally agreed to write this chapter, I planned to describe the intersection of feminist and public relations theory. At the time, it seemed to me that feminist theory and public relations theory were two sides of the same coin. On the one side, public relations had become a predominantly female profession, giving feminists (a.k.a. rebels) like myself a way to channel energy inside the system. On the other side, feminist and public relations theory appeared to share a common goal: transforming the organization to serve the needs of community.

I thought I had a clear vision of how the two worldviews intersected because I had driven through—or ridden through—their intersection. I had spent 15 years as a public relations practitioner, and 10 as a public relations professor, where I had discovered feminist theory. So I presented a draft version as a conference paper last July. Returning to it several months later, however, I found my vision was fogged in with rhetoric. I had forced the two theoretical traditions together, supporting the idea of common goals with a plethora of references.

I completed three more drafts of the chapter, but none fit with what I was experiencing personally. Something about writing that chapter seemed threatening. It wasn't that the intersection had moved; rather, I had moved on. I had become an administrator, the director of a school of journalism and mass communications. I hadn't realized how profoundly the move had affected my vision and my voice.

Vision

Research tells us that much of our vision depends upon how the brain interprets visual information. It tells us that not everything we see reaches the brain for cognitive processing. No one knows, however, how much of what we see actually is stored somewhere in the brain ready to be processed when some emotional event triggers a synapse.

As I recall, I started wearing glasses in junior high. It was traumatic. Our family optometrist devastated me with the news that I would have to cover my eyes with glass every day. He told me in technical jargon that I had a distorted focal image that did not allow me to see distinctly at distances. He was correct. By the time my 11- or 12-year-old rebel child recognized a gendered world, I needed corrective lenses to bring it into focus.

My current eyes aren't any better either. My latest optometrist describes my vision as myopic and astigmatic. To comply with her diagnosis, I wear soft, extended wear, hydrophilic contact lenses through the day, and after I'm safe at home put on ultralight, plastic glasses, with lenses that still resemble the thick, opaque glass bottom of a Coke bottle.

My corrected vision allows me to do my duty, to serve a world that otherwise I would see as shortsighted and distorted.

Psychophysicists, scientists who attempt "to bridge the gap between the physics of light and the behavior of living organisms" (Sinclair, 1985, p. xvii), have spent a great deal of time researching vision and perception. They have made an interesting discovery.

Wild birds have acute vision and can see the stars, while domesticated birds can become nearsighted. Their discovery doesn't come as much of a shock. When puberty forced me to become domesticated in ways that I never imagined, I too lost sight of where I could go somewhere in the distance.

Increasingly of late, I find myself gazing at the world without corrective lenses. The gaze has an artistic dimension—a vaguely recognizable blur of shapes and colors resembling a Renoir or Monet. This uncorrected view of the world is also frightening. Although such fear stopped me in the past from walking down an unfamiliar street or from diving into a familiar body of water, naming it has fed my determination to regain my way of knowing.

Voice

My father suffocated from emphysema. My mother labors for breath in cold weather because she lost a lung to cancer. Regaining my voice in a family value system that taught me to avoid conflict and confrontation at all cost has not been easy.

Women gained a voice, the right to vote, when Edward Bernays, the double nephew of Sigmund Freud whom textbooks call the "father of modern public relations," first described the emergence of a new profession. He called it "counsel on public relations," which was designed "to meet the needs of an increasingly complex society" (Bernays, 1978, p. 15). Some 60 years later, women held the majority of public relations practitioners' jobs in the United States. In 1987, *Business Week* went so far as to warn that U.S. public relations was in danger of becoming the "Velvet Ghetto of affirmative action."

I entered the field in 1971, slightly ahead of the female equivalent of a tsunami, or tidal wave. A career in public relations appealed to me for several reasons. I liked to write, and writing was considered to be an essential skill. In journalism school, I had learned that I liked helping people communicate about their successes, their needs, and their desires. I wanted to help people get their needs met. I wanted to serve. In poet Sexton's chronology, I was entering my servant phase. In public relations, I could use my writing ability to serve the needs of an organization.

Today, public relations is growing exponentially in the global marketplace. Even countries with strict press controls and with rigid gender roles appear to be eager to communicate and present the "right" image. China, for example, reportedly has 500,000 students taking public relations courses at 400 universities (Chen, 1994). I spent several weeks in 1994 working with the United Arab Emirates University in the Middle East because the university's administration had decided to institute a public relations degree program for women only (Creedon, Al-Khaja, & Kruckeberg, 1995). The public relations program was one of five majors being added to the curriculum for women, who constituted 75% of entering freshmen. Not a surprise, the other majors were education, family studies, international relations, and social work.

Before I understood the organizational servitude aspect of the field, I thought that women's participation in the global growth of public relations might be an opportunity for redefining the nature of organizational communication and giving voice to those who have suffered in silence. Instead, the most obvious result of women's numerical presence has been a not-too-covert attempt by organizations to co-opt the four "Cs" ascribed to women in Western culture—that is, caring, cooperation, compromise, and communication. As a former employee communication specialist for a *Fortune* 100 corpo-

ration with 60,000 employees around the globe, I confess to writing copy for a value system that justified company cars as essential executive perks and considered child care a women's issue.

I don't think my brain cognitively processed this experience as servitude. I know I never openly voiced such an opinion, but I did decide to move on. I was hired as an assistant professor at a major U.S. public university in 1984. Not such a surprise, in feminist theory I began to find a rebel voice that I hadn't heard in a long time. The world started to make sense. Anne Wilson Schaef's (1981) book *Women's Reality* was a marker, as it has been for so many white, middle-class women like me. My own writing gave me a chance to explore this voice.

Adam's Rib

And the rib, which the Lord God had taken from the man, made he a woman, and brought her unto the man. And Adam said, This is now bone of my bones, and flesh of my flesh: she shall be called Woman, because she was taken out of Man. (Genesis 2:22-23)

For 2,000 years, the Hebrew creation myth in which Eve is created from Adam's rib—a useless, arched bone pulled from his chest cavity—has been used in various ways to justify women's second-class status as men's servants. Women throughout Western history have been barbecued by the mainstream interpretation of this anomalous account.

A woman in the colonial days, for example, who lived outside of a patriarchal family and did not conform to a masculine view of society, could be persecuted openly as a witch. The third stanza of Sexton's "Her Kind" describes a witch on her way to burn at the stake. Even Sexton, who committed suicide in 1974, was "burned" after her death by her psychotherapist Martin Orne. He violated her confidence and released 300 audiotapes to her biographer, which indicated that she was sexually abused as a child and attempted suicide numerous times (Middlebrook, 1991).

Battles over women's second-class status provided good story lines for Hollywood. I was only 2 years old when Spencer Tracy and Katharine Hepburn squared off in the courtroom in the 1949 movie *Adam's Rib*. Hepburn and Tracy played lawyers married to each other. Hepburn's character defends a woman accused of shooting her husband, portraying her as the symbol of downtrodden women everywhere (Rosen, 1973). When she wins the case, the loss humiliates the assistant district attorney, played by Tracy, who asks for a divorce.[2] Hepburn's character learns her lesson quickly. She must be punished for verbally beating up on her husband.

From the beginning of Christian time, women have found it necessary to present their arguments in terms that were acceptable to men. The more confident I became with my voice, however, the more I refused to pay homage to this maxim. In one instance, I found myself publicly confronting male colleagues who had no pangs of conscience about presenting a convention paper with my name on it as a coauthor, despite the fact that I had never read the completed manuscript. Ethical considerations aside, my concern centered on the fact that the use of my name implied a feminist endorsement of their findings on salary differences between male and female faculty.

In another instance, I challenged a program of research by two males on public relations practitioner roles, building on my career experience and the writings of other feminist scholars. I attempted to point out some of the myopia reflected in this large body of work (Creedon, 1993).

In this research program, females were described as predominantly filling a technician's role, while males filled the manager's shoes. Earlier feminist critiques had suggested that roles research dichotomized, homogenized, and trivialized practitioner roles (e.g., Creedon, 1991; Ferguson, 1987; Grunig, 1988; Rakow, 1986; Toth, 1989). I contended that the acceptance of societal values underlying

the roles should be questioned because, although American women have legal guarantees of career choice and mobility, such choice is gendered. Susan Kaufman (1992) calls it the holographic effect—three-dimensional images of happy, strong superwomen in the media who have free choice, who have it all, but who, when put under the lens of women's lived experience in American culture, look miserable and surreal and all but disappear.

The researchers responded by focusing on my concern over their choice of the term *technician*. I argued that using the term *technician* to describe the role of most women in public relations work was pejorative, akin to calling them housewives. It trivialized the myriad tasks performed in the role, such as its creative dimension and decision-making function. The male research team responded that my concern over the use of the term had "little to do with feminism" (Dozier & Broom, 1995, p. 21). The politics of naming, however, has long been a central area of concern in feminist scholarship. Dale Spender's (1985) classic *Man Made Language* explains:

> To live in the world, we must *name* it. Names are essential for the construction of reality for without a name it is difficult to accept the existence of an object, an event, a feeling. Naming is the means whereby we attempt to order and structure the chaos and flux of existence. . . . By assigning names we impose a pattern and meaning which allows us to manipulate the world. (p. 163, italics in original)

In response to my concerns, they used this analogy: "Studying the day-to-day tasks in caring for an infant does not trivialize or denigrate parenthood. Extending the same analogy, arguing that women should have the choice to work inside or outside of the home does not denigrate or trivialize motherhood" (Dozier & Broom, 1995, p. 20).

Why didn't they argue that men should have the same choices as women? Why did they present the idea of combining a career and family as an issue for women, rather than for men? Simply put, "They just don't get it." Paraphrasing Gloria Steinem (1994), they have for so long looked at their subject through male eyes that they need remedial vision, which, for women, would mean looking at the world as if women mattered, and for men, as if they were women (p. 14).

Specifically, their analogy did not acknowledge that choosing what has value is gendered. It did not address the gendered value system or infrasystem that makes choice a gendered issue. The infrasystem is a set of "institutional values and norms that determine an organization's behavior and its response to changes in its environment" (Creedon, 1993, p. 160).

The infrasystem is not an abstract academic concept. It is an effective system of controlling those who deviate too far from the norm. It affects women of various colors, classes, and orientations. It has been, and is, used to justify rape, domestic violence, sexual harassment, the glass ceiling, and pay inequity. Feminists watched in anguish as Anita Hill, Lani Guinier, and Joycelyn Elders were sacrificed for speaking truth from prominent political positions. We listened in disbelief as President Clinton retreated from a gay rights activist into the Whitewater rhetoric of "don't ask; don't tell."

Despite all this, I was encouraged because I had used my voice to expose a value system that cuts deep enough, and spreads wide enough, to be confused by some researchers with the laws of nature. Their response gave status to a feminist's voice, which challenged empirical data with statistical significance, by attempting to refute it in a journal article.

The Rib Syndrome

Eve, the rebel, who sought knowledge and food, may have been the first woman openly told that her life's role was to be a servant of man.[3] Ever since, pioneering women, who attempted to bite the apple of knowledge, or crack the rib of patriarchy, have fallen victim to the Rib Syndrome. The Rib Syndrome is, simply, *The Reason Why*. It's a pervasive virus with complicated, often undetectable, symptoms that infect every aspect of our lives. It destroys the living tissue in our bones and makes us vulnerable to osteoporosis. It explains why history books focus on the lives and wars of dead white men. It explains why the architectural wonders of the world are massive monuments to pharaohs, kings, and popes, rather than homes. It explains why intricate embroidery has little status in the art world. It explains why women earn 70 cents to a man's dollar. It explains why, in the United States, every 12 seconds a man beats up his current or former wife or girlfriend (Jones, 1994).

It explains why I'll never forget a confrontation with my dad. In my hometown of Mentor, Ohio, the Boy Scouts always marched at the front of the Memorial Day parade and the Girl Scouts brought up the rear. When I was 12 or so, I thought I could change the parade order. My dad, a highly decorated World War II Army veteran, had sole responsibility for deciding the order of march, so I asked him to let the Girl Scouts march at the front for a change. "No," he said, it could not, and would not, be done. The reason? "Because I said so, that's why." No two ways about it. Conversation concluded. Discussion over. There is a gender order and that's that.

"Because I said so, that's why." It's the most vivid recollection I have of being taught *The Reason Why* (TRW).

Today, I find contemporary "how-to" manuals for women attempting to climb the career ladder all infected with the "TRW" virus associated with the Rib Syndrome. Popular book titles for women aspiring to management positions, such as *Breaking With Tradition* (Schwartz, 1992) and *Breaking the Glass Ceiling* (Morrison, White, & Van Velsor, 1992), make it clear that women must be willing to break, crack, or sacrifice some part of their physical or psychic bodies to climb the ladder of success. Many women, myself included, survive these fractures by blurring—

not really seeing, not cognitively processing, not feeling—the injuries.

Instead, we drain our energy healing ourselves from bruises, broken bones, and internal injuries. It leaves us with little energy to begin the transformation of the organizational infrasystem built on the values of "competition, aggression, control, and rationality" (Rakow, 1992). Of course, as many feminists have reminded us, women do not "naturally, inevitably, or biologically, have the values of cooperation, nurturance and an ideology of communal good and egalitarianism" (Rakow, 1989, p. 293). Women can be as competitive as men, we just aren't socialized that way. I totally agree. To achieve positions of power, many women buy into gender-linked behaviors within the gendered value system. Many believe it's a survival technique.

Cracking the Rib Syndrome

I was struck by the "Garden of Eden" drawing that appeared on the cover of the spring 1990 issue of the *Gannett Center Journal* (now the *Freedom Forum's Media Studies Journal*). A journalist, a.k.a. Eve, naked, with long, wild hair and a naive facial expression, plucks the "apple" in the form of a press release from the serpent coiled around the tree.[4]

The journal's focus was on publicity and public relations as Original Sin. Extending this analogy, Eve takes the rap for moving public relations from its natural state to an evil force threatening humanity, much as she brings shame to our nakedness in the Bible story.

Feminists, however, have re-visioned Eve as a powerful and independent woman, who consciously chooses to take a bite from the apple in the Garden of Eden. Rather than serving as a cultural symbol for eating disorders, Eve is empowered.

The woman [Eve] is fully aware when she acts, her vision encompassing the gamut of life. She takes the fruit and she eats. The initiative and decision are hers alone. There is no consultation with her husband. She seeks neither his advice nor his permission. She acts independently. (Trible, 1979, p. 79)

Feminist scholars of the Gnostic Gospels offer even more powerful visions of Eve:

Eve, who has been told that she was created from a disposable part of the male body, touches the divine fruit and discovers the Mother Goddess. . . . Eve bites, she chews, she takes into herself that female creative power which has been left out of the Genesis story, except for the obscure symbol of the fruit tree. (Chernin, 1987, p. xix)

Feminists have reinvented an independent Eve. A creative Eve. A powerful Eve. An Eve that is no longer man's servant, or disobedient rebel. Is it possible that these visions of Eve suffer from a different strain of the Rib Syndrome virus? I'm not so sure that I still have the clear feminist vision of the transforming world about which I used to write.

When I read about an empowered Eve, I wax cynical. I too am no longer either rebel or servant. I direct a journalism and mass communications program with 800 students, 19 full-time faculty, and a budget of $1.7 million. I make decisions about how others will serve the general good. I influence what students learn. I allocate resources according to a sense of priority, a ranking, ultimately a hierarchy. I make choices between security and taking risks, between loyalty and self-development, between submission and personal power. I feel in control; I don't feel second class; and I feel that I am willingly and consciously playing the game.

By no means am I the first woman in journalism and mass communications administration. Ramona Rush pioneered in 1977 as the first dean of a college of communications in a major university. Yet without much hesitation, I could still probably name all of those who have survived, those who have been set up to fail, and those who have quit. A study in the early 1990s showed that about 11% of the deans, chairs, and directors of U.S. journalism and mass communications programs are women—a number that has increased at least a few percentage points since then (Kaufman, 1992).

Ramona Rush (1989) described an *intersection* as a crossroads "where a gender gap in values and modes of thinking has been revealed" (p. 8). I've reached that intersection with the conscious knowledge that fellow travelers—men and women, black and white, old and young, straight and gay—have equally significant destinations and reasons to be heading in differing directions. However, if I assume that everyone else at this intersection will act from a sense of public good or social responsibility, I'm likely to be no more than roadkill on the so-called information superhighway.[5]

Nor can I assume that females—as a sex, a gender, a sex role, or as situated knowledge—will give me the right of way.

> Intersections are inherently dangerous places. On the road, nasty collisions regularly happen at intersections. Different people heading in different directions with different purposes all attempt to pass through. . . . Stop signs, yield warnings, traffic lights, and protected turn lanes all tell us that when we enter an intersection we are not entering a natural place. (Wenner, 1993, p. 75)

When I started my job as director of the Kent State University School of Journalism and Mass Communication last August 1, the first graduate student that I met was editor of the *Daily Kent Stater,* the university's student paper. She stopped by the office to introduce herself and meet me. By the end of August, she had asked me to serve on her thesis committee. I knew her as a serious, responsible, quietly competent student.

I read her thesis proposal in October. We quibbled a bit over her use of masculine pronouns, so we talked a bit about feminism.

She defended it in December. In March, she collided with a tractor trailer at an intersection about three miles from the university. Her body had to be cut from the mangled car. Because her family was in another state and she had no roommate, the call to identify her body at the hospital morgue came to my office.

Another graduate student, who knew the victim very well, volunteered to go to the hospital morgue with me. However, a male faculty member intervened, and told the student that he would go instead because it would "be too much for her." As he spoke those words, I was looking directly at her, and I saw both her eyes turn white with fury. I felt weak; I did not countermand his directive.

When we returned, I sought her out to ask her what she felt when she was told that she could not go to the hospital. "I felt rage," she said.[6] I told her that I saw that rage in her eyes, but I did nothing. I apologized because I had done nothing. I had given control of the situation to my male colleague.

I'm still sorting out what happened to my emotions that day. I know I felt angry because my moment of indecision was seized by a patriarchal moment, an anachronistic moment of chivalry. My feminist sensibility told me that I had been victimized by the infrasystem. Yet, for some reason, I still don't feel right about standing this moment on end, critiquing it as a feminist issue. Rather than see it as a moment of victimization, my focus seems to be shifting.

From the beginning, something about writing this chapter has seemed threatening to me. I've spent the last 10 years of my life trying to discover myself apart from the woman I have presented to the world. I originally wanted to title the chapter, "Cracking the Rib Syndrome." I wanted to describe having reached the place where no one could make me submit to *The Reason Why.*

Instead, I've come to an intersection, which feels very unfamiliar and dangerous. I've lost the sense of chronology presented by Sexton's rebel, servant, and victim stanzas. I can experience all three separately, or in the same instant or instance. I can rebel and feel intense anger about constraints and inequities. I can serve an institution whose values I agree and disagree with. I can be victimized by the gendered infrasystem or by myself. I can feel powerful, insightful, and creative, as well as powerless, inept, and empty in the span of minutes. Perhaps I'm experiencing life as it is, not virtual or constructed; rather, seamless. Life in a seamless world may be making the distinctions, which have affected my vision and shaped my voice for nearly five decades, less important, while making my understanding of them more complex and diverse.

Notes

1. A biographer of Sexton saw the three stanzas as representing a witch (stanza one), a housewife (stanza two), and an adulteress (stanza three) (Middlebrook, 1991).

2. The movie has a "Hollywood" ending. Tracy and Hepburn reconcile the next day in their accountant's office and hurry off to a romantic weekend.

3. It appears that the Gnostic Gospels tell quite a different story of Eve (e.g., Chernin, 1987). However, the virus associated with the Rib Syndrome was not eradicated with the discovery and publishing of these suppressed texts.

4. It is interesting to note that the first woman mentioned in several public relations texts is Lady Godiva, whose nude horseback ride (c. 1040-1080) to convince her husband, the Earl of Coventry, to lower taxes on his subjects is characterized as a publicity stunt (Wilcox, Ault, & Agee, 1989, p. 36).

5. Linda Lazier must be credited with my first exposure to this extension of the intersection metaphor. She used the expression "roadkill on the information superhighway" to explain how a message was lost in cyberspace in an Internet message.

6. She has since left our graduate program.

References

Bernays, E. L. (1978, Spring). Defining public relations. *Public Relations Quarterly,* p. 15.

Chen, N. (1994). Public relations education in the People's Republic of China. *Journalism Educator, 49*(1), 14-22.

Chernin, K. (1987). *Reinventing Eve.* New York: Times Books.

Colburn, S. E. (1989). "This is my tale which I have told": Anne Sexton as storyteller. In L. Wagner-Martin (Ed.), *Critical essays on Anne Sexton* (pp. 166-177). Boston: G. K. Hall.

Creedon, P. J. (1991). Public relations and "women's work": Toward a feminist analysis of public relations roles. *Public Relations Research Annual, 3,* 67-84.

Creedon, P. J. (1993). Acknowledging the infrasystem: A critical feminist analysis of systems theory. *Public Relations Review, 19*(2), 157-166.

Creedon, P. J., Al-Khaja, M. A. W., & Kruckeberg, D. (1995). Women and public relations education and practice in the United Arab Emirates. *Public Relations Review, 21*(1), 59-76.

Dozier, D. M., & Broom, G. M. (1995). Evolution of the manager role in public relations practice. *Journal of Public Relations Research, 7*(1), 3-26.

Ferguson, M. A. (1987, May). *Utility of roles research to corporate communication: Power, leadership and decision making.* Paper presented at the International Communication Association, Montreal.

Grunig, L. A. (1988). A research agenda for women in public relations. *Public Relations Review, 14*(3), 48-57.

Jones, A. (1994, March 10). Crimes against women: Media part of the problem for masking violence in the language of love. *USA Today,* p. 9A.

Kaufman, S. J. (1992). *Developing administrative leadership among women in journalism and mass communication programs: A conceptual model.* Unpublished doctoral dissertation, Indiana State University, Terre Haute.

Middlebrook, D. W. (1991). *Anne Sexton: A biography.* Boston: Houghton Mifflin.

Morrison, A. M., White, R. P., & Van Velsor, E. (1992). *Breaking the glass ceiling.* Reading, MA: Addison-Wesley.

Rakow, L. F. (1986). Rethinking gender research in communication. *Journal of Communication, 36*(4), 11-26.

Rakow, L. F. (1989). From the feminization of public relations to the promise of feminism. In E. L. Toth & C. G. Cline (Eds.), *Beyond the velvet ghetto* (pp. 287-298). San Francisco: International Association of Business Communicators.

Rakow, L. F. (1992, May). *Public relations: Masculine or feminine talk?* Paper presented to the International Communication Association, Miami, FL.

Rosen, M. (1973). *Popcorn Venus.* New York: Avon.

Rush, R. (1989). Communications at the crossroads: The gender gap connection. In R. R. Rush & D. Allen (Eds.), *Communications at the crossroads: The gender gap connection* (pp. 3-19). Norwood, NJ: Ablex.

Schaef, A. W. (1981). *Women's reality.* New York: HarperCollins.

Schwartz, F. N. (1992). *Breaking with tradition.* New York: Time Warner.

Sexton, A. (1960). Her kind. In *Anne Sexton: To bedlam and part way back.* New York: Houghton Mifflin.

Sinclair, S. (1985). *How animals see.* London: Croom Helm.

Spender, D. (1985). *Man made language* (2nd ed.). London: Routledge Kegan Paul.

Steinem, G. (1994). *Moving beyond words.* New York: Simon & Schuster.

Toth, E. L. (1989). Whose freedom and equity in public relations? The gender balance argument. *Mass Communication Review, 16*(1-2), 70-76.

Trible, P. (1979). Eve and Adam: Genesis 2-3 reread. In C. P. Christ & J. Plaskow (Eds.), *Womanspirit rising: A feminist reader in religion* (pp. 74-83). San Francisco: Harper.

The velvet ghetto of affirmative action. (1987, May 8). *Business Week,* p. 122.

Wenner, L. A. (1993). Intersections as dangerous places: Theories and role models in sports studies. *Journal of Sport and Social Issues, 17*(2), 75-76.

Wilcox, D. L., Ault, P. H., & Agee, W. K. (1989). *Public relations: Strategies and tactics* (2nd ed.). New York: Harper & Row.

PART
III

Transformative
Communications

21

The Birth, Success, Death, and Lasting Influence of a Feminist Periodical
New Directions for Women (1972-1993-?)

Paula Kassell[1]

The whole idea for starting *New Directions for Women* in New Jersey grew out of a conference of the same name in the spring of 1971, sponsored by a coalition of women's rights groups in New Jersey. The proceeds of the conference ($240) were dedicated to starting a newspaper to "keep communicating" with the 300 women who had attended and to reach other potential feminists. Formerly a social worker and then a technical editor at Bell Telephone Laboratories, I was appointed editor and launched the publication with a volunteer staff in my Dover, New Jersey, home, working in two bedrooms furnished as offices and pasting up the newspaper on the dining room table.

The first issue, the first statewide feminist periodical in the United States, came out in January 1972. Consisting of 14 mimeographed pages with a cartoon, it had a press run of 2,000 and was distributed, in addition to the feminist groups, to the presidents of as many different types of women's clubs in the state whose names we could get.

That first issue was very well received and highly praised. And we thought we would just have to sit back and the subscriptions would come rolling in—that anybody reading it would be inspired to write us a check for $3 for a year's subscription. But unfortunately, only 85 people were so inspired. (As we learned later, 4.25% actually was a respectable return.)

And it never even occurred to us that we should have an aggressive circulation promotion policy. We talked about getting advertising for future issues without knowing how to go about it.

So, although we were supposed to be a quarterly, eight months went by before the idea came to me that would get us enough money to put out another issue.

I began to see that if real changes were ever to take place, the women's movement would have to back up into the school system with a vigorous attack on the way schools were shunting girls into certain occupations and boys into others, starting in the very early grades. We decided to put out an education issue in the fall of 1972 and distribute it free at the state teachers' convention to push the idea of equality in vocational education.

It was this burning desire to communicate our story to thousands of people that gave us our handle, both on increasing circulation and on selling advertising. It suddenly came as a flash of inspiration that these two elements had to go together, that because we were distributing to teachers, librarians, and library users, we had an ideal audience for book publishers. From this narrow base, we were able to put together several hundred dollars worth of advertising from book publishers and a few feminist businesses.

We published an eight-page typeset tabloid with pictures, ordered a press run of 53,000, trucked it down to Atlantic City, and ended up with a deficit of only about $140.

The next issue, Winter 1973, was then created on the same principle. A special issue on employment and child care, we arranged to distribute it free to all members of the American Association of University Women (AAUW) and the Business and Professional Women (BPW) in the state and the personnel managers of all the New Jersey companies employing 500 or more, a total of about 350 companies. This time, we were able to sell several hundred dollars more in advertising than the previous issue, and this distribution increased our subscriber list severalfold.

By 1975, we felt restricted in scope and potential subscribers by our statewide status, and decided to go national in coverage and circulation. We dropped "in New Jersey" from our logo. And with the Winter 1979-1980 issue, we moved up to a bimonthly schedule after six years as a quarterly.

Our idealism was the secret of our success. *New Directions for Women* and all periodicals are always faced with two questions: Whom do we reach? What do they want to know? The marketplace gives one answer, of course—the only answer sought by periodicals whose purpose is to make money. But *New Directions for Women* was organized as a nonprofit corporation run by an unpaid board of trustees. It always had to be operated in a businesslike manner—subscriptions and advertising space had to be sold or the bills would not be paid and the venture would fail and disappear. But earnings and contributions were devoted solely to carrying out its ambitious objectives. Here is the "Statement of Purpose" published in the Fall 1972 issue:

> *New Directions for Women* is a consciousness-raising organ published to inform women about equal rights.
>
> *New Directions for Women* is directed to all women, not just feminists.
>
> It is filled with hard news and reports on the issues that concern women rarely found in the standard press.
>
> It is written to energize women to take action to advance their position.
>
> *New Directions for Women* believes that when women understand sex discrimination, they will reach for the tools to combat it.

The key to the whole operation is to be found in the second paragraph of the "Statement of Purpose": "*New Directions for Women* is directed to all women, not just to feminists." We always tried to reach women who did not yet quite understand the feminist movement, a lack of understanding that often led to fear.

Since its beginning in the mid-1960s, the feminist movement has suffered from inadequate and inaccurate reporting and false interpretation by the standard media. The first and most notorious instance was the report that bras were burned in a demonstration at a Miss America contest in 1968. This episode *never took place,* yet feminists are still trying to live down the epithet "bra burner." The important reason for the action that *did* take place: Girdles, bras, and lipsticks were tossed in a barrel as symbols of the unnatural distortions of body, face, and mind that constrict women.

Page after page could be filled with further examples of inept or distorting coverage (or noncoverage) of women's events and issues in books, newspapers, magazines, radio, and TV—and perhaps especially in advertising.

New Directions for Women was founded because constant, accurate, in-depth coverage of the issues as they surface and develop is possible only in a woman-run publication; our activism and contacts with feminists and feminist groups throughout the country enabled us to scoop the mainstream press time after time.

An excerpt from a successful subscription promotion letter of the mid-1970s tells the heartwarming story of our inspiration and devotion:

RECIPE [by Brenda Turner]

1 cup crushed ego
1 teaspoon job discrimination
¼ teaspoon chauvinism
1 well-beaten path to the washing machine
½ teaspoon grated nerves
1 pinch from a man in the street
1 dash from the dentist to the babysitter
    Mix all ingredients, one on top of the other, and stir violently. Cook until you feel a slow burn and add one last straw.
    Serves: 53 percent of the population

Women are becoming aware of the ingredients that make up their daily lives, and many questions are rising to the surface.

The staff of *New Directions for Women* is dedicated to finding some answers and creating a newspaper that will affect every woman who reads it. . . . That is why we are trying to reach the woman who recognizes herself as a person,

with her own rights even though she may have heavy responsibilities for others.

New Directions for Women, a nonprofit organization, is funded by subscriptions, advertising, a federal grant, and donations from feminist groups and individuals who want news about the women's movement to reach more women.

Of course, we rely heavily on advertisements, but we do have a firm policy to never accept one that we do not believe would be of positive value to our readers.

Most of our staff are volunteers: teachers, homemakers, lawyers, politicians, and secretaries, who joined us after reading *New Directions for Women.* Many are professional writers or artists who donate their work to us because they know they are helping other women.

The unusual dedication of the staff is one of the reasons why our subscribers feel a personal relationship with the women whose words they are reading.

We are reaching intelligent, concerned, involved women. A survey of our readers indicates that 79 percent are college educated, and 60 percent of these have continued their schooling in postgraduate work. 66 percent of our readers are employed full- or part-time. 49 percent are married.

In the survey our readers most often voted for our articles about Legal Rights, Job Opportunities, Legislation, and New Life Styles.

We are not afraid to publish articles on controversial subjects . . .

"Volunteerism—The Still Sizzling Bomb." The debates and demerits of volunteering, and the difference between unpaid work that is "service-oriented" and "change-directed."

"Conference MDs Equate Menopause With Sickness." A report on the meeting that prompted our series on the menopause.

"How to Say No to a Rapist." There are two schools of thought: some believe a woman should resist violently; others say a woman must try to appease a rapist.

In the very first issue (January 1972), we reviewed 1971 rulings about abortion in New Jersey, and told of President Richard Nixon's veto of a comprehensive child care bill that had passed both houses of Congress after much lobbying by women's groups (to this day, 23 years later, Congress has not passed another). The Spring and Summer 1993 issues carried helpful articles about divorce and alimony written by an attorney. Coverage of domestic violence started in 1976. Almost every issue from the beginning delineated the pervasive discrimination against women in employment but stressed earning money and getting ahead as the basis of women's liberation. Not forgetting the housewife, the Winter 1973 issue assessed her economic value in view of the 12 jobs she filled, which came to $1,000 per month in 1972 dollars for the more than 28 million working at the job.

Throughout its life, the paper acted as a consciousness-raising conduit to the women's movement, covering the issues, always giving names and addresses of organizations to help women get involved and become activists. At the same time, every issue had helpful information about personal problems—alcoholism starting in the Spring 1973 issue, sexual harassment as early as the Spring 1979 issue, questioning estrogen use in Summer 1974. Older women were given regular coverage starting with the Winter 1974 issue, and in 1978, *Prime Time,* a newsletter for older women, was absorbed by *New Directions for Women,* and coverage of aging and ageism was increased.

The women who managed and wrote for the paper through the years were as varied as the people who read it, most strikingly in the age range—from the teens through the seventies. Many of the writers and staff gained professional stature and self-confidence. Learning to put out the paper was a growth experience no matter what the age or background. It would be safe to say that no woman who gave herself to the venture was untouched by the experience.

The same could be said for hundreds, perhaps thousands, of *New Directions for Women* readers, judging by the flood of letters they sent throughout the years: "My feelings about myself have changed since I've read this paper." "Your paper has been most helpful to me in determining my future goals in life." "After reading your publication, I am sure I will find a way I might be able to assist in the efforts of other women." This letter illustrates the conduit to activism at work.

Now that I've painted that rosy picture, I must admit there are two very serious flaws in it.

We survived only because, through most of our years, the staff was almost entirely unpaid, and all the writers gave us their work free, even some professionals. They worked for *New Directions for Women* for nothing because of their strong convictions of its importance to the women's movement. But their paid work took precedence regardless of our deadlines. We had to increase our budget severalfold to pay for staff work, pay our reporters, and pay for creative work (verse, cartoons, drawings, and photographs).

The financial problem was tied in closely with our other major difficulty. Among the hundreds of women who have written or worked for *New Directions for Women,* hardly anyone aside from myself took responsibility for the business side of the publication, the areas usually under the jurisdiction of the publisher rather than the editor.

Recognizing the imperative for women to face and learn to operate in the business world, in 1976 *New Directions for Women* organized a conference, "New Directions for Women in the Media: How to Market Your Executive Talents and Your Writings in Books, Newspapers and Magazines." This conference also featured presentation to five women of the *"New Directions for Women* Positive Image of Women Award" and presentations of awards to the winners of our first essay contest,[2] "A High School Student Looks at Equal Rights for Women."

We tried to use the media conference to recruit women to help on our business side, but this did not work out.

In spite of our business-side staffing problem, in its first few years the publication expanded in size, reaching 20 pages by November 1975. The size of each issue depended on the advertising space sold; the printing bill for each issue was covered by its ad revenue. Because paid subscribers now numbered in the thousands, and tens of thousands of copies of each issue were distributed free for circulation promotion, the ad rate was raised to $400 per page.

Our ad rate structure was unusual, devised in 1972 by my son, who was in advertising. On the assumption that most of the ad spaces we sold would probably be 8 column inches or less, we needed to promote maximum revenue from small ads. So, rather than the usual flat rate per column inch, it was based on a sliding scale (the larger the ad, the lower the rate per inch). Advice from a woman buying advertising space for a major book publisher suggested a salable price for a typical book ad in a periodical such as ours, and the rates above and below were extrapolated from that marker. Prices ranged from the minimum size offered (2 column inches) for $30 to a full page (a total of 80 column inches) for $320. My knowledgeable son's theory proved to be correct, and the sliding scale was retained as the full-page rate was raised:

- to $400 per page in 1975 (circulation promised: 30,000, except education and book issue: 50,000)
- to $500 per page in 1976 (same circulation figures)
- to $550 in 1987 (circulation promised: 55,000)
- to $600 in 1991 (circulation promised: 65,000)
- to $675 in 1992 (same circulation figure)

Subscription rate changes were much more modest to keep the paper as affordable as possible. When we published our first issue in 1972, *New Directions for Women* (then a quarterly) was $3 per year. In 1977, we increased the price to $4 per year, or $1 per issue. When we went bimonthly in 1980, our annual rate went to $6, the price per issue remaining $1. Because of skyrocketing increases in the costs of doing business (printing, postage, mailing services), we raised the subscription rate to $10 per year in 1982. Starting to pay the staff in the mid-1980s increased the budget by $1,000 an issue, and the subscription price was raised to $12 per year in 1989. In the late 1980s, we started to pay writers (who got two cents a word), artists, and photographers, and in 1993 the subscription rate was raised to $16.

During the seven years that *New Directions for Women* was published in my home, I employed one paid clerk-typist, half-time. Late in 1975, we obtained a federal Comprehensive Education and Training Act (CETA) grant administered by the county for one full-time employee, salary and payroll taxes paid. We contracted to train a woman in the business side of publication and put the new staff member to work soliciting advertising and writing subscription and renewal letters. Because so much of the work involved book advertising, at the end of the grant period, she found a responsible supervisory position in the advertising/publicity department of a book publisher.

By 1977, I was suffering from a painful muscle spasm in my back, diagnosed as due to tension, and could no longer take responsibility for editing and publishing the paper. The offices were moved to rented quarters in Westwood, New Jersey, initially set up with borrowed card tables and chairs. Several volunteers who lived nearby agreed to run the paper cooperatively. Decisions were made by an editorial board and a board of trustees. I remained a member of both boards and continued to write for the paper. By 1978, after some of the women started full- or part-time paid employment, Vivian Scheinmann was appointed managing editor, with overall responsibility for both the business and the editorial aspects. Scheinmann had a Masters in Library Service from Columbia University and administrative business experience. She had been children's book editor and then book editor of *New Directions for Women*.

"In retrospect," Scheinmann says, "we were very courageous, considering we were working with an unsalaried staff and with minimal advertising. However, the consensus was that we had to grow or we would stagnate; we knew we would also have to expand our coverage and proceed to a bimonthly publishing schedule." (January-February 1980 was the first bimonthly issue.)

At the time of the move, the paper had about 8,000 paid subscribers—one third on the East Coast, one third on the West Coast, and the rest scattered across the country in every state. It was also sold in feminist bookstores.

Additional CETA grants were obtained through 1980 to train five minority women and displaced homemakers in the publishing business. One was responsible for subscription records; one learned to sell advertising space and greatly improved the revenue; one was office manager; a fourth did clerical work; and the fifth learned to be the bookkeeper. The subscription base and readership grew as the CETA staff applied themselves to succeeding in their individual goals and in those we had set for the paper. When the CETA grants ended, three of the employees found jobs in the private sector doing work for which we had trained them, and two became paid employees of *New Directions for Women.*

Vivian Scheinmann expended much time and effort to find new grant money. The stumbling block was that most foundations did not fund periodicals as a matter of policy. When she put together the training of women along with the expansion of *New Directions for Women* as a tool for education, however, the Ford Foundation approved a three-year grant totaling about $60,000. It was for a subscription campaign among minority women and to strengthen our financial position. Using the grant, the publication was sent free to women in prisons and mental institutions as well as to university women's centers and women's clinics.

During Scheinmann's regime, a successful contribution campaign was carried on through ads in the paper requesting tax-deductible donations. A number of premiums were pictured: a see-through bubble umbrella with the *New Directions for Women* logo for a $25 contribution, a canvas tote bag with the logo for $35, a pen on a marble stand engraved with either the logo or the donor's name for $50, a zippered leather case with 10 carpentry tools and the logo for $100, and a collapsible director's chair with steel frame and canvas seat and back for $500.

For the January-February 1982 issue, the trustees revised the "Statement of Purpose" to reflect the coming of age of the Second Wave of the feminist movement:

> *New Directions for Women* is committed to publishing the many voices of feminism. We believe the diversity of the women's movement must be seen as one of its strengths.
>
> *New Directions for Women* is a national feminist periodical written for feminists and committed to reaching out to those not yet dedicated to a feminist future.
>
> *New Directions for Women* believes when we understand the pervasive force of sexism, we will act to effect change.

In addition to a strong book review section for adults', children's, and young adults' books and broad coverage of women in the arts, the paper covered, among other feminist issues, child abuse, domestic violence, prostitution, rape, homophobia, sexuality, politics, and local and national feminist actions and events. Columns took up health, legal, employment, and tax issues affecting women.

Although it always provided a feminist perspective, the paper was never allied with any particular group within the women's movement and sought to offer a broad spectrum of opinion, particularly on controversial issues such as pornography.

In 1983, Vivian Scheinmann left the paper to open a feminist bookstore with Pamela Sheldrick, who had been doing *New Directions*'s layout for several years. The paper moved its offices to an old building in Englewood, New Jersey, renovated for the Women's

Rights Information Center of Bergen County. Phyllis Kriegel, a graduate of the women's history program at Sarah Lawrence College, became managing editor. According to Kriegel, when she took over, the publication had an annual budget of $43,000 compared with an annual budget of $157,000 in its final year. The increase reflected Kriegel's decisions to compensate staff members and contributors.

"We started to pay the staff in the mid-1980s, and in the late 1980s we started to pay writers (who got two cents a word), artists and photographers," she said in an interview in 1995. Although no one was ever employed more than part-time, "we were paying out an added cost of $1,000 per issue," she said. "We felt we could no longer ask women to be volunteers on a continuing basis. The times had changed. A lot of good writers we wanted wanted a token that they were professionals, and we honored that," she explained.

Even though articles were written by professionals, "we were careful to make the copy tight and lively," Kriegel commented. Unlike some other feminist newspapers that run submissions word for word, "we felt we had a literary and grammatical standard. We cared passionately about writing and how it sounded."

Kriegel said she contributed her own funds to hire a staff and to "help leverage other funds." Some years, she said, she gave a "significant amount—$25,000 to $30,000. It was my life and I was delighted that I could do it."

By 1993, *New Directions for Women* had a readership of some 65,000 (a combination of paid and free distribution) and was a nationally and internationally recognized and respected agent of social change. Its size had grown to between 44 and 48 pages, with up-to-date style and professional design and layout by computer. This was accomplished, in part, by grants from the Ms. Foundation for Education and Communication, the Funding Exchange, ADCO Foundation, the Sophia Fund, North Star, the Foundation for a Compassionate Society, and the Harbach Foun-

dation. But grants were sporadic and small. "A $2,000 to $3,000 grant for us was handsome," Kriegel said.

One gift was more substantial. *New Directions for Women* was distributed internationally starting in 1989-1990 through a $30,000 grant for two years from Genevieve Vaughan, a philanthropist. The grant financed an international pull-out section called "Country of Women" that ran for three years and included material from a women's newspaper in Italy on feminist conferences in Europe. The section featured a quotation from Virginia Woolf: "As a woman I have no country. As a woman I want no country. As a woman my country is the whole world." *New Directions for Women* had a correspondent in eastern Europe at the time of the collapse of communism reporting on its effects on women.

A "Twentieth Anniversary Benefit Concert" was produced in 1991 at Steinway Hall in New York City. The Mannes Trio (the all-woman trio in residence at the Mannes College of Music) donated its services for an evening of classical "Music by Great Women Composers." After expenses, which were largely donated, the concert added $2,250 to the paper's coffers.

Under Kriegel's leadership, *New Directions for Women* ran a valuable intern/co-op program, drawing students of diverse backgrounds from many colleges and universities who were then trained and supervised by staff. The program was valuable to the paper, to the students, and to the community. Many of the interns went on to work for social change in the Peace Corps, politics, religious organizations, city government, hospitals, and clinics as well as in journalism with mainstream magazines, newspapers, and publishing houses.

Beset by rising production costs and falling subscriptions, which had declined to about 3,500, *New Directions for Women* was forced to fold with the September-October 1993 issue. (Subscription fulfillment was taken over by another fine feminist periodical, *On the Issues*.) The subscription price, held at

$10 for most of Kriegel's tenure, was $16 a year at the time publication ceased. Kriegel, who had prepared a business plan at the request of a woman's foundation, decided to end the operation, which advertised a total circulation of 65,000 (because of free distribution) after she failed to get expected funding.

Under Kriegel's leadership, the paper stressed more investigative journalism. "We were far ahead of other publications," Kriegel feels. "We had a wonderful issue on women in prisons in the early 1990s. We were the ones telling the story of the grassroots woman's movement at a time when people said it was dead. We tackled what feminist think tanks say about feminists. We wrote about women's funding sources, social change, women's health, women losing their children. That was part of the problem—people said reading it was a downer. We were bringing a lot of bad news." The paper also regularly covered lesbians, peace activism, and spirituality. A New York Metro Area Supplement was added in 1989, and news from the Women's Action Coalition was carried regularly starting early in 1993.

Kriegel believes lack of promotion led to the demise. "We never had enough money or talent to get on radio programs and be visible. I couldn't do it and run the paper," she said. "Book advertising was the largest source of advertising [and] we went up to $5,000 an issue in ads." Tying into editorial themes, the publication solicited advertising for issues on special topics like women's history, black history, and women's spirituality. Yet *New Directions for Women* lacked local circulation and, consequently, failed to attract local advertising.

Another problem was its newspaper format. Even though its bimonthly publication schedule made it hard to cover news events, "We attempted to be timely," Kriegel said. "We were a news magazine." Kriegel believes a gap has been left in the media since *New Directions for Women* went under.

But *New Directions for Women* will have a lasting influence on its staff, on its writers, and on the changed lives and minds of its readers.

Almost unbearably touching were the many letters received after our final issue. A few excerpts: "Oh woe, alas—such sad news. I can only imagine what the loss is to you, for us it is a cruel cut indeed." "I wept when I read your letter yesterday. You have been friends of long-standing to me (collective 'you') for all the years as I read and watched *New Directions* evolve and become the excellent publication that it was." "It just breaks my heart to see such a wonderful periodical run out of funds and have to stop publishing." "No words I can think of will say what I felt when I read your letter about *New Directions for Women* lying down to rest. It's been a good friend for so long I never considered living without it." "For me your closing the windows is a cause for mourning. You have opened the many windows to the world's women for me. You have been my companion." "From my selfish perspective I'm grateful that you were around during the years I was most isolated in Topeka and *New Directions for Women* was my lifeline."

New Directions for Women has published two cumulative indexes of its complete contents: the Ten Year Cumulative Index of Volume 1 Number 1 through Volume 10 Number 6 (January 1972 through November-December 1981), and the Twelve Year Cumulative Index of Volume 11 Number 1 through Volume 22 Number 5 (January-February 1982 through September-October 1993, the final issue).

The first index was compiled entirely by volunteers, with printing and binding donated by a major New Jersey corporation. Compiling the second index was partly paid work but mostly volunteer. Printing, binding, and marketing funds were raised with a letter to *New Directions for Women*'s loyal supporters.

Arranged chronologically by subject, the indexes provide a running account of feminist actions, philosophies, and feelings, issue by issue, year by year. Hundreds of articles are listed in the indexes under more than one subject to facilitate research on every aspect of the movement. In the first index, there are 131 subject headings, 52 subject cross-references, listings of over 600 reviewed books (adults', children's, and young adults'), over 300 advertisers in *New Directions for Women,* profiles of almost 50 feminist organizations, and over 100 biographical profiles.

The second index adds many subjects that surfaced since 1981, such as Addictions, AIDS, Backlash, Courts, Disabilities, Homelessness, Hunger, Incest, Peace Activism, Spirituality.

Both indexes include the columns and regular features, such as Media Watch, Women in the Arts, Equal Pay, Your Legal Problems, International Round-Up and Country of Women, the Metro Section, Keeping Tabs on Our Health, Editorials, Calendar.

They list (by name) the work of all our writers and graphic artists.

We believe this is the only cumulative index by subject of the many issues of the women's movement as they were documented by a feminist periodical. Evidence that the indexes and back issues are used rests with the hundreds of dollars of royalties *New Directions for Women* is still receiving from University Microfilms International.[3]

The archives of *New Directions for Women*— virtually the complete contents of all our files—are being deposited in the National Women and Media Collection at the University of Missouri School of Journalism in Columbia, Missouri, where these records will afford valuable insight into the workings of feminist journalism.

SO THE LEGACY OF *New Directions for Women* WILL LIVE ON.

When we started our feminist newspaper in 1971, we didn't realize we would be running a business, unbelievable as that seems to us today. In the 22 years we managed to keep publishing, we did a remarkable job of learning all the aspects of the business, but we never had the time, energy, funds—or inclination—to do all the necessary publicity and circulation promotion. Putting out the next issue always came first. And that is what finally brought us to our downfall in 1993.

We offer, to those who come after us, this detailed history of why we started and how we learned to become the most successful feminist newspaper in the country (called by *Magazines for Libraries* "the leading feminist newspaper in the United States"). Just as important to understand are the factors that thwarted us throughout our long history and that ultimately led to our demise as a publishing venture.

We hope that this chronicle of *New Directions for Women* will encourage, not dispirit, women who may be contemplating a new feminist periodical or are now publishing one. We hope that others will be inspired by the idealism that inspired us, by the conviction that accurate, in-depth coverage of women's lives and feminist issues as they surface and develop is possible only in a woman-run newspaper.

Notes

1. With invaluable contributions from Maurine Beasley, Phyllis Kriegel, Vivian Scheinmann, and Lynn Wenzel.

2. The second essay contest, in 1982, on the subject, "What Do You Have to Say About Feminism," was a double contest—for women never before published and for high school students. The third essay contest, in 1989, called a "feminist essay competition," specified: "You may write about anything you wish, but it must be from a personal perspective."

3. The indexes are available from *New Directions for Women,* c/o Paula Kassell, Index Editor, 25 West Fairview Avenue, Dover, NJ 07801-3417, U.S.A. The Ten Year Cumulative Index is $10 plus $3 shipping and handling; the Twelve Year Cumulative Index is $20 plus $3 S&H; both indexes ordered together are $25 plus $3 S&H. Most issues are available from the same address at $6 per issue. Both indexes and all issues are available in micro form from University Microfilms International, 300 North Greeb Road, Ann Arbor, MI 48106-1346, U.S.A.

22

Women and International Communication
The Story of *WIN News*

Fran P. Hosken

First, a definition of what we are talking about, and—most of all—why. If you have nothing of substance to say, the most sophisticated communication system will be of no use. In all this rush for ever more efficient tools, do we have time to look at content? Just what are we communicating, and why?

Looking at the international political scene, communication does not seem to make any difference to the continuous bloody conflicts all over the world. Yet one of the most important potential contributions of communication is to prevent or settle conflict. From Africa, where constant ethnic warfare is raging in at least a dozen countries, to the former Yugoslavia, Afghanistan, Russia, and much of the Middle East, Kashmir, and Tibet, the ability to communicate directly and instantly

does not seem to have changed anything. This, quite aside from the growing number of terrorist groups who seem to prefer violence to discussing anything.

The basic purpose of communication is to create understanding, cooperation, and peace. The objective is for people to talk together and to share their ideas to achieve joint human goals. But communication has not really accomplished that, although we are now able to learn instantly what is happening all over the globe.

Perhaps we need to ask another question: Who is sending the messages to whom and therefore making decisions for all involved? One thing becomes clear: International communication and the tools used are almost exclusively male prerogatives. No doubt many will reject this idea, but I believe it is important to examine this question carefully with an open mind.

I believe we must be aware of how gender affects the message in many ways: Messages of "importance" are communicated mostly by men. In turn, the technology used to transmit the message, which often affects its form, is for the most part designed by men. The continuously changing communication tools have been elevated to special status together with their designers. But what mostly concerns us here is content. Most of the information is selected and communicated from the viewpoint of men and, in turn, communicated to men.

What is more, the language that shapes our thoughts and gives them form in order to communicate is basically a tool designed by and for men. A lot of work has recently been done for the feminization of language, which faces different problems depending on the particular language involved. For instance, in French as well as German, the situation is especially difficult as words are gender linked. In a recent study, "Women and Language," in *Women of Europe* (Niedzwiecki, 1993), the relationship of language and behavior of women and men is analyzed. The Council of Europe in a recent recommendation states that the public sector should adopt a new form of nonsexist language "to create the most favorable sociocultural conditions for the achievement of equality" (p. 50).

It is also a sobering consideration when talking about international communication, its technology, and tools to inject this reality: The majority of women in Africa, in large parts of Asia, and in many rural areas all over the world can neither read nor write. Literacy in Southeast Asia and in India is quite limited among women, and even in China today a large percentage of women cannot read. Remedying this situation should be a priority, as women are the majority affected who are left out and left behind. Any serious discussion of communication by, for, and about women must be built on the participation of all women.

U.N. Conferences Provide International Personal Contacts

When International Women's Year (IWY) was planned by the United Nations for 1975, including the first World Conference for Women in Mexico City, women in the United States at first paid no attention. Very few international women's organizations were active then. Most women thought IWY had no meaning for their lives.

Not only are governments overwhelmingly male dominated, but the prestigious job of being sent as a delegate to the United Nations is a domain men like to keep for themselves. Women are not only a tiny minority among delegates, but the U.N. Commission on the Status of Women was mostly ignored. It was therefore quite remarkable that the commission succeeded—working in the shadow of this male-dominated world—to persuade the General Assembly, the main decision-making body, to support a world conference and a year for women. By then, world conferences had started to be organized around global issues as a method to gain support for joint action, with the first Environment Conference in 1972 in Stockholm, followed by the 1974 Population Conference in Bucharest.

To plan and organize such a world meeting is an enormous task, given that more than 150 countries had to be mobilized. First of all, their governments had to be persuaded to participate. That was not an easy task for a women's conference; the male-dominated governments of most countries hardly considered women a priority and certainly did not want to change their patriarchal systems.

The objectives of International Women's Year were summarized as "equality, development, and peace." But before anything else, it was necessary to marshal global support, and for that the media were essential. Before a world conference can even begin to develop a plan, media support has to be assured around the world to gain political support.

Needless to say, the issue became a field day for male reporters and editorialists to express their opinions on why or why not to hold this conference, patronizing women all the way. These were the good old days, when the male-dominated press could publish anything about women unchallenged, when there were hardly any feminist publications and very few women reporters or editors, especially not in international affairs.

Women were generally excluded from all international professional positions. Only very few worked as diplomats or at the United Nations and its agencies, or had any experience with daily life in different parts of the world. Although today one can find women from all over the world studying at universities in Europe and the United States, this is quite a recent development. That is, any direct contact or communication between women from different parts of the world was rare when IWY was organized in the early 1970s. As a result, international communication and information depended largely on the professional press.

Newspapers and newsmagazines, radio and television traditionally report political problems, natural and man-made disasters, conflicts, and wars. There is very little reported on the life of the people—least of all women— in the limited space allotted by most publications to international affairs.

Since I attended both the 1972 Environment Conference and the first Population Conference in Bucharest in 1974 as a U.N.-accredited journalist, I was familiar with the complicated and confusing U.N. conference system. What is more, I had extensively traveled in Asia, Latin America, and Africa and had prepared the first-ever global directory of women's organizations for the U.S. Agency of International Development (USAID) (Hosken, 1977),[1] which was their contribution to IWY. To be sure, it was an important communication tool, but unfortunately, the agency took more than two years to print it. It was finally published in 1977 and was distributed free to all women's organizations listed all over the world and many in developing countries, but to no one in the United States. This directory could have been very useful for women's organizations in the United States to set up direct communication with like-minded groups; but it was not printed at the time of the conference.

As a journalist, I fully appreciate the importance of open communication so as to work for joint goals. But before one can even talk about goals and objectives, it is essential to build networks of direct communication based on free exchange of information, independent of the male-dominated international press.

Due to lack of communication, the vast majority of women who went to the IWY conference in Mexico City had quite unrealistic expectations and lacked any basis for mutual support. Most women had no idea about the way of life, background, or environment of the other women from so many different countries they were meeting for the first time at that world meeting.

Nor was it made clear that in fact there are always two conferences: one by the United Nations for government delegations, the other called Forum or Tribune organized by nongovernmental organizations (NGOs) accredited at the United Nations. The U.N., or governmental, conference is open only to governmental delegations and press, as well as a few NGO representatives as observers; it is at that meeting where a plan of action and major world documents for governments are voted on for the coming years. At the nongovernmental meeting, anyone can organize a session with advance registration for meeting space assignment, which then appears in the conference calendar. The NGO meeting offers many opportunities to make issues heard and to freely exchange information. It is also possible to invite delegates from the government conference to come to meetings and/or speak at the Forum, where communication is open and participatory and not limited to the conference plan, which has already been discussed at the regional preparatory meetings.

However, the open Forum meetings do not lend themselves to developing any formal action plans and can also be abused for political purposes. In 1975 in Mexico City, for instance, women from some countries of South America came with instructions by political parties and took over some of the largest meeting rooms, after shouting down and removing the scheduled speakers, so as to proceed with political speeches that had nothing to do with women.

In Copenhagen in 1980, at the Mid-Decade World Conference of Women held as part of the "Decade for Women," 1975-1985, the Forum was similarly used for political propaganda, for instance, by the Iranians. In 1985, at the End-of-Decade U.N. World Conference of Women held in Nairobi, Kenya, political groups went from room to room propagating a male political agenda. Such methods attract attention and became part of the patriarchal press agenda reporting, "Well, it is clear that women from different countries cannot work together."

The Nairobi Forum in 1985 was the start of many ongoing activities shared by women from different countries and continents, for instance, DAWN (Development Alternatives for Women for a New Era)[2] or GROOTS (Grassroots Organizations Operating Together in Sisterhood),[3] both organizations based on extensive grassroots networking and direct communication to achieve shared objectives.

The International Women's Tribune[4] is probably the most successful example of productive and constructive international communication among women. The Tribune was organized in the late 1970s following the Mexico City U.N. conference; its Centre is located in a building facing the United Nations in New York that also houses many other NGOs. At the 1985 Forum in Nairobi, under the leadership of Anne Walker, the Tribune organized a formidable exhibit and series of meetings on appropriate technology for women. The Tribune Centre has produced large numbers of excellent educational publications and newsletters over the years and has become a unique resource for women's groups everywhere, especially in developing countries, providing effective advice on how to organize, on legal affairs, on publishing, and many other subjects of importance for grassroots-level organizations.

It is clear that world conferences are unique communication and organization tools for women's rights. The importance of personal contact for establishing women's networks cannot be overemphasized as this eliminates dependence on the patriarchal press and communication systems.

Founding *WIN News* for International Communication

Based on the contacts I had made by developing the global women's directory, my extensive travel as a journalist all over the world during which I met with women's organizations, and my experience at the first two U.N. world conferences, on environment and population, I decided to launch *Women's International Network (WIN) News*.

With the IWY scheduled for 1975 offering unique opportunities, it was essential to develop a global communication system by, for, and about women, to which women and women's organizations everywhere had ready access to speak for themselves. It was to enable women to communicate about their own concerns and issues regardless of political barriers and of manipulation by mainstream media.

Thus, in the autumn of 1974, I organized, with legal assistance, the necessary formal basis for a nonprofit educational corporation, Women's International Network (WIN), to publish the first issue of *WIN News* in January 1975. My training as an architect and designer was useful in creating the logo and format. My experience with publishing also helped; I had prevailed on my publishers (McMillan and Weatherhill) to let me do the layout of the books I had recently published with them (Hosken, 1968, 1972, 1974).

There was no chance of receiving any grants for international projects; there was no time, nor did I want any interference in what to publish, which would have accompanied most grants. Though I am grateful to many women for much useful advice and help, there was no time to organize a formal group, given the very uncertain chance of success. That left no alternative but to finance the initial issues myself, before getting any subscriptions.

The first three issues of *WIN News* were published before the July 1975 IWY conference in Mexico City. They resulted in enough subscriptions and responses from women all over the world to indicate that such a publication really filled a need.

When I first started to publish *WIN News,* I expected that some of the international women's organizations working with the United Nations and the Commission for Women would take it on and continue to publish it after 1975. But by the end of the year, I was unable to find any group that was willing or able to continue *WIN News* as a global network from a feminist view. Although several thousand copies were sent out to all women's groups accredited at the United Nations and working internationally, and to everyone mentioned in each issue, this was still a very limited effort that depended mostly on subscriptions for financing. The purpose was to develop a global network to deal with an enormous problem: worldwide communication by, for, and about women.

As a network, *WIN News* is a vehicle for women and women's groups to contact each other. Therefore, names and addresses are given with all articles to enable readers to make their own contacts with women in all parts of the world and to exchange information as well as gain access to publications and information of interest to themselves or their group. Programs and projects from all over the world are outlined in each issue of 80 pages, published quarterly, so that women reading *WIN News* in India, for instance, can make contact with a like-minded group or with a program they might want to explore in Africa or North America.

In addition to its major section on the United Nations, *WIN News*'s objective was to report from a female perspective all international decisions and affairs that affect women, as well as about international organizations that influence women's lives.

For more than 20 years, for example, *WIN News* has continuously published about successful women's development programs. The strategy is to search out and publish summaries of successful development programs by and for women that set an example and advance the status of women, excerpting from the hundreds of publications and reports that *WIN News* receives from all over the world, translating information from French, German, Spanish, and Italian sources.

I initially experimented with publishing a summary in Spanish and French, but this unfortunately turned out to be unrealistic and quite beyond our means. *WIN News* encourages women's organizations that receive the publication to translate and publish information provided in each issue. Language is a limitation, but internationally English has become the lingua franca that is understood in most areas of the world.

WIN News encourages participation by offering free copies to anyone who contributes information. The objective is for women's groups to send information about their own organization and activities and their community and country, whatever they consider important and want to share with women in other parts of the world. On every cover of *WIN News,* these objectives are summarized as follows: "*WIN News* is a worldwide open communication system by, for, and about women of all backgrounds, beliefs, nationalities, and age groups."

To participate effectively in international decision making, it is essential to have the facts, to know who makes the decisions, and to know what the objectives and alternatives really are. International decisions that women do not know about greatly affect women's lives. For instance, the decisions made by the World Bank on economic restructuring or adjustment have had a devastating effect on women's lives in many countries of the developing world. Yet women were never informed, let alone consulted, on these decisions that so drastically influence and often damage their lives.

In addition to reporting on the United Nations, other regular sections are "Women and Development," "Women and Health," "Women and Media," and "Women and Genital Mutilation." Gradually more sections were added on violence and environment. It was essential to organize by subject matter because *WIN News* began to receive a huge amount of international material. What did not fit under the subject headings was organized geographically under regions and countries. A final section of each issue covers international affairs, which includes conferences and international initiatives.

"Women and Human Rights" was added as a separate section in 1978. Every spring for the last 10 years, this special section has reported on the *Country Reports on Human Rights Practices* published by the U.S. State Department. During the Carter administration, these *Country Reports* assumed special importance. And I lobbied for years for the inclusion of women in the reports of every country. In the past five years, women have had a special section in each report. The coverage is quite comprehensive, including female genital mutilation, family violence, and abuse of women by men.

Exposing the Facts on Violence Against Women Worldwide

As an international journal, *WIN News* planned from the start in 1975 to report on male abuse of women. But initially it was quite impossible to get any facts. Therefore, in 1977, I sent out questionnaires all over the world, asking women and women's groups and media contacts to provide what information they had. I received few replies, and those who answered stated "we have no information."

The first documented facts on wife abuse came from Britain. Erin Pizzey first started to shelter a few abused women and their children in her home, and then opened the first women's shelter—despite strenuous opposition by the London housing authorities, who took her to court. This made headlines. After she published some articles and, in 1974, a book, the issue suddenly surfaced all over Britain and shortly after that in the United States. All this was reported in *WIN News* beginning in 1977. In the United States, information and statistics on wife abuse suddenly began to be published by women, but it took a long time for information to appear in the mainstream press. Large numbers of research papers followed and then more and more books. Reporting on wife abuse that had started in the United Kingdom was taken up all over Europe, Canada, and Australia, and shelters for abused women and children began to be established and funded as well as telephone hot lines—although for a long time it was impossible for *WIN News* to get any information from developing countries.

In the early 1980s, abuse and violence by men against women suddenly broke out of the patriarchal media control. Women began not only to speak up about it but to organize support systems and shelters literally all over the world. Many different forms of abuse perpetuated against women are now reported everywhere: The damaging media control of this issue has been broken.

Facts are reported, but actions to stop the abuses by men are slow or often do not exist at all. Southeast Asian women are traded as "brides" to European and Australian men. Sex tourism to Southeast Asia, a favorite recreation of Japanese, European, and Australian men, continues to grow as it is incredibly lucrative for the male entrepreneurs, despite the increasing spread of AIDS.

Wife abuse in Africa is regarded as a normal part of family life; for instance, in Kenya, parliamentarians demanded that their traditional right to beat their wives be written into the new family laws, as documented in parliamentary debates in the late 1970s. Abuse of women in Latin America is part of the macho code, and in Russia the huge divorce rate was and is propelled by male violence, which under the present so-called democratic conditions is rapidly increasing together with all other forms of sexual exploitation and violent crime.

Male violence against women and children is a global cancer. I recently stated in an editorial in *WIN News* (vol. 20, no. 3, Summer 1994) what a conservative politician pointed out: "It is a cowardly act for a man to abuse and attack a woman whom he can easily overpower due to his greater body strength." This truth should be broadcast all over the world: Only a coward attacks someone less strong than himself.

Why is this very obvious fact about attacking women never mentioned by the male-dominated press when in sports and everywhere else competition is strictly regulated to be between equals? Branding as cowards all men who attack their wives and children would put quite a new light on this issue and would finally lead to the exclusion of such men from peer groups.

Currently, just the opposite is true. Men are admired for wife abuse by other men in all societies backed up by the male press, which evidently considers violence against a woman who cannot defend herself to be a hallowed male right. What is more, violence against women in advertising, in countless films, and in videotapes has become a most lucrative business along with violent pornography. The fact that violence and exploitation of women and female children are considered entertainment by and for "real men" has provided a source of millions of dollars to international media moguls. Their huge international businesses yield enormous profits for which women are victimized and often made to pay with their lives.

Unless and until the partnership model, as brilliantly documented by Riane Eisler (1989),[5] is firmly established to assure real equality, sharing, and mutual support, starting with the family and throughout society, the family

home is a dangerous place where male violence often rules.

The contributions of the women's press reporting on male violence have been groundbreaking. Without media women persistently pursuing this issue, the male press would have continued to conceal the facts, aided and abetted by male physicians, male police, and male judges.

Reporting on Female Genital Mutilation

In the summer issue of 1975, I began a section reporting on female genital mutilation (excision and mutilation of the female genitalia).[6] This was still a taboo subject; no one in international affairs or working with the United Nations would report on this. Only by continuing to publish myself was it possible to regularly report on this subject of such vital importance to women.

I started my investigation of female genital mutilation in 1973, when I visited 15 countries in sub-Saharan Africa, where I first learned about the practice. Although as a journalist I knew how to get information, it was impossible at first to get any solid facts: everyone turned me away or sent me on to another source that was another dead end.

The one reliable source was the midwives in the maternity sections of large hospitals where women from all ethnic groups delivered. On many subsequent trips, I visited hospital maternities and talked to midwives and doctors working there. What I learned was horrendous—but evidently nobody had ever bothered to find out about women's reproductive health by going to maternity hospitals. This was confirmed by the very few medical articles that I found after spending days in medical libraries and writing to health ministries all over Africa.

Both the World Health Organization (WHO) and the U.N. Children's Fund (UNICEF) had refused to provide any information. The director of UNICEF claimed that female genital mutilation is a practice "in a few remote areas"; the agency had other more important issues to deal with and, in any case, "the practice was disappearing," which is contrary to all facts, as is confirmed now. For many years, WHO claimed this was a "cultural issue" and refused even to do research, although they have resident representatives in every African country. Because it was impossible to persuade international organizations and agencies working in Africa, including the U.S. Agency of International Development (USAID), to take the problem seriously, it was essential to publish the information I had gathered from hospitals in Africa; they were sources that could not be denied.

But no matter how I tried to get my research published in many different forms in newspapers and magazines of all kinds, and despite my extensive experience as an international journalist, it was quite impossible to do. "This topic is not suitable for our publication" was the usual response, including from European publications. Most just returned my articles without a word.

Finally, an African library collection in California published a comprehensive article of mine—because they found in their files a letter on female genital mutilation written by a British physician from colonial times.

Then, a new women's health journal published by the State University of New York accepted an extensive research article ("Women and Health," 1976), which was subsequently translated and published by feminist journals in Germany, France, and Italy. This article also led to my being invited by the editor of the *Tropical Doctor,* the prestigious international medical journal published by the British Royal Society of Medicine, to write an article, "The Epidemiology of Female Genital Mutilations," which they published in July 1978. I documented with fieldwork and numerous firsthand citations of gynecologists I had talked to in Africa as well as midwives that far from an "isolated practice

in a few remote areas," female genital mutilation was a major public health problem that affected a huge region of Africa, including many major cities and involving tens of millions of women, that must be dealt with by health authorities.

It was this article, published in 1978 and circulated all over the medical world, that persuaded WHO to no longer evade their responsibility, and to organize the 1979 WHO-sponsored seminar in Khartoum, Egypt, "Traditional Practices Affecting the Health of Women and Children," to which I was invited to present the opening paper on the global distribution and spread—that is, the epidemiology—of female genital mutilation.

Yet the conspiracy of silence maintained by the media in the United States continued. No one was even willing to accept an article about the WHO seminar in Khartoum. The UNICEF media director who had retired in the meantime used his press connections to publish an article in a widely read journal in Britain, attacking me personally, as editor of *WIN News,* as a crazy American feminist who was trying to "interfere in hallowed African tradition."

When I tried to publish my research on Africa in book form, I was turned down again by every publisher and agent. They simply refused to take on a book on "such a subject." This, despite the fact that I had previously published books with three major publishing houses. Finally, after every university press as well had turned down the subject, no matter what the documentation, I decided to publish *The Hosken Report: Genital and Sexual Mutilation of Females* myself, and have done so ever since (the fourth edition was published in January 1994) through *WIN News.* The report is now in major libraries all over the world.

But it has been a sobering experience documenting the patriarchal control by the press where issues of concern to women are involved. As a nonprofit organization, Women's International Network is perfectly capable of publishing books of different kinds as well as magazines such as *WIN News*. We also publish the *Childbirth Picture Book/Program (CBPB)*,[7] which was first developed in 1980 as a teaching tool to prevent and stop female genital mutilation. The CBPBs are now printed in English (two versions), French, Spanish, Arabic, and Somali with a distribution of more than 60,000 books. The book is also printed in India in eight Indian languages by a women's health group, as well as in Nepal, the Marshall Islands, and most recently Senegal. The entire commercial mainstream publishing establishment has been avoided.

Having also published with well-known international publishers, I believe it is more efficient and less time-consuming for women to publish their work themselves, to keep control, and to be free of outside interference.

Outlook

WIN News now goes to more than 100 countries all over the world and reports from many more. Universities and libraries worldwide subscribe to *WIN News* as a research source; women's organizations use the information by networking. Development agencies of many European countries as well as Canada and Australia and their missions in developing countries maintain subscriptions as a source of information, as do most U.N. agencies.

The record over the years shows that *WIN News,* with no subsidies from foundations, which do not recognize the importance of publishing international information by, for, and about women, has not only been able to survive to its 22nd year, but has grown steadily, overcoming political and man-made barriers, and is increasingly recognized as a unique source of information. Most important, *WIN News* over the years has provided information to enable women to participate and to be heard, trying to make the democratic process a reality.

Publishing *WIN News* for more than two decades has been a unique experience that has been greatly enhanced by participation in the U.N. world conferences for women. The record of the major world press at these global meetings, though the press is given every opportunity to learn about the issues by special press seminars held before each conference, has been dismal, confirming that an independent press and communication system by, for, and about women is essential to get balanced information and to learn the real facts that promote our cause.

The most comprehensive international studies on women and the media over the years have been made by Margaret Gallagher. The first-ever international examination of the influence by the media on women and the treatment and employment of women by the media was the 1981 report *Unequal Opportunities: The Case of Women and the Media,* which was published by UNESCO. This was followed by an unpublished UNESCO report by Gallagher in 1985.

Recently, Gallagher, together with Lilia Quindoza-Santiago, produced *Women Empowering Communication: A Resource Book on Women and the Globalisation of Media* (1994).

The most remarkable media development of the last two decades is the proliferation of women's publications with literally hundreds of feminist magazines and newsletters in all languages—with new ones being created all the time, as reported in the *WIN News* section "Women and Media." These women's publications are able to provide direct contact with women's organizations and activities by and for women in each country.

Publishing and journalism are very important professions for women, and recently women have begun to gain much more influence in these professions. The new electronic media offer an opportunity for women, but I do not believe that print media will disappear, as some claim—and certainly not in the developing world or for the majority of people. Publishing offers women a real voice, including political influence and control.

The time has come to challenge the male-dominated newspaper, publishing, and communication industry and/or to infiltrate the patriarchal media, to build an internal power base to demand change and a decision-making editorial voice.

We have yet to recognize the real power women potentially have by organizing women's media globally in support of basic goals. The Decade for Women and the four women's conferences, including most recently the 1995 U.N. conference in Beijing, have opened up enormous opportunities for women through personal contacts and developing shared initiatives and networks for collaboration of women all over the world.

We share so many experiences, objectives, concerns, and goals. But no matter where we live, we also share the same patriarchal control and exploitation: The global cancer of male violence against women must be eradicated. We shall succeed by planning and working together for the love of our children, which brings women together all over the world. The goal is to develop a more equal and caring society that is shared and supported, rather than dominated, by men. Communication is the means to that end.

Notes

1. In the 1980s, I repeatedly tried to get U.S. publishers interested in updating this directory after USAID refused, but all major houses that dealt with directories declared such a venture would not pay and turned it down. Many years later, Longman Group UK Ltd., a publisher of reference books, finally published a comprehensive world directory of women's organizations to which I contributed the survey of the United States (Shreir, 1988).

2. Development Alternatives With Women for a New Era (DAWN): The University of West Indies, School of Continuing Studies, Pinelands, St. Michael, Barbados, W.I. Contact: Peggy Antrobus.

3. Grassroots Organizations Operating Together in Sisterhood (GROOTS): GROOTS International, One Sherman Sq., #27L, New York, NY 10017.

4. International Women's Tribune Centre, 777 United Nations Plaza, New York, NY 10017.

5. Eisler's *The Chalice and the Blade* has been translated into many languages.

6. Female genital mutilation: *Excision* is cutting off the clitoris and often all external genitalia; *infibulation* occurs after excision when the entrance to the vagina is closed by sewing or scarification.

7. The *Childbirth Picture Book/Program* is produced in English/French/Spanish/Arabic/Somali. Additions are included to prevent excision and infibulation. Flip charts and color slides are available from *WIN News*, Women's International Network, 187 Grant Street, Lexington, MA 02173.

References

Eisler, R. P. (1989). *The chalice and the blade: Our history, our future.* San Francisco: Harper & Row.

Gallagher, M. (1985). *Unequal opportunities: The case of women and the media.* (Available from UNESCO, 7 Place de Fontenoy, 15700 Paris, France)

Gallagher, M., & Quindoza-Santiago, L. (Eds.). (1994). *Women empowering communication: A resource book on women and the globalisation of media* (4th ed.). London/Manila/New York: World Association for Christian Communication/Isis/International/International Women's Tribune Centre.

Hosken, F. P. (1968). *The language of cities.* New York: Macmillan.

Hosken, F. P. (1972). *The functions of cities.* Cambridge, MA: Schenkman/General Learning Corp.

Hosken, F. P. (1974). *The Kathmandu Valley towns: A record of life and change in Nepal.* New York: John Weatherhill.

Hosken, F. P. (Ed.). (1977). *International directory of women's development organizations.* Washington, DC: U.S. Agency for International Development.

Hosken, F. P. (1978). The epidemiology of female genital mutilations. *Tropical Doctor, 8,* 150-156 (London: Royal Society of Medicine).

Hosken, F. P. (1994). *The Hosken report: Genital and sexual mutilation of females* (4th ed.). Lexington, MA: Women's International Network.

Niedzwiecki, P. (1993, August). Women and language. *Women of Europe, 40* (Code 10/0341/93 EN, Orig fr). (Available from the European Commission, Rue de la Loi, 200, B-1049 Brussels, Belgium)

Shreir, S. (Ed.). (1988). *Women's movements of the world: An international directory and reference guide.* Harlow, U.K.: Longman Group UK Ltd.

Women and health. (1976). *Issues in Women's Health Care, 1*(1), 3-11 (Biological Sciences Program, College at Old Westbury, State University of New York).

23

The Founding of WINGS (Women's International News Gathering Service)
A Story of Feminist Radio Survival

Frieda Werden

In mainstream media, the force for growth is the mogul; in feminist media, it's the maniac. By "maniac," I mean the woman who, working independently or with like-minded others, refuses to stop communicating with and about women, even if she's told she's destroying her chances for a career, even if no one will fund her, even if she knows she's heading hell-bent for burnout, and family members or potential lovers warn her it's impossible to love someone so obsessed with the feminist movement and the long stressful hours of media work.

Fortunately, a few people do manage to love or to fund the feminist media maniacs from time to time, despite their insufferability as human companions. Even the names of maniacs are preserved mainly by others of their ilk. Dale Spender revived Rebecca West in the book *Time & Tide;* Maria Luisa Bemberg restored the voice of Sor Juana Inés de la Cruz in the film *Yo, la peor de todos;* Judy Chicago set a place in her "Dinner Party" sculpture for tenth-century canoness Hrotswitha—the first playwright of the Christian world, whose plays honored "the faithfulness of woman" . . .

The name I lift up here is that of Katherine Ann Davenport, cofounder of WINGS: Women's International News Gathering Service. A tall, Dianic westerner who came to New York as media co-coordinator of the first March on Washington for Lesbian and Gay Rights (1979), she became coproducer with Judie Pasternak of the two weekly women's programs on WBAI-FM: the one-hour *Velvet Sledgehammer* and the half-hour *51%: The Women's News* (this was in the early 1980s, and not to be confused with the program titled *51%* distributed in the 1990s by WAMU-FM and funded by Gannett).

Judie was Women's Department Director at WBAI, the Pacifica station in New York, for the even-then minuscule salary of $15,000 a year. She and Katherine lived together on that salary in Judie's rent-controlled Manhattan apartment, working together on shows.[1]

Katherine had a great nose for news, going after the breaking issue of the day as it related to women. She also knew many sectors of the women's community, and had produced live events with such stars as Roseanne Barr and Z Budapest in New York, Seattle, and Denver. I was a radio and events production maniac too, having produced my first syndicated series (about the women's movement in Texas) as a volunteer at Longhorn Radio Network (Austin, Texas) in 1972-1973. In the 1970s, I did more radio, copublished a feminist magazine, and produced events such as the first Austin women's music festival. By 1983, I was working for National Public Radio managing a massive docudrama project, but was not too busy for the fun (and unpaid) job of reporter for *51%*—and for KPFA's *Majority Report* when Katherine moved to the San Francisco Bay area.

Near the end of 1985, Western Public Radio, a training and production facility on San Francisco Bay, hired me as operations manager. The deal had been sweetened with a promise I could develop any project I wanted, and I hovered between women's drama and women's news until Katherine and I got together and began planning a news program. The Decade for Women was just ending, and with my background in women's history (I'd also been associate curator of the Texas Women's History Project, 1979-1981), I was all too aware that the little splash of coverage the mainstream media had given the international women's movement would soon disappear without a ripple. Both Katherine and I were then reading Dale Spender's *Time & Tide,* so we were clear about the value of politically independent feminist media.

After the first couple of times we got together, I realized Katherine had no place to live. She'd been in the Bay Area two years, had just turned 43 years old, and was perhaps the most active unpaid reporter at KPFA (in Berkeley), as well as an unpaid adviser to the women's program at college station KALX; but she was laying her sleeping bag on the floor of a friend's apartment that had no working toilet. Often she spent the night at the radio station, where late night was the most likely time to get studio time to produce. (Another very active feminist reporter was living the same way—they had sacrificed ordinary life to concentrate on reporting.) I got her to move in with me, and started taking her to my workplace to work on our project.[2]

Katherine and another independent producer, Augusta Del Zotto, and I met over a period of six months to design and produce a pilot for the women's news project. Initial research was conducted through international women's publications and organizations, domestic and foreign radio stations and radio organizations, women's studies scholars, and producers experienced with international radio and independent news services. Some good groundwork had already been laid, for example a list of producers from a women's radio meeting held at the Peace Tent at the U.N. Women's Conference in Nairobi, Kenya, earlier that year, and a current list of women's radio programs at U.S. community radio stations from the National Federation of Community Radio Broadcasters.

The principles we laid down for WINGS were influenced by my having read the *Media Report to Women* newsletter, but also seem typical of women's news programs around the world. We wanted to emphasize women from the regions covered speaking for themselves, while also focusing on "hard news," which is rarely associated with women by the other media. Shortly after we came on air, we got this comment from a listener in Buffalo, Kristen Reilly: "Though I've been involved in women's issues for years, I was still struck by the contrast of your broadcast to the news we are usually hearing—news reflecting male interests in a basically male world. Women's affairs are a hidden current in the flow of world events."

To be heard by listeners, we were dependent on being picked up by radio stations, so we made the format flexible—able to be aired as a half-hour continuous newscast or as news "modules" one story at a time in other programs (including between the songs on women's music shows—the most common type of woman-controlled program). This meant that if the program director of a station wasn't interested, we still had a market selling direct to producers of local women's and current affairs shows. We also agreed that contributing reporters would be paid for their work, because women deserved that respect—although financial limitations keep the actual figures low. As the years passed, we found that WINGS has often been the first paid job for women in community radio who go on to become paid producers for other services.

WINGS received start-up funds from National Public Radio's Satellite Program Development Fund (now no longer extant), a $2,000 discretionary grant from then-director Sandra Rattley, which paid for our outreach and a prototype program to be released on public radio satellite in May 1986. That first half-hour audio newscast contained 13 stories by and about women from around the world. Over the years, the number of stories gradually shrank to 5, because of continued complaints that the program was too crowded. But there was so much to tell!

Once the pilot was out, we had a dilemma: The outreach we'd done was still working! Fascinating tapes kept coming in from women around the world. Yet money for regular production and distribution would take months, perhaps years to develop. If in the meantime WINGS stopped producing, major news stories would be lost; enthusiasm would pall, contacts fall away; and the tide of public interest from the Nairobi meeting would continue receding.

Augusta was living on her freelance earnings and had to drop out, but Katherine and I decided we would keep producing as long as possible and live on my salary while we tried to get another grant. We took sample cassettes to Vancouver for the AMARC conference (French initials for the World Congress of Community-Oriented Community Radio Broadcasters), met a lot of broadcasters and reporters who were interested in the project, and came back to discover I'd been fired in absentia. At that point, the project moved into the living room, where luckily I had a good open reel tape machine I'd bought while working at NPR, which we could edit on. We hired women engineers who had access through their other jobs to commercial radio studios that let us record continuity and mix there (eventually we got enough equipment and expertise to do our own engineering). We figured out the best deals on tapes and the cheapest ways to mail things; I took a part-time job as a tele-fund-raiser for the San Francisco Symphony (and, later, similar jobs), and WINGS became the focus of our lives.

In fall 1992, my former boss Leo Lee came up to me at a meeting where WINGS was honored and said, "I hope there are no hard feelings." I told him the truth, which was, "If you hadn't made me so angry, I don't think we could have kept the program going for seven years." As I write this, WINGS has passed the nine-year mark, which is an advanced age for any independently produced program. It survived six moves, an earthquake, and Katherine's death[3] from leukemia in September 1992. We added weekly current affairs program service in 1988, to meet station demand; and we've released a variety of one-hour specials, including live multicity discussion programs using advanced technologies. The newscast goes regularly to about 130 subscribers, with some specials passing the 160-station mark. There are now 26 stations subscribing to the weekly programs—more than one-quarter of them outside the United States.

Money has never been abundant. The annual WINGS budget hovers around $25,000 a year (a similar project distributed by NPR, *Crossroads,* spends more than $400,000 a year to fill the same amount of time). Almost all the grants have been from small social-change-oriented foundations, in amounts ranging between $1,000 and $10,000. Other than that, funding for women's media seems regularly to fall in a crack between the very slim resources of the women's funds, which all say they don't fund media, and the media funds, which have deeper pockets but don't fund women. Once, in 1987, a proposal by WINGS got as far as committee at the Corporation for Public Broadcasting Radio Fund, and the comments reported back were things like the following: "This is an idea whose time has passed." "Can't men listen to this?" and "In a better world, these things would be reported on 'All Things Considered.' "

WINGS did receive a handful of personal donations from women even in its first year. The first donor was Genevieve Vaughan, who has become a long-term supporter of the project and has probably been the largest single funder of alternative women's media projects in the world. (She is now looking for additional funders to join her in this endeavor.) Since 1993, I've received a salary from Genevieve's Foundation for a Compassionate Society for duties including training women in radio production and recording foundation events. WINGS gets the use of the foundation's media studio for training, interviews, and meetings as well. It's called WATER (Women's Access to Electronic Resources, 109 W. Johanna St., Austin, TX 78704).

Subscribing stations also send WINGS some of our budget (although many poor stations and women's collectives continue to receive the monthly newscasts free as long as they will air them). The weekly subscribers pay $99 a quarter for 13 programs, which is a large commitment for a low-budget station—especially in a market where there is a lot of "free" programming that is either grant funded or thrown in with the price of the membership fees of the major noncommercial networks. The fact that stations continue to pay is the biggest compliment WINGS gets.

One thing that attracts some stations is that WINGS is very different from both commercial and public radio. I like to say that we use radio as Marshall McLuhan described it—as a "hot" medium, compared with television ("medium cool"). The NPR news style makes radio more like television: The reporters write long word pictures and stay detached. They also make much of the appearance of balance. Anything that suggests change, especially, they feel must be balanced with a statement from the status quo. On the other hand, commercial radio is "hot" in presentation, but it uses such brief sound bites (10 seconds is a long one!) that there is no context, and consequently a lot of distortion of the message.

The favored WINGS style is to use a short, factual script to set up the story in universal terms—so that it can be understood by listeners in New Zealand as well as the United States—and then to let the women being covered speak for themselves. We don't allow editorializing by the reporters, but we do allow it by the subjects, which is different from both commercial and noncommercial media. We like to showcase new information, new analyses, and passion—the thing that comes through the voice regardless of what language is being spoken (the thing radio does so much better than print!). Whereas NPR doesn't allow cuts from public addresses, speeches are the most common source of WINGS tapes. We like the energy that comes out when a woman is speaking to an audience—so much stronger than an interview in a studio! And one of the great secrets in this world is that there are many, many wonderful women orators with important things to tell.

Another drawback financially is our emphasis on news. News is very time-consuming to produce, compared with live or live-on-tape programs, and it's especially time-consuming to do intensive editing as WINGS does to keep as many of the woman's actual words as possible and make the story flow, instead of just picking out a 10-second sound bite and writing a script. Furthermore, news is not the sort of thing to generate a lot of paid tape orders from listeners. What audiences will buy on cassette most often falls into four categories—music, self-help, celebrities, and conspiracy theories—whereas the topics we find through the international women's movement are in such areas as politics, environment, labor, human rights, health, food security, community building, war and peace, sovereignty, and the like.

Our commitment to the news format came especially from Katherine, who really knew what was a hot story. She was a news junkie, following television, shortwave, and alternative sources; she'd written and taken photos for alternative print media; and she had a talent for taking a topic that the journalistic world was scrambling for and turning it on its ear to get a women's angle. She was a fast editor, used to working on deadlines, and her scripts were terse and elegant. She had a light Dallas accent despite decades away from her birthplace; her voice was deep for a woman's, and her delivery was both clear and deadpan, reminiscent of *Dragnet*'s Joe Friday. We took a lot of criticism for her delivery style from people who thought we should try to sound like NPR, but her distinctive sound also drew recognition and fans.

The talents I brought to WINGS included a dramatic flair and an ability to figure out what was needed to make the story comprehensible to various audiences. I had experience as a performance poet, print journalist and editor, literary critic, rhetoric teacher, docudrama producer, and historian. Katherine used to say to me, "This is a news program, not a history lesson," because I was always trying to cram more background into the stories. And unlike her, I'd agonize over every cut I had to make in the tape of the women's voices—we called it "falling in love with the tape"—and I still do it today.

Sometimes people tell me it's wonderful that WINGS is filling the need for women's international news programming, and I have to say that WINGS is nowhere near filling the need—just a drop in the bucket. But at least when there's a drop in the bucket you know what water is. For one of our first programs, I remember phoning a woman reporter we'd heard about in Sweden and asking her out of the blue, "What's the hot women's news in Sweden?" She told us there was a great new American diet plan! So we had to explain that that wasn't what we meant by women's news, and as a matter of fact, there'd been women's news in Sweden that week that none of the media there had covered: All the women in the Swedish parliament had gotten together across party lines to try to pass a bill that criminalized the patrons of prostitutes.

From the beginning, we were able to get many exclusive stories and scoops just because of our angle: *cherchez les femmes*. For example, WINGS scooped *Nightline* by seven months on the German radioactive milk powder controversy after Chernobyl: Suzanne Seeland from the women's radio program *Zeitpunkte* in Berlin sent us tapes of the first women's demonstrations on this issue. In another case, *20/20* executives kept sitting on a TV segment they had bought about the Pacific island nation of Palau, so WINGS broke the story of the draconian measures being used to repeal the world's first antinuclear constitution, which had been written by elder women who'd seen the results of Pacific testing. When *MacNeil-Lehrer* slid right over the fact that the U.S.S.R. had its first woman on the Politburo of the Central Committee in 25 years, WINGS used our female networking to get an exclusive interview with Alexandra Biryukova and an analysis of sex discrimination in the (then-still-closed) Soviet Union. After our first year in production, WINGS won the National Federation of Community Broadcasters Golden Reel Award for coverage of major women's conferences around the world.

One of the surprising things about doing women's media has been how long it takes to gain acceptance as real media. Feminist organizations still often fail to put us on their media lists—although they've grown more used to seeing us tape at events. Quite often, WINGS is the only media at a women's event—and sometimes the organizers say to our faces, "Too bad no media showed up!"

Somehow the idea of "women's" anything carries with it a low status marker. Both WINGS and Australia's weekly *Women on the Line* program, for instance, got attacked from the beginning on grounds of "quality"; even some women producers who started to file with us were scared off by a man saying WINGS was "not very good." The best argument for our quality is our survival. I love it that younger women now come here to learn from this venerable feminist institution.

The other argument we still hear against our existence is that "we don't want to ghettoize women's programming." But I say if we don't yet have our fair share of space in the mainstream, then I definitely want to have the ghetto. Not only to have at least some space, but also because the act of bringing together women's stories from different parts of the world builds up such an invaluable picture of a complex international movement.

For every newscast, we have the fun of seeing themes emerge from the material. For example, after a story about U.S. women trying to get the women's vote out now that we've felt the backlash of 1994, I included a story about how Swedish women counteracted their country's antifeminist, antiliberal backlash in the last election and got 50% of the cabinet positions in the bargain. Another program had several stories about transnational corporations, including one about laid-off U.S. garment workers fighting back and one about a U.S. company taking out a patent on a traditional plant remedy used for thousands of years by grandmothers in India. Another recent program had views on reproductive issues by disabled feminists in the United States, Polish women parliamentari-

ans, and fundamentalist Muslim women in Karachi!

Some of the themes for which WINGS continues to take special responsibility because they are so important to women and so seldom covered elsewhere include the links between environmental factors, especially radiation, and cancer and birth defects; the unrecognized importance of women's unwaged work in the economies of every country; the struggle between rights of corporations and governments and rights of traditional communities; women's experiences of war and efforts against it; varieties of institutional sexism and successful tactics to use against them; antiracism and antisexism movements; and the ways that women organize for effective change.

Dealing with stories about women is sometimes terribly depressing; for example, after the World Conference on Human Rights and its Tribunal on the Violations of Women's Human Rights, it was really brought home to me that there is still a worldwide war against women, and no government in the world is adequately addressing the violence we face.

On the other hand, WINGS is very much about staring women's issues in the face and finding hope, anger, initiative, and successes: If we leave you laughing or cheering or thinking about something you can do to help, then we're succeeding in our mission as constructive media.

I really treasure a comment from a producer in New Zealand, Nikki Reece, whose station Plains-FM is a long-term WINGS subscriber. Along with the tape she sent, she wrote: "WINGS is at different times horrifying, exciting, funny, eye-opening, and definitely inspirational."

Now, doesn't that make it all worthwhile?

Postscript

I can't conclude this chapter without saying something about access to media and how essential it is to fight for it, not just for women but for the public at large and for all forms of alternatives to self-serving corporate information.

Many people in the United States know that Congress is threatening to cut public funding to public radio and television. Personally, I think these institutions will survive, whether publicly or privately funded, although increasingly sidling up to the forces that oppose them.

What is more immediately at risk in the United States is the network of stations called community stations that provide airtime to the local community and to alternative programs such as WINGS. In the summer of 1995, the federally funded Corporation for Public Broadcasting signaled its intention to fund only one radio service per community— the largest one. Many community stations are second services in their communities, and that includes all of the five Pacifica-owned radio stations, whose national programming dollars are used to support the national Pacifica program service (serving about 60 stations across the United States with daily news programming out of Washington).

Noncommercial radio in the United States has been almost uniquely fortunate in the world to have exclusive access to the left side of the FM band (below 92). In many other countries, people are going to prison for trying to get the right to community airtime. In the Reagan era, however, the Federal Communications Commission ruled that religious stations may compete for this space, and with their greater access to money, they have been steadily gobbling up these frequencies, as well as most of the AM dial and most of the shortwave dial. (For more information on the shortwave problem, write "Right Wing Radio Review," Radio for Peace International, Box 88, Santa Ana, Costa Rica.)

The following are the ways to keep these windows open and accessible to feminists and others not on the right: (a) Listen to community radio stations: Don't just keep your radio on one station and think "NPR" is all there is. (b) Support them; give them your money and your time. (c) Use them: Ask to appear as a guest, ask them to carry WINGS or other national and international women's programs—and ask repeatedly until they do it. Start a local women's program (community stations are the only place ordinary people can get the simple training needed to get on the air). (d) If there's no community radio station in your area, get a group of people together to form a nonprofit organization and start one, just as hundreds of other community groups have done.

The same goes for any other outlets you can find. Cable access TV programming is threatened by a combination of right-wingers using this outlet very enthusiastically and by corporations wanting to get out of the onerous requirement to provide community access facilities and channel time. Demand your cable company keep access: Praise it. Watch it, and think about how it could be improved by your input. (I've recently started a local cable access program called *Women's News Hour,* and every time I see a mistake we've made on screen I just consider that this is an hour a week that isn't occupied by the right wing.) My friend Trella Laughlin has been producing a cable access program called *Let the People Speak!* for 15 years, starting with a program produced by white people wanting to contradict the Ku Klux Klan's access program; today her shows are seen on quite a few cable systems around the country.

We have to stop cynically saying "freedom of the press belongs to those who own the press," and start making the most of the public resources that are actually there for us in many communities. Don't let the access be taken away from you before you even know it's there.

In addition to making women's media programs, I urge you to save and archive your tapes. One of the mottoes I made up for WINGS is, "Today's news is tomorrow's history: Keep women's actions on the record!" If you have women's media, there are several archives that would probably accept them, including the Center for American History at the University of Texas at Austin, which houses the WINGS archive; the Women's Studies Archive at Duke University; and the women's media archive at University of Missouri at Columbia.

Despite all the warnings I've listed, I still see a number of hopeful signs in women's media. One is the creation of FIRE: Feminist International Radio Endeavor in 1991 by Genevieve Vaughan. It offers two hours a day, seven days a week, of feminist programming on shortwave (via Radio for Peace International out of Costa Rica), and has even become very popular with the mostly male shortwave audience as well as drawing women listeners. The program is repeated twice daily, so you can actually catch it during six hours of the day. WINGS also airs on Radio for Peace, in its own slot as well as in the FIRE programs. (Note: WINGS is popular with men listeners, as well—they account for half our listener cassette orders.) Another hopeful sign is the development of audio capability on the World Wide Web. WINGS is putting our own programming on a Web site, which, as the technology becomes more widely available, will allow women around the world to listen to feminist programs through their computers at times of day they choose, even where their local radio stations are not carrying the programs. I don't think this kind of listening will replace local radio in the near future, but it will revolutionize audio distribution to eliminate both messy cassette mailings and the problem of getting subscribing stations to all hustle and catch a feed off of a satellite at a fixed moment.

Finally, I'm hopeful because access to media has finally gotten on the international women's movement agenda. It was one of the 12 critical areas of concern on the agenda at the Fourth World Conference on Women in Beijing. Although I doubt that there will be any immediate useful steps taken by governments, it's about time that this was recognized as an essential issue. Without communication, we can't learn from each other, and we're condemned to keep reinventing the wheel.

For WINGS producers' guidelines and information about programs, write to WINGS, P.O. Box 33220, Austin, TX 78764, U.S.A.

"This is the Women's International News Gathering Service."

Notes

1. Just now in 1995, the last of the Pacifica radio station women's departments, at KPFA-FM, has been dismantled. This fact grieves me because I think that special outreach to women is still absolutely essential for community radio stations; unless women are specifically invited to join in and resources reserved for them, most of them will step aside for the men who are always there ready to claim space.

2. One reason that so few women participate in community media compared with men (and I've never heard of a radio station with more than 30% of its airtime filled with women's voices—most are well below 15%) is that their lives are so crowded with responsibilities and they make so little money. In trying to fund-raise for any women's project, the impact of women only controlling 1% of the world's resources (as the United Nations has said) becomes abundantly clear. It is my fond wish that a day will come when women's media can be operated by reasonable women living balanced lives and working normal hours on reasonable budgets. I've just never seen it happen. Even where I've found women salaried to produce women's programming, the women seem always to have extra duties that a man with the same production responsibilities wouldn't have.

3. In 1993, I created the DAWN prize—Katherine A. Davenport Award for Women's News. This is an annual cash award of $100 for the hottest women's radio news story of the year. Tapes may be sent at any time during the year, and will also be considered for airing on WINGS on a nonexclusive basis. Contact: WINGS, P.O. Box 33220, Austin, TX 78764, U.S.A.

24

Feminist International Radio Endeavor—FIRE

Maria Suarez Toro

Feminist International Radio Endeavor (FIRE) is a women's radio project founded in May, 1991 with support from the Foundation for a Compassionate Society. FIRE broadcasts a two-hour daily program (one hour in Spanish and one hour in English) on the shortwave radio station, Radio For Peace International (RFPI) in Costa Rica, and is heard in over 100 countries around the world.

Our daily FIRE programs address diverse themes from a gender perspective. These include structural adjustment, women's human rights, the environment, racism, militarism, sexuality, education, art, and culture. We report on the situation in areas such as Haiti, former Yugoslavia, and Guatemala, as well as from events around the world, for example, the Latin American Caribbean Black Women's Conference (Dominican Republic) and the World Conference on Human Rights (Vienna, Austria). All of this and more, from women, to women, and to everyone.

FIRE brings you into direct contact with diverse women's voices via special live broadcasts from women's activities and conferences, such as the V International Interdisciplinary Congress on Women (Costa Rica), the VI Latin American and Caribbean Feminist Conference (El Salvador), V World Association of Community Radio Broadcasters Conference (Mexico), the U.N. Human Rights Conference in Vienna 1993, the U.N. Population and Development Conference in Cairo 1994, the U.N. Social Development summit 1995, the South African Women's Health Conference 1994 and others.

- March 1995—UNESCO selected two FIRE productions to present in Beijing:

EDITORS' NOTE: Frieda Werden, Producer of WINGS, Women's International News Gathering Service (see Chapter 23), is interviewing Maria Suarez of Feminist International Radio Endeavor—FIRE.

1. The series: Radio Tribunal on Violations of Women's Human Rights in Latin America and the Caribbean, 1993.
2. The series: History of Gender in Central America, 1992.

- February 1995—WINGS awarded FIRE the Katherine Davenport Award for its coverage of the U.N. Conference on Population and Development.
- November 1994—The Peace Power Foundation for support of women.

The following interview by WINGS reflects this experience and is presented here as an illustrative example of the use of feminist radio in advocacy of women's concerns at the level of consideration by the United Nations:

WINGS: Shortwave is a truly international means of communication. Its radio signals bounced off the ionosphere can be received by shortwave radios in far distant parts of the world. FIRE, Feminist International Radio Endeavor, uses shortwave to give worldwide coverage to the global women's movement. Their live broadcasts and radio tribunals have become a familiar part of the action at conferences from Austria to South Africa, Thailand to Argentina. FIRE played an especially crucial role as activist media covering the United Nations Conference on Population and Development held in September 1994 in Cairo, Egypt. FIRE producer Maria Suarez explained to WINGS that the work began in April 1994 in New York City at the final preparatory meeting for the population conference.

Maria Suarez: I believe that the third preparatory conference was key because it is there where the States draft the document that will be approved in the final conference and that the main debates take place. That is where they put in brackets the sentences that are not of consensus and approve the things upon which they have already built consensus. So the women's movement that has been involved in all the conferences knows that this is the main battleground—and that the

final conference is more of a formality and a propaganda thing.

So this is the framework of that third preparatory conference where women knew that we were going to face many opposing forces, especially to what was one of our major objectives in that conference, which was changing the focus of population policies from fertility control and regulation to rights, especially reproductive and sexual rights and also policies around the empowerment of women to have control and participation in the decision making.

So what happened at that preparatory conference was that the women's movement brought an agenda and lobbied the state delegates to have an influence in that agenda. I guess FIRE was invited by the Latin American and Caribbean Women's Health Coalition, both because of the work that FIRE had been doing in previous conferences—like the Earth Summit in 1992 and also the Human Rights Conference—but also because women have a better understanding of the role that an alternative media, that is, activist media, can play to support their agenda, their lobby, and their efforts in this kind of conference.

For example, when the Caucus got together to develop its strategies, FIRE was asked to interview Mr. [Nicolaas] Biegman, who was chairing the main committee where the debates on sexual and reproductive rights were held. And what we wanted to know from him was what was going to be his attitude toward the straight opposition of the Vatican. And what the women wanted him to know through FIRE was that the Caucus was not willing to allow the chair of such a meeting to be lax with the Vatican. So that he was not only able to know what the position of the Women's Caucus was, but also feel the strength of our Caucus that had assigned me to go and interview on its behalf. I also had to let him know that I wasn't coming as a journalist but as a communicator involved in the strategies of the Women's Caucus and the women's movement. One of the interesting things about that interview was that he started telling me off the record some stories about how he had learned why women's rights were important to the issue of population. That's because I always ask women in the interviews: How did you personally get involved? When I interviewed this man I also asked him. He told me the story about his first mission from the government of the Netherlands to Egypt about 25 years ago and what he was able to learn about the women there.

WINGS: I understand that you were also able to put together events between women at the conference and that these events had a kind of catalyzing effect. Would you describe some of that?

MS: At one point the Latin American Women's Caucus asked Feminist International Radio Endeavor to convene an encounter between the hardest delegation from Central America, which was a woman who was representing the Honduran government, which became famous in the prepcom because of their hard positions. The Opus Dei is the equivalent to the right-to-lifers. And she was representing her government and she had a voice, a very strong voice, in the official plenary of the meeting, whereas the nongovernmental organizations did not have a voice at the meeting. So the Women's Caucus wanted her to have to listen to what the women were saying. At the same time, the Caucus wanted to know her logic behind being so strong against women's rights. So I convened this interview with her and again I let her know that it wasn't only my idea or it wasn't only for the radio but that it was for the Women's Caucus. It was an interview and a debate that took place between the coordinator of the Latin American and Caribbean Women's Health Network, Amparo Claro from Chile, and this woman from Honduras that everybody knows as Lorena. The interview started with the issues of the separation between State and Church. And I remember that Lorena said that it wasn't that she was following the

Vatican's position but that the Vatican was following her position because she spoke before the Vatican. And Amparo was able to explain that when we said that she was following the Vatican, we meant that the Vatican had this same position for at least 200 years, yet the Honduran government had approved the recognition of women's rights as human rights in the Vienna conference just two years before.

So she had to listen to the arguments of the Women's Caucus and we were also able to systematize and organize the logic behind her position, which was the logic of the Opus Dei or the right-to-lifers, but also a logic that women were called to be the saviors of humanity—that the salvation of humanity was based on the sacrifice of women, even if it had to do with the sacrifice of our lives in danger—for example, the need of an abortion, where the woman and the fetus life was in danger. She said that if we lose the sacrifice of maternity all of humanity was lost. It was very important for us to understand that there was no possibility of dialoguing and understanding with such a position with her, the people of her kind, that were just following the Vatican. We just had to expose her and there we had an interview that we could use.

WINGS: There was another type of event?

MS: Yes. When the Vatican at that preparatory conference put in brackets the use of condoms, there was an outrage both by many of the official delegates and especially by the NGOs listening in to the official meeting. It was an outrage that I call historical, because they had bracketed the safe motherhood; they had bracketed sexual and reproductive rights. But to bracket condoms, even in this day and age with the epidemic of AIDS, was an outrage. It was very close to noontime, and there was going to be a lunch break, and we had to have strategies for how to react immediately that afternoon. Because if we lost that one, we were going to lose everything else that was going to be discussed.

So FIRE convened a panel, and 25 women came together from all the countries of Latin America. You have to remember that Latin America was the battleground for the support of the Vatican at that conference. The women came together with FIRE's microphone and they were able also to systematize, to hold their voices, to listen to each other. Alongside the expressions of outrage were all the arguments about not only AIDS but how women had the sole responsibility of the use of contraceptives. The women came up with the strategies on how to articulate a reaction to that. It came out very fluidly because they were able to put out the rage and to listen to themselves and to each other.

So an hour and a half later, we had a whole proposal to bring to the Women's Caucus, the worldwide women's caucus, on how to deal with this. And it was very important because it was an event that articulated the possibility of elaborating strategies on the spot and getting them going in the afternoon.

WINGS: So that you think that by it being on media it was given extra power?

MS: Well, yes, because media brings women together. They would have talked to each other bilaterally in the halls. I don't doubt that women talk to each other outside of media. But media, especially women's media when we are there with the movement, it creates the opportunity of bringing people together. As many as are needed and in the moment and in the places where it can be most necessary.

WINGS: I know that you were broadcasting live from this preparatory conference over Radio for Peace International. That you were doing it through telephone lines. And that you were able to get the information out that was not very well known anywhere else. But after you broadcast live, what did you do with the information?

MS: Well, let me brief you about the live broadcast, because it took place after the panel, the first one. I brought women together and I remember the woman from the U.S. delegation, who is a Puerto Rican, came on the live broadcast. She expressed her view about the same issue that the Latin American women had talked about in the FIRE panel. Everybody started applauding. So besides putting it out on the air, on Radio for Peace Broadcast, there was an audience right there around the live broadcast.

After the preparatory conference, both the Caucus and we at FIRE decided that one of the things that was our responsibility is getting that whole process of the voices of the States, the voices of the Vatican, the voices of the women, the State delegates that we had interviewed, the panel and some data, indicators about the issues that were discussed. That we had the responsibility of producing a documentary that would become a popular education instrument, that would allow anybody who wasn't there to come in there into that process. It's called Yemanya's Sparrows of All Evil. Yemanya is the Goddess of Fertility and the Goddess of the Oceans. And it's that. It's a documentary that gives you, with no mediation, the States' voices, the Vatican's voices, the women's voices, the interviews, the panel, parts of the live broadcast so that anybody could have access to it. And we used it when we had to go back to our countries and lobby our local delegates that were going to Cairo.

For example, in Costa Rica, we went to a meeting with the government but they said, No, the Costa Rican delegate did not bracket safe motherhood—I just put on the tape and it was her voice. And it was her voice, in the context of the voices of all the Central American delegates, which was sided with the Vatican. It was very scary for the government here to know that the Costa Rican government was in such a position. Then they sat down to dialogue with us and to see if we could work on a better position.

WINGS: Wow. Would you just tell me briefly as an aside what safe motherhood is?

MS: Safe motherhood is a definition by the World Health Organization which is all the conditions necessary so that women can develop their motherhood in safety. It doesn't include reproductive rights before birth but it's all the conditions of health care, food, and medical, psychological and physical attention to a woman and her young baby so that she can develop motherhood in safety. And that was placed in brackets, you know.

WINGS: Was that eventually part of the document that came out of the final event in Cairo?

MS: We worked very hard to get safe motherhood out of brackets and it came out of brackets very soon because it was ridiculous. The argument that that same Honduran delegate had used together with the Vatican to say that if you opened up to safe motherhood it could mean opening up to abortion. The problem that they had is that they were looking into anything and seeing the ghost of abortion in everything. Those were definitions we had already gained, and that we had to fight to hold within the U.N. definitions; and it stayed in, and it's a very important issue.

WINGS: OK, so when you got to Cairo you had to try to set the scene to get your point of view across. What were some of the things you did?

MS: Well, for one thing, when we got to Cairo now it was myself and also Nancy Vargas. We had also strengthened our links with ISIS in Chile and with other women in media, because we knew it was going to require a broader team to do the work that was expected of us, both because of what had been created as an expectation in the prepcom and because there was a lot more promotion in media, between both conferences, of the position of the Vatican and the Islamic

fundamentalists and not so much the voices of women. And that's what we had to bring out. When we got to Cairo, first of all we found a lot of media. In no conference before had there been 3,000 journalists that made themselves present there to cover that conference. That conference had a very high profile in media like no other one. The Earth Summit had 2,300 and this one had 3,000. So one of the things that we did is for FIRE, which is an alternative media, to go and visit all the media outlets that were there in their little offices and let them know that we were there, that we were going to do media work for the Women's Caucus and that they could count on us for any contacts with anybody from the Women's Caucus—but that we were also expecting that they put the voices of women in their media outlets. So it was very interesting because it happened with the *Earth Times,* which is the official paper of the United Nations in those conferences, with IPS, with French media, media in Spain, media in the U.S. And finally when the debate started and they would look for the women's voices from the different countries that had positions of opposition or positions of support of what was on the agenda, then they started looking for us to get the women that they wanted— and that they probably would have spent three or four days looking for who they should get, and so on—but we were able to provide it, but also demanding of them that they put women's voices in articles that we were writing in their media. It created a different context for us in being able to collaborate with commercial media.

WINGS: I understand that you also got involved as a media president in your own right as a spokesperson for the women's movement position?

MS: The Latin American Women's Caucus was asked by the *Christian Science Monitor* to select some woman to have a debate with the delegate of the Pope for their shortwave radio program, and the Women's Caucus selected me. I believe it was because they knew that I was somebody because of the work of FIRE and the links to their movement, somebody who had gathered a lot of information from all angles to be able to debate such a person as the Pope's delegate. It was Bishop [James] McHugh. You all know him in the States because he was on the air more times than anybody else between the prepcom and Cairo. I have seen him on television and I had learned his tricks. Now this was a guy who would look both at the audience straight in the eye when he wanted to get his message to the audience and to the persons he was debating straight in the eyes the whole time. So when I prepared for that debate I said I'm going to get this guy to not be able to look at me in the eyes so that I can look at him. Looking at him in the eyes has nothing to do with radio. The audience wouldn't be able to catch that, but I know how powerful that was when I saw him on television.

So we went onto the debate and it just so happened that two hours before the debate on the radio the plenary session of the official meeting had approved the Article 821, which is the famous article on abortion which recognizes that abortions should be recognized as a health issue. He was quite upset, but when he came to the debate he came with all his prepared things and he looked me straight in the eyes and asked who I was. When the *Christian Science Monitor* opened that microphone and asked me to present myself, I said I want you to know that I'm not here only as a representative of the Women's Caucus but also as a former nun and a present feminist. And that did it to him with the eyes. He couldn't look at me straight in the eyes again. The debate went on, especially highlighting what the Caucus had highlighted. Why is the Vatican even a State within the United Nations, and especially the only State in the world that doesn't have any women or children in it, to be so outspoken about women's and girls' rights? And this stopped him to the point where he told us that he wasn't there so

much as a State but as a moral and religious force. And if it was moral and religious force, there's a lot of other groups should have seats in the United Nations.

And the other role I think we were able to play is that at one point in the middle of the conference, when the debate was very hot at the official conference and at the Non-Governmental Organizations Forum, the Women's Caucus organized a press conference. Because the press was wanting to interview individual women from specific countries to counteract their positions with the official delegates positions, we had decided that we were going to organize a small press conference with three women speakers and then we would move to another room and each woman had a sign which she posted on her dress that spoke to the country where she came from, so that the media could look for the women that they wanted without having to spend too much time asking who they were and who was from where.

There were about nine right-to-lifers that were actually interrupting the interviews between mainstream media and the women's NGOs. Very aggressive. So I looked around and I said, Well, there has to be a way in which this can't happen—this is our moment in mainstream media. So I went to the tallest and the most outspoken right-to-lifer, who was a woman from Canada, and I guess I'll never forget her because she was so aggressive. And I went and I very loudly said to her, "For Feminist International Radio Endeavor, I want to know what your position is about the right to development," because they were saying that it was "development" and it shouldn't be reproductive rights and so on. Well, let me tell you that the moment she heard "Feminist International Radio Endeavor," she started fighting with my microphone. She wasn't even talking to me. I grabbed that microphone and I pulled it off from my body because I thought she was going to hit it at some point. It was like she was fighting with a feminist tape recorder and a feminist microphone. I kept asking her questions louder and louder, and they are so fanatic that in less than three minutes I had the nine of them around my microphone, talking and screaming and bringing their positions. I would tell them, how can you talk about development, where have you been when we have manifested in front of the Monetary Fund and the World Bank. I never saw you in the Social Summit and I never saw you in the Vienna conference. You've only been here in the Population Conference. Why is that? So they stayed there for about 45 minutes in this big debate with our program while the media and the women were able to talk in peace. Let me tell you, Frieda, that after 45 minutes they discovered what was happening and they were so angry that I have a picture where one of them has her hand trying to go towards my camera, because they realized—but that nobody had kept them there, you know. I mean, they were freely onto fighting with the feminists' microphone.

WINGS: So you feel that the Conference on Population and Development was a success from the feminists' point of view?

MS: Well, I think that the success is still to be measured in what happens in the implementation for the Plan of Action. As you know, they decided to postpone the discussion about the amount of funding that will be given for the implementation towards the Social Summit, so it's still a challenge. And I do believe that in terms of shifting the language of the Plan of Action for the next 20 years, it was a success for the women, because there is a shift in the overall philosophy of the relationship between population and development. The major shift in the philosophy is that now women are not as often blamed for the population explosion, as they call it, but it is the poverty, lack of develop-

ment, lack of opportunities and reproductive and sexual health and reproductive rights and the empowerment of women. And an emphasis on education and an empowerment of women and girl children, who are recognized as the major policy. I say that it's partial success because it is in the implementation and in our ability so that all women know what these new rights are for them and can organize to fight for them—that is where real success takes place. This is what the challenge is ahead. But I also think we have a very special challenge of media, as media women, because even after Cairo most of the mainstream media have tried to co-opt what we won in Cairo and what we went to Cairo for—saying that the women made a big contribution to make policies to reduce fertility more humane. That's not what we went to Cairo for. We went to change the paradigm of the relationship between population and development, recognizing for example that empowerment of women is not a means to achieve an end of reduction of population, but that the empowerment of women is a right in itself.

WINGS: Maria Suarez is one of the producers of FIRE, Feminist International Radio Endeavor, a daily shortwave program on Radio for Peace International out of Costa Rica. For schedule and frequency listings, write to RFPI, Box 88, Santa Ana, Costa Rica. A cassette of this program may be ordered for 9 U.S. dollars from WINGS, P.O. Box 33220, Austin, Texas 78764, U.S.A. Both FIRE and WINGS received support from the Foundation for a Compassionate Society. The WINGS sound logo is from Libana album "A Circle Is Cast." I'm Frieda Werden and this is WINGS, the Women's International News Gathering Service.

25

Women Communicating Globally
Mediating International Feminism

Annabelle Sreberny-Mohammadi

As a woman I have no country; as a woman, my country is the whole world.
Virginia Woolf, Three Guineas (1990)

Current global media dynamics reveal some paradoxical tendencies. On the one hand, there is the process of conglomeration of the cultural industries into global transnational corporations, which sometimes employ more people than live in some small countries. Recent examples of this tendency, taking advantage of the prospect of new cross-ownership rules in the United States, is the summer 1995 purchase by Disney of the ABC television network and the possible merger of Time-Warner and Turner Broadcasting. On the other hand, there is the dynamic of democratization and participation in community-controlled media and the production of politically progressive messages and culturally sensitive programs. Such media, broadly labeled

"alternative," are usually positioned as either against big transnational capital or against big states (Lewis, 1993; Sreberny-Mohammadi & Mohammadi, 1994).

But another form of communication is also burgeoning globally, and has received far less empirical and theoretical attention. It is the range of media broadly positioned against patriarchy, made mainly by women for women, and often forming the basis for feminist solidarity and global linkages that are unprecedented. Patriarchal media—which can operate at both local and international levels—can be typified by its output of sexist imagery constructed to suit the male gaze, by its representation of women in traditional social roles, by its organizational structure and gendered hierarchies with few women occupying top decision-making roles and few women in creative positions (Creedon, 1993; van Zoonen, 1994). Perhaps even more important, patriarchal media may be integrated with transnational capital at the global level, making money out of sexploitation, or with repressive state formations at the national level, maintaining the sociopolitical and cultural gender imbalances. Thus, almost by dint of their existence alone, autonomous media controlled by women with women-defined output offer a challenge to existing hierarchies of power; when these media take up specific issues and campaigns, and align themselves with larger social movements, their political potential is significant.

This chapter, predominantly descriptive in nature, maps out some of these new women-centered media, concentrating mainly on those operating in the South, or the southern hemisphere, as examples of the transformations in communications that women are effecting. This writing is based on research undertaken for UNESCO in May 1994 in preparation for the 1995 Beijing conference (Sreberny-Mohammadi, 1995a, 1995b). I end by asking some analytic questions that might ground future research in this area, and by suggesting some practical strategies that might be pertinent to further developing women's communication activities.

Print Media

The most common form of communication now includes newspapers, journals, magazines, newsletters; occasional monographs and leaflets; well-established publishing houses and distribution outlets. The most numerous (Allen, 1988) as well as some of the longest running are in the United States and Europe, but there is now significant development across the South. Already in 1990, ISIS International had a directory, *Third World Women's Publications*, which then listed more than 300 publications. Some new publications include *Sister,* Namibia; *Speak,* South Africa; *Sauti ya Siti,* Tanzania; and *Asmita,* Nepal, although such publications can be found in all regions.

The *Tamania Mars* (March 18th) Magazine Collective in Morocco is an interesting example of the dilemmas facing women when they begin to organize and implicitly—if not always explicitly—challenge the gendered status quo (for an extended discussion, see Lewis, 1993). *Tamania Mars* was begun in November 1983, published monthly till 1989, ceased for a year, then reappeared as a monthly journal. Founded by women members of a left-wing political party plus a number of independent women, it was organized democratically, was open to all women, and published articles by men. The *Tamania Mars* collective aimed to provide information to women, to establish a rallying point to fight against patriarchy, specifically the personal statutes of Moroccan law, and to work for human rights and a more just and egalitarian society. The group intended to build a self-reliant united women's democratic mass movement, addressing intellectual and working women, and students and schoolgirls from the Moroccan middle and lower classes. It helped to define a new agenda of women's issues, running discussions and symposia on the origins of women's subordination in Morocco and discussing previously taboo topics such as prostitution and repudiation. The group also conducted research, carrying out surveys and opinion polls and examining the broader contexts of the situation of women as in the family, the economy, education, and legal structures. It also supported lectures, meetings, literary gatherings, cultural festivals, and other kinds of actions, which culminated in the establishment of the Women's Action Union in 15 locations across Morocco. It was the inspiration for the establishment of other publications such as *Nissa al Maghrib* (Morocco), *Nissa* (Tunisia), and *Fippo* (Senegal).

The *Tamania Mars* collective continually struggled to maintain its financial base, an experience that is common not only to women's activism but to popular movements as a whole. This raises an issue about the appropriate choice of medium, particularly about the use of print in a context of massive female illiteracy, and hence also issues about the potential for dialogue across class and urban-rural divisions of women. Much development literature agrees that continued high levels of illiteracy are among the biggest obstacles to women's involvement in development (Bellara, 1991). The production of materials pertinent to women's concerns might be exactly the kind of materials around which new literacy campaigns could grow; or these publications might only circulate in narrow literate circles, creating a female leadership without much of a popular base. While the development of *Tamania Mars* shows the many struggles involved in women's right to speak, to argue, to occupy public space and open up public debate, and how much can be done, it also raises new critical questions that should be pursued.

Press Services

With the growth in a diverse feminist press, news services that support these—and also try to get women's issues and concerns into the mainstream media—also have developed around the world. There are now a number of women's press services such as DepthNews in Asia, the Women's Feature Service, based in New Delhi, WINGS in the United States, and a women's news agency, FEMPRESS, in Chile.

The Women's Feature Service (WFS) based in New Delhi became independent from Inter-Press Service, the progressive news agency, in 1991. The Women's Feature Service offers a syndicated feature service worldwide, using more than a hundred women journalists based around the world to provide copy for the mainstream media. The focus of these features is the examination of development from perspectives of progressive women. De-

velopment is broadly defined, and can include both micro- and macro-level foci, depending on the particular circumstances. Often the subjects are not novel in themselves, but WFS attempts to write with a gendered perspective to balance that traditionally mainstream dominance. The WFS strategy is to get more feminist news and analysis into mainstream media to prevent them remaining marginal, arguing that mainstream media have the power to transform peoples' opinions, as well as to legitimize issues. Its work practices support the promotion of women journalists in mainstream media, and WFS also offers journalist training programs, comprising theoretical and practical curricula from a gender perspective (Anand, 1994; also Women's Feature Service, 1993).

One of the main issues surrounding such news services is how much of this material circulates internationally and whether it makes its way into the mainstream press—indeed, whether such stories become useful pegs for more media material and discussion about the situation of women. Monitoring studies of the gendered representation of news are growing, including the one-day global media monitoring organized by MediaWatch, Canada (Global Media Monitoring Project, 1995). A major multicountry study of international news (Sreberny-Mohammadi, 1995b), which includes the Beijing conference in its time frame of content analysis, should provide solid empirical evidence about the news representation of women's issues.

Broadcasting, Film, and Video

Although women have been using electronic media in North America and Europe for some time, it is increasingly available in all regions and used for many different purposes.

Media are used in local contexts to help women develop skills and lose their fear, to remember and to build for the future, as with video use by the Self Employed Women's Association (SEWA) in India (Bali, 1993;

see Stuart and Bery's Chapter 32 in this volume), or the use of video and radio among indigenous women in Bolivia and other parts of Latin America (Rodriguez, 1994; Ruiz, 1994). In addition are Radio Tierra in Chile, and FIRE (Feminist International Radio Endeavour), Costa Rica, which aims to "give voice to those who never had one." The FIRE collective conceives of radio as a process of meeting, dialogue, and participation with other women and puts great store on the transformational power of women's personal testimonies. (See Suarez Toro, Chapter 24.)

Yet other radio projects are oriented toward more specific development needs and empowering women to play a role in development planning, for example, the Development Through Radio Project. In 1988, the Federation of African Media Women—Zimbabwe (FAMWZ) began to provide rural dwellers with access to national radio by giving them the opportunity to participate actively in the preparation of development-oriented programs based on their own needs and priorities. The programs constitute part of the regular schedule of the national education and development channel of Zimbabwe Broadcasting Corporation.

Radio listening clubs were organized in rural areas, with overwhelmingly female membership, aiming to deal with the imbalances in the distribution of and access to resources, from land to decision making, which women faced, and to see if media could be used to promote greater access to other resources. Clubs listen weekly to a half-hour tape prepared by the broadcasters compiled from tapes submitted by all the clubs. After discussion on the topics raised and suggesting their own topics, clubs will record their own responses, which are collected, and listened to, and then the relevant government minister or official, businessperson, donor agency representative, or other appropriate person will be invited to record responses and suggestions to the issues raised.

There are now 45 radio listening clubs in four of nine provinces in Zimbabwe, and a desire to expand to other areas, to include more men and adolescents in the clubs and communities also (Moyo & Quarmyne, 1994).

Radio remains one of the cheapest and most widespread of forms in the South. The Development Through Radio Project has developed a unique way of communicating horizontally among communities in Zimbabwe as well as vertically up to responsible officials and back down and out to the rural areas, yet its very success and desire for expansion threaten to overburden the system in terms of demands on resources and personnel. It is a fascinating model of how to foster participation of women within their communities and how to link media to development efforts, one of the few precise examples of the women-media-development nexus.

Women are active across many other media also. Latin America is home to Cine Muher, a collective of women filmmakers—film being well-established and popular in many regions and all too often omitted from media analysis. Satellite EVE, based in Buenos Aires, Argentina, has a national focus and aims specifically "to stimulate women's creativity and ability to organize and use the power of the media toward the construction of a more pluralistic, equitable, and just society," using video, photography, and investigative journalism as its main vehicles. A satellite project in Canada, WETV, was launched in conjunction with the Beijing conference. The intention of its organizers was to provide "an alternative global television service available on every continent through international satellite services, providing the first global access television service"; it was to broadcast southern nations' programming, and claims a particular concern for women. The World Association of Community Radio Broadcasters, AMARC, based in Montreal, is a network of communicators who "identify themselves with the construction of a new world order in communication and in society," which also has initiatives to support women's voices on the global airwaves.

Live Locally, Think
and Act Globally Too

Women have shown ourselves to be excellent networkers, living locally, but both thinking *and* acting globally, extending solidarity across national and other boundaries. There are numerous networks that specifically focus on media such as CAFRA, Trinidad and Tobago; WAND, Barbados; SISTERLINK, Australia; IWSAW, Lebanon; and FEMNET, Kenya.

Organizations such as the International Women's Tribune Center (IWTC), New York, act as central clearinghouses of information about women's activities globally. IWTC ran the Global Faxnet of information about activities, planning, and registration for the Beijing conference, and maintained a faxnet commentary throughout the NGO conference. The center also publishes the *Tribune* and manages Women, Ink., a marketing and distribution service funded by the U.N. Development Fund for Women (UNIFEM), which publishes *Unifem News.* Distribution to the South is subsidized by sale of publications in the North. Another very active network, ISIS International, operates out of Santiago, Chile, and Manila, the Philippines. It was established as an NGO in 1974 as a women's information and communication service, supporting "the empowerment and full participation of women in development processes through the formation of networks and channels of communication and information." ISIS has more than 50,000 contacts in 150 countries, and produces a directory of publications as well as *Powerful Images* (1986), a catalogue that lists over 600 films, videos, and slide shows by Third World women.

On many continents, specifically regional networks of women have developed. For example, the Asian Network of Women in Communication (ANWIC), New Delhi, publishes *Impact* and aims "to mobilize Asia women, through communication, to achieve a more equitable and just social order recognizing the diversity present in the region." And there are networks operating within a religio-cul-

tural milieu, such as Women Living Under Muslim Law (WLUML, headquartered in France with offices throughout the Muslim World), an international network of solidarity that publishes a quarterly news sheet as well as monographs on varied topics, including violence against women, reproductive rights, and disenfranchisement. The WLUML network has strong links with women's groups in the North (e.g., Women Against Fundamentalism in the United Kingdom) whose focus is on the dilemmas of women in minority ethnic groups whose voices are often not heard by the dominant culture.

Networking is also facilitated by the use of the Internet and e-mail transmission, with the Women and Environment Network (WEDNET) forging links between its Canadian base and African researchers. Mujer a Mujer, a Mexican-based women's collective concerned with free trade and structural adjustment, coordinates projects in Mexico, Canada, the United States, and Nicaragua. There are a variety of electronic bulletins (Women Envision by ISIS; SEAWIN, South East Asian Women's Information Project in the Philippines), feminist listservs, and discussion groups such as FEMISA, many under the aegis of the Association for Progressive Communication (APC). These are just beginning to be analyzed for their political potential (Balka, 1992; Sreberny-Mohammadi, in press). World Wide Web (WWW) sites were set up under the aegis of APC and GreenNet to provide those who could not attend the U.N. conference in Beijing with up-to-date information, documents, and analyses of events at the NGO Forum and at the official proceedings; much of this information remains available at on-line sites. Feminist academics and researchers have also established international networks, such as Womennet of the International Association of Media and Communication Research (IAMCR). Electronic mail can be cheaper than the telephone, faster than snail mail, more efficient than fax, and many women's groups are providing training for women activists and organizations on computers, e-mail, and creative use of the Internet.

Indigenous Culture and Performance

One other area of communicative activity that often gets overlooked but may be of special relevance for women is the use of and support for folk cultures and oral traditions in development-oriented and participatory communication projects (e.g., dance in Tanzania, see Mlama, 1994; storytelling of African American women, see Dyer-Bennem, 1994). These are no-cost or low-cost practices with low technology inputs. They may ensure that we build on the past and develop existing female knowledge and skills, creating dialogue and equal relations and not separating media makers from media consumers (Bhasin, 1994). Indigenous culture and modes of performance can also be used as a bulwark against the products of Western cultural industries by encouraging women to take pride in their own culturally authentic forms of expression.

For example, Sistren Theatre Group, developed in the democratic socialist environment of Manley's Jamaica, was founded by a group of women in 1977. Shaped by common experiences of poverty, rural life, and often single parenthood, the group draws on personal problems that are connected to broader social themes. Their technique develops scripts out of improvization and African oral traditions. The aim is to address women, particularly in working-class communities, to mobilize themselves and to organize for a stronger voice about issues that concern them. Sistren has diversified into textile design and into production of a magazine three times a year. It has also developed a research and documentation center and has considerable experience in identifying problems of working-class and rural women and helping them to establish their own community groups.

The Sistren collective set out to weave performative narratives out of ordinary women's lives. Their experience also raises many issues about the financing of women's groups, here from external sources, and the need to become self-sufficient. Their honest analysis also provokes examination of the dilemmas of self-management and internal democracy, specifically the emergent class differences among women, which arose particularly in discussion about Creole versus English language use in Sistren's theatrical performances.

The Rise of Global Women's Media

With the rise of so much and such varied activity, the distinction between commercial media and the new global women's media seems increasingly blurred. A feminist publishing house, which struggles at one time to survive financially, to build a reputation and an audience, and to find manuscripts, may at another time become so successful that the main factor that distinguishes it from any other publishing house is that it is run by women, albeit an achievement in itself. Kali for Women in New Delhi started in 1984 by fund-raising for each publishing venture to support writing by and about women in the Third World; by 1994, it was financially solvent and sometimes copublishes with progressive publishers around the world. The Women's Press, Virago, and Sheba in Britain were the first to publish women's writing, yet that is now increasingly taken on board by malestream established publishers and booksellers, a supreme indication of the success of the earlier ventures in gaining acknowledgment for women's writing. Recently, one of the first feminist bookshops in London, SisterWrite, and one of the first feminist magazines, *Spare Rib,* ceased their activities, eclipsed by transnational media economics.

What little literature exists on this topic (Allen, 1988; Riaño, 1994) tends to suggest that feminist media share certain characteristics:

They produce different output, often materials on issues pertinent to women that receive short shrift in patriarchal media. They are run by women for women, often with a nonhierarchical and collective structure. They often have an activist orientation, combining theory and practice, trying to integrate the personal and the political, because giving women a chance to find and articulate their voices is often the precondition for and a precursor to developing a political voice at local, national, and international levels. Yet some of the most successful of such projects—the ones that endure for the longest time, that secure a funding base for their activities, and that find audiences for their particular assortment of cultural products—sometimes find themselves having to develop more formal structures. Attempts to make sharp distinctions between "alternative" and "mainstream" feminist media sometimes obfuscate the complex realities, the different socioeconomic contexts of North and South, and the varied political-cultural milieus in which women struggle. It is more productive to ask how linkages between North and South can be forged and maintained, and how women in different locations can support each other.

Strengthening Women's Voices

The focus on women's media, however, may help us think through and make both analytic and practical linkages with other new social movements (Wignaraja, 1993); antiwar and peace movements; and ecological, labor, and revolutionary movements (Peterson & Runyan, 1993). We need to unpack the various meanings of *empowerment* and critically examine how and if media/communicative empowerment feeds in to economic and political empowerment. The most recent *Human Development Report* (1995) indicates just how severe the global gender imbalances remain in so many basic areas of social life. Partly this means rescuing "alternative media" from a narrow media-centric focus and

taking up much broader perspectives in feminist work in this area.

It is useful to try to formulate some recommendations for ways in which some of the issues can be taken forward and acted upon by pressuring international organizations, national development foundations, media organizations, and so on. My focus here remains predominantly—but not solely—on activities supportive of development in the South (see also Sreberny-Mohammadi, 1994, 1995a).

Although women's work in media has shown remarkable progress over the last 15 years, it needs to be further strengthened in terms of financial, moral, and intellectual support and, where feasible and appropriate, these efforts should be integrated into development planning efforts. As women's media activities expand, further support should be given to initiatives that encourage a range of women's expression and creativity within all kinds of media operations at national, regional, or global levels.

There is increasing understanding of the crucial link between the situation of women and the dynamics of development (e.g., Massiah, 1993; Moser, 1993; Mosse, 1993), and there is better awareness of the role that the media can play in challenging sex role stereotypes and promoting women's concerns. The two foci are rarely brought together in the understanding that media, both malestream and women's, may play a role in improving the gendered processes of development. External funding organizations and technical agencies should positively support those projects that try to strengthen and secure positive and public roles for women in media and development.

Other Practical Strategies for Change

The considerable amount and array of women's media production (film, video, photographic, audio, print, and so on) needs to be archived and catalogued, which is perhaps best done on a regional basis. This would offer a huge source of broadcast material for use by all media channels, as well as useful materials for training purposes, which could be used to foster cross-cultural understanding and solidarity and to inspire other women through examples of best practice.

Similarly, despite the increase in research and publishing on women and media, much of it is inaccessible, particularly to women in the South. There is an urgent need for the further development of regional documentation centers and libraries, the publication of bibliographies on international research work on gender, media, and communication, and the wider dissemination of research findings.

If women are better at nonhierarchical working, then we could also be better at crossing disciplinary and occupational divides. We need to make, and find support for, better links among grassroots activists, media researchers, NGOs and advocacy groups, and policymakers as well as across sectoral divides (media workers, development workers, health workers, and so on). If media can play useful functions in specific campaigns, and women are active in producing media content, then instead of putting up new structures, existing positive activities could be directed to new issues and concerns. Women media activists also need to explore links to other progressive groupings working for a new communication environment where gender blindness still exists, such as the movement toward a People's Communication Charter and the ongoing discussions of the MacBride Round Table.

Better links need to be forged with networks of development planners and researchers, so that they too come to understand the potential contribution of media in the development process and the empowerment of women through media activities. If the redefinition of development focuses on human needs and empowerment, then women and media need to be recognized as key elements of that redefinition.

Functional literacy is key to social and economic development. Thus priority must be given to those programs and projects that seek to strengthen the basic education and training of girls and women, preparing them to fulfill more dynamic roles in the development process in general and in media production in particular. Media can also be used in more innovative ways to deliver adult literacy support.

Various international bodies, such as UNESCO and the European Community (EC), have already made useful initiatives in support of women's activities, including the range of consultations and working groups building toward draft documents and participation at Beijing. It is important to consolidate this work with adequate resources. A percentage of development agency funds should be earmarked for women's activities, given the trickle-up effects that these can have through all the social networks of which women are a part. Because the U.N. system at large, and UNESCO in particular, act as significant international forums for discussion of women's issues and for implementation of initiatives on such issues, it is important that the United States, the United Kingdom, and Singapore rejoin UNESCO, and that all those countries with significant outstanding debts to the United Nations pay them quickly.

There are numerous international conventions—including human rights conventions—with gender implications that need to be adopted by more countries. The United States, as well as other nations, has not ratified the Convention on the Elimination of All Forms of Discrimination Against Women (CEDAW), one of the major international instruments that seeks to feminize the existence and enunciation of human rights; there was strong concern that the politics of the September 1995 Beijing conference would weaken CEDAW rather than strengthen it, and international pressure was summoned for the NGO Forum in Beijing to proclaim the universality of the human rights of all women (Global Faxnet, August 21, 1995). At the time of this writing, support was growing for an annual International Day of Protest Against Violence Against Women, as well as support for a Global Tribunal on Violations of Women's Rights, with action to ensure that the media would cover and debate the issues that lie behind such actions. Women made enormous efforts to make the global media aware of the multiple preparations for the Beijing conference, and of the global female audience interested in the event. A measure of how far we have come will be found in the analysis of how much media coverage the Beijing conference received, as well as what financial and resource commitments were made by international agencies as well as states to follow through on the Beijing declarations.

Some Tentative Conclusions

We need to be wary of a universalizing notion of women that produces simplistic, quantitative solutions to gender inequality and to development. Women—and feminists—around the world have different priorities, strategies, and purposes as well as different paths to solutions, although mutual support and learning from others is vital. Although I do think it's important to celebrate, support, and foster the variety of activities that women are undertaking worldwide, we must remain critical as to what we hope to achieve. Specifically, we need more critical analysis about these alternative media in the South: Do they "empower"—how and whom? How does empowerment function, as a psychological state, as collective power, with cultural or social or political consequences? Are such media activities the sites for learning democratic participation, collective action, political strategy—and can such lessons be transferred to other social locations? The efficacy of specific media activities must be analyzed within their particular situated contexts of economic, political, and cultural concerns, and it is women in the South who will be the best judges of the nature and extent of their achievements.

In writing this chapter, I have had cause once again to reflect on my own position of privilege in relation to the issues I describe. In writing for a predominantly North American and European readership, I can hope that my articulation of issues is new and interesting and perhaps provocative. I can also hope that, in another sense of articulation, I help to make connections and strengthen the weak links in our knowledge and understanding of the huge range of communicative forms worldwide by which women act through speaking and speak through action.

References

Allen, M. (1988). *The development of communication networks among women 1963-1983.* Unpublished doctoral dissertation, Howard University, Washington, DC.

Anand, A. (1994, February). *The Women's Feature Service: A news alternative.* Paper presented at the Women Empowering Communications conference, Bangkok, Thailand.

Bali, N. (1993). Video as a means of training and organising: The experience of SEWA [Women's Experiences in Community Media: Special issue]. *Women in Action* (ISIS International).

Balka, E. (1992). *Womantalk goes on-line: The use of computer networks in the context of feminist social change.* Unpublished doctoral dissertation, Simon Fraser University.

Bellara, M. (Ed.). (1991). *Women and literacy.* London: Zed Books.

Bhasin, K. (1994). Women and communication alternatives: Hope for the next century. *Media Development, 41,* 2.

Creedon, P. (Ed.). (1993). *Women in mass communication* (2nd ed.). Newbury Park, CA: Sage.

Dyer-Bennem, S. (1994). Cultural distinctions in communication patterns of African-American women. In P. Riaño (Ed.), *Women in grassroots communication* (pp. 65-83). Thousand Oaks, CA: Sage.

Global Media Monitoring Project. (1995). *Women's participation in the news.* Canada: MediaWatch.

Kerr, J. (Ed.). (1993). *Ours by right: Women's rights as human rights.* London: Zed Books.

Lewis, P. (Ed.). (1993). *Alternative media: Linking global and local* (Reports and Papers in Mass Communication, No. 107). Paris: UNESCO.

Massiah, J. (Ed.). (1993). *Women in developing economies: Making visible the invisible.* Providence, RI: Berg/Paris: UNESCO.

Mlama, P. (1994). Reinforcing existing indigenous communication skills: The use of dance in Tanzania. In P. Riaño (Ed.), *Women in grassroots communication*. Thousand Oaks, CA: Sage.

Moser, C. (1993). *Gender planning for development*. London: Routledge Kegan Paul.

Mosse, J. C. (1993). *Half the world, half a chance*. Oxford: Oxfam.

Moyo, M., & Quarmyne, W. (1994, February). *The Development Through Radio (CTR) Project (Zimbabwe)*. Paper presented at the Women Empowering Communications conference, Bangkok, Thailand.

Peterson, V. S., & Runyan, A. S. (1993). *Global gender issues*. Boulder, CO: Westview.

Riaño, P. (Ed.). (1994). *Women in grassroots communication*. Thousand Oaks, CA: Sage.

Rodriguez, C. (1994). A process of identity construction: Latin American women producing video stories. In P. Riaño (Ed.), *Women in grassroots communication*. Thousand Oaks, CA: Sage.

Ruiz, C. (1994). Losing fear: Video and radio production of native Aymara women in Bolivia. In P. Riaño (Ed.), *Women in grassroots communication*. Thousand Oaks, CA: Sage.

Sreberny-Mohammadi, A. (1994). *Women, media and development in a global context*. Paris: UNESCO.

Sreberny-Mohammadi, A. (1995a, February). *Women, media and development in a global context*. Paper presented at the UNESCO International Symposium, Women and Media: Access to Expression and to Decision-Making, Toronto.

Sreberny-Mohammadi, A. (1995b). International news flows in the post-cold war world: Mapping the news and the news producers. *Electronic Journal of Communication, 5*(2-3).

Sreberny-Mohammadi, A. (Ed.). (in press). International feminism(s) [Special issue]. *Journal of International Communication*.

Sreberny-Mohammadi, A., & Mohammadi, A. (1994). *Small media, big revolution: Communications, culture and the Iranian revolution*. Minneapolis: University of Minnesota Press.

van Zoonen, L. (1994). *Feminist media studies*. London: Sage.

Wignara, P. (Ed). (1993). *New social movements in the south: Empowering the people*. London: Zed Books.

Women's Feature Service. (1993). *The power to change: Third World women shaping their environment*. London: Zed Books/Kali for Women.

Woolf, V. (1990). *Three guineas*. London: Virago.

26

Reclaiming Language

Casey Miller
Kate Swift

"Sex!" the man shouted—and the Class of 1967 broke into giggles and grins, smiles and smirks. "I'm going to say the magic word," he had told them, "then I'll shoot."

Whatever that "magic word" conveyed to each of the 50-some high school girls and boys who had gathered for their class picture, the photographer caught the spontaneous facial expressions he wanted when he clicked his shutter.

Sex was out in the open. It was cool. It was fun. It could be enjoyed by everybody, whether or not they went "all the way." For the generation then coming of age, *sex* meant erotic pleasure first and foremost—as distinct from the historical meaning of the word reported in standard dictionaries such as Merriam-Webster's Seventh *New Collegiate* of 1963, where the entry for *sex* began: "either of two divisions of organisms distinguished respectively as male or female."

When did the connotations of pleasure, desire, and passion so completely override the sense of the word as a division of organisms as to change the meaning *sex* communicated? Could the photographer have elicited the same reactions from the students by shouting "girls and boys"?

As long as *sex* was defined by males for males, its erotic connotations could remain covert. Until well into the twentieth century, entries for the word in standard dictionaries omitted any reference to emotions or behavior, but they did include, among other definitions, "women." For example, the 1913 edition of Funk & Wagnalls *New Standard Dictionary of the English Language* defined *sex* as "1. The physical difference between male and female animals. . . . 2. Either of the groups into which organisms are thus divided. . . . 3. Women in general; womankind as distinguished from man: generally with the definite article, as, a devoted admirer of *the sex*."

Encoded in part 3 of that definition was the frisson experienced by members of one group of human beings, the dominant one, when contemplating the physical differences from themselves of members of the subordinate group—subordinate not only in the minds of men but in the minds of most women and in the structure of almost every human society. The definition took no account either of the responses of those in the subordinate group or of the feelings of dominant group members who were sexually attracted to one another. The patriarchal perspective thus expressed persisted in dictionaries published into the 1960s, including the last edition of Merriam-Webster's Second *New International,* which included a note on *the sex,* defining the term as "the female sex; women, in general."

But usage was already changing to reflect female perspectives, including women's long-denied and often-suppressed enjoyment of sex. A different word was required to replace the term in its formerly primary sense of "either of two divisions of organisms," and *gender* was at hand to fill the need. Ruth Bader Ginsburg, when writing briefs for sex discrimination cases being argued before the Supreme Court in the 1970s, deliberately chose to use *gender* after her secretary, who was typing the briefs, pointed out that the constant repetition of *sex* on every page must create distracting associations for the nine justices on what was then an all-male court (as reported in the *Hartford Courant,* November 21, 1993, p. A2).

Grammarians objected to the use of *gender* in such contexts. The *New York Times*'s in-house usage expert, Theodore Bernstein, stated the rule succinctly in his 1965 book *The Careful Writer* and in the same breath confirmed the by-then primary meaning of *sex.* "*Gender* is a grammatical term," he wrote. "It is not a substitute for sex (but, then, what is?)" (p. 199).

Bernstein and other language professionals notwithstanding, *gender* was in widespread use by the 1980s to indicate female-male distinctions in political, economic, and other cultural contexts, such as "gender studies," "gender roles," and "the gender gap." Far from minor, the shift was emblematic of the linguistic upheaval in which English usage would finally begin to reflect more evenly the perceptions of both divisions of the human organism. Although the male bias of English had been the subject of occasional comment in previous centuries, only with the Second Wave of feminism did awareness of the oppression of women through language reach the critical mass necessary to generate responsive changes in common usage.

Our personal history as writers and editors provides a paradigmatic example of how individual awareness can merge with and help to synergize a groundswell of new perception. Growing up in the 1920s and 1930s, both of us had been taught to appreciate the English language and to respect its lexical subtleties. Later, when each worked with words professionally, we were frequently troubled by the stereotypes and distortions of meaning conveyed by some forms of standard usage, including the cognitive exclusion of females perpetuated through what is supposed to be generic use of masculine-gender nouns and pronouns. But like thousands of educated women before us, we continued to accept as practical conventions and useful shortcuts the "rules" that rendered us invisible or, at best, second class.

By the 1960s, American society was undergoing a major if largely still unrecognized sea change with regard to women's expectations. Thus, when in 1970 we formed an editorial partnership, we discovered almost immediately that our individual concerns about the male bias of English had not been idiosyncratic. But it wasn't until we tried to figure out what was skewing the otherwise straightforward content of a sex education manual we were copyediting that the depth of the problem struck us. This was a routine assignment, or it seemed routine until the moment we realized that although the author apparently intended to convey one message—the sexes are equal and deserve equal respect—his language was telegraphing the opposite—males are more important than females and more deserving of respect. The significance of what now seems so obvious it scarcely bears repeating had up to that moment eluded us: Standard English usage said males are the norm, females a lesser breed.

Specifically, this author's conventional use of *man* and *he* when generalizing about human behavior either rendered his observations ambiguous or screened out half the people he intended to include. His consistency in giving precedence to males in such phrases as *men and women, husbands and wives,* and *male and female* signaled secondary status for those in the number two spot. Even more subtle was his use of the terms *feminine* and *masculine* in ways that conveyed societally sanctioned stereotypes. If the author's objective was to describe real teenagers, it seemed to us he had an obligation to make clear that all girls are not gentle, delicate, and self-indulgent, any more than all boys are strong, brave, and domineering.

Our immediate job, of course, was to suggest ways around such pitfalls in the manuscript. But, as though we had tasted the forbidden fruit, we found we could no longer ignore the implications of what at the time seemed like a unique discovery. From our newly acquired perspective, we decided that our task was to capture the attention of ordinary speakers and writers of English, convincing them through everyday examples that many of the grammatical and lexical conventions we had learned in school—and which we felt great pressure to continue observing—were irrational at best and damaging to the self-image of women and girls at worst. Even if we had been familiar with the work scholars were already doing in the field, our aim would still have been to re-create the epiphany we had both experienced when we suddenly saw what our native tongue had been saying to us and about us as female human beings from the time we had first learned to speak.

The legitimacy of such an anecdotal approach to understanding the subliminal messages encoded in language is controversial. Linguists and grammarians, the former trained in technical analysis, the latter in a reverence for tradition, tend to discount such seat-of-the-pants methods. But given the rootedness of language in human experience and its consequent reflection and perpetuation of the human perceptions of any given time, we wanted to challenge people's unthinking acceptance of the grammar and vocabulary we had inherited. What we failed to realize was that such a direct attack would be lost without concomitant changes in society itself. As is now clear, however, the societal changes even then occurring were so widespread that, unlike our precursors, what we and others were saying about the subliminal messages in standard English not only found fertile ground but helped to explain and extend the changes already occurring in the language of ordinary people if not, as yet, in the rules expounded by usage mavens.

The apparent absence from English of a singular pronoun designating a person of either sex struck us as a major stumbling block to linguistic equity, and we decided to write an article on the subject. Although we were aware that many well-spoken people used *they* with singular or indefinite antecedents, we still thought it unacceptable in writing, not knowing that *they* as a singular pronoun had been accepted English usage until the nineteenth century, when prescriptive grammarians ruled it out and invented the "generic" *he* to take its place. Nor did we know then that proposals for new, inclusive pronouns had been showing up in newspapers and magazines for at least 100 years. Two of them, *he'er* and *thon,* had appeared in the 1913 Funk and Wagnall's dictionary, and the latter was even included in the last printing of Merriam-Webster's Second *New International* in the 1960s.

Our first published effort to analyze and, we naively thought, to correct this lack was an article subtitled "Desexing the Language," which appeared in *New York Magazine* in late 1971 and in the first issue of *Ms.* in the spring of 1972. In it we proposed that a set of invented words—*tey, ter,* and *tem*—be adopted as the singular counterparts of *they, their,* and *them* (a suggestion which suffered the same fate as its predecessors).

Early in 1972, we were asked by the *New York Times Magazine* to write a general article on sexism in English. That article, published under the title "One Small Step for Genkind," was a breakthrough in that, as far as we know, it was the earliest substantive piece on linguistic sexism to appear in a large-circulation, mainstream publication.

From the responses to those two articles, we learned that a great many people, including scholars, were interested in and actively exploring the subject of linguistic sexism. The role of androcentric language in the power structure had been among the concerns exposed and analyzed in women's movement periodicals, pamphlets, and flyers. *Male chauvinism, sexism,* and other new terms had emerged in these discussions and were moving rapidly into everyday discourse. Soon, an interdisciplinary journal, *Women and Language,* founded in 1976, would begin recording the growing body of research in the field as well as reporting on courses and conferences.[1]

Meanwhile, the initial refusal of most of the mainstream media to acknowledge the male bias of English took the form of ridicule and satiric wordplay designed to inhibit reasonable dialogue. The title of a full-page essay in *Time* magazine (Kanfer, 1972), "Sispeak: A Msguided Attempt to Change Herstory," was typical of the superficiality accorded the subject, although the amount of space devoted to similar putative jocularity—entire columns by prominent syndicated pundits, William Buckley (1972), Russell Baker (1973), and George Will (1974), for example—revealed a motivation that seemed more akin to anxiety than amusement. At the same time, serious commentary on the subject continued to appear as other respected popular publications acknowledged linguis-

tic sexism as a legitimate concern. When our book *Words and Women* was published in 1976, a number of thoughtful male critics were genuinely persuaded—apparently to their surprise—of the validity of its reasoning.

In *Words and Women,* we tried to show how English usage had evolved over the past 1,000 years to reflect a patriarchal culture, supporting and perpetuating the assumptions, both conscious and otherwise, of male superiority and of a male norm representing the human species. The evidence we cited included, among other things, the arrogation to males of *man,* in Anglo-Saxon English a gender-inclusive designation for any male or female person; the history of terms such as *harlot* and *virago,* once used benignly of men but devalued in meaning when applied, and eventually limited, to women; and the addition of *-ess, -ette,* and similar suffixes to gender-neutral agent nouns, a device that serves no function in modern English except to identify girls and women as deviant or substandard beings, thereby reinforcing the assumption of the male norm. Having learned that linguistic change rarely comes about through fiat, we avoided prescribing remedies. Instead, we assumed that if our evidence was convincing, readers who agreed with us would find their own way. In any case, others were already offering specific alternatives to androcentric terminology, including major textbook publishers who began in the early 1970s to provide their authors with explicit guidelines on how to avoid sexist usage.

Our *Handbook of Nonsexist Writing,* first published in 1980, was addressed to writers, editors, and speakers. In addition to suggesting possible solutions to the most common problems we and others had identified, it again used historical evidence in an effort to confront head-on the conviction of many educated people that grammar and vocabulary are sacrosanct. What we wanted to demonstrate was that linguistic change is not only needed but natural and inevitable—the very lifeblood of a living language.

These efforts and the proliferating contributions of other nontechnical writers were striking deep chords of recognition, and the implicit messages encoded in standard English were no longer going unchallenged. Both in print and on radio and television, careful writers and speakers were shunning as imprecise the so-called generic use of masculine-gender words. Women who had once accepted titles like *chairman* and *congressman* were now insisting on being called either by neutral terms or by terms that, in explicitly recognizing their gender, simultaneously acknowledged their presence in positions of power. When women in the acting profession began to refer to themselves as *actors* rather than *actresses,* they were merely extending to the latter term their recognition of the secondary status implied by such similar putdowns as *poetess* and *authoress.* No longer was *heroine* adequate to explain, for example, young girls' attraction to toys like Power Rangers, which come in both sexes. As an analyst of the toy industry explained, "These [Power Ranger] girls are heroes!"

Predictably, opposition continued, with charges of "political correctness" and "word policing" largely replacing overt ridicule as a weapon. Devotion to the patriarchal assumption of the male norm remains conspicuous in occasional efforts to revive what that preeminent usage guru of the early twentieth century, H. W. Fowler (1950), called "sex words." In defending the addition of *-ess* endings to agent nouns such as *author* and *poet,* Fowler wrote, "Far from needing to reduce the number of our sex words, we should do well to indulge in real neologisms such as *teacheress, singeress, & danceress*" (entry "Feminine Designations," p. 176). His use of *sex* in this context to mean women was echoed in 1995 by a latter-day Fowler, William Safire, who blamed the "language police, sex-eraser squad" for the decline of gender-marked job titles. Abolishing the *-ess* suffix, he wrote, "tells the reader or listener, 'I intend to conceal from you the sex of the person in that job' " (p. 10).

The Fowler-Safire claim that common-gender words must be modified so as to evoke "the sex" in the mind of a reader or listener illustrates not only the irrational notion that males have exclusive rights to certain agent nouns but the underlying myth that women are deviations from a human standard.

In the communications revolution, the spoken and written word remains what it has always been, the most effective medium for sharing information and ideas. Perhaps never before have people in general been so aware of linguistic change in the making. Advances in science and technology create their own new vocabularies, which the general public accepts with varying degrees of interest or indifference. But the appearance of new words generated by the recognition of women's full humanity will continue to be controversial, with arguments pro and con occurring within the ranks of those comfortable with change as well as those who almost automatically oppose it. Whether, like *man,* a word has narrowed in meaning; or, like *esquire* when used of an attorney, has lost its gender exclusivity; or, as some would argue of *fellow,* is regaining its former gender inclusiveness—changes are taking place regardless of the approval or disapproval of individuals.

Guy is another case in point. In the 1990s, its application to a girl or woman has been largely confined to the spoken word. Yet no matter how visceral or logical the arguments claiming the exclusive right of males to the term, *guy* is now being used freely and naturally of both genders—perhaps because it reflects an image of females as ordinary people. Whether this change will survive is still a question, but the need for words that convey the primacy of personhood and of the human qualities shared by female and male alike may be stretching the meaning of many gender-associated words beyond traditional concepts of "masculinity" and "femininity."

In the wake of such changes comes the added responsibility not to use gender-neutral words in ways that may obscure the presence of women and girls. A case in point was a news story about a coeducational program at a local YMCA which relied exclusively on the term *youths* without specifying that female as well as male youths were included. Those aware that the YM in the organization's title stands for "Young Men's" were understandably confused. In this case, the cognitive exclusion of women was probably inadvertent, but as many have pointed out, gender-inclusive language can be and often is used to camouflage sexism. Because no user of language can expect to be understood without an effort at exactness, however, to give up gender-neutral terminology because it can be misused seems rather like cutting off one's nose to spite one's face.

Acceptance of fairness and precision as basic standards for discourse can be measured by the growing number of individuals who have adopted nonsexist and gender-inclusive alternatives to the male-oriented "standard" usage of a few decades ago. And at last many of the changes in English usage that have occurred in response to the experiences and insights of women are being documented in new editions of standard dictionaries. Among these is the third edition of the *American Heritage Dictionary* (1992), whose editors noted that "feminism has had more extensive consequences for questions of usage than any other recent social movement" (p. xxx).

The rapidity of change in women's roles, status, and expectations during the past 25 years provided us, as editors and writers, with the opportunity to observe and report on the widely accepted theory that linguistic change, responding to the need for new terminology, follows social change. At the same time, it led us to support the less widely accepted theory that, by altering people's perception of reality, linguistic change contributes in its turn to further social change.

Note

1. *Women and Language,* first published as *Women and Language News* in 1976, is an interdisciplinary research periodical affiliated with the Organization for the Study of Communication, Language and Gender (OSCLG) and currently published by the Department of Communication at George Mason University, Fairfax, VA 22030-4444.

References

American Heritage Dictionary (3rd ed.). (1992). Boston: Houghton Mifflin.

Baker, R. (1973, March 4). Observer: Nopersonclature. *New York Times,* p. E13.

Bernstein, T. M. (1965). *The careful writer: A modern guide to English usage.* New York: Atheneum.

Buckley, W. F., Jr. (1972, November 30). On the right: Who's beautiful? *Middletown Press* (Connecticut), p. 12.

Fowler, H. W. (1950). *A dictionary of modern English usage.* New York: Oxford University Press.

Kanfer, S. (1972, October 23). Sispeak: A Msguided attempt to change herstory. *Time,* p. 79.

Miller, C., & Swift, K. (1971, December 20). The urban strategist: Desexing the language. *New York Magazine,* p. 103.

Miller, C., & Swift, K. (1972a, Spring). De-sexing the English language. *Ms.,* p. 7.

Miller, C., & Swift, K. (1972b, April 16). One small step for genkind. *New York Times Magazine,* pp. 106 ff.

Miller, C., & Swift, K. (1976). *Words and women: New language in new times.* Garden City, NY: Anchor/Doubleday. (Updated ed., New York: HarperCollins, 1991. Published in Great Britain by Victor Gollancz Ltd, 1977, and Penguin, 1979)

Miller, C., & Swift, K. (1980). *The handbook of nonsexist writing: For writers, editors, and speakers.* New York: Lippincott & Crowell. (2nd ed., New York: Harper & Row, 1988. British ed. published by the Women's Press Ltd, 1981; rev. eds., 1989 and 1995)

Safire, W. (1995, January 1). On language: The concealment of sex. *New York Times Magazine,* p. 10.

Will, G. F. (1974, September 20). Sexist guidelines and reality. *Washington Post,* p. A29.

27

African American Women and Mass Communication Research

Jannette L. Dates
Carolyn A. Stroman

Although research on African Americans and mass communication has shown progress over the years, it is clear that communication researchers have devoted little attention to African American women and communications. Indeed, a title used by Marilyn Fife (1981), "The Missing Minority in Mass Communication Research," aptly describes the status of African American women in mass communication research. A massive bibliography on African Americans and the media, which lists sources published since 1978, contains more than 300 entries (Williams, 1990), but less than 10% focus specifically on African American women.

This chapter identifies what we consider to be the published major historical and em-

pirical research on African American women and mass communications, to date. To place the research in perspective, we have included works that focus on African Americans generally, rather than solely on African American women, because such works often highlight black women.

Intended as a representative, though not an exhaustive, overview of both historical and empirical research, it examines the scholarly literature for its historical or critical analyses of African American participation in four areas: motion pictures, radio, television, and print journalism. After highlighting the available empirical literature, the chapter concludes with an agenda for future research on African American women and mass communications.

Historical/Critical Research

Until recently, African Americans were perceived by scholars, historians, and the public as not having strong participatory roles in the creation and development of American mass media.

Recent works have filled in some of the gaps in the literature concerning the contributions of African American women and men to media development. African American involvement in various areas of the mass media, including the music and recording, film, commercial and noncommercial radio, commercial and public television, print journalism, broadcast journalism, advertising, and public relations industries, was critically analyzed in Dates and Barlow's (1993) *Split Image: African Americans in the Mass Media*. Wilson and Gutierrez's works *Minorities and Media* (1985) and *Race, Multiculturalism, and the Media: From Mass to Class Communication* (1995) each discusses African, Latino, and Native American participation. Kern-Foxworth's (1994) *Aunt Jemima, Uncle Ben, and Rastus: Blacks in Advertising, Yesterday, Today, and Tomorrow* details the complex relationship between African Americans and the advertising industry, and the activism that precipitated changes in the portrayal of African Americans in advertising. Patricia A. Turner's *Ceramic Uncles and Celluloid Mammies: Black Images and Their Influence on Culture* (1994) offers a disturbing cultural criticism of antiblack images as she documents the strategies employed by black people to counter those images.

Recent works focus specifically on the contributions of African American women to the growth of American mass media. A wealth of historical information on African American women communicators is contained in Darlene Clark Hine's mammoth work *Black Women in America: Historical Encyclopedia* (1993). Numerous women television personalities, print and broadcast journalists, filmmakers, and entrepreneurs are profiled in this work, including the widely known Ida B.

Wells-Barnett, Charlayne Hunter Gault, and Oprah Winfrey, as well as lesser-known figures such as Charlotta Bass and Julie Dash. Other historical works that give meaning to the lives of African American women from various professions include Davis's (1982) *Contributions of Black Women to America* and Hine's (1990) Black Women in United States History Series.

Three recently published, edited books on women and communications contain chapters focusing on African American women; included in Creedon's (1989, 1993) *Women in Mass Communication* are two chapters on strategies for studying African American women (Matabane, 1989; Rhodes, 1993). Rakow's (1992) work, *Women Making Meaning,* focusing on new feminist directions in communications, contains Jane Rhodes's chapter, "Mary Ann Shadd and the Legacy of African-American Women Journalists." Lont's (1995) work, *Women and Media: Content, Careers, and Criticism,* contains four chapters pertaining to African American women and the media: (a) "Activism Through Journalism: The Story of Ida B. Wells-Barnett" (Rhodes, 1995); (b) "Caroline Jones: Advertising Agency Executive" (Dates, 1995); (c) "The Debbie Allen Touch" (Merritt, 1995); and (d) "African American Women and the Oscars" (Stubbs, 1995).

The Motion Picture Industry

An entry in *Black Women in America* (Hine, 1993, p. 428) details the history of the image of African American women in films; it characterizes the relationship between African American women and film as a constant tension between an overwhelmingly white Hollywood and a largely male independent scene, both situations representing the dual oppression faced by black women in American society as a whole and in the black community in particular.

Among the works on film that focus specifically on African American women are

Bogle's *Brown Sugar: Eighty Years of America's Black Female Superstars* (1988b); Mapp's "Black Women in Films" (1973); Stubbs's (1995) "African American Women and the Oscars"; Stubbs and Freydberg's (1994) "Black Women in American Films"; and Freydberg (1995) "Sapphires, Spitfires, Sluts, and Superbitches: Aframericans and Latinas in Contemporary American Film."

African American women's reactions to their portrayals and characterizations in films are articulated in Jacqueline Bobo's (1988) "Articulation and Hegemony: Black Women's Response to the Film *The Color Purple*."

The works of historians Thomas Cripps and Donald Bogle dominate the list of scholarly books about African American women and men in the motion picture industry. Cripps's (1976) *Slow Fade to Black: The Negro in American Film—1900-1942* and *Black Film as Genre* (1978) and Bogle's (1989) *Toms, Coons, Mulattos, Mammies, and Bucks: An Interpretive History of Blacks in American Films* and *Blacks in American Films and TV* (1988a) are stellar works that contain information about African American women. There are also works by James R. Nesteby, including *Black Images in American Films, 1896-1954: The Interplay Between Civil Rights and Film Culture* (1982).

With painstaking care for detail, Thomas Cripps describes, analyzes, and gives historical contexts to his masterful studies of African Americans in the motion picture industry in a series of articles, book chapters (e.g., "Amos 'n Andy and the Debate Over American Racial Integration," 1983, and a chapter in Dates and Barlow's *Split Image*, 1993), as well as in his own books, as noted above.

In the 1990s, Cripps has two new publications on this subject: For the Johns Hopkins University Press American Moment Series (in press), he wrote *The History of Classical Hollywood*, which includes an examination of motion pictures and commercial television, and for the Oxford University Press, he wrote *Making Movies Black: The Hollywood Message Movie From World War II to the*

Civil Rights Era (1993). For Indiana University Press, Cripps worked on a revision of the second edition of the highly respected *Black Film as Genre*, which was out of print for some years.

Popular historical works about motion pictures that examine African American participation include *Blacks in American Films and Television: An Encyclopedia* (1988a) by Bogle; Daniel Leab, *From Sambo to Superspade: The Black Experience in Motion Pictures* (1975); John Gray, *Blacks in Film and Television: A Pan-African Bibliography of Films, Filmmakers, and Performance* (1990); and numerous collaboratively written popular books by film director Spike Lee about work on his films (e.g., *Do the Right Thing, School Daze,* and *Malcolm X*).

A recent work, Reid's (1993) *Redefining Black Film,* offers a new perspective on African American film.

The Radio Industry

Little was published about African Americans in the radio industry: Eric Barnouw's *A History of Broadcasting in the United States* (vols. 1, 2, and 3) and *Tube of Plenty* (1982) include some information, as does J. Fred MacDonald in *Don't Touch That Dial: Radio Programming in American Life, 1920-1960* (1979). In *Split Image,* Dates and Barlow critically assess the radio industry's portrayal of African Americans since the 1920s, the limited nature of black participation in the industry, and the role African Americans have played in fashioning radio's black audio images. Dates and Barlow show how the usual pattern of white control in African American radio operations had changed by the 1990s, particularly in the 50-odd noncommercial black university and community radio stations that were established after the 1960s.

In the popular arena, there is Mark Newman, *Entrepreneurs of Profit and Pride: From Black-Appeal to Radio Soul* (1988), and Louis Cantor, *Wheelin' on Beale* (1992), the story of WDIA-Memphis, the first black radio station that is distinct for having originated the "sound" of contemporary radio.

An entry titled "Radio" in *Black Women in America* (Hine, 1993) provides an overview of African American women radio personalities and managers and owners of radio stations.

The Television Industry

Several works critically examine African American women's portrayals on television. Included are Rhodes's (1991) "Television's Realist Portrayal of African-American Women and the Case of *L.A. Law*"; Matabane's (1982) "Black Women on Commercial Television"; and Dates's (1987) "Gimme a Break? African American Women on Prime-Time Television." Bogle (1988a) provides a comprehensive alphabetical listing of blacks who appeared on television from its beginning.

In her study, Stroman (1983) assesses the role of approximately 20 black women characters featured on television between 1968, when *Julia* premiered and the 1980s series *Gimme a Break.* Dates (1987) critically analyzes the roles of black women in primetime television from 1950 to the mid-1980s. She focuses on the motivations of the image makers (producers, writers, sponsors) and the effects of those images on viewers' perceptions of black women.

Eric Barnouw, in *Tube of Plenty* (1982), includes discussions of African American participation in television as an integral part of his descriptions of American media history. Other scholarly discussions of black people's participation in television include J. Fred MacDonald, *Blacks and White TV: Afro-Americans in Television Since 1948* (1983/1992); Melvin Moore, in the chapter "Black Faces in Prime Time" (1980); Nancy Signorielli, *Role Portrayal and Stereotyping on Television* (1985); and Douglas Gomery, "Brian's Song: Television, Hollywood, and the Evolution of the Movie Made for Televi-

sion" (1987). Douglas Gomery's "Brian's Song" is a solid example of how mainstream publications can include the contributions of African Americans in media histories and analyses. Gomery used the essay to comment on social and cultural forces, as reflected in the television industry.

In *Split Image*, Dates (1993) provides a listing by show, years, and network of black actors who appeared on television between 1950 and 1993. Black women with leading roles are among the group. Here, Dates examines the portrayals and the effects of the performances of black women on primetime television. She also focuses on the portrayals of black women and their significant contributions to the industry—from Louise Beavors on *The Beulah Show* to the *Oprah Winfrey Show*.

Mark Crispin Miller, in *Boxed In: The Culture of TV* (1989) also demonstrates how critics in mainstream publications can incorporate information about groups other than those in the white mainstream. Here Miller's analyses of commercial television's advertisements and programs featuring black characters show insight and depth.

Melvin Patrick Ely, in *The Adventures of Amos 'n' Andy: A Social History of an American Phenomenon* (1991), traces the history of the popular radio show, using it as a prism through which to view American racial attitudes and issues. Ely concludes that the United States always attempted to ignore the hard questions about racial issues and, in the nation's mass entertainment programming, pretend there were no problems.

Numerous articles appeared in scholarly journals about African Americans and commercial television (e.g., Herman Gray's, "Television, Black Americans, and the American Dream" [1990]. In his works, Gray examines the twin representations of fictional and nonfictional television as a part of the public discourse about American race relations. He argues that these twin representations erroneously organize viewers' perceptions about black middle-class success and black underclass failure—and implicitly and incorrectly place the blame for underclass failure on those African Americans who fail to integrate. In media presentations, the system that separates and penalizes black people is not regulated or scrutinized. Gray sees this as a major flaw in society, and in media systems and their products.

In the popular arena, there is Bogle (1989), *Blacks in American Films and Television: An Encyclopedia;* George H. Hill and Sylvia Savers Hill (1983), *Blacks on Television: A Selectively Annotated Bibliography;* and Cynthia E. Griffin and George H. Hill (1985), *History of Blacks on Television*; and Hill et al.'s *Black Women in Television: An Illustrated History and Bibliography* (1990). Hine's (1993), *Black Women in America: Historical Encyclopedia* contains a detailed entry on television and black women, as well.

Print Journalism

It is in the field of print journalism that the participation of African American women is covered most in the literature. Two communication history researchers, Jane Rhodes (Indiana University) and Rodger Streitmatter (American University), have diligently worked to set the record straight on the history of African American women journalists. Included in the impressive work that Jane Rhodes has produced are her award-winning dissertation, *Breaking the Editorial Ice: Mary Ann Shadd Cary and the "Provincial Freeman"* (1992a); "Mary Ann Shadd and the Legacy of African-American Women Journalists" (1992b); and "Activism Through Journalism" (1995). Streitmatter's exemplary record of documenting the legacies of African American women journalists includes "Gertrude Bustill Mosell: Guiding Voice for Newly Freed Blacks" (1993a); "Alice Allison Dunnigan: Pioneer Black Woman Journalist" (1990); *Raising Her Voice: African-American Women Journalists Who Changed History* (1994b); and Streitmatter and Diggs-Browne's *Marvel Cooke: An African-American Woman Journalist Who Agitated for Racial Reform* (1991).

Streitmatter has also written about Ethel L. Payne (1991) and Delilah Beasley (1994a).

Frankie Hutton's (1990) work on free women and the antebellum press, Sealander's (1982) "Antebellum Black Press Images of Women," and an entry titled "Journalism" in Hine (1993) contain historical information on African American women in journalism. A number of reference works also contain historical data on African American women communicators, including Davis (1982).

Other works that speak specifically to the experiences of African American women in mass communications include the biography (Thompson, 1990) and autobiography of Ida B. Wells-Barnett (Duster, 1972); Snorgrass's (1982) "Pioneer Black Women Journalists From the 1850s to the 1950s"; Wade-Gayles's (1990) "Black Women Journalists in the South, 1880-1905"; Streitmatter (1992) "Economic Conditions Surrounding Nineteenth-Century African-American Women Journalists"; and Diggs-Browne's (1992) *Phillipa Duke Schuyler*.

Popular autobiographical works of African American women currently employed as journalists include Charlayne Hunter-Gault's *In My Place* (1992); *Volunteer Slavery* by Jill Nelson (1993); and *Laughing in the Dark* by Patrice Gaines (1994). Sources that include information on African American women and men journalists include Martin E. Dann, *Black Press: 1827-1890—The Quest for National Identity* (1972); Penelope Bullock, *The Afro-American Periodical Press, 1838-1909* (1977); Roland Wolseley, *The Black Press, U.S.A.* (1971/1990), and Clint C. Wilson II and Felix Gutierrez, *Minorities and Media* (1985); Potter's (1993) *A Reference Guide to Afro-American Publications and Editors;* and Streitmatter's (1993b) *African American Women Journalists and Their Male Editors.*

Other works include Hutton's (1993) *The Early Black Press in America, 1827-1860;* the chapter "Print Journalism" in Dates and Barlow (1993); and Clint C. Wilson II, *Black Journalists in Paradox: Historical Perspectives and Current Dilemmas* (1991). Here,

Wilson presents a historical context for his targeted readers—young journalists. He begins with communications systems in Africa, profiles important past African American journalists, and finally discusses problems of the 1990s and challenges for the future. Among the African American women presented in vignettes are Ida B. Wells-Barnett, Victoria Earle Mathews, Ethel Payne, Charlayne Hunter-Gault, and Susan L. Taylor.

Empirical Research

Empirical research on African American women and mass communications is scarce. Kern-Foxworth, Gandy, Hines, and Miller's (1994) study of African American female public relations practitioners is in a class by itself. That is, it is one of the few communications studies in which the sample solely comprises African American women. Similarly unique is Bramlett-Solomon's (1991) content analysis of newspaper coverage of Fannie Lou Hamer, one of America's most influential civil rights leaders.

The bulk of the empirical research on African American women and mass communications, like most of the research on African Americans, focuses on portrayal. Included among the works that examine solely the portrayal of women are the following: Sheperd's (1980) "The Portrayal of Black Women in Ads of Popular Magazines" and Stroman's (1983) *From "Julia" to "Gimme a Break": The Portrayal of Black Womanhood on Prime-time Television.*

A number of studies, in examining gender and race, have focused some attention on African American women (e.g., Northcott, Seggar, and Hinton's, 1975, "Trends in TV Portrayal of Blacks and Women," and the U.S. Commission on Civil Rights' groundbreaking works, *Window Dressing on the Set: Women and Minorities in Television,* 1977, 1979). Other studies in this vein include the following: Seggar and Wheeler (1973); O'Kelly and Bloomquist (1976); Donager,

Poulos, Liebert, and Davidson (1976); Lemon (1977); Culley and Bennett's (1976) "Selling Women, Selling Blacks"; Seggar (1977); Seggar, Hafen, and Hannonen-Gladden's "Television's Portrayals of Minorities and Women in Drama and Comedy Drama" (1986); Brown and Campbell's "Race and Gender in Music Videos" (1986); Dodd, Foerch, and Anderson's "Content Analysis of Women and Racial Minorities as News Magazine Cover Persons" (1988); and Riffe "Females and Minorities in Television Advertisements in 1987 Saturday Children's Programs" (1989).

Recent works that examine both race and gender include Brown and Schulze's "The Effects of Race, Gender, and Fandom on Audience Interpretations of Madonna's Music Videos" (1990); Atkin and Fife's (1993-1994) "The Role of Race and Gender as Determinants of Local TV News Coverage"; and Cowan and Campbell's (1994) "Racism and Sexism in Interracial Pornography."

Some studies have examined African American women incidentally while examining African Americans generally. Included among these are Hinton, Seggar, Northcott, and Fontes's (1974) "Tokenism and Improving Imagery of Blacks in TV Drama and Comedy"; Baptista-Fernandez and Greenberg's (1980) "The Content, Characteristics, and Communication Behaviors of Blacks on Television"; Martindale's (1985) "Coverage of Black Americans in Five Newspapers Since 1950"; and Stroman, Merritt, and Matabane's (1989-1990) "Twenty Years After Kerner: The Portrayal of African-Americans on Prime-Time Television."

Several studies shed light on African American women's employment in the media, including Bramlett-Solomon's (1993) study, which examines job appeal and job satisfaction among female and male Hispanic and African American journalists; Kern-Foxworth et al.'s (1994) study; Stone's (1988) "Trends in the Status of Minorities and Women in Broadcast News"; and Lafky's (1993) "The Progress of Women and People of Color in the U.S. Journalistic Workforce."

A fascinating description of the history and philosophy of a company that publishes the writing of "Third world women of all racial/cultural heritages, sexualities, and classes" is provided in Barbara Smith's (1989) "A Press of Our Own: The Story of Kitchen Table: Women of Color Press."

Research Agenda

African American women and mass communications is a fairly unexplored research topic; therefore, much research needs to be conducted if we are to understand this aspect of our history. This section provides a research agenda that helps structure our understandings in this area; it suggests several issues and areas of study that should receive high priority in future research.

Much of the communications research on African American women has focused on portrayals in various media. However, we need to look beyond portrayal and also examine the impact of portrayals or coverage of African Americans on African American women's beliefs, values, and attitudes. How, for example, does the presence or absence of African Americans on national news programs, in entertainment television, and in films influence African American women's perceptions and attitudes? What meaning is attached to media content as it relates to African American women's cultural experiences? Future studies should also examine the processes within the systems that create images of African Americans. For example, what are the production factors in news media that determine how African Americans are depicted, and how does the absence or presence of African Americans at various points in the production influence character development?

Almost nothing is known about how African American women function in white media organizations. With few exceptions, we know little about job-related issues and their effects on black women. We need to examine the effects of minority status on attitudes, beliefs, and job performance.

How does ownership by African American women change the mass communication process? Kathy Hughes, owner of WOL and WKYX in Washington, D.C., as well as WERQ and WOLB and WWIN(AM/FM) in Baltimore, should be used as a case study of how African American women can maneuver in the white male-dominated media industries.

The question of ownership becomes more critical in view of the emergence of the nation's information superhighway. For example, where will African Americans in general and African American women in particular position themselves for active participation in meeting their needs on the information superhighway? How can society embrace diverse voices that cross gender, race, and class within the new technologies?

Health communication is another fertile area for research on African American women. What kinds of health communication messages appeal to African American women? What is the most effective manner in which to relay persuasive health information to African American women?

Although this chapter has identified many historical studies of African American women journalists, there is still an abundance of historical research to be undertaken in this area. Sorely needed also are studies that use an African American womanist/feminist research perspective (Stanback, 1988-1989). As Saunders (1995) cogently noted: The use of feminist theory will move communication scholars toward a more accurate understanding of African American women's communication within a framework that is grounded in their communication experience and world of meaning.

The topics that could be researched are unlimited; so too are the theoretical frameworks and perspectives that could be used to guide research in this area. What is clear is that a great amount of research is needed if we are ever to obtain a comprehensive understanding of the relationships between African American women and mass communications.

References

Atkin, D., & Fife, M. (1993-1994). The role of race and gender as determinants of local TV news coverage. *Howard Journal of Communications, 5*(1/2), 123-137.

Baptista-Fernandez, P., & Greenberg, B. (1980). The content, characteristics, and communication behaviors of blacks on television. In B. S. Greenberg (Ed.), *Life on television: Content analysis of U.S. T.V. drama.* Norwood, NJ: Ablex.

Barnouw, E. (1966, 1968, 1970). *A history of broadcasting in the United States* (Vols. 1-3). New York: Oxford University Press.

Barnouw, E. (1982). *Tube of plenty: The evolution of American television* (rev. ed.). New York: Oxford University Press.

Bobo, J. (1988). *Articulation and hegemony: Black women's response to the film "The Color Purple."* Unpublished doctoral dissertation, University of Oregon, Eugene.

Bogle, D. (1988a). *Blacks in American films and television: An encyclopedia.* New York: Garland.

Bogle, D. (1988b). *Brown sugar: Eighty years of America's black female superstars.* New York: Continuum.

Bogle, D. (1989). *Toms, coons, mulattos, mammies and bucks: An interpretive history of blacks in American films.* New York: Bantam.

Bramlett-Solomon, S. (1991). Civil rights vanguard in the deep South: Newspaper portrayal of Fannie Lou Hamer, 1964-1977. *Journalism Quarterly, 68,* 515-521.

Bramlett-Solomon, S. (1993). Job appeal and job satisfaction among Hispanic and black journalists. *Mass Communication Review, 20,* 202-211.

Brown, J., & Campbell, K. (1986). Race and gender in music videos: The same beat but a different drummer. *Journal of Communication, 36,* 94-106.

Brown, J. D., & Schulze, L. (1990). The effects of race, gender, and fandom on audience interpretations of Madonna's music videos. *Journal of Communication, 40*(2), 88-102.

Bullock, P. (1977). *The Afro-American periodical press, 1838-1909.* Baton Rouge: Louisiana State University Press.

Cantor, L. (1992). *Wheelin' on Beale.* Mahwah, NJ: Pharos.

Cowan, G., & Campbell, R. R. (1994). Racism and sexism in interracial pornography. *Psychology of Women Quarterly, 18,* 323-338.

Creedon, P. (1989). *Women in mass communication: Challenging gender values.* Newbury Park, CA: Sage.

Creedon, P. (1993). *Women in mass communication: Challenging gender values* (2nd ed.). Newbury Park, CA: Sage.

Cripps, T. (1976). *Slow fade to black: The Negro in American film—1900-1942.* New York: Oxford University Press.

Cripps, T. (1978). *Black film as genre* (1st ed.). Bloomington: Indiana University Press.

Cripps, T. (1983). Amos 'n Andy and the debate over American racial integration. In J. E. O'Connor (Ed.), *American history/American television: Interpreting the video past* (pp. 33-34). New York: Fred Ungar.

Cripps, T. (1993). *Making movies black: The Hollywood message movie from World War II to the civil rights era.* New York: Oxford University Press.

Cripps, T. (in press). *The history of classical Hollywood* (American Moment series). Baltimore, MD: Johns Hopkins University Press.

Culley, J. D., & Bennett, R. (1976). Selling women, selling blacks. *Journal of Communication, 26,* 160-174.

Dann, M. E. (1972). *Black press: 1827-1890—The quest for national identity.* New York: Capricorn.

Dates, J. (1987). Gimme a break? African American women in prime time television. In A. Wells (Ed.), *Mass media and society.* Lexington, MA: D. C. Heath/Lexington.

Dates, J. (1995). Caroline Jones: Advertising agency executive. In C. M. Lont (Ed.), *Women and media: Content, careers, and criticism.* Belmont, CA: Wadsworth.

Dates, J., & Barlow, W. (1993). *Split image: African Americans in the mass media* (2nd ed.). Washington, DC: Howard University Press.

Davis, M. W. (Ed.). (1982). *Contributions of black women to America* (Vol. 1). Columbia, SC: Kenday.

Diggs-Browne, B. (1992, August). *Phillipa Duke Schuyler: African American woman journalist.* Paper presented to the Association for Education in Journalism and Mass Communication, Montreal.

Dodd, D., Foerch, B., & Anderson, H. (1988). Content analysis of women and racial minorities as news magazine cover persons. *Journal of Social Behavior and Personality, 3*(3), 231-236.

Donager, P., Poulos, R., Liebert, R., & Davidson, E. (1976). Race, sex, and social example: Analysis of character portrayals on inter-racial television entertainment. *Psychological Reports, 37,* 1023-1034.

Duster, A. (1972). *Crusade for justice: The autobiography of Ida B. Wells.* Chicago: University of Chicago Press.

Ely, M. (1991). *The adventures of Amos 'n' Andy: A social history of an American phenomenon.* New York: Free Press.

Fife, M. (1981). The missing minority in mass communication research. In H. Myrick & C. Keegan (Eds.), *In search of diversity: Symposium on minority audiences and programming research: Approaches to application.* Washington, DC: Corporation for Public Broadcasting.

Freydberg, E. H. (1995). Sapphires, spitfires, sluts, and superbitches: Aframericans and Latinas in contemporary American film. In K. M. Vaz (Ed.), *Black women in America.* Thousand Oaks, CA: Sage.

Gaines, P. (1994). *Laughing in the dark: From colored girl to woman of color—A journey from prison to power.* New York: Crown.

Gomery, D. (1987). Brian's song: Television, Hollywood, and the evolution of the movie made for television. In H. Newcomb (Ed.), *Television: The critical view.* New York: Oxford University Press.

Gray, H. (1990). Television, black Americans, and the American dream. In R. K. Avery & D. Eason (Eds.), *Critical perspective on media and society* (pp. 294-305). New York: Guilford.

Gray, J. (1990). *Blacks in film and television: A pan-African bibliography of films, filmmakers, and performance.* New York: Greenwood.

Hill, G., et al. (1990). *Black women in television: An illustrated history and bibliography.* New York: Garland.

Hine, D. C. (1990). *Black women in American history: From colonial times through the nineteenth century* (Black Women in United States History series, Vols. 1-4). Brooklyn, NY: Carlson.

Hine, D. C. (1993). *Black women in America: An historical encyclopedia.* Brooklyn, NY: Carlson.

Hinton, J., Seggar, J., Northcott, H., & Fontes, B. (1974). Tokenism and improving imagery of blacks in TV drama and comedy: 1973. *Journal of Broadcasting, 18,* 423-437.

Hunter-Gault, C. (1992). *In my place.* New York: Farrar Straus Giroux.

Hutton, F. (1990, August). *Free women and the antebellum black press: The gender oppression view reconsidered.* Paper presented at the Annual Convention of the Association for Education in Journalism and Mass Communication, Minneapolis.

Hutton, F. (1993). *The early black press in America, 1827-1860.* London: Greenwood.

Johnson, R. (1980). Blacks and women: Naming American hostages released in Iran. *Journal of Communication, 30*(3), 58-63.

Kern-Foxworth, M. (1994). *Aunt Jemima, Uncle Ben, and Rastus: Blacks in advertising, yesterday, today, and tomorrow.* Westport, CT: Greenwood.

Kern-Foxworth, M., Gandy, O., Hines, B., & Miller, D. A. (1994). Assessing the managerial roles of black female public relations practitioners using individual and organizational discriminants. *Journal of Black Studies, 24,* 416-434.

Lafky, S. A. (1993). The progress of women and people of color in the U.S. journalistic workforce: A long, slow journey. In P. J. Creedon (Ed.), *Women in mass communication* (2nd ed.). Newbury Park, CA: Sage.

Leab, D. (1975). *From Sambo to Superspade: The black experience in motion pictures.* Boston: Houghton Mifflin.

Lemon, J. (1977). Women and blacks on prime-time television. *Journal of Communication, 27*(4), 70-79.

Lont, C. (Ed.). (1995). *Women and media: Content, careers, and criticism.* Belmont, CA: Wadsworth.

MacDonald, F. (1979). *Don't touch that dial: Radio programming in American life, 1920-1960.* Chicago: Nelson-Hall.

MacDonald, F. (1992). *Blacks and white TV: Afro-Americans in television since 1948* (rev. ed.). Chicago: Nelson-Hall. (Original work published 1983)

Mapp, E. (1973, March-April). Black women in films. *Black Scholar,* pp. 36-40.

Martindale, C. (1985). Coverage of black Americans in five newspapers since 1950. *Journalism Quarterly, 62,* 321-328, 436.

Matabane, P. (1982). Black women on American's commercial television. *Western Journal of Black Studies, 6,* 22-25.

Matabane, P. (1989). Strategies for research on black women and mass communication. In P. J. Creedon (Ed.), *Women in mass communication: Challenging gender values.* Newbury Park, CA: Sage.

Merritt, B. (1995). The Debbie Allen touch. In C. M. Lont (Ed.), *Women and media: Content, careers, and criticism.* Belmont, CA: Wadsworth.

Miller, M. C. (1989). *Boxed in: The culture of TV.* Evanston, IL: Northwestern University Press.

Moore, M., Jr. (1980). Black face in prime time. In B. Rubin (Ed.), *Small voices and great trumpets: Minorities and the media.* New York: Praeger.

Nelson, J. (1993). *Volunteer slavery: My authentic Negro experience.* Chicago: Noble.

Nesteby, J. (1982). *Black images in American films, 1896-1954: The interplay between civil rights and film culture.* Washington, DC: University Press of America.

Newman, M. (1988). *Entrepreneurs of profit and pride: From black-appeal to radio soul.* Westport, CT: Greenwood.

Northcott, H., Seggar, J., & Hinton, J. (1975). Trends in TV portrayal of blacks and women. *Journalism Quarterly, 52,* 741-744.

O'Kelly, C., & Bloomquist, L. (1976). Women and blacks on TV. *Journal of Communication, 26*(4), 179-192.

Potter, V. R. (1993). *A reference guide to Afro-American publications and editors.* Ames: Iowa State University Press.

Rakow, L. (1992). *Women making meaning: New feminist directions in communication.* New York: Harper & Row.

Reid, M. A. (1993). *Redefining black film.* Berkeley: University of California Press.

Rhodes, J. (1991). Television's realist portrayal of African-American women and the case of L. A. Law. *Women and Language, 14*(1), 29-34.

Rhodes, J. (1992a). *Breaking the editorial ice: Mary Ann Shadd Cary and the "Provincial Freeman."* Unpublished dissertation, University of North Carolina.

Rhodes, J. (1992b). Mary Ann Shadd and the legacy of African-American women journalists. In L. Rakow (Ed.), *Women making meaning: New feminist directions in communication.* New York: Routledge Kegan Paul.

Rhodes, J. (1993). Falling through the cracks: Studying women of color in mass communication. In P. J. Creedon (Ed.), *Women in mass communication: Challenging gender values* (2nd ed.). Newbury Park, CA: Sage.

Rhodes, J. (1995). Activism through journalism: The story of Ida B. Wells-Barnett. In C. M. Lont (Ed.), *Women and media: Content, careers, and criticism.* Belmont, CA: Wadsworth.

Riffe, D. (1989). Females and minorities in television advertisements in 1987 Saturday children's programs. *Journalism Quarterly, 66,* 129-136.

Saunders, D. K. (1995). *A multi-stage analysis of the communication of African American women in a public transit setting.* Unpublished dissertation, Howard University.

Sealander, J. (1982). Antebellum black press images of women. *Western Journal of Black Studies, 6,* 159-165.

Seggar, J. (1977). Television's portrayal of minorities and women. *Journal of Broadcasting, 21,* 435-446.

Seggar, J., Hafen, J., & Hannonen-Gladden, H. (1986). Television's portrayals of minorities and women in drama and comedy drama, 1971-1980. *Journal of Broadcasting, 25*(3), 277-288.

Seggar, J., & Wheeler, P. (1973). World of work on TV: Ethnic and sex representation in TV drama. *Journal of Broadcasting, 17,* 201-214.

Sheperd, J. (1980). The portrayal of black women in ads of popular magazines. *Western Journal of Black Studies, 4,* 179-182.

Signorielli, N. (Ed.). (1985). *Role portrayal and stereotyping on television: An annotated bibliography relating to women, minorities, aging, sexual behavior, health and handicaps.* Westport, CT: Greenwood.

Smith, B. (1989). A press of our own: The story of Kitchen Table: Women of Color Press. In R. Rush & D. Allen (Eds.), *Communication at the crossroads: The gender gap connection.* Norwood, NJ: Ablex.

Snorgrass, J. W. (1982). Pioneer black women journalists from the 1850s to the 1950s. *Western Journal of Black Studies, 6*(3), 150-158.

Stanback, M. H. (1988-1989). Feminist theory and black women's talk. *Howard Journal of Communications, 1*(4), 187-194.

Stone, V. (1988). Trends in the status of minorities and women in broadcast news. *Journalism Quarterly, 65*(2), 288-293.

Streitmatter, R. (1990, August). *Alice Allison Dunnigan: Pioneer black woman journalist.* Paper presented to the Association for Education in Journalism and Mass Communication, Minneapolis.

Streitmatter, R. (1991). No taste for fluff: Ethel L. Payne, African-American journalist. *Journalism Quarterly, 68,* 528-540.

Streitmatter, R. (1992). Economic conditions surrounding nineteenth-century African-American women journalists: Two case studies. *Journalism History, 18,* 33-40.

Streitmatter, R. (1993a). Gertrude Bustill Mosell: Guiding voice for newly freed blacks. *Howard Journal of Communications, 2*(4), 317-328.

Streitmatter, R. (1993b). African-American women journalists and their male editors: A tradition of support. *Journalism Quarterly, 70,* 276-286.

Streitmatter, R. (1994a). Delilah Beasley: A black woman journalist who lifted as she climbed. *American Journalism, 11*(1), 61-75.

Streitmatter, R. (1994b). *Raising her voice: African-American women journalists who changed history.* Lexington: University of Kentucky Press.

Streitmatter, R., & Diggs-Browne, B. (1991, August). *Marvel Cooke: An African-American woman journalist who agitated for racial reform.* Paper presented to the Association for Education in Journalism and Mass Communication, Boston.

Stroman, C. (1983, November). *From "Julia" to "Gimme a Break": The portrayal of black womanhood on television.* Paper presented at the Middle Atlantic Writers Association Fourth Annual Conference, Washington, DC.

Stroman, C., Merritt, B., & Matabane, P. (1989-1990). Twenty years after Kerner: The portrayal of African-Americans on prime-time television. *Howard Journal Communication, 2*(1), 44-56.

Stubbs, F. M. (1995). African American women and the Oscars. In C. M. Lont (Ed.), *Women and media: Content, careers, and criticism.* Belmont, CA: Wadsworth.

Stubbs, F. M., & Freydberg, E. H. (1994). Black women in American films. In D. Carson, L. Dittmor, & J. A. Welsh (Eds.), *Multiple voices in feminist film criticism* (pp. 481-491). Minneapolis: University of Minnesota Press.

Thompson, M. (1990). *Ida B. Wells-Barnett: An exploratory study of an American black woman, 1893-1930.* Brooklyn, NY: Carlson.

Turner, P. A. (1994). *Ceramic uncles and celluloid mammies: Black images and their influence on culture.* New York: Anchor.

U.S. Commission on Civil Rights. (1977). *Window dressing on the set: Women and minorities in television.* Washington, DC: Author.

U.S. Commission on Civil Rights. (1979). *Window dressing on the set: An update.* Washington, DC: Author.

Wade-Gayles, G. (1990). Black women journalists in the South, 1880-1905: An approach to the study of black women's history. Reprinted in D. C. Hine (Ed.), *Black women in United States history.* Brooklyn, NY: Carlson.

Williams, M. (1990). *Blacks and the media: Communications research since 1978.* Washington, DC: Howard University, Center for Communication Research.

Wilson, C. (1991). *Black journalists in paradox: Historical perspectives and current dilemmas.* Westport, CT: Greenwood.

Wilson, C., & Gutierrez, F. (1985). *Minorities and media: Diversity and the end of mass communication.* Beverly Hills, CA: Sage.

Wilson, C., & Gutierrez, F. (1995). *Race, multiculturalism, and the media: From mass to class communication.* Thousand Oaks, CA: Sage.

Wolseley, R. (1990). *The black press, U.S.A.* Ames: Iowa State University Press. (Original work published 1971)

28

Women at Hearst Magazines
A Case Study of Women in Magazine Publishing

Barbara Straus Reed

Magazines in America Today

Almost all Americans read magazines—166 million adults, or 88% of the U.S. population age 18 or older (*The MPA Magazine Handbook,* 1994-1995, p. 46). Moreover, they each read an average of 12 different issues every month. Women, who have always been inveterate magazine readers, read more than men, and more magazines monthly too. Eighty-nine million adult women, or 91% of U.S. women, read at least one issue, whereas 77 million adult men, or 86% of U.S. men, read one issue, at least (data from Mediamark Research, Inc., New York, spring 1995).

The number of U.S. magazines has grown, from about 7,000 in 1950 to more than 11,000 in 1990; moreover, the number of those independently audited for circulation has grown

from 250 in 1950 to about 650 in 1995 (Audit Bureau of Circulations, New York, circulation data, July 1, 1995; *Consumer and Agri-Media,* various years). Moreover, there are more women's magazines than men's (Sean Brevick and Jeff Baron, client service representatives, MRI, personal interviews, August 31, 1995).

Magazines are an expanding, dynamic business where career opportunities exist. This can be seen especially at women's magazines. The median age is comparatively lower than in other media, according to Charles Rodin, independent magazine consultant (personal interview, August 23, 1995).

Moreover, a rapid transformation has occurred as women have been promoted and now stand among the top ranks of the magazine industry pyramid. Movement has turned to momentum in the last twenty years; in the last five years, women have been moving steadily upward. They are not only editors but also publishers, sellers, and ad directors. Women will be at higher levels still in years to come as the industry looks around for the best persons to promote (Rodin, Green, Ricks, and Jorgensen, personal interviews, August 1995). Resistance does not matter; a group head, if bright and ambitious, will see the good of potential employees. For graduates coming out of journalism and mass communications programs, magazines offer the promise of prosperity, and the younger the person, the more likely she is to get parity.

Furthermore, among the top-20 magazines in revenues and circulation, seven were women's, and of the top-10 titles with the biggest gains in total revenues for 1994, the first is *Better Homes and Gardens* followed by *Martha Stewart Living* and *Family Circle* ("Folio 500," 1995). Although circulations declined in the 1980s, the big magazines still report circulations in the millions (Carmody, 1990).

Although statistics can be found for circulation, ad pages, cover prices, gains in paid subscriptions or ad pages—and magazine companies are only too happy to gloat at any increases—they do not keep (or perhaps reveal) personnel statistics (Carmody, 1994).[1] Neither of the two magazine trade associations, the Magazine Publishers Association or the American Business Press, keeps precise count of gender and ethnic minority employment.

Hearst Magazines: A Case Study

Although much can be said pointing to deficiencies in American magazines for women (Douglas, 1994; Steiner, 1995; Whelan, 1992), a publishing company that has been accessible to women and not afraid to promote them to the ranks of either editor or publisher is Hearst Magazines International, based in New York City. Hearst is the largest producer of

monthly magazines in the world, and one of the largest producers, if not the largest, of women's titles (*Bacon's Magazine Directory,* 1995; Ricks, personal interview, 1995). In fact, Hearst magazines enter 40% of American households.

Hearst publishes *Redbook, Good Housekeeping, Cosmopolitan, Country Living, House Beautiful, Colonial Homes, Harper's Bazaar, Town & Country, Victoria,* and *Marie Claire.* In addition, Hearst produces *Esquire, Popular Mechanics, Sports Afield, Smart Money,* and *Motorboating and Sailing* as well as quarterlies, semiannuals, and annuals such as *Colonial Homes*'s *Kitchens & Baths* and *Cosmopolitan*'s *Life After College.* Yet, the magazines all operate differently, said Gloria Ricks (personal interview, 1995), vice-president for public affairs. The staffs of the various magazines work separately, in three different buildings in Manhattan, and on different floors of those buildings.

Internationally, Hearst has 85 magazines in 29 countries and is expanding. Women are in top positions around the world too. For example, in the Far East, Hearst has a woman at the top of a staff of 14, all of whom are women. In France, Hearst has published *Marie Claire* for years and only recently brought it to American readers. Not one man is on the staff. Hearst is partners with L'Oreal, the cosmetics company there. In Taiwan, a woman owns the company that coproduces with Hearst *Cosmopolitan, Esquire,* and *House Beautiful.* In Hong Kong, the publisher and editor are women for both *Cosmopolitan* and *House Beautiful.* Women dominate as editors at *Esquire* around the world. In the United Kingdom, a woman publishes *Esquire* jointly with Hearst. Women are in charge in Holland, Japan, and Thailand, although a male is in Korea (Green, personal interview). This sample of titles typifies the Hearst scene internationally.

Although Hearst is probably not an extreme case, it represents a sign of the times: As women have been hired at the first tier, into editorial positions, they have risen to the second tier, to become editors and publishers, as well as taking other positions on the editorial and business sides, both once the domain of men. Indeed, the position of publisher had been exclusively male.

Some believe that women have a natural affinity for magazines; they make permanent connections to their publications. Many more women are successful to a greater extent in magazines, whether in management or as staff members, compared with newspapers (Cleere, personal interview, August 23, 1995).

Women in the magazine business at Hearst are effective, outstanding, creative. The company gives them the franchise to operate, and they do not do so on a casual basis. The cardinal rule is to produce, but that is the basis on which one is judged—nothing else. Women produce. In tight economic times, good producers get the job, and the last five years represent a time when many magazines died (Magazine Publishers Association). Concurrently, women have risen significantly in the same five years. Hearst hires people to get the job done, not people with whom the male executives are comfortable because they resemble themselves. In fact, all of a sudden, women are moving forward.

Women at Hearst sacrifice and put in extra hours to make a difference (Fuchs, Sperling, personal interviews). "If I am not selling, I am not doing anything," said one. They work hard, show commitment, and bring results. These qualities are not ignored by upper-level management. Certain women at Hearst could have left for more money, they said, but they chose to stay because of a welcoming, supportive atmosphere.

Agreeing is George Green, director of Hearst Magazines International and executive vice-president of magazines. With 30 years in publishing, 10 of them with the *New Yorker* as publisher, Green has witnessed enormous changes. During his 11 years with Hearst, Green said he has seen women hired and promoted and said more women have been able to rise higher in the corporation, and there will be more of them in high-level positions.

Green started in 1962, when the magazine industry was primarily a male business, in terms of senior people. There were influential women editors at lower positions such as departments or sections within a magazine but not at the editor in chief or executive editor ranks. During his years at the *New Yorker,* he recalled one woman in a high position there: Myra Friese served as chief financial officer. She was the first woman financial officer of an American magazine (Green, personal interview, August 24, 1995).

Green acknowledged that magazines are talent driven; he doesn't know or care whether a man or a woman is at the helm. What counts is the effort they bring to the business side; women are given opportunities because they've produced, and men know women can do the job, he said.

Women succeed for themselves, Green said. They can take rejection and try to overcome it; they persevere and succeed. He cited Helen Gurley Brown, editor of *Cosmopolitan* since 1965. She began at Hearst in a secretarial pool, then became a copywriter, and then a writer. She wrote a book, which became a movie. Her husband worked with a Hearst magazine consultant who saw the couple's new idea for a magazine; they took a new concept and applied it to an old magazine. Looking at the staff of *Cosmo,* one sees that all editors are women, both for the domestic version and around the world as well. The magazine is primarily a women's product.

Women understand better what other women want—it is a woman's business, Green said. Men are not there because they don't understand the needs of women; they have been intimidated out of it. Women work harder, are tougher, and aggressively want to succeed, more than males today, Green said. They are effective in their work. When Green began his career in the magazine publishing industry 30 years ago, a club atmosphere prevailed, with alcohol being a major aspect of day-to-day life. One could never do any business in the afternoon, as the men might not have been sober. By contrast, women were never big drinkers. Now it is not acceptable to imbibe a large quantity during the business day, and only social drinking is legitimate. "That eliminated the bonding aspect of [the drinking]," he said. Primarily, women are productive and creative, and men are smart enough to see their own careers enhanced by the women working with them. Men overcame their initial prejudices because they saw that women were willing to sacrifice to be successful professionally and be seen as successful in every way. The women sensed they were the underdogs, and did more.

Women in Power at Hearst

Currently, a glass ceiling has cracked at the corporate level, and women in the pipeline have reached the top echelons of the Hearst Magazines Division: Anne Sutherland Fuchs is senior vice-president, group publishing director; Anne Holton is group publishing director of the Hearst Home Resources Group. The company replaced D. Claeys Bahrenburg, as president of Hearst Magazines, in December 1995, with Cathleen Black of the National Newspaper Association, the first woman on the corporate level, thereby breaking the glass ceiling.[2] In addition, of the 17 Hearst magazines, there are currently six women publishers. Thus, meetings of publishers are male dominated, but women at Hearst said they feel comfortable because they are treated professionally.

Ken Feldman, human resources director at Hearst, does not believe the company shows preferential treatment to women. They do not view any position as a "woman's job" when they are hiring. Jobs are not designed for women, he maintained, and the company sees itself as competitive (Feldman, personal interview, August 22, 1995).

Hearst just hired the first woman publisher at *Cosmopolitan,* Donna Kalajian Galotti, formerly vice-president and publisher of the *Ladies' Home Journal,* and she is the first woman publisher of the magazine ever ("New Publisher," 1995). "She was the best qualified candidate; her salary and benefits package would not be different were she a male," said the director of human resources. The day she officially became *Cosmopolitan* publisher, August 23, Galotti was rumored to be receiving between $200,000 and $600,000, depending on the person speaking at Hearst (anonymous publishing individuals, personal interviews).

According to Feldman, big changes began at Hearst 15 years ago, as Hearst became a melting pot of the best and most talented people from the rest of the magazine industry. He said, "We are not luring them with pockets of gold [although he refused to reveal salary ranges or any salaries whatsoever], or gigantic cash outlays, but with the integrity of the magazines, their reputations, and the power of Hearst. (Hearst is the largest privately held communications company.)" Feldman said, "We don't have people raising a feminist flag; we don't fill a quota. It is the best qualified person who gets the job, who gets the promotion."

According to Feldman, women just happen to be better. There is no "us and them" mentality. The director said gender is not ever an issue, in hiring or promotion. There is no pay differential. He seeks the "best players" and tries to attract notable people.

He cited the changes in *Redbook,* which Hearst bought in 1982, with the new vision and viewpoint of Editor Ellen Levine, formerly editor of *Women's Day* and now the editor of *Good Housekeeping,* Hearst's flagship magazine. Now *Redbook* Editor Kate White, formerly of *McCall's, Working Mother, Child,* and *Mademoiselle,* has put her stamp on the publication. Feldman also noted Ed Kosner, the current editor of *Esquire,* who, before coming to Hearst, was editor of *New York* and who had been at *Newsweek,* and Liz Tilberis, who came from *British Vogue* to edit *Harper's Bazaar.*

Feldman also acknowledged women founders of Hearst magazines who have earned internal promotions by their work at Hearst over many years: Editor Rachel Newman of *Country Living* and Editor Nancy Lindemeyer of *Victoria* built their magazines from the ground up. Annette Stramesi, longtime staff member, became editor of *Colonial Homes,* and Jeanette Chang, publisher of *Harper's Bazaar,* came from *Cosmopolitan* and, before Hearst, *Reader's Digest.* Although *Harper's Bazaar* dates to 1867, she is its first female publisher. "We have nothing but stars heading up the magazines," Feldman bragged. All Hearst women's magazines have female editors, except *House Beautiful,* which is edited by prize-winning Louis Oliver Gropp, formerly of *House & Garden.*

Probably the highest ranking woman at Hearst, Anne Sutherland Fuchs, senior vice-president, group publishing director, has the business responsibility for four publications, with their publishers reporting to her. Fuchs began at the *New York Times* selling advertising. She was also the publisher of seven different magazines during the 1970s (Fuchs, personal interview, August 23, 1995).

Fuchs said she believes that women are successful in the magazine business because of the kind of impact they make. Women, she said, bring different qualities to management decisions than men do. Women have the advantage in handling people, in being sensitive to men and other women. Women can be characterized by their positive reinforcement of people, and although it may be prototypical, women bring to management a quality of dealing with people positively. So it's a great advantage of being female, she said.

Fuchs said she firmly believes in a team concept of management: "The better my team is, the better I am; we all win. I've always been one to have people around me who want my job; I like that, people who want to move on. I've hired a lot of stars." Fuchs had been running *Vogue* for more than three years when Hearst offered her the group publishing position, involving then three magazines, or brands, as she calls them. She runs each business separately, sees them as separate businesses, but likes them "to work off each

other, learn from each other, create an ongoing team," she said.

When a new magazine is created at Hearst, chances are that many women will be involved, in all capacities. For example, *Victoria* has only one man on its editorial staff: Daniel D'Arezzo, deputy editor. Another man on the staff, the advertising director, left recently. Even the 24 contributing editors are all women, as is the sole contributing writer. Although the staff does use male photographers, they use more female photographers. On the business side, women hold 15 of the 18 slots (D'Arezzo, personal interview, August 23, 1995).

Editor Nancy Lindemeyer worked on Hearst Special Publications, the magazines that appear annually or semiannually, and headed that group. She saw the need for a book that touched women in a way other Hearst publications did not. The male executives at the company perhaps failed to understand her vision and wanted to produce another shelter magazine, a publication about the home. Nevertheless, they gave her backing for one issue; it promptly sold out, as did the second issue too. It was a different magazine than anything else around, D'Arezzo said. Deputy Editor D'Arezzo, who is called Nancy's alter ego, said, "Success has a thousand parents; failure is an orphan. Only one person is responsible for the creation of *Victoria*—Nancy."

Cindy Sperling, first publisher of *Victoria,* finds no difference in treatment between women and men at Hearst. She noted that women sometimes blame their failure on their gender; they attribute failure to the fact that they are women. She disagrees vehemently with this, suggesting it is really hard work that pays off (Sperling, personal interview, August 24, 1995).

Sperling began at *Cosmopolitan* in Chicago, selling ads for the midwest region with two people reporting to her. Then she was promoted to national sales manager for *Cosmopolitan* at age 24, which necessitated a move to New York. Only four months later, she learned she was being considered for publisher of *Victoria* but had to wait another month to find out if she got the position.

Sperling finds Hearst corporate executives supportive. In fact, she had lunch recently with Gilbert Mauer, number two at the company, who acts as her mentor. Although she dresses well and is well groomed, she said she never had "to lose her femininity to get somewhere."

Another publisher, Adrienne Cleere of *House Beautiful,* was vice president of international marketing at Bloomingdale's before she came to Hearst two and a half years ago. She was also vice president of retail marketing for American Express and bought advertising in magazines. In the 1980s, she was publisher of *W* magazine for Fairchild, when men were in charge at *Elle, Vogue,* and *Bazaar.* She wanted to embark on a career in magazine publishing with a publication whose primary audience was women.

Anne Holton is group publishing director for Hearst Home Resources Group and, as such, does special interest publications. Her books include *House Beautiful, Colonial Homes,* and *Good Housekeeping* special interest publications. She prepares larger home packages into monthlies and coordinates everything. It is a challenge, and Holton looks to the next century doing on-line service, a home arts site on the World Wide Web that makes a more powerful buy for advertisers who also place print ads with various Hearst magazines. She coordinates corporate packages for home advertisers, which means they get discounts for corporate buys; in other words, they receive deeper discounts by advertising in more Hearst magazines, so that Hearst obtains as much of their business as possible.

Holton started in 1975 at *Rolling Stone* with D. Claeys Bahrenburg, former president of Hearst Magazines Division. Then she went to *Ms.* magazine from 1977 to 1982 as a salesperson and became New York manager. In 1982, she went to Condé Nast as marketing director, where she found a woman ad director to be the only other female (Mary Beth Russell of *Glamour,* the first woman

director of advertising). There were no women publishers, no women senior managers, and only one or two New York managers. She worked for *Gentleman's Quarterly,* where she was told, "because you are a woman, you can't [sell certain kinds of advertising]." In 1985, after her stint at *GQ,* she moved to *Parade* (owned by Condé Nast at the time), where she became vice-president and advertising director. She then spent two and a half years as publisher of *US,* which Jan Wenner published in addition to *Rolling Stone.* In 1990, she became advertising director of *Country Living* and was promoted to associate publisher in 1992. In December 1994, she was promoted to her current job (Holton, personal interview, August 25, 1995).

Holton had a staff of 20 at *Parade* and found she worked well with older men. The president was intense and a difficult person, but she got along well with him because she realized what he wanted: no pretense, that is, people who are straight about problems; people who aren't afraid (of him). Men saw she could make their lives easier and began to respect her. At *GQ,* she had "felt totally inadequate" because it was a boys' club—a not particularly happy one at that—whereas at *Parade* she was respected for what she accomplished, not because she fit gender specifications. She encountered impatience and unfairness but found the men evolving over time.

Holton, a feminist, said that as women have gone from one woman to many at a magazine, they have become empowered by their sheer numbers, and it was a natural process to bring other women along with them. Working at *Ms.* made a huge difference to Holton, for she learned she could make mistakes and not think it was because she was a woman. She never questioned: Did I really do that wrong, or did that occur because I'm a woman? She could evaluate her experiences differently, more realistically. Women have wondered why they "screwed up" when they were not given a fair chance during a formative period. Holton knew she did not fail because she was a woman or young; she developed a sense of self-value that transcended differences. She spoke out, saying her mind, believing people should know what she was thinking. That was what coworkers really wanted to know, she said.

When working for someone smart, intense, with a temper, such as the legendary Carlo Vittorini, then *Parade*'s publisher and someone considered difficult, Holton found she still got along with him. He urged her to speak up, suggesting she did not work for him but for the company, and she needed to tell him what she thought. She had to carry out his decisions regardless of what she thought, but he did not want a "yes" person around. She had to be prepared to do battle; maybe he would rethink his decision and change his mind. But her job was not about making him, someone in senior management, feel comfortable.

She learned when to be delicate about saying what she thought, and she tried to do the right thing for the company. She recognized that people not only hear what you say but also what they hear. Men often present their position as an attack; she learned to address an idea and offer another perspective without diminishing the idea. She found she could disagree in a rich and dynamic environment, but she had to make decisions with information. Holton finds it is easier for women to disagree with men as many women have built-in politeness, and are conditioned to be sensitive and better in assessing people. She now takes advantage of that skill and shares her views, because they are valuable. She is able to assess the psyches of folks, she said.

Holton characterizes her five and a half years at Hearst as a place for camaraderie. Hearst, a huge company, can be a chauvinistic place. Legacies exist, but Hearst brings in people from the outside. As a result, people need to reach out to other people, not to form a segregated clique but to find someone new to embrace, to show them "the ropes." "Most of us understand that we are not going to get there by being the only girl in the club," said

Holton. "That comes from maturity, from the sense of 'we're in this together.'"

Holton cited a young woman who was treated like a mascot by upper-level male executives. She was their associate, yet they flew on airplanes first class while she flew coach. ("A dog goes in baggage and is not part of the team," Holton said.) For some, it is harder, but ultimately more rewarding, when all can be enriched by diversity. It means recognizing what a valuable person can contribute. People are always going to hire others like themselves, people with whom they are familiar, Holton remarked, so affirmative action remains important, mandating diversity, forcing employers as much as possible to think of qualifications.

She exemplified her value in discussions about the rate-base downsizing at Hearst; in other words, Hearst magazines began offering smaller circulation guarantees in the fall of 1995. Holton had the same experience at *Ms.* in 1980. "It was a no-brainer for me; I could say that cutting the rate base was workable, and here is why," she said. Everybody was concerned and talking, and she had something to add from her experience. Changes are occurring because people recognize an individual's worth.

Peg Farrell is publisher of Hearst's newest domestic magazine venture, *Marie Claire*. She began at BBDO advertising as secretary of the media department in 1971; in three months, she was promoted to spot TV buyer and then to media research, where she did an annual cost guide. She then worked at Vitt Media, a buying service in New York, earning more money and having the camaraderie of two men she had worked with at BBDO. She spent two years in each place. Then she became associate manager for media services for the Gillette Company and worked on personal care products and the Papermate Pen Division, where she was liaison between product managers and agency personnel for media decisions.

Changing jobs again, she went to Time, Inc., in 1976, where she was offered the job of salesperson, and spent the next 15 years there. She was one of the first women hired who had grown up within the company, the first woman to come up through the ranks, she remarked. After six years at Time, the company launched *TV&Cable Week* and she participated in its short life; it folded a year later. Another Time, Inc., product, *Sports Illustrated,* offered her a position in 1984. She left two years later and, in 1987, was invited back as New York divisional manager, with six people working for her. Her children were born in 1984 and 1988, which prevented extensive travel. She became eastern sales manager and remained at *SI* until 1990. In December of that year, she became associate publisher/advertising director at *Reader's Digest,* where she stayed two years. Then Hearst called.

She talked with corporate executives and said she wanted to be on the staff of a magazine she could relate to. She became associate publisher of *Cosmopolitan* and, after two years, became publisher of *Marie Claire.* She said the magazine business is based very much on reputations, "the way you approach business, and how intelligent that approach is." She was not brought in by a mentor or a friend. She had to hire a staff, start from scratch (Farrell, personal interview, August 25, 1995).

Farrell believes that women, fortunately, have come to a place right now where they bond on a professional level, "on what we've achieved, not because I'm a woman." Working mothers at Time, Inc., came together years ago as women needing support. Now, at Hearst, a nice camaraderie has developed where women have lunch together, "respect each other as professionals and not as women." Farrell admitted that when she was having children, she was conscious of needing to do something for women, to make strides, instinctively, for women, to help women. "You were careful not to screw up," she said.

Now the climate is different; women do not perceive themselves as female first, editor in chief (or whatever their title) second;

rather, they're professionals who strive to make an impact as professionals. Hearst is "no girls' club" (Stramesi, personal interview, 1995). Nor does one exist at women's publications, as men interested in fashion, architecture, or antiques, for instance, are welcome. Being a female does not enter into the job at all, according to women at Hearst. People in the field know each other but don't discuss their concerns as women. Women editors are of various ages, and that might have something to do with not relating in a woman-to-woman fashion (Stramesi, personal interview, 1995). Farrell herself does not think about making decisions that could have an impact on women. Rather, she makes decisions for the magazine, determining what is right and will be successful. Everything else falls into place. She has "the chance to do for women" but does not see herself as role model. Women understand networking, and they are more astute in trying to pick people's brains. Women must learn how to do expense accounts. "They cannot be spoon-fed," Farrell said. They seek out someone to help them. This still happens, informally, when someone asks for advice or an opinion, or how to approach a problem.

Farrell had to work hard to establish respect. She was not taken "under someone's wing" as some men are; nor was she a younger version of someone older who then could relate to her easily. Moreover, she learned from the beginning not to flirt, not to indicate any interest in a man. Sexual harassment has not been a problem for Farrell, who never wanted it to happen and behaved accordingly. Men simply don't approach her improperly, she said. Women may get their first job on their looks, Farrell said, but they must work hard or they will have to move on and won't succeed.

Annette Stramesi represents another woman who has succeeded at Hearst as the newly appointed editor of *Colonial Homes.* She has moved up the career ladder during 16 years at Hearst. First, Stramesi did publicity for eight years at a few private agencies. Many times she was assigned clients she had to be enthusiastic about and had to suppress her dislikes. Then, she wrote a paperback book about carpeting for one client and did publicity for another in the home furnishings business. She felt no kinship with them and decided she needed to change direction, so she sold freelance articles to the *New York Times* travel section. Her initial piece dealt with Belgian castles; her husband, an amateur photographer, provided the pictures. Then she wrote for the *Times* about shopping in the street markets in Palermo, Italy; again, her husband took pictures to illustrate her article.

Stramesi decided that if she could write for the *Times,* she could write for magazines (Stramesi, personal interview, August 25, 1995). She believes in "taking the bull by the horns yourself," avoiding personnel agencies ("they can be devastating and often screen on the wrong stuff"). Going her own way, she learned that the two freelanced articles helped her get a job. She answered an ad in the *Times* and got a job at *Colonial Homes.*

Colonial Homes came as a special publication from an issue of *House Beautiful.* After college graduation, she went to the New York School of Interior Design and spent evenings earning an associates degree, realizing she should know something about design. She liked the magazine's subject matter and the company, so she didn't move. As senior editor at first, she was promoted subsequently to editorial director, then executive editor, and now is the first female editor.

Stramesi never saw working as an editor as something impossible to achieve. She recalls thinking what a wonderful job it would be, especially as represented in the movies of the 1950s, citing those with Rosalind Russell and Lauren Bacall. She never had aspirations to work at news weeklies, thought being an editor was do-able, and chose the fashion field. However, her work as a publicist gave her a taste of it, which she did not like. So she wanted something that would allow her to use college studies and at the same time show her parents that she could do well in the business world. Her biggest problem now, professionally, is controlling her day; she is constantly trying to catch up on her work, which is interrupted with many meetings.

Ellen Kunes, executive editor of *Redbook,* embarked on a writing program while at college. She got an internship at *Boston* magazine and then went to New York. Beginning in 1981 as an editorial assistant at *Mademoiselle,* she then worked as a freelance writer for four years for magazines, earning as much as $85,000 a year. She freelanced her own column in *Mademoiselle,* became a contributing editor, wrote for *Omni* magazine, and did articles for major women's and heath magazines. Specializing in health and environmental issues, she could be both a technical writer or a generalist when needed.

She even wrote for *Parenting* magazine about children, although she has none, and also wrote a book, *How to Live Well or Even Better on Less.* She joined *Seventeen* as articles editor but was offered more money at *Family Weekly* (now *U.S.A. Weekend*). She was senior editor at *Self* and then *Lifestyles;* eventually becoming director at *McCall's,* where she oversaw beauty, food, fashion, and decorating sections. She came to Hearst when Kate White became editor of *Redbook* (Kunes, personal interviews, August 24, 26, 1995).

As executive editor at *Redbook,* Kunes said that everyone on the editorial side reports to her. She reads every story, approves writers and topics, works on the lineup of articles for each issue, and writes cover lines. She said she must have a good overview, knowing what works and what doesn't.

Redbook suggests how far women have come in magazine publishing. It has no male editors but 27 female editors; two or three men are in production. Kunes said a few men were at *Self,* and *Mademoiselle* had male editorial assistants, art department personnel, and a male fashion editor. Kunes has never worked with a lot of men; even at *Omni,* males and females were of equal number, and the editor in chief was a woman.

Kunes said men are not interested in and do not want to work on a woman's magazine.

Irene Copeland, senior articles editor at *Cosmopolitan,* has been at Hearst for 15 years (Copeland, personal interview, August 27, 1995). *Life After College* is an annual she produces for *Cosmopolitan,* and special sections, such as "Mothers at Work," come under her purview as well. She said she enjoys creating a special book for college-age students.

She set out to be in journalism and joined a magazine publishing company producing quarterlies and bimonthlies featuring beauty and hairstyles for consumers. She became an expert in beauty and extremely knowledgeable about the industry, and was then hired at *Seventeen* as beauty editor. She worked with advertisers and public relations practitioners to learn how companies decided to introduce products. Fascinated by the advertising side, she called someone she knew at an ad agency, who suggested meeting for lunch, whereupon she was offered a job. It proved to be a coincidence; she just happened to be there, and so she became an account executive for Cover Girl cosmetics. She became bored, however, and was fired in 1975, when a depression hit the ad industry.

She decided not to work full-time, and for five years she freelanced, doing well enough to continue but not embarking on a career option although several job offers came her way. Joining *Cosmopolitan* in September 1980, she wrote the advertorials that ran in the magazine. She was offered the job because of people at *Cosmo* she had known when she had been beauty editor at *Seventeen.* As often happens in any kind of career, most jobs are found through networking or people you know, she said.

Copeland is used to working for and with women and never had a male assistant. She worked with a male managing editor for many years, however, and the publication used to have a male associate art director as well. Individuals are hired if they fit appropriate criteria, and Copeland believes Publisher Donna Galotti was an outstanding candidate and a natural choice for *Cosmopolitan,* where most of the staff is female. At the lowest levels, men don't try to be assistants, probably because they don't want those jobs, Copeland said. Most men do not rise through the ranks that way.

Kate White, editor of *Redbook,* said she believes that in women's magazine journalism, women have the required expertise, comparing it with the specialized knowledge some people possess about sports. Even when men edited women's magazines, women were the support players (Kate White, personal interview, August 31, 1995). *Redbook* had a male editor and a male articles editor for many years. "They knew what we wanted better than we did," White said sarcastically.

Women at their own magazines brainstorm from their own experience. Women have succeeded at magazines because their best idea wins, which is not the case in other endeavors, such as politics. White likened being at a women's magazine to being at a women's college: A woman can be most proactive and innovative; she can reap rewards, not jockey for position. Newsweeklies, by contrast, have shown resistance to women through the years, White said.

White related the story of when she worked with a man who could not make eye contact with women if other men were in the room. He felt more comfortable with men coming in to his office for a chat, for boys' talk, she said. Women there realized they would have a hard time getting on the inside track. At the New York Times Magazine Division, she encountered two men of a different breed: She never had a sense they had any kind of bias toward women. The men in the field become somewhat gender-blind if they associate with women's magazines, White said. By contrast, when she was on a magazine in the 1970s and announced she was leaving for a more prestigious magazine, she was told her title would change and she would receive more money if she stayed. She did stay but found out the corporate executives had no intention of letting her run the magazine. She was passed over and decided to leave for better opportunities.

White served as *McCall's* editor in chief for four years, *Working Mother* editor in chief for two years, and *Child* magazine editor in chief. Before that, she was executive editor at *Mademoiselle*. She became editor in chief at *Child* when she was seven and a half months pregnant. No one asked her about being pregnant during the interview, and when she brought it up, the men said they were sure she would "work out" her scheduling problems, and promptly offered her the job. White said that men at women's magazines are different, more understanding and flexible in their thinking; at least, that has been her experience.

The *Redbook* editor doesn't care when her staff comes in or when they leave. If a staff member has to bring a child in one day, that is considered all right. It is environmental policy, not corporate policy, she said. She recalls being scolded for leaving at 5 p.m., and had input into changes in maternity policy at the New York Times Magazine Division: "They had a terrible policy," she said. She had to sense the need to live and breathe what was in the magazine, which was easier to do with a lot of women on the staff.

What happens when you're understanding with women? White asked rhetorically. You get paid back in performance. Some people worry about not giving an inch or the staff will take a mile, but that is not realistic, White found. She saw job-sharing at other magazines and dealt with such issues a lot "under the table." "We were like an underground railroad, with extended maternity leave. We were ahead of corporations, which had to catch up," she said. She remarked she knows how to get the most from her staff.

Success and Promotion

More than 50 women hold the rank of publisher at major American magazines (Jorgensen, 1995). These include women's maga-

zines (those created by and produced for women readers primarily), general interest magazines such as *People,* news weeklies, health magazines, city magazines, opinion magazines such as the *New Republic,* magazines for seniors, and young people's periodicals such as *Sports Illustrated for Kids.* Some women have risen to group publisher, such as chief executive officers, chief operating officers, and co-owners (Anne Sutherland Fuchs at Hearst, Christie Hefner of Playboy Enterprises, Linda Johnson Rice of Johnson Publishing, and Marie Clapper of Clapper Communications, respectively).

An examination of selected women's magazines at Hearst suggests the changes in male and female staff.

• *Town & Country* in 1985 had a male editor, publisher, editorial director, as well as male directors of production, marketing, and advertising. The same pattern emerged in 1990, but in 1995, both editor in chief and publisher were women, as were the managing editor, senior editor, creative director, art director, all department editors, and six subeditors. Men occupied the roles of deputy editor, editor at large, and four subeditors.

• *Cosmopolitan* in 1985 had a male publisher, managing editor, account manager, entertainment editor, sellers, and representatives. Ten years later, a female publisher had been hired, and editorial and business side operations were performed by women.

• The *Harper's Bazaar* staff in 1980 had a male editor, as did the 1990 *Bazaar,* which also had a male publisher, art director, and advertising director. Five years later, both editor and publisher were female, as were most staff members.

• *House Beautiful* in 1985 had a female senior editor, business and promotions managers, special marketing and marketing directors. In 1990, both editor and publisher were male, but by 1995, a female publisher was in place.

Thus women are making their presence felt as top editors and in the publishing ranks. Women are entering the senior levels of their corporate management.

Women in Corporate Life at Hearst

Although there are women on the Magazines Division level, only one woman is on the corporate level. Most people at Hearst do not see anyone at Hearst Magazines moving into high-ranking positions, at least not in the foreseeable future. In fact, Executive Editor Kunes noted the "window of time" women had open to them. In the magazine industry, she said, a person should be on staff by their twenties and thirties, and they must be editor in chief by age 40 or so. That position requires drive and energy, and people tend to burn out. The job is harder to do after 40, she said.

In hiring a new publisher of *Cosmopolitan,* the corporation went outside. Commented one person bitterly, "You're not appreciated here till you leave. They want no home-growners." Another said, "You cannot be a prophet in your own land." Women may experience that on the corporate level.

Women also won't move into upper ranks of management at Hearst right away because men head and are second in command at the other divisions within the corporation. Indeed, the hiring of Cathie Black, an outsider, supports this idea. In addition to magazines, there are newspapers, books, entertainment, real estate; Hearst is partners with Disney, Lifetime, ESPN, and A&E, and Hearst owns King Features Syndicate. Upper-level management might come from those divisions. Women will move into management positions of different groups, for executives are not resistant to women, but women are not positioned to move there yet. That will evolve. Women will be replacing the men at the top eventually, however, but that will take time (Ricks, D'Arezzo).

Women in Sales

Magazine consultant Charles Rodin related that, in 1969, when he was at Time, Inc., it was conventional wisdom, "it was ingrained," that women would not be invited to a sales meeting that took place in Portugal.

Publishing Director Anne Holton has had opposite experiences as she has gone through cultural and age-related changes: from *Rolling Stone,* where she worked out of her "hip pocket," to *Ms.,* which had no budget, to Condé Nast, where "to move a plant from one place to another required permission"—from having access to Gloria Steinem to suddenly being just "one of the little kids" was as much a shock as being excluded from the boys' club, Holton said.

At *Rolling Stone,* Holton sold advertising for wearing apparel, cosmetics, grooming products, and musical instruments. When the magazine decided to solicit ads for liquor, tobacco, and imported cars, she asked for the imported car category, to no avail. She was told they couldn't put a woman on imported cars and then put a man with less experience on it. She was 26 at the time and couldn't believe the discrimination. "Tell me I could not do it because I was inexperienced but not because I was a woman. That incensed me." It proved an epiphany for her; no one had ever said that to her in her entire adult working life. It was a shock for her when gender became an issue.

Indeed, she could prove she could sell better, and had done so with "dog categories." People were still caught up in the stereotype; what fit their image was a young salesman. She did not fit the "guy image." What are you going to do? Someone asked her sarcastically, "Get a job at *Ms.*?" So she did. Being at *Ms.* to her was like going to a women's college where you can fail or succeed not based on gender.

Now 60%-70% of the ad directors are women, and at least half the group heads and the publishers are, and no magazine company would hold such beliefs today, Rodin said.

Women in Sales at Hearst

Independent analyst Charles Rodin said women have increasingly come to magazine sales, and from that vantage point they have moved into higher staff positions. This is true not only at Hearst but at all magazines. At all of Time, Inc., publications 25 years ago, only one woman, Susie Schwartzman, sold ads— for *Life* magazine. Less than 25 years ago, a woman became the first seller for *Newsweek,* Valerie Salembeier. Her mentor was Cathie Black, now President of Hearst Magazines. Few women sellers were in the field. Looking at big magazines, one could count women in sales positions on one hand.

Yet, once given the chance, women earned reputations as being highly successful in sales, according to Publisher Adrienne Cleere. Being in sales calls for certain techniques and negotiating skills. Women have sensitivities and attitudes that help them a great deal in sales. They can be very dogged in their approach, repeatedly returning whether or not a person is rude. They exemplify what's practical and can nurture, suggesting what is best for a client in a sincere way, Cleere said.

Women are rewarded for their productivity in sales and publishing. During the last 20 years, they have been accountable, trackable. Women have found a great way to be rewarded, with clear-cut criteria. Direct rewards are given for efforts, and women can be financially successful. An accepted equality exists for women in sales, who now stand toe-to-toe with their male counterparts.

In fact, although males dominated the sales staffs in the 1970s, today that is not so at the agency end or the magazine end, said Ken Feldman of Human Resources. Group Publishing Director Anne Holton agrees. From a handful of women selling in the 1970s, the field has grown so that 80% of sellers are women, she said. Trying to find a male seller is difficult these days. Magazines prefer diversity in their sales staffs, are richer for it. Yet in the 1990s, for every adequate and acceptable male trying for a job selling advertising, for each one who would qualify for a second interview, there are ten women.

Women dominate the sales staffs at Hearst for women's books. For example, *Redbook,* 26 to 1; *Country Living, Cosmopolitan, Bazaar,* 3 to 1; *House Beautiful,* 2½ to 1; and *Town & Country,* 2 to 1. (However, the use of initials or names such as Sugar, Kersti, Leslie, V. Lee, and Kit makes staff gender determination difficult.)

In sum, women have made strides at magazines, especially at women's magazines. They have been able to enter the business side of magazine publishing in addition to the editorial side, and they have reached the highest levels, the top of the masthead, as the case study of Hearst Magazines suggests. Nevertheless, this process is under way and women still encounter the problems of 15 and 20 years ago.

Women have forged new career paths in the magazine industry. Their method of succeeding has been hard work, dedication, and willingness to make sacrifices. At Hearst, no one has made mention of any special treatment, although senior-level male executives occasionally function as mentors for some women publishers. No women's group exists where women can air problems, but there is a willingness, on the part of some editors, to be flexible for the schedules of childbearing women staff. It appears that two paths exist for promotion: remaining at the company and working one's way up or affiliating with other magazine corporations and being hired away. Either demands solid performance.

Women seem to be listening to readers' views, and readers are writing to complain about, as well as compliment, editorial and advertising material. If readers are distressed with the content of these magazines, let them raise their voices; they will be heard, now perhaps as never before.

Notes

1. Comment by Everette E. Dennis, executive director of the Freedom Forum Media Studies Center at

Columbia University: "I think the magazine industry is, the worst in keeping records, and in not caring. They just sort of tuned out." The Audit Bureau of Circulations (ABC) established independent audits of newspaper and periodical circulation when it was formed in 1914. Its total membership of 4,225 publishers, advertisers, and advertising agencies makes ABC the world's first and largest circulation auditing organization. ABC maintains the world's foremost electronic database of audited-circulation information, and offers reports and services in a variety of print and electronic formats—including CD-ROM.

2. For Christmas 1995, Black gave editors and corporate executives "White House" towels. She found the extra-special Christmas gift not by raiding the White House linen closet but at a gift shop in Washington, DC, and had them shipped to New York—80 of them, complete with the words "White House" stitched on them along with the executive mansion insignia. At a lunch in her honor at New York's 21 Club, she held up a towel and told everyone that "Clinton wept into it when the Republicans swept into office in November."

References

Bacon's magazine directory. (1995). Chicago: Bacon's.

Carmody, D. (1990, August 6). Identity crisis for "seven sisters." *New York Times,* pp. D1, D12.

Carmody, D. (1994, July 18). Magazines try to fill a void in minority hiring. *New York Times,* p. D6.

Consumer magazine and agri-media source. (various years, September issues). New York: Standard Rate and Data Service (SRDS).

Douglas, S. (1994). *Where the girls are.* New York: Times Books.

Folio 500, juggling act. (1995, July 1). *Folio,* pp. 49, 51.

The MPA magazine handbook. (1994-1995). New York: Magazine Publishers Association.

New publisher for Cosmopolitan. (1995, August 23). *New York Times,* p. D7.

Steiner, L. (1995). Would the real women's magazine please stand up . . . for women. In C. M. Lont (Ed.), *Women and media, content, careers, criticism* (pp. 99-108). Belmont, CA: Wadsworth.

Whelan, E. M. (1992, September 8). Alarm clocks can kill you: Have a smoke. *New York Times,* p. A24. (Responses to article on September 25, 1992, p. A24, by the editors in chief of *Family Circle, Redbook, New Woman, McCall's, Glamour,* and *Self*).

Personal Interviews

Brevick, Sean, and Jeff Baron: Client Service Representatives, Mediamark Research, Inc. (August 31, 1995).

Cleere, Adrienne: Publisher, *House Beautiful* (August 23, 1995).

Copeland, Irene: Senior Editor, *Cosmopolitan* (August 27, 1995).

D'Arezzo, Daniel: Deputy Editor, *Victoria* (August 23, 1995).

Farrell, Peg: Publisher, *Marie Claire* (August 25, 1995).

Feldman, Kenneth: Human Resources Director, Hearst (August 22, 1995).

Fuchs, Anne Sutherland: Senior Vice-President, Group Publishing Director (August 23, 1995).

Green, George, President, Hearst Magazines International (August 24, 1995).

Holton, Anne: Group Publishing Director, Hearst Home Resources Group (August 25, 1995).

Jorgensen, Judith S.: Magazine Publishers Association (August 25, 1995).

Kunes, Ellen, Executive Editor, *Redbook* (August 24, 26, 1995).

Ricks, Gloria: Vice-President of Public Affairs, Hearst (August 21, 1995).

Rodin, Charles: independent magazine consultant (August 23, 1995).

Sperling, Cindy: Publisher, *Victoria* (August 24, 1995).

Stramesi, Annette: Editor, *Colonial Homes* (August 25, 1995).

White, Kate: Editor, *Redbook* (August 31, 1995).

29

Television's Transformative Role in Courtroom Justice for Women and Children

Elizabeth Dodson Gray

First, there was great consternation at a woman "daring" to cut off her husband's penis after he had raped her. Were you then surprised (as I was) that Lorena Bobbitt was tried—and acquitted? She was acquitted by a mixed jury of both males and females, with a nice-looking early-thirties male as foreman of the jury.

What a surprise that acquittal was! And how was it possible, when her husband's body provided indisputable evidence of her deed?

Then there were the Menendez brothers, Erik and Lyle. Once again, there was no doubt they had murdered their parents. As with Lorena Bobbitt, their guilt was not contested. What was at issue was the interpretation to be given to that guilt, and what was to be a suitable punishment.

The outcome, once again, was a surprise. The first trials of each of the brothers resulted

in "hung" juries. Again, how could that be possible in a popular culture in which Hillary Clinton's work with the Children's Defense Fund on behalf of the legal rights of children has been widely viewed with apprehension, one media pundit speculating that "soon your children will sue you if you ask them to take out the garbage"! So how could two separate juries not return verdicts of guilty against the Menendez brothers?

The larger question is this: What has recently intervened in our culture to make such verdicts possible now?

It seems to me the likely answer is a decade of TV talk shows and news shows about, among other topics, domestic violence against women and children. Ten years ago, I think such jury verdicts would have been impossible.

But by the early 1970s, increasing numbers of women were being employed in the industry, and many of them were working internally to get greater visibility in news and programming for events and issues affecting women. Even that would not have been enough, had there not also been the focus on these issues by the emerging organizations and media of the women's movement itself also beginning in the early 1970s. What the issue-oriented women's activist organizations provided was something for the TV women to find and then lobby to get on the air.[1]

So finally television gave voice to enough human experience of domestic abuse, including marital rape and the sexual abuse of children by their parents, to make a defense based upon those realities credible to jurors. Let us look now at selected examples of how television coverage contributed to this change.

Night After Night, Day After Day

First, there has been the ordinary nightly news. The local evening news not only convinces viewers of the reality of crime in our society, but in these last years it has served also as witness to the increasing numbers of brutal murders coming out of so-called domestic violence.

Watching either the early or the late local news regularly, you hear not only of drive-by shootings on urban streets but also again and again of a husband (or boyfriend) who kills his wife, his children, himself, his girlfriend, her sister's family when he cannot find her, or he kills those with whom she has taken refuge. One recent spring in Boston over a period of a few weeks, we learned of three teenage girls killed by their boyfriends when the girls tried to break off the dating relationship, in one case after three weeks since its inception. One girl was shot to death, another knifed to death, a third beaten to death with a baseball bat!

The night-after-night repetitions of variations on this same theme finally convince you as a viewer that this is not fantasy or nightmare. This is the reality of everyday life for some people in this culture of ours.

You-the-Viewer Meet "Experts" and Participants

If you come from these nightly accounts at all confused and asking, "What is going on in our culture, that such things can be happening?"—other aspects of TV media step in to interpret for you. We now have a growing genre of hour-long TV news magazines: *60 Minutes, 20/20, Prime Time Live, Dateline NBC, 48 Hours.* Most of these programs have done segments on domestic violence and domestic abuse, exploring both events and the issues with commentary by anchor people, in-depth psychological interpretation by visiting "experts" with psychological training, and sometimes even interviews with couples themselves.

Exposure to even a few of these news-magazine segments lets you begin to perceive an emerging picture that has been hidden in that euphemistic cover-up phrase *domestic violence* (as though the walls were turning in and beating up women and children). It is a nasty picture of male violence to women and children, violence repeated in home after home, city after city, town after town, in all social classes.

Then there are the TV talk shows. Watch Phil Donahue, Oprah Winfrey, Geraldo Rivera, Sally Jessy Raphaël, Montel Williams, Jerry Springer, Vicki, Rolanda, Maury Povich, or their more recent colleagues in this competitive genre—and you will see again and again the real-life stories of battered women. The women talk of being beaten, kicked, knifed, threatened with being killed. They tell 10 or 20 million television viewers of their experience of marital rape with a brutally invasive penis or with a Coke bottle or a curling iron or whatever.

"You don't have to be a rocket scientist to understand" that sex with a violent man would never be erotic; it would be simply brutal. And you hear these women's sobbing voices and see their faces, and you begin to believe what would have seemed to many of us unbelievable 10 years ago.

Then you watch two-hour made-for-television movies, often fact-based (or so *TV Guide* tells you) and you see all these same stories again. This is a typical *TV Guide* listing: *Shattered Dreams* (1990), a fact-based movie recounting the 17-year ordeal of the battered wife (Lindsay Wagner) of a prominent Washington, D.C., lawyer (Michael Nouri).

You see Farrah Fawcett star in *The Burning Bed,* and you watch with sickening horror as her abuse continues and increases and crescendos until she finally does burn the bed. And you hear about the Framingham Eight, who are some of the women in prison in Massachusetts who finally did kill their abusive, stalking, threatening, restraining-order-ignoring former husbands and boyfriends. Now you can see that battered women are white and black, Hispanic and Asian, rich and poor, society matron and blue collar.

Without Reading the Book

Whether you have ever read Lenore Walker's classic *The Battered Woman* (1979)—whether you have ever heard her on a TV talk show or TV newsmagazine focused on battered women—whether or not you have ever heard the phrase *battered woman syndrome*—you as a viewer of present-day television, you understand. You are ready, whether male or female, to be on Lorena Bobbitt's jury. Television has opened up to you, in living color, the reality of battered women in today's culture.

Television has given battered women faces you have seen. And it has given them voices, so they speak to you of this awesomely terrible life experience that for hundreds of years in patriarchy has been silenced, suppressed, covered up. Oh, the valiant and determined Victorian women of the Women's Christian Temperance Union (WCTU) knew of these realities. But given the conventions of their day, they could not speak them. They could only inveigh against the evils of what they called "drink," knowing (as their audiences also knew) that drunken angry men

often came home to beat and abuse their children and wives. But the women of the WCTU could only speak against alcohol, not against these unspeakable abuses themselves.

A lot of that covering up has been ripped away. Now all of us who have not experienced such abuse personally can see the reality of those who have, and we can tremble for what we have missed.

Beholding the Crucifixion of Children

Not only battered wives but abused children have become visible through the miracle of television. I think we all naively assumed for "all" families a "normative" decent pattern of child rearing. This included some degree of disciplinary "spanking." But it certainly did not extend to behavior such as burning a child's skin with a hot cigarette, or breaking a child's arm or leg or ribs, or throwing the child down a flight of stairs, chaining a child to a water pipe or radiator, or locking a child up in a basement, starving a child, and so on.

Yet recently we have seen all this on the evening news, happening sometimes in unknown families, sometimes in much heralded ones, as in the Lisa Steinberg case in New York City. Can anyone doubt such abuse happens, when you see it not only on the evening news but read about it over breakfast on the front page of the *New York Times* (which promises you "all the news that is fit to print")?

There have also been talk shows where we have seen with our own eyes many women (and some men) recall, and recount to us, their experiences of being sexually abused many years earlier. We search their faces: Are they really telling us the truth? Could any parent in this culture (usually a male) do this to his child (usually a female)? It boggles our minds, but we realize eventually that when we have difficulty imagining something, it does not mean that it is not true.

We watch their eyes, we see their tears, we begin to feel their pain. We begin to believe. We also see their diversity—again, white and black and Hispanic and Asian—again, rich and middle class and poor.

We watch that terribly attractive former Miss America, Marilyn VanDebur, look directly into the camera's eye as she tells us how her father, the Denver socialite, a pillar of society, a seemingly upright man, "pried her legs open at night" to molest her. She tells us how she repressed those "night memories" but became too terrified to sleep in her too-tightly clamped muscles of resistance—until years into her marriage, she "fell apart" in midlife and regained those memories. We sense as we hear her speak her deep commitment to making everyone understand that it happens, and what it means to those children to whom it happens.

Other Prominent Voices Speak Out

Even if we have never read Harvard psychiatrist Judith Herman's classic *Father-Daughter Incest* (1981), with its profile of the incestuous father as "good provider, pillar of the church, pillar of the community," we begin to believe that sexual abuse and incest can happen. We begin to understand that it does happen. We have taken into our minds and hearts the sickening reality of child sexual abuse—the reality of incest.

Then media celebrities such as Roseanne Arnold and Oprah Winfrey add their voices to the chorus, and we marvel at their courage to join poet Maya Angelou in letting us see into the violence they have experienced earlier in their lives in such a private way.

Word gradually leaks out about scandals in churches and sexual abuse by priests, first in the *National Catholic Reporter* and the specialized religious press. Then suddenly it is on the nightly television news and we are watching arrests and allegations and court trials. Then we see survivors speaking out on talk shows and television newsmagazines—especially the men, lots of men, confessing their shame and lifelong trauma from being sexually abused—sodomized—as young schoolboys by their priest, their "Father in God." And we exclaim, like Marie Fortune, "Is nothing sacred?"[2]

In a follow-up story on a TV newsmagazine, we see the journalist who first broke into print with accounts of pedophilia by priests. He has been following this diocese by diocese, and he tells how many million dollars Roman Catholic dioceses in the United States have spent paying off survivors and "settling" out of court in return for survivors' silence. Then he and Roman Catholic priest-sociologist Andrew Greeley are on the *Phil Donahue Show*.

The film *The Prince of Tides* was in movie houses across the country a year or more before. Even though the novel does not culminate in the sodomy-rape of the son, the movie does. It helps us begin to believe that child sexual abuse happens to little boys as well as little girls, and that when it happens, it is as life-distorting, as traumatic, and perhaps even more deeply repressed with men than with women.

Now we are ready to sit through the Menendez brothers' trial as jurors, and at least consider seriously the possibility that their father's sexual abuse through the years could indeed have made the brothers fear for their own lives and have driven them to murder in self-defense.

TV as Ally in Feminist Consciousness Change

How does all this make me feel as a feminist who is interested in consciousness change? It makes me feel we should "thank our lucky (feminist) stars!" that we live in a TV age.

Television has taken parts of the reality of women's lives and it has made them "seen and heard" as a part of the visible and taken-seriously reality of our culture. It has taken women's experience, aptly named by sociologist Elise Boulding "the underside of history" (1976/1992), and made it noteworthy, even with patriarchy's determination only to focus only on male experience as normative and visible. It has allowed the voices of women and children, long silenced as victims of abuse, to resonate loud and clear until we can hear them as survivors and not just as victims. It has done this with male talk show hosts (Donahue, Geraldo, Montel, Jerry, Maury), with male commentators on newsmagazines (Sam Donaldson, Hugh Downes, Stone Phillips), and with a male news anchor as host of a TV special on rape (Peter Jennings).

I do not think I will ever forget the incredible feeling I had when Peter Jennings in the ABC rape special (March 1992) looked directly into the camera and said that rape is a man's problem because we men are always doing it to women! Men like Peter Jennings bring a huge reservoir of credibility to a women's issue because when important men declare an issue to be important and urgent, it *becomes* important and urgent in the male world that dominates our public life.

What to Make of O. J. Simpson?

For millions of sports fans, the struggle originally was whether they could imagine that their beloved O. J., the sports hero and superior athlete of almost mythic dimensions, actually could have committed such a violent and awful crime—the double murder of Nicole Brown Simpson and Ronald Goldman. But television—because it cares about ratings and money, and not because it cares particularly about women's issues—was to cover every moment of the trial it was allowed to, bringing out every gory detail a million times on every TV station and every newsmagazine. That O. J. might have done it became thinkable. At the start, it appeared that the hyper-coverage might accomplish what the women's movement by itself could

never have accomplished. It appeared that this trial might finally make it commonplace in our culture to perceive the relationship between the macho sports male mystique and violence itself, not just in our sports but in our personal relationships.

At about that time, I saw at my supermarket checkout the latest issue of the *National Enquirer,* with a full-page article by two men, Reginald Fitz and John Blosser (1994), on what they are now calling the "Super Jock Syndrome." The title of the article promises to tell its readers "why O. J. and other sports stars turn violent toward women." "Many sports figures have shown signs of the syndrome," the article continues, "including Sugar Ray Leonard who confessed to punching his wife; Mike Tyson, convicted of rape, and San Francisco Giants slugger Darryl Strawberry who admitted beating his spouse" (p. 41). The more recent book, *Sex, Violence and Power in Sports: Rethinking Masculinity,* by Michael Messner and Donald Sabo (1994), is also concerned to investigate this connection between athletes and violence to the women in their lives.

Finally Racist Violence Overwhelmed Sexist Violence

The yearlong O. J. trial developed a complexity all its own, in which the focus shifted away many times from the dead victims. The lawyers defending O. J. attacked the forensic procedures and conclusions of the Los Angeles Police Department. With a screenwriter's disclosure that LAPD detective Mark Furman had been talking to her on tape for a decade, it almost became the Mark Furman trial, for on the tapes Furman described how officers fabricated evidence to convict defendants, beat up blacks, and administered street justice in a racially biased and hostile way.

At the end of the trial, the acquittal of O. J. Simpson still seemed unthinkable and unjust to a substantial majority of white America.

But for a jury of mostly black women, this was a trial about the long history of violence and injustice of whites toward blacks, rather than of men toward women. There was, in their judgment, "reasonable doubt," and the media focus shifted to explore another dark and dangerous tradition of violence, that of whites against blacks. Violence has moved along racial as well as sexual divisions, and both are important, both need to be understood and acknowledged—and both need to cease.

"Go, Tell It on the Mountain"

In ancient times, people would seek the height of mountaintops to help them amplify their voices and help in getting their message out: "Go, tell it on the mountain, / Over the hills, and everywhere. / Go tell it on the mountain." Television has provided contemporary feminism, and now American blacks, with a modern equivalent of such a mountaintop, providing just such an amplifying voice for at least certain of our messages about women's (and blacks') experience in this culture.

I do not say that television does this for love of women or affection for the women's movement. Rather, the driving forces are more likely television news managers' and network managers' insatiable needs for news that is highly visual and also emotionally powerful and very involving for their viewers—a large number of whom are women. Networks and stations are also driven by concerns about advertising revenues and market share, and so they are constantly creating and showing whatever is the hottest and latest issue or newest trend. This means that, in the midst of television's coverage of issues which concern and affect women, it also continues to show and maintain the old stereotypes of women and it has all the other flaws of a well-invested patriarchal institution.

But despite itself, television as the great amplifying voice of our time has made pos-

sible some unexpected and truly incredible cultural leaps in consciousness symbolized by Clarence Thomas, the priestly pedophile Father Porter, Lorena Bobbitt, and O. J. Simpson. These leaps of consciousness on the issues of wife battering, incest and sexual abuse of children, violence to women, and sexual harassment could not have been produced by the women's movement alone, or by the courts alone. A crucial role is played by the harsh glare of publicity and celebrity, the amplifying "voice" of television.

The extent of these changes in consciousness, and in general awareness of these issues, is suggested by the jury verdicts in the Lorena Bobbitt and first of the Menendez brothers trials, and perhaps by white America's willingness to consider an exemplary black sports hero a batterer and then the murderer of his wife.

The Continuing Struggle to "Name" What Is Happening

Where such a cultural shift takes place, providing a gain in cultural power for some group, the shift often provokes a backlash. I take *The Abuse Excuse: Cop-Outs, Sob Stories and Other Evasions of Responsibility*, by Harvard law professor Alan M. Dershowitz (1994), to be an expression of just such a patriarchal backlash against these very real recent gains for women and children in a still violent patriarchal culture. I think the publication of *The Abuse Excuse* indicates that my quick sketch of women's and children's recent search for safety and justice is not the end of the story. On the contrary, we all know such violence will continue. But there is, for me, clear evidence in the publication of this book, by such an eminent defense lawyer, that a lot of progress has indeed already been made, perhaps more than we noticed. We need to appreciate that progress, and honor the women in the women's movement and in the communications industry whose efforts made it possible.

Notes

1. For a more detailed account of the history of how this happened, see Donna Allen (1989). Also see Allen's Chapter 34 in this volume.

2. Marie Fortune is a United Church of Christ minister and a consultant on preventing clergy sexual abuse and on procedures for dealing with it when it does occur. See Fortune (1989).

References

Allen, D. (1989). From opportunity to strategy: Women contribute to the communications future. In R. Rush & D. Allen (Eds.), *Communications at the crossroads: The gender gap connection* (pp. 59-79). Norwood, NJ: Ablex.

Boulding, E. (1992). *The underside of history: A view of women through time* (rev. ed.). Thousand Oaks, CA: Sage. (Original work published 1976, Boulder, CO: Westview)

Dershowitz, A. (1994). *The abuse excuse: Cop-outs, sob stories and other evasions of responsibility.* Boston: Little, Brown.

Fitz, R., & Blosser, J. (1994, August 2). Why O. J. and other sports stars turn violent toward women. *National Enquirer*, p. 41.

Fortune, M. (1989). *Is nothing sacred? When sex invades the pastoral relationship.* San Francisco: HarperSanFrancisco.

Herman, J. L. (M.D.). (1981). *Father-daughter incest.* Cambridge, MA: Harvard University Press.

Messner, M. A., & Sabo, D. F. (1994). *Sex, violence and power in sports: Rethinking masculinity.* Freedom, CA: Crossing Press.

Walker, L. E. (1979). *The battered woman.* New York: Harper & Row, Colophon.

30

Filipino Women in Communications
Breaking New Ground

Florangel Rosario-Braid

Women's impact in the field of communication did not happen overnight. Early activities in this field were dominated by men, and, as in many other areas, the approach has been that of a demand for equal rights.

The common perception was that breaking through the glass ceiling necessitates setting up adversarial relationships. The women's liberation movement that picked up steam in the late 1960s was about women asserting their rights. Today, however, women have gained more experience and confidence; men are getting used to the idea of sharing power and responsibility, and thus the relationship is now moving toward partnership and complementarity. The demands of a sustainable society require leadership that is guided by the perspectives of both sexes. A feminist author puts this argument quite simply: "It is not about women taking over, but women

and men together expressing their full potential—neither superior nor inferior" (Eisler, 1987, cited in Aburdene, 1992, p. xxvii).

Women leaders, and the more sensitive menfolk, now realize that sustainable development can only come about through cooperation. The culture of competition and conflict resulted in ideological schisms, ecological disasters, racial and ethnic strife, and economic stagnation. Power and domination characterize the current mode of decision making and this may be attributed to the predominance of men in the arena of politics. But in many parts of the more developed societies, the old power structures are being rearranged as they enter the information-driven twenty-first century. There is now wider sharing of knowledge and information; profit-motivated corporations now realize that, to survive, they must restructure existing monoliths to smaller autonomous units.

These developments require changes in management principles from consolidation of authority toward more democratic participation in decision making. The emphasis on decentralized decision making and a new pluralism has crystallized the need for women's participation in promoting stability. When peace and the development of human potential, rather than war, become society's central agenda, women's natural disposition for caring, nurturing, and compassion will be an indispensable complement in governance. This chapter demonstrates the value of the feminine perspective in the transformation of contemporary Philippine society. The challenge of developing mechanisms and structures for partnership and cooperation requires creativity, innovation, and resiliency.

Women in Journalism: A Historical Overview

In the field of journalism, Filipino women are not only writing the news, they are also coauthors in the writing of the nation's history. Philippine media are perceived as enjoying unbridled freedom (it is known as the freest and liveliest in Asia). Another perception is that women communicators belong to a privileged circle. These circumstances, however, were not achieved overnight. From the Spanish colonial era to the Marcos dictatorship, it has been a constant struggle for the few courageous souls who had to contend with traditional barriers: (a) breaking into the macho-dominated culture of media, (b) proving that one is worth one's salt, and (c) guarding one's freedom and independence.

Because women journalists were not in the mainstream, this hostile environment may have created a distinct women's media culture—evidenced in innovation, risk-taking, perseverance, and a high sense of justice and equity.

At the village level, women leaders are using indigenous communication channels such as street theater, blackboard newspaper (peryodikit), and folk literature to mobilize the community toward communal projects on health, nutrition, livelihood, and environment.

Communication schools were founded and are now staffed by women—as administrators or teachers. At least four women academics, whose successors were also women, introduced and expanded the concepts of development communication, process reporting, and social mobilization. Process reporting could revolutionize the teaching of journalism. *Events reporting,* which dominates present-day journalism, deals with concrete events using the five Ws and one H as standard formula and focuses on the unusual, sensational, and bizarre such as man-bites-dog stories. Events reporting, or "he said, she said journalism," however, may not suffice in covering today's complex issues. *Process reporting,* on the other hand, examines issues in relationship with other events and the larger environment. It examines the whys and hows of events but does not dichotomize or fragment the various components of an event. Issue-oriented stories look back at the past, examine the present, and provide options for the future. It focuses beyond what is manifest or visible to the naked eye. Priority national programs such as the peace process and sustainable environmental development can best be communicated through process reporting.

Advertising has also become more gender sensitive. The number of women advertising executives is on an upswing compared with a decade ago when the field was primarily male dominated. But it is in the telecommunications sector where women's absence of leadership is more visible. Perhaps the unattractiveness of this industry of the future to women is due to perceptions of how this industry operates. Telecommunications is perceived as laden with political and economic intrigues and shady deals. Technical courses such as electronics and communications engineering remain male dominated.

Current environmental conditions have also forced women communicators to be quite unorthodox. Many have taken the lead in advocacy for hard issues such as the environment, debt problems, land reform, crime and violence, in addition to the traditionally perceived soft issues of education, health, and nutrition. Dissatisfied with current media fare, many have ventured into innovative approaches in news gathering. Women journalists have become risk-takers in dealing with unfriendly establishments (e.g., autocratic regimes) and in testing the limits of what is considered to be within the purview of national security.

Whether women can become full partners in the socioeconomic and political life of a nation, and now of the global economy, will be determined by their integration in today's information society. As futurist Alvin Toffler (1990) reminds us in *Powershift:* "The highest quality-power will come from the application of knowledge rather than from the will of force or wealth" (p. 15). Women in all fields could remain marginalized unless they gain access to information and, as the saying goes, "own half of the (satellite) sky."

Topping the agenda of women's networks worldwide is the desire to bring about a realization that the world's survival will depend on partnership between women and men. In the communication field, however, this partnership is not happening quickly enough. Leadership is still adversarial, with either men or women in charge, and does not involve partnership where women and men take charge together. The history of the Philippine mass media is silent on the initial role of women, especially in the struggle for Philippine independence against the Spanish colonizers. In particular, *La Solidaridad,* recognized as the mouthpiece of the revolution, which first appeared in 1889 and lasted until 1895, was dominated by men who were acknowledged as national heroes—Jose Rizal, Marcelo H. del Pilar, Mariano Ponce, Graciano Lopez Jaena, among others (Corpuz, 1989, pp. 166-174).

Although Filipino women during the Spanish colonial period were held in high esteem, their activities were confined to religion, art and culture, and the traditional household chores. Not having adequate access to higher educational opportunities limited their par-

ticipation in affairs such as politics. The participation of women in mainstream media started in 1891 when *El Bello Sexo* (The Fair Sex), an illustrated weekly, was first published. It contained sections on fashion, morals, literature, and history. This weekly lasted for nearly two years. Another women's magazine was published a year later, *Madrid Manila.* The first women's journal, *El Hogar* (The Home), was first published in January 1893 and was supposed to be staffed only by women (Lent, 1966, pp. 57-58). The stereotyping (or even trivialization) of the interests and concerns of women readers is evident in the content of these early publications.

The American commercial media system in the early 1890s facilitated the entry of more women journalists. With improved educational opportunities, more women joined media establishments, although a majority were confined to the so-called lipstick beat—coverage of home and society, fashion, food, lifestyle, and so on. Positions of power and influence, however, remained male dominated. The highest position that women journalists could aspire to was the editorship of lifestyle or society pages. This marginalization of women was to continue for decades, despite the fact that the postwar period (1945-1971) is best remembered as the golden age of Philippine journalism. The press during this time functioned as a watchdog of the government—sensitive to national issues and critical of government mistakes.

It seems ironic that the liberation of women journalists from traditional roles would come during the repressive years of the Marcos regime starting with the declaration of martial law in 1972. Women journalists, more than their male counterparts, proved to be more daring and independent in their writing. In those times of living dangerously, women journalists become innovative and creative in their writing style to avoid direct confrontation with the establishment, thus enabling the women to remain in circulation. Many ventured into innocuous writing—use of metaphor, fable, barbs, euphemisms, and so on to send messages (while readers read between the lines). The more daring ones continued to write exposés on injustices, human rights abuses, graft and corruption, crime and violence, and military abuses.

The emergence of the so-called alternative press came about essentially through the efforts of women such as Eugenia D. Apostol, Betty Go-Belmonte, and Letty J. Magsanoc, who served as founders, publishers, journalists, and managers. Among these publications were *Mr. and Ms.,* a women's magazine, and three national newspapers—*Veritas, Malaya,* and the *Inquirer.* For not toeing the official line, that is, writing and publishing only about the "true, the good and the beautiful," several women journalists were subjected to harassment, threats, and intimidation by the military. They were often invited into military camps for "interviews." Multimillion peso libel suits were filed against them, and there were constant threats of dismissal and forced resignations. Among these courageous journalists were Letty J. Magsanoc, Domini Torrevillas, Ceres Doyo, Sheila Coronel, Alice Villadolid, Sylvia Mayuga, Arlene Babst, and Ninez Cacho-Olivares. As expected, the struggle for press freedom often centered on women journalists aptly portrayed as martyrs or victims of the autocratic regime. A national crusade against the dictatorship and all forms of oppression was waged by the Concerned Women of the Philippines, who used letter-writing as an effective lobby mechanism.

During the historic 1986 People Power Revolution, women journalists were again at the forefront. Millions of Filipinos followed the historic event from the clandestine Radyo Bandido anchored by a woman broadcaster, June Keithley. The station, along with church-owned Radio Veritas, was credited with mobilizing people power to support the rebel soldiers against Marcos's military power. To a great extent, the politicization of the masses, the discontentment with the discredited regime, and the call for social reform that culminated in the 1986 EDSA Revolution (for Epifanio DeLos Santos Avenue, the site of the con-

flict) were fired up by the writings of these women journalists.

Why were these women journalists so brave? A freelance journalist, Neni Sta. Romana-Cruz, believes that "unlike the men who usually think of their jobs, their future, and their families, we (women) are not the breadwinners (and therefore our jobs and incomes can be risked)" (Fernandez, 1987, p. 185).

An American media scholar observed:

Women journalists, remained uncompromised by the close association with [Marcos] government sources . . . allowing them to emerge as effective adversaries when the opportunity presented itself. Furthermore, many of the powerful anti-Marcos male journalists were fired, jailed, or otherwise rendered ineffectual as Marcos increasingly assumed direct or indirect control of the nation's press. It was therefore an opportune time for women journalists to take the lead in the struggle for freedom and democracy. (Shafer, 1994, p. 24)

Doreen G. Fernandez, a communications professor at a Catholic university in Manila, herself a journalist, attributes women's bravery to cultural factors, particularly the multiple roles of Filipino women in society:

The women journalists who were so militant about freedom of expression were fighting as journalists barred from writing the truth, as wives of men threatened by the regime, as mothers of children who would inherit it, as citizens of a nation oppressed by dictatorship, as individuals with private battles and problems—all at the same time, without separating levels of commitment or risk. (Fernandez, 1987, p. 186)

Perhaps another cultural factor is how society regards women. Any (physical) attack on a woman by a man is a serious social offense. Thus the Marcos regime, at least initially, treated women journalists with kid gloves and tried to ignore them until their criticism had become too frequent and intense. After the 1986 Revolution, there was no turning back for women journalists. They had become prominent, influential, and credible. Many of the so-called hard beats such as defense, politics, police, and business gradually became staffed by women reporters. At least two major dailies, *Philippine Daily Inquirer* and *Manila Times,* have women as editors in chief—Letty J. Magsanoc and Ma. Lourdes Mangahas, respectively. The chief operations officer of a TV network is a renowned broadcast journalist, Tina Monzon-Palma. Two of the largest advertising agencies have women as chief executive officers (CEOs). With the restoration of democratic space, the next step for women journalists is to reform media through more responsible, ethical, and professional reporting.

A common criticism against local media is the lack of depth and their inability to delve into the causes and broader implications of issues and events. Thus, in 1991, the Philippine Center for Investigative Journalism (PCIJ; in Manila) was founded by nine Filipino journalists, mostly women, who were prominent during the antidictatorship campaign. The center provides readers with a knowledge base for decision making through investigative articles on current issues. It has investigated controversies on environment issues, human rights, agrarian reform, and government bureaucracy. The center was the first to publish news of the rumored illicit love affair of a top government official. Another organization, the Center for Media Freedom and Responsibility (CMFR; in Makati, M.M.), as its name connotes, focuses on the upgrading of professionalism and responsibility of media workers. Staffed by women journalists, the center publishes the *Philippine Journalism Review,* which monitors media performance and credibility. CMFR also sponsors regular forums on media and development issues. The ability to delve into latent issues, as well as greater attention to details, patience, and perseverance in following through stories that could have been relegated to the dustbin—these are some of the outstanding journalistic qualities of some of these women. These qualities are also illustrated in two

award-winning television public affairs programs—*The Probe Team* and *The Inside Story*—produced and hosted by broadcast journalists Cecilia Lazaro and Loren Legarda, respectively. Another award-winning television show on entrepreneurship was the brainchild of Zenaida Domingo and Rebecca Smith. Journalist Melinda de Jesus and this author are painstakingly rewriting the newswriting formula—from traditional events-oriented to *process-oriented* stories.

As one of those involved in initial efforts to democratize elitist media ownership, I served as a founder and first president of the *Philippine Daily Inquirer,* the first ever national daily envisioned to be a cooperatively owned newspaper. However, cultural differences and vested interests prevailed and the venture failed. Some provincial women journalists in Mindanao have pursued the dream. A cooperative media service has been set up in Davao City while a cooperative television station, also spearheaded by a woman, has been in operation for some time in Zamboanga City.

Advocating for a New Communication Order

It is inevitable that advocacy for structural reforms to correct existing imbalances and disparities in media ownership, content, flow or dissemination of messages, and technology transfer should be perceived as a priority area for reform. The author, as an appointed member of the Constitutional Commission that drafted the Constitution, was involved in this breakthrough in policy advocacy resulting in 13 communication-related provisions in the 1987 Philippine Constitution.

The constitution is perhaps one of the few to declare outright that "the state recognizes the role of women in nation-building and shall ensure the fundamental equality before the law of women and men" (Article II, Sec. 14).

I was also responsible for convening over a dozen forums that attempted to evolve comprehensive communication policies and define operational ones. Representatives from government, industry, academe, and social institutions (people's organizations, church, labor, farm, and cultural communities) participated in drafting recommendations on needed policies in communication. The framework included issues of access, balance, equity, diversity, ethics, and right to communicate. Communication-related legislation was then drafted by the author working with other women leaders in the communication sector. These efforts have been sustained through lobbying.

The alternative press during the Marcos regime drew heavily on the talents of women journalists. Today, alternative programming such as the two top-rated public affairs TV programs and the children's educational program, *Batibot,* provide models for quality programming here and abroad. The use of broadcast media for education was pioneered by women educators including the two existing science-oriented school-on-the-air programs for teachers and elementary students.

The first-ever educational cable TV was set up in 1993 at the Philippine Women's University (PWU), which is now managed by educator Amelou B. Reyes and broadcast journalist Olive Villafuerte. A woman legislator, Senator Anna Dominique Coseteng, who hosts a women's program on TV, initiated the 1991 Manila international conference on women, media, and advertising, which stressed that women's issues are everybody's issues, and that the woman's perspective is often lacking in international discussions. Women in media were individually and collectively asked to shift their struggle from the personal to that of the collective needs of society.

Social Transformation Through Community Communication

In remote coastal villages, marginalized fisherfolk actively participate in the production of mimeographed newsletters, poems, songs, posters, street theater, and sound slides. These community channels are used in or-

ganizing, mobilizing, and educating fisherfolk and their families on issues such as illegal fishing, pollution, peace and order problems, and the lack of access to basic services. This participatory approach in small media production has enabled people to be conscious of and to reflect upon the richness of their experiences. The popularization of community media was initiated by Mina Ramirez, who heads a Manila-based social institute that also initiated the Tent School. The latter uses a methodology of individual sharing and group reflection among students and marginalized groups (Pablo, 1994, p. 2).

In Central Visayas, a World Bank-funded community-based resource management project mobilizes community participation through indigenous channels such as street theater, "barefoot" technicians, mobile posters, and folk literature. Again, the strategy was conceptualized and managed by development communication specialist Conchita Bigornia. This project is now recognized by the World Bank as a "model" in community resource management worldwide. Philippine folk media were able to withstand the onslaught of modern technologies through the dedication of women folk media researchers and practitioners. For decades, the government information arm, Philippine Information Agency (then the National Media Production Center), maintained a puppet-theater group that performed nationwide with messages highlighting such development concerns as health, nutrition, population, and so on. This theater group was initiated by Rebecca Smith and Lolita Aquino. A national network of development communication practitioners, mostly women, have sustained the use of various forms of folk media in popularizing agricultural innovations and technologies.

New Communication Technologies and the Women's Response

Telecommunications today is the world's most visible and powerful industry as it is responsible for processing, transmitting, and interpreting all types of information and knowledge, which is the new currency of the business world.

Although women have a foothold in local industry, they are few and far between, because the industry is capital-intensive and often laden with economic intrigues. It is also ominous that an industry that relies heavily on women to manufacture the lifeblood of its existence—the computer chip—does not involve more women in the upper echelons of vision and direction setting.

The Internet and the information superhighway will open wider horizons for women. But, again, these are technologies in which the male imprint is more visible. In developing countries, the majority of the users of these technologies are men.

Women in Communication Education

Communication education is one area where women have or have had a significant impact. Most communication schools today are headed by women who also constitute their core faculty. The ratio of women to men faculty is approximately 70:30. The first deans of four communication schools were Gloria Feliciano, Nora Quebral, Josefina Patron, and the author. Communication concepts such as development communication, social mobilization, and process reporting have been initiated by women educators. Nora C. Quebral and Ely Gomez of the University of the Philippines at Los Banos (UPLB) were mainly responsible for giving shape and form to the concept of development communication (Devcom). Today Devcom is a distinct discipline recognized not only in developing and Asian countries but even in the United States.

Development communication has also found its way into other parts of the world, especially Asian and developing countries including Malaysia, Thailand, Indonesia, Sri

Lanka, Papua, New Guinea, India, Kenya, and Nigeria. The "missionaries" of Devcom in these countries are UPLB graduates. Communication (including marketing) research has among its leading practitioners women academics and researchers. The two pioneer communication (media) research institutes were also founded by women. Social mobilization was conceptualized in the late 1980s by the United Nations' Children's Fund (UNICEF) as a support strategy to rally multisectoral support at all levels for its social goals using various communication strategies. The Philippine experience in social mobilization, particularly in such programs as immunization, rights of the child, and education for all, is now considered to be a model worldwide. At the forefront is Ofelia Valdecanas, who introduced innovative strategies and expanded the concept using local experiences. Likewise, through her efforts, a social mobilization course has been integrated into local communication schools.

Women as Advocates of Development Programs

Cooperatives are another area where women have used communication channels to demonstrate their leadership capacity. Much of the advocacy in mobilizing government and other sectors of society to expand and strengthen cooperatives is done by women. Here women have demonstrated the importance of innate values in cooperativism that are essential to national survival—nonadversarial mechanisms in conflict resolution, democratic participation, resource conservation, and savings consciousness.

A woman legislator, Senator Leticia Shahani, has led the way in the National Moral Recovery Program, which is anchored on positive values. Women peace advocates are often heard leading the call for peace talks among government and rebels of the left and the right. Teresita Ang-See, a Filipino-Chinese woman, leads a crusade against violent crime and has used marches, demonstrations, and the traditional media to get her ideas across. Local tribeswomen have literally laid their lives on the line in Mindanao to prevent illegal loggers from cutting down trees. This captured a lot of media space, but media's short attention span needs sustainability, and this can be done only by shifting from events to process reporting. Some controversial issues where women advocates have gained considerable headway are in foreign debt servicing, tax reforms (e.g., value-added tax), and the recent Uruguay Round-General Agreement on Tariff and Trade (UR-GATT). In these economics-related areas, the advocacy leader is Professor Leonor Briones. Even in the police and military, traditional areas dominated by men, women have dramatized critical community concerns by using communication channels. Mary Grace Tirona, commissioner of the National Commission on the Role of Women advocated the creation of a woman's desk for handling gender-related complaints.

Philippine Development Plan for Women

A concrete action plan to alleviate the plight of Filipino women is found in the Philippine Development Plan for Women. Its media section aims for a level playing field between men and women media practitioners, and advocates the following: (a) Images of women must veer away from the discriminatory and derogatory to what is realistic and positive in terms of women's roles. (b) Media must be used to advocate women's issues and to promote further access to the urban poor, grassroots, and cultural communities. The media plan also hopes to build a database containing story lines on women, a directory of women government and non-government experts to provide a women's perspective in various disciplines, and an updated listing of government services offered to women. Because English is identi-fied with the elite, the use of Filipino and other local dialects is advocated for public affairs programs. (c) Alternative media such as street theater, puppets, verse contests, and video-slide presentations are proposed.

In culture and arts, the plan calls for consciousness-raising among women artists on gender-sensitive issues. Women's portraits in the various artistic roles are, in fact, the root of media's portrayal of women as fragile, passive, and mindless. From sculpture to music, to theater and literature, few images show women as being strong.

Women Empowering Communication: The Bangkok Declaration

In February 1994, the historic forum "Women Empowering Communication" in Bangkok, Thailand, was organized by the World Association for Christian Communication (WACC), ISIS International, and International Women's Tribune Center with more than 400 women communicators from some 80 countries representing women's groups and networks, mass and alternative media, and development groups. The conference identified strengths and weaknesses of communication initiatives, explored areas of possible empowerment of women in and through media, and encouraged and expanded networking and solidarity among women's groups.

Here are excerpts from the Bangkok Declaration:

The so-called "mainstream" media are a male-dominated tool used by those in power. At the global level, they are controlled by the North; nationally they are in the hands of the local elite. As they are now structured, the media propagate unsustainable lifestyles, militarism, growing pauperization and consumption patterns which turn people into consumers not only of good ideas and ideologies; women, children, and the majority of men are invisible and their voices are unheard. There is particular lack of respect for the integrity and dignity of women: stereotyped and dehumanized, we have been turned into commodities. The excessive use of violence in these media is destroying the sensibilities of humanity.

For all these reasons it is essential to promote forms of communication that not only challenge the patriarchal nature of media but strive to decentralize and democratize them: to create media that encourage dialogue and debate; media that advance women and peoples' creativity; media that reaffirm women's wisdom and knowledge, and that make people into subjects rather than objects or targets of communication. Media which are responsive to people's needs. In the years since the Nairobi World Conference on Women, which closed the United Nations Decade for Women in 1985, our networks and levels of organization have grown. We have made many interventions and taken many actions at all levels: local, national, regional, and international. Yet despite our achievements, negative global trends have become more powerful.

Several strategies aimed at strengthening and empowering women in communications include:

- Strengthening people's, and more specifically women's media, including storytelling, visual and performances arts, which build on their knowledge, wisdom and creativity.
- The integration of humane values into our media creations such as harmony with nature, cooperation, nurturing, caring, love and compassion, and our struggles for freedom, to ensure that our alternatives do not become hierarchal, undemocratic and elitist.
- Education and training methodologies to access existing media for women's organizations and community groups in order that they can effectively communicate their own messages and concerns.
- The incorporation of gender-sensitivity, local history and cultural diversity in the education and training of professionals in the field of communication.
- The development of national curricula that encourages critical thinking among future generations through formal and nonformal education.
- Building links and solidarity between women and gender-sensitive men working in media at all levels and in all conditions.

- Pinpointing special networking considerations and strengthening information exchanges between urban and rural groups and organizations, across language barriers, at varied levels of consciousness and access to technology, in oppressive conditions.

Retooling for the Twenty-First Century

Women's issues are no longer women's issues exclusively. Such issues as women's rights, children's rights, human rights, and environment are world issues that demand the attention of both men and women together in partnership. This partnership must extend to the creation of national agendas and policies that are often left to government and business sectors. The creation and strengthening of society's third sector—the civil society, primarily consisting of nongovernmental organizations—should actively involve women. There is a need to shift leadership and management styles from the male command-and-control model to the more feminine communicate-and-inspire model. This is an area where the female perspective, with its value on consensus, can actively contribute. In doing so, let us work within the framework of the Bangkok Declaration, which suggests building links and solidarity between women and gender-sensitive men working in media. This could be the beginning of the partnership that we envision.

Margaret Thatcher and Golda Meir and, in the Asian context, Corazon Aquino and Aung San Syu Kyi offer images of women who have made an impact in the international scene. The growing globalization of media and world trade will require women's perspectives in reshaping economic political and social institutions.

Survival in the twenty-first century and beyond will depend on partnerships between men and women, on creative and innovative ideas and institutions, and on the creation of a culture of peace. The Bangkok Declaration from the "Women Empowering Communication" international conference sums it up succinctly: "If our [women's] interests are met, the interests of all humanity will also be satisfied."

References

Aburdene, P. (1992). *Megatrends for women.* New York: Ballantine.

Bangkok Declaration. (1994, February 17). Produced at the Forum, "Women Empowering Communication," Bangkok, Thailand.

Constitutional Commission of 1986. (1987). *The Constitution of the Republic of the Philippines.* Quezon City: Author.

Corpuz, O. D. (1989). *The roots of the Filipino nations.* (Vols. 1, 2). Quezon City: Aklahi Foundation Inc.

Eisler, R. (1987). *The chalice and the blade: Our history, our future.* San Francisco: Harper & Row.

Fernandez, D. G. (1987). Women in media in the Philippines: From stereotype to liberation. *Media Asia: An Asian Mass Communication Quarterly, 14*(4), 185-186 (Singapore).

Lent, J. (1966). *Philippine mass communication: Before 1811 after 1966.* Manila: Philippine Press Institute.

Pablo, L. D. (1994, September). Strengthening poverty-stricken families. *Asi Option* (Manila).

Shafer, R. (1994). Women's page editors as agents of political change in the Philippines. *Media Asia: An Asian Mass Communication Quarterly, 21*(1), 24 (Singapore).

Toffler, A. (1990). *Powershift.* New York: Bantam.

United Nations Children's Fund. (1992). *Situation of children and women in the Philippines, 1992.* Manila: Author.

31

The Washington Press Club Foundation's Oral History Project

Getting Women Journalists
to Speak of Themselves,
for Themselves,
for Herstory's Sake

Peggy A. Simpson

The Washington Press Club Foundation's (WPCF) oral history project provides primary source material on the lives and achievements of women in journalism. Some of the material is dramatic, some subtle in its impact. Collectively, the oral histories fill a vacuum. Only recently have there been magazine articles and books on the women who broke barriers in covering the news.

There is no comparable oral history project on women journalists. The 56 women interviewed had experiences in various media for more than 70 years, surviving and many times prospering in an often hostile world. The years covered included those of especially dynamic changes in the lives and work of women. The women both covered those changes and were themselves affected by them.

Women journalists, through their reporting, often illuminated issues in society that had been given short shrift before. They legitimized many issues, by their coverage. They gave serious news coverage to stories that either were not covered or were covered flippantly. As editors, they assigned reporters to look into stories that the male editors had not even considered stories. Among these issues were sex education, birth control, child abuse, women in the workforce, pay inequities, women in politics, women and credit, and the economic status of older women and women after divorces.

The women who assigned and who wrote these stories had rarely been interviewed. Among the topics explored in the oral histories are their experiences, including disputes with bosses over their coverage of these issues, instances when what they wrote was not printed or broadcast, or cases when they were asked to act in ways that violated their ethical code or to cover stories that represented a boss's stereotypical view of women.

The interviews with the 56 women were conducted in 301 interview sessions, by 11 different oral historians. Transcripts were translated by professional oral history transcribers. The total original-source material comes to 8,700 pages, including indexes and appendixes. One interview session with each of 41 women was videotaped. In addition, three broadcast interviewees (Sylvia Chase, Connie Chung, and Charlayne Hunter-Gault) provided video clips of major stories from their broadcast careers.

Background

The WPCF was created in 1985 after the merger of the Washington Press Club with the National Press Club. A predecessor organization, the Women's National Press Club, had been founded in 1919 for the small but growing number of women journalists covering national news. It served as a news-gathering forum for women excluded from the major journalism organizations in Washington—the National Press Club and the Gridiron Club—until they dropped their male-only policies in the early 1970s.

My inspiration for the WPCF's oral history project came partly from a course I audited at Harvard while on a Nieman Fellowship in 1978-1979. It was about "women in the workforce, 1850-1950," taught by Barbara Solomon. At one point, she drew upon oral histories that were the basis for a documentary called *Rosie the Riveter,* about five women who had worked in wartime factories, liked the work and the wages but who lost those jobs when men came home from the war. They never again used those skills or got those high wages although most of the five continued to work.

I realized at that moment that the women journalists who were my role models and were 15 to 20 years older probably had similar stories. It occurred to me that, if this postwar profile of women in industry was in any sense mirrored in journalism, that might go a long way to explain why there were so few women editors or reporters in "hard news" fields when I got out of college and took my first jobs as a weekly newspaper editor, then as a desk editor, and later statehouse reporter for the Associated Press (AP).

I wanted to go ask my older colleagues and mentors about their stories but never found the time. Six years later, when a group of former presidents of the Washington Press Club debated what to do with the new foundation being created, I suggested we should find a way to record, for ourselves and also for future generations, the stories of our own pioneers, the women who had broken barriers in journalism. Some of them had been members or presidents of the Women's National Press Club but others probably had compelling stories to tell if only we knew how to track them down. At that meeting, I talked about the Barbara Solomon course and the oral histories of the World War II "riveters" that had helped scholars re-create the picture of women and work in that era. We, too, could document the track record of women in journalism in these past decades, while these women were able to tell us their stories.

None of us knew what an oral history interview was like, how it differed from the journalism we all practiced every day, or who could advise us on this. First, we needed to know if anyone already had done this. After a few telephone calls, it was clear this was new turf. Few oral history interviews had been done on women journalists, the experts said.

I was surprised and pleased by the enthusiastic reaction from some leading scholars when they heard what we contemplated undertaking. My long-distance call to Columbia's oral history program stands out, still, as a turning point. Ronald Grele had taken over the collection only months earlier and had found very few interviews of women of any category, let alone women journalists. He not only urged us on, he offered help in shaping the project and said Columbia probably would be very interested in housing the originals.

His enthusiasm as well as his nuts-and-bolts guidance proved invaluable. The oral history committee I had formed ultimately presented an ambitious but credible proposal to the WPCF board, where a minority of members were skeptics and feared that the oral history project would bankrupt the foundation or would lead to disputes about selection decisions.

Financing was a big issue. We were journalists, not academics used to raising outside money with grant proposals to foundations. It was news to us that people would pay you to do a project like this. The WPCF put in the initial money to start interviews and hire our first part-time oral historian, Margot Knight, while we undertook fund-raising campaigns with media foundations. Our first major grant was $50,000 from the Gannett Foundation (now the Freedom Forum). This opened doors elsewhere but raising money and keeping costs down remained a struggle throughout the project, which ended four interviews short of the targeted sixty interviews. The final fund-raising tally was $570,000 spread over seven years.

We had minimal overhead and minimal staff. The policy direction and fund-raising campaigns and selection of interviewees were done by our task force of working journalists. We worked for months, and then years, to be clear about our goals and to develop structures to enable us to carry them out.

The initial oral history task force under the WPCF did praiseworthy work in planning and then launching the project, squeezing the strategy and problem-solving sessions into our frenetic work schedules as reporters or TV producers. The initial task force members were Lyle Denniston of the *Baltimore Sun,* Clare Crawford-Mason of CCM Productions, Sara Fritz of the *Los Angeles Times,* Dorothy Gilliam of the *Washington Post,* Finlay Lewis of Copley News Service, and Eileen Shanahan, at that time with *Governing* magazine.

In addition to Grele, who remained but a telephone call away, we hired part-time professional oral historians, starting with Margot Knight, then Fern Ingersoll, and ending with Donita M. Moorhus.

It was an easy call to start with "oldest first." The catalyst for persuading the foundation board to put up the initial money and give the policy go-ahead was our discovery that a woman on our "A" list, Beth Short, had cancer and already was very weak. She had been one of the first women to welcome me when I came to Washington as an AP reporter in early 1968 although by that time she had been gone from the AP for decades. It was only after I read the transcripts that I learned she had specialized in her early years in Oklahoma City as a "stunt girl"—and as something of an investigative reporter, living at one point on 25 cents a day to tell readers what real poverty tasted like.

As we educated ourselves, we developed an idea of what should come next, in our attempt to give a picture of the evolution of women in the media, who were struggling to find their own footing in the overwhelmingly male world of journalism, while their reporting often broadened the scope of what was considered "news."

From the first, we had been determined to search out minority women, and Ethel Payne was an obvious choice for our first group. She was known by all of us in Washington as the *Chicago Defender*'s Washington correspondent, covering everything including foreign policy. Kay Mills of the *Los Angeles Times* told us of Marvel Cooke, a long-retired reporter who had worked both for the *Amsterdam News* and briefly for one of the mainstream New York dailies. We learned about a powerful yet self-effacing woman from a black newspaper in St. Louis, Lucile Bluford, who not only recalled 1930s lynchings but also was a witness to much of the growth of the NAACP.

We set a priority on finding minority journalists, knowing that they were doubly invisible. Little had been written about women journalists in general; next to nothing had been done on minority journalists, including those of such high reputations among their peers as Payne, Cooke, and Bluford. Our judgment calls proved correct: The transcripts of the black women were among the most widely used in the early days, filling a vacuum in basic information about minority women in the media.

We sometimes skipped over journalists who were famous, many of whom had written their own autobiographies or collections of columns, to choose women who were not name brands but had made unusual breakthroughs for women in the media, such as sports reporters. We opted to pursue some famous journalists because we wanted to ask them our questions about their very special place in the media today; Ellen Goodman was an example of this. A few people turned us down, including war correspondent Martha Gelhorn, who feared we would consider her mostly as a Hemingway wife; another reason might have been her own forthcoming book. Some people never said yes, never said no, and we eventually went on to others; UPI's venerable White House correspondent Helen Thomas was in this category.

There were some heartbreaks, none more so than the fact that the oral history interview with Isabelle Shelton was in the beginning stages when she had a stroke and subsequently died. She had an invaluable window on the 1950s-1980s era when women emerged from the shadows, in the overall society and to

some extent in the media. As a reporter for the *Washington Star* and then a syndicated writer for a features service, she chronicled many of the cutting-edge collisions in which women earned their political spurs and a larger "place" in society.

The Political *Is* Personal!

I had never met a reporter before I became one. I worked on the weekly newspaper at North Texas State University but couldn't find summer internships on daily newspapers like my male J-school colleagues. I later worked one summer on a weekly paper and, after a summer as a chambermaid in a hotel in Germany, came back to edit another weekly paper in southwest Texas, the *Hondo Anvil Herald*. My first boss, William Berger, gave me free rein.

I didn't realize until much later how unusual it was that he gambled on me. I never felt any restraints connected to my sex. There were plenty of economic constraints on him, as owner, including a showdown with the city council, which demanded I stop quoting council members and just print the minutes. The problem was I had quoted them too accurately and had caught the nuances, as well. That caused not just discomfort in a town of 5,000—but when Berger refused to keep me from covering the council meetings as I saw fit, it caused an advertising boycott by leading merchants, which cost him thousands of dollars each week.

He never urged me to leave and we've kept in touch, during these past three decades. But I decided I'd move on. I wanted to cover national politics, to be a foreign correspondent, to cover what was happening, wherever it was happening. My role model, if I had one, was Pauline Frederick of NBC's *Nightly News,* who reported from the United Nations. I had listened to the NBC news every night since the seventh grade (it came on before a radio soap opera favored by my mother). It never occurred to me there would be any problems with my following in the path of a Pauline Frederick, with a bit of gumption and hard work.

My next job was with the Associated Press in Dallas. One of my North Texas professors had worked at the AP and I recalled that he seemed to warn women away from the AP: they'd be treated as badly as men. That was fine with me; I didn't want any special favors. I joined the AP as a vacation relief temporary for nine months in Dallas, then got a second temporary job for six months covering the state legislature in Austin. And then I got a permanent job, back at the Dallas editing bureau. It astounded me that the AP did not credit my 18 months as editor of a weekly newspaper and started me at the base pay of $75 a week. But my complaints (and those of my weekly publisher) were ignored and I was too busy to bother, relishing the sink-or-swim challenges of coping with a 24-hour news operation where mistakes got you fired and extra effort, maybe, got you to Washington. I was sure that was where I wanted to go next.

I was the only woman with the AP in Texas, out of perhaps 40 reporters, editors, and support staffers, and I knew few women who were "hard news" reporters on the Dallas or Austin papers. One woman I admired, and watched from afar, was *Dallas Times Herald* society editor Vivian Castleberry. She seemed to get the most interesting stories in print, about reproductive health, about child abuse, about women on the move. Later, she was one of our unanimous choices for a WPCF oral history interview. She exceeded expectations, with a spectacular glimpse into how she had managed to cover cutting-edge issues in a very conservative city. She had assigned her reporters to the stories but often didn't run them until the top bosses were out of town. She had much autonomy and used it, to broaden the public "space" for all women.

When President Kennedy was assassinated in Dallas, I had been on the streets monitoring the parade through Dallas, waiting to fly to Austin, where I had been persuaded by my

bureau chief to get a date with a bachelor state legislator to gain entrée to the invitation-only dinner that night by the governor.

Instead, I spent most of the weekend at the city jail, monitoring the comings and goings of Lee Harvey Oswald. And, on Sunday, I was with other reporters in the basement, monitoring Oswald's transfer to a county jail, when nightclub owner Jack Ruby emerged from our midst to fatally wound Oswald.

After that tumultuous series of events, when White House AP correspondents assured me that at the age of 24, I'd covered what would be the biggest story of my lifetime, I began to question what I wanted to do next. I had no doubts about the AP or about my commitment to news. Although I had filled out the personnel forms saying I wanted a transfer to Washington, I decided to explore other options that also intrigued me, such as becoming a foreign correspondent or bureau chief, or possibly helping run the AP itself someday. If I needed to do something different to position myself to compete for those jobs, I wanted to know while there was still time to change.

I took my bureau chief to lunch for a reality check on my ambitions. His view of reality was not mine. Becoming a foreign correspondent was out of the question because women didn't work in other countries so the AP couldn't risk sending a female correspondent overseas—it was possible that nobody would talk to her. Being an AP bureau chief wasn't feasible either because, first, you had to sell the AP's services to members—to persuade a radio station manager or a newspaper editor to sign up for extra photo or news wires—and he knew what that entailed because he'd done it. It meant drinking the editors or broadcast managers under the table—and their wives wouldn't like it if the AP sent a woman out to do that job. Somehow, it had never dawned on me that I also had to compete with the wives.

But my bureau chief assured me that I was a terrific reporter and that he'd make sure I got that transfer to Washington, if I kept doing work beyond the norm. I did and he kept his word, with a transfer to Washington in January 1968, covering five southwestern states on what the AP then called its regional staff at the U.S. Capitol. I didn't dwell on the painful lunchtime conversation; I didn't think about doors closing; I was too busy walking through the one that was open, as an AP congressional reporter.

The Associated Press gives its reporters much autonomy. You have a beat and you decide how to cover it. You tell the assignments editor what you're doing on any given day, rather than taking orders from above, with obvious exceptions for AP member requests or breaking news events that require all hands on board. Any other "enterprise" stories you develop are gravy. If the stories are picked up by many AP papers, you have free rein to keep developing more of them— as long as they don't interfere with your bread-and-butter beats. Covering the southwestern congressional delegations could be done in any number of ways, as long as it included oil and gas and the heavyweight politicians from those states. I developed many other specialties.

One was a continuation of stories I had begun while in Texas, on grassroots campaigns by Hispanics that involved better education, more jobs, a larger role in politics. They also launched national campaigns demanding that the marketing and advertising campaigns for major corporations stop stereotyping them as "lazy Mexicans" or as "Frito bandito" outlaws.

In addition, I began to cover Indian rights campaigns that were emerging partly from New Mexico, partly from South Dakota, which focused on getting back land rather than money and at one time involved an occupation of the Bureau of Indian Affairs building.

As a congressional reporter, and as one of the few women covering "hard news" in the nation's capital in the late 1960s and early 1970s, I also had a good window on the drama of women's efforts to expand their roles in society.

With a handful of other women, I began tracking the women's political movement, as it emerged. Other colleagues were Eileen Shanahan, who then covered taxes for the *New York Times;* Kay Mills then of Newhouse; Vera Glaser of Knight-Ridder; Isabelle Shelton of the *Washington Star.*

The mid-1971 founding of the National Women's Political Caucus was covered by White House correspondents Frances Lewine of the AP and Helen Thomas of UPI, who helped put the caucus on the map by their next-day question about it to President Nixon. His jesting remark about never being fond of women in trousers made headlines. But White House reporters don't have time for second-day stories; other people do the follow-ups.

In this case, a young woman named Debbie Leff, who had taken a leave from the first class of women at Princeton to work as press aide for the NWPC, lobbied me to cover a Capitol Hill news conference aiming to persuade Democratic presidential contenders to choose more women as their convention delegates for the 1972 nominating conventions. The draw at the news conference was Fannie Lou Hamer, a Sunflower County, Mississippi, civil rights activist, making the point that the women's political movement represented many colors and kinds of people, not just middle-class whites. That news conference was my first of many efforts to tracking the twists and turns of the contemporary women's movement. (Debbie Leff went on to get a law degree, work as press officer for the Federal Trade Commission, take a two-thirds cut in salary to learn the ropes of television production, move up the ranks rapidly in ABC to be senior producer for *Nightline* and later foreign producer, then scrap all that to become president of the Chicago-based Joyce Foundation. She was one of the women interviewed in the "door-opening" phase of the WPCF oral history project.)

Shanahan and I and others had sources who alerted us to stories. It was essentially a nonassignable beat; we usually were several jumps ahead of any assignment editors.

We covered congressional hearings into pay inequities, credit discrimination, women and sports, pregnancy medical leave, "displaced homemakers," women and pension inequities, poverty and older women. We covered the fledgling women's political movement, as many new groups were formed in the early 1970s to educate each other about how to find their footing in national politics. They learned how to develop issues, find money and political support, and analyze why voters were so critical of women candidates. Our day-to-day stories became a chronicle of seismic changes occurring, which sometimes were more after the fact.

Our stories about these changes became, simultaneously, a catalyst for further change. Sometimes we did roundups, tracking the cumulative effect of these disparate events. Sometimes those never made it into print. One such roundup I orchestrated on election campaigns in which women were major contenders in statewide or congressional elections in the mid-1970s was spiked by the AP political writer, Walter Mears. He said he didn't care if a dozen AP bureaus had contributed to the roundup, the story wasn't going to run. He tossed it back to me with the sarcastic jibe, "Sell it to *Ms.*"

In 1975, the AP sent me to cover the International Women's Year conference in Mexico City, one of few Western reporters. By the time I arrived, the local staff had already written stories about incoming delegations—asking these women if they were "bra-burners" and then writing stories saying they weren't. It was a disconcerting start. Later, a desk editor altered my opening-session story to insert up high several paragraphs on what was worn by the Soviet cosmonaut.

During the next two weeks, we ran many substantive stories on the economic and political challenges facing women, worldwide, and these got good play in thousands of papers in the United States and elsewhere. It was a jolt, then, to be ordered by the AP foreign desk one day to scrub my scheduled interview with Fidel Castro's sister-in-law to go ask Burt Reynolds what he thought about bra-burners. He and Liza Minnelli were in town for a movie and had a photo-op with the Mexican media. She thought I was ridiculous; he mumbled something about how, actually, he preferred women who were independent to those who were too dependent.

Back at the bureau, I told New York I would leave right then if their idea of covering the conference was to try and get a movie star to ridicule it. They calmed me down, assured me the stories were getting good play, and told me to keep on writing.

The final insult came from a photo. I was having a rare meal out when I got an urgent page from New York to provide a story to go with their very dramatic picture of women fighting each other at the IWY conference. After hours of telephone calls, I figured out what had happened. More than 3,000 women who represented nongovernmental organizations had met with a top U.N. official in a big auditorium—no fireworks there.

As the crowd left, about eight women were grabbing for a microphone at the front of the hall, arguing about which small caucus was slated to go next. The photographer had caught that moment. There was no story. But the damage was done: The AP already had sent the photo around the world with a caption that read something to the effect of "Women Fight at U.N. Conference." That proved to be the most widely used photo of the two weeks in Mexico City, making not just daily newspapers but the weekly newsmagazines as well. The photo confirmed the stereotype—although not the reality—that women can't be in the same room together without getting into a catfight.

Looking back, it is remarkable to reflect on the way women were seen at the time, not just by the media but by the principal actors in business and politics, who had a huge influence on the economic status of women. Here are some of my broad-strokes recollections of the assumptions about women then:

• They were considered potential wombs, by employers and bankers; if they weren't married, they certainly would be. When they got married, they certainly would become pregnant. When they gave birth, they certainly would quit their jobs. With those assumptions firmly in place, it was seen as fruitless to (a) give women a scarce slot in Ivy League professional schools, even if they scored high on entry exams; (b) give women a job with "ladders" for promotion; better to put her in one where she could train the men in the basics, before *they* climbed the ladder; (c) approve women for credit cards, mortgages, business loans, or lines of credit.

• Women were fragile flowers who had to be protected. They were protected right out of the good jobs, under the 1930s labor laws, which by the 1960s had become limitations on women's ability to compete for jobs with heavy lifting, late hours, or travel. This kept them in jobs with less pay and less potential for promotion. The first lawsuits under the 1964 Civil Rights Act's Title VII prohibitions on employment discrimination were brought by blue-collar women challenging just such factory-floor restrictions.

• Women did not have voices deep enough, faces serious enough, to (a) do the news, (b) handle voice-overs on lucrative commercials, (c) have on-camera credibility in national news or commentary programs. Consumers wouldn't buy products; viewers would switch channels, it was said.

• Stereotypes abounded about women in general: They were Queen Bees who liked being the only woman around. When they made it, they pulled the ladder up with them to block competitors from coming aboard. Women couldn't work with each other. They were terrible bosses. And this was not even counting the George Gilder stereotypes, from his *Wealth and Poverty* book, which says in essence that since the time of cavemen, women have existed mostly to tame men's sexual urges. They make lousy employees, however, because they're always worried more

about the kids they've left at home than about the job at hand in the office.

In short, women were not seen as serious, long-term players. They could be marginalized with no loss to society overall, it was assumed. Special rationales for doing this could be developed without much thought. This was dramatized in the early 1970s in the "raging-hormones" proposition put forth by Hubert Humphrey's political colleague and physician, Edgar Berman. His views mattered because he was big at the Democratic National Committee.

When Congresswoman Patsy Mink asked why so few women were being named to top jobs in government, he said that would be too risky—because women suffered from "raging hormones" once a month that skewed their judgment. This caused lots of snickering. But the Women's National Press Club picked up the issue and sponsored a debate between Berman and Georgetown University physician Estelle Ramey. Several hundred people showed up to watch the show. Berman didn't fare well in defending his raging-hormones theory.

Ultimately, more women were appointed to top jobs—a few, then a flood tide by two decades later. And "raging hormones" is a description that has no application anymore, except as a historical marker in the formative stages of the women's political movement. The women journalists, in this case, not only served as reporters but provided the forum for ventilating the issue, for exploring in public a policymaker's excuse-of-the-moment for keeping women at bay.

Two decades later, a similar role was played by an organization called Women, Men and Media, cochaired by Nancy Woodhull and Betty Friedan. Among its activities, it has supported an annual survey, originated and conducted by M. Junior Bridge since 1989, on the front pages of a dozen U.S. newspapers to assess how the media cover women. The research counts the number of times women are quoted as sources, named in headlines, or bylined reporters or photographers. In 1990 for the second year in a row the *New York Times* had the lowest percentage of references to women on the front page out of 20 newspapers surveyed. This was noted in a news release about the survey.

Eleanor Randolph, then covering the media for the *Washington Post,* called the editor of the *New York Times* to talk about the survey and ask how this could be, in the 1990s. He said the *Times* covered serious issues, not tea parties. That caused a firestorm in the *Times*'s newsroom and the next day hundreds of male and female *Times*'s reporters showed up with a tea bag on their lapel. Eight hundred women attended a subsequent meeting with the editor to talk about the reality of women's status at the *Times,* which had been revealed by his candid quip to Randolph.

Personal Actions and Reflections

My thinking about the U.S. women's movement and the lasting impact it has made on the United States was shaped by my 35 years as a reporter: 15 years with the Associated Press, including a decade covering the Congress; freelance magazine writing, including six years as a Washington columnist for *Working Woman;* and, finally, as a Washington bureau chief for *Ms.* magazine between 1988 and 1990.

My coverage of the women's rights struggle made me more conscious of the circumstances in my own organization. I had been at the AP for more than a dozen years when I read that a sex discrimination complaint had been filed against the AP by Shirley Christian and other AP employees. I knew her only as a famous byline, covering the United Nations. Asking about the suit didn't get me much information, in Washington, where merit pay supplements the basic salary. I was shocked that a lawsuit could emerge right under my nose, without my knowing about it. But I didn't even call Christian to find out more. I went back to basics: coverage of Congress, including many legislative

attempts to improve the status of women—and the beginning of backlash from the religious right against that.

It was several years later when I got a call from Virginia Pitt, who worked on the AP's general desk in New York, a nerve center of the overall system. She and the lawyer for the AP suit, Janice Goodman, were coming and wanted to meet with the ten women (of 100 people on the Washington bureau staff) if I could help arrange it. About half the women agreed to meet. Ultimately, I became one of seven named plaintiffs in the sex and race lawsuit against the AP, in the second stage of the post-EEOC legal proceedings that took place in federal court. Shirley Christian was the only remaining plaintiff from the original complaint.

Many of my colleagues and mentors with the AP in Washington were flabbergasted and dismayed. I had had a spectacular career as a congressional reporter; there would only be more of the same if I didn't rock the boat. I'm not sure I thought through all the pro-and-con options. But I felt I knew too much, having covered so many of the sex discrimination legislative hearings, having seen the struggle for legitimacy by the fledgling feminist groups trying to help women get an even shake in politics. I also had my own experiences, none of which in the past I had labeled but that, upon reflection, I knew were reflections of the AP institutional thinking about the relatively limited "place" given women in the AP, compared with men.

In two days of depositions, I went back to some of those early AP experiences, including the initial salary dispute (it turns out nearly all men hired off of weekly papers had been credited with that time) and the door-closing conversations with my Texas bureau chief. The lawsuit ultimately was settled with an out-of-court consent decree in which the seven named plaintiffs divided $70,000; a similar amount went to the limited number of blacks who had ever been with the AP; and every woman who had worked at the AP in the past 10 years got a per capita sum of money reflecting back-pay adjustments for every year worked there. The salary discrepancies had proven to be considerable. The AP had to pay the legal costs, which ran into the millions. An affirmative action program was launched for minority journalists; the AP already had begun hiring major numbers of women, after the lawsuit was filed, and also made some of them domestic and foreign correspondents, for the first time.

I was long gone by the time the lawsuit was settled, having been assured by Walter Mears, in effect, that if I was stupid enough to return to the AP after my Nieman Fellowship year, I would cover the Congress forever—unless I wanted to cover the weather. I joined the *Boston Herald* as their national political correspondent, traveling much of the time covering the 1980 presidential campaigns and then national politics out of Washington. Before the paper was sold to Rupert Murdoch, I had quit to take a new position created in the Hearst Newspapers' Washington bureau, covering national economics and politics. And, in early 1988, I was recruited by the two Australian women, Ann Summers and Sandra Yates, who had bought *Ms.* magazine, to open a Washington political bureau for them.

They lost their ownership less than two years later and I lost my job, after an advertising boycott launched by religious right groups based in Indiana got more than $25 million in ads canceled that were slated to run in *Sassy,* a teenage magazine launched by the Australians. The protesters said the magazine was promoting promiscuity for teenagers by talking about sex (in reality, by talking about contraceptives, if readers were having sex, to avoid becoming yet another pregnant-and-poor teenager).

After teaching magazine writing at Indiana University, I pursued what seemed to be a fascinating adventure: covering what happened next after the collapse of Communism, including what workers thought of the "workers' revolution" and how highly educated and skilled women in countries like Poland would fare in the market economy.

I have written this book chapter from Poland, where I have lived mostly full-time since late 1991. Sometimes it feels like a flashback to the 1960s and the debates about "women's place." There is much pressure here for women to leave their jobs and go home and be full-time wives and mothers, to focus on "culture" rather than on careers, to shed the drabness of their workaday lives and to become more "sexy" and consumer oriented, now that these options are available.

There are differences, of course, including the confrontation with the Catholic Church on reproductive rights, which in retrospect seems to have been a catalyst for jump-starting a fledgling women's rights movement here that is gaining both savvy and a measure of credibility from the media. These collisions and the consciousness-raising within the media, and by the media, have raised the public awareness about "women's place" issues in the broadest sense.

In early 1995, there was a front-page debate in the leading national Polish newspaper, *Gazeta Wyborcza,* about a Mobil Oil billboard that became tagged as the "woman as idiot" advertisement. It featured a panicky woman clutching the steering wheel of her car while her bemused husband cocked an eyebrow with a (familiar, to U.S. audiences) patronizing "there she goes again" smirk on his face. The message read, in essence, "even she can't ruin your car if you use Mobil Oil."

Somebody had defaced one of the billboards, substituting "he" for "she" and the newspaper had been alerted to the incident and then went on to critique its message as sexist. (Mobil initially said this was just one of a series, that a "man as idiot" was due next; that didn't happen, naturally, and a Mobil spokesman said the original "woman as idiot" billboard was being sought by men, and women, who wanted to put it on their walls at home.)

The details differ; the debate continues. But there is no debating the fact that there have been fundamental shifts not only in the attitudes about contemporary women but in the public space they can claim as their own. This is a result of a combination of forces, including antidiscrimination laws and their enforcement, grassroots activists, the growing credibility of women in high places in politics, business, and government—and in the coverage of all this by the media, by now, by educated and committed male reporters, who have expanded the job of reporting "women's place" issues begun by those pioneering women journalists of two decades ago.

Appendix: Facts About the WPCF, Project Goals

The WPCF was created to promote equality and excellence in journalism. The oral history project became its first major venture, in addition to its continuing sponsorship of an annual "salute to Congress" dinner that the previous WPC and the earlier National Women's Press Club had begun decades earlier.

The oral history project set these goals:

- to record the influence women have had on the designation of what is "news" and the way it was covered;
- to document the opportunities and barriers for women regarding pay, assignments, and advancement in journalism;
- to document the contributions to journalism of minority women serving in both minority media and the mainstream media;
- to create a new, accessible resource for biographers, teachers, writers of women's studies curricula, and students;
- to encourage changes in curricula of journalism and women's studies to include the roles and achievements of women in journalism.

The project was divided into three phases. The first focused on pioneers in the field: interviews with 20 women who entered journalism before World War II. Phase II documented the experiences of 20 women whose careers began between World War II and the passage of the Civil Rights Act of 1964—the

generation of women who became a critical mass in the profession. In the 1940s, women not only staffed newsrooms when men went off to war but assumed jobs as broadcasters and foreign correspondents. Their struggle to secure their places often intensified after the war, when some of them lost their jobs or were put in jobs with less scope than before. Phase III targeted women who opened doors for others: those who, between the Civil Rights Act of 1964 and the present time, helped create more opportunities and advance equal treatment for women in both print and broadcast journalism.

Oral history is a relatively new field, not more than 40 years old, but already is seen as invaluable for observing how large social forces converge at key moments and for reflecting how those influences play out in the lives of an individual, often transforming her life.

The WPCF project goal was designed to create primary source material with the broadest possible future use, by doing full-life oral history interviews. This captures, in the woman's own words, the many interwoven threads of her lifetime. Her personal recollections can be recorded verbatim, including her observations about experiences in historical movements of her time as well as reflections on the core issues outlined in the project goals. Open-ended questions are used. Scrapbooks, journals, and the journalists' own papers are collected, when possible, as backup documentation for the taped oral history interviews.

In addition to videos with 41 of the women, there also was a video interview with a group of four women who were part of Eleanor Roosevelt's women-only press conferences. It has been deposited with Roosevelt papers in Hyde Park, New York, and also has been used by journalism classes at the University of Maryland.

The interviewers conducted extensive research about the woman being interviewed, including from her published articles, speeches, and scrapbooks, to talks with her peers. Interviews often were conducted over a period of months, giving both the woman being questioned and the oral historian time to reflect and to consult more sources.

The topic guidelines developed by Sherna Berger Gluck for use in women's oral history were adapted to the lives of women journalists. This makes comparisons possible not only between the generations of the women journalists interviewed but with other women's oral history projects.

Interviews ranged from 12 hours to 25 hours, usually in periods of 2 hours at one session. Professional oral history transcribers worked with the interviewer in comparing the transcript with the taped recording.

Transcripts of the interview sessions average 140 single-spaced pages although several are nearly double that length. In addition, each interview is indexed by proper names of people, newspapers and newspaper chains, wire services, and broadcast outlets and stations. For print journalists, samples of the woman's work are included. A brief biography of the woman is included at the end of the transcript.

In three instances, the entire transcripts have been sealed for specific periods of time, at the request of the interviewee.

Usage

Master copies of audio- and videotapes, photographs, biographical materials, and transcripts have been deposited with the Columbia University Oral History Research Office in New York City. Copies of both audio- and videotapes have been deposited in the National Press Club Library, in a climate-controlled room. Other repositories making the transcripts available to researchers include the National Women and Media Collection at the University of Missouri, the Schlesinger Library on History of Women in America at Radcliffe College, and many schools of journalism.

The completed transcripts already have been in much demand by independent researchers, journalism professors and students, and authors.

Some of the usage, so far, includes the following:

• The first interviews with African American journalists were requested for a classroom textbook by Maurine Beasley and Sheila Silver Gibbons, *Women in Media: A Documentary Source Book*, published by the Women's Institute for Freedom of the Press (1977).

• Maurine Beasley and Sheila Gibbons used several transcripts in their book *Taking Their Place: A Documentary History of Women in Journalism*.

• The interview with Ethel Payne of the *Chicago Defender* provided the basis for a traveling exhibition on her that was featured at the opening of Afro-American History Week in 1991.

• A Library of Congress exhibit, "The American Journalist: Paradox of the Press," used a picture and information from the interview with Lucile Bluford of St. Louis.

• The Lucile Bluford and Marvel Cooke interviews were the basis for scholarly papers presented at meetings of American Journalism Historians and the Association for Education in Journalism and Mass Communication.

• Interviews with Dorothy Jurney and with Marjorie Paxson are primary source material for Sharon Nelton in her biography of Dorothy Jurney, a pioneering women's page editor with Knight-Ridder who influenced many other editors on coverage of cutting-edge news affecting women.

• Audrey Moore, of California State University, used oral histories on black women journalists for a project called "Black Women, the Quiet Crisis."

• Sigrid Bathen is writing a dissertation on Mary Ellen Leary, a former Associated Press reporter.

• The oral history interview with Sarah McClendon was the basis for a presentation on her by the Women's Research and Education Institute.

• Leonard Teel, of Georgia State University, used Lucile Bluford's recollections of a lynching in Missouri for an *Atlanta Constitution* article on the 1930s movement for a federal anti-lynching law.

• The interview with Mary Garber was used by Carol Reuss, of the University of North Carolina, for a presentation on women writers of that state. The same transcript was used by Arlene Shulman for an article in the *Village Voice* on women sports writers.

• The National Portrait Gallery used the Helen Kirkpatrick oral history and photo for a 1994 exhibit on World War II correspondents.

• The Kirkpatrick history and that of Ruth Cowan Nash were used by Nancy Sorel for her essay, "The Women Who Wrote the War" for Time Books.

• And Simpson has used it for a book chapter on women's movement/oral history of women journalists/legislation affccting women in the 1970s-1980s.

References

Beasley, M., & Gibbons, S. (1977). *Women in media: A documentary source book.* Washington, DC: Women's Institute for Freedom of the Press.
Beasley, M., & Gibbons, S. (1993). *Taking their place: A documentary history of women and journalism.*

32

Powerful Grassroots Women Communicators
Participatory Video in Bangladesh

Sara Stuart
Renuka Bery

Prologue

When Bulu, a village woman, was young, she was deserted by her husband, who had tried to sell her "like a cow." Now, she is an organizer with years of experience and a steadfast commitment to legal aid for grassroots women. She works at Banchte Shekha, a women's organization in western Bangladesh.

Bulu's involvement in participatory video began in 1992 when she joined a workshop with 14 other Banchte Shekha group members and field-workers. She wanted to make a tape that would tell Nasima's story—a story of domestic violence. Although it would have been easier to interview Nasima at Banchte Shekha's office to avoid crowd control problems, Bulu said no. She hoped that by taping in the village, word would reach Nasima's husband and that this would make him worry.

Bulu made this tape simply—editing in the camera. She completed the recording in less than three hours and played it back immediately to Nasima and the members of her *somiti* (women's group). They were excited and inspired by seeing themselves and the story of their sister on a television screen. They gave feedback and permission to show it elsewhere.

Bulu's strategy for using the tape was clear: She planned to show it to Nasima's husband's neighbors to keep Nasima's experience and perspective alive in their minds, as well as to put pressure on them not to give false testimony in the village court where Nasima's case would be heard. In most domestic cases, the court in the husband's village has jurisdiction. As women generally marry outside their own villages, they have very little influence in that court, while their husbands' families may have a great deal. The tape about Nasima gave her a stronger voice in a situation where she would otherwise have had very little power. In addition, the tape is used to raise awareness among Banchte Shekha members and workers about violence against women and women's human rights.

Since 1992, Bulu has used video extensively in Banchte Shekha's legal aid activities. She taped a village court case about a man who had disavowed paternity and refused to give financial compensation. In the village court, he reversed his position and promised child support rather than face a suit in the local government court. In another case of desertion, the mere mention that Banchte Shekha planned to make a tape about a particular woman's experience motivated her husband and his family to negotiate a settlement. They didn't want to be embarrassed in front of their neighbors.

In Bulu's hands, a camcorder is a powerful tool to advocate for women's human rights. Her access to and skills with this tool have given her elevated status in the community, just as being associated with an organization that owns these tools has given all Banchte Shekha members increased status in their communities. Her tapes illustrate to grassroots men and women how their sisters, who have been abandoned or abused, have gained justice through village-level mediation or through the formal courts.

Bulu's experience demonstrates the potential and power of grassroots women communicators. She and her sisters in Bangladesh have mastered not only the technical skills, they have integrated participatory communication methods and strategies into their own organizations.

Introduction

Participatory video is a methodology developed over 25 years of experience. Communication for Change (formerly Martha Stuart Communications) began its work keenly aware of the disadvantages inherent in centralized control of media making and media dissemination. In exploring less brokered forms of communication, we produced programs with real people speaking from their own experience on issues of general concern. This approach challenged the norm, where experts or journalists reported on an issue. We also questioned the concept that communication is a product. We consider it a process—a means, not an end. Our work has evolved, through experimentation, into what we call participatory communication.

At Communication for Change (C4C), we define "participatory communication" as a process that allows people to speak for themselves. Although the modes of communication vary, in participatory communication the people who control the tools are community members—not outsiders who mediate information and representation. Participatory communication is an exchange among individuals that values each person's perspective and voice. Such communicators can mobilize constituencies and give a stronger collective voice for change at many levels of society.

Communication for Change forms collaborative relationships with people's organizations that are working successfully at the grassroots level on issues of importance to their members or constituents. Together we introduce communication tools and methods to their workers, members, and community organizers. This, we believe, establishes a model for communication that strengthens local communities through their organizations and inspires social and economic change.

The objectives and strategies of participatory communication share a great deal with the methods for achieving change that have been developed through the global women's movement. The inclusive stance of the women's movement, which values each woman's perspective and experience, and which seeks out and embraces diversity, is consonant with participatory communication. Participatory communication methods enhance the bottom-up strategies used by women's organizations around the world and aid their efforts to leverage their experience to influence the mainstream.

It is a mistake to ask, "What is the women's agenda?" We cannot expect a single agenda for half the world's population. There will never be a unified women's front or an equivalent of the World Bank representing women's interests around the world. Diversity must enrich and strengthen the women's movement or we will have no movement at all.

Given this fluidity and preference for autonomy, women are becoming, by necessity, skilled networkers and coalition builders—active in many alliances. For these strategies to succeed, the movement requires a multitude of participatory communicators.

Participatory Media

Participatory communication focuses on who is communicating. Why? Because whoever creates the message shapes its content, perspective, and impact. Participatory media are a subset of direct media, which are distinct from mass media. We consider mass media as "big" in terms of budget and numbers of people who can receive the messages (e.g., broadcasts aimed at an audience of millions and mass-market videocassettes). Direct media are smaller on all these scales; here, the elements of choosing to participate or self-determination are strong, and these forms of communication often enable feedback or exchange. Participatory communication is two-way. It involves dialogue, collaboration, and group decision making. This classification system is not perfect; as the technology changes rapidly, there are more and more hybrids and we must adapt definitions.

To grasp the characteristics and impact of participatory media, it is best to start without preconceived ideas. Assumptions based on the expectations created by mass media are often incorrect. For example, a participatory videotape can be considered successful and even cost-effective by reaching and motivating a handful of viewers. This small audience would be considered a resounding failure in the mass media.

Participatory media have a function in the larger process of organizing, training, or advocacy. The goal of such communication might be mobilizing, or awareness raising, or confidence building—not a finished program. We find that the value and impact of a tape is rarely determined by technical quality. Grassroots organizers with little formal education are often the most effective producers.

With participatory media, people first learn to operate the equipment. They participate in planning and making productions about their own concerns. Seeing their situations framed on a video screen, their perspective on these issues changes. Afterward, they show their programs to their peers and members of their communities. Such activities are profound experiences for the small media maker. They have the potential for great impact, before one considers the value of the recorded program to its viewers. The mass media maker's job is finished once he or she files the story or delivers the final edited tape. But the participatory video maker's work is just beginning. He or she will be involved in facilitating playbacks of the tape, in building on the insight, motivation, and understanding the tape creates, and in continuing to work toward the goals that the tape is serving. Participatory media are practically oriented and build on the strengths of local organizers. They can succeed even when time and resources are constrained.

Bangladeshi Nongovernmental Organizations

Bangladesh has a large, vital, and mature community of nongovernmental organizations (NGOs) that have played a critical role during the years of authoritarian rule and in the transition to democracy. They address many areas of social concern, which includes coordinating relief efforts for the natural disasters that routinely occur and speaking strongly against religious fundamentalist forces that try to infiltrate government structures at all levels.

Since 1989, Communication for Change has introduced participatory video to several Bangladeshi NGOs. This chapter documents and analyzes the experience of Banchte Shekha and Proshika, two such organizations.

Proshika, the third largest NGO in Bangladesh, has more than half a million members in villages and urban slums throughout the country. The basic organizing unit is a group of up to 20 men or women members. Women constitute a slight majority of Proshika's membership. Human development is the core of Proshika's work. Members begin by raising consciousness, analyzing the causes of poverty, initiating collective saving, and developing income-generating activities. Over a period of years, group members have achieved sustainable improvements in income, health, education, social issues, environment, and other areas. They also participate actively in local and district levels of decision making and planning.

Proshika's work is broad and therefore difficult to summarize in brief. As the groups form alliances, their collective strength grows. They have opposed powerful interests and exposed inequity and corruption in their communities and on the part of local authorities. They have learned the value of collective strength in the face of conflict. In their work on the environment, the organization has pioneered sustainable agricultural practices and opposed the importation of pesticides that are banned in developed countries. In some cases, by gaining access and rights to public resources, such as water, the poor have increased their income while protecting their environment.

Banchte Shekha is a women's organization with more than 20,000 members in sev-

eral districts of western Bangladesh. Banchte Shekha began by working with poor, rural women who were struggling to survive on their own. They had experienced violence, desertion, and dowry abuse; often their families were unable or unwilling to support them. Banchte Shekha's numerous program activities reflect their commitment to giving poor women, through awareness raising and skills building, the right to live with dignity.

As with Proshika, Banchte Shekha's central organizing unit is a group of 20-25 members. Their programs in savings, credit, training, and income generation assist the members to become solvent. Their literacy, health, and legal advocacy programs assist the women in recognizing and demanding their legal and human rights. Banchte Shekha's legal aid program has become a formidable force in the area. Their reputation in the communities is that the cases supported by Banchte Shekha never lose in government courts.

Planning

Planning is crucial when developing participatory approaches. Considerable attention and time was given to forming collaborative relationships with Proshika and Banchte Shekha. Participatory video challenged existing assumptions and structures. Banchte Shekha had almost no previous experience with any communication technology. Like rural women in many parts of the world, Bangladeshi village women have very limited access to information and most have little formal education. The mass media in their country do not represent their experience or issues. Therefore, the opportunity to share relevant experiences of peers inside and outside the organization was compelling.

In 1991, Banchte Shekha sent two young women to a 20-day participatory video workshop for workers from smaller NGOs. They returned to make their productions with Banchte Shekha members. As a result, many people in the organization gained exposure and firsthand experience with participatory video. Despite this exposure, some found it difficult to separate their thinking about participatory video from promotional video. They saw video as a tool to promote the organization's public image.

In Proshika, it was different. Although not everyone understood it, some field-workers and members immediately recognized the potential of this tool and methodology for strengthening their work. During an exploratory visit to Bangladesh, C4C spent a day with 12 village women. With Proshika's video team, we introduced the basics of video equipment and discussed some experiences of grassroots producers.

This first exposure generated a great deal of excitement, ideas, and energy. The women had no fear of the equipment and eagerly gave it a try. We screened these recordings with several Proshika workers who were at the center that day. The men were impressed. They had not thought village women could use sophisticated technology.

After the screening, the village women talked about their ideas for using video; their thoughts were insightful. They proposed making tapes to expose exploitation in their communities. One woman wanted to interview leaders making promises. By showing the tape to the communities, she felt their group could put enough pressure on the leaders to fulfill the promises they so often break. These women also felt that video could be a very good channel for sharing experiences between communities and for elevating women's status in society.

Their visions convinced all who were present of the value and potential these tools offer. It is one thing to be fascinated and enthused by a new technology; it is quite another—after your first exposure—to have formulated a strategy to apply this technology with potentially far-reaching impact.

Implementation

Both Proshika and Banchte Shekha committed themselves to train grassroots members and field-workers. By learning to shoot in-sequence, they avoided the time and expense of editing. The simple methods made it possible for those directly involved to participate in the decision-making process—participatory video. Proshika chose to establish independent rural production units based in seven of their sixty Area Development Centers (ADCs). Each ADC-based team was equipped with a VHS camcorder, a battery monitor, a set of playback equipment, a generator, and accessories. Banchte Shekha established a single video team at their office. They have one complete set of equipment and use Hi8mm as their recording format rather than VHS.

In both organizations, grassroots members and full-time field-workers received training and access to the equipment. Few of the participants had prior experience with video or any other electronic technology; they all learned by doing. Some participants were skeptical; others were frightened of electronic technology—but all were very curious to try these new tools. A pioneering spirit grew in the groups; we felt we were doing something new in Bangladesh.

The grassroots participants were eager for the workshop to address their issues and social change concerns. Muriam, an organizer who distributes loans, wanted to learn video and train her *somiti* sisters with it. Aklima is the first of nine wives. Deserted by her husband, she struggled to support herself and her three children. She wanted to make tapes about women's legal rights. Tuli, a group leader, had some experience with popular theater and saw video as another method for increasing the status of women. Their ideas and others ensured that participatory video grew into a relevant and locally valuable process.

During the three-week workshops, the trainees were introduced to participatory video strategies. Each participant learned to operate the equipment, that is, to make simple programs edited in the camera, to conduct playbacks, and to lead discussions about the tapes and the issues in their communities. The trainees returned to their villages to make a video program on an issue directly related to their own individual work. They also led community screenings of these productions. Through these activities, they gained a powerful, new kind of literacy.

The training was intensive. The women participants grew bolder as their self-confidence grew; they deferred less to the men and relied on their own judgment. They were better able to assert their ideas. They often admonished the men for being clannish or insensitive. This change was more evident after six months of practice. The technical quality of their programs had improved but, more important, their ability to conceptualize issues and use video to communicate these issues had developed as well.

Often training is conducted far from the environment where the new skill is to be applied. Thus, when the trainees return home, they face the difficult task of introducing something new, and convincing their peers of its merit. The experience of bringing these new skills to their communities during the training was important. There is no substitute for showing your program to your peers. It is at once humbling, empowering, and intensely motivating. Muriam organized all the women in her *somiti* to help with her production on nutrition. The villagers were impressed and suggested other programs she could make. In Hassina's village, the men were extremely critical because they were jealous of the women who were learning new skills that they themselves wanted. The participatory video trainees completed their training as confident and experienced teams of producers and communicators whose work was, at least partially, understood by their communities.

Decentralization, Participation, and Empowerment

Proshika's participatory video program is groundbreaking. We know of no other rural development communication initiative that compares in its scope and its level of decentralized grassroots participation. Although occasional follow-up training and technical support is available from Proshika's communication unit in Dhaka, the participatory video teams' work is locally focused and integrated into the overall work of the ADCs.

Video team members in Proshika and Banchte Shekha consult with their peers about important issues in the communities. They discuss how a videotape could assist them in pushing for change and solving problems. In some cases, workers and members from outside the video team initiate ideas for tapes. This type of collaboration increases the scope of the video program.

For example, a participatory video team documented the destruction of the social forestry income-generating projects of many Proshika members. Tree plantations along the roadside were cut down to widen the road. The members had used many tactics to either stop the road or get compensation, but to no avail. Then they taped the destruction and interviewed people who had lost their livelihood. This video was used successfully to gain just compensation from the local government for the lost trees. The experience won many supporters among the local population and Proshika staff members. They are convinced that grassroots members with access to video have greater power to solve local problems.

Members and workers report that video is a valuable tool because it can make people conscious; when people can visualize, they understand. They say, "Video cannot be bribed, and it tells our stories honestly."

Video is also a valuable tool for documenting injustice and harassment. As Bulu's experiences illustrate, this application of participatory video is useful in efforts to gain equitable settlements and to protect the rights of women. The potential to be exposed or embarrassed by video in front of one's peers is enough to motivate changes in behavior, gain financial redress, and prevent further acts of violence. Thus video becomes a powerful deterrent. Peer pressure is an effective force for change and video can help to release this force.

During a cholera outbreak, one video team produced a health tape about the causes of diarrhea. The video devoted attention to insects as a vector for spreading bacteria, and showed flies on the food available from street vendors and restaurants. Community screenings of this tape educated the population about the causes and remedies for diarrhea, but they also influenced the owners of restaurants and sweet shops to improve sanitary conditions because their clientele refused to purchase food from unsanitary vendors.

Playbacks in the centers, during trainings, and in villages can unleash the drive and commitment to work for meaningful change. One worker explained, "We get instant consciousness with video playbacks. It works very rapidly. People come thinking it will be a movie, but when they see that the tape is about their lives, they ask to see the tape again and again. They raise lots of questions and get more conscious." Village playbacks and the discussions that follow offer rich opportunities for organizing and mobilizing. For example, Shameema and Lailee led a discussion with the villagers after viewing a tape about bamboo handicrafts. The women were amazed to see their sisters in another village working in an occupation traditionally reserved for men. They were excited by this tape and talked about getting a loan from their *somiti* to start a bamboo handicrafts trade. Suddenly they realized they could expand their ideas to include any occupation. Their range of options increased dramatically through this experience.

In addition to introducing new ideas and stimulating consciousness in a group, grassroots videotapes make a strong impression. They are so easy to understand and so relevant that viewers absorb a great deal. One playback in a village attracted more than 200 people to watch the tapes. Everyone came— from small children to village elders. After

watching three tapes, the video team led discussions with different groups from the audience. One worker spoke with a 12-year-old boy, who, having seen *The Life Struggle of Aleya,* recited the entire story of Aleya's life. He made connections about how the practice of giving dowry is harmful to all levels of society and said he would not ask for a dowry when he gets married. In another conversation, some of the men teased another man about his marrying a 12-year-old girl. People in this village were more conscious about issues portrayed on the tape after the playback session.

Participation takes place at many levels: in planning strategies, in making productions, in showing them, in leading discussions, in managing the video work. Although many organizations are reluctant to decentralize responsibility for communication resources, Banchte Shekha and Proshika are doing it.

Banchte Shekha's video team has instituted a policy aimed at increasing the participation and leadership capacity of the grassroots members. There is a rotating "presidency" for participatory video. The president ensures that the participatory video activities are implemented. She mediates problems within the group, and refers them to the participatory video supervisor if necessary. The president keeps the records and documents the activities with the help of someone more educated.

She assigns tasks and responsibilities among the team during her term. This process has stimulated some positive competition. Everyone wants her reports to be the best.

Proshika has also made strides in solving institutional and management issues arising from the ADC participatory video work. New policies have been adopted that give greater status and accountability to these activities. They have defined participatory video in such a way that it relates to the organization's core mission. They agreed on the following 10 goals for participatory video:

1. to awaken people's human and ethical values,

2. to ensure the participation of poor villagers and to value their thoughts and beliefs,

3. to disprove the popular belief that poor villagers cannot use sophisticated technology and to create skill among these target people,

4. to project the viewpoints of the villagers about social issues and to ensure their participation,

5. to point out the reasons the poor are deprived and robbed of power,

6. to ensure that participatory video remains true to life rather than being created as entertainment,

7. to uphold the views of people who are alienated by the mass media,

8. to show that grassroots people are capable of expressing their feelings and their problems,

9. to raise people's consciousness by exchanging video programs among people of various regions,

10. to show the processes from which people conquer poverty and to show the causes of poverty.

Proshika has redefined participatory video as its own. This ownership extends from the tools, methods, and management all the way to the ideology and ethic.

Other organizations accomplish a great deal without finding it necessary to digest and institutionalize participatory communication to such an extent. Still, these 10 goals indicate the degree to which Proshika has successfully integrated participatory video.

The themes of decentralization, participation, and empowerment are interdependent. True participation can lead to empowerment, but without significant decentralization and scope for self-determination, the grassroots people we seek to empower will not be able to participate.

Participatory Communication and Leadership

Although there are people who are natural or gifted communicators, most of us develop our communication skills through education and practice. Generally, when we describe the benefits of participatory video, we focus on empowerment training, self-representation, and advocacy outcomes. Participatory video training provides a forum to learn and use new communication skills. These are all ingredients of leadership.

When people learn to make a meaningful and compelling video program, to master a new and sophisticated tool, or to facilitate a group discussion after viewing a relevant video program, they develop communication skills that increase their visibility in the community. Even after putting down the camera, cassettes, and VCR, participatory video producers remain experienced communicators. Exercising these communication skills to effect change requires vision and strategy. We see among our partners a growing and strong strategic sensibility—another key element of leadership. As the people we train become more skillful communicators, and thus more capable leaders, they will take more responsibility for the goals of their organizations. Strategic thinkers and communicators are important and valuable assets, not only to their organizations but to their communities and nations as well. They are the ones who will ask challenging questions and inspire others to make changes to improve their lives.

Reaching Beyond the Local Level

Once local-level participation and empowerment have taken root and are succeeding, it is possible to add a second objective for participatory communication: to serve as a channel to communicate beyond the local area. Tapes can flow horizontally from one village to another. This mode of distribution could, if carefully managed, challenge the prevailing top-down flow of media and information in society.

One videotape exchange created healthy competition and increased motivation among

Proshika workers for prompt delivery of services. The participatory video team in one ADC documented the ceremony honoring the installation of the 45th sanitary, deep-tube well in the area. When this tape was shown to a number of Proshika field managers, they were impressed. They felt that if their peers had distributed 45, then they could certainly do as well or better.

Tapes from Banchte Shekha and Proshika have been screened locally, nationally, and internationally. Such recognition and distribution can have both positive and negative outcomes, as Shahnaz Begum's experience illustrates. She is a village woman who was trained in participatory video at Proshika. In 1993, Shahnaz was among eight winners of the British Council's Women in Development video competition. Her production, *The Life Struggle of Aleya,* is a powerful tape. It was one of 78 entries from 23 countries. This award illustrated the strengths of participatory video and gave the communities in South Asia, Bangladesh, and especially Proshika a concrete reason to acknowledge it as a viable and important communication model.

Shahnaz made the tape about her neighbor, Aleya. Despite being poor, uneducated, and abandoned by her husband, Aleya struggled hard and successfully to educate her daughter. Shahnaz felt that her own possibilities in life were greatly limited by her lack of schooling. She wanted the tape to be a positive example to encourage other parents to educate their daughters, even in hard times.

Shahnaz went to Delhi to a screening of all the winning tapes. It was her first time out of Bangladesh and her neighbors warned her to take care not to get kidnapped and sold. "I was scared at first but then I felt strong. I was afraid I would not be able to walk with the people I met in Delhi because they would be more educated and well dressed. But going to Delhi was one of the greatest experiences in my life!"

Not being able to talk directly with anyone else was the most difficult problem she faced. Shahnaz has lots of new ideas about how video can be used as an organizing and mobilizing tool. In Delhi, she saw a tape about people who came together to fight the police. "In this tape the people were so united the police couldn't do anything. Unity is so important." While sharing her experiences with the other Proshika video teams she said, "All the other tapes in this competition used lots of make-up and acting. My tape was about the real life in Bangladesh."

Although the award brought greater legitimacy to participatory video at Proshika, it has taken attention away from participatory video as a movement by highlighting one tape, one style, and one person. It created problems in Shahnaz's community, where Aleya and others accused Shahnaz and Proshika of reaping benefits from Aleya's personal story. Proshika has had to work hard to reemphasize the value of the methods and process of participatory video, and not just the accomplishments of one tape or story.

While it is important to balance the demands of advocacy and broader distribution to retain the benefits of participation and local empowerment, there are times when the former reinforces the latter. The Self-Employed Women's Association (SEWA), for example, has been a leader in advocating for inclusion of the self-employed in national labor policy. Their video unit, Video SEWA, supported them in motivating and educating the women of Gujarat State to stand up and have their work counted in the 1991 census. Video SEWA's 15-minute edited program, *My Work, Myself,* reached an audience of approximately half a million women through community playbacks and was broadcast on Gujarat State television three days before the census was taken.

Proshika will have the capacity and the structure to undertake this sort of advocacy communication campaign. They are establishing an advocacy unit that will receive participatory videotapes on specific issues. They may use excerpts in their campaigns and lobbying initiatives. For instance, the advocacy unit might request grassroots testimony on chemical pesticides for use in lobbying or to bring the issue to broader public attention. With finite human resources, a balance must prevail to ensure that the work retains its participatory dimension and services the needs of both the larger organization and the grassroots communities.

Conclusions

NGOs are working in many areas for increased education, human rights, gender equity, a sustainable environment, freedom, and economic self-sufficiency. To achieve fundamental change in these areas, organizations created by and for grassroots women and men have a critical leadership role to play. These NGOs are pioneers and advocates. They must create programs that address the realities of their constituents' needs. To succeed, these organizations—and through them their members—need to communicate for themselves. They cannot reach their goals without communication skills and tools.

Participatory communication skills can elevate women's status in their communities by strengthening women's voices. With powerful voices, women can organize, train, take collective action, and ultimately build communities and a society based on self-determination. These actions form a chain. Participation leads to empowerment. Proof of empowerment comes from exercising collective strength. Effective deployment of collective strength opens the doors for self-determination. We believe that as individuals and communities become self-determining, they have the capacity to gain social and economic justice in all areas of their lives. They have the strength and experience to demand that their governments and other authorities be responsive and responsible in their policies and decision making. Our experiences in Bangladesh point to some effective and powerful methods.

Bibliography

Devine, B. (1994). Training for social activism. *Community Media Review, 17*(2), 15-18.
Fuglesang, A. (1982). *About understanding: Ideas and observations on cross-cultural communication.* Uppsala, Sweden: Dag Hammarskjold Foundation.
Higgins, J. W. (1993). Visions of empowerment, media literacy and demystification. *Community Television Review, 16*(3), 17-19.
Protz, M. (1989). *Seeing and showing ourselves: A guide to using small format videotape as a participatory tool for development.* New Delhi: Centre for Development of Instructional Technology.
Rahaman, R. S. (Ed.). (1986). *A praxis in participatory rural development.* Dhaka, Bangladesh: Proshika MUK.
Rao, A. (Ed.). (1991). *Women's studies international: Nairobi and beyond.* New York: Feminist Press.
Riaño, P. (Ed.). (1994). *Women in grassroots communication furthering social change.* Thousand Oaks, CA: Sage.
Rose, K. (1992). *Where women are leaders: The SEWA movement in India.* New Delhi: Vistaar.
Rush, R. R., & Allen, D. (1989). *Communications at the crossroads: The gender gap connection.* Norwood, NJ: Ablex.
Shramshakti: Report of the National Commission on Self-Employed Women and Women in the Informal Sector. (1988). New Delhi: Akashdeep Printers.
Video for the people [Special issue]. (1989). *Media Development: Journal of the World Association for Christian Communication, 36*(4).

33

Multicultural Literacy
Communicating in Culturally Diverse Organizations

Marlene G. Fine

Shortly after the middle of the next century, non-Hispanic whites will no longer be the majority cultural group in the United States. Although whites will remain the largest racial group in the United States throughout most of the next century, a large and growing proportion of them will be ethnic Hispanics. In fact, the U.S. Census Bureau projects that the non-Hispanic white population will stop growing after 2030 (Day, 1993). The black population in the United States is growing at twice the rate of growth as the white population, and Asians and Hispanics are increasing their numbers even faster (Day, 1993). Coupled with the increasing number of women who are entering the workforce (U.S. Bureau of the Census, 1991), these demographic trends are creating a culturally diverse labor pool. During the 1990s, the majority of people entering the U.S. labor force will be women, people of color, and immigrants (Johnston & Packer, 1987). To remain economically viable, U.S. organizations must find ways to enable all employees to work to their full potential and to enable them to work with each other.

In this chapter, I try to frame a theoretical perspective and define one set of practices that can guide organizations in the search for ways to encourage the full productivity of a culturally diverse workforce. In developing this perspective and its practices, I adhere to four of the commitments[1] of women's theorizing that Rush (1996) identified in her chapter in this volume. My theoretical frame (a) moves beyond dualistic thinking and action, (b) is inclusive and diverse, (c) is healing and liberatory, and (d) shows concern and respect for global citizens and world opinion.

Most organizational policies and practices in the United States, in both private and public sector organizations, reflect white, male cultural values and behaviors. White male norms are embedded in organizations in forms that range from corporate dress codes to military discourse to rationalistic modes of decision making. Although professional women are no longer prisoners of a "dress for success" code (Molloy, 1977) that required a navy blue suit, white shirt, and navy midheeled pumps, they are still bound to hierarchical organizational structures, dispassionate discourse, the dualistic assumption that family and professional life are separate spheres, and definitions of business based on sports and war metaphors. Members of racial and ethnic minorities face similar constraints.

In the past, organizations insisted that employees who were neither white nor male either assimilate into the existing corporate culture or seek employment elsewhere. Forcing all employees to fit the white male mold has proven highly dysfunctional, however, for both the individuals who are forced to conform and the organizations that employ them. Denying and suppressing one's genuine self in the workplace create enormous personal stress that has damaging psychological and physiological consequences for women and people of color. I have talked with many African Americans who describe organizational life as "crazy-making" because of the way in which their perceptions and understandings of their experiences are either ignored or denied by white members of their organizations. Many women and members of ethnic minorities, especially recent immigrants, are choosing to leave or not to enter organizations; instead, they are creating small businesses in ever increasing numbers (see, for example, *Survey of Minority-Owned Business Enterprises,* 1991; Taylor, 1986; U.S. Bureau of the Census, 1992).

Beyond the loss of individual productivity, organizations are also hurt by the loss of different perspectives in organizational decision making and problem solving. Diverse cultural perspectives are important in helping companies gain access to new markets, develop products designed for people other than white males, and create more alternatives for solving business problems. Several years ago, I had a delightful cocktail party conversation with several other women who all shared their joy at driving Japanese cars, which they had purchased recently. Each agreed that her new car was the first one she had ever owned in which her feet comfortably reached the gas pedal, brake, and clutch, and her head sat comfortably above the steering wheel. We joked about oversized American cars that are built by and for tall American men.

As the workforce becomes increasingly culturally diverse, organizations must "re-vision" themselves, creating organizations that reflect multicultural rather than monocultural assumptions. Multicultural organizations:

1. value, encourage, and affirm diverse cultural modes of being and interaction;
2. create organizational dialogues in which no one cultural perspective is presumed to be more valid than other perspectives; and
3. empower all cultural voices to participate fully in setting goals and making decisions.

Creating multicultural organizations requires a broad range of interpersonal and organizational changes, encompassing every aspect of organizational life.[2] This chapter focuses solely on changes in interpersonal relationships in organizations and suggests a set of personal attitudes and skills that will enable people in organizations to create organizational discourses in which no one cultural voice is privileged over another and all voices participate equally. These attitudes and skills are the components of multicultural literacy; they are the literacy skills that are necessary to function successfully in the workplace of the twenty-first century.[3]

Multicultural Literacy

For employees and employers to negotiate a diverse workplace in mutually productive ways, they must acquire multicultural literacy.

The definitions of both terms, *multicultural* and *literacy,* are central to understanding the concept.

Multiculturality

Culture is the "patterned ways of thinking, acting, feeling, and interpreting" of particular groups (Ting-Toomey, 1985, p. 75). Culture guides our understanding and behavior; it shapes how we approach the world. In the various literatures on culture, being *multicultural* generally refers to the ability to move from one cultural system to another with relative ease. In this conception, a multicultural person is "a native of many homes" (Hall, 1992). The concept is an extension of a more familiar term, *biculturalism,* or the ability to move easily between two cultures. Businesspeople who maintain business dealings in the United States and another country are sometimes referred to as bicultural because they are comfortable doing business in both countries. When African Americans became a more visible presence in the managerial ranks of U.S. organizations, they were often described as bicultural because they were compelled to follow white organizational norms in the workplace and then switch to black cultural norms at home. Sociolinguistic research suggests that some African Americans move from speaking Black English Vernacular in their own communities or when they are with other African Americans to speaking Standard English in white institutional contexts such as school or work.

Defined as "a native of many homes," the multicultural person is a problematic concept for a diverse workforce. It suggests that at any given point in time, an employee has a cultural home that has a relatively stable, enduring set of cultural assumptions. Defined this way, multiculturalism carries the same admonition as standard cross-cultural training for managers: When in Rome, do as the Romans do.

The problem is that in a diverse workplace, where is Rome? Organizations in the United States represent a microcosm of the cultural dynamics of the country as a whole. People of many different cultural backgrounds come together to re-create, on a continuing basis, our national (and organizational) culture and identity. We don't move from place to place; rather, we continually reinvent home. Eva Hoffman, who emigrated from Poland to Canada as a teenager and then to the United States as a young woman, described coming to contemporary America as an immigrant and facing "the blessings and terrors of multiplicity" (Hoffman, 1989, p. 164). Hoffman said she stepped "into a culture that splinters, fragments, and re-forms itself as if it were a jigsaw puzzle dancing in a quantum space" (p. 164). In a culture of multiplicity, being multicultural represents an attitude of openness toward expressions of different cultures while simultaneously engaging in an ongoing process of creating and re-creating a multicultural culture. This resulting multicultural culture maintains the integrity of many cultures while incorporating them into a whole that is greater than the sum of its parts. It is a "superculture," as one of my students so aptly put it.[4]

In everyday usage, literacy is generally understood to be the ability to read and write; it is considered a sign of an educated person. This understanding of literacy dates back to the late 1800s, when the combination of industrialization and immigration created national concern about having a workforce with basic reading and writing skills (Michaels & O'Connor, 1990). By the 1930s, educators and employers were concerned with the reading and writing skills people needed to function effectively on the job and in their daily lives. *Functional literacy* was defined as "the ability to decode and comprehend text at a certain grade-level of difficulty" (Michaels & O'Connor, 1990, p. 3). As technology increased the complexity of work, functional literacy was extended to include the *complex* reading and writing skills required in work and daily life.

In an information society in which change is constant, literacy takes on an added dimension. People not only need to know how to understand complex texts, both oral and written, they also need to know how to learn from those texts and how to create new meanings in different situations. Michaels and O'Connor (1990) say that literacy is now "less about reading and writing *per se* and is rather about ways of being in the world and ways of making meaning with and around text" (p. 11).

Although we tend to identify people as literate or illiterate, *literacy* is a relative term that is culturally bound. A person may be literate in one culture and language, and illiterate in another, a condition that is often true of immigrants to the United States and also true of the vast majority of Americans. In other words, a person who is fluent in Spanish may be able to produce sophisticated written and oral texts in Spanish while simultaneously being unable to read, write, or speak a word of English, or vice versa.

The cultural boundaries of literacy are more sharply illuminated in a multicultural society because people confront daily the limits of their literacy as they move from encounters in which they can understand the discourse to those in which they cannot. These encounters are especially problematic when the participants share the same (or a very similar) linguistic system but not the same cultural system. Because the utterances they produce appear or sound familiar, the people may assume that they are capable of understanding each other when they are not. Individuals in a multicultural society are simultaneously literate and illiterate; they are "faced with an array of alternative methods and contents representing different views of literacy" (Ferdman, 1990, p. 188). In this kind of society, literacy "becomes an interactive process that is constantly redefined and renegotiated, as the individual transacts with the socioculturally fluid surroundings" (Ferdman, 1990, p. 187).

Definition of Multicultural Literacy

Multicultural literacy in a multicultural society is the ability to participate in a collective process of redefining and renegotiating the texts (e.g., written documents, conversations, nonverbal cues, social arrangements, organizational expectations, and so forth) that constitute the public world. *Literacy,* in the sense that I am using it here, has to do with the ability to read and write the different texts through which people develop, maintain, end, and re-create their relationships with each other. Because these texts are both oral and written and use verbal and nonverbal symbols, the definitions of reading and writing are expanded beyond the ability to read and write a particular language; literacy incorporates the skills necessary to learn different cultural discourses, or different ways of thinking, acting, and valuing (Michaels & O'Connor, 1990). In a multicultural society, multicultural literacy is essential for survival, and is the cornerstone of ensuring the productivity of a culturally diverse workforce.

The interpretation and creation of texts require using verbal and nonverbal symbols to create shared meanings both orally and in writing; multicultural literacy therefore is grounded in communication and communicative processes. It has five components, each of which is centrally related to communication: (a) the ability to recognize cultural differences, (b) a knowledge of cultural differences, (c) the ability to discover particular cultural meanings when they are unknown, (d) the ability to negotiate shared meanings, and (e) the ability to accommodate multiple meanings. In reading and creating multicultural texts, people must acknowledge and recognize cultural differences in order to avoid the error of reading, or assuming that others will read, a text from a particular cultural vantage point. Having knowledge about cultural differences allows people to both read and create texts from other cultural perspectives. Because multicultural societies are in flux, however, people in them must also know how to learn how to read and create texts when they encounter unfamiliar cultures. Negotiating shared meanings is essential to ensuring that people understand one another. Finally, accommodating multiple meanings is an indispensable element of multicultural literacy, for multicultural societies, by definition, include multiple ways of thinking, acting, feeling, and interpreting.

Cultural Sensitivity

Underlying the knowledge base and skills that define multicultural literacy is an attitude of cultural sensitivity. Cultural sensitivity has three components, each of which builds developmentally on the previous component: (a) recognition of cultural differences, (b) knowledge about cultural differences, and (c) suspension of judgment about cultural differences. The first two components are also part of multicultural literacy and were briefly discussed in the previous section.

The first component of cultural sensitivity is the recognition that cultural differences exist. For example, when I teach courses in public speaking, my students generally agree that good speakers maintain eye contact with the audience. They say that speakers who do not maintain eye contact give the impression either that they are untrustworthy or that they are not knowledgeable about their topic. Students are surprised when I tell them that eye contact is a culturally based behavior, and that, in some cultures, direct eye contact, especially with superiors or others who are in authority, is a sign of disrespect or an invitation to conflict.

Recognizing cultural differences is often very difficult, however, because culture tends to be out of our conscious awareness. As are many other national cultures, the United States is highly ethnocentric. We tend to believe that the way we conduct our lives is the only way to do so.

Several years ago, I did a values clarification exercise with some of my M.B.A. students in which the students rank-ordered 10 concepts in terms of each concept's importance in making decisions in their work lives. Then they formed small groups and were instructed to achieve consensus on the relative importance of the concepts. One small group had several U.S. students and one woman from Pakistan. The group members began arguing loudly almost as soon as the group discussion began, and I was finally forced to intervene. The conflict was both simple and profound. One of the concepts that students had to rank was religion. Not surprisingly, all of the students from the United States placed religion at the bottom of their lists, saying that religion had no influence on their business decisions. The student from Pakistan, on the other hand, ranked religion first and said that all of her business decisions were determined by her religious beliefs. The U.S. students not only were astounded by her statement, they also refused to believe her, even after she provided several examples. The examples, in fact, only served to heighten the U.S. students' disbelief. Their disbelief was based not only on their surprise that someone would allow religious beliefs to affect business decisions but, more important, on their inability to envision how religion could affect business decisions. Despite her insistence that religious prohibitions against usury meant that banking was not based on charging interest, the other students refused to believe her because they could not imagine how a bank that did not charge interest could be a bank.

My students further demonstrated the difficulty of seeing cultural differences when I asked them to write about their cultural backgrounds. International students and students who had recently emigrated to the United States were able to do the assignment easily. They could describe their own national or ethnic cultural backgrounds by contrasting them to U.S. culture. U.S. students, on the other hand, were generally unable to do the assignment. Recognizing difference is often a function of juxtaposing something against that which it is not.

Our inability to see cultural differences in the United States is strengthened further by our belief in equality, which is embedded in

American culture. Believing that all people are equal often leads us to conclude that all people are alike; that conclusion leads us to deny differences even when they are apparent. Equating equality with sameness comes from the false assumption that quality (because equality is really a statement of equal quality) is a relative and comparative condition. In other words, something must be better than something else, and only one thing can be the best. Given that assumption, people who are equal must be the same. In the current debate over affirmative action policies in the United States, opponents of affirmative action often point to examples of women and people of color who were selected over white men who scored higher on preliminary exams or who had other qualifications that exceeded those of the women or people of color who were hired. Their arguments are premised on the assumption that equality is based on similarity, an assumption that undermines efforts to build culturally diverse organizations.

The second component of cultural sensitivity is knowledge about cultural differences and the ability to read those differences. Reading cultural differences involves knowing the meanings that others ascribe to their behaviors. For example, my colleagues often bemoan the fact that many of their Asian students dislike participating in class discussions. They have told me that they have given the students lots of encouragement and support, but despite their best efforts, the students still refuse to speak up. The problem my colleagues have is based on a misreading of the students' behavior. They are assuming that the Asian students are not speaking up in class because the students are either shy or insecure about their oral facility with English. That reading is often incorrect, however. Asian students frequently do not participate in class discussions because speaking up in class draws attention to themselves, making them stand out and above other students. That behavior is culturally inappropriate for them.

The last component of cultural sensitivity is the willingness to suspend judgment about culturally different behavior. The willingness to suspend judgment is based on the recognition that "different" does not equal "deficient," and that things that are equal do not need to be the same. People can achieve the same ends in entirely different ways. Culturally sensitive managers recognize that employees may have culturally different ways of accomplishing their work. These managers nurture and encourage the best work in all employees, not just those who conform to the managers' expectations of how work should be accomplished. To do this, these managers need to have what Hoffman (1989) calls a "multivalent consciousness" (p. 274). Hoffman says that the contemporary world is geographically decentered and "in a decentered world we are always simultaneously in the center and on the periphery, that every competing center makes us marginal" (p. 275). Competing methods of accomplishing work decenter our own methods. That decentering does not diminish the value of what we do and how we do it; it simply recognizes the value of alternative methods. Managers need to remain centered in the sense that they recognize the integrity of their own ways of accomplishing work; at the same time, they need to be comfortable when their ways of doing work are marginalized by the recognition of the integrity of other ways that their employees might use.

Organizational Training

To ensure that employees become multiculturally literate, organizations need to develop and implement training programs in multicultural literacy. The five components of multicultural literacy that I described earlier should be used to focus, frame, and develop the content and teaching methods of those training programs. In terms of content, for example, a training program should provide specific knowledge about several cultures so that workers will have a shared knowledge base. The program should also include training in specific skills, such as asking questions, recognizing different cultural frames (i.e., the perspectives different cultures bring to interpreting and understanding experience), knowing how to make judgments within different cultural frames, and negotiating. In terms of teaching methods, a training program should emphasize problem-solving exercises that are highly ambiguous and have no "correct" answers, and learning techniques that allow participants to engage in consensus building and shared decision making.

Training programs in multicultural literacy should be specifically tailored to the needs of a particular organization. If a company is based in a region of the country where its customer base is heavily Hispanic, or if its workforce now has or is projected to have large numbers of Hispanic workers, then its training program should include content about various Hispanic cultures. Because U.S. population and workforce demographic characteristics are in flux, and will most likely remain in flux over the next century, no training program can provide knowledge about all of the cultures workers may encounter in the workplace. In developing the content of specific programs, however, trainers can emphasize those cultures that predominate in a particular organization. That information becomes the base on which employees can build their skills for learning about new cultures that they may encounter. Ultimately, the success of training in developing employees' multicultural literacy depends on instilling particular attitudes about difference, ambiguity, and the willingness to ask questions.

Feminist Transformations

As I said at the beginning of this chapter, my approach to understanding cultural diversity in organizations is consistent with the tenets of women's theorizing laid out by Rush in Chapter 1. The approaches currently used in organizational theory and practice generally are not.

White male theories of organizations take a dualistic approach to understanding cultural diversity in the workplace. They force individuals to suppress their cultural identities and assimilate into the existing organizational culture. Organizations tend to hire and promote people who look and act like those people who are already in the organization, a phenomenon noted by Wilbert Moore (1962) when he characterized the organization as a kinship system based on homosexual reproduction. Kanter (1977) agreed with this characterization, saying that the structure of organizations makes social similarity important; thus "the men who manage reproduce themselves in kind" (p. 48).

By calling for an attitude of openness toward difference and by recognizing the integrity of multiple ways of being and behaving in the workplace, multicultural literacy moves organizational theory beyond dualistic assumptions. These features also create an approach to diversity in the workplace that is inclusive, diverse, healing, and liberatory. People can choose to retain their cultural identity without fear of losing their economic and professional opportunities; those who are "different" do not need to sustain the psychological and physiological damage that occurs when people are forced to repress their genuine selves.

Multicultural literacy also provides individuals in organizations with the cognitive and behavioral skills to be good global citizens. Just as the culturally diverse workplace is a microcosm of the culturally diverse communities that now represent the United States, the culturally diverse organization is a microcosm of the world economic community. Cultural sensitivity and a multivalent consciousness force individuals to recognize the constant shifting in world attention that characterizes a global economy. The economic center and its margins are in perpetual motion, and depending on one's global vantage point, it is possible to be simultaneously in the center and on the margin.

In addition to the feminist commitments Rush articulates, multicultural literacy meets the feminist commitment to revolutionary pragmatism (Fine, 1993a). Feminist theories are about change, about ways to empower the powerless and to allow all people to express fully their human potential. Multicultural literacy empowers all employees to participate in creating and re-creating organizational discourses. It offers a pragmatic, yet revolutionary way to re-vision organizational discourse and our everyday work lives.

In this chapter, I have tried to offer an alternative vision of organizational life, one that not only accommodates the cultural diversity of our population but also values, nurtures, and sustains that diversity. We need many such re-visionings if we are to ensure our economic future and that of our children.

Notes

1. In an earlier essay on feminist research (Fine, 1993a), I identified five epistemological and methodological commitments of feminist research. I called these features of feminist research "commitments" rather than "assumptions" because feminist researchers are personally committed to the ways in which we do our research and the ways in which we come to understand and know our world, and we acknowledge those commitments throughout the research enterprise. Feminist theories include similar personal commitments, such as the features Rush identifies.

2. The issues involved in creating multicultural organizations are complex and require much greater analysis and development than are possible in this chapter. Although many public and private organizations in the United States are beginning to address issues of cultural diversity, most of their efforts are directed at valuing diversity. Organizational practices here range from displaying holiday cards from different countries to playing ethnic music in the company cafeteria. Creating organizational dialogues in which all employees are included is more difficult.

And more difficult yet is designing policies and practices that not only include all employees in decision making but also enable employees to discover and use their genuine voices. In other works, I have described the constraints people encounter in articulating ideas and positions that reflect their own experiences and opinions rather than those they believe are expected or correct (Fine, 1992, 1993b). The power of patriarchy and other systems of dominance lies primarily in their ability to control not by physical coercion but through internaliza-

tion of the dominant group's way of understanding the world—thus the conclusion of some African Americans that life in corporate America is crazy-making because it denies the validity of their own experience and makes them doubt their sanity. For a more detailed analysis of the issues involved in building multicultural organizations, including developing multicultural literacy, and suggestions for changing organizational policies and practices, see Fine (1995).

3. This analysis of multicultural literacy is equally applicable to other areas of life in the United States. For example, as the population of the United States becomes more diverse, school curricula will need to adapt. In recent years, we have seen an explosive growth in bilingual education in the United States; in addition, the literary and historical works that students are expected to study have expanded beyond the Western canon, which is primarily white and male, to include works by women and people of color from around the globe. I believe that schools now need to address more personal issues of teaching students the skills necessary to live and work with culturally diverse peoples.

4. I am using *super-* here in its double meanings of (a) extra or additional and (b) excellent. In other words, a multicultural culture is a *superculture* in that it is larger than the individual cultures it encompasses and it is a terrific culture. I am not using *super-* to mean superiority or placement above the individual cultures. My intent is not to re-create the ethnocentric assumption of the superiority of U.S. culture within the concept of multiculturalism. The term *superculture* is meant to identify the inclusivity and positive attributes of multiculturalism.

References

Day, J. C. (1993). *Population projections of the United States, by age, sex, race, and Hispanic origin: 1993-2050* (U.S. Bureau of the Census, Current Population Reports, P25-1104). Washington, DC: Government Printing Office.

Ferdman, B. M. (1990). Literacy and cultural identity. *Harvard Educational Review, 60,* 181-204.

Fine, M. G. (1992, May). *Negotiating multicultural communication in the workplace: A case study in failure.* Paper presented at the annual meeting of the Eastern Communication Association, Portland, ME.

Fine, M. G. (1993a). New voices in organizational communication: A feminist commentary and critique. In S. P. Bowen & N. Wyatt (Eds.), *Transforming visions: Feminist critiques in communication studies* (pp. 125-166). Cresskill, NJ: Hampton.

Fine, M. G. (1993b, November). *Participatory discourse and the redistribution of power: A case study of alternative organizing.* Paper presented at the annual meeting of the Speech Communication Association, Miami, FL.

Fine, M. G. (1995). *Building successful multicultural organizations: Challenges and opportunities.* Greenwood, CT: Quorum.

Hall, B. J. (1992). Theories of culture and communication. *Communication Theory, 2,* 50-70.

Hoffman, E. (1989). *Lost in translation: A life in a new language.* New York: Penguin.

Johnston, W. B., & Packer, A. E. (1987). *Workforce 2000: Work and workers for the 21st century.* Indianapolis, IN: Hudson Institute.

Kanter, R. M. (1977). *Men and women of the corporation.* New York: Basic Books.

Michaels, S., & O'Connor, M. C. (1990, July). *Literacy as reasoning within multiple discourses: Implications for policy and educational reform.* Paper presented at the Council of Chief State School Officers Summer Institute, Mystic, CT.

Molloy, J. T. (1977). *The woman's dress for success book.* New York: Warner.

Moore, W. (1962). *The conduct of the corporation.* New York: Random House/Vintage.

Survey of minority-owned business enterprises: Asian Americans, American Indians, and other minorities. (1991). Washington, DC: U.S. Bureau of the Census.

Taylor, A. (1986, August 18). Why women managers are bailing out. *Fortune,* pp. 16-23.

Ting-Toomey, S. (1985). Toward a theory of conflict and culture. In W. B. Gudykunst, L. P. Stewart, & S. Ting-Toomey (Eds.), *Communication, culture, and organizational processes* (pp. 71-86). Beverly Hills, CA: Sage.

U.S. Bureau of the Census. (1991). *Statistical abstract of the United States: 1991.* Washington, DC: Government Printing Office.

U.S. Bureau of the Census. (1992). *Statistical abstract of the United States: 1992.* Washington, DC: Government Printing Office.

34

Women and Technology
Transforming Communication and Democracy

Donna Allen

W omen are the key players in a transformation of communication that is
rapidly moving the world toward a democracy based on everyone being heard. This
democratizing process is new—only 3 or 4
decades old, following the post World War
II development of highly accessible communications technology, principally the offset
press—but it has already begun to have re-
percussions greater than the invention of the
printing press in the 1450s. The printing press
led to the period of the Enlightenment out of
which came the idea of democracy. This new
communications technology is now at last
bringing the reality of democracy: for the
first time in history, long-unheard information—the experience and opinions of millions
of people—is now being taken into account
in national and world decision-making.

This process of being heard and having
one's information taken into account is occurring with every group in the population—
and is of no less importance to each group
and to society—but women, as 53% of the
population, are the major factor in the new
democratization. Furthermore, because women
are half of every race, creed, color, ethnic
origin, and other minority group identity they
thus speak out of their experience as members of those groups as well. Therefore, their
effect on communication goes far beyond the
addition of the essential information inherent
in their female experience.

However, within this broader diversity that women represent, it is still the information unique to them as women (different experience, different perspectives, arising from different hormones) that transcends their other cultural identities and it is this unique female information now being heard by the world for the first time in history that is causing the drastic changes in the decisions being made in every country. Although just beginning, the process has indeed begun and is irreversible, as irreversible as the new communications technology that made it possible.

To illustrate the dramatic changes in participation in political decision-making that have occurred just in the last two decades, compare 1974 when women were no part of the first United Nations world population conference in Bucharest with the September 1994 UN population conference in Cairo, where it was clear to everyone that women helped shape the decisions. The *New York Times* acknowledged that "bringing women to the center of family planning was the major change since 1974."

Examination of no more than four decades from the 1960s to the 1990s shows how the change came about. It was caused by women acquiring and using communication technology we never previously possessed, enabling millions more, worldwide, to take part in political decision-making. It was, in short, a revolution in both communication and democracy.

Male Ownership of Mass Media Is Incompatible With Democracy

Democracy requires equality of outreach to the public so the public is able to take into account everyone's information in its decision-making. Most people agree that democracy is equal citizen participation in decision-making. Equal participation is achieved by everyone having their viewpoints equally heard and considered by all of the others. We see this process most clearly in small group meetings where a vote is not taken until everyone

has had his or her say and been heard by all of the others. In a whole nation person-to-person communication cannot reach everyone. Yet the principle is still the same: equal participation in decision-making is achieved by everyone being able to reach the whole public to have their views equally taken into account, whether then accepted or rejected.

For the mass audience of a nation, clearly some technical/mechanical method equally available to all citizens is needed to distribute each one's information beyond the person-to-person reach of one's voice. When the First Amendment was written in 1789, the press was the only such mechanical means of distributing one's information to the rest of the public. Today we have many other technical/mechanical and electronic devices for distribution of our views, but however information is distributed, the democratic principle holds for an entire nation: the greater the number of people who can communicate their information to the whole public, the more workable will be the decisions. Viable decisions are the goal of democracy.

The First Amendment to the U.S. Constitution, written as a citizen right to protect the communication seen as essential to the success of the new democracy, lists four person-to-person means of communication—petition, assembly, speech, and religion (which also uses the others)—and one mechanical means—"the press"—of reaching the public beyond those four one-on-one contacts.

The First Amendment reads: "Congress shall make no law respecting an establishment of religion, or prohibiting the free exercise thereof; or abridging the freedom of speech, or of the press; or the right of people peaceably to assemble, and to petition the Government for a redress of grievances."

Today we have many and vast technologies for the wide distribution of information, many of which are also put to the service of the person-to-person means of communication—large assemblies have microphones and religious services are broadcast. But in that day when the printing press was the only wide-distribution mechanism, the First Amendment authors made no distinction between "the press" and the other four protected communication rights; all were listed together as being equal citizen rights of the individual. It was only the subsequent invention of new communications technology that increasingly divided First Amendment communication rights into two kinds: equal citizen rights for individuals and unequal (since based on wealth) property rights for owners of distribution technologies.[1]

In 1789, the writers of the First Amendment knew only the press technology of their time. It was so simple (virtually the same as in the 1450s when Johann Gutenberg invented his press) that almost anyone (generally white and male) could own a press. We have all heard of the "poor printer" of colonial days. The owner of a press, whether rich or poor, could print only about 300 papers a day, raising and lowering the press and pulling out each printed sheet by hand. To this extent, then, equality of the press did exist at that time—in both outreach and ownership.

The reality, violating the principle of democracy, has been extreme inequality: Only a few wealthy white men are able to reach the majority with their information. Not long after the First Amendment was written, high speed presses and other new printing technologies began arriving on our shores. Very shortly, not hundreds but thousands of papers could be printed per day. In 1833, Benjamin Day's *New York Sun* "penny press" was printing 5,000 copies daily. From then on, print run numbers rose steadily. Mass media had arrived. The "poor printer" became an employee of the well-to-do owner of the costlier high speed presses.

The press owner's political power grew as he significantly increased the number of people he could reach with his opinions, compared to the number non-press owners could reach with other viewpoints.

"The press" had now ceased to be a First Amendment citizen right equally available to all, even potentially. It had become a property right totally based on one's wealth. While not royalty or religion, which possessed the only means of reaching the majority of people for thousands of years, mass media owners still have been nearly all men. They conveyed information men considered important for the public to know—and, if about women, information that men deemed suitable for or wanted the public to know or believe about women. Citizens of ordinary means could no longer distribute their information for the public to take into account, except to the few they could reach in person or with small-circulation media.

It is a thousand times worse today. Newspapers and broadcast stations cost millions of dollars. Television networks cost billions. The half dozen networks together reach 98.6% of the public. The nation's mass media reality is that only a few individuals (a tiny fraction of 1% of the public), who are appointed by the leaders of financial corporations that own and vote nearly all of the stock of the major television networks, are able to reach the majority of Americans, 24 hours a day, 7 days a week. By contrast, the total circulation of all women-owned media at its peak reached fewer than 5% of the public. Thus, more than 90% of the public hears no alternative viewpoints from women and probably assumes that what they hear day in and day out from male-owned media is true.

Since political power can be measured by the number of people we each can reach with our information, this gross inequality of outreach results in grossly unequal political power—anathema to democracy. It has enabled a few men to spread the information on which the vast majority of the public bases its judgments. In the absence of other information for the public to consider, these few men thus have the power (1) to determine the issues for the nation, (2) to set the parameters of debate on those issues, and (3) to decide who can be heard by the majority. With such vast political power, mass media have become a means of governing, not a means of communication for the public.

If only men, but not women, can be heard, then obviously, even though women are the majority, their problems and opinions will not reach the public or be reflected in the decisions. Thus, and simply, the nation's decisions cannot be viable. Women must be able to communicate with each other if they are to discover that there are others of similar experience with whom to take action. Hearing instead the claim that these male-owned media are also speaking for women, individual women would conclude that their different viewpoints must be wrong. They fear trusting their own judgment though it is based on their own experience. The effect is to silence women and to prevent joint corrective action. The woman who is beaten, for example, but does not know that any other women suffer such attacks, knows she cannot alone (and so will not) take corrective action, or even speak up about it. If other women do not hear her, they cannot assist her or tell others of the need for corrective or supportive action.

Regardless of the citizen right the First Amendment guarantees, if only the wealthy can exercise it while we are isolated from each other by not having our own means of communication, we cannot assemble the body of common knowledge that is a prerequisite to collective action. Instead, women must base their decisions on the men's information that male-owned mass media have made the public's common knowledge.

Until now, that has been the reality. But today's reality is also that that day is gone. A new reality is in hand.

How Women Are Transforming Communication and Expanding Democracy

What has changed the prospects for democracy so drastically is that the owners of mass media no longer have sole control of the content of the media they own, and it is the expanded content that is making possible more democratic decision-making. Men still own the mass media, nationally and internationally. That has not changed. It has grown even more extensive and more concentrated. But their sole ability to provide the common knowledge on which the public bases its political decisions has been broken by women creating their own media, as also by other unheard people, using the new communications technology to offer the public new and very different information.

The result has been astonishing. Less than four decades after the offset press technology drastically reduced the cost of printing, women were able to reach enough of the public to significantly reverse three principal male viewpoints that had silenced women for thousands of years, effectively excluding them from political participation:

1. silencing women by threat of violence (justified in the male mass media viewpoint as being a minor problem, and acceptable because such violence is "natural" and therefore unavoidable),
2. silencing women by threat of social disapproval of political participation (justified by the male viewpoint that women's place is in the home, not in politics), and
3. silencing women by exclusive male control of the only means of reaching the majority of the public (justified by the male viewpoint that men can and are speaking for women).

We know that throughout history, women have written and published with considerable impact on society. In a few periods women were able to maintain distribution of their ideas long enough to win significant progress, such as the right to vote. But we also know from the "waves" of the women's movement that women were unable to sustain their outreach to the public because they did not own the distribution technology. In one way or another, they were dependent in whole or in part on men for their media access to the public, and even for access to each other.

For example, the media space given to women during World War II to enlist their support for the war effort disappeared immediately after the war ended. Coverage in both news and features, as measured in the *New York Times Index,* dropped from 4½ pages under "Women" headings in the mid-war year 1943 to 1¾ pages in 1950. In the *Readers Guide to Periodical Literature,* listings dropped from seven pages of articles under "Women" in 1943-1945 to only three pages in 1949-1950. At the same time, the content changed to domestic and family issues with the single viewpoint that women should stay home, care for family, and leave other matters to men.

But that male media effort to determine women's role was doomed. Women immediately took advantage of the newly available offset press technology. By establishing their own new media and expanding their existing organizational periodicals, they coordinated a surge of lobbying activities on behalf of women's rights. Federal and state commissions for women were won in the early 1960s. Still more periodicals were founded to support commission-recommended actions. When the Equal Employment Opportunity Commission didn't take strong enough action, women in 1966 created the National Organization for Women. Its chapters quickly established their own periodicals across the country, reaching thousands more women and greatly widening the pressure for EEOC action and other gains. Women in civil rights groups, including Freedom Summer in 1964, circulated position papers and other publications that laid the basis for a major new part of the growing women's movement. The 1960s witnessed dozens more arise: the first newspaper, *Voice of the Women's Liberation Movement;* the first journal, *No More Fun and Games;* magazines, *Lilith* in 1968 and *Women: A Journal of Liberation* in 1969; and the first and famous KNOW press. The movement had arrived—with the arrival of our own means of communication to each other. Women's periodicals sparked and fueled the movement and recruited others into its organizations and public actions.

Hundreds more arose in the 1970s—500 by 1972—newsletters, newspapers, magazines, and quarterly journals—*Womyn's Press, off our backs, New Directions for Women, Ms.* magazine, to name only a few. Publishing houses like The Feminist Press in 1970 and news services like HER SAY all stimulated further communication by women who took their message into other media forms as well, for example, more book publishers and ad agencies, broadcasting, video, film, music—women's own bands, recording companies, and distribution companies—art and theater. There were women's sports periodicals, health journals, filmmakers' magazines, political newspapers, literary journals, as well as periodicals for women in religion, art, self defense, and women's studies. The female majority of the population was beginning to be heard—first by each other and then by others.

From the beginning, women conveyed information that had never been heard by most people, but which spread rapidly because it had the ring of truth that comes from women speaking for themselves. Other women recognized the information as their own. Lindsy Van Gelder noted that the early papers were "minutely-dissected, dog-eared and smeary" from being passed from hand-to-hand to all the women who had never seen such material in print before. Here were ideas, information, and viewpoints that women heard from no other source, information that, by confirming their own experience and viewpoints, offered opportunities to take action and make changes that they believed should come in society. By creating their own media, women were able to establish their own common knowledge. Then as they raised each issue to sufficient visibility by reaching enough people, the mass media were forced to pick it up. Thus it became the whole public's knowledge upon which new judgments were based, different from those that had previously been based only on male viewpoints.

FIRST Male Viewpoint: Violence Against Women Is Acceptable.

It took just two decades for women to win adoption of their viewpoint that violence to women is far more than a minor problem affecting only a few. Women reversed the long-held male viewpoint that violence to women is natural and unavoidable and therefore acceptable.

Women's viewpoint on violence against women is now official U.S. policy. Congressional passage of the Violence Against Women Act in 1994 is the most stunning illustration of women's success in reaching enough of the public to replace the male viewpoint that prevailed for thousands of years. In authorizing nearly 2 billion dollars over a six-year period, the law firmly acknowledges that violence to women is a major not a minor problem, and that violence is not acceptable. The law also affirms the women's viewpoint that because violence against women is not "natural," it is avoidable. It does this by authorizing more than one billion dollars for law enforcement training grants, and for education and training of state and federal judges, and for youth education and community programs on domestic violence, to name a few among numerous other programs, such as working with offenders and establishing a domestic violence hotline.

It may yet take a long time to eradicate violence against women or, still more difficult, the threat of violence to women so pervasive in all forms of media (from news stories reporting what a raped woman was wearing to advertising magazines as "male entertainment" that show violence to women). Nonetheless, this official and legal acknowledgment of the women's view that violence to women is wrong and intolerable indicates that the male viewpoint will never again become the accepted view that it was for thousands of years. Too many people have now learned such facts as the FBI data that every 15 seconds a woman is assaulted in the United States and that every day four women are killed by male batterers.

An irreversible change in attitude has occurred and it took just a few decades. How did that happen?

Despite the mass media silence on violence to women, many individual women who saw such violence in their own experience began to speak about it to each other, first in the person-to-person communication of consciousness-raising groups, speakouts, conferences, and demonstrations, and then by establishing organizations, founding periodicals, and writing books. Following Erin Pizzey's visit telling of her first battered women's shelter in Britain, women in 1975 formed the first organization in the United States for battered women, Abused Women's Aid in Crisis. In 1976 Del Martin wrote the first book addressing this problem, *Battered Women,* and in 1977 women formed WAVAW, Women Against Violence Against Women. The National Coalition Against Domestic Violence was established in 1978. Thereafter, more such organizations arose each year, each publishing one or more periodicals and related publications, reaching still more women.

Each different form of violence was combatted by its own rapidly expanding communication network. Rape crisis centers were established, for example, and published their periodicals in a nationwide network. Susan Brownmiller's book, *Against Our Will: Men, Women and Rape,* appeared in 1975. *Take Back the Night: Women on Pornography,* edited by Laura Lederer was followed by many "Take Back the Night" demonstrations regularly scheduled throughout the nation up to the present day. Organizations were formed to combat pornography, two in New York City alone and many others across the country. They published periodicals and journals, such as the *Women Against Violence in Pornography and Media Newspage* in San Francisco. News services like Backlash Times were started. Many books came out on the harm pornography does to women, by Diana Russell, Andrea Dworkin, and others. The organization, Women Hurt in Systems of Prostitution Engage in Revolt, made up of women who experienced prostitution as violence against women, has published its periodical *WHISPER* for more than a decade. The solution to pornography will come in the same way as for other violence to women—when enough information from women telling about its harm reaches other women and the public.

These touch only the surface of the growing national and worldwide revolt of women against the silencing of their problem by the male media. With women now able to publish their own viewpoints, all forms of violence from rape and incest to sexual harassment are being discussed and have become the public's common knowledge. It is no surprise that Anita Hill felt it her duty to report sex harassment to the Senate Committee considering the confirmation of Clarence Thomas to the Supreme Court, that women in the Navy Tailhook incident initiated 12 lawsuits, that the police felt it their duty to air the tapes of Nicole Brown's protest against O. J. Simpson's battering, and that Congress in 1990 began legislative consideration of the Violence Against Women Act. Anita Hill forever changed the public's understanding of sexual harassment when she shattered a male media imposed silence and freed thousands of women to follow her lead and speak out.

Women with their own media were clearly transforming communication. By raising their issues to wide visibility, they were enabling millions of women to be heard and their information to be taken into account in making new political decisions not only crucial to the safety of women, but beneficial to the whole society. Inclusion of those millions more viewpoints in the national decision-making process strengthens democracy.

SECOND Male Viewpoint: Women's Place Is in the Home.

In scarcely two decades women have also reversed a second long-disseminated male viewpoint that silenced women for centuries. Women have been able to reach the public with new information that disproves the male assertion that women's "place" is in the home and not in politics. The new information revealed that such a view was not the reality of American life.

More women are registered and more women vote than men do. That is the reality. We also know that women play a larger role in political party activities than men do and, in fact, that significant numbers of the public actually prefer women in public office. This public acceptance of the women's thinking, replacing the long-disseminated view that women did not belong in politics, was clearly evidenced in a *Woman's Day* poll of 115,000 readers in 1984. Respondents believed by 2 to 1 that women in political office are "more effective in getting things done," by 9 to 1 that women in politics "are more responsive to constituents' concerns," and by 20 to 1 that "women in public office are more honest." Then in 1984 as if to seal the acceptance of women belonging in politics as well as in the home, a woman, Congresswoman Geraldine Ferraro, was nominated for the second highest office in the nation and won significant support from the public. In an April 1995 Louis Harris poll, 75% of the public (men and women) said it was very important or somewhat important that more women be elected to office. With respect to the long-promoted view that women's place is in the home, the poll found that two-thirds (66%) disagree "that women should return to their traditional role in society."[2]

How did this reversal of the male mindset, held for thousands of years, come about in only the few decades since the 1950s when it was doctrine in all mass media?

Even with that 1950s rhetoric about women's "place" still ringing in their ears, women in traditional organizations began in the late 1950s and early 1960s to build a political network by expanding their periodicals, and creating new ones. They lobbied the administration for federal and state commissions on women to help win a greater political role in government and lobbied the Congress for equal pay and other political equality legislation. In 1970 women founded the National Women's Political Caucus and published *Women's Political Times*. This was followed by other new periodicals, such as the *Women's Washington Representative, Women's Lobby Quarterly, The Woman Activist,* and dozens more through the 1970s and 1980s. Women networked politically through numerous coalitions, such as ERAmerica and The Vote Project and continue today expanding their communication outreach by not only desktop publishing but also use of facsimile (for example, Washington Feminist Faxnet) and electronic mail (like Political Woman Hotline). Periodicals and organizations such as The Feminist Majority, Women's Campaign Fund and Emily's List have wide and growing networks, both partisan and non-partisan, assisting the participation of women in the political arena in all ways, including running for office.

THIRD Male Viewpoint: Male Owned Media Can Speak for Women.

New information reaching the public from women also is replacing a third long-disseminated male mass media assertion: that male-owned media can speak for women (or for anyone other than themselves), that they mirror society or that they do, or can, reflect or represent the population. Or that they can tell the whole public, including its female majority, "what it needs to know."

Despite the wide prevalence of that male view and even before the decade of the 1950s had echoed away, millions were buying Betty Friedan's *The Feminine Mystique,* documenting the evidence that men could not speak for women. And millions again in the 1990s kept Susan Faludi's *Backlash* on the best-seller list, exposing to ridicule the efforts of men in the mass media to persuade the public that women themselves wanted men to resume dominance.

As opinion polls show, the public knows that women's views are enough different that men cannot accurately speak for them. In each election, gender gap data continues to show sharp differences between men and women in their preferences on certain issues, policies, and candidates. The 1984 *Woman's Day* poll had also shown by a huge ratio of 74 to one, for example, that respondents believed women "were more oriented toward peace" than men are. Polls consistently show women hold a different view than men on military spending. And a recent poll has shown that 80% of women believe that violence on television contributes to violence in society.

How did this irreversible recognition that men in mass media cannot speak for women come about in so few decades?

Dissatisfaction with portrayal and news coverage of women began building up during the 1960s, expressed by women both outside and inside mass media. Widely discussed in women's media, it laid the basis for a common knowledge that led to the 1970 sit-in at the *Ladies Home Journal*—and to similar demonstrations and visits to other of the "women's" magazines. In addition, throughout the 1970s and beyond, a number of other print media (*Newsweek, New York Times, Reader's Digest,* Associated Press, and others) were sued by their women employees and community groups, citing employment discrimination and stereotyping of women.

In the early and mid-1970s, broadcast license renewals were challenged at all three major networks and at numerous television and radio stations. Actions to improve employment of women, and especially broadcast programming both public and commercial, continued through the 1970s and 1980s.[3] Even now in the 1990s there are coalition efforts to protest and reverse the occasional views by the Federal Communications Commission and the courts holding, despite evidence to the contrary in all of women's broadcast programming, that women broadcast station ownership would not add diversity to programming.[4]

For four decades, studies monitoring media have documented the inability of male-owned media to portray or even to cover the news of women accurately.

Nearly all of the hundreds of women-owned media that have arisen since the 1950s were founded expressly to convey information men's media did not provide, from the *Black Women's Log* to the *Women's Health Network News.*[5] More than a dozen of them, in fact, were begun specifically to discuss remedies for the shortcomings of mass media and to help expand women's media. These ranged from *Media Report to Women,* published by the Women's Institute for Freedom of the Press beginning in 1972, which based its philosophy on the principle that all people should speak for themselves, down to today's *Action Agenda* co-published by Media Action Alliance and Media Watch; *Challenging Media Images of Women* published from 1988 through 1994; the Women's Desk of Fairness and Accuracy in Reporting (FAIR); the public broadcasting show "To the Contrary" by Women Are Good News (WAGN); and a growing number of others. Periodicals of professional media women's organizations, who had long concerned themselves with both the reporting and representation of women, such as Women in Communications, Inc. (WICI), were joined by newly established groups, for example, Women, Men and Media, Journalism and Women Symposium (JAWS), and others.

This wide recognition that the male-owned media do not and cannot speak for women is also irreversible.

Attempts to backlash will still be made, as they currently are, but they can no longer return women to the silence of the 1950s. It is too late. Each of the silencers that male media imposed on women for so long was broken by women creating their own media using the new technology and getting their information to each other and the public.

Further progress for women toward equality will come the same way: by making their issues heard speaking for themselves in their own media through 1) increasing their use of the existing technology of print and desktop publishing, broadcasting, cable, music, film, and phone, 2) expanding their use of facsimile and electronic mail networks, and 3) quickly participating in each new technology as it arises in order to affect how accessibly it develops.

The Future

The future offers the potential of women's leadership in creating a new communications system for the world. Indeed, as the majority of the world's population, women have an obligation to do so. There is considerable evidence, both scientific and practical, indicating that women may be particularly suited to lead the way toward a more equitable and more democratic system of communication than the one run by men for thousands of years. An important part of women's success in turning back the three long-prevailing viewpoints that silenced millions of people has been due, in fact, to certain characteristics that make women natural communicators. In addition to their recognized higher scores in verbal abilities, the media that women establish reveal, according to studies of four decades of women-owned media, that their way of communicating is very different from that of male-owned media.[6] These differences include, for a few examples, women's preference for a sharing over a competitive media structure, their more customary creation of a cooperative rather than a hierarchical media structure, their characteristic reporting of information in the first person which lets people speak for themselves, and their preferring an open forum—to expand the choice of viewpoints—by helping others be heard instead of deciding for others what they need to know and think.

These criteria would more equitably restructure the communication system on democratic principles, enabling the information of more people to be taken into account in political decision-making. A system that would share communication technology equally as a citizen right—not a property right, based on a person's wealth—could then be devised to work on the same common carrier basis as the telephone, or the U.S. or other postal service. It would, like the phone or mail, separate the distribution mechanism from the message and thereby protect the message from interference, censorship, or political dominance by the firm that is the message distributor. The wealthy distributor, like the major stockholder/owner of the phone company, would wait in line for his turn to convey his individual message—like the rest of us who desire to have our views be heard and taken into account equally by as many of the public as can be reached by current technology.

A new democratic structure for communications is in fact already in the making everywhere. Communication worldwide and in every country by both women and the other long-unheard parts of the population is incredibly greater now than ever in all of past history—and it is continuously increasing through use of the new media technology. This too cannot be turned back as it marches inevitably toward the common carrier basis that will permit all people to be heard speaking for themselves to each other. However long it takes, or slow or fast it moves, this is its irreversible course.

Building such a system is and has been women's work. Their qualities are needed to more equitably restructure the communication system. It is the most important "women's work" that women as the world's majority have ever had the opportunity to contribute to democracy, especially being also the majority of each group of other unheard people in the world.

If women continue the present course of expanding communication to each other and the public, it will only be a matter of time, however distant it may seem now, until we will have created a new world communication system that, by equalizing communica-

tion to all of us, equalizes the political power we define as democracy.

Notes

1. The very common use of the term "free speech," which everyone acknowledges is a citizen right exercised by all, is often substituted as a synonym for "free press," perhaps to cover up the absence of equal exercise of "free press" as a citizen right. Use of the word "speech" as being the same as the word "press" renders the word meaningless. After all, speech is also exercised in petition, assembly and religion as well as press. It makes sense that the First Amendment writers included it in the list not as a synonym but on its own merits as verbal communication by voice, apart from and in addition to writing or printing, or even to speaking in a public assembly. Calling "free press" "free speech" does not eliminate the need for citizens in a democracy to have some print, electronic, or other means of reaching the public beyond person-to-person communication in order to contribute views and information they wish the public to take into account in the nation's decision-making.

2. Lou Harris and Peter Y. Harris Research Group, Inc., "The 1995 Women's Equality Poll," conducted for the Feminist Majority Foundation, 1600 Wilson Blvd., Suite 801, Arlington, VA 22209. (703) 522-2414. Fax (703) 522-2219.

3. Lewis, C. (1986). *Television License Renewal Challenges by Women's Groups.* Ann Arbor, MI: UMI. Also, see listings under the category, "License Renewal," in the *Index to Media Report to Women* (1977, 1982, Washington, DC: Women's Institute for Freedom of the Press) for more than 30 stories reported in *Media Report to Women* from 1972 to 1981, providing the text and outcome of the license challenges by women.

4. Such a coalition has been assembled, for example, by the Citizen's Communication Center Project (of the Georgetown University Law Center's Institute for Public Representation) and the Media Access Project to submit a Response to the Federal Communications Commission's Proposed Rulemaking of December 15, 1994.

5. Allen, M. L. (1989). *The Development of Communication Networks Among Women, 1963-1983.* Ann Arbor, MI: UMI. See also Allen, M. L. (Ed.) (1989). Celebrating the Unique Characteristics of Women's Media, in 1989 *Directory of Women's Media.* Washington, DC: Women's Institute for Freedom of the Press. (pp. 72-82). Also annual editions of the *Directory* since 1975; *Media Report to Women* since 1972 and *Index to Media Report to Women,* 1972 through 1987.

6. Ibid.

Author Index

Aburdene, P., 280, 289
Ackerman, D., 17
Agee, W. K., 195n, 196
*Alert for Action of Women Living Under Muslim
    Laws*, 39n
Alfaro, R. M., xv, xviii
Al-Khaja, M. A. W., 190, 195n
Allen, D., ix-x, xi, xviii, 3, 4, 18, 39, 39n, 40, 83, 84,
    91, 93, 279, 279n, 312
Allen, M., 234, 238, 241
Allen, M. L., 331n
Allen, P., 104
Altschull, H., 172, 180, 180n
American Council on Education, 171, 181
American Heritage Dictionary, 248
Anand, A., 235, 241
Andersen, M. L., 9, 17
Anderson, D. F., 113, 117
Anderson, H., 254, 256
Anzaldúa, G., 111, 117
Applebome, P., 171, 181
Argyris, C., 50, 56, 58
Arnold, J., 105
Asante, M. K., 60, 61, 70n, 71
Association for Education in Journalism and Mass
    Communication, 151
Atkin, D., 254, 255
Atwood, M., 23, 27

Audit Bureau of Circulations, 259
Ault, P. H., 195n, 196

Bacon's Magazine Directory, 260, 272
Bagdikian, B., 4
Baker, P. Q., 45, 47
Baker, R., 246, 248
Bali, N., 235, 241
Balka, E., 237, 241
Bangkok Declaration, 289
Baptista-Fernandez, P., 254, 255
Barlow, W., 70n, 71, 250, 251, 253, 256
Barnouw, E., 251, 252, 255
Baron, J., 259, 272
Barry, D., 32, 39
Barstow, A. L., 31, 39
Bataille, G., 143n
Baum, C., 92, 93
Baumann, M., 15, 16, 17
Bearden, J., 70n, 71
Beasley, M., 302
Becker, H. S., 111, 117
Bekerie, A., 60, 71
Belkin, N., 86, 93
Bellara, M., 235, 241
Bemberg, M. L., 218
Benjamin, J., 85, 93

NOTE: Page references followed by *t*, *f*, or *n* indicate tables, figures, or notes respectively. Page references in *italics* indicate photographs.

Subject Index

AAF. *See* American Advertising Federation
AAUW. *See* American Association of University
    Women
ABC, 108, 130, 233
Abortion:
    Article 821, 230
    right-to-lifers, 227-228, 231
    Yemmanya's Sparrows of All Evil, 229
Abstracts:
    Communication Abstracts, 154-158, 160
Abuse:
    child, 275-276
    investigating, 147-150
    Mengele twins, 123-131
    sexual, 99, 137
    verbal, 32-33
    wife, 213-214
The Abuse Excuse (Dershowitz), 278
Abused Women's Aid in Crisis, 327
Academia, 144-152, 165
    assistant professors, 161-169
    proactive approaches, 151-152
    related issues, 150-151
    salary reports, 147
    tenure, 146-150
Access:
    definition of, 57
    fee for, 91

    to technology, 89-90
Accrediting Council on Education in Journalism and
    Mass Communications (ACEJMC), 145-146
    Standard 12, 146-147
ACEJMC. *See* Accrediting Council on Education in
    Journalism and Mass Communications
ACP. *See* Association for Progressive Communication
Action.
    affirmative, 180, 299
    self-esteem and, 99
Action Agenda, 330
Action research, 49-58
Activists, 102
Actuality:
    local, 84-85
Adam's rib, 190-192
Adam's Rib, 191, 195*n*
ADCO Foundation, 205
ADCs. *See* Area Development Centers
Addictive System, 75
Administrator's association (ASJMC), 146
Advertising, 271
    dog categories, 270
    woman as idiot, 299
    women in, 271
Advocate, 13
Advocates, women, 286-287
A&E, 270

NOTE: Page references followed by *t, f,* or *n* indicate tables, figures, or notes respectively. Page references in *italics* indicate photographs.

Committee to Protect Tacoma Human Rights, 119
Country Reports on Human Rights Practices (U.S. State Department), 213
Human Rights Ordinance of the City of Minneapolis, 138
Humanity, journalism of, 25
Hunger strikes, 127
Hunter-Gault, Charlayne, 250, 291
Hutchins Commission. *See* Commission on Freedom of the Press

IAMCR. *See* International Association of Media and Communication Research
Idiot era, 108
IMF. *See* International Monetary Fund
Impact, 237
In These Times, 13
Incest, 276
Incidentalism, 85
Inclusivity, suggestions for, xvii
Indexes:
    Communication Abstracts, 154-158, 155f, 156t, 160
    keywords related to gender, 157
    keywords related to gender differences, 157
    New Directions for Women, 206-207, 207n
    New York Times Index, 326
    Readers Guide to Periodical Literature, 326
Industrial Revolution, 91
Information revolution, 89-93
    dangers, 89-92
    in library, 87-89
    opportunities, 89, 92-93
    participation in, 89-90
Information superhighway, 3, 92-93
Information technology, 90
Infrasystem, 192
Ingersoll, Fern, 292
Initiatives, 240
Inner child movements, 102
Inquirer, 283
The Inside Story, 284
Intellectual diversity demonstrations, 170-181
International Association of Media and Communication Research (IAMCR), 237
International communication, 208-217
International Communication Association, 150-151
International Day of Protest Against Violence Against Women, 241
International feminism, 233-242
    strategies for change, 239-241
International Monetary Fund (IMF), 34
International Women's Tribune, 211
International Women's Tribune Center (IWTC), 217n, 237, 287
International Women's Year (IWY), xv, 209
    conference, 296

Internet, 88, 90, 237
InterPress Service, 235
Intersections, 194
Interviews, 226-232, 272, 283
    WPCF oral history project, 290-302
IPS, 230
ISIS International, 39n, 229, 234, 237, 287
IWSAW, 237
IWTC. *See* International Women's Tribune Center
IWY. *See* International Women's Year

Jaena, Graciano Lopez, 282
JAWS. *See* Journalism and Women Symposium
The Jeffersons, 109
Jeffrey, Robert, 179
Jennings, Peter, 277
Jewish press, 130
Jewish scripture, 25
Journalism:
    antilynching, 65
    entertainment, 71n
    environmental, 44
    global, 15
    of humanity, 25
    Philippine, 282
    principles of, 15
    print, 253
    spicy, 65
Journalism and Women Symposium (JAWS), 330
Journalism education:
    diversity in, 171-172
    hegemony in, 170-181
    Latinas in, 170n
Journalists:
    black female, 59-72, 253
    Filipino women, 281-284
    Latinas in, 170n
    minority participation, 175, 177
    WPCF oral history project, 290-293, 300-302
Journalist's creed, 20, 25
Joyner-Kersee, Jackie, 113
Juan, Don, 35-36
Jurney, Dorothy, 301
Justice:
    courtroom, 273-279
    definition of, 13
    Simpson trial, 109, 227-278, 328

Kali for Women, 238
Kassell, Paula, 199
Kennedy, Flo, 122
Kerner Commission. *See* National Advisory Commission on Civil Disorders
Kiethley, June, 283
King, Billie Jean, 113

Shallower Communications, 7, 12
Shanahan, Eileen, 292, 295
Sheba, 238
Sheldrick, Pamela, 204
Shelton, Isabelle, 293, 295
Short, Beth, 292
Shulman, Arlene, 302
Silvera, Marissa, 176, 178
Simmons, Reverend William J., 65
Simpson, Nicole Brown, 109, 277
Simpson, O. J., 109, 277-278, 328
Simpson, Peggy A., 291-300, 302
Simpson, Roger, 122
Sinclair, Upton, 121
Sister, 234
SISTERLINK, 237
SisterWrite, 238
Sistren Theatre Group, 238
Situated knowledge, perspective of, 42
60 Minutes, 129, 274
Skinhead terrorism, 31
Smart Money, 260
Smith, Adam, 29, 38n
Smith, Rebecca, 284-285
Social action research, 10-11, 24
Social science, applied, 50
Social subordination, 139
Social transformation, 285
Socially constructed realities, ix-xi
Society and Nature, 6
Sociological theory, feminist, 83-94
Sojourner: The Women's Forum, 13
Solomon, Barbara, 291
Sophia Fund, 205
Sorel, Nancy, 302
The Sound of Soul (Garland), 69
South East Asian Women's Information Project
    (SEAWIN), 237
Space, new, xviiin
Spare Rib, 238
Speak, 234
Speech:
    free, 37, 171, 331n
    of pornographers, 140-141
Speech Communication Association, 150
Sperling, Cindy, 263-264
Spicy journalism, 65
Spinsters, xiii-xviii
Spirituality, 9-10, 23, 78
Sports:
    championship games, 112
    feminine *vs* masculine, 113
    Gay Games IV, 111, 113
    media coverage of, 111-117
    Olympic games, 115
Sports Afield, 260
Sports Illustrated, 112-113

Sports Illustrated for Kids, 269
Springer, Jerry, 274
Stanton, Elizabeth Cady, 29
Steinberg, Lisa, 275
Steinem, Gloria, 95-105
Stephenson, Jan, 113
Stereotypes, 30-31, 297
Stories, 98-100
Stramesi, Annette, 263, 266-267
Strawberry, Darryl, 277
Suarez Toro, Maria, 226-232
Submission, 139
Subordination, 138-140
Success:
    in magazine publishing, 269-270
    tenure, 146-150
Summers, Ann, 299
Superculture, 315, 320n
SuperJock Syndrome, 277
Superwoman syndrome, xiv
Swift, Kate, 246
Systems theory, 30

Tailhook, 328
Take Back the Night March, 132n, 327
Talk shows, 33, 277-275
Tape, "falling in love with," 222
Taylor, Alana, 176
Teaching:
    education of the painter approach, 184
    media technology, 182-187
Teague, Robert, 108
Technicians, 191, 285
Technology, xiv, 322-331
    accessibility of, 89-90
    community, 285-286
    earmarks of envisionary media, 16
    Industrial Revolution, 91
    information revolution, 87-93
    and public libraries, 83-94
    teaching, 182-187
    used for this book, xvi
Teel, Leonard, 302
Tejas, 175-180
Television, 110, 273-279. *See also specific shows,
    stations*
    abused children on, 275-276
    African Americans in, 70n, 252
    commercials on, 108
    gender imbalances, 35
    idiot sitcoms, 108
    news magazines and talk shows, 274-275
    news shows, 274
    reformist era, 108
    station ownership, 109
    violence on, 30-33

About the Authors

Donna Allen founded, in 1972, the Women's Institute for Freedom of the Press, which, among other activities, published the annual *Directory of Women's Media,* books, and the monthly *Media Report to Women,* which she edited and indexed during its first 15 years, and for which she is now a columnist. She is the author of *Media Without Democracy and What to Do About It* (1991). In 1989, she coedited *Communications at the Crossroads: The Gender Gap Connection* (Ablex). An economist and historian who taught for Cornell University, she has written books and monographs on economics, media, and women and has spoken at national and international conferences. In the early 1970s, as Associate Professor, she taught media economics and women and media for Antioch College, Baltimore Media Studies Center. She received the 1979 Headliner Award, Women in Communication, Inc.'s highest honor, the Wonder Woman Award in 1983, and, subsequently, awards from the Association for Education in Journalism and Mass Communications and from American Journalism Historians Association. She has judged media awards, including the NAB Crystal Radio Awards, and was the keynote speaker at the spring 1990 meeting of the Association of Schools of Journalism and Mass Communications, "Women, Minorities and Freedom of the Press," and at the 1992 Mass Communications Conference at Jackson State University, "Women in Communications." She has been a speaker at press accountability conferences in Madrid, Nice, Paris, Manila, Montreal, Moscow, Prague, and Kiev.

Renuka Bery is a project director and development video trainer with Communication for Change, New York City. She worked on family planning and adolescent health issues with Columbia University in New York and the Association for Reproductive and Family Health in Ibadan, Nigeria, while getting an M.A. in public health. She has also advised Apple Computer's Multimedia Lab on the Visual Almanac, developed international networks at Internews, assisted the introduction of video teleconferencing at Kaiser Permanente in Oakland, California, and consulted the PBS series *Where in the World Is Carmen Sandiego?* She has lived, worked, and traveled extensively in Asia, Africa, Europe, and the United States.

Christy C. Bulkeley, an independent scholar and consultant, holds a Master of Theological Studies from Wesley Theological Seminary, Washington, D.C. She engaged in theological studies after more than 20 years as a daily newspaper reporter, editor, and publisher for Gannett Co., Inc., and seven years as a foundation officer developing and administering grant-making programs intended to accomplish change. Her interests include the intersection of journalism, religion, and public policy as well as news media content and community-building.

Kathryn Cirksena is the Director of Studies for the National Election Studies, Center for Political Studies, University of Michigan. She holds M.A. and Ph.D. degrees in communication from Stanford University and a B.A. in motion pictures and television from UCLA. She has worked on feminist analysis of communciation since the 1970s. Prior to joining NES, she taught at the University of Iowa, East Carolina University, and Russell Sage College for Women; she was a Fulbright Lecturer in Romania in 1991-1992. She co-chaired the Feminist Scholarship Division (then interest group) from 1988 to 1990. In addition to her work at NES, she continues to pursue projects related to women's political communication.

Judith Cramer is a lecturer in the Communication Department at Buffalo State College/SUNY. She is studying for her Ph.D. in mass communication and cultural studies at The Union Institute in Cincinnati. She earned her M.A. in applied communication from the University of Hartford in Connecticut. Her B.S. is in sports information/journalism from Keene State College in New Hampshire. She has worked for 10 years as a news and sports reporter, news director, talk show host, and producer in commercial and public radio in New England, Ohio, and New York. She has written several articles and is the author of chapters in *Women in Mass Communication: Challenging Gender Values* (Sage, first published in 1989) and *Women, Media and Sport: Challenging Gender Values* (Sage, 1994).

Pamela J. Creedon, Director of the School of Journalism and Mass Communications at Kent State University, practiced corporate and nonprofit public relations for 14 years before joining the Ohio State University in 1984. She is the editor of *Women, Media and Sports: Challenging Gender Values* (Sage, 1994) and *Women in Mass Communication: Challenging Gender Values* (Sage, first published in 1989). She also has served as a curriculum consultant to the Department of Mass Communication at the United Arab Emirates University in Al Ain.

Jannette L. Dates is acting Dean in the School of Communications at Howard University. She served as Associate Dean at the school for nearly five years. The book for which she served as senior editor and major contributor, *Split Image: African Americans in the Mass Media* (1993), received a national award, and has been adopted by more than 70 universities. She completed research for a new book, *The Image Shapers,* during the year she served as a Fellow at the Freedom Forum Media Studies Center. She has a Ph.D. from the University of Maryland.

Mercedes Lynn de Uriarte is Associate Professor in Journalism and Latin American Studies at the University of Texas—Austin. She is currently completing a book on diversifying the news product. She received her Ph.D. in American Studies from Yale in 1996. She was a 1991-1992 Research Fellow at the Freedom Forum Media Studies Center in New York and a Visiting Scholar at the Center for Social Sciences at Columbia University. She worked for eight years at the *Los Angeles Times,* where she was Assistant Editor for the *Opinion* section, assigned to open the editorial pages to commentary on Latin American, U.S. Latino, and minority issues. She has served as a journalism education diversity consultant for the Ford Foundation

and a consultant on diversification of the news product for the Austin *American-Statesman* and other newsrooms. She served two terms as Chair of the Association for Education in Journalism and Mass Communication (AEJMC) Commission on the Status of Minorities. She received an M.A. in American studies from Yale. She has two B.A. degrees—in American studies and comparative literature—from California State University, Fullerton. She has received fellowships from the Freedom Forum, Alicia Patterson, and Ford Foundations as well as from the Social Science Research Council and the American Association for the Advancement of Science. She was awarded a 1986 Fulbright to Peru.

Andrea Dworkin is a radical-feminist activist and author who has helped break the silence around violence against women. With Catharine A. McKinnon, she authored pioneering ordinances that define pornography as a civil rights violation. Her books—translated into Japanese, Korean, and Chinese, as well as European languages and published worldwide in their English editions—include *Women Hating; Intercourse; Pornography: Men Possessing Women,* and the novels *Mercy* and *Ice and Fire.* Her latest nonfiction work is *Letters From a War Zone* (1993, Lawrence Hill).

Edna F. Einsiedel is Professor of Communication Studies in the Graduate Program in Communication Studies and also serves as Coordinator of the Development Studies Program at the University of Calgary, Calgary, Alberta. She has a Ph.D. in communications from Indiana University. She has worked on a number of development projects funded by the Canadian International Development Agency (CIDA) and the International Development Research Centre (IDRC). Her research interests include the public understanding of science, risk communications, and issues of gender and development communications.

Riane Eisler is the author of *The Chalice and the Blade: Our History, Our Future* (1987), a fundamental reexamination of Western culture translated into 15 languages, including Russian, Spanish, Japanese, German, and Chinese. Her new book, *Sacred Pleasure: Sex, Myth, and the Politics of the Body* (1995), provides a blueprint for a society where pain, domination, and violence can be overcome by pleasure. She is cofounder of the Center for Partnership Studies (P.O. Box 51936, Pacific Grove, CA 93950) and has taught at UCLA and Immaculate Heart College. Her books include *Dissolution* (1977) and *The Equal Rights Handbook* (1977) and journal publications include *Political Psychology,* the *Human Rights Quarterly,* the *International Journal of Women's Studies, Futures,* and *Behavioral Science.*

Marlene G. Fine is Dean of Graduate Studies and Professor of Communication Studies at Emerson College. She received a B.A. in speech from the University of Massachusetts, Amherst, an M.A. in speech communication from the University of Minnesota, and a Ph.D. in communication as well as an M.B.A. from the University of Massachusetts, Amherst. Her research interests include cultural diversity in the workplace; gender, race, and communication; and feminist theory and research. She is the author of *Building Successful Multicultural Organizations: Challenges and Opportunities* (Quorum, 1995). She has also published articles in a variety of books and journals, including the *Journal of Language and Social Psychology, Public Personnel Management, Journal of Communication, Quarterly Journal of Speech, Women's Studies in Communication, Journal of Multilingual and Multicultural Development, HR Horizons,* and *Phylon.*

Elizabeth Dodson Gray is a feminist theologian and environmentalist. Since 1978, she has been coordinator of the Theological Opportunities Program at Harvard Divinity School and codirector of Bolton Institute for a Sustainable Future. She is the author of *Green Paradise Lost* (1979), *Patriarchy as a Conceptual Trap* (1982), the editor of *Sacred Dimensions of Women's Experience* (1988), and the author of *Sunday School Manifesto* (1994). In 1989, the National Film Board of Canada released a 19-minute film, *Adam's World,* about her work and thought-world. She has taught at MIT's Sloan School of Management, Williams College, Boston College, and Antioch-New England Graduate School.

Fran P. Hosken, founding editor/publisher of Women's International Network News (WIN News) since 1975, was born in Vienna, Austria. She received a B.A. at Smith College in 1940 and an M.A. in architecture in 1944 from Harvard University's Graduate School of Design. She continued postgraduate work in city planning at the Massachusetts Institute of Technology after raising three children. Before organizing WIN News, she worked in architecture and as a journalist in international urban affairs, writing for U.S. and international papers and magazines. She was correspondent-at-large for the *Architectural FORUM.* From her worldwide traveling, she assembled a large collection of architectural color slides used by universities around the

world. She has reported on urban affairs and women's development on every continent, and has taught urban studies at the University Without Walls in Boston. Among her five books, numerous research studies, and reports on urban affairs and women's development are *The Language of Cities; The Functions of Cities; The Kathmandu Valley Towns; The International Directory of Women's Development Organizations; The Hosken Report: Genital and Sexual Mutilation of Females;* and *Stop Female Genital Mutilation: Women Speak.*

Frankie Hutton worked her way through North Carolina A&T University in the public affairs office on campus and as a copyperson at the Greensboro *Daily News,* where she interned. During her undergraduate years, she was also managing editor of the *A&T Register* campus newspaper. She earned an M.A. in journalism at the University of South Carolina, Columbia, in 1971, and has since worked in industry and academy. For WBTV in Charlotte, North Carolina, she produced a pilot minority affairs show. She has since served as a gubernatorial appointed member of the Commission on Sex Discrimination in the New Jersey Statutes. She has taught journalism at Hampton University, the University of Virginia, and at Lehigh University. She was awarded the Ph.D. in American his-

tory at Rutgers University in 1990 and is author of *The Early Black Press in America 1827-1860* and a number of scholarly articles and reviews.

Paula Kassell was the founder, in 1971, and editor until 1977, of *New Directions for Women,* the national U.S. feminist newspaper. In 1993, when the paper ceased publishing, she was the senior editor and a trustee. She is now editing and preparing for publication a 12-Year Cumulative Index (1982-1993), a cross-referenced listing of the entire contents of *New Directions for Women,* which is a sequel to the 10-Year Cumulative Index (1972-1981). She is also preparing the archives and papers of *New Directions for Women* for donation to the National Women and Media Collection at the University of Missouri School of Journalism. She is vice president of the Women's Institute for Freedom of the Press and its representative at the United Nations,

where she convened the Communications Task Force of the Committee on the U.N. Decade for Women and was a member of the Forum 85 Media Committee. She was a member of the media working group for Beijing 1995 of the United Nations Non-Governmental Organizations Committee on the Status of Women.

Susan J. Kaufman is Professor of Journalism at Eastern Illinois University. She is Director of Education and Outreach for WEIU-TV. She is a former cochair of the Commission on the Status of Women of the Association for Education in Journalism and Mass Communication (AEJMC). In 1985, she helped coordinate women journalists in development of a Women's International News Service to cover the U.N. Decade for Women Conference in Nairobi, Kenya. She has a Ph.D. in educational administration and an M.S. in speech communication from Indiana State University as well as a B.A. from Michigan Technological University. She studied journalism at Marquette University. Her professional experience is in commercial and public radio, television, and print operations in

Wisconsin, Michigan, Indiana, and Illinois. She and two women partners founded and operated an advertising agency in Michigan's Upper Peninsula in the 1970s.

Jane Kirkpatrick is Chief Executive Officer of the Stratford Public Library, Stratford, Ontario, Canada. She has a B.A. in literature from the University of Guelph and an M.A. in library science and a Diploma in Public Administration from the University of Western Ontario. She has worked in public libraries in both Canada and the United Kingdom and has served as President of the Administrators of Medium Public Libraries of Ontario and on the Council of the Ontario Public Library Association.

Patricia Madoo Lengermann is currently Research Professor at the George Washington University, where she has taught as Professor of Sociology and Director of Women's Studies. She holds a B.A. in history from Oxford University and a Ph.D. in sociology from Cornell University. She is the author of *Definitions of Sociology: A Historical Approach* and coauthor (with Ruth Wallace) of *Gender in America,* and with Jill Niebrugge-Brantley of several papers and chapters in feminist theory. She is currently working with Niebrugge-Brantley on a book-length manuscript, *Ex Femina: Feminist Reworkings of Sociology,* involving feminist reevaluations of the sociology of organizations.

Casey Miller and **Kate Swift** are freelance writers and editors. Their interest in language grew out of editorial work in a wide range of fields, including science, religion, history, and the arts. Miller was curriculum editor of the Seabury Press for 10 years. Previously, she had been an editor at Appleton-Century, later heading the publications department of Colonial Williamsburg, Inc. She holds an A.B. degree in philosophy from Smith College and studied graphic arts at Yale. Swift was a science writer and editor with the American Museum of Natural History and later with the Yale School of Medicine. She had previously been a newspaper reporter and editor. She earned her B.A. in political science from the University of North Carolina at Chapel Hill. Since 1970, when they formed a freelance partnership, Miller and Swift have written and edited publications for a variety of clients, mainly in the field of education. In addition, their articles have appeared in the *New York Times Magazine,* the *Washington Post, Ms.,* and *New York Magazine,* among others. Both are photographers, and they have done photo essays for *Nature* and *Science, Medical World News, National Fisherman, Antiques,* and other publications. Their first book, *Words and Women,* was published in 1976 by Anchor Press/Doubleday & Company and in a slightly revised paperback edition in 1977. Victor Gollancz Ltd, London, published a hardcover edition in 1977, and Penguin brought out the British paperback in 1979. In 1991, HarperCollins

published an updated edition of *Words and Women,* with a foreword by Catharine R. Stimpson. *The Handbook of Nonsexist Writing,* a guide and reference work for writers, speakers, and editors, was first published in 1980 by Lippincott & Crowell. It was reissued in a revised and enlarged edition in 1988 by Harper & Row (now HarperCollins) and simultaneously in Canada by Fitzhenry & Whiteside Ltd, Toronto. The book is used in numerous college and professional school courses and is recommended by the *Chicago Manual of Style* "for useful and sensible suggestions on how to avoid sexist connotations." The third British edition was published in 1995 by the Women's Press, London.

Sandy Nelson is a 1979 graduate of the University of Washington School of Communications. She has worked at daily newspapers in Washington since March 1980, when she went to work for the *Daily World* in Aberdeen. In 1983, she was hired by the *News Tribune* to write features; she moved to education reporting in 1987. She won a second-place award in social issues writing in a regional Society of Professional Journalists' contest in 1985 and shared a second-place SPJ award with other *News Tribune* writers in 1989. She is an organizer for Radical Women and the Freedom Socialist Party. Backed by the ACLU of Washington, she has sued the *News Tribune* for reinstatement as a reporter.

Julianne H. Newton (Ph.D.) is head of photojournalism, at the University of Texas at Austin Department of Journalism, and specializes in visual ethics. She has more than 20 years of journalism experience, including reporting and/or editing for the Fort Worth *Star-Telegram*, Waco *Tribune-Herald,* and Austin *American-Statesman* as well as public radio and television. She is director of a research project begun in 1994, "The Burden of Visual Truth," examining the role of photojournalism in mediating reality. Her photographic work has been shown in more than 50 exhibitions in the United States and Mexico. Born in Dallas, Texas, she spent the early part of her life in Colombia and Ecuador. She is particularly fond of watching eagles soar—and soaring herself.

Jill Niebrugge-Brantley has been Professor of Communications and Human Studies at Northern Virginia Community College and has taught at American University, George Mason University, and the George Washington University, where she developed the undergraduate Women's Studies minor and is currently research associate in sociology. Her B.A. in English is from Pomona College and her Ph.D. in American Studies is from the University of Kansas. She has written extensively with Patricia Lengermann on feminist theory, including major chapters in sociology's leading theory texts, *Sociological Theory* (by George Ritzer) and *Frontiers of Sociological Theory* (an edited collection of essays).

Barbara Straus Reed (Ph.D.), Associate Professor of Journalism, Rutgers University, previously worked at the Associated Press and for Young & Rubicam, Inc., advertising agency. She did public relations for the first national conference on children and television in Philadelphia, and served as assistant editor of *Journalism Quarterly* and as assistant producer at KCET-TV 28, public television in Los Angeles. She wrote and continues to produce updates for a chapter on women and the media for the Emery and Smythe reader. She has taught a class with women from the Screen Actors Guild (SAG), the American Federation of Television and Radio Artists (AFTRA), and the Writers Guild at UCLA Extension on women in media including film. She headed the Committee on the

Status of Women in the Association of Education in Journalism (AEJ) in 1978, and currently is co-chair of its successor Commission. She is known as a researcher on women and media—including receiving a research grant from an archive in Ohio to study the life and work of one female magazine editor/publisher. She has published, and continues to publish, articles and book chapters stemming from that research.

Florangel Rosario-Braid is the President and Executive Dean of the Asian Institute of Journalism and Communication, located in Manila, the Philippines, an institution offering graduate degrees in journalism and communication management, as well as undertaking development and communication research and consultancy. She has a B.A. from the University of the Philippines and her M.S. and Ph.D. from Syracuse University. She was Senior Researcher at the East West Communication Institute and taught graduate courses at the University of Hawaii, University of the Philippines, and other universities. As a member of the 1986 Constitutional Commission, she wrote provisions on communication, nonformal education, coop-

eratives, science and technology, and NGOs. Her publications include *Communication Strategies for Productivity Improvement; The Philippines at the Crossroads: Some Visions for the Nation; Development Issues: Constitutional Response, Communication, and Society;* and *Social Responsibility in Communication Media.* She writes on communication and development for professional journals and national dailies. She was president and founding director of the *Philippine Daily Inquirer.* A UNESCO adviser to Sri Lanka on population communication, she is also a member of the UNESCO National Commission and a Commissioner of the National Centennial Commission. She has consulted on development projects for FAO, UNICEF, the World Bank, USAID, as well as for the government.

Ramona R. Rush, Professor and the first Dean in 1977 of the College of Communications at the University of Kentucky, is coeditor of *Communications at the Crossroads: The Gender Gap Connection* (Ablex, 1989). Her latest work involves global eco-communications (a conceptual/philosophical framework grounded in environmental and ecological communications), peace education, and conflict resolution. She was named the Outstanding Woman in the Field by the Association for Education in Journalism and Mass Communication's (AEJMC) Committee on the Status of Women in 1990. In 1991, she received the career achievement alumni award from the Department of Radio and Television, University of Kansas, where she

received a B.S. and an M.S. She holds a Ph.D. in international and mass communication from the University of Wisconsin, and an A.A. in journalism from the Hutchinson (Kansas) Community College. She is a native of Little River, Kansas. She has served as an administrator and on the faculty at the Universities of Florida, Tulsa, and Kansas State, and worked as a professional communicator in political communications, public relations, and commercial television.

Sharon A. Russell is Professor of Communication and Women's Studies at Indiana State University. She received her A.B. from Bryn Mawr College and her M.A. and Ph.D. from Northwestern University. She teaches film theory and production. She has published extensively in various areas of popular culture. She has written several articles on the role of women in mystery and horror fiction including contributions to *Great Women of Mystery, Women Times Three,* and *In the Beginning.* She is also an editor and contributor to the forthcoming book, *The Dog Didn't Do It: Animals in Mystery.*

Annette J. Samuels has had more than 25 years' experience as an administrator and communications specialist. She was the first African American woman to serve as a spokesperson for the president of the United States (Carter administration) and the first fashion editor for *Essence* magazine. She is a past executive director for the D.C. Commission on the Status of Women and served for a brief time as the D.C. ombudsman. Prior to that, from 1981 to 1987, she was the Director of Communications and press secretary to the former mayor of Washington, D.C., Marion Barry, Jr. During the mid-1970s, she was the executive editor of the Community News Service, which at the time was the nation's only minority news service. It was formed on the recommendation of the 1968 Kerner Commission report. She has a Master in Public Administration from the John F. Kennedy School of Government at Harvard University.

Anne Wilson Schaef (Ph.D.) is an internationally known writer, lecturer, organizational
consultant, philosopher, and workshop leader.
She has a doctorate in clinical psychology
from the Union Institute and did her graduate
work at Washington University, St. Louis,
Columbia University, Union Theological Seminary, and Teacher's College, Columbia, with
an internship at Bellevue Hospital in New
York City. She has been conducting yearlong training groups in Living in Process
Facilitation in the United States and in Europe
for 10 years and is starting groups in New
Zealand and Australia. She has been working
in the field of addictions for many years, and
describes herself as a "recovering" psychotherapist. Her books include *Women's Real-*

ity (1981), *Co-Dependence: Misunderstood, Mistreated* (1986), *When Society Becomes an
Addict* (1987), *The Addictive Organization* (with Diane Fassel; 1988), *Escape From Intimacy*
(1989), *Meditations for Women Who Do Too Much* (1990), and *Laugh, I Thought I'd Die . . . If
I Didn't* (1990). Her most recent book, *Beyond Therapy, Beyond Science* (1992), deals with
shifting scientific paradigms and new forms of working with people that are congruent with a new
paradigm.

Peggy A. Simpson has been a reporter, editor, and university instructor over the past 35
years. She worked as a reporter and editor
with the Associated Press in Texas and in
Washington, D.C., and has covered national
politics and economics for national newspapers and magazines, and was *Ms.* magazine's
Washington bureau chief. Since late 1991,
she has reported on the economic psychology
of post-Communist Poland. She has taught at
Indiana University and at Warsaw University
(Poland), was a Nieman Fellow at Harvard and
a visiting scholar at the Woodrow Wilson
Center. She is contributing editor of the *Warsaw Business Journal* and of *Ms.* magazine
and a regular contributor to *Business Week*
and *Business Central Europe.* In addition,
her articles have appeared in the *Washington*

Post, the *Chronicle of Higher Education, On the Issues, Theatre Annual,* the *Journal of
Women's History* as well as in books on the media published by the University of Georgia.

Annabelle Sreberny-Mohammadi is Professor and Director of the Centre for Mass Communication Research at the University of Leicester, Leicester, England. She was educated at Cambridge (M.A., history) and Columbia University, New York (Ph.D., sociology). She lived in Iran from 1976 to 1980, where she taught sociology and mass communications and was the founder-editor of *Communications and Development Review.* She lived in the United States from 1985 to 1992 and directed the Graduate Program of the Department of Communication Arts and Sciences, Queens College/CUNY, New York. Major publications include *Questioning the Media* (Sage, second edition 1995),

Small Media for a Big Revolution: Communication, Culture and the Iranian Revolution (University of Minnesota Press, 1994), and *Globalization, Communication and Transnational Civil Society* (IAMCR/Hampton, forthcoming). She is currently preparing a special issue of the *Journal of International Communication* on "international feminism(s)" and imagining a book on international communication and gender.

Gloria Steinem is one of the country's most widely read and critically acclaimed writers and editors. She travels as a lecturer and feminist organizer, and appears frequently on television and radio as an interviewer and spokeswoman on issues of equality. She is currently an editorial consultant and writer for *Ms.* magazine, the international feminist bimonthly that she cofounded in 1972. Her most recent book, *Moving Beyond Words,* a collection of essays, was published by Simon & Schuster in 1994. Her best-seller *Revolution From Within: A Book of Self-Esteem* was published in 1992 by Little, Brown. Other writing is also available in *Outrageous Acts and Everyday Rebellions,* a best-selling collection published by Holt, Rinehart & Winston in hardcover and Signet in mass paper-

back. Her book about Marilyn Monroe, *Marilyn: Norma Jeane,* was published in 1986 by Holt, in hardcover and paperback. Her writing has also appeared in *New York Magazine*—a weekly she helped to found in 1968 and served as political columnist for until 1972—and in many other magazines, newspapers, and anthologies here and internationally. After growing up mainly in the Midwest, she graduated Phi Beta Kappa from Smith College in 1956. She then lived in India for almost two years as a Chester Bowles Asian Fellow and a writer for Indian publications. In 1978, she took a year off from traveling and lecturing to study the impact of feminism on the premises of political theory as a Woodrow Wilson Scholar at the Smithsonian. She is especially interested in the shared origins and parallels of caste systems based on sex and race, in nonviolent conflict resolution, and in organizing across national boundaries for social justice and peace.

Susan Holly Stocking is Associate Professor in the School of Journalism at Indiana University in Bloomington, and coauthor (with Paget H. Gross) of *How Do Journalists Think? A Proposal for the Study of Cognitive Bias in Newsmaking.* A former journalist with the Associated Press, the *Minneapolis Tribune,* and the *Los Angeles Times,* she writes poetry and personal essays and publishes widely on science and media issues.

Carolyn A. Stroman is Associate Dean in the School of Communications at Howard University. Since receiving her Ph.D. from the Maxwell School at Syracuse University, she has written extensively on African Americans and mass communication. Her current research interests are centered in the area of health communication, especially the effects of exposure to health content on behavior among African Americans.

Sara Stuart heads Communication for Change, a New York City-based not-for-profit organization that has led participatory communication projects in Asia, Africa, and the Caribbean. Currently, she is involved in projects that use participatory communication methodologies to further social change work in the fields of women's economic empowerment, reproductive health, and protection of the environment. Recent publications include "Training and Organizing for Change in India: Video as a Tool of the Self Employed Women's Association" in *Women's Studies International,* edited by Aruna Rao (1991) and "Access to Media: Placing Video in the Hands of the People" in *Media Development* (no. 4, 1989).

Maria Suarez Toro is a Puerto Rican and Costa Rican feminist, teacher, and women's human rights activist. With Katerina Anfossi, she produces FIRE: Feminist International Radio Endeavor at Radio for Peace International. She was formerly Coordinator of the Human Rights Popular Education Secretariat at CODEHUCA (the Central American Human Rights Commission) from 1988 to 1991, during which time she initiated the Women's Human Rights Project, "Los Derechos de las Humanas." A teacher of literacy in Honduras, Costa Rica, Nicaragua, and El Salvador, she was Professor in the University of Costa Rica School of Education from 1974 to 1982. An accredited teacher in New York state and in Costa Rica, she has an M.A. from the State University of New York at Albany.

JoAnn Myer Valenti, Professor of Communications at Brigham Young University in Provo, Utah, received her Ph.D. in natural resources specializing in environmental communication at the University of Michigan (1983), and both an M.A. in mass communication (1969) and a B.S. in journalism (1967) at the University of Florida. An educator for more than 15 years, she is a charter member of the Society of Environmental Journalists (SEJ) and was corecipient of the Olive Branch Award for outstanding reporting on the nuclear arms issue in 1987. She is cochair of the Association for Education in Journalism and Mass Communications (AEJMC) Commission on the Status of Women. Her work appears in numerous publications including *Public Understanding of Science, Health Education*

Quarterly, Public Relations Research Annual, and recent contributed chapters in *Media Ethics: Issues and Cases* (1994, William C. Brown) and *Encyclopedia of Environmental Control Technology* (Vol. 7, 1995, Gulf). A Florida native, she now lives with her husband and two children in Salt Lake City and is active with Great Old Broads for Wilderness.

Frieda Werden has produced for five noncommercial radio networks, including National Public Radio. In 1986, she cofounded WINGS: Women's International News Gathering Service, an independently syndicated news and current affairs program by and about women around the world. In 1991, she helped the Foundation for a Compassionate Society and Radio for Peace International develop Feminist International Radio Endeavour (FIRE), a daily two-hour shortwave program out of Costa Rica. She still produces for WINGS, contributes to FIRE, and teaches at Women's Access to Electronic Resources (WATER) in Austin, Texas.